POLITICAL LEADERSHIP

Political Leadership

Themes, Contexts, and Critiques

MICHAEL FOLEY

11/19/14
WW
$ 99.00

OXFORD
UNIVERSITY PRESS

Great Clarendon Street, Oxford, OX2 6DP,
United Kingdom

Oxford University Press is a department of the University of Oxford.
It furthers the University's objective of excellence in research, scholarship,
and education by publishing worldwide. Oxford is a registered trade mark of
Oxford University Press in the UK and in certain other countries

First Edition published in 2013

Impression: 1

Published in the United States of America by Oxford University Press
198 Madison Avenue, New York, NY 10016, United States of America

British Library Cataloguing in Publication Data
Data available

Library of Congress Data available

ISBN 978-0-19-968593-6

Printed in Great Britain by
CPI Group (UK) Ltd, Croydon, CR0 4YY

In memoriam—Thomas H. Foley
A distant yet always present inspiration

Contents

List of figures and tables

List of boxes

List of abbreviations

BNP	Bangladesh Nationalist Party
BRICS	Brazil, Russia, India, China, and South Africa
CGI	Clinton Global Initiative
CSO	civil society organization
EHRC	Equality and Human Rights Commission
ERM	Exchange Rate Mechanism
IAEA	International Atomic Energy Agency
ICBL	International Campaign to Ban Landmines
ICC	International Criminal Court
ICISS	International Commission on Intervention and State Sovereignty
IMF	International Monetary Fund
MBTI	Myers–Briggs Type Indicator
NGO	non-governmental organization
NMF	Nelson Mandela Foundation
NTC	National Transitional Council
OCA	operational code analysis
R2P	Responsibility to Protect
RPF	Rwandan Patriotic Front
RUF	Revolutionary United Front (Liberia)
SCSL	Special Court for Sierra Leone
UNESCO	United Nations Educational, Scientific, and Cultural Organization
UNHCR	United Nations High Commissioner for Refugees
WEF	World Economic Forum
WFP	World Food Programme
WHO	World Health Organization
WSSD	World Summit on Sustainable Development
WTO	World Trade Organization

1

Introduction: Approaching the study of political leadership

'Inevitably, it seems, the study of leadership becomes an examination of the nature of individuals, their virtues or vices, their gender, their ambitions or goals, their "authenticity" and "transformative" or "transactional" dispositions. Or it becomes an examination of the place or context of leadership—the historical, political, cultural, religious and institutional factors that shape and influence leaders. Perhaps the most telling sign of the chameleonic nature of leadership is that if you gaze on it for too long it disappears altogether, revealing—followers.'

Haig Patapan[1]

PREAMBLE

Leaders matter; but political leaders matter more than most and for more reasons than most. Even set against a world of increasing complexity, the clean lines of leadership continue to make their presence felt in the profiles of politics and governance. Far from being subsumed within the diffuse assemblages of contemporary political organization, or marginalized by transnational and global developments, or dislocated by the multiple cross-pressures and intractable problems that distinguish modern politics, leaders and leadership have retained their central significance in the operation and understanding of political engagement. Arguably, they have even enhanced their status as material and conceptual expressions of the political sphere.

At a foundational level, leaders serve to populate the political landscape with conspicuous centres of functional value and public attention. They amount to such a self-evident feature of associational life that every form of social and political organization has some sort of facility both for producing leaders and for establishing the terms and conditions of leadership. Leaders provide a prodigious range of roles and functions that would otherwise be depleted or even lost without the direction and focus of exerted leadership. The responsibilities ascribed to leadership range from performing executive and administrative duties to

---

[1] Haig Patapan, 'On Leadership', University of Sydney, *Australian Review of Public Affairs*, August 2011.

shaping policy agendas and making key decisions; from providing a sense of strategic direction to using political communications to convey organizational responsiveness; and from offering a navigational channel of political explanation to providing a material expression of common points of accord (e.g. shared values, the public welfare, the national interest). At one and the same time, leaders are expected to ensure they are both guarantors of continuity and the main instruments of necessary change.

Notwithstanding their considerable obligations, the utility of leaders is not solely confined to a set of clearly defined political tasks. Leaders are often distinguished by their ability to offer a variety of more visceral, symbolic, and emotive levels of political engagement. It is noteworthy, for example, that children are generally introduced to the world of politics through the actions and reputations of past and present leaders. For many children, their foundational and cultural understanding of politics is formed through the agency of leaders and their ability to evoke on the one hand rich symbolic associations with large themes and powerful concepts, and on the other a personal linkage to the largely impersonal world of political interplay.[2] Just as leaders offer simplifying narratives, so their young audiences are invited to adopt the suggested dichotomies between good and bad leaders—between the heroically protective and the self-serving antagonist.

It is equally noteworthy that the intermediary agency of leaders is retained in adult life where the individual's engagement with politics remains strongly influenced by the reference points of different leaders and leaderships. In many respects, the interconnections are even stronger than they are during childhood. This is partly because adults have simply experienced longer periods of conditioning into the political medium of leadership claims and reputations. But it is also because of the way that political complexity has become increasingly reconfigured into a leader-centred forum of public expression and opinion formation. This is especially so in advanced liberal democracies, where the provision and management of leadership are taken to be the litmus test of organizational sophistication. Just as political debate is increasingly dominated by competing claims to leadership, so the terms and language of political engagement have become permeated by references to the location and relative merits of different available leaderships. Within these systems, profound social and political issues become routinely translated into conflicts between incumbent leaders and alternative leaderships. In like manner, policy prescriptions become refracted through the lens of an enabling leadership to such an extent that the constitutive elements of leadership and the differential appeals of competing leaders come to pervade both the marketing of parties and the presentation of their credentials in respect to organizational integrity and governing competence.

---

[2] Fred I. Greenstein, 'The Benevolent Leader: Children's Images of Political Authority', *American Political Science Review*, 54(4) December 1960: 934–43; Fred I. Greenstein, *Children and Politics* (New Haven, CT: Yale University Press, 1965), pp. 27–54; David Easton and Jack Dennis, *Children in the Political System: Origins of Political Legitimacy* (New York, NY: McGraw-Hill, 1969); Gunnel Gustafsson, 'Political Socialization Studies in Scandinavia', *International Political Science Review*, 8(3) July 1987: 225–33; Karen Orren and Paul Peterson, 'Presidential Assassination: A Case Study in the Dynamics of Political Socialization', *Journal of Politics*, 29(2) May 1967: 388–404.

In the same way that political conflict and policy differences can be projected onto the competition for leadership authority, so the forms and mediums of leadership exchange can be closely related to the substance of public argument. This is particularly the case in a social era which is noted for its near obsessive interest in the personal, psychological, and physical attributes of leaders, and for the way that media agendas are dominated by the need to cover the minutiae of leaders' public and private actions. It is also an era which is characterized by the way that political leaders increasingly seek to advance their claims to power and to legitimize their positional status through ever more personalized forms of out-reach and public engagement. These individualized appeals to what can often be described as populist sentiment have encouraged the creation of a dynamic in which the public comes to expect leaders to be both the guarantors and embodiments of their own prospectuses. Given this emergent syndrome of leadership projection, together with the highly conspicuous, intensive, and sustained attention devoted to leaders within the management of news cycles, it becomes possible to speculate on the extent to which individual citizens have now come to rely upon leaders not just in providing a plausible depiction of the political realm but also in offering a type of proxy involvement in the political process.

The effective recruitment of leaders and the provision of leadership have become recognized as a thoroughly conventional requirement of all stable political systems. Stability has in many respects become synonymous with a system's capacity to resolve leadership issues without excessive strain and disruption. In the same way that a leadership crisis normally denotes the existence of a profound systemic or constitutional dysfunction, so the peaceful and orderly transfer of power from one leadership to another has become a major test of a system's capacity to withstand pressure and to minimize the disruption caused by the installation of a new leadership. This being so, the availability of alternative leaderships is now in many systems a key ingredient of the normal processes of political dispute. Such is the faith in the prospect of leadership provision that in many modern systems it appears to be the case that there is practically no problem that cannot be attributed to an alleged failure of leadership, and no solution that cannot be achieved through an alternative leadership.

It is clear that leaders occupy a pivotal position not just within their own political contexts but also within their respective cultural landscapes. Far from being mere functionaries who perform a set of predetermined roles and who possess nothing more than a derivative position and authority, many political leaders are distinguished by the way that they offer alternative sets of categories and themes by which public life and even social existence can be characterized. For example, it is common for political time to be measured in terms of a succession of leaderships. Political leaders generate their own fabric of periodic episodes. As a consequence, a particular leadership will often mark and define a particular era. Because historical time is almost habitually broken up and organized through the lives, and terms of office, of contemporary leaders, it is common for a new leadership to be measured both in relation to its predecessors and in respect to its position in the evolutionary development of the society involved. In similar vein, immediate and long-term social futures are also commonly demarcated by references to the availability of possible future leaders who can give some prospective political shape and meaning to the unknown.

Another example of the expansive and assimilative properties of leadership significance is provided by the way that a leader can evoke a sense of social solidarity and cultural identity. The representative components of many leaders are not confined to purely political factors. They can extend to the way that past triumphs, historical grievances, recent strains, or contemporary challenges can be expressed through leadership narratives and converted into focal points of cultural awareness and social mobilization. In this guise, leaders can summon up a symbiosis between historical memory and collective identity on the one hand, and the promotion of their own leadership resources on the other so that the provision of leadership becomes a signature of a society's own integrity.

THE ALLURE OF LEADERSHIP

The high demands and enhanced visibility afforded to political leaders have created a pronounced cultural resonance surrounding the theme of leadership in contemporary life.[3] This has served to underline the social presence of leaders and the public and private roles that they are expected to fulfil. However, while it can be argued that the prominence and status of leaders have increased in scope, the precise nature of their claims to leadership has become more open to question. This is not least because of the emergence of new sources and expressions of leadership within society. While it can be acknowledged that different spheres of leadership have always coexisted in modern society, a growing trend can be discerned not just towards the conscious development of publicly projected leadership within other fields of organizational activity but to a sustained focus upon the provision and utility of leadership as a key requirement for achieving any kind of large-scale objectives. Many areas of conspicuously high priority leadership can be observed and, although they are not normally in a position of open competition with the structures of political leadership, they do serve to compound the problems of defining the boundaries and meaning of leadership within the political context.

Of the many alternative bases of leadership provision that now tend to crowd around the more conventional locations of political leadership, there can be little doubt that the most significant and most influential contemporary source lies within the sector of business organization. It is indisputable that no other sector sets such store in the value of leadership, and no other sector assigns so many resources and such lavish rewards to the establishment and promotion of leadership. It does so as a matter of course in recognition of the functional effectiveness that is assumed to inhere in the capacity of leaders to act as a counterweight to the deficiencies of any organization. In the world of business, there are no apologies for leadership. The only apologies in this respect are reserved for those occasions when there has been an egregious lack of leadership within an organization.

[3] Michelle C. Bligh and James R. Meindl, 'The Cultural Ecology of Leadership: An Analysis of Popular Leadership Books', in David M. Messick and Roderick M. Kramer (eds.), *The Psychology of Leadership: New Perspectives and Research* (Mahwah, NJ: Lawrence Erlbaum, 2005), pp. 11–52.

Leadership is a prized resource within business models for a host of different reasons.[4] Leaders can offer, or at least indicate, a sense of hierarchy within which a command structure is afforded a clear sense of direction and an established set of priorities. An effective leader can not only infuse energy, innovation, and responsiveness within a business enterprise, but can provide a focus for coordination, planning, implementation, and accountability. Leaders are valued for their capacity to act as strategists, enforcers, team builders, production maximizers, task-induced facilitators, and agents of conflict resolution and accommodation.

Large-scale commercial and financial activities are regularly attributed to individual leaders who are personally reputed to having reassured, or alternatively having disturbed, the markets. Just as the markets scrutinize the appointments and track records of corporate executives, so productivity, profitability, and share values are widely assumed to be closely aligned to the quality of leadership within the enterprises under examination. Individual leaders are seen as catalysts that can turn entire companies around, or else precipitate their decline and even collapse. Even in an era of downsizing, outsourcing, and various forms of organizational 'flattening', there continue to be multiple claims relating to the central significance of leadership and to the need for leadership resources, training, and remuneration to be in line with the demands and stakes attendant upon the role of leadership within the contemporary corporate culture.

Businesses not only have to demonstrate an ability to recruit leaders but also to provide the conditions and training opportunities to produce leadership qualities on a regular basis. Within business culture, the notion that leadership is a form of transferable knowledge has prompted the establishment of an entire industry geared to the analysis of leadership and to the enhancement of leadership skills. Books, articles, journals, CDs, audio cassettes, podcasts, DVDs, and video channels on the subject of leadership are complemented by numerous leadership institutes, schools, courses, programmes, conferences, and seminars run by analysts, exponents, coaches, and even leadership gurus.[5] The emphasis given to the need for individuals to be able successfully to demonstrate leadership behaviour and to fulfil leadership roles has now reached such a level that the once venerable distinction between leadership and management has increasingly been eroded by the sheer weight of managers who now wish to be designated as leaders. In an era when the chief executive officers of major corporations occupy key positions in celebrity culture, and when a belief in the transformative power of individual corporate leaders has become established as a popular orthodoxy, the social currency of organizational leadership has in turn become more marked and more penetrating as a widely subscribed role model.

What can justifiably be termed a cult of economic leadership has helped to propagate similar forms of status enhancement for leaders within other organizational structures. Whether it be in education, health, and social services or in

---

[4] For a representative sample of what is a huge corpus of literature on business leadership, see Henry Mintzberg *et al.*, *Harvard Business Review on Leadership* (Boston, MA: Harvard Business School Publishing, 1998); Robert H. Rosen with Paul B. Brown, *Leading People: The 8 Proven Principles for Success in Business* (New York, NY: Penguin, 1996); Daniel Goleman *et al.*, *HBR's 10 Must Reads on Leadership* (Boston, MA: Harvard Business School Publishing, 2010).

[5] See Chapter 6.

sports, entertainment, and the arts, the emphasis has become one not merely of facilitating the establishment and projection of leadership skills but also of changing organizations through leadership positions to allow for the infusion of business models into the operational processes. The shift to 'new public administration', or 'new public management', in the 1980s and 1990s, for example, was designed to modernize the public sector through the introduction of market-based reforms that instituted executive agencies and promoted internal competition, devolved responsibilities, established incentive structures and business 'best practice techniques'.[6]

The model placed a distinctive emphasis upon the role of administrative heads as the main agency and chief beneficiary of the strategic managerial shift. The heads of public agencies were granted extensive autonomy and with it the responsibility for producing the required objectives and targets. Like their private sector counterparts, the virtues of vision, drive, and inspiration were considered to be essential to the integrity and productivity of the operation. Agency heads were granted extensive autonomy and with it the responsibility for producing the required objectives and targets. Accountability now became segmented across different compartments of public administration. This *de facto* privatization of government has continued to be exemplified by the proliferation of leadership positions that often acquire a high public profile and an equally conspicuous salary level in recognition of the market rate assigned to their leadership value.[7]

Another notable source of leadership presentation and discussion has come in the international dimension. This includes the sustained increase in the number of nation states and with it a further deepening of the correlation between leaders and the effective expression of national interests and cultural identities. But developments within the international sphere also incorporate trends towards structures of regional integration, global governance, and multilateral agreement that again tend to generate leading players and figures of representational, symbolic, and occasionally pioneering substance. Given parallel advances in the global integration of broadcasting and the continuing profusion of media outlets, many leaders in an array of different contexts find that they have an international or at least a transnational exposure both of their policy agendas and of their personal characteristics. This prominence becomes even more acute in those situations that are assigned the provenance of crisis and with it the commensurate level of attention given to the roles and expectations of responsive leadership.

The varied depictions of leadership, in combination with the onset of multiple reference points of leader activity and the close proximity of leadership clusters across different sectors of public life, have led to an enhanced awareness of the social significance of leaders but at the same time to a high level of confusion over their meaning and place in society. More leaders have in many respects led to a

[6] See John R. Greenwood, Robert Pyper, and David Jack Wilson, *New Public Administration in Britain*, 3rd edn. (Abingdon: Routledge, 2002); Anthony King, *The British Constitution* (Oxford: Oxford University Press, 2009), ch. 9.

[7] The rise in designated leadership positions in the UK public sector is reflected in the estimated 9,000 employees in this category earning salaries in excess of the prime minister. See BBC *Panorama* survey in BBC *Panorama*, 'Public Sector Pay: The Numbers', 20 September 2010. Report accessed 24 September 2011 at: <http://www.bbc.co.uk/news/uk-11319918>.

diminished understanding of the phenomenon. The high incidence of leaders as well as the salience attached to leadership issues have not only reaffirmed the complexity of the field but have exacerbated the problem of making sense of the subject. The contingent and mutable nature of leadership status and effectiveness— together with the cross-currents and synergies between different leaderships, and the varied contextual bases of leadership location and function—has always imposed limitations at arriving at a workable overview of the terrain. Recent conditions and developments have merely compounded the problem.

LEADERSHIP AND ANALYTICAL INHIBITION

One factor in particular stands out as being peculiarly significant in the challenge to reduce the subject to some degree of explanatory order. This relates to the extraordinary diffidence exhibited by political analysts and even participants towards approaching the theme of political leadership in any kind of coherent and inclusive manner. Indeed, it can be claimed that in the main the study of contemporary political leadership is afflicted by a conspicuous anomaly. As leaders assume a greater presence across an increased range of societal sectors, the characteristic response is less one of concerted analysis and more a case of either confining the field into discrete studies of individual leaders or studiously marginalizing the subject area into a set of peripheral or derivative issues. Accordingly, the popular fixation with leader-centred parties and high-profile leadership politics is not reflected in the level of attention given to the close analysis of leadership. In effect, the political salience of leadership is not matched by its position on the agendas of political inquiry and research.

Very few systematic studies of political leadership exist and those that do tend to be severely constrained by the contested nature of the subject. In general, the study of leadership has suffered from the standard operating principles of political science. Research design and hypothesis formulation are governed primarily by the impulse to elicit regularities and generalizations from a diversity of separate cases. One of the chief problems raised by the subject of leadership in this context, therefore, is one of extremes. Individual political leaders are notably limited in number. Furthermore, their distinctive appeals and comparatively isolated status mean that there is very little in the way of aggregate materials to support the advance of systematic analysis. Since analytical effort is related to explanatory potential, the study of political leadership has tended to be ignored or assigned a secondary status.

The marginalization of leadership as a key field of political inquiry can be observed in the limited space that is accorded to the subject in many general textbooks on political science. For example, in a sample of ten popular texts in the UK on the study of politics, only five had any indexed references to the subject of leadership. Even in these volumes, the number of page references amounted to only 35 out of a combined total of 1,927 pages[8] (i.e. 1.82 per cent). If those

---

[8] Excluding the pages carrying the indexes.

Table 1.1 Volume of indexed references to *leader(s)* and *leadership* in a selection of UK textbooks on politics

Title	Number of indexed page references to *leader(s)* and *leadership* / total number of pages per volume	Indexed page references to *leader(s)* and *leadership* as % of total pages per volume
Kenneth Minogue, *Politics: A Very Short Introduction* (Oxford: Oxford University Press, 2000)	0/128	0%
Barrie Axford, Gary K. Browning, Richard Huggins, Ben Rosamond, and John Turner, *Politics: An Introduction*, 2nd edn. (London: Routledge, 2002)	0/624	0%
Peter Calvert, *Comparative Politics: An Introduction* (Harlow: Longman, 2002)	8/351	2.28%
Colin Hay, *Political Analysis: A Critical Introduction* (Basingstoke: Palgrave Macmillan, 2002)	0/328	0%
Adrian Leftwich, *What is Politics? The Activity and Its Study* (Cambridge: Polity Press, 2004)	0/224	0%
Kenneth Newton and Jan W. van Deth, *Foundations of Comparative Politics*, 2nd edn. (Cambridge: Cambridge University Press, 2005)	0/472	0%
Andrew Heywood, *Politics*, 3rd edn. (Basingstoke: Palgrave Macmillan, 2007)	15/496	3.02%
Robert Leach, *The Politics Companion* (Basingstoke: Palgrave Macmillan, 2008)	6/328	1.83%
Isaac D. Balbus, *Governing Subjects: An Introduction to the Study of Politics* (Abingdon: Routledge, 2009)	2/288	0.69%
Rod Hague and Martin Harrop, *Comparative Government and Politics: An Introduction*, 8th edn. (Basingstoke: Palgrave Macmillan, 2010)	4/464	0.86%
Cumulative total	35/3703	0.95%

volumes with no entries at all on leaders or leadership were to be included in the total, then the proportion of page entries in the combined sample slips to less than 1 per cent (Table 1.1).

Another indicator is provided by *The Oxford Handbook of Political Science*[9] which is widely cited as an authoritative compendium—incorporating 52 separate

[9] Robert E. Goodin (ed.), *The Oxford Handbook of Political Science* (Oxford: Oxford University Press 2011).

contributions by high-profile specialists. And yet, in a volume of 1,312 pages, there are no indexed page references to either leaders or leadership. These measures serve to underline what is a very common disjunction between on the one hand what might be termed an acute cultural fascination with the theme and operation of political leadership, and on the other hand an enduring cognitive bias and analytical deficit that works to move the subject to the periphery of concerted inquiry.

If only by default, a developed interest in leaders is mostly confined to the genre of political biography. This mode of inquiry can provide illuminating insights into the conditions and contingencies of particular leaderships. At the same time political biography has by its very nature a narrow focus which tends to perpetuate a highly individualized approach to the subject of leadership. Individual leaders are embedded within their own separate and largely idiosyncratic contexts. The *raison d'être* of a biography is to relate selected leaders to the specific situations within which they have to operate. As a consequence, biographies normally do very little either to develop a basis for comparison or generalization, or to draw together the separate strands of materials relevant to a more holistic conception of leadership within the field of political study.

Arguably, a far more potent factor in the limited stature of political leadership as a core theme of political analysis has been its ambiguous relationship with the dominant contemporary paradigm of liberal democracy. There remains a deep ambivalence in the role and authority of leaders within democratic systems. In one respect, political leaders can be depicted as the logical extension of a party-based democracy. The leaders of winning parties assume the position of prime minister or president. In doing so, they recharge the executive authority of such roles with their own projection of electoral consent. They are seen to be representative figures that have a functional utility in structuring the policy agenda, mobilizing political action, and securing a programme of policy changes in accord with public needs and preferences. In another quite different guise, leaders can pose serious questions over the reach and limits of democracy. For example, it is possible to argue that democracies should neither allow nor require individual leaders to function effectively. To the extent that leaders achieve prominence within a democracy, then this could be construed as a widening of the gap between government and the governed. Inevitably, this might well indicate a reduction both in the diversity of opinion presentation and in a government's level of political responsiveness. While leaders may be accepted on the grounds of their utility to governance, democracies regard the concomitant notions of 'followers' and 'the led' with considerable normative and conceptual discomfort.[10]

A further caveat over the role of democratic leaders centres upon the implications of leadership within such a context. Contemporary leaders both generate and receive exaggerated forms of public attention. They claim exceptional insights into the condition of the people and into their anxieties, hopes, and demands. They employ an array of techniques to develop the perception that they not only represent the public interest but in fact embody it. The need to pursue such

---

[10] See James M. Burns, *Leadership* (New York, NY: Harper & Row, 1979), pp. 18–23, 129–37, 169–200.

presumptions and the extent to which they are developed in an environment of democratic competition can be said to generate a profusion of undemocratic and even anti-democratic implications. Some contest the negative constructions of these developments and consider the emergence of what is termed 'leader democracy' as amounting to a contemporary reconciliation of elite political theory, concepts of democracy, and the virtues of representation, in which responsible government is achieved through a mass-mediated process of leadership selection.[11] Others remain unconvinced and view leader-centred politics as regressive and even disruptive forms of governance. Such political tactics are typified by leaders organizing populist campaigns to circumvent institutional channels of democratic expression and in the process to marginalize intermediary agencies, thereby fostering suggestions that leaders do indeed provide forms of surrogate popular participation—even substitutes for, and antidotes to, conventional democratic activity.[12]

The variable outlooks upon democratic leadership are further compounded by the way they are often fused together within political cultures and institutional frameworks. As a consequence, the democratic response to leadership is notoriously disjointed. More often than not, it generates a profusion of persistent dualities—empowerment and constraint; hopes and fears; benefits and dangers; modernity and mystique; majoritarian right and minority rights; trust and suspicion; direction and dissent; functional need and political complaint. These contrary impulses and traditions run parallel to one another in a complex and unresolved set of tensions that do not readily admit to a clear exposition on the role and place of leadership within the ethos and operation of liberal democracy. They generate a perplexing, and often bewildering, process of high leadership expectations intertwined with high leadership antipathy. Each liberal democratic system has had to find a workable accommodation through which these tensions can be contained. The British system provides an illustrative example of how this aggregate outlook has been traditionally maintained within the parameters of liberal democratic framework.

DUAL PERSPECTIVES: THE CASE OF BRITAIN

The British system is traditionally noted for the centrality of parliament and cabinet government, and for a host of supportive traditions that contribute to an operational ethos of collegiate conventions, corporate action, and collective responsibility. The properties of this structure have almost invariably resisted any

---

[11] See András Körösényi, 'Political Representation in Leader Democracy', *Government and Opposition*, 40(3) Summer 2005: 358–78; Jan Pakulski and John Higley, 'Towards Leader Democracy?' in John Uhr and Paul 't Hart (eds.), *Public Leadership: Perspectives and Practices* (Canberra: The Australian National University Press 2008), pp. 45–54; Jan Pakulski and András Körösényi, *Toward Leader Democracy* (London: Anthem Press 2012).

[12] For a recent overview of this phenomenon, see Matthew A. Crenson and Benjamin Ginsberg, *Downsizing Democracy: How America Sidelined its Citizens and Privatized its Public* (Baltimore, MD: Johns Hopkins University Press, 2002).

notion that individualized leadership should or does play a prominent role in British government. A characteristic feature of British exceptionalism therefore has been the unexceptional and even prosaic role that is formally ascribed to the prime minister's position in the UK constitution. This is not to deny that individual prime ministers can develop and have developed strong centres of power within the framework of government. However, these developments always provoke political and constitutional unease, especially if a particular incumbency is portrayed as a personalized and autonomous agency of political will. The few wholly exceptional leaders that have punctuated the collective continuities of British political history have been closely associated with the extraordinary conditions of wartime. With the resumption of peacetime conditions, the leadership position of prime ministers has generally returned to the constitutional norm of a provisional and collegiately based semi-prominence. Peacetime prime ministers do occasionally transcend the constitutional wiring and rise to positions of conspicuous exposure but such a distinction is usually seen as a temporary and even an aberrational departure from the norm.

The conventional ethos of British governance leaves very little room either for the idea, or for the practice of, leadership. The prime minister is generally taken to be a given unit of authority situated within a pluralist system of multiple power centres where organized power comes only through disciplined parties and collective policymaking. Political leaders have to operate through party organizations. Formally, prime ministers occupy the role of *primus inter pares* and are confronted with the continuities of the government machine and political tradition. In accordance with this conception of the office and of the orderly system that reputedly surrounds it, the role of personal leadership has often been dismissed as something of a digression to an understanding of British politics.[13]

This British bias against elevated forms of leadership has a number of foundations. At its root is an orthodox liberal suspicion towards the accumulation of power, especially when it is portrayed or deployed in the kind of concentrated and centralized manner that is suggested by the presence of a dominant leader. In its most basic sense, strong leadership constitutes an overt form of individual political inequality. This arouses a basic liberal bias against the presumption of hierarchy and enforced direction. It prompts a concern for how civil liberties and individual rights can be compromised and undermined by a leadership's policy programme, even one promoted under the auspices of popular consent. The traditional liberal concerns for the rule of law, checks and balances, due process, constitutional constraints, and plural power centres sit uneasily with the ingredients and imperatives of leadership.

The hallmark of political leadership is conventionally one of challenge and a reordering of priorities. A highly effective leader can push novelty to the point of transcending old constraints and of developing a power base separate in character to the established sources of authority and political channels within a political

---

[13] For example, see Vernon Bogdanor (ed.), *The British Constitution in the Twentieth Century* (Oxford: Oxford University Press, 2003). In a volume of 799 pages, no single chapter is assigned to the prime minister's position within the UK system of government. See also G. W. Jones, 'The Prime Minister's Power', in Anthony King (ed.), *The British Prime Minister*, 2nd edn. (Basingstoke: Macmillan, 1985), pp. 195–220; Simon James, *British Cabinet Government* (London: Routledge, 1992).

system. Effective political leadership, therefore, carries the implication of a significant reduction in the effectiveness of political constraints upon government. Claims of electoral legitimacy do not diminish the liberal anxieties induced by strong leaders. The liberal ethos fosters a basic discomfort with leaders claiming to speak for and to act on behalf of the people and the nation. It is not merely that such a privilege always remains open to empirical disputes, but that it is contestable on normative grounds for challenging the moral autonomy of the individual and the principles of volunteerism within a liberal society.

Another source of bias against accepting strong leadership as a normative requirement to conventional political activity is based more specifically upon Britain's particular constitutional traditions. The viability of an unwritten constitution is widely seen to be a reflection of a set of binding social and political conventions that support a culture of collective self-restraint. British political stability, therefore, is largely based upon the intuitive understandings of its constitution and upon the acquired capacity of the political participants to conform to the spirit of those understandings. This idea of a political community working within its own constitutional norms is further endorsed by a traditional dependence upon certain types of political leader—i.e. those whose social backgrounds evoke public trust in their leaders' individual sense of propriety and their deference to established standards of political conduct. This conspicuously benign outlook upon appropriately socialized leaders and leadership has also been fostered by the orthodox view of British political history. This interprets Britain's parliamentary democracy as the outcome of a long historical process of graduated evolution and adaptation. A state of democracy was achieved without recourse to democratic revolutions, or to popular leaders inciting historical discontinuities from outside the governing structures. Democracy came gradually. By emerging through the established institutions, it had the effect of enhancing the integrity of these traditional structures and of underlining the supremacy of parliament and its collective disciplines.[14]

As a consequence of this constitutional context, any individual leader finds it difficult enough to prevail within a party—let alone to exert leadership within a governing structure that reserves personal symbolism to the crown and which emphasizes the ethos of multiple and mutual restraint. In Britain, leaders are always in a position of having to confront other leaders of comparable, or potentially comparable, stature. It is difficult to make a decisive break from the pack. A prime minister has no ministerial department or even a fully recognizable job description. Premiers are always confronted by the prospect of competitors within their own parties. Their rarity value as leaders is also diminished by the presence of an institutionalized alternative prime minister in the form of the Leader of Her Majesty's Opposition, complete with a shadow cabinet on permanent standby to provide a replacement government. The wider structural context of adversarial parties, combined with a highly pragmatic constitutional culture, means that the aspiration to personal leadership can appear to be not merely a fatally immodest trait but a distraction that will be politically counterproductive.

---

[14] See such classic texts as Samuel H. Beer, *Modern British Politics* (London: Faber & Faber, 1969); A. V. Dicey, *Introduction to the Study of the Law of the Constitution*, 8th edn. (Indianapolis, IN: Liberty Fund, 1982); O. Hood Phillips, Paul Jackson, and Patricia Leopold, *O. Hood Phillips and Jackson, Constitutional and Administrative Law*, 8th edn. (London: Sweet & Maxwell, 2001).

A further source of antipathy against the presumptions and accoutrements of leadership is provided by Britain's historical reactions to the rise of European fascism and to the onset and course of the Second World War. Just as British governing institutions and arrangements represent the core element of its national identity, so Britain's experience in the war has remained the litmus test of both its constitutional ethos and its sense of national autonomy. The nation's adversary was not merely an enemy but the pre-eminent symbol of a philosophy and organization of government that amounted to an anathema to British conceptions of the state.

The danger was defined and the nation's existence was threatened by the Axis powers, whose destructive forces were reducible to the individual figure of Adolf Hitler. The predominant view within British public opinion saw Hitler as a leader who had utterly perverted all the liberal premises of democratic leadership. He did not ask for the curtailment of individual freedoms as a temporary measure or as an instrumental device. The subjugation of the individual was an end in its own right and a defining theme of the regime. Hitler demanded the complete abandonment of the individual's free will and moral autonomy. His leadership existed to receive the people's surrender, submission, and sacrifice in the name of a higher obligation that recognized only one individual and one will. To Hitler, this absorption of the citizen into the state was an imperative precondition to the fulfilment of an historic destiny that fused national mythology, racial superiority, and demagogic leadership: 'Nature is cruel; therefore we are also entitled to be cruel. When I send the flower of German youth into the steel hail of the next war without feeling the slightest regret over the precious German blood that is being spilled, should I not also have the right to eliminate millions of an inferior race that multiplies like vermin?'[15]

Hitler threw into high relief what liberal constitutionalism and representative democracy were designed to prevent. He did not merely personify the failure of the democratic experiment of the Weimar Republic; he was an active agent in its destruction. Hitler's *raison d'être* was to use a cult of leadership in a crusade to supersede conventional politics and to raise his own person as the supreme embodiment of the nation and the state. In achieving this objective, he epitomized the destructive potential of unregulated political leadership, the excesses of concentrated power, and the capriciousness of a totalitarian order. Hitler evinced a kind of irrationalism and mysticism that led to government by prophetic visions and to explicit notions of messianic providence. The instinctive British reaction to the metaphysical character of such leadership extremes is typified by the comments of Ian Kershaw: 'More than any other political leader, Hitler stands for the dangers of unlimited power and the horrors of war and genocide. Our moral revulsion at Hitler is greater than that attached to any other figure of the 20th century. Hitler's face is arguably the most unmistakable face of the century. For most people, it is the face of a monster, the face of evil.'[16]

[15] Adolf Hitler, quoted in Joachim C. Fest, *Hitler* (New York, NY: Vintage Books Edition, 1974), pp. 679–80.
[16] Ian Kershaw, 'Making of a Monster' (Review of Ron Rosenbaum, *Explaining Hitler: The Search for the Origins of Evil* and John Lukacs, *The Hitler of History: Hitler's Biographers on Trial*), *The Observer*, 18 July 1998.

Hitler it was who exemplified the lengths to which a leader could go and the magnitude of unaccountable power that a leader could amass. Even in a modern state and a mass democracy, the public could be aroused and mobilized by the highly emotional appeals of a charismatic leader. From a liberal democratic perspective, it was evident that the illiberal and psychotic properties of a population could be brought to the surface by a psychotic leader, who in turn could represent, extend, and magnify those properties into a regime of raw coercive power. In terms of British conventions of statecraft and British principles of liberal democracy, Hitler remains the consummate cautionary tale of excessive personal prominence within a political arena. He remains fixed in the public's imagination as a leader who not only depicted evil but who embodied the evils of perverted leadership.

The social catharsis incited by Hitler within Germany turned into the international catharsis of the Second World War, which culminated in the physical destruction of Hitler and the Third Reich. Since that conflict, Hitler has remained the defining benchmark of what a political order should endeavour to avoid at all costs. Following the demise of his regime, the figure of Hitler succeeded in generating a host of structures and processes designed to prevent any recurrence of such leadership excess. Much of the post-war reconstruction of Europe was guided by this reaction against the democratic and liberal perversions of strong leadership. During the Cold War, this revulsion against Hitler became fused with an abhorrence of Stalin and the Soviet regime. This was fuelled by successive revelations of the various purges subsumed under what became known as the 'Great Terror'.[17] The myriad instruments of social control and political coercion collected together under the aegis of another personality cult had the effect of reinforcing the equation of dictatorial leadership with an extreme abuse of power that unleashed destruction on a scale comparable to that of Nazi Germany.[18]

Accordingly, Stalin joined Hitler in providing another archetypal lesson of history into the dangers posed by advanced political leadership to the normal functioning of any political order. Stalin reaffirmed the psychotic tendencies of a leadership driven by chronic insecurities into an instrument of social and political domination. The pathologies of fascist and communist leadership jointly fostered a set of post-war initiatives (e.g. European Economic Community, European Convention on Human Rights) that in large part were designed to prevent the new European democracies from subsiding into forms of leadership-induced extremism. In similar vein, the meaning and identity of the West became bound up with the need to avoid any repetition of the 1930s appeasement policies and to make the crusade against authoritarian control into a defining narrative of the 'free world'. This Cold War posture has been extended into the post-Cold War era through such themes as the prospectus of the European Union as a 'civilizing power'. This injunction relates to the EU's adoption of a role not just of 'resolutely

[17] See Anne Applebaum, *Gulag: A History* (London: Allen Lane, 2003); Donald Rayfield, *Stalin and His Hangmen: An Authoritative Portrait of a Tyrant and Those Who Served Him* (New York, NY: Random House, 2005); Robert Conquest, *The Great Terror: A Reassessment* (London: Pimlico, 2008).
[18] See Alan Bullock, *Hitler and Stalin: Parallel Lives*, 2nd edn. (London: Fontana, 1998); Richard Overy, *The Dictators: Hitler's Germany and Stalin's Russia* (New York, NY: Norton, 2004); Timothy Snyder, 'Hitler vs. Stalin: Who Was Worse?', *New York Review of Books*, 27 January 2011.

doing battle against all violence, all terror and all fanaticism',[19] but also of working to advance democratic values, human rights protection, social justice, and good governance within the international environment.[20]

The net effect of these influences has reinforced a sense of British exceptionalism not just in relation to European social history but also in respect to continental-style excesses outside Europe. The programmes and power of highly personalized leaderships in some emergent or developing nations, for example, are taken to signify the presence of political instability and an immaturity in the institutions and processes of governance. In extreme cases—for example Abdul Nasser (Egypt), Idi Amin (Uganda), Saddam Hussein (Iraq), Robert Mugabe (Zimbabwe), Charles Taylor (Liberia)—leaders have been commonly portrayed as monstrous, thereby allowing for an ease of political mobilization against them amongst the British public. Even in post-Cold War Europe, the parity value of Hitler and Nazism continues to be the standard of choice by which to compare and to condemn an objectionable regime. For example, during the conflict over Kosovo in 1999, the US and British mass media directly and indirectly equated the Serbian leader, Slobodan Milošević, with Adolf Hitler.[21] The same usage of the Hitler analogy was prevalent in the build-up to the Iraq war in 2003.[22] This impulse not only sharpened the terms of disparagement but also assisted in summoning up a strong liberal democratic reaction against a leadership that had been permitted to lapse into tyranny. A similar piece of analogical mapping[23] occurred in the military conflict in Libya during 2011. Opinion formation in the United States was influenced through the numerous cross-references that were made either suggesting or asserting a close similarity between Colonel Gaddafi and Adolf Hitler.[24]

---

[19] European Council, *Declaration on the Future of Europe*, Laeken, 15 December 2001. Accessed 27 November 2011 at: <http://european-convention.eu.int/pdf/lknen.pdf>.

[20] See Ian Manners, 'Normative Power Europe: A Contradiction in Terms?', *Journal of Common Market Studies*, 40(2) 2002: 235–58; Ian Manners, 'Normative Power Europe Reconsidered: Beyond the Crossroads', *Journal of European Public Policy*, 13(2) 2006: 182–99; Ben Tonra, 'Conceptualizing the European Union's Global Role', in Michelle Cini and Angela K. Bourne (eds.), *Palgrave Advances in European Union Studies* (Basingstoke: Palgrave Macmillan, 2006), pp. 117–30.

[21] BBC News, 'Britons "support Nato strikes"', 28 March 1999. Accessed 2 October 2011 at: <http://news.bbc.co.uk/1/hi/uk/306010.stm>; Nick Gillespie, 'Führer Furor: Is Milošević a Hitler?', *Reason*, June 1999. Accessed 15 August 2011 at: <http://reason.com/archives/1999/06/01/fhrer-furor>.

[22] Seumas Milne, 'The opponents of war on Iraq are not the appeasers', *Guardian*, 13 February 2003; *CNN World*, 'Blair likens Saddam to Hitler', 1 March 2003. Accessed 2 September 2011 at: <http://articles.cnn.com/2003-03-01/world/sprj.irq.blair_1_prime-minister-tony-blair-weapons-inspections-more-time-adolf-hitler?_s=PM:WORLD>; David Remnick, 'War without end?', *The New Yorker*, 21 April 2003.

[23] The concept is explored in Barbara A. Spellman and Keith J. Holyoak, 'If Saddam is Hitler then who is George Bush? Analogical Mapping between Systems of Social Roles', *Journal of Personality and Social Psychology*, 62(6) 1992: 913–33; David P. Houghton, *Political Psychology: Situations, Individuals, and Cases* (New York, NY: Routledge, 2009), ch. 9.

[24] 'Libya protests: Gaddafi will die like Hitler, says ex-Libyan minister', *Daily Telegraph*, 24 February 2011; Bill Varner, 'Libyan Envoy, Comparing Qaddafi to Hitler, Seeks UN Sanctions', *Businessweek*, 26 February 2011; ABC News, '"New Hitler" Gaddafi rounding up opponents', 7 March 2011. Accessed 24 September at: <www.abc.net.au/news/2011-03-03/new-hitler-gaddafi-rounding-up-opponents/1966478>. Lindsey Graham, 'Gadhafi is like Hitler', *Salon: War Room*, 6 July 2011. Accessed 20 November 2011 at: <http://www.salon.com/news/politics/war_room/2011/07/06/lindsey_graham_gadhafi_hitler>.

LOST IN TRANSLATION

The British example is not atypical of the complex dynamics that are generated by the theme of democratic leadership in systems with a long tradition of successfully managing power relations. In such systems, it is common for leaders to occupy positions of both licence and restriction at the same time. Just as the activities and claims of leaders continue to arouse contrary responses, so the disjointed perspectives upon leadership continue to afflict the operation of high-level governance—as well as the attitude structures surrounding the conduct of politics—even in highly advanced and stable liberal democracies. There remains a nostalgic affection for past leaders and a promiscuous fascination for charisma. Politics may be increasingly structured around demands for leadership and the rival claims of leadership. Leadership may also be widely cited as the antidote to the gridlock and inertia of contemporary democracy. And yet, very few leaders are permitted to match up to the inflated public expectations of leadership.

Leadership remains a painful and public form of diminishing returns, in which the heavily contingent nature of leadership authority is progressively eroded away. The dominant and recurring characterization of leadership within these contexts is one of paradox; not simply one clearly delineated paradox but a matrix of multiple paradoxes pivoting upon the provision of responsibility and the denial of power.[25] Far from a pantheon of heroic leaders, therefore, most liberal democracies are characterized by a landscape of frustrated leaders and broken leaderships. For every new leader, there is the unfulfilled promise of a displaced leader. The passage of political time can almost be marked by the regular cycle of unlikely ascents followed by the normal anticlimax of deep descents with ex-leaders complaining about precarious support bases, capricious publics, and the limits of politics.

As we have already noted, the complex status of leaders and leadership within liberal democracies is projected onto our analytical approaches of the subject which can be characterized as segmented and eclectic at best, and as confused and incoherent at worst. The subject of political leadership continues to evoke intense interest not least because of its associations with entirely legitimate features of public life and political activity. By contrast, it is also a theme that often produces ambivalence and even suspicion. Leadership can be construed as being in close proximity to notions of extreme inequality, prerogative rights, executive privilege, arbitrary rule, unbalanced power relations, and even forms of mysticism and irrationality. The natural appeal of political leadership is one of concentrated meaning and while this usually embraces such positive features as vitality, action, responsiveness, and strategic vision, it can also insinuate far more negative categories like those of distrust, suspicion, fear, and danger.

It is these negative categories which have largely conditioned the adoption of approaches to the study of political leadership. In many ways, this is because it has been liberal democratic societies that have mostly been responsible for allocating

---

[25] For a classic study of this phenomenon, see Michael A. Genovese and Thomas E. Cronin, *The Paradoxes of the American Presidency*, 2nd edn. (New York, NY: Oxford University Press, 2004).

resources to political research and for establishing agendas of political inquiry. In this field, liberal curiosity has been closely connected to liberal suspicion. The concerns over correlations that connect normalities of leadership with abnormal politics are well captured by Jean Blondel:

> One reason why political leadership has not been systematically analyzed is the *fear* which it has provoked among generations of liberal thinkers. Alongside a few 'good' leaders, so many have been ruthless in controlling their subjects and in acquiring territories, usually by force, that enthusiasm for leadership has been limited, to say the least... The deeds of many twentieth-century leaders, both before and after the Second World War, did not help to modify the pessimistic view. Hence the widespread belief that leadership was essentially bad—a belief shared by many among the political elites of democratic countries, especially of those countries, on the Continent of Europe and in Latin America, where the population suffered particularly from the excesses of rulers.[26]

Although Blondel acknowledges the progressive development away from such fearful scepticism, it has at the same time been a slow release from past anxieties. As a consequence, the movement towards dispassionate analysis has not only been guarded in tone, it has been conditioned by the need to combine empirical analysis with a strong normative basis.

The reflexive inhibitions that have characteristically surrounded the theme of political leadership have also had to contend with the constraints imposed by the emergence of disciplinary boundaries and the analytical biases that accompany them. Over the second half of the twentieth century, systematic forms of social inquiry developed along different lines of subject identification and methodological approach. In the resultant differentiation and separation of disciplinary rationales, political science formed a set of agendas with a strong orientation towards rigorous empirical investigation, quantifiable evidence, testable hypotheses, acquired generalizations, and cumulative knowledge bases. The phenomena of leaders and leadership did not readily conform to the preferred paradigm of positivist and structural explanation.[27] In fact, the subject area was widely thought to be at variance with the discipline's prevailing ethos. Leaders were considered to be too variable; leadership was regarded as excessively concerned with the lure of agency over structure; its study was necessarily interpretive, variable, and unreliable in nature; and its corollary of followers smacked of properties that could not be construed as strictly rational. As a consequence, 'the mainstream of the political science profession has remained sceptical about the concept of leadership and has retained a lingering antipathy to addressing the phenomenon of leadership'.[28]

These inhibitory factors have eased over recent years with a renewal of interest in the role and agency of leadership especially within transformed socio-economic

---

[26] Jean Blondel, *Comparative Government: An Introduction* (Hemel Hempstead: Prentice Hall/ Harvester Wheatsheaf, 1995), p. 301.

[27] For a succinct summary of the way that political science has in the past marginalized the study of leadership, see Gillian Peele, 'Leadership and Politics: A Case for a Closer Relationship?', *Leadership*, 1 (2) June 2005: 187–204. See also Glenn D. Paige, *The Scientific Study of Political Leadership* (New York, NY: Free Press, 1977), chs. 1, 2.

[28] Peele, 'Leadership and Politics: A Case for a Closer Relationship?', p. 190.

structures operating in conjunction with complex matrices of contemporary forms of governance. Nevertheless, the conditioning effects of the old landscapes are still in evidence. As a consequence, the situation is now one in which leadership occupies very variable positions that range from intense salience to marginal significance; from high exposure to low public presence; from a sharply defined individual phenomenon to an opaque and indeterminate theme; and from its accepted status as a systemic requirement to an altogether darker reputation as an agency of defective governance and as an object of disputed legitimacy. Unsurprisingly, the examination of political leadership has been one of extraordinary dissipation. It generates not only a profusion of different signals and approaches, but a veritable blizzard of discrete cases and items. The subject has its own grand disputes but it is also known to spill over into many debates more normally located within other areas and disciplines. While leadership has its more prosaic properties in the shape of procedures, rules, traditions, conventions, and routines, it is primarily known for its dramas and narratives, as well as for its dilemmas and ethical disputes.

It would not be unfair to conclude that the subject of political leadership has suffered from its very own abiding properties—or more accurately from those with which it has come to be most closely associated. These can be reduced to such succinct terms as power, control, authority, action, movement, decision, change, responsiveness, expectation, and culpability. Leadership implies mobilization and synergy, even volatility and flux. Almost inevitably, the study of leadership has reflected the immediate and transient character of the way it is normally observed as an everyday occurrence. Disproportionate attention upon leaders and leaderships has led to a corresponding lack of focus upon what leaders in general do and what leadership is, or might be. The result is a bewildering dissonance in which the subject becomes fractured into a multiplicity of concentrated sub-items—very often with little sense of the possible connection that they may have to one another. As the observer becomes increasingly disorientated, so the nature of the subject field, its main themes and boundaries, together with its signature questions is inclined to be overlooked in the general desire to hold on to selected particulars.

APPROACHES TO POLITICAL LEADERSHIP

The study of political leadership remains something of a paradox. At first sight, the subject seems to possess a self-evident focal point of analytical inquiry. The very notion of leadership evokes properties of clarity, settlement, and order. The subject area is usually distinguished by its inherently singular nature and by the capacity of its practitioners to evoke themes of organizational solidarity, political cohesion, and collective identity. In addition to its universally acknowledged value as a functional requirement of governance and its developed role as a representative and symbolic device, the value of leadership is intuitively related to the negative features that are generally ascribed to its absence. By reputation, effective leadership does not just resolve political issues and channel political energies into purposive action, it establishes or at least reaffirms a framework of agreed status, authority, and legitimacy. Political leadership, therefore, seems to lend itself to an almost natural form of symmetry which combines a clear rationale with a defined centre of power and a signature profile of reductionist order.

On closer inspection, however, the subject of political leadership is far more complex and imprecise than its logic might infer. Instead of orderly hierarchies of indisputable leadership authority, there are contested and mutable frameworks of position in which leadership resources can be both elusive and volatile. In place of fixed and final conceptions of leadership, the predominant conclusion is one that is replete with caveats, qualifications, exceptions, and nuances. Political leadership is a subject so conditioned by a profusion of contingency-based and contextual factors that it is widely seen to be an inherently multidimensional phenomenon. Far from being a simplifying construction of social organization, leadership can present itself as an extraordinarily elusive, and even inaccessible, set of imprecise dynamics. As a consequence, a disjunction exists between the commonplace prominence of individual leaders and the far more opaque properties associated with the general field of leadership. Instead of affording easy access to analysis, the subject is usually characterized as one that generates more questions than answers. In short, the biodiversity of leaders is more than matched by the points of inquiry prompted by the diffuse nature of the research area.

Leaders, and the issue of leadership, propagate a series of often highly fractured agendas that revolve around a proliferating array of issues. At one level, the questions posed can be apparently straightforward, relating to where leaders come from, who they are, and how they succeeded in securing their positions. In another guise, even these questions possess deeper dimensions. For example, the issue of who leaders are and where they come from opens up such areas as the personal, psychological, and social origins of leadership. It also leads to speculation over the extent to which leaders are born, or whether leadership can be acquired and learnt as a transferable skill. The process of elevation to a leadership position also raises the issue of how leadership decline can be defined and explained.

Inquiries of this kind will sooner or later unearth even more problematic areas of analysis that revolve around such areas as why leaders take up the task of leadership and why followers agree to follow. The reasons why individuals aspire to leadership positions and undertake the responsibilities that accompany them will in many respects to be connected to the impulse amongst many others to afford such an influential position to leaders. It may even be said that the status and authority of leaders are closely correlated to a common susceptibility towards authority in the form of a collective impulse on the part of ordinary citizens towards a state of 'followership'. In this sense, leaders can be seen as merely adjuncts to a general inclination to social conformism around a central figure of unified expression. In another sense, the way that leaders exert leadership over others can be seen to be a far more subtle mix of incentives involving layers of joint enterprise spanning tradition, custom, persuasion, duty, conditioning, identification, manipulation, mobilization, and even coercion.

These more contingent forms of behaviour bear witness to the relational nature of leadership in both conceptual and practical terms. In other words, the position of leaders and the exertion of leadership are inherently related to one another in respect to their meaning and operation.[29] The relational aspect is also evident in the interaction between leaders and notions of leadership on the one hand, and the different contexts and situations within which leadership activity is conducted on the other. How leadership is done is a highly variable and contingency-based method that is deeply rooted in the profusion of variables that are inevitably attached to its exercise. Attempts to impose some explanatory order upon the diversity of leadership situations have prompted the usage of selected criteria by which certain relational aspects of different leaderships can be assessed against some ascribed common standard. In this way, some behavioural, stylistic, and operational categories can be employed to distinguish separate sets of contextual dynamics within different leaderships. One commonly used frame of reference, for example, is based upon the concept of 'fit'—i.e. the extent to which a leadership can be considered to possess the optimum fit in respect to the requirements of the context within which that leadership has to operate. Using this kind of device does permit leaders to be judged in a way that touches directly upon the quality of their connection to the wider aspects of their political circumstances.

The study of leaders in relation to various roles and positional types is not limited to the dimension of leadership activity. It can be extended to the field of ethics. Leaders are studied and assessed in terms of the principles they adhere to, both in the roles they adopt and in the outcome of their decisions. This theme often serves to deepen even further the problematic properties that inhabit the subject of leadership operation in relation to differences in contexts. When the context is widened out to include references either to indigenous conventions and models of leadership, or to external leadership norms and standards, the effect is to magnify the number and complexity of the analytical categories surrounding the general issue of political leadership.

The subject of leadership does not merely offer a potent access point into the relationship between power and ethics, it imposes a demanding agenda of inquiry into the area. It generates a host of questions into the ethical implications of strong leadership but also into the penalties of weak leadership. It raises difficult issues over the extent to which leaders are supposed to be pragmatic or principled in their behaviour—and over the circumstances that should define when there is a need for one characteristic or another to prevail. If leadership requires principles, then the question shifts to which principles are pertinent in such a situation. It may be necessary to go on and to formulate the very simple but awkward question of whether a bad person can be a good leader and vice versa. While some will argue that the personal and the political occupy different ethical realms, others will disagree and see a direct and necessary connection between the two. For example, in a well-known and widely used text on leadership, it is established at the outset that a distinction should be made between coercion and leadership.

---

[29] For example, see Ronald Heifetz, *Leadership Without Easy Answers* (Cambridge, MA: Belknap, 1994); Keith Grint, *The Arts of Leadership* (Oxford: Oxford University Press, 2000); Robert K. Greenleaf, *A Journey into the Nature of Legitimate Power and Greatness* (Mahwah, NJ: Paulist Press, 2002); Daniel Goleman, Richard E. Boyatzis, and Annie McKee, *The New Leaders: Transforming the Art of Leadership* (London: Time Warner, 2003); Roger Gill, *Theory and Practice of Leadership* (London: Sage, 2006); Barbara Kellerman, *Followership: How Followers are Creating Change and Changing Leaders* (Boston, MA: Harvard Business School Press, 2008).

Coercion is described as the use of force to achieve change through manipulation, threats, punishment, and 'negative reward schedules'. As a consequence, 'coercive people will not be used as models of what ideal leadership is about'.[30] The reason is one of simple ethics:

> Our definition suggests that leadership is reserved for those individuals who influence a group of individuals toward a common goal. Leaders who use coercion are interested in their own goals and seldom are interested in the wants and needs of subordinates. Using coercion runs counter to working with followers to achieve a common goal.[31]

This may be a commendable outlook and one that has a distant resonance with medieval notions of good kingship. Nevertheless, no matter how laudable such a position may be, it neither diminishes the complex cross-currents that pervade the relationship between leadership and ethics, nor clarifies the ethical standards by which leaders are to be judged in terms of their leadership techniques, performance, and objectives.

The challenges associated with the study of leaders and leadership are made more severe by the difficulty of establishing any settled methods on how the subject field should be approached. For example, enormous potential for confusion always lies in the connection between the two principal elements of leaders and leadership. These two components of the subject constitute a duality of sorts but it is one in which neither element is assigned any clear sense of logical or analytical priority. As a result, leadership studies are marked by a variety of departure points that are governed by what the nature of the subject is considered to be, and by what is thought to be the most appropriate way of acquiring an understanding of it. On the whole, most of these approaches have an affinity with one or other of two analytical strategies.

One approaches the subject from the point of view of leadership as a set of generic characteristics from which it is subsequently possible to examine and to assess a succession of specific leaders. In contrast to this deductive strategy, an inductive approach is designed to gather empirical evidence from a host of particular sources and to move cautiously towards some form of limited generalizations on the subject of leadership. While this *modus operandi* looks to expand upon the evidence of individual leaders in order to enlarge the explanatory orbit, the former is more reductionist in spirit in that it is geared to move from the general to the particular in its quest for a more reliable guide to the subject. In reality, each strategy borrows something from the other. Nevertheless, the distinction does exist and it is not only relevant to leadership analysis but can be far-reaching in its effects.

Probably the most damaging—yet ostensibly the least conspicuous—effect of this duality of approaches is the way that they tend to interact with one another and create in the process a form of circular logic. Thus, 'leadership' comes to be defined in terms of the activities of 'leaders', while at the same time 'leaders' come to be defined by reference to the apparent abstraction of 'leadership'. In the same

---

[30] Peter Northouse, *Leadership: Theory and Practice* (Thousand Oaks, CA: Sage, 1997), p. 7.

[31] Northouse, *Leadership: Theory and Practice*, p. 7. The same condition is laid down in another seminal text: 'Coercive strategies need not detain us here, since we exclude coercion from the definition of leadership.' Burns, *Leadership*, p. 417.

way that it is practically impossible to disentangle a dance from a dancer in strict logical terms, so it is that leaders and leadership seem similarly locked within a tautology of their own dance. The relationship between leaders and leadership is often couched as something approximating to a virtuous circle. Be that as it may, it is important to note that the relationship can also be compared to a vicious circle in the way that it can wrap premises and conclusions into a tight analytical bind.

A much-used device by which to reduce the complexities of the subject area and to achieve at least a partial escape from its many traps has been to project the theme of leaders and leadership through the lens of a particular analytical discipline. By adopting the orderly approach of an established tradition of inquiry, it is possible to reduce, and arguably even to resolve, many of the disputes that surround the field. This is because a particular discipline is likely to have its own conception of what it is that requires explanation and how such an understanding is to be secured. Clarity of objective and methodology is acquired by confining the subject into pre-set and discipline-centred parameters. By the same token, the various constituents and themes associated with the subject allow for a wide circle of subscribers from different schools of inquiry. In fact, the area of leaders and leadership often proves to be something of a stimulant to an array of different disciplines each of which sees the subject as exemplifying a core strand of its own analytical agenda. Paradoxically, while the nature of the subject area may infer a singularity of focus and agency, its compulsive attractions as an object of inquiry have resulted in a confusing plurality of iterations which allows the nominally centripetal logic of leadership to become suffused with a host of centrifugal lines of inquiry.

For example, in the view of many historians, leaders have offered not only a way of structuring the passage of time and of shaping the accounts of developing social orders but also of illustrating the continuities of historical tradition. While it would be a distortion to claim that historical analysis is always closely aligned with a leader-centred view of events and developments, there exists a strong historical inclination to delineate periods and epochs by reference to leaders. Just as leaderships are commonly explained in respect to historically conditioned contexts, so they also come to signify and even to embody such contexts. This dynamic is particularly prevalent within the genre of individual histories that come in the form of biography and autobiography.[32]

A psychologist on the other hand would have quite a different disciplinary predisposition towards the study of leadership. Within this perspective, the study of leaders and leadership tends to give emphasis to the mental processes and personal behaviour patterns of those individuals who either inhabit leadership positions or who are connected to them in some way. Very often this perspective settles upon agendas that give analytical priority to the origins and effects of a leader's personality. This can embrace investigations into its conscious and unconscious dimensions as well as how these can relate not just to past and current experiences but also to the way that a leader adjusts to the demands of the

---

[32] See the section in Chapter 3 on the relationship between the genre of biography and the study of political leadership.

position. Other strategies of psychological inquiry focus more on the perceptual and cognitive processes of leaders, or on the physiological and neurological aspects of individual behaviour, or on the dynamics of social interaction between leaders and other co-participants in a polity.[33] While such an approach can yield valuable insights into the sources and operation of leadership, it can also lead to a reconfiguration of the subject area itself. It does so by the way that the discipline's foundational premises as well as its explanatory and methodological priorities can skew the study of political leadership towards a distinctive set of agendas compared to those of other approaches. This inherent bias was captured by the rueful observation of Nevil Johnson in a review of an edited work on ageing and political leadership: 'It becomes clear that most contributors are less concerned with the political actions and achievements of their subjects than with claiming to prove with the aid of limited biographical data the relevance or reliability of propositions drawn from experimental psychology.'[34]

This distinction between history and psychology is by no means the only source of fragmentation in the study of leadership. An organization theorist, for example, would interpret the issue of leadership from quite a different standpoint. Here the analytical emphasis would be weighted towards examining how successful a leader needs to be in order (i) to maintain or improve the level of integration within a system; (ii) to regulate the core functions of an organization; (iii) to facilitate effective decision-making; and (iv) to provide strategic guidance in response to adaptation challenges. Again, such a perspective would be at variance from the analytical priorities of other disciplines. A sociobiologist would approach the social and individual traits of leaders as a conspicuous example of the way that genetic patterns of behaviour can become socially embedded through the selective process of evolutionary development. Within such a framework of understanding, the social role and status of leadership are conceived as a consequence of long-term human evolution and are therefore a subject area that is susceptible to generalized study across different cultures. A sociologist on the other hand would be likely to view the phenomenon of leaders and leadership as part of a wider context relating to social stratification and class formation in general, and to the status and influence of elites within social and cultural hierarchies in particular. Even in the hybrid field of political sociology, the subject of leadership is normally marked by its conspicuous absence. For example, in one highly authoritative work on political sociology running to 838 pages, there were no index references to 'leader' or 'leaders' and only one reference to 'leadership'.[35]

From even this brief review of a selection of approaches, it is clear that there are as many variations in structuring the study of leadership as there are disciplines and sub-disciplines in the humanities and social sciences. The fissiparous tendencies of both the subject area itself and the disorder of analytical strategies

---

[33] See Chapters 3–5.

[34] Nevil Johnson, review of Angus McIntyre (ed.), *Aging and Political Leadership* (Sydney: Oxford University Press, 1988), *International Affairs*, 66(1) January 1990: 155–6.

[35] Thomas Janoski, Robert R. Alford, Alexander M. Hicks, and Mildred A. Schwartz (eds.), *The Handbook of Political Sociology: States, Civil Societies, and Globalization* (Cambridge: Cambridge University Press, 2005).

attracted to it constitute a key organizing element of a commonly observed bipolarity in the field of leadership studies. At one end is the material reality of individual leaders whose visceral properties possess an immediate appeal to a particular genus of understandings that are usually related to the specifics of discrete figures. At the other end is the enduring presumption of leadership's susceptibility to extensions of an ever widening range of analytical frameworks whose primary rationale is often only marginally related to the political sphere. As a consequence, the subject area tends to migrate, or be colonized, into a strain of different generic perspectives in which leaders and leadership more often than not assume the status of derivatives or corollaries of wider systems of social, psychological, or organizational explanation. These combinations of multiple specifics can offer an array of separate insights but they can also amount to an amorphous remit set within a disaggregative logic that is only partially effective in offering a coherent perspective of the subject.

The contention is that the study of what is a compulsive and demanding, yet also elusive and mercurial, subject has been increasingly hollowed out by the joint preponderance of the biographical genre on the one hand and the usage of leadership as a sub-theme within broader complexes of social inquiry on the other. The cumulative effect—albeit inadvertent and unconscious—is one in which leaders and leadership become increasingly presented as incidental parts of a disaggregated array of separated viewpoints. All too frequently this treatment of leadership overlooks both the intrinsic political substance of the role and its wider significance in respect to governing power and political conflict.

It is true that the general phenomenon of leadership continues to generate a vast literature that now requires the navigational assistance of extensive reference guides and heavyweight compilations of selected source materials. However, most of these handbooks are still distinguished by their lack of engagement with the theme of political leadership. In *The Sage Handbook of Leadership*,[36] for example—a text of 38 chapters covering 531 pages—only one entry specifically covers the field of political leadership. The authors underline their outsider credentials: 'The leadership literature has tended to be dominated by studies from the business and organizational fields, with managers as the key role examined in theory and empirical research ... Few books or articles on leadership analyse political leadership at all.'[37] Even though the handbook-companion format has very recently shown signs of being opened up to the area of political leadership, its overall design does not break with the anthologizing logic of the genre.[38] This is because the purpose of the enterprise is not to provide an antidote to the subject's segmentation so much as to act as a positional hub for its multiple contents and plural foci of analysis.

---

[36] Alan Bryman, David L. Collinson, Keith Grint, Brad Jackson, and Mary Uhl-Bien (eds.), *The Sage Handbook of Leadership* (London: Sage, 2011).

[37] Jean Hartley and John Benington, 'Political Leadership', in Bryman *et al.* (eds.), *The Sage Handbook of Leadership*, p. 203.

[38] For example, see Joseph Masciulli, Mikhail A. Molchanov, W. Andy Knight, and W. Andy Knight (eds.), *The Ashgate Research Companion to Political Leadership* (Farnham: Ashgate, 2009).

PUTTING POLITICAL LEADERSHIP BACK TOGETHER

This present study proceeds on the grounded premise that the dynamic of diffusion can and should be corrected by a strategic readjustment that focuses explicitly upon the field of political leadership in its own right rather than an exclusive engagement with either individual leadership practitioners or derivative sub-themes from different disciplines. The guiding objective is to focus upon political leadership as an authentic field of inquiry in its own right. In doing so, it will reduce the negative effects that accompany the current trend towards bifurcation. By reversing the normal pattern of diffusion, the project deliberately sets out to focus on leadership's own indigenous political components and dimensions and, thereby, to reveal its wider significance in respect to the sourcing, securing, and sustaining of political power. Accordingly, the emphasis is on leaders firmly embedded in their political contexts and unequivocally connected to high-level issues of political location and status; political leverage and legitimacy; and political functions and action.

In essence, the project's design is governed by precisely the relational ethos that is almost invariably cited as a cardinal feature of leadership practice. In this case, the relational approach is deployed back to the task of analysing leadership itself. As such, the rationale is consciously geared to facilitating a coherent exposition on political leadership that is consistently centred upon those core elements and themes that are integral to the subject—e.g. the interaction between different leaders and notions of leadership; the dynamics of variable situations within which leadership activity is conducted; and the factors shaping the conduct of leadership in highly mutable and contingency-based contexts.

The main analytical thrust will be to engage with the largely ignored middle ground that lies between the two standard approaches to leadership studies. It is possible to claim that the intermediate area between these two positions has rightfully been marginalized in terms of analytical attention and significance. However, it is the contention of this study that such a position would constitute a premature and largely misplaced conclusion. Far from settling for an allegedly impoverished zone of analytical potential, the inquiry proceeds upon the proposition that it is precisely this intermediate area which offers extensive scope for improving our grasp of what is a complex field. Moreover, it is claimed that this area of engagement offers not only a viable medium of inquiry but arguably the most productive means by which to examine the phenomenon.

By focusing upon this middle ground, the study opens up tracts of empirical, conceptual, and interpretive space within which it is possible to identify and track the multiple cross-currents of activities, contexts, and contingencies that characterize leadership's own authentic repertoire of dynamics. This is not to deny the value and traction of the two predominant perspectives. On the contrary, this study draws extensively on the materials and insights of both forms of inquiry. Nonetheless, the primary objective of the approach adopted by this study is to be strategically selective in the use of materials considered to be directly pertinent to the central focus of the subject. In effect, the objective is to advance the thematic coherence of a field that almost invariably subsides into a condition of deep segmentation—facilitating an ever expanding space for both an immense bio-diversity of leader-centred biographies and a burgeoning literature on leadership presented as a disaggregated set of analytical sub-genres in which it is taken as read that compilations and anthologies constitute the primary strategy of elucidation.[39]

By reoccupying the notional 'empty quarter' between the two conventional elements of the leadership studies duality, it is possible to exploit the location's considerable potential for creating productive inroads into the interior of the subject. In doing so, the study sets out to acquire an assimilative perspective that will cultivate a measure of containment and coherence in a subject noted more for its congested specialisms than for any real sense of clarity and understanding. In these circumstances, the objective is not that of simply resisting the customary flow of diffusion in the area but more of seeking to confine it to some semblance of order within a remit that is centred upon the field of political leadership in its own right rather than a collection of derivative sub-themes from different disciplines. The purpose of this study therefore is one of reducing the negative effects of the disaggregative processes that normally characterize the subject. The guiding object-ive is one of providing something akin to a map which can act as a guide both to the different elements of the subject and to their relationships to one another. The study aims not only to acquaint the interested observer with the foundational properties of the subject along with the major questions and disputes raised by it, but also to seek to explain the significance of new developments and recent research to the overall theme and changing terrain of leadership within a political setting.

As a consequence, a signature aspect of the exploration will be to ensure that the *political* character of the subject is kept securely in the foreground. The analysis of leadership is drawn increasingly away from its explicitly political role within the broader reaches of governance and society. What has become a sprawling expanse of multidisciplinary studies into numerous sub-categories and alleged derivatives of leadership has had the effect in many ways of inadvertently diminishing the field's political components and, thereby, its wider significance in respect to governing power and political conflict. This current excursion into the field is therefore designed to maintain a clear emphasis upon leaders firmly embedded in their political contexts and viscerally connected to high-level issues of political location and status, political power and legitimacy, and political functions and action. This is not to say that research findings or interpretive insights drawn from other disciplines will be excluded. But it is to underline that every attempt will be made to ensure that such resources remain directly pertinent to the theme of leadership within established or emergent polities—as well as activities and organizations engaged in relationships between such entities.

THE AGENDA

Part I (Chapters 2–5) focuses on the main elements and defining characteristics of the subject field. It examines how leaders acquire their positions; how they work to

---

[39] For example, see Barbara Kellerman (ed.), *Political Leadership: A Source Book* (Pittsburgh, PA: University of Pittsburgh Press, 1986); Masciulli *et al.* (eds.), *The Ashgate Research Companion to Political Leadership*; Bryman *et al.* (eds.), *The Sage Handbook of Leadership*; David S. Bell (ed.), *Political Leadership*, Sage Library of Political Science (London: Sage, 2011).

sustain their access to the resources of leadership; and how they invariably come to the point where they have to relinquish their power and authority in what can be seen as akin to a generic life cycle. This section surveys the problems and challenges entailed in fulfilling the requirements of political leadership, as well as in coming to terms with the nature of the contextual circumstances which condition the operational and behavioural dimensions of such a role. In locating the primary categories and dynamics of leadership it will be possible not only to outline the contingent aspects of the subject but also to establish the relational features of its interior and exterior logics. The main emphasis of this section will be that of specifying some of the key factors in the leadership phenomenon—ranging from the operational and conditional aspects of exercising leadership to the causes and composition of leaders' inner drives, outward styles, and political objectives; and from the close interdependency between leaders and non-leaders to the opportunities and limitations of leadership politics. This initial scoping of the subject field will offer a means by which to arrive at an improved sense of its thematic richness while at the same time conveying an informed awareness of its complex relationships, its problematic properties, and its contested criteria for assessment and evaluation.

Part II (Chapters 6–8) goes on to examine the variations and trends in the matrix of leadership politics. It directs attention to modes of leadership appeal and techniques of political communication; to emergent forms of representational claims and outreach obligations; and to shifts in leadership-related political alignments and narratives. The aim of these chapters is to draw out the nature and implications of contemporary leadership dynamics and especially the way that leaders and their conceptions of leadership adjust to changing conditions and to altered points of social and cultural reference. By being attentive to the influence of contextual landscapes—and in particular to the different leadership sectors, paradigms, and spheres of activity as well as to the changing profiles of leadership sources and recruitment—this section will work to convey both the multidimensional and synergistic character of the subject area.

Part III (Chapters 9 and 10) engages with a dimension of leadership which at one and the same time gives full expression to its potential as an organizing device but also coveys the expansive nature of its problematic and contingent properties. In a context-centred field of inquiry, the international sphere offers serious challenges related to the applicability—or otherwise—of those leadership modes, resources, norms, and explanations normally associated with state and sub-state levels of governance to the transnational and global categories of political activity. The appeal and responsibilities attached to those policy areas connected to national security and foreign policy have long offered political leaders a defining rationale for their role and for the symbolic assets, political traction, and prerogative powers that customarily go with it. And yet, the international sphere also constitutes a context that has been described as functionally anarchic as it has severe deficiencies in political settlement, jurisdictional authority, and operational capability. Political leadership in these surroundings attracts a characteristic ambivalence in that it is routinely cited as being both a key reason for the underdevelopment of an international order capable of addressing global issues, and yet also identified as the main solution to the specified disorders at regional and international levels.

It is for these reasons that the international medium can throw additional light upon the inherent and developmental remits of political leadership. In examining the relationship between the concept and practice of leadership and this broader context of engagement, it will be possible to acquire a clearer understanding of the adaptive reach and capacity of leadership and the extent to which new meanings, sources, and iterations of leadership can be—and are being—assimilated into notions of global governance and into innovative formulations of international leadership. In the same way that the latter can open up the complex demands and contingencies of the former, so the international can disclose the challenges of an increasingly interdependent and interconnected world to the capabilities and resources of leadership adaptation.

The final section is divided into two reflective parts. Chapter 11 examines the changing landscapes of contemporary leadership activity. It surveys the form and significance of some of the more recent developments that influence the formation of leadership positions, roles, and responsibilities within increasingly changeable matrices of political engagement. In focusing upon certain key aspects of leadership construction, it is possible not only to trace the emergence of noteworthy developments in the subject field, but also to discern the adaptive properties, the altered rationales, and the innovative expressions of leadership provision set against more complex and fluid hinterlands.

Chapter 12 reviews the aggregate components, themes, and issues emerging from the previous sets of analysis. It offers ways of coming to terms with a subject field which is notorious for the number and diversity of its points of access, lines of interpretation, and migrations of usage. By providing an informed retrospective of the main features of leadership operations and constructions—as well as insights into the sustained ecology of leadership's problematic properties, and explorations into the possible utility and trajectories of leadership deployment— this section will allow for a more integrated grasp of the place, the status, and the potential of political leadership set within contemporary conditions. The modest, yet ambitious, aim is to arrive at an approach to the subject that is grounded within its own indigenous properties and circumstances, and in doing so, to secure a surer understanding not just of what kind of phenomenon it is but what makes it such a demanding, contested, and urgent prospectus of inquiry.

Part I

Core Elements and Relations

2

Doing leadership: Types, styles, and contingency

'What makes statesmen, like drivers of cars, successful is that they do not think in general terms—that is, they do not primarily ask themselves in what respect a given situation is like or unlike other situations in the long course of human history... Their merit is that they grasp the unique combination of characteristics that constitute this particular situation—this and no other. What they are said to be able to do is to understand the character of a particular movement, of a particular individual, of a unique state of affairs, of a unique atmosphere, of some particular combination of economic, political, personal factors; and we do not readily suppose that this capacity can literally be taught... [It entails] an acute sense of what fits with what, what springs from what, what leads to what; how things seem to vary to different observers, what the effect of such experience upon them may be; what the result is likely to be in a concrete situation of the interplay of human beings and impersonal forces—geographical or biological or psychological or whatever they may be.'

Isaiah Berlin[1]

'Great leaders are both born and bred. They need to be brave and endowed with extraordinary political instincts, but they also have to be armed with a range of skills if they want to carry people with them. In order to come to power, they need to be blessed with fortune and to know how to take advantage of her. But, if they are to stay in power, they have to have steel in their soul.'

Jonathan Powell[2]

PREAMBLE

Activity lies at the heart of all notions of leadership. The overriding implication of leadership is one of conscious agency in which decisive movement of one sort or another becomes attributable to an identifiable centre of authoritative influence.

---

[1] Isaiah Berlin, 'Political Judgement', *New York Review of Books*, 3 October 1996.
[2] Jonathan Powell, *The New Machiavelli: How to Wield Power in the Modern World* (London: Vintage, 2011), p. 56.

Leaders are inherently associated with the theme of causality. As key participants, they are expected to take action and as a result to have a disproportionate effect upon their surroundings. In any political system, leaders are assigned roles and perform functions that are invariably related to such vigorous terms as initiative, direction, decision, coordination, intervention, advocacy, strategy, oversight, coherence, control, and executive action. When leadership is construed in this light, there appears to be a direct and necessary linkage between position and performance. Given that a leader is expected to act as a catalyst precipitating a set of intended measures, then it follows that such an individual has the capacity and the associated responsibility to fulfil the role.

In essence, leadership infers both the occupancy of a position and the possession of power by which to substantiate it. In this way, leadership can often appear as a closed system of political behaviour and explanation in which questions have necessarily been resolved in favour of a clear rationale of relationships. The air of finality is further enhanced by the conventional depiction of leadership as a vertically driven top-down organization aligned along a simple axis of communication and authority. The ostensible finality of such a one-dimensional command structure allows much of leadership behaviour to be couched not in the complex terms of *how* decisions are made, but according to the more prosaic properties of simply *what* decisions have been taken.

As we have already noted, such an attractive simplicity is a chimera both in the normal exercise of political leadership and in any serious study of the phenomenon. Leadership is an inherently contested, contextual, and contingent variable dependent upon a multiplicity of factors. Therein lies its challenge to analysis. Nevertheless, despite the underlying complexity of the subject area, leadership does have a compelling and enduring overlay of elegance that is drawn from its abiding association with a singular entity that conveys the idea of leadership within any structure. In many ways, leadership has a binary quality to it in which the multiple grounding of a leadership situation coexists with the singular rationale of a leadership identity. In other words, leadership comprises a complex set of dynamics, while at the same time supporting the idea of a leader that is in part a summation of those dynamics but also an antidote to them in the form of a countervailing dimension of political focus.

A leader therefore is at a junction point between an individual identity that is a political resource in its own right and a set of surrounding factors that impinge upon and condition the political usage and value of the personal remit. While a leader will have a presumptive claim to leadership authority based upon an initial power flow, or on a more formal transfer of governing status, such a position will be conditioned and dependent upon a leader's awareness of the synergies that are not only possible but necessary between the two domains. In other words, for any individual to substantiate and to retain a claim to leadership, it is necessary for them to understand the interplay between their own resources and those that lie outside their immediate sphere. In effect, it is only by engaging effectively with the wider political environment that a leadership can maximize the influence of its own individual marque within government and advance the causes which give that leadership its distinguishing purpose. The key issue of what it is that leaders do therefore is not so much about *what* decisions are made but rather *how* leaders reach a position to make the decisions, and *how* they maintain that position.

Studies on leadership tend to be about specific leadership positions and resources. Their general orientation is usually one of laudatory celebration. Moreover, they are generally instructive in tone and message. The great bulk of such studies are drawn from individual cases that are analysed for insights into the experience of leadership and into how the role can be successfully performed. Whether they are CEOs, generals, or archbishops, the theme is generally one of accounting for their rise to prominence and of conveying their leadership experiences and techniques. Self-help prescriptions concerning the ways of leadership follow on either implicitly or explicitly for those seeking bespoke advice on emulation.[3] While these individual case studies can be highly informative and can even serve the interests of wider studies, they are nevertheless heavily case-centred and tend to have an idiosyncratic character based upon the particular context of the leadership in question.

MACHIAVELLI AND THE TECHNIQUES OF PRINCELY POWER

More systematic analyses of leadership try to combine individual studies with a more generalized overview of the subject so that each element can serve to inform the other. The celebrated pioneer of this approach and the person who set the pattern for numerous subsequent studies on leadership is Niccolò Machiavelli. In his world of sixteenth-century Florence, Machiavelli witnessed at first hand the fecklessness and duplicity of individuals, and the fragility of states and the treacherous nature of allies. He identified different types of principality but was mostly interested in that type which constituted the greatest challenge to a prince's statecraft—namely those principalities that were newly established and therefore highly reliant upon a leader's ability to acquire and to sustain an organizing power that would compensate for a lack of tradition and established civic roots.

From his observations of various contemporary leaders, Machiavelli was aware that different leaders had different styles that reflected their individual outlooks and temperaments. But to Machiavelli the most important characteristic which would determine the effectiveness of a prince and the criterion by which he should be judged above all others was his ability to withstand the twists and turns of fortune. The notion of *fortuna* is a central component of *The Prince*. The term conveys the wanton and unreasonable nature of violent and disruptive forces with which leaders necessarily have to engage with both wisdom and adaptive skill in order to maintain their positions and achieve their objectives.[4] Despite its mythical roots, *fortuna* is used by Machiavelli to rationalize the need for a thoroughgoing realism in the practice and study of leadership. Given the volatile nature of *fortuna*, operating within the realm of power politics at both an individual level and in respect to kingdoms and principalities, Machiavelli believed that a

---

[3] See Chapter 6.
[4] Niccolò Machiavelli, *The Prince*, translated and introduction by George Bull (Harmondsworth: Penguin, 1966), ch. 25.

successful leader had to have the personal skills and appropriate motivations to overcome the difficulties of what we would now term circumstances or events. In other words, a prince could not depend upon providence or formality or trust to secure his goals. He had to put his faith in his own instincts for power and in his own ability to respond to the needs of individual situations.

Machiavelli's emphasis upon the leader's central role in maintaining the integrity and stability of the principality has far-reaching implications for the values that were customarily attached to princes and their duties. From various classical, humanist, and Christian sources, a literature on kingship had developed that underlined a set of key principles that had acted as a contemporary moral guide to the processes of leadership. Good kings and princes were expected to epitomize the values of nobility, honesty, and a truthful adherence to the principles of kingship. Apart from their being above reproach, it was considered rightful that they should temper their rule with demonstrations of clemency, mercy, and generosity of spirit. Controversially, Machiavelli was not prepared to give such ethics the priority that they had been afforded by other writers at the time. On the contrary, many of his pronouncements on the correct conduct of princes were prompted by the view that an attachment to such codes of princely honour risked jeopardizing not merely their thrones but the viability of their entire polities (Box 2.1).

Machiavelli did not openly refute the principled prescriptions of kingship, so much as ignore them in his effort to give emphasis to the primary need of princes to secure social order by maintaining the integrity of their claims to leadership positions—if necessary by deception, duplicity, and occasional cruelty. The contemporary significance of Machiavelli's iconoclasm is captured by Quentin Skinner: 'Machiavelli's criticism of classical and contemporary humanism is thus a simple but devastating one. He argues that, if a ruler wishes to reach his highest goals, he will not always find it rational to be moral.'[5] In respect to the Christian position that such an outlook is not only socially wicked but personally foolish from the point of view of the ruler's own soul, Machiavelli makes it clear that he is indifferent to the injunction: 'His silence is eloquent, indeed epoch making; it echoed around Christian Europe, at first eliciting a stunned silence in return, and then a howl of execration that has never finally died away.'[6] So intent was Machiavelli on redefining the required virtues of kingship in the light of the necessities of acquiring and sustaining princely power that he was prepared to diminish the reach of ethical codes and traditions originating outside the explicit realm of leadership imperatives.[7]

Machiavelli's descriptions of, and prescriptions for, the behaviour of princes are founded upon the premise that the generation, maintenance, and distribution of political power are governed by human calculation. Instead of writing about politics as one might wish politics to be in some abstract sense, Machiavelli analysed politics as it was and is—namely through the realism of historical fact

---

[5] Quentin Skinner, *Machiavelli: A Very Short Introduction* (Oxford: Oxford University Press, 1981), p. 42.

[6] Skinner, *Machiavelli: A Very Short Introduction*, p. 42.

[7] Quentin Skinner, *The Foundations of Modern Political Thought: Volume 1, The Renaissance* (Cambridge: Cambridge University Press, 1978), pp. 113–38; Anthony J. Parel, *The Machiavellian Cosmos* (New Haven, CT: Yale University Press, 1992).

Box 2.1 Machiavelli: Observations on the acquisition and maintenance of leadership power

---

'[I]t would be most laudable if a prince possessed all the qualities deemed to be good... But, human nature being what it is, princes cannot possess those qualities, or rather they cannot always exhibit them... [H]e will find that some of the things that appear to be virtues will, if he practises them, ruin him, and some things that appear to be wicked will bring him security and prosperity.'[8]

'A prince... need not necessarily have all the good qualities... but he should certainly appear to have them. I would even go so far as to say that if he has these qualities and always behaves accordingly he will find them ruinous; if he only appears to have them they will render him service.'[9]

'Everyone sees what you appear to be, few experience what you really are... The common people are always impressed by appearances and results.'[10]

'[A] prince should not worry if he incurs reproach for his cruelty so long as he keeps his subjects united and loyal.'[11]

'[A] prince... should learn from the fox and the lion; because the lion is defenceless against traps and a fox is defenceless against wolves. Therefore one must be a fox in order to recognize traps, and a lion to frighten off the wolves. Those who simply act like lions are stupid. So it follows that a prudent ruler cannot, and should not, honour his word when it places him at a disadvantage and when the reasons for which he made his promise no longer exist. If all men were good, this precept would not be good; but because men are wretched creatures who would not keep their word to you, you need not keep your words to them.'[12]

'But, confining myself to particular circumstances, I say that we see that some princes flourish one day and come to grief the next, without appearing to have changed in character or any other way. This I believe arises, first, for the reasons discussed at length earlier on, namely, that those princes who are utterly dependent on fortune come to grief when their fortune changes. I also believe that the one who adapts his policy to the times prospers, and likewise that the one whose policy clashes with the demands of the times does not.'[13]

Source: Niccolò Machiavelli, *The Prince*, translation and introduction by George Bull (Harmondsworth: Penguin 1966).

---

and what we would call human behaviour and psychology. To Machiavelli, politics is a self-contained world with its own system of causes and effects that can be observed and appraised. Politics and power are about a system of human dynamics that is universal and timeless. *The Prince*, therefore, is a treatise on the arts, and artfulness, of government based upon embedded experience. The emphasis is laid not on the propriety or ethics of the techniques used, so much as upon their overall effect to the stability of the state and the security of the population. Results are everything for Machiavelli's prince. It is not that politics is amoral; it is that political power possesses its own morality—especially when the destructive and violent consequences of a naïve and ineffectual prince are considered. In effect, there is a substantive difference between what is morally

---

[8] Machiavelli, *The Prince*, pp. 91–2. [9] Machiavelli, *The Prince*, p. 100.
[10] Machiavelli, *The Prince*, p. 101. [11] Machiavelli, *The Prince*, p. 95.
[12] Machiavelli, *The Prince*, pp. 99–100. [13] Machiavelli, *The Prince*, p. 131.

acceptable in respect to princely conduct and what is more widely applicable in moral terms to the external field of social conduct.

In the field of leadership, Machiavelli's legacy has been highly influential because it made the relationship between the leader and its contextual position central both to the role and obligations of leadership and to the safety and welfare of the social entity in which the leader is located. To Machiavelli, a princely leader could not simply rely upon formal position or moral character or even luck to substantiate his leadership. It needed a particular kind of temperament and method that could maximize the possibility that his competence would reach a level comparable to that of his onerous responsibility as leader. In effect, there needed to be a match between a leader's style and the circumstances of the leadership.

STUDYING LEADERS (I) TRAITS

Today, the influence of Machiavelli is readily discernible in the mainstream approaches to the subject of leadership. This is evident in the volume of work on the identification and assessment of leadership qualities. Almost invariably these studies proceed on the same basis as Machiavelli in that they are designed to answer the question of what it is that makes an individual into an effective leader. The most basic contemporary approach to this inquiry is termed trait analysis. Its rationale is one of examining known leaders with the objective of discovering patterns of common characteristics between them.

In essence, the study of traits begins and ends with leaders. It works backwards from assessments of who leaders are—and what leaders have to be and what they have to do—in order for them to have achieved the positions that they hold. At its heart is an empirical investigation into the observable traits of leaders that will lead to generalized conclusions concerning those elements that are most closely associated with the presence and exercise of leadership. Trait analysis offers a way of accessing a broad range of leadership data and of reducing it to manageable proportions by concentrating upon discrete components, and that allows for the systematic study of multiple leaderships and what it takes to engage in leadership activities. In proceeding upon this lateral course of inquiry, trait analysis often carries with it the assumption that leaders are different from their followers, and that the analytical purpose of the exercise is to locate those factors that distinguish them from the mass.[14]

The most basic form of trait analysis is founded upon factors that are most susceptible to precise measurement. Scanning leaders on the basis of such categories as gender, age, height, weight, race, ethnicity, and religious affiliation can

---

[14] See Ralph M. Stogdill, *Handbook of Leadership. A Survey of Theory and Research* (New York, NY: Free Press, 1974); Bernard M. Bass, *Bass and Stogdill's Handbook of Leadership: Theory, Research and Managerial Applications* (New York, NY: Free Press, 1990); Shelley A. Kirkpatrick and Edwin A. Locke, 'Leadership: Do Traits Matter?', *Academy of Management: Executive*, 5(2) 1991: 48–60. Accessed 27 August 2012 at: <http://sbuweb.tcu.edu/jmathis/Org_Mgmt_Materials/Leadership%20-%20Do%20Traits%20Matgter.pdf>.

yield some interesting results on the broad profile of leader characteristics. For example, surveys show that leaders are normally individuals in good health; that they usually originate from upper socio-economic levels; that most leaders are above or below average height; and that they tend to come from those religious, ethnic, and racial groups which are dominant within their respective areas. The problem with such results is that the characteristics identified are normally too common to provide any real sense of distinction between leaders and ordinary group members.

The answer to such complaints has been both to widen the expanse of the net and to reduce the size of its mesh in the hope of isolating more distinguishing features. These broader-based studies are inevitably oriented towards more complex traits. As a consequence, many characteristics have been cited as being central to, or closely associated with, the incidence of leadership. Trait analyses commonly include the following types of category:

Dominance
Persistence
Drive
Confidence
Intelligence
Responsibility

This is not to say that all the studies identify these same traits or even give those that they do equal weighting. Far from it. In fact, it is very rare for any two trait analyses to emerge with the same set of key leadership characteristics. This has led to attempts to reduce the confusion by the formulation of an overall synthesis of traits in the form of an aggregate collection of the most cited traits. Peter Northouse,[15] for example, cites:

Intelligence
Self-confidence
Determination
Integrity
Sociability

Helpful though such tabulations may be, they suffer from being highly generalized in nature. This can create further problems, firstly in respect to the nature of relationships between different traits and secondly in reference to the exact meanings attached to each set of traits in the context of different leaderships. The trait of intelligence, for example, can arouse disputes over what kind of intelligence is being cited (e.g. social intelligence; technical intelligence; emotional intelligence; cultural intelligence; contextual intelligence[16]) and over the priority that is placed on intelligence in leadership profiles over and above other related traits (e.g. common sense; competence; judgement).

---

[15] Peter Northouse, *Leadership: Theory and Practice* (Thousand Oaks, CA: Sage, 1997), p. 17.

[16] See Daniel Goleman, *Emotional Intelligence: Why It Can Matter More than IQ—10th Anniversary Edition* (New York, NY: Bantam, 2006); Daniel Goleman, *Social Intelligence: The New Science of Human Relationships* (New York, NY: Bantam, 2006); Joseph S. Nye, Jr., *The Powers to Lead* (New York, NY: Oxford University Press 2008), ch. 4.

Box 2.2 John Gardner: Evidence-based leadership attributes

Gardner studied a large number of North American organizations and leaders and came to the conclusion that there were some qualities or attributes that suggested a leader in one situation could lead in another.

These included:

- Physical vitality and stamina
- Intelligence and action-oriented judgement
- Eagerness to accept responsibility
- Task competence
- Understanding of followers and their needs
- Skill in dealing with people
- Need for achievement
- Capacity to motivate people
- Courage and resolution
- Trustworthiness
- Decisiveness
- Self-confidence
- Assertiveness
- Adaptability/flexibility

Source: John Gardner, *On Leadership* (New York, NY: Free Press 1989).

Given the lack of consensus on the precise operational implications of these studies, several analyses have sought to offer greater clarity by once again widening the net and making the mesh even smaller. An example of what such analysis can generate is provided in Box 2.2.

These kinds of trait lists do offer more in the way of detail but it is equally the case that they do so by including categories that are often imprecise and open to question. For example, many of these types of trait are subjectively based in that they are open to interpretation rather than to reliable measurement. In the example given in Box 2.1, it is evident that the list includes various forms of behaviour ranging from particular skills to specific forms of outlook and temperament. It also incorporates aspects of intelligence and character. It may well be the case that these attributes are important to leadership, but in simply citing them as significant such a trait list does not demonstrate the connections between specified attributes and the exercise of leadership.

On closer inspection, it is evident that these types of enumerated characteristics are not merely attributed by observers to leaders—and remain highly contestable as a result of their subjective nature—but are almost invariably depicted as positive virtues or at least neutral categories. Apart from giving an overlay of morally defensible properties, these kinds of trait surveys often appear to dismiss the darker arts of leadership. This may indicate a certain element of ethical screening in what are nominally descriptive exercises but also ones which usually imply a prescriptive code of behaviour. On the other hand, the priority given to positive or neutral attributes may also be more apparent than real. It is possible to conceal the more chilling aspects of leadership in the warm glow of such references as 'skill in dealing with people', 'need for achievement', 'capacity to motivate people', and 'assertiveness'.

There are other reservations and objections against such extensive lists of traits. For example, it can be claimed:

- that they offer patterns of incidental rather than substantive features;
- that because so many traits are specified, the possession of all of them becomes an impossible norm;
- that single traits offer only a segmented and disaggregated perspective of a subject that is inherently organic and relational in character;
- that numerous traits generate inconsistencies and contradictions between them;
- that extensive lists of traits generate exceptions to any implied norm or aggregate rule;
- that because no single list will be comprehensive in its range of traits, it will always be possible for a specific leader to demonstrate the possession of alternative leadership properties;
- that trait analysis tends to privilege exterior phenomena over the formative experiences that give rise to such characteristics;
- that leadership traits infer a steady-state existence for leaders in an occupation that is notorious for its instability and insecurity;
- that leadership decline cannot easily be explained in terms of static traits;
- and that it is possible for many leaders not to possess some of the major nominated traits but nevertheless to remain effective leaders—and vice versa.

A particularly revealing caveat to the significance attached to trait analysis is given by Stephen D. Reicher *et al.* who assert that 'no fixed set of personality traits can assure good leadership because the most desirable traits depend on the nature of the group being led. Leaders can even select the traits they want to project to followers.'[17] Perhaps the most telling complaint in the end is the simple claim that trait analysis is distinguished by an inherent limitation in which a process of proliferation compounds rather than clarifies the subject under examination. Although John P. Frank is describing another aspect of political analysis, his account of it as 'more amenable to description by infinite itemization as by generalization'[18] is remarkably apposite in this respect.

One way of diminishing some of these problems has been to concentrate upon various combinations of leadership traits in order to fine-tune the relationship between different characteristics and different forms of leadership. It is true that such an option can be seen as compromising the main thrust of trait analysis which is based upon the rationale that there is a consistent and universal set of traits that differentiates leaders from other members of a group. According to the aggregate logic of trait analysis there can really be only one field of leaders—not a

---

[17] Stephen D. Reicher, S. Alexander Haslam, and Michael J. Platow, 'The New Psychology of Leadership', *Scientific American Mind*, August/September 2007, p. 24.

[18] John P. Frank, 'Political Questions', in Edmond Cahn (ed.), *Supreme Court and Supreme Law* (Bloomington, IN: Indiana University Press, 1954), p. 36.

set of different leadership sub-fields. Nevertheless, by turning the attention towards how traits relate to different themes and contexts of leadership, it allows for a greater degree of adaptability in the usage of traits as an analytical tool. In essence, it permits traits to be more firmly embedded in a conception of leadership analysis that is more sensitive to the operational realities of leadership in respect both to the variation in styles and to the diversity of situations within which leaders are required to exert themselves.

STUDYING LEADERS (II) STYLES

The usage of style as an instrument in the examination of leadership is partly the result of the limitations of trait analysis. The investigation of leadership styles allows for a broader basis of investigation. But more significantly, it opens up the analysis to what is arguably leadership's most recognizable characteristic—namely the actual behaviour of leaders engaging in the business of leadership. Machiavelli operated on the premise that the most important aspect of leadership is the doing of it. By the same token, the most important explanation of leadership centres upon its actual exercise and the effects that can be achieved by it. Style analysis follows in the same Machiavellian mould. In contrast to the study of single traits, the categorization of leaders by reference to styles is not dependent upon the identification of individual characteristics but rather upon leadership activity and the behaviour of leaders in relation to non-leaders. Of course to some extent an individual's leadership style will be influenced by who that person is in terms of various personal traits. Nevertheless, the study of style remains a distinctive strategy because it operates on the basis, and through the medium, of complex units of analysis that take into account the variability of leadership resources, objectives, and outcomes.

Many types of style have been advanced as being generic in nature. Different aggregates of leadership behaviour have been used to characterize leaders as falling within such designated style categories as 'facilitators', 'drivers', 'integrators', 'strategists', 'thinkers', and 'exemplars'.[19] Although styles are essentially composed of aggregates of multiple strands of behaviour, nominated styles themselves have also tended to multiply as analysts have used varied organizational strategies by which to rationalize different schemas of style. This in turn has led to attempts to make sense of the proliferation of assigned styles within organizations by seeking to isolate the central distinguishing properties of different styles.

In the fields of business and management, the search for these properties has settled in the main upon two signature styles of leadership. On the one hand is leadership activity that can be categorized as being task oriented; on the other hand is behaviour that can be characterized as serving the priority of organizational cohesion. A similar division is made between what is often termed 'directive or authoritarian leadership' and 'participative or democratic leadership'. The

---

[19] For example, see the report on the survey of 400 directors in top UK companies conducted by Michael Knight (partner of head-hunter firm CCG Ward Howell International) and Brenda Bell (industrial psychologist) in Judi Bevan, 'Four profiles of the perfect chairman', *Sunday Telegraph*, 26 October 1997.

former is a style demonstrated by those leaders who tend to take decisions with little consultation with, or concern for, subordinates or followers. The latter is a style oriented towards sharing information and maintaining an inclusive outlook upon the business of leadership. Because both these sets of categories have a close association with one another, they are often combined to form either one continuum of aggregated leadership style, or else two keynote components that can be used to generate graphs and grids of leader styles.

The appeal of the notion of a continuum of leadership styles is reflected in Table 2.1 adapted from Charles Handy's study in *Understanding Organizations*. Here Handy juxtaposes the conclusions of several studies in order to reveal a consistent pattern of leadership styles along a spectrum positioned between 'autocratic' and 'democratic'. The meanings ascribed to the variation of styles

Table 2.1 Spectrum of ascribed leadership styles

AUTOCRATIC ⇐══			══⇒ DEMOCRATIC
Harbison & Myers[1]	'Autocratic'	'Paternalistic'	'Consultative'	'Participative'
Tannenbaum & Schmidt[2]	'Leader control'	'Shared control'	'Shared control'	'Group control'
Vroom & Yetton[3]	'Leader decides'	'Leader consults'	'Leader shares'	'Leader accepts consensus agreement'
Blake & Mouton[4]	'Produce or perish'/ 'Dictatorial'	'Status quo'/ 'Middle of the road'	'Country club'/ 'Accommodating'	'Sound'/'Team'
Ohio State Studies[5]	'Task oriented'/ 'Initiating structure'			'People-oriented'/ Consideration'
Hersey & Blanchard 1[6]	'Telling'	'Selling'	'Participating'	'Delegating'
Hersey & Blanchard 2[7]	'Directing'	'Coaching'	'Supporting'	'Delegating'
Bolman & Deal[8]	'Authoritarian'	'Impoverished'	'Socialite'	'Team leader'
Wright[9]	'Directive leadership'	'Concern for task'	'Concern for people'	'Participative leadership'

[1] Frederick Harbison and Charles A. Myers, *Management in the Industrial World: An International Analysis* (New York, NY: McGraw-Hill, 1959).

[2] Robert Tannenbaum and Warren H. Schmidt, 'How to Choose a Leadership Pattern', *Harvard Business Review*, 36(2) 1958: 95–101.

[3] Victor Vroom and Phillip Yetton, *Leadership and Decision-Making* (Pittsburgh, PA: University of Pittsburgh Press, 1973).

[4] Robert R. Blake and Jane Mouton, *The Managerial Grid III: The Key to Leadership Excellence* (Houston, TX: Gulf Publishing, 1985).

[5] Edwin A. Fleishman, *Leadership Climate and Supervisory Behavior* (Columbus, OH: Personnel Research Board, Ohio State University, 1951); Edwin A. Fleishman 'Twenty Years of Consideration and Structure', in Edwin A. Fleishman and James G. Hunt (eds.), *Current Developments in the Study of Leadership* (Carbondale, IL: Southern Illinois University Press, 1973), pp. 1–37.

[6] Paul Hersey and Kenneth H. Blanchard, *The Management of Organizational Behaviour*, 3rd edn. (Upper Saddle River, NJ: Prentice Hall, 1977).

[7] Kenneth H. Blanchard, Patricia Zigarmi, and Drea Zigarmi, *Leadership and the One Minute Manager: Increasing Effectiveness through Situational Leadership* (London: HarperCollins, 1994).

[8] Lee Bolman and Terrence Deal, *Reframing Organizations* (San Francisco, CA: Jossey-Bass, 1991).

[9] Peter L. Wright, *Managerial Leadership* (London: Routledge, 1996), pp. 36–7.

along the continuum are indicated by the cited characteristics specified in the individual studies. This kind of chart offers a clear framework for positioning leaders in accordance with a set range of commonly observed styles.

The advantage of apparent clarity, however, is offset by the disadvantage of an emergent ambiguity. Because the spectrum is largely defined by the polar opposites of autocracy and democracy, it is dependent upon two extreme conditions of leadership—neither of which is regarded as a sustainably viable form of leadership activity. In other words, the notionally 'pure' forms of leadership by which all other leaderships are to be measured and assessed can be claimed to be in fact highly unstable types which are not even functionally operational in the long term. The other problem with this kind of asserted continuum is one of ambiguity. It is not clear whether the intermediate points are clearly definable, or whether they are depictions of a pragmatic and adaptable approach to leadership.

One of the most common ways of reducing the difficulties associated with the spectrum model is to separate the main categories into two coexistent measures. Thus, it is possible to have an axis upon which styles can be allocated a place based upon the extent to which they are seen as being either more or less concerned with the stated tasks and objectives of leadership. In similar fashion, a second axis can be used to locate leaderships in relation to whether they reveal a greater or lesser interest in organizational solidarity, fairness in operational methods, and collective self-esteem. The two measures are used to create various cross-tabulations and graphs that can generate a broader range and more precise definition of styles. Many examples exist of this more calibrated approach to style types.[20]

It will be evident from such an example that this kind of style analysis is most commonly used in relation to business structures whose parameters are more defined than large-scale political entities. It might also be argued that the emphasis laid upon style analysis in economic organizations is geared to the functional objective of eliciting the best style for maximizing the efficiency and profitability of the structure in question. Given the premise that leaders can influence the environment in which both they and their companies operate, style analysis becomes highly significant in attempting to locate those leaders with the most appropriate style to serve the interests of the organization. In the field of business leadership, 'the assumption behind these theories is that employees will work harder—and therefore more effectively—for managers who employ given styles of leadership than they will for managers who employ other styles of leadership'.[21]

And yet notwithstanding the strong association between style analysis and the business sector, the study of styles has been a popular genre in the political field. Once again, such an analytical tool is limited firstly by the relatively small sample size upon which to build a typology, and secondly by the high incidence of complex factors pertaining to a political environment. Nevertheless, several

---

[20] See Robert R. Blake and Jane S. Mouton, *The New Managerial Grid* (Houston, TX: Gulf Publishing, 1978); Robert R. Blake and Anne A. McCanse, *Leadership Dilemmas: Grid Solutions* (Houston, TX: Gulf Publishing, 1991); P. Wright, *Managerial Leadership* (London: Routledge, 1996); Paul Hersey, Kenneth H. Blanchard, and Dewey E. Johnson, *Management of Organizational Behavior: Leading Human Resources*, 8th edn. (Upper Saddle River, NJ: Prentice Hall, 2001), chs. 7, 8.

[21] Charles Handy, *Understanding Organizations*, 4th edn. (New York, NY: Oxford University Press), p. 100.

studies have tried to devise a typology of political styles by which individual leaders can be categorized in relation to one another by virtue of their location on a grid of differentiated leadership styles. Some of them deal with broadly conceived styles that relate to what is considered to be an individual's characteristic signature in social, organizational, cognitive, and emotional categories of behaviour. Others classify leaders in terms of an overall or aggregate portrayal of style that seeks to provide a defining summation that permits leaders to be assigned to a singular type (e.g. 'manager', 'strategist', 'visionary'[22]).

As alluded to above, the study of political leaders has not been immune to the classic business model of adopting two key variables (e.g. concern for task objectives; concern for support base) and positioning them on two axes to create four-cell tables in which individual styles can be assigned on the basis of how each leader negotiates the two values. Several variations of this deceptively simple device have been devised in order to provide a more sensitive measure of style descriptions and assignments. The schema employed by Lance Blakesley illustrates both the initial thrust of the four-cell logic and also the drive for elaboration.[23] In his study of presidential leadership, Blakesley uses two variables drawn from the social behaviour of leaders—i.e. (i) expressive responsiveness towards others; and (ii) directive assertiveness over others—in order to devise not merely a fourfold table of social styles but one in which each cell is broken down into two 'sub-quadrants' (see Figure 2.1). Presidents are assessed against these social criteria and thereupon assigned to that leadership style deemed to be most closely correlated with its social style equivalent.[24]

Another variant is offered by Margaret G. Hermann *et al.*[25] In this case, leadership style is in the first instance taken to be a derivative of two variables— namely (i) responsiveness to constraints; and (ii) openness to information. The mix of these two measures generates four types so that the behavioural profiles of individual leaders in respect to the two measures give a high probability that they will be inclined to operate as a 'crusader', a 'strategist', a pragmatist', or an 'opportunist'. Having established this fourfold typology, Hermann *et al.* then run each of the types through additional criteria based on motivation in respect to what are designated as 'problems' and 'relationships' which bear a close resemblance to the more conventional split between task orientation and interpersonal value. The overall result of this hybrid in which each of the four types is subdivided into two variants is presented in Table 2.2.

Other examples can be cited of the way that variants and derivatives of commonly nominated criteria are used to devise schemes of leadership style categorization.[26]

---

[22] For example, see Kent J. Kille, *From Manager to Visionary: The Secretary-General of the United Nations* (New York, NY: Palgrave Macmillan, 2007).

[23] Lance Blakesley, *Presidential Leadership: From Eisenhower to Clinton* (Chicago, IL: Nelson-Hall, 1995), pp. 32–66.

[24] Blakesley subsequently examines these conjoined types in relation to three specified requirements of what is termed strategic leadership versatility at the presidential level (i.e. (i) self-awareness and self-monitoring; (ii) development and use of sub-leaders; and (iii) leadership style modification).

[25] Margaret G. Hermann, Thomas Preston, Baghat Korany, and Timothy M. Shaw, 'Who Leads Matters: The Effects of Powerful Individuals', *International Studies Review*, 3(2) Summer 2001: 83–131.

[26] For example, see John D. Stoessinger, *Crusaders and Pragmatists: Movers of Modern American Foreign Policy* (New York, NY: W. W. Norton, 1979); Margaret G. Hermann and Thomas Preston,

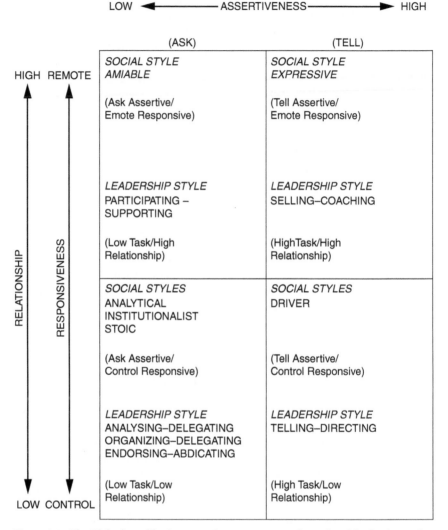

Figure 2.1. The Blakesley table depicting the conjunction of social and leadership styles Blakesley studied the social and leadership styles of Presidents Eisenhower, Kennedy, Johnson, Nixon, Ford, Carter, Reagan, Bush 1, and Clinton. The study goes on to examine these styles in relation with specific elements of presidential strategic leadership versatility.

Source: Lance Blakesley, *Presidential Leadership: From Eisenhower to Clinton* (Chicago, IL: Nelson-Hall, 1995).

'Presidents, Advisers, and Foreign Policy: The Effect of Leadership Style on Executive Arrangements', *Political Psychology*, 15(1) March 1994: 75–96; Margaret G. Hermann and Charles W. Kegley, Jr., 'Rethinking Democracy and International Peace: Perspectives from Political Psychology', *International Studies Quarterly*, 39(4) December 1995: 511–33; Juliet Kaarbo, 'Prime Minister Leadership Styles in Foreign Policy Decision-Making: A Framework for Research', *Political Psychology*, 18(3) September 1997: 553–81; Jonathan W. Keller, 'Leadership Style, Regime Type, and Foreign Policy Crisis Behavior: A Contingent Monadic Peace?', *International Studies Quarterly*, 49(2) June 2005: 205–32.

Table 2.2 Leadership style as a function of responsiveness to (i) constraints, (ii) openness to information, and (iii) motivation

Responsiveness to constraints	Openness to information	Motivation	
		Problem focus	Relationship focus
Challenges constraints (Becomes a crusader)	Closed to information	*Expansionistic* (Focus is on expanding one's power and influence)	*Evangelistic* (Focus is on persuading others to accept one's message and join one's cause)
Challenges constraints (Is generally strategic)	Open to information	*Incremental* (Focus is on maintaining one's manoeuvrability and flexibility while avoiding the obstacles that continually try to limit both)	*Charismatic* (Focus is on achieving one's agenda by engaging others in the process and persuading them to act)
Respects constraints (Inclined towards pragmatism)	Closed to information	*Directive* (Focus is on personally guiding policy along paths consistent with one's own views while still working within the norms and rules of one's current position)	*Consultative* (Focus is on monitoring that important others will support, or not actively oppose, what one wants to do in a particular situation)
Respects constraints (Is usually opportunistic)	Open to information	*Reactive* (Focus is on assessing what is possible in the current situation given the nature of the problem and considering what important constituencies will allow)	*Accommodative* (Focus is on reconciling differences and building consensus, empowering others, and sharing accountability in the process)

Source: Margaret G. Hermann, Thomas Preston, Baghat Korany, and Timothy M. Shaw, 'Who Leads Matters: The Effects of Powerful Individuals', *International Studies Review*, 3(2) Summer 2001: 83–131.

The benefit of these exercises in style typing is that they offer the prospect a more granular approach to the study of leadership. However, it is equally important to note that these studies suffer from a number of inherent drawbacks.

While the concept of style types offers the prospect of a more calibrated approach to the study of leadership, it also suffers from a number of inherent drawbacks. For example, in trying to rationalize the differences between various leaders, style surveys often generate only very limited numbers of style types. It is true that these offer the benefit of an aggregative perspective upon leadership, but it is equally the case that they are often thought to work within confined parameters of leadership possibilities. One egregious feature of these studies has been the near uniform tendency to prioritize style characteristics that are seen to be male-oriented in character—and to do so to such an extent that both men and women have difficulties in perceiving leadership as a gender-neutral position.[27] We will

---

[27] See J. B. Rosener, 'Ways Women Lead', *Harvard Business Review*, 68(6) November/December 1990: 19–25; J. B. Rosener, 'Sexual Static', in Keith Grint (ed.), *Leadership: Classical, Contemporary, and Critical Approaches* (Oxford: Oxford University Press, 1997), pp. 211–23.

address the issue of gender and leadership in Chapter 8, but for our purposes at present it is sufficient to note the way that style categories can become circular and self-affirming through their focus upon successful leaders in the past.

Other criticisms include the inherent convergence of personal style with leadership style. Just because an individual is a leader, it does not necessarily follow that all aspects of his or his personal outlook or working methods can be converted into a leadership style. In the same vein, some elements of style analysis are in effect externally devised assessment criteria related to success or otherwise of leadership output which are then ascribed to measures or portrayals of leadership style. One study, for example, works backwards from the scope and type of change associated with well-known leadership figures to arrive at a typology of styles evoked from a consequentialist calculation based on the logic of an imputed cause and effect.[28] Another variation is one in which a leadership position is analysed historically and functionally in terms of a set of required skills. The respective styles of individual office-holders are then assessed and rated against a set of criteria that represents the components of an implied preferred style match.[29]

In addition, while an emphasis upon the description and effects of individual style can at one level induce a nuanced grasp of different leaderships and, thereby, a proliferation of separate styles, it usually in fact presages a marked contraction of ascribed styles for the purposes of analytical focus. While the style approach shows that there are no fixed patterns of leadership, the aggregative nature of styles usually fails to produce many variants. In essence, style analyses are criticized for dealing with a number of styles that are considered to be too few to account for the diversity of leaderships.

Another common complaint centres on the way that style analysis is founded upon categories that are not merely ambiguous and subjective, but are insufficiently specific to demarcate clear boundaries between different nominated styles. Notwithstanding the reservations over the techniques of differentiation, this kind of analysis usually carries the implication that styles are mutually exclusive: i.e. that any individual leader is necessarily rooted in one static style and one style only. The investigation of styles was originally prompted by the drive within organization theories and business schools to isolate and define the optimum type of leadership. Like the originators of the trait approach, the guiding logic was one of eliciting the best type of leadership from the behaviour of successful leaders. It would then be up to others to emulate the model drawn from experience. The implication was that a successful leader in one sphere would always exhibit the same universal style as effective leaders in other spheres. By the same token, the premise was that a style could be adopted on the basis of a free choice of leadership behaviour—as if leaders were fully autonomous individuals.

---

[28] Jean Blondel, *Political Leadership: Towards a General Analysis* (London: Sage, 1987). From this analysis, Blondel identifies nine leadership types based upon their scope of political engagement and the degree of advocated change (i.e. 'managers'; 'adjusters'/'tinkerers'; 'innovators'; 'comforters'; 'redefiners'; 'reformists'; 'saviours'; 'paternalists'/'populists'; and 'ideologues').

[29] Fred I. Greenstein, *The Presidential Difference: Leadership Style from FDR to George W. Bush*, 2nd edn. (Princeton, NJ: Princeton University Press, 2004).

In this respect, both personal trait and leadership style perspectives can be described as top-down explanations. They both suffer from the lonely planet syndrome in that neither of them pays much attention to the organizational context of leadership—i.e. the extent to which leaders necessarily operate and exert leadership within a group or social environment. This aspect is even more important in political leadership where the context involves not only larger numbers than any other environment, but more co-participants engaged explicitly and implicitly in the competition for power and in the resistance to power. The limitations of both the trait and style approaches prepare the ground for a third point of access into the study of leadership which seeks to incorporate a much greater sensitivity towards the changing contexts and to underline the need for leaders to adapt themselves and their styles to differing conditions.

STUDYING LEADERS (III) CONTINGENCY/SITUATIONAL LEADERSHIP

A third variant of leadership analysis seeks to compensate for the deficiencies of the other two forms of inquiry. In particular, it attempts to make the study of leadership as dynamic and responsive as the subject matter itself. It does so by giving emphasis to the way that the nature of leadership is conditioned by the specific context within which a leader has to operate. The contingency or situational approach to the study of leadership operates on the premise that different patterns of leadership behaviour are required in different contexts. In essence, leadership has to be conceived by reference to the demands and opportunities inherent in different situations. In contrast to trait or style approaches that tend to focus upon on what leaders do, the contingency outlook is more inclined to look at why leaders behave as they do. This perspective literally situates leadership firmly within a context of dependency relationships in which leaders have to negotiate between variables that interact with one another.

The contrast with the two previously cited methodologies is an important one to note. A leadership style normally implies a fixed property that style analysis can elicit from contemporary or historical evidence. The defining objective of style analysis is to assign a leader to a particular set of categories that collectively denote a recognizable style. In contingency theory, there is no such point of finality. The contingency approach uses style as the basis from which to proceed. Far from being the finishing point, styles become a set of options with which each individual leader has to negotiate on the basis of context in order to maximize the chances of achieving or maintaining the status of effective leadership. Within such a schema, leadership is not only an open-ended concept but also a variable set of practices that involve the need for style changes on the part of individual leaders in response to the shifting circumstances in which they find themselves. Style and contingency analyses are both classified as behavioural approaches to the study of leadership. But while the former is concerned with locating the best match between the collection of evidence and the assignment of a set style to a particular leader, the latter emphasizes the need of an individual leader to achieve the optimum fit between context and leadership behaviour. This infers that the former is primarily static and descriptive in nature, whilst the latter is flexible in operation and strongly prescriptive in tone.

As with so many forms of leadership study, the contingency approach originated in the managerial sector and in particular the spheres of industrial and organizational psychology. Here the emphasis lay with training leaders to be adaptable to changing situations in order to maximize the effectiveness of their leadership function. It is widely considered to be important for a leader not merely to make the right decisions but to make the right choices as to what kind of leader to be in given situations. In a pioneering study, Fred E. Fiedler pointed to the analytical importance of taking full account of the interdependency between a leader's style and the ways in which context shapes a leader's control and influence. Fiedler emphasized the relationship between leaders and followers, the nature of the leader's specified agendas, and the positional variables experienced by a leader operating within an organizational setting.[30] Many others have followed Fiedler's steer in embedding leadership deep within conditioning matrices of determinate and indeterminate constraints. The prescription has remained that a leadership style should vary with the circumstances in which leadership is possible. A leader would need to choose which style to employ in response to the differing contexts of each task. In business terms, a leader would be required to adopt the most productive style in line with the difficulty of the task and with the competence and experience of the subordinates.[31]

In the field of political leadership, various models have been devised to identify different situations and the related leadership styles that are considered to be congruent with each context. The most common formats are those based on precisely those categories drawn from style analysis—namely directive/consensual; task driven/cohesion; innovation/consolidation. The usage of these measures leads to various iterations of the classic four-cell table already alluded to above. The key difference in contingency theory is that leaders are not assigned to one style type based on temperament and outlook, but are encouraged to move across style types in response to the shifting requirements of different situations. On some occasions leaders will have to judge whether the situation warrants being decisive, single-minded, and forceful. In other instances, a leader will need to be cautious, consultative, and collaborative. In all circumstances, leadership is taken to mean the capacity to play out different roles dependent upon the parameters set by the main contextual factors.

The conditioning influences of context upon the exercise of political leadership will include the relationship between a leader and his or her subordinates; the nature of the task involved; the degree to which an organization is accustomed to

[30] Fred E. Fiedler and Joseph E. Garcia, *New Approaches to Effective Leadership: Cognitive Resources and Organizational Performance* (New York, NY: John Wiley, 1987). See also Fred E. Fiedler, 'Situational Control and a Dynamic Theory of Leadership', in Grint (ed.), *Leadership: Classical, Contemporary and Critical Approaches*, pp. 126–48.

[31] Paul P. Hersey and Ken H. Blanchard, *The Management of Organizational Behaviour*, 3rd edn. (Upper Saddle River, NJ: Prentice Hall, 1977); Paul P. Hersey *The Situational Leader* (New York, NY: Warner, 1984); William J. Reddin, *How to Make Management Style More Effective* (New York, NY: McGraw-Hill, 1987); L. G. Bolman and T. E. Deal, *Reframing Organizations: Artistry, Choice and Leadership*, 2nd edn. (San Francisco, CA: Jossey-Bass, 1997).

performing such actions; the susceptibility of conditions to leadership initiatives; and the level of internal legitimacy conferred upon a particular leader or a leadership position in respect to a specific set of objectives. In effect, although a leader will necessarily be conditioned by the material and social properties of a working environment, an accurate understanding of the varied characteristics within that environment will allow a leader to alter styles in accordance with the exigencies of each organizational challenge. As a consequence, contingency leadership is both confined by the situation in which it is positioned, and at the same time expanded by it through the recognition that leaders can be strategically empowered by adaptive shifts in style.

This form of leadership analysis can offer a more supple approach to a subject that is inherently multidimensional in nature. It can more easily accommodate the varied forms of activity and behaviour that leaders have to demonstrate in the multiple roles that are either ascribed to them or which are claimed by leaders themselves. The contingency approach is arguably a more layered, more inclusive, and more sensitive analytical strategy than other approaches because it has a direct affinity with the relational spirit of leadership behaviour.[32] In terms of organizational inquiry, it is claimed that contingency studies have a strong pedigree of practical significance not only because they are strongly grounded in research but also because of their functional utility in leadership training. Integral to the contingency approach is an asserted realism which takes as its key premise the notion that there is no one model of leadership—only different ways for a leader to operate in order to achieve effectiveness. Two corollaries follow on from this precept. The first is that organizations should endeavour to match different types of leaders to those task areas most appropriate to their attributes. The second is that no single leader or type of leader should be expected to undertake a raft of different leadership roles to match widely varied situations.

Notwithstanding the analytical and operational virtues of the contingency approach, it does suffer from a number of drawbacks. Paradoxically for a form of inquiry founded upon the realities of doing leadership, it does tend to suffer from critiques that are similarly based upon the actual circumstances and interpretive conclusions associated with leadership activity. For example, in giving appropriate empirical and normative weight to the need for leaders to be adaptable to the contexts within which they find themselves, the contingency approach does have a tendency to consign leadership to nothing more than a reactive agency. Put more strongly, when leadership is refracted through the lens of contingency, it risks becoming redefined in terms of organizational properties and structural limitations. As such, leaders increasingly become seen as facilitators while leadership is translated into a passive and malleable entity based upon circumstances and environmental constraints. In recognizing the significance of environment in the construction of leadership options, the contingency approach can induce a conception of leadership that reduces it to the level of being a functional extension of the environment. This is particularly the case if the

---

[32] For example, see Erwin C. Hargrove, 'Presidential Personality and Leadership Style', in George C. Edwards III, John H. Kessel, and Bert A. Rockman (eds.), *Researching the Presidency: Vital Questions, New Approaches* (Pittsburgh, PA: University of Pittsburgh Press, 1993), pp. 69–109.

parameters of the environment are set too narrowly by reference, for example, to an inner group or a leadership circle.

Another critique of this approach features the complaint that while it can point to correlations between styles and situations, it cannot explain the nature of these relationships. In other words, it is not able to account precisely for the reason that one style rather than another will be more effective in any given context. Thus, the approach can be accused of being motivated and characterized by prescriptions on leadership that are very often based not so much upon precise and generically valid information, but on intuition and personal experience. A further problem lies in the necessary emphasis upon the exigencies of location and time. While these variables are prioritized within the logic of the situational approach, they can overlook the ability of leaders to shape their environments through their own choices and their adaptive capacities to play different roles under different conditions. There is also the risk that a close analytical dependency upon the multidimensionality of context can lead to the myopic conclusion that no two contexts are the same—thereby offering no durable basis for comparison.

Arguably a more serious criticism relates to the way that the contingency approach legitimizes established patterns of leadership recruitment and behaviour. Even though this category of leadership analysis is arguably more sensitive to change and to the need for leadership to be contextually responsive, it nevertheless is seen as a way of reaffirming the traditional practices and cultural predispositions surrounding leadership within its established spheres. One of the most conspicuous examples of the way that such an analytical strategy can foreclose options comes in the field of gender. Because leaders are almost invariably male, leadership styles can easily be seen to be inherently male in inception and nature. The established repository of case materials cannot help but to generate male-dominated continuities in respect to situational styles. The same circumscribed outlook can also be ascribed to other culturally sanctioned attributes.[33] As a consequence, the categories of leadership analysis and evaluation can come to reflect a distinctly Western set of values and customs primarily because this is the region that has generated the dominant corpus of leadership analysis.

TRANSFORMATIVE LEADERSHIP

A fourth approach to the study of leadership embraces the idea that there is a premium form of the subject that supersedes all the other perspectives in the way that it evokes leadership as an extraordinary centre of creative force which is not reducible to the standard and more limited experiences of leadership activity. Arguments abound over whether this type of leadership is an extension or a variant

---

[33] Expectations of leadership roles and behaviours will vary according to cultural traditions and practices. These will condition both the assignment of leadership, the conduct of leaders, and the responses to their position. While some cultures are individualistic in outlook, others are more communal or bureaucratic or hierarchical in their attitude structures. Such characteristics as deference and respect will also have an impact on leadership styles. See Gary A. Yukl, *Leadership in Organizations*, 7th edn. (Paramus, NJ: Prentice Hall 2009), ch. 15.

of more common forms, or whether it represents a qualitative shift into an entirely separate category of relationships. Notwithstanding the debates over the existence or otherwise of a leadership continuum, one conclusion remains clear and this is the recognition that there are leaderships which fall outside the normal remit and provide a concentrated form of the phenomenon. It is seen as constituting a level of leadership that offers the prospect of defining a kind of pedigree benchmark or a catalyst of meaning against which other less advanced or more qualified types of leadership can be assessed. Just as leadership is generically connoted with ideas of change, so by inflating the scale of change it becomes logically plausible to claim the existence of an advanced or even ideal state of leadership. The fundamentalist character of this kind of leadership is normally associated with unusual and even exceptional circumstances, and is more often than not motivated by the desire or need to mobilize resources in the cause of extensive change. It is for this reason that leaders operating in these conditions and with these motivations are widely characterized as engaging in transformative leadership.

The customary way of defining transformative leadership is to contrast it with the more conventional forms of leadership which are normally referred to as being transactional in nature. The main constituent features of the latter are the cultivation of influence through the processes of social exchange, negotiation, and coalition building. In these circumstances, leaders have a limited reach. They are surrounded by those with access to resources of their own which can be deployed to impose limitations upon the choices and activities of leaders. Transactional leadership therefore casts the leader in the role of a broker who is required to work within customary constraints and to attempt to change the behaviour of others through incremental means via arguments, inducements, concessions, rewards, sanctions, and agreed compromises between positions. Leaders who engage in transactional behaviour necessarily have to match their activities to the given environments in which they operate. In this sense, they are grounded in the normal dynamics of situational leadership. Transformative leadership on the other hand represents in many ways a frontal assault upon the roles and techniques associated with the transactional norms of conventional leadership modes.

One of the major theorists on leadership, James MacGregor Burns, was the first to give prominence to what he regarded as the conceptual and empirical distinction between transformative and transactional leadership.[34] In his view, transformative leaders are different not just because they typify heroic notions of leadership or because they exemplify the notion of leadership as an instrumental force, but because they lead by breaking out of their environments and altering previously established ground rules and norms. To Burns, transactional leadership can produce changes through the give and take of negotiated engagements. But transformation is not the same as the accumulation of minor changes. It is much more profound: 'It is to cause a metamorphosis in form or structure, a change in the very conditions or nature of a thing, a change into another substance, a radical change in outward form or inner character . . . It is change of this breadth and depth that is fostered by transformative leadership.'[35]

[34] James MacGregor Burns, *Leadership* (New York, NY: Harper & Row, 1979).
[35] James MacGregor Burns, *Transforming Leadership* (London: Atlantic, 2003), p. 14.

The notion of transformative leadership offers something approaching an ideal type which allows for a point of reference to be established concerning the meaning and value of other forms of leadership. Burns's concept manages to combine the fullest expression of both the integrative and purposive elements of leadership with a strong ethical dimension to make the ensuing power output a matter of moral enhancement. Burns gives emphasis to the importance of identity and values, as well as needs, motives, expectations, and aspirations, in the formation of a symbiosis between the leader and the led.

> Such leadership occurs when one or more persons *engage* with others in such a way that leaders and followers raise one another to higher levels of motivation and morality. Their purposes, which might have started out as separate but related, as in the case of transactional leadership, become fused. Power bases are linked not as counterweights but as mutual support for common purpose.... The relationship can be moralistic, of course. But transforming leadership ultimately becomes moral in that it raises the level of human conduct and ethical aspiration of both leader and led, and thus it has a transforming effect on both.[36]

The scale of the synergies released by such a process of leadership can have profound effects upon the structural and normative elements of a social order. It is because some leaders are able not only to exploit the opportunities for collating need and value hierarchies together in support of a higher-level sense of purpose, but also to respond to any breakdowns in the more normal patterns and traditions of political engagement in order to turn conflict into a more productive use of social resources. For Burns, transforming leaders are able to locate the roots of cohesion through calibrated appeals to needs but particularly to the motivational force of values and the arousal of value-based movement driven by exercises in the raising of social and moral consciousness. A skilful leader will be able to create the conditions 'so that higher motivations will arise to elevate the conscience of men and women'.[37] In effect, Burns is advocating leadership as a device for conflating political and moral impact. As such, high-elevation leaders can come to fuse their own identity with that of their followers and vice versa— thereby generating leadership that 'asks sacrifices *from* followers rather then merely promising them goods'.[38]

This normatively informed account of leadership has been highly influential in the study of the subject area. The weight given to the mobilization of needs and values through the agency of gifted individuals has provided an explanatory device by which leadership can be cast as medium of reconfigured perceptions and consolidated purpose. This mode of leadership has been used to explain the extraordinary shifts in social and political landscapes associated with such central figures as Charles de Gaulle, Franklin Delano Roosevelt, Winston Churchill, Nelson Mandela, Gandhi, Martin Luther King, Václav Havel, and Mao Zedong. The analytical absorption with such leaders and with their emblematic properties as instruments of transformation has led to a variety of different forms of refinements to Burns's original exposition—most notably by Bernard Bass who advances the proposition that transformative leadership can be broken down into different component parts: namely idealized influence, inspirational motivation,

---

[36] Burns, *Leadership*, p. 20.   [37] Burns, *Leadership*, p. 43.   [38] Burns, *Leadership*, p. 455.

intellectual stimulation, and individualized consideration.[39] While it may be claimed that Bass's main sphere of interest lay in the fields of business management and organization theory, rather than the sphere of high politics and grand historical cases, it has nonetheless added considerable appeal to the notion of a chemistry between particular personal characteristics and social contexts susceptible to being galvanized into large-scale positive change.[40]

While transformative leadership is usually depicted as having favourable associations, it does have a number of negative connotations. It tends to be suggestive of a form of leadership that relies less on such soft power devices as productive dialogue, collaborative enterprise, and collective identity, and much more upon the driving energies of hard power in pursuit of a set of non-negotiable objectives. In short, a transforming leader can be synonymous with an enhanced form of domination over subordinates and even as a device by which increased numbers of people—including individuals and agencies of comparable status—are reduced to a position of subjection. Because such leaders operate at different levels of scale and intensity, they are often characterized as altering the parameters of the political realm in ways that allow benefits to accrue to the leadership and which enhance its capability of securing higher than normal levels of compliance. This leads to concerns that such rationales of leadership can generate excessive concentrations of power which in their turn arouse complaints over the ways in which transformative leaders seek not merely to supplant the customary processes of checks and balances, but to supersede the conventional dynamics of political negotiation and accommodation. In addition to the charges of elitism, detachment, and lack of responsiveness, transformative leadership is also criticized for the way it is often embedded (i) in the leader's own personality and individual sense of vision, (ii) in the inspirational and emotional attachment that is fostered around the figure of the leader, and (iii) in the agitated character of the commitment engendered by the imperative requirements of the leadership's programme for change.

On a more positive note, transformative leadership can be depicted as constituting the very essence of what leaders can achieve in their adopted roles. When the notion of transformation is linked to leadership in this way, it is not used merely to convey the possible scale of change associated with an enabling leadership. The term suggests that it is only through the agency of leadership that radical systemic change can be precipitated. Moreover, it imputes that the full potential of leadership can only be gauged by such an outcome. In this way, transformative leadership can imply a pure form of the leadership function because it suggests a direct relationship between disproportionate influence and disproportionate

---

[39] Bernard M. Bass, *Leadership and Performance Beyond Expectation* (New York, NY: Free Press, 1985); Bernard M. Bass, *Transformational Leadership: Industrial, Military, and Educational Impact* (Mahwah, NJ: Erlbaum, 1998).

[40] For an overview of this genre of leadership study, see Bernard M. Bass and Bruce J. Avolio, 'Transformational Leadership: A Response to Critiques', in Martin M. Chemers and Roya Ayman (eds.), *Leadership Theory and Research: Perspectives and Directions* (San Diego, CA: Academic Press, 1993), pp. 49–80; James G. Hunt, 'Transformational/Charismatic Leadership's Transformation of the Field: An Historical Essay', *Leadership Quarterly*, 10(2) Summer 1999: 129–44; Jay A. Conger, 'Charismatic and Transformational Leadership in Organizations: An Insider's Perspective on these Developing Streams of Research', *Leadership Quarterly*, 10(2) Summer 1999: 145–79; John van Maurik, *Writers on Leadership* (London: Penguin, 2001), pp. 99–186.

effect. Transforming leaders, therefore, are those that transcend established systems and rules in the cause of purposeful action that would otherwise lie outside the parameters of possible action and the constraints of more limited interests and perspectives. Such leaders not only generate a profusion of associations between their active involvement and the achievement of radical change, but foster an explanatory ethos in which transforming developments cannot be satisfactorily accounted for without the input of the sponsoring leadership.

In this more constructive light, transformative leaders can provide the necessary means for a renewal of collective identity which comes with an enhanced sense of autonomy and direction. This kind of leadership can be seen not as a higher order of top-down influence, but as a fusion of leader and followers in the cause of a collaborative partnership. The defined purpose and the leadership agency connected to it are set at intense levels of stimulation and motivation so that no clear distinction remains between leader and non-leaders. The interplay between them becomes the motor of a heightened state of organized mobilization in the pursuit of a common and idealized set of objectives. According to this perspective, the mutual needs and emotional demands of both the leader and the followers become instrumental in the reordering of organizational structures and social architectures. This synergy incorporates not only the notion of followers becoming empowered by the processes of transformative leadership, but also the theme that such leadership imposes more complex demands upon the leader than the normal run of transactional processes. Far from inflating leadership status for its own sake and for reasons of enlarging the sphere of coercive power, transformative leaders can be perceived as dealers in soft power. Relying on their own special resources in the way they are able to cultivate support through the advocacy of cultural values and other techniques of aroused affinity,[41] it is possible for the exponents of transformative leadership to be interpreted as exercising entirely legitimate forms of large-scale mobilization.

In spite of the benefits that are commonly attributed to it, transformative leadership remains a controversial construction of the subject area. It has self-evident connotations with high-risk strategies, disruptive behaviour, and unpredictable results. It can be associated with sweeping challenges to the status quo, with an insurgency approach to established rules and processes, and with the usage of high emotions and even irrationality in the pursuit of leadership agendas. Although there is no necessary connection between transformative agency and charismatic leadership, the impression of just such a direct linkage remains strong, which in turn fosters the view that radical change is dependent upon the special qualities, emotive traction, and distinctive appeal of a particular individual as the primary components in securing a new order.[42] The emotive, ritualistic, and even passionate properties of charismatic influence offer further indictments of the kind of leadership that most

---

[41] See Howard Gardiner, *Leading Minds: An Anatomy of Leadership* (London: HarperCollins, 1996), chs. 1–3.

[42] Charles Lindholm, *Charisma* (Cambridge, MA: Blackwell, 1990); Jay A. Conger and Rabindra N. Kanungo, *Charismatic Leadership in Organizations* (Thousand Oaks, CA: Sage, 1998); see also Max Weber, *From Max Weber: Essays in Sociology*, trans. and ed. H. H. Gerth and C. Wright Mills (London: Routledge, 1998) ch. 9; Christopher Adair-Toteff, 'Max Weber's Charisma', *Journal of Classical Sociology*, 5(2) July 2005: 189–204.

easily comes to be linked to this type of support structure. Even if it is accepted that transformative leaders can establish an organic fusion of interests and identities with their followers, leadership of this kind is not noted for its orientation towards mutual accommodation and negotiated compromise. On the contrary, it is seen as being fuelled by notions of personal vision and compulsive destiny, and by the requisite need to act out of the ordinary, to be iconoclastic and to operate on a plane that supersedes the normal dynamics of organizational and political life.

Transformative leaders are most adept at changing the conditions within which leadership is allowed to exist and operate. But in doing so, they run the risk of creating a system of unrestrained coercive power increasingly committed to a progressively wider remit of large-scale change. This can bring in its wake charges not merely of an abuse of power but of a regime with a pronounced lack of institutional and even moral perspective. The complaint thus returns to one of unpredictability with the possibility of excess and even indiscriminate destruction. While some transformative leaders have a laudable reputation for necessary organizational adaptation in the face of altered conditions, others stand accused of engaging in wholly abnormal leadership behaviour leading to organizational dislocation and institutional disarray. When the sphere is enlarged to that of society as a whole, then the complaints are as serious as any political indictments can be. Many transformative leaders stand accused of engaging in wholly abnormal leadership behaviour leading to serious social dislocation, political violence, and centralized repression (Box 2.3). On some occasions, transformative behaviour can be associated with the more positive values of great leadership, but on others it can rank as the concomitant of dangerous extremism and with it the corruption of both the leadership's authority and the integrity of the polity itself.

In many ways the issue of transformative leaders typifies the problems that cluster around the entire subject area of leadership and its analysis. The interest, and also the discomfort, that is regularly prompted by such an uncompromising form of leadership reflects many of the responses to the issues surrounding the social position of leaders. Great leaders are almost invariably associated with one kind of transformation or another. But by the same token, transformative leadership also carries a close correlation with reckless, repressive, and violent regimes.

In the sphere of business, a similar mix of attitudes surrounds the notion of transformative leadership. It can signify the collective organizational benefits that may be accrued from pioneering leaders set on a course of necessary innovation and restructuring. But it can also refer to institutional disarray, to structural instability, and to potentially disastrous forms of decision-making and agenda setting. It is for this reason that there is a long-running dispute within business education over whether transformative leadership should be, or even can be, a taught subject. On one side is the argument that this type of leadership has a role to play at almost every level of management because it can be seen as a particular form of situational leadership that can be applied at different levels. In opposition is the view that for the most part transformative leadership is an atypical and even abnormal form of leadership. In this light, it is confined to extreme circumstances and dependent upon wholly exceptional leaders with a strategic vision and with the drive to carry their plans through to implementation.

The implication of the latter viewpoint is that transformative leadership is dependent upon those individuals at the strategic centre of organizations who

Box 2.3 The danger of transformative leadership: The case of the Great Leap Forward

Between 1958 and 1962, China suffered from a famine that has been described as not merely the greatest catastrophe in the country's history but the worst known famine in the experience of the world. Moreover, it was an event that was entirely man-made in that it followed from a political and ideological experiment that sought to transform China's largely peasant economy into an industrial-urban powerhouse capable of surpassing Britain in steel production and the Soviet Union as the showpiece of communism. The programme of the Great Leap Forward was driven by the leadership of Mao Zedong and his ambition both to restructure China's society and economy, and to reinforce his personal hold on the political cadres of the communist regime. As millions were forced off the land and out of their farms in order to boost industrial production, food production was made dependent upon an extreme form of collectivization imposed by methods that were as brutal as they were dysfunctional. The net effect was one in which millions suffered starvation, especially in the central and southern provinces.

Revolutionary farming techniques also devastated the land, creating severe soil erosion, landslides, floods, droughts, and insect infestations. But it was the effect upon the people that was most noteworthy. As agricultural production plunged, the posture of the communist leadership became increasingly violent against vast swathes of the country. Recent archival work is only now revealing the scale of the deprivation. As the grain stores emptied and the land reduced to a wilderness, large numbers were left to eat tree bark, leaves, plants—even leather and mud. People sold relatives for handfuls of food. Cannibalism became rife with human flesh traded on the black market. Reports of the disaster were either dismissed by Mao, or used to invoke even more severe measures against behaviour that was deemed to be counter-revolutionary. A close study of the crisis concludes that the scale of the disaster was much larger than was originally thought. It is estimated that as a direct consequence of Mao's project, at least 45 million people died from starvation, neglect, and persecution—including at least 2.5 million who experienced violent deaths and 1–3 million who committed suicide.

Although Mao eventually conceded the need to amend the programme, it is thought that he had used the disaster to purge or threaten his rivals into final submission—allowing him to assume even greater power than before. His psychopathic obsessions with power maximization, as well as his attachment to the techniques of coercion, fear, and terror used during the famine, were later to be revived during the next experiment in transformational catharsis—i.e. the Great Proletarian Cultural Revolution.

Sources: Jasper Becker, *Hungry Ghosts: Mao's Secret Famine* (New York, NY: Henry Holt 1996); Frank Dikotter, *Mao's Great Famine: The History of China's Most Devastating Catastrophe, 1958–62* (New York, NY: Walker & Co 2011).

have an exceptional trait geared to the unconventional and idiosyncratic properties of creating drastic change. In short, there is the assumption of an equation in which exceptional innovation is correlated with the existence of leaders who are essentially out of step with conventional practices. In other words, the process of transformative leadership is taken to be grounded in an individual trait that cannot be provided by training or experience. For many organizations, it is important that attempts to engineer the introduction of such types of leader should be studiously avoided. For the most part, therefore, transformative leadership does not sit easily within the realm of normal organizational operations. Another constituent feature of this caution within business and organizational spheres is the view that transformative leadership has a more natural resonance with the medium of high politics and with the extraordinary scale of societal change that can be secured through the exercise of an energetic and visionary form of political leadership.

CONCLUSION

It is evident that far from providing a definitive model of the subject area, the phenomenon of transformative leadership serves instead to throw into high relief most if not all the problematic and controversial features associated with the phenomenon of leadership as a focal point of political agency. On the one hand, it can be construed as a quintessential expression of leadership. On the other hand, it can be perceived as an atypical outlier or even a deviant and extreme form of leadership. Whatever the case, it highlights the difficulties of clarifying the meaning of political leadership and of explaining its operational dynamics. Its apparent simplicity and pretensions to clarity belie as many analytical challenges as other less pristine models of leadership. In spite of its reputation for clean lines and intense appeal, transformative leadership is far from being as conceptually precise and politically autonomous as it is often portrayed to be. On the contrary, it might be said to throw into high relief the extent to which even this ostensibly pure-bred conception of leadership is functionally dependent upon highly subjective forms of interpretive judgement involving contestable issues, intersubjective perspectives, and variable constructions of political meaning.

Just as the behaviours and judgements of leaders in relation to contexts are not susceptible to objective criteria, so the attributed solidity of context appears on closer inspection to be grounded less in material reality and more upon malleable depictions of political environment. This property of contingency and interdependency is equally evident in the sectors of traits and styles. In the same way that style analysis can be seen as a derivative of traits, so both can have an impact upon the definition and meaning of situation.[43] In many ways, leadership traits and styles are made manifest through the dynamics of situation, and while traits and styles are often conceived as fixed properties they are both amenable to the political properties of adjustment and flexibility in the face of contextual constraints.

Even in the sphere of apparent transformative agency, leadership retains its property of being a mutually constitutive and therefore highly relational process of cultural and political negotiation. It is for this reason that it becomes necessary to return to the initial point of access to the subject and to begin to unpack both sides of the relationship between individual leaders and those who are prepared to be led. But before the study proceeds to the side of what is often perceived to be a stimulus–response equation, it is first necessary to look more closely at the leaders themselves and the relationship between what they do and who they are.

---

[43] For an illustrative example of how these analytical categories can fold into one another, see Margaret G. Hermann, 'Assessing Leadership Style: A Trait Analysis', *Social Science Automation 1999*; revised 2002. Accessed 13 July 2012 at: <http://www.socialscience.net/Docs/LTA.pdf>.

3

Being a leader: Personal interiors and political externalities

'Johnson's career was marked by a continuing effort to avoid confrontation and choice, to prevent passionate and emotional divisions over issues. This inclination can be understood as a response to his particular family situation. From his earliest days . . . he had learned that if he chose his father, he might jeopardize the love and respect of his mother: if he chose his mother, his identity as a man would be in danger. The challenge then as always, was to find a method of satisfying both . . . to find consensus.'

Doris Kearns[1]

'Most public men share the Caesarian habit of detaching themselves to admire their own figures on the world stage, but Stalin's detachment was a degree greater. His adopted son Artyom Sergeev remembers Stalin shouting at his son Vasily, for exploiting his father's name. "But I'm a Stalin too", said Vasily. "No, you're not," replied Stalin. "You're not Stalin and I'm not Stalin. Stalin is Soviet power. Stalin is what he is in the newspapers and the portraits, not you, no not even me!"'

Simon Sebag Montefiore[2]

PREAMBLE

Even though leadership is not necessarily synonymous with the existence of a specific leader, it is almost invariably the case that the theme of leadership is treated as being analogous to a distinctive and primarily individual point of origin. Whether this is because leadership lends itself to an instinctive logic of concentrated focus that can be best expressed in individual terms, or whether it is more that notions of leadership become culturally and traditionally equated with narratives of leaders, the effect is one of a habitual resonance between leadership and individual leaders. That being so, there has always been a close interest in the identity of leaders, in how leaders succeed in acquiring such positions, and in what

---

[1] Doris Kearns, 'Lyndon Johnson's Political Personality', *Political Science Quarterly*, 91(3) Autumn 1976: 389.

[2] Simon Sebag Montefiore, *Stalin: The Court of the Red Tsar* (London: Phoenix, 2004), p. 4.

personal properties they bring to their respective positions. Partly because of their social prominence but also because of the attributions of causality and responsibility that they attract, leaders become a natural focus not just of everyday politics but also of sustained analysis and assessment in which the personal and the political become closely entwined.

While leaders provide an explicit point of reference for framing an approach to the subject of leadership, their natural focus does not always convert into a readily coherent structure of examination. Contrary to appearance, their accessibility is far less clear than the initial position would imply. It is the case that leadership is generally seen as a behavioural characteristic by which one individual has the ability to influence others. Outstanding leadership is accordingly construed as the product of exceptional leaders. Leaders are regarded as individuals who make the key decisions, who precipitate movement, and who therefore make a significant difference. Once this position is accepted, it becomes a matter of course to turn one's attention to the individual leader as a primary subject for analysis.

It should be recognized at this point that examining the individual properties of leadership does not preclude the structural, constitutional, and cultural milieu within which any particular instance of leadership is situated. On the contrary, it is acknowledged that leadership will always be shaped and conditioned by the conditions of its inception and by the systemic features of its location. For example, the affinity between leadership and the presence of a clearly demarcated individual leader will be strongly influenced by the nature of the political system. A case in point would be a system where there exists a formally constituted presidential office with a substantial allocation of powers. Given the primacy of such an office, it becomes much more likely that any analysis of political leadership will quickly follow a line of progression from the individualized nature of the office on towards the nature of the individual and that person's own background and leadership style. The logic of a personal office like this tends to facilitate a particularly individualized approach towards the study of leadership in which institutional features become enfolded into personal histories and outlooks.

Different systems of government, of course, have different traditions. Some may possess a well-established disposition towards giving priority to strong and even authoritarian leadership over the claims of institutional or legal constraints. Although other systems will have a more pronounced and settled constitutional structure with a greater collective basis to representation and decision-making, even they have a capacity for high-profile leadership geared to political need and opportunity. Notwithstanding the huge variations in political structures and traditions, it is generally the case that all systems in one way or another, and with varying intensity, raise the issue of leadership in terms of a connection between its thematic nature and the properties of individual leaders. Even in highly advanced mass societies, it is the norm for the concept of political leadership to be constructed around the theme of an individual in whom so much organizational and explanatory weight is invested.

The emphasis given to the individuality of leadership even within well-established and complex systems inevitably raises questions over the most appropriate ways of approaching the theme as a subject of analysis. To begin with, there is always the general difficulty of giving appropriate recognition to the cultural context of leadership while at the same time differentiating the leader as a distinctive property that is in some way separate from the rest. Other prominent and highly problematic issues also serve to colour the landscape. For example, while the notion of leadership provides the prospect of an apparently unified subject for investigation, it also propels the study of leadership into a profusion of variables generated by a multiplicity of different exponents of leadership. It might be thought that directing attention to the individual leader would afford the prospect of analytical focus, but in doing so it risks fragmenting the study of leadership into a disparate set of as many discrete parts as there are different individual leaders. The position is further compounded by the way that the apparently objective and material reality of a person is conjoined to what are often highly subjective criteria relating both to the nature of personality and to the categories of leadership.

MOVING TOWARDS THE PERSON

One way of approaching the subject is to resort to a device discussed in Chapter 2. The identification and analysis of traits relating specifically to individual characteristics has been a common form of assembling data on leaders both past and present. In fact, the technique allows for leaders from different eras to be compared through the same medium of 'historiometric' measurement. On the debit side, however, is an extensive list of reservations and objections over the validity of much of this kind of data collection. As noted earlier, the main concern is that while it relies upon a methodical consistency across standardized units of analysis, the categories themselves are normally very limited in scope. It is acknowledged that these types of category represent hard data that are directly derived from the behaviour of each individual. As a consequence, they can be used to support the proposition that the subject matter of analysis is a set of objective entities susceptible to measurement and in particular to the relationships between different specified variables. On the other hand, these units of analysis can be viewed as being driven more by the availability of the data rather than from their analytical significance. As a result, the subsequent analyses are either confined to general commonalities in the surface features of individual leaders, or to more ambitious analyses which are nevertheless based upon what are arguably more tenuous grounds of statistical inferences and associations.

In summary, trait studies of individual leaders do succeed in operating at the level of observable and verifiable units of analysis. In doing so, they can generate a profusion of connections between variables. The main criticism is that these studies are lateral in their scope and thin in their operation. In other words, they cover large numbers of leaders but at the cost of contextual and analytical depth. In essence, trait studies are accused not only of evading most of the problematic issues surrounding leadership analysis, but of filtering out many of the intangible and interpretive properties of leadership that so characterize the subject area.[3] In seeking to achieve a more expansive grasp of individual leaders and to give greater grounding to their particular contexts, other strategies of inquiry have been utilized. One of the most popular devices has been the sharp focus given to individual lives in the genre of biography and autobiography.

The biographical approach has had far-reaching effects upon the study of leadership. It possesses an apparently compulsive logic that operates on the guiding premise that the best way of analysing the properties of a being a leader is to focus upon the issue of who the leader is as a person and how that individual interacts with the conditions with which he or she is presented as a leader. The corollary is that by concentrating the field of vision upon a single person, the resultant examination will elicit a wealth of formative, contextual, and interpretive material that will disclose a detailed picture not merely of the individual but of the individual in a leadership position. Thus, given that a life is lived by an individual and that leadership is primarily conceived as being centred upon an individual, biographical methodology can conflate the personal and the political within a unity of purpose.

It is certainly the case that biography has had a long historical affinity with leadership figures—stretching from Suetonius's *The Twelve Caesars*[4] and Plutarch's *Parallel Lives*[5] through to such notable examples of the genre as Isaac Deutscher,[6] John Grigg,[7] Ian Kershaw,[8] and Robert Caro[9] with their magisterial studies of Leon Trotsky, Josef Stalin, Adolf Hitler, and Lyndon B. Johnson. The attachment of biographical modes of study to the topic of individuals in power shows no signs of declining in terms of intensity and scale. On the contrary, the production of biographical studies in this field continues to grow at almost exponential levels. Table 3.1 lists a selected sample of biographically based publications relating to some notable political leaders that are currently available for purchase at the time of writing.

---

[3] See Chapter 2.

[4] Suetonius, *The Twelve Caesars*, ed. James Rives (London: Penguin, 2007).

[5] Plutarch, *Plutarch's Lives Volume 1*, ed. Arthur Hugh Clough (New York, NY: Modern Library/Random House, 2001); Plutarch, *Plutarch's Lives Volume 2*, ed. Arthur Hugh Clough (New York, NY: Modern Library/Random House, 2001).

[6] Isaac Deutscher, *Stalin: A Political Biography* (New York, NY: Oxford University Press, 1967); Isaac Deutscher, *The Prophet Armed: Trotsky 1879–1921* (London: Verso, 2003); Isaac Deutscher, *The Prophet Unarmed: Trotsky 1921–1929* (London: Verso, 2003); Isaac Deutscher, *The Prophet Outcast: Trotsky 1929–1940* (London: Verso, 2003).

[7] John Grigg, *Lloyd George: The Young Lloyd George* (London: Faber and Faber, 2010); John Grigg, *Lloyd George: The People's Champion, 1902–1911* (London: Faber and Faber, 2011); John Grigg, *Lloyd George: From Peace to War, 1912–1916* (London: Faber and Faber, 2011); John Grigg, *Lloyd George: War Leader, 1916–1918* (London: Faber and Faber, 2011).

[8] Ian Kershaw, *The 'Hitler Myth': Image and Reality in the Third Reich* (Oxford: Oxford University Press, 1987); Ian Kershaw, *Hitler 1889–1936: Hubris* (London: Allen Lane 1998); Ian Kershaw, *Hitler: A Profile in Power*, rev edn. (Harlow: Pearson Education, 2001); Ian Kershaw, *Hitler 1936–1945: Nemesis* (London: Allen Lane, 2000).

[9] Robert A. Caro, *The Years of Lyndon Johnson, Vol. 1: The Path to Power* (New York, NY: Vintage, 1990); Robert A. Caro, *The Years of Lyndon Johnson, Vol. 2: Means of Ascent* (New York, NY: Vintage, 1991); Robert A. Caro, *The Years of Lyndon Johnson, Vol. 3: Master of the Senate* (New York, NY: Vintage, 2002); Robert A. Caro, *The Years of Lyndon Johnson, Vol. 4: The Passage of Power* (New York, NY: Knopf, 2012).

Table 3.1 Search results for published works currently available on selected leaders

Leader	No. of results
Franklin D. Roosevelt	35,864
Ronald Reagan	11,878
Winston Churchill	9,566
Saddam Hussein	9,225
Josef Stalin	5,939
Mikhail Gorbachev	3,804
Nelson Mandela	2,864
Vladimir Putin	2,526
Hugo Chávez	1,597
Silvio Berlusconi	812
Total	*84,075*

Source: Amazon.com accessed 24 March 2012.

The sheer volume of publications provides an illustrative indication of the extraordinary appeal that this genre has not just in the professional and academic field but also amongst the general reading public.[10]

A number of compelling reasons exist to account for this voluminous outpouring of biographical material. These can range from a desire to celebrate uplifting and inspirational figures to an impulse to subject leaders to close and critical scrutiny; from the appeal of revealing the private dimensions of public figures to the promise of acquiring deeper explanations of historical events; and from a desire to know more about potential or incoming leaders to the task of recovering lost or overlooked leaders and adjusting their reputations and legacies accordingly. The aggregate effect of this prodigious interest in leader-centred biography is one of continuing controversy. From the standpoint of historical study, the medium of biography has a strained relationship that is characterized by a series of complaints that are rooted in conflicting views over the relationship between biography and historical analysis. Most exponents of the biographical genre assert that the two areas of activity are intimately and inextricably linked to one another.

Practitioners claim that biography can be an instrument in opening up enriched understandings of cultural and social contexts—especially in the way that a focus upon the individual can offer a 'prism of history' which can draw readers into altogether larger spheres of understanding.[11] The counterclaim is that biography is not an authentic form of historical analysis. This view is based on various critiques that cite biography as being necessarily subjective in its outlook, selective in its use of materials, speculative in its judgements, and driven by a sentimental and even emotional attachment by biographers towards the individual merits of their chosen subject matter. The issue of bias is also extended to what is taken in many quarters to be the controlling bias of the genre—namely, that the

[10] David Marquand, 'Biography', in Matthew Flinders, Andrew Gamble, Colin Hay, and Michael Kenny (eds.), *The Oxford Handbook of British Politics* (Oxford: Oxford University Press, 2009), pp. 187–200.

[11] Barbara W. Tuchman, 'Biography as a Prism of History', in Marc Pachter (ed.), *Telling Lives: The Biographer's Art* (Philadelphia, PA: University of Pennsylvania Press 1985), pp. 132–47.

character, motivation, and behaviour of individuals are given an inflated emphasis that far exceeds their significance when set against more structural, sociological, and cultural forces at work within historical explanation.[12]

One response to these indictments has been for biographers to make an explicit turn towards the rigour of behavioural sciences by adopting a much more exploratory approach to the interior origins and dynamics of individual perspectives, impulses, and behaviour. The onset of the psycho-biography that attempts to engage with the formative influences of familial and sexual experiences upon the conscious and subconscious mind has helped to enhance the analytical and theoretical credentials of a medium that has commonly been taken to be instinctive in spirit.[13] It has led to the emergence of an entire sub-genre of in-depth studies of leaders that rely upon the analysis of psychological influences and the operation of various psychodynamics for their explanatory traction.[14] Another response has been to confront the disparity between the high popularity of biography and the low regard with which it is held in so many professional sectors. Some practitioners of biography have consciously sought to distance themselves from the implicit apologias that can be inferred from the many silences surrounding the biography's contribution to historical understanding.

This more robust justification of the genre is well conveyed by the historian Ben Pimlott who argues that biography is the key to understanding the exchange between an individual and a wider social and cultural realm.[15] Intricate continuities and subtle changes can be registered by the 'exploratory possibilities of biography, and its potential as a way of describing and evoking the past'.[16] Far from seeing the necessary focus upon an individual as a constraint, Pimlott claims that biography has an extraordinary explanatory appeal because it is based precisely upon the way all of us structure our own sense of conscious identity.

> Biography deals with a cosmically arbitrary, but biologically simple, unit of time and psychic space. The basic idea of taking a single human span from cradle to grave . . . is

---

[12] The position is exemplified in E. H. Carr, *What is History?* (Basingstoke: Palgrave Macmillan, 2001), pp. 25–49.

[13] See Bruce Mazlish, 'Toward a Psychohistorical Inquiry: The "Real" Richard Nixon', *The Journal of Interdisciplinary History*, 1(1) Autumn 1970: 49–105; Robert Tucker, 'The Georges' Wilson Reexamined: An Essay on Psychobiography', *American Political Science Review*, 71(2) June 1977: 606–18; Avner Falk, 'Aspects of Political Psychobiography', *Political Psychology*, 6(4) December 1985: 605–19; Alexander L. George and Juliette L. George, *Presidential Personality and Performance* (Boulder, CO: Westview, 1998), chs. 1, 3; William Todd Schultz, *Handbook of Psychobiography* (New York, NY: Oxford University Press, 2005); David P. Houghton, *Political Psychology: Situations, Individuals, and Cases* (New York, NY: Routledge, 2009), especially ch. 7.

[14] Bruce Mazlish, *In Search of Nixon: A Psychohistorical Inquiry* (New York, NY: Basic Books, 1972); Alexander L. George and Juliette L. George, *Woodrow Wilson and Colonel House: A Personality Study* (New York, NY: Courier Dover, 1964); Robert G. L. Waite, *The Psychopathic God: Adolf Hitler* (New York, NY: Da Capo Press, 1993); Erik H. Erikson, *Gandhi's Truth: On the Origins of Militant Nonviolence* (New York, NY: Norton, 1993); Leo Abse, *Tony Blair: The Man Behind the Smile* (London: Robson Books, 2001); Theo L. Dorpat, *Wounded Monster: Hitler's Path from Trauma to Malevolence* (Lanham, MD: University Press of America, 2003); Dan McAdams, *George W. Bush and the Redemptive Dream: A Psychological Profile* (New York, NY: Oxford University Press, 2011).

[15] Ben Pimlott, 'Is Contemporary Biography History?' *Political Quarterly*, 70(1) January 1999: 31–41.

[16] Pimlott, 'Is Contemporary Biography History?', p. 36.

not only easy to comprehend; it is fundamental to the way everybody leads their own life . . . Every sentient and intelligent being is an instinctive biographer and autobiographer. Biography is about memory and expectation. Only human amoebae fail to construct a chronology of both their own lives, and those of the people around them, as a frame through which to view contemporary events.[17]

It is this simplicity of purpose that allows biographers to establish a conversation with another person and in doing so to gain access to a different time and place—along with a way of acquiring a closer understanding of that individual's significance. Although Pimlott and others have criticized the often highly conventional architecture of biographical studies, they mostly adhere to the substantive and interpretive utility of the genre in situating individuals within the various constructions of contextual meaning.[18]

The dispute within the historical profession over the methodology and purpose of biography is highly instructive in approaching the issue of political leadership. In many ways the genre of biography has acquired a similarly ambivalent reputation in the field of political explanation—namely that in focusing upon the individual it precludes comparative, systemic, or theoretical forms of explanation. The defensive riposte to this dismissive attitude is virtually indistinguishable from the response made on behalf of biographical historians by Pimlott and others. The same significance is afforded both to the individual leader as the primary object of analysis and to the milieu in which that person was located. It is the case that the selection of subjects is driven by the identity of their political positions and by the specifically political nature of their social and professional contexts. Nonetheless, the premises, methodologies, and adopted styles bear a very close resemblance to one another. Where there are important differences, they lie more in some of the consequential and instrumental aspects of the genre's attachment to political leaders and the theme of leadership.

A particularly significant outcome of the high volume of leadership biographies is the way that such publishing activity reinforces the phenomenon of leaders being regarded as extraordinarily suitable cases for biographical study. Biographical producers and consumers essentially vote with their feet. In essence, both parties to this synergy reaffirm the existence not merely of a compulsive human interest in those who occupy leadership positions but also of an implicit recognition that leaderships always evoke demands for extensive explanations. The embedded sequence of biographies and autobiographies following on from the completion of leadership tenures provides an added stimulus to the appeal of studies that purport to show what gives rise to leaders and the factors that lie behind their decisions. Given that biography proceeds on the basis of a compelling focal point of attention, political leaders always offer a ready-made purpose in studying an individual life. Leaders provide a rich prima facie agenda with which to engage in narrative and analytical excursions. In doing so, they progressively advance the circularity of the dynamic that fuses leaders and biographies together

[17] Pimlott, 'Is Contemporary Biography History?', pp. 34–5.

[18] For example see Ben Pimlott, 'The Future of Political Biography', in Ben Pimlott, *Frustrate Their Knavish Tricks: Writings on Biography, History and Politics* (London: HarperCollins, 1994), pp. 149–61; R. A. W. Rhodes, 'Theory, Method and British Political Life History', *Political Studies Review*, 10(2) May 2012: 161–76.

in a self-fulfilling remit concerning the importance of the subject and the appropriateness of the genre. Far from raising doubts over their explanatory contribution, the proliferation of biographies on the same subject merely legitimizes the continuing exploration for new materials, insights, interpretations, and assessments that will embellish the aggregate portraiture of a leader.

An emphasis on instrumentalism is another distinctive aspect of political biography. Many forms of the biographical genre do seek to place their subjects in a wider sphere so that their achievements can be more readily identified. But it is political biography that more often than not affords this contextual aspect a notably high priority. Because the *raison d'être* of a political leader is mainly understood by reference to the expansive nature of the effects ascribed to a singular entity, a biographer operating in such a field will almost be bound to use the selected individual both as a signifier and as an instrument of social change. In this way, it is normal for political biographers—either consciously or intuitively—to reflect and to endorse the view that leaders themselves are not merely emblems of contextual conditions but are inherently active agencies of change. Just as leadership is widely depicted within political commentary as a medium of cause and effect, so biography follows the pack in being drawn to those who are assumed to be shapers of their respective worlds. In doing so, political biographers tend to conflate the instrumentalism of their wider analytical objectives with the ascribed instrumentalism of leaders in exerting change upon others.

Historical biography can be of immense value in building up a store of raw materials and background information—as well as insights and assessments—on individual leaders and on the way that they can illustrate cultural contexts and social connections. Nevertheless, in the same way that biography is often disputed as serious historical inquiry, so the genre is equally subject to scepticism in the category of political analysis and even in the sub-field of leadership studies. Despite the developments made in biographical conventions to include childhood, gender, and psychosexual dimensions, political analysis has retained a conspicuous scepticism of the genre. This is based upon a variety of objections. For example, it is commonly thought that biography's logic of having to work within the constraints of a singular subject renders it necessarily one-dimensional in substance. In being distracted by the narrative of a particular persona, it is possible to claim that the genre gives priority to the idiosyncrasies of individual figures rather than to any underlying or recurrent factors of explanation. In terms of the general area of political leadership, the charge is that biography concerns itself with an atomized perspective of leaders rather than with any kind of organized overview of them. In effect, despite its engagement with a variety of behavioural sciences, the *sui generis* character of biography is thought to be deficient both in its attentiveness to the key analytical category of political power, and in its lack of ambition in developing anything approximating to a systematic or overarching study of political leadership.

INTO THE INTERIOR

The deficiencies of the trait and the biographical approaches are addressed in another and far more extensive avenue of examination. In many ways it seeks to combine the merits of both by incorporating the breadth of the trait analysis with the depth of the biographical genre. Its premise is based upon the individual nature of leadership. Given that the core basis of leadership is rooted in the properties and characteristics of leaders, then the optimum explanation of leaders and their positions is considered to lie in an understanding of them as individuals and to be grounded in those sets of analytical criteria and layers of meaning that can be assigned to a personal frame of reference. This approach to the whole theme of being a leader steers analysis firmly towards the role of psychology in leadership and to its contribution in being able to identify the sources of leaders' outlooks, drives, behaviour, and decisions. It can be claimed that such an orientation to the subject is set within the logic of leadership itself. The practice and study of leadership invariably centre upon the notion of causality in the way that leaders are seen as instrumental agents of decision, movement, and direction. In many respects, the adoption of a psychological standpoint extends the logic of causality back to the origins, components, and subsequent operation of leaders' personalities. The dominant psychological approach within this subject field is one that investigates the sources and development of leadership personalities, and locates linkages between formative experiences and subsequent leadership behaviour set within a contextual framework of political interrelationships.[19]

Despite its apparent elegance, the psychological approach is marked by a profusion of disputes concerning the ways and means of putting it into operation. There may be general agreement that each leader will bring to the position a cluster of particular skills, competences, outlooks, and weaknesses which will have some influence upon each leader's performance. What is far more open to question is the causal significance of these identified factors and the way they can be used to explain leadership performance and policy outcomes. Different forms of analysis operate on different premises and in relation to different explanatory logics. It is not so much that leaders and leadership generate these strategic divergences and priority disputes; it is that the subject area often brings to the surface and exemplifies generic controversies within the discipline of psychology itself.[20] The field of

[19] See Fred I. Greenstein, *Personality and Politics: Problems of Evidence, Inference and Conceptualization* (New York, NY: Norton, 1975); Jerrold M. Post, 'The Seasons of a Leader's Life: Influences of the Life Cycle on Political Behavior', *Political Psychology*, 2(3/4) Winter 1980: 35–49; Margaret G. Hermann, *Handbook for Assessing Personal Characteristics and Foreign Policy Orientations of Political Leaders* (Columbus, OH: Mershon Center, 1987); George and George, *Presidential Personality and Performance*; Stanley Renshon and John Duckitt (eds.), *Political Psychology: Cultural and Cross-Cultural Foundations* (New York, NY: New York University Press, 2000); George R. Goethals, 'The Psychodynamics of Leadership: Freud's Insights and Their Vicissitudes', in David M. Messick and Roderick M. Kramer (eds.), *The Psychology of Leadership: New Perspectives and Research* (Mahwah, NJ: Lawrence Erlbaum, 2005), pp. 97–112; Jerrold M. Post (ed.), *The Psychological Assessment of Political Leaders* (Ann Arbor, MI: University of Michigan Press, 2005); Houghton, *Political Psychology*, especially chs. 7–11; Martha L. Cottam, Beth Dietz-Uhler, Elena Mastors, and Thomas Preston, *Introduction to Political Psychology*, 2nd edn. (New York, NY: Psychology Press, 2010) especially ch. 5.

[20] For example, see John L. Sullivan, Wendy M. Rahn, and Tom Rudolph, 'The Contours of Political Psychology: Situating Research on Political Information Processing', in James H. Kuklinski (ed.), *Thinking about Political Psychology* (Cambridge: Cambridge University Press 2002), pp. 23–47; Wendy M. Rahn, John L. Sullivan, and Thomas J. Rudolph, 'Political Psychology and Political Science', in Kuklinski (ed.), *Thinking about Political* Psychology, pp. 155–86; Joe C. Magee, Deborah H. Gruenfeld, Dacher J. Keltmer, and Adam D. Galinsky, 'Leadership and the Psychology of Power',

leadership inquiry throws into high relief several deep questions over the usage and application of psychological concepts and techniques. It raises key methodological and epistemological issues surrounding the questions that can or should be posed concerning an individual's personality; along with the highly problematic challenges associated with how it might be possible to elicit such knowledge. Similarly important controversies are evoked by what it is that we need to know; and indeed how we will know when the requisite level of information has been acquired. There again, questions are raised over what may be said to be relevant and over what it takes to arrive at such judgements. All these kinds of queries pose substantial problems which very often lead to severe analytical logjams.

Before examining this signature analysis, it is necessary to outline the premises and logic of this kind of approach. The skills that any individual brings to a position of political leadership will be influenced by that person's political experiences and by the nature of what has been a learning process prior to acquiring office. The cumulative effects of a political life will shape and direct the leader's view of the role of the office and the political purpose of his or her presence within it. It is accepted that external forces like the state of the economy, or the balance of the parties, bureaucratic structures, previous commitments, or the onset of issues will be significant factors in the exercise of leadership. But even these elements will be perceived, conditioned, appraised, and acted on in accordance with a leader's political experience, and in relation to the lessons learnt during the process of a political apprenticeship.

The more individualized the office, or the more individualized the style adopted by a leadership, the greater will be the salience of the leader's own history as a political participant. In the case of the US presidency, there exists an evident resonance between the office and the individual occupant. Historically, the position has always had a very close connection to the idea that there is a *prima facie* relationship between the incumbent and the structure, direction, and decision-making processes of the US government. The singularity and centrality of the position, combined with its political significance and its ascribed role in the developmental dynamics of American governance, make it a conspicuous point of analytical focus for those who are concerned with the causes and effects of personality upon government and politics.[21] Throughout the history of the office, it has long been recognized that individual presidents have had different views in relation to what they wished to achieve and in respect to how they sought to attain their goals. It is recognized that a president's choices and actions will be

---

in Messick and Kramer (eds.), *The Psychology of Leadership*, pp. 275–95; David G. Winter, 'Personality and Political Behavior', in David O. Sears, Leonie Huddy, and Robert Jervis (eds.), *The Oxford Handbook of Political Psychology* (New York, NY: Oxford University Press, 2003), pp. 110–45.

[21] This subject has generated a very large body of analytical studies. For example, see Alexander L. George, 'Assessing Presidential Character', *World Politics*, 26(2) January 1974: 234–82; George C. Edwards III, Bert A. Rockman, and John H. Kessel (eds.), *Researching the Presidency: Vital Questions, New Approaches* (Pittsburgh, PA: University of Pittsburgh Press, 1993); George and George, *Presidential Personality and Performance*; Stanley A. Renshon, *The Psychological Assessment of Presidential Candidates* (New York, NY: Routledge, 1998); Fred I. Greenstein, *The Presidential Difference: Leadership Style from FDR to George W. Bush* (New York, NY: Free Press, 2000); James P. Pfiffner, *The Character Factor: How We Judge America's Presidents* (College Station, TX: Texas A&M University Press, 2004).

constrained by contextual conditions, political circumstances, and institutional constraints. Nevertheless, the imprint of the individual upon the office remains a vitally important element in understanding the operation of the institution. Far from being marginalized in the modern organizational complexity of the presidency, the individual remains at the centre of its meaning and operation. Moreover, it can be claimed that the study of the presidency has increasingly incorporated factors related specifically and explicitly to the individual occupants of the Oval Office—namely their personal backgrounds and motivations as well as their individual dispositions and attributes.

Of course, the views of individual incumbents on the appropriate nature of the president's role in the political system have always been a necessary feature of understanding not just the variation in the office but also the nature of its historical development. Indeed, the history of the presidency can in many respects be seen to be contingent on the way in which different presidents have interpreted their constitutional powers in the light of contemporary public attitudes and prevailing social conditions. More contemporary approaches, however, have taken the personal perspective much further than merely acknowledging that President Theodore Roosevelt, for example, had an activist and expansionist view of the presidency while his successor President William H. Taft had a far more restricted conception of the presidency's constitutional role.[22] Different presidents have differing views of the roles and priorities of the office; they make decisions in different ways; they have distinctive methods of organizing the White House; and they introduce different perspectives, agendas, and responses. Analysts have asked why it is that different presidents do have different views of the office and behave differently within it.

In the study of such a position, it is implausible that any two presidents would arrive at exactly the same decision in exactly the same way. Of course, the precise nature of the variation is impossible to calculate. There always remains an element of indeterminacy. However, this indeterminacy does not support the counter-argument that individual differences between leaders are immaterial because they are not reducible to material distinctions. On the contrary, the prevailing assumption of presidential analysis is that the individual is the root of both the office and its explanation.

> The job of the president is extraordinarily ill-defined and ambiguous . . . On a continuum from ambiguity to structured constraint, the presidency is as close to the former as repetitive assembly-line work is to the latter. And the more ambiguous the definition of a role, the more it will of necessity be shaped by the personal makeup of the individual who fills it.[23]

---

[22] President William H. Taft objected to President Theodore Roosevelt's appropriation of the title 'steward of the people' and his stated view that a president could take whatever action necessary for the public good unless it was *expressly* forbidden by law or the Constitution. In Taft's view, the right approach to take was one in which a president could only exercise those powers which could rightly drawn from a specific provision in the US Constitution. As a consequence, there is 'no undefined residuum of power which he can exercise because it seems to him to be in the public interest' (see William Howard Taft, *Our Chief Magistrate and His Powers* (New York, NY: Columbia University Press, 1916), pp. 139–40).

[23] Fred I. Greenstein 'Toward a Modern Presidency', in Fred I. Greenstein (ed.), *Leadership in the Modern Presidency* (Cambridge, MA: Harvard University Press, 1988), pp. 4–5.

[I]t would be unrealistic to overlook the importance of personality in trying to understand the presidency because this office imposes fewer constraints on the occupant's behaviour than any other in American government. In other words, there is enormous opportunity for presidents to be themselves in performing their day-to-day responsibilities'.[24]

Presidential analysts, biographers, and historians now proceed on the clear premise that a strong interdependency exists between the presidency and the individual properties of the presidents themselves. Because the office has no fixed form and changes in composition with new incumbents, studies in this field suggest that the variety in the definition of presidential roles, in the style and organization of government, and in the selection of policy priorities is to a large extent determined by the individual occupant of the White House.[25]

It is significant that Richard Neustadt's iconic study of the presidency draws particular attention to the central significance of the individual in what is a long-established and highly institutionalized office. Neustadt concludes that it is the individual incumbent who has to shape the administration and to turn the provisional nature of the presidency's powers into a substantive force.[26] In this process, leaders are influenced by the social and political contexts within which they have to operate and to exert leadership. But leadership is also shaped by the leaders themselves and what they bring to the challenge of developing and maintaining the political resources of their positions. This dimension includes the consequences of prior political life, which is often construed in retrospect as constituting a preparation for leadership. However, it also includes much more than this. If the leader is a central component of leadership, what might be said to follow from this proposition? It must be that the personal and psychological composition of the individual leader is central to any understanding of leadership and also to the variability between different leaders and their administrations.

A leader is not just a person, but a personality. Leadership draws on a personality and also draws out a personality. A political life, therefore, extends much further back and embraces a far wider field of influences than any narrow apprenticeship. A political life reaches into the leader's character, into its constituent elements and into its formative processes and the behavioural ramifications of such processes. It includes the role of emotional reactions, physical drives, and developmental crises. In effect, it means that to understand leadership, it is necessary to identify who the leader is; what accounts for that person's entry into public life and for the individual's investment in politics; and what explains a leader's desire, or even need, to be a leader.

---

[24] Norman C. Thomas and Joseph A. Pika, *The Politics of the Presidency*, 4th edn (Washington, DC: CQ Press, 1996), p. 161.

[25] The classic statement of this view is that of Woodrow Wilson—'The President is at liberty, both in law and conscience, to be as big a man as he can. His capacity will set the limit.' Woodrow Wilson, *Constitutional Government in the United States* (New York, NY: Columbia University Press, 1908), p. 70.

[26] Richard E. Neustadt, *Presidential Power: The Politics of Leadership—With Reflections on Johnson and Nixon* (New York, NY: John Wiley, 1976).

THE SEARCH FOR CHARACTER

The pursuit of the relationship between leadership characteristics and the characters of leaders has a long history of analysis. The influence of Sigmund Freud, Carl Jung, and other pioneers in the field of psychoanalysis began to make itself felt in the area of political analysis during the 1930s and 1940s. The work of Harold Lasswell was particularly noteworthy in this respect. In *Psychopathology and Politics* (1930),[27] Lasswell made an explicit attempt to apply Freudian concepts and techniques to the study of politics and to the possibilities of a more scientifically based political order. His conviction in the utility of psychological analysis to the creation of a broad base of political knowledge was exemplified in his explicit adoption of psychoanalysis in the study of political leaders. He sought to show that the childhood experiences of leaders would disclose direct causal connections between their developmental pasts and their basic behavioural orientation as leaders—i.e. a linkage between formative experiences and leadership postures (e.g. revolutionaries, radicals, and conservatives).[28]

Because Lasswell tried to enfold these innovative departures into a much wider and altogether more speculative set of ideas relating to an overarching conception of politics and to a need for social psychiatry to replace political philosophy, his insights into leadership became marginalized for many years in the curricula of political analysis. They were revived by a number of theorists and analysts who sought to use some of Lasswell's work on leadership character, and the interconnections between politics, psychology, and leadership, in order to devise a narrower and more focused set of inquiries on the character and significance of political leaders.

Arguably, the best known and most influential of these analysts has been James D. Barber. From the first of many editions of *The Presidential Character: Predicting Performance in the White House*,[29] Barber's study has been regarded as a pioneering exposition designed to undertake a specifically psychological approach to leadership in a coherent and systematic manner. His theory of political personality and his deployment of comparative biography exemplify the premises, approaches, and objectives of this type of analysis. Barber's work has not only demonstrated the potential and reach of personality inquiry, but has succeeded in raising its public profile to such an extent that his psychological terminology and personality typology have become part of the political discourse on the US presidency. At the same time, it is important to note that his work has also served to underline the limitations and contested nature of this genre of analysis.

James Barber's point of departure is that the US presidency can best be explained by analysing not merely the political performance of individual presidents, but also the formation and composition of their personalities. According to

---

[27] Harold D. Lasswell, *Psychopathology and Politics* (Chicago, IL: University of Chicago Press, 1930).

[28] See also Lasswell's study of the connections between personality characteristics and patterns of legal decision-making in Harold D. Lasswell, *Power and Personality* (New York, NY: Norton, 1948).

[29] James D. Barber, *The Presidential Character: Predicting Performance in the White House* (Englewood Cliffs, NJ: Prentice Hall, 1972). The most recent edition was published by Pearson/Longman in 2008.

this perspective, presidential character becomes the guiding force that shapes behaviour, perceptions, and decisions. According to Barber, a president's character is the critical factor in understanding the office. He states at the outset that 'the connection between his character and his presidential actions emerges as paramount'.[30] The basic objective of Barber's type of analysis, therefore, is to trace the line of causation from childhood to adulthood, from personality to action, and from the subconscious to political decision. This form of study attempts to go one step further than conventional biography by seeking to explain the developmental process in character formation and then to examine the ways in which character or personality influence a president's actions in office. Barber's framework of analysis is based upon a general theory of political personality that can be subdivided into two component elements.

First is the relationship of the individual's psychological composition to its surrounding environment. Learning how to react to what is a shifting context constitutes what can be termed a developmental process of adjustment. Barber refers to three elements in an individual's psychological history. Initially, it is 'character' that is formed. This is determined largely in childhood and provides a basic outlook upon life, experience, and personal self-worth. Building upon the foundations of character is the formation of a 'world view'. This embraces wider ideas of cause and effect in society and conceptions of human nature and moral conflict. According to Barber, this outlook on the world is normally formed by the end of adolescence. The final constituent is 'style'. This is closely associated with early adulthood and relates to a person's habitual way of performing roles that he or she has adopted or has been allocated to. Style takes into account the ways in which individuals adapt to positions where other people have expectations of them and make judgements about them. Although the three elements are claimed to 'fit together in a dynamic package',[31] Barber gives primary significance to character. 'It is what life has marked into a man's being . . . character is a person's stance as he confronts experience'.[32] As a consequence, it is character that provides the key to understanding the behaviour of an individual in such an isolated leadership position as the presidency. Where a president is concerned, personal history and political behaviour are closely aligned with one another.

The *second* element of Barber's analytical structure is derived from the proposition that there exist four types of political personality. While being attentive to the biographical diversity of individual presidents, Barber asserts that in the final analysis, any president can be assigned to *one, and only one*, of four types of personality. The typology is derived from the interplay of two criteria—namely the amount of energy a president invests in the office (active or passive), and the degree of emotional satisfaction derived from his political activity (positive or negative). These two axes produce a fourfold table to which all presidents can be allocated on the basis of a biographical investigation into the formation of their characters (Figure 3.1).

---

[30] Barber, *The Presidential Character*, p. 445. See also Michael Nelson, 'The Psychological Presidency', in Michael Nelson (ed.), *The Presidency and the Political System*, 8th edn. (Washington, DC: Congressional Quarterly, 2006), pp. 170–94.

[31] Barber, *The Presidential Character*, p. 6.

[32] Barber, *The Presidential Character*, p. 8.

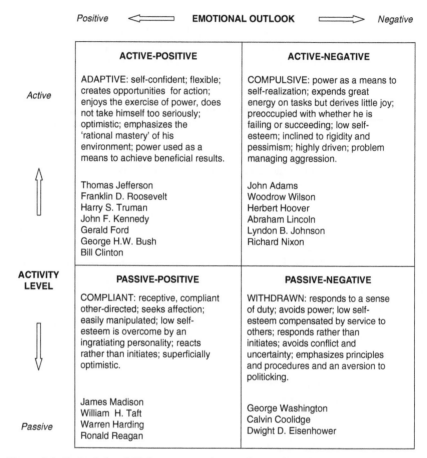

Positive ⟸ **EMOTIONAL OUTLOOK** ⟹ Negative

ACTIVE-POSITIVE

Active

ADAPTIVE: self-confident; flexible; creates opportunities for action; enjoys the exercise of power, does not take himself too seriously; optimistic; emphasizes the 'rational mastery' of his environment; power used as a means to achieve beneficial results.

Thomas Jefferson
Franklin D. Roosevelt
Harry S. Truman
John F. Kennedy
Gerald Ford
George H.W. Bush
Bill Clinton

ACTIVE-NEGATIVE

COMPULSIVE: power as a means to self-realization; expends great energy on tasks but derives little joy; preoccupied with whether he is failing or succeeding; low self-esteem; inclined to rigidity and pessimism; highly driven; problem managing aggression.

John Adams
Woodrow Wilson
Herbert Hoover
Abraham Lincoln
Lyndon B. Johnson
Richard Nixon

ACTIVITY LEVEL

PASSIVE-POSITIVE

COMPLIANT: receptive, compliant other-directed; seeks affection; easily manipulated; low self-esteem is overcome by an ingratiating personality; reacts rather than initiates; superficially optimistic.

James Madison
William H. Taft
Passive   Warren Harding
Ronald Reagan

PASSIVE-NEGATIVE

WITHDRAWN: responds to a sense of duty; avoids power; low self-esteem compensated by service to others; responds rather than initiates; avoids conflict and uncertainty; emphasizes principles and procedures and an aversion to politicking.

George Washington
Calvin Coolidge
Dwight D. Eisenhower

Figure 3.1. Barber's fourfold character typology with presidential examples

Source: James D. Barber, *The Presidential Character: Predicting Performance in the White House* (Englewood Cliffs, NJ: Prentice-Hall, 1972) and succeeding editions.

The matrix of these four character types differentiates four alleged strategies that are employed by those individuals who are drawn to politics by their respective political personalities. Within the remit of Barber's analytical logic, politics has an evident appeal to those individuals with high self-esteem. The success which such individuals have had in relating to their environment and in overcoming the various crises of psychological development leads them to aspire to the highest levels of social influence. But politics also has a special appeal for individuals with low self-esteem. Taking his cue from Lasswell's construction of the 'political man', Barber develops the idea that some of those who enter politics do so because they are chronically deficient in confidence and self-worth. The impulse here is to seek attention and power in order to secure a partial substitute for poor self-esteem and to acquire a position whereby private needs can be displaced onto public objects. They are thought to do so by one of three character-driven strategies for compensation—namely:

1. by appealing for the affection of others through compliant and agreeable behaviour;
2. by invoking a sense of duty and usefulness;
3. or by seeking the deference that emanates from a sense of control and direction over other people.

These different reactions to low self-esteem drive Barber's typology. The 'passive-positives' (e.g. Warren Harding, Ronald Reagan) are the affection-seekers; the 'passive-negatives' (e.g. Calvin Coolidge, Dwight Eisenhower) are those drawn to duty and a sense of public obligation; the 'active-negatives' (e.g. Lyndon Johnson, Richard Nixon) are the compulsive power seekers who tolerate the frustrations of office for the assets of personal power. The 'active-positives' are those who already have a highly developed sense of self-esteem and, as a consequence, bring a confidence and an adaptable outlook to the role of leadership. The 'active-positive' character is well adjusted to its environment and as a result is able to operate flexibly in a grounded way that allows for adjustment within a strong framework of personal objectives. Barber considers 'active-positive' presidents to have the 'virtues of omission'—i.e. they succeed in avoiding 'both obsession and lassitude'. Their energies are positively driven in the way they 'seek out—even create—opportunities for action, rather than waiting for action to come to them'.[33] In so doing, a synthesis is formed between the properties of personality and the nature of presidential office.

As political character is taken to be a fixed property, a president cannot avoid revealing the inner strengths and weaknesses of character when situated in such a highly pressured and exposed position as the White House. The way that a president relates to the tasks and pressures of leadership will reflect the nature of that person's developmental legacies and psychological strategies acquired in dealing with people and situations. The fixity of character means not only that any president will necessarily approximate to one of the four personality types, but that each president's assignment to a type will be permanent and irreversible.

Barber's innovative and influential work has been widely commended on the grounds that it provides a systematic way of focusing on the role and significance of political personality in the presidency. It offers a clear theory and the means to apply it across different presidencies and different periods of time.[34] In alluding to the psychological components of successful presidents and unsuccessful presidents, Barber also provides criteria for comparative evaluation and normative recommendation. The maturity, confidence, and flexibility of the *active-positives* make them the preferred option for the presidency. By the same token, the type most ill-suited to such a high leadership position is the *active-negative*. Their deficiencies in security and self-esteem mean

---

[33] Barber, *The Presidential Character*, p. 210.

[34] The sustained resonance of Barber's work is reflected in the way that it continues to be used as a foundational point of departure in many contemporary analyses of political leadership. For example, see Stephen J. Wayne, 'Presidential Character and Judgment: Obama's Afghanistan and Health Care Decisions', *Presidential Studies Quarterly*, 41(2) June 2011: 291–306.

that their ambition is fuelled by a compulsion for domination and control. Politics becomes a means of compensation for personal inadequacies and while this can generate exceptional leadership, it can also lead to destructive behaviour under pressure.

It can be argued that because of the nature of their position, political leaders have the potential and very often the capacity to incur extraordinary levels of disruption and harm to any social order. This being so, the study of leadership is often premised on the importance of identifying, and where possible avoiding, a situation where an ill-suited individual is placed in a leadership position. Barber's analysis is noteworthy therefore not just for alluding to the positive elements of balanced leadership but for alerting his readers to those personality types who are not only wholly unsuitable and possibly even dangerous candidates for leadership positions, but who are drawn to such sources of compensating status and dominance. For Barber, there is no doubt that those candidates for high office who display signs of having *active-negative* personalities should be avoided as they inevitably will become severely neurotic and dysfunctional in such positions.

An *active-negative* personality is brittle and, therefore, will be unable to adapt to the difficulties and disappointments of office. The occurrence of unexpected developments will almost invariably be interpreted as threats or the equivalent of threats. As a consequence, this personality type is likely to demonstrate a pattern of rigid defensiveness that produces aggression towards opponents and the translation of leadership into fixed positions of intransigence. According to Barber, the records of *active-negative* presidencies can all be characterized by an obstinate persistence in pursuing disastrous policies. Whether it is Woodrow Wilson's intransigence over the League of Nations, or Herbert Hoover's policy reactions to the Great Depression, or Lyndon Johnson's adherence to the Vietnam War, or Richard Nixon's stonewalling during the Watergate crisis, the behaviour pattern is the same. Namely, an inability to acknowledge that a course of action is not working and that a change of direction is required. To have acknowledged such mistakes and changed course may have been politically prudent, but for all such active-negative types such a course would also have been psychologically destructive. It would have subverted their entire sense of control and, thereby, undermined their personal security within the leadership role.

Barber concludes that *active-negative* types pose a danger both to themselves and to the government as a whole for they are likely not only to pursue failed policies but also to undermine the system's democratic processes and norms in an attempt to retain their personal authority. Accordingly, Barber regards it as essential that the presidential selection process should ensure that it successfully identifies the presence of candidates who are active-negative types so that voters can ensure that they are prevented from reaching the White House—a task made more difficult by the fact that it is precisely the active-negatives who invest the most compulsive energy in the drive for office.[35]

---

[35] Barber, *The Presidential Character*, chs. 3, 10, 11, 12.

ASSESSMENTS AND ALTERNATIVES

Barber's investigation of presidential character offers a valuable point of access to the subject of leadership personality. The study looks behind the behaviour, techniques, and styles of leaders at what impelled them into politics in the first place, and what the psychological determinants are of such behaviours, techniques, and styles. Barber provides a set of criteria and a methodology for differentiating and comparing presidents on the grounds of their basic outlook upon the world and of their personal strategies for coping both with themselves and with others around them. Apart from offering a highly suggestive and relatively comprehensive model of the 'psychological presidency', Barber reintroduces a concern for the moral integrity of individual power in general and of presidential leadership in particular. He underlines the importance of the influence of an individual's experiences, responses, and needs upon political motives and choice. In doing so, he draws attention to the existence of connections between personal temperament and political action. Barber implies that there is a personality type that best fits the roles and demands of the presidency. By the same token, he asserts that there are proactive yet emotionally negative political types who should be screened out of the selection process by an alert media and a concerned public.

In addition to issuing a warning against active-negative types in the White House, Barber's typology includes a strong predictive dimension—namely that by analysing the matrix of known personality traits together with the pressures of the presidency, it is possible to establish a profile of probabilities in respect to presidential behaviour. Given the background and temperament of Richard Nixon, for example, Barber claims that an issue like the Watergate scandal was always a probability. In a White House constructed around the insecurities and anxieties of an 'active-negative' personality like that of Nixon, it was always likely that the presidency would become engulfed by controversy born out of an over-reactive sense of defensiveness. In conclusion, it can be said that Barber's work has come to typify an analytical approach that has gained enormous social currency in the United States. Even a confident and secure president like Ronald Reagan felt compelled to take public issue with being categorized as a 'passive-positive' personality in Barber's typology of presidential character.[36] The classification of character types continues to arouse interest and is often to be found in analyses and evaluations of recent and current holders of the presidency. The place of George W. Bush within the typology, for example, has provoked widely different estimations that have variously assigned him to the active-positive, the passive-positive, and the active-negative categories.

Barber's pioneering study of political personality and its presentation of a four-fold typology of presidential character has also provoked considerable analytical controversy. For every plaudit, there has been an equally vigorous critique that points to aspects of analysis in this area that remain deeply problematic and therefore unresolved. The complaints tend to come in three main forms. The first

---

[36] Robert Shogan, *The Riddle of Power: Presidential Leadership from Truman to Bush* (New York, NY: Plume, 1992), p. 244.

is those in which the type of psychological analysis is disputed. The second relates to questions over adopted methodologies. And the third is the more generic objection that raises doubts over the role and reach of any kind of psychological analysis in such an area. A selected sample of some of the main critiques is listed in Box 3.1.

Box 3.1 The Barber exposition on political personality and presidential character: Key analytical objections and critiques

- The study largely assumes what it has to prove—i.e. that three levels of analysis (phenomenological; psychodynamic; psychogenetic variables) can be fused together to generate an explanatory logic that demonstrates how character can shape individual behaviour and political action.

- The fourfold typology is condemned as narrow, unsophisticated, and unproven in that it not only implies certainties from probabilities but creates an artificial symmetry of four types from two categories to cover an array of different individuals.

- The analysis is accused of being too deterministic in the way it assigns present and future behaviour to past personal experiences, thereby ignoring a host of other more contemporary influences. Thus although the typology rests on notions of causality, the causal chains are not conclusive.

- In necessarily precluding any movement by an individual between what are taken to be pure types, the study is said to ignore the possibility (i) that genuine hybrids might combine the properties of two or more types; (ii) that character trends from different types might coexist together in the same person; and (iii) that character adjustment through social learning and professional experience might allow for a conditioned response to the demands of a leadership position.

- Barber is also criticized on the grounds of data collection and assessment in that the evidence supporting his classification is highly subjective and based upon narrow and selective constructions of biographical interpretation. Despite the appearance of an inductive exercise of analysis, Barber is accused of selecting evidence to fit a preconceived typology.

- It can be claimed that leadership behaviour cannot always, or even primarily, be reduced to the results of an individual's inner drives, needs, and coping mechanisms. Barber's schema can be said to offer a very opaque conception of the difference between what is 'political' and what is 'personal'; and what is public and what is private.

- The demarcation of 'active-positive' types as the best fit between character and the office of the presidency can be taken as indicating the presence of a normative political bias in that his ideal president is Franklin D. Roosevelt while his 'active-positives' are predominantly liberal Democrats with a reformist and expansive view of the state.

- Subsequent archival research can reveal dimensions to, and properties of, a president and a presidency that may have been largely inaccessible to Barber's techniques of biographical inference. Fred I. Greenstein's study of Eisenhower, for example, challenges Barber by showing that a 'passive-negative' personality could in fact be a highly effective president whose behaviour and achievements could be construed as out of synch with the psychological premises of such a type.

- The deployment of 'ego defence' strategies (e.g. denial, suppression, rationalization, projection) by a leader cannot necessarily be equated with evidence of an individual under so much stress that he or she is unable to operate rationally or effectively. On the contrary, the usage of such strategies can be synonymous with intelligent and well-adjusted coping mechanisms for individuals in challenging situations.

- The exclusive emphasis on character fails to compensate for an inadequate consideration of the role of belief systems and cognitive styles.

- Even if Barber's typology of characters were proved to be accurate in accounting for differences in presidential personalities, the issue remains of whether it amounts to a satisfactory explanation of presidential actions and decisions—i.e. whether it explains the character of a presidency set within the constraints of a political environment and whether all presidential behaviour can be reduced to the category of 'personality'.

Sources: Alexander L. George, 'Assessing Presidential Character', *World Politics*, 26(2) January 1974: 234–82; James H. Qualls, 'Barber's Typological Analysis of Political Leaders', *The American Political Science Review*, 71 (1) March 1977: 182–211; Fred I. Greenstein, *The Hidden Hand Presidency: Eisenhower as Leader* (New York, NY: Basic Books, 1982); Erwin C. Hargrove, 'Presidential Personality and Leadership Style', in George C. Edwards III, Bert A. Rockman, and John H. Kessel (eds.), *Researching the Presidency: Vital Questions, New Approaches* (Pittsburgh, PA: University of Pittsburgh Press, 1993), pp. 69–109; Michael Nelson, 'The Psychological Presidency', in Michael Nelson (ed.), *The Presidency and the Political System*, 8th edn. (Washington, DC: Congressional Quarterly, 2006), pp. 170–94.

Barber's study of presidential character, therefore, is very useful from the point of view of disclosing not merely many of the objections to this kind of analysis but in highlighting the scope for deeper reflection on the issues of leadership and personality. Very often Barber is used to introduce the significance of personality as a category of examination only for the analysis to go on to specify the limitations of Barber's own methodology and typology. The work of Fred I. Greenstein, for example, goes to great lengths to underline the complexity of analysing personality. He draws attention to the different dimensions and bases of the subject field that ranges from socializing processes and environmental influences to the realm of conscious orientations (e.g. opinions, attitudes, beliefs, values, ideology); and from the functional bases of such predispositions (e.g. cognitive structures, needs, defences, strategies of mediation between the self and others) to the biological underpinnings of personality in terms of genetic inheritance and physiological attributes.[37]

The eminent presidential scholar Erwin C. Hargrove summed up the problem of opening up this complex area of political personality to concerted inquiry by pointing out that different models of personality could account for any given action by a leader: 'There is no agreement in personality theory on the inner dynamics of human beings . . . Everyone knows that presidential personality is a crucial independent factor, which is clear in the analysis of specific decisions and actions, but few know how to deal with this factor systematically and weigh its effect in relation to other factors.'[38] Hargrove's conclusion is that the personality of the leader remains a highly significant analytical factor but one which is plural in nature and elusive in terms of arriving at generalizations: 'The personality of

[37] Fred I. Greenstein, 'Can Personality and Politics Be Studied Systematically?', *Political Psychology*, 13(1) March 1992: 105–28. See also George and George, *Presidential Personality and Performance*, *passim*.

[38] Erwin C. Hargrove, *The Power of the Modern Presidency* (New York, NY: Knopf, 1974), p. 69.

each individual is a gestalt, a unique configuration of variables, and there are few general propositions about the links between personality and political style that will apply to a number of people. There will be too many variables of complex possibilities.'[39]

The scale of these constraints, and the multiple disputations that arise from them, have not noticeably inhibited the drive towards increasing numbers of personality-based studies of leaders and leadership. On the contrary, critiques have only prompted fresh attempts to correct, refine, and extend previous strategies of inquiry. Some have sought to introduce more sophisticated typologies of leadership personality or individual styles using a range of different analytical categories to devise allegedly more precise and nuanced registers of leadership forms. Such analyses often draw upon established psychometric models used to differentiate individual perceptions of the world and personal approaches to role definition and decision-making. The Myers–Briggs Type Indicator (MBTI) system, for example, offers one type of resource base for establishing methodologies that engage in distinguishing different forms of leadership behaviour by reference to sixteen different psychological types based upon a series of self-identified categories or preferences—i.e. introversion, extroversion, sensing, intuition, thinking, feeling, perception, and judgement.

Another increasingly prominent approach has been the study of leaders' belief structures and the cognitive frameworks that support them. In a system of assessment termed operational code analysis (OCA), individual leaders are differentiated from one another by their attributed responses to a set of questions designed to elicit two sets of beliefs[40]—namely (i) *philosophical beliefs* (core assumptions concerning the fundamental nature of political life; the balance of conflict and harmony; the character of one's opponents; the extent to which society is predictable and controllable) and (ii) *instrumental beliefs* (more specific operational dispositions concerning approaches, objectives, methods, and timing). From its early applications in political science, OCA has been progressively refined to become a popular analytical model of leadership dispositions and behaviour alignments.[41] The technique places particular emphasis upon examining the connections between what are taken to be coherent and usually resilient systems of belief on the one hand, and leaders' perceptions of, and engagements with, their political environments on the other. The information drawn from

---

[39] Hargrove, *The Power of the Modern Presidency*, pp. 72–3.

[40] This method allows for 'analysis at a distance' through the tracking of leaders' views normally disclosed through the medium of written statements, prepared comments, and set piece speeches.

[41] Alexander L. George, 'The "Operational Code": A Neglected Approach to the Study of Political Leaders and Decision-Making', *International Studies Quarterly*, 13(2) June 1969: 190–222; Stephen G. Walker, 'The Evolution of Operational Code Analysis', *Political Psychology*, 11(2) June 1990: 403–18; Stephen G. Walker, Mark Schafer, and Michael D. Young, 'Systematic Procedures for Operational Code Analysis: Measuring and Modeling Jimmy Carter's Operational Code', *International Studies Quarterly*, 42(1) March 1998: 175–89; Stephen G. Walker, Mark Schafer, and Michael D. Young, 'Profiling the Operational Codes of Political Leaders', in Jerrold M. Post (ed.), *The Psychological Assessment of Political Leaders* (Ann Arbor, MI: University of Michigan Press, 2003), pp. 215–45; Mark Schafer and Stephen G. Walker (eds.), *Beliefs and Leadership in World Politics: Methods and Applications of Operational Code Analysis* (New York, NY: Palgrave Macmillan, 2006); Houghton, *Political Psychology*, pp. 108–13.

operational coding is not normally seen as providing indicators of personality per se. Coding indicators are primarily cognitive constructs grounded in the identification of private and subjective principles that order relationships with surrounding contexts. The OCA process has been used to examine the belief systems of several world leaders and in particular the actual or predictive effect of these dispositional structures upon their reactions to foreign policy conflicts, crisis decision-making, and the international system as a whole.[42]

Other studies have used different analytical approaches and research methodologies that are centred upon more explicit connections between character analysis and leadership actions. An illustrative case is provided by the work of Graham Little on leadership types. In an approach that bears some similarity to that of Barber, Little focuses upon biographical and psychoanalytical techniques to generate a tripartite classification of leadership repertoires. But in contrast to Barber, his work incorporates a psycho-social dimension that engages with the generative aspects of the interrelationships between leadership styles on the one hand and the conscious and unconscious needs and impulses of the wider cultural milieu on the other. Based upon the different reactions to the 'self–other dilemma',[43] Little posited the existence of three distinct 'ensembles' of self–other dispositions that allowed for three correlated patterns of viable leadership.[44]

The *strong leader* is related to a 'structure' ensemble which is drawn from an 'us versus them' societal outlook based upon structured competition and the need to contain rather than to resolve conflict. Such a matrix accommodates a disciplined command style of leadership in line with the need for tough decisions and, if required, the issuing of threats. A 'group' ensemble of unconscious perspectives is aligned with a leadership that is consultative in style and concerned for the dependency of others upon the leader's position. The *group leader* therefore is sensitized towards shared needs and experiences; is concerned for the needy and disadvantaged; and evokes a self-effacing outlook based upon trust and a respect for tradition.

The third variant emanates from what Little terms 'the Ensemble' which is largely reducible to a mix of the previous ensembles in that it posits a solution to the self–other problem in the form of a constructive balance between the two elements in which each is enhanced by the presence of the other in an ongoing mutual relationship. The *Ensemble leader* in this format is an imaginative and innovative individual looking beyond established structures and traditions in the

---

[42] For example, see Stephen G. Walker and Mark Schafer, 'The Political Universe of Lyndon B. Johnson and his Advisors: Diagnostic and Strategic Propensities in their Operational Codes', *Political Psychology*, 21(3) June 2000: 529–43; Huiyun Feng, 'The Operational Code of Mao Zedong: Defensive or Offensive Realists', *Security Studies*, 14(4) Summer 2005: 637–62; Akan Malici and Johnna Malici, 'The Operational Codes of Fidel Castro and Kim-Il Sung: The Last Cold Warriors?', *Political Psychology*, 26(3) June 2005: 387–412; Mark Schafer and Stephen Walker, 'Democratic Leaders and the Democratic Peace: The Operational Codes of Tony Blair and Bill Clinton', *International Studies Quarterly*, 50(3) September 2006: 561–84; Akan Malici and Allison L. Buckner, 'Empathizing with Rogue Leaders: Mahmoud Ahmadinejad and Bashar al-Asad', *Journal of Peace Research*, 45(6) November 2008: 783–800.

[43] The self–other dilemma relates to the problems incurred in discovering ways to resolve the psychological conflict between the sense of ourselves as individuals, and the presence, needs, and demands of others.

[44] Graham Little, *Political Ensembles: A Psychosocial Theory of Politics and Leadership* (Melbourne: Oxford University Press, 1985).

cause of positive and improving change. All three types possess their own characteristic strengths and weaknesses. As a consequence, each of the three leadership styles and their constituent ensembles can attract critiques drawn from the other two ensemble relationships and the reflexive drives that lie at the core of their respective dynamics.

Graham Little's work not only opened up leadership study to a wider remit of psychoanalytical approaches but in doing so deployed the analysis of political leadership itself as an instrumental agency in the deeper development of the discipline's theoretical and operational resources. In addition, Little set in train a particular style of conceptually informed and innovatively configured biographical studies which subjected such figures as Margaret Thatcher, Ronald Reagan, Malcolm Fraser, and Jeff Kennett to close scrutiny.[45] The modus operandi of these studies acted as a stimulus to the emergence of what became known as the Melbourne School of political psychology whose cultivated interest in the political self set within the grain of personal and social conflicts has generated a continuing engagement with both political leadership and the genre of political biography.[46]

A quite different type of analytical engagement with the subject field is provided by the work of Margaret Hermann and her associates who have developed techniques for identifying and assessing the leadership styles of heads of government and the way that these can impact upon key decision-making processes, especially in the spheres of foreign policy and crisis management. As shown in Chapter 2, Hermann's system is based upon a multi-category matrix of observed traits in order to create a way of classifying different leadership styles. The composite model of style construction, based upon leaders' attitudes to restraints, their responses to incoming information, and their overall rationales of political engagement, has generated a large dataset covering the personality profiles of over 300 leaders.[47] These facilitate the analysis of leaders' probable and actual

---

[45] Graham Little, *Strong Leadership: Thatcher, Reagan and an Eminent Person* (Melbourne: Oxford University Press 1988); Graham Little, 'Malcolm Fraser: A Strong Leader Revisited', in Judith Brett (ed.), *Political Lives* (Sydney: Allen & Unwin, 1997), pp. 52–70; Graham Little, 'Celebrity Leadership', in Brian Costar and Nicholas Economou (eds.), *The Kennett Revolution: Victorian Politics in the 1990s* (Sydney: New South Wales Press, 1999), pp. 15–26; Judith Brett, 'Graham Little's Theory of Political Leadership', *International Journal of Applied Psychoanalytic Studies*, 6(2) March 2009: 103–10.

[46] See Brett (ed.), *Political Lives*; Judith Brett, *Australian Liberals and the Moral Middle Class: From Alfred Deakin to John Howard* (Cambridge: Cambridge University Press, 2002); Judith Brett, *Robert Menzies' Forgotten People* (Melbourne: Macmillan, 2003; Judith Brett, 'Exit Right: The Unravelling of John Howard', *Quarterly Essay*, 28 2007: 1–96; James Walter, *The Leader: A Political Biography of Gough Whitlam* (Queensland: University of Queensland Press, 1980); James Walter, 'Howard's Strength', *Journal of Australian Studies*, 31(91) 2007: 59–68; James Walter, 'Political Leaders and their Publics', *International Journal of Applied Psychoanalytic Studies*, 5(3) September 2008: 153–70; James Walter, 'Political Biography', in R. A. W. Rhodes (ed.), *The Australian Study of Politics* (Basingstoke: Palgrave Macmillan, 2009), pp. 97–106; James Walter and Paul 't Hart, 'Political Psychology', in Rhodes (ed.), *The Australian Study of Politics*, pp. 356–65.

[47] Hermann, *Handbook for Assessing Personal Characteristics and Foreign Policy Orientations of Political Leaders*; Margaret G. Hermann, *Workbook for Developing Personality Profiles of Political Leaders from Content Analysis Data* (Columbus, OH: Mershon Center, 1987); Margaret G. Hermann 'Assessing the Foreign Policy Role Orientations of Sub-Saharan African Leaders', in Stephen G. Walker (ed.), *Role Theory and Foreign Policy Analysis* (Durham, NC: Duke University Press, 1987), pp. 161–98; Margaret G. Hermann, *Assessing Leadership Style: A Trait Analysis* (Columbus, OH: Social Science Automation, 1999).

interactions with other leaders and with the situational contexts of norms, rules, and principles. As a result, Margaret Hermann has become associated with a prodigious set of analytical and comparative outputs examining the constituent elements of leadership styles and their effects upon role definitions, policy orientations, and decision-making. In contrast to Barber, Hermann's work is based upon a far wider set of variables that allow for a more nuanced set of role orientations, leadership conditionalities, and predictive probabilities.[48] Their reach is reflected in Hermann's grid of personality orientations (Table 3.1).

Another analyst who has been instrumental in moving the study of leadership personality to higher levels of empirical and theoretical rigour is David Winter. His main point of departure is that too much weight had previously been assigned to individual traits in conveying the core of personality. Although traits represent a significant, observable, and largely consistent element in the composition of personality, Winter criticized the way that traits were often used indiscriminately in ways that gave the impression that personality was reducible to traits and their stylistic expressions. In Winter's view, personality is a much more complex amalgam of properties and characteristics.[49] It includes not only cognitive repertoires (values, beliefs, moral codes) that form the main mediating devices through which the individual negotiates with the wider world, but also the accumulated effects of experienced multiple social contexts.

The fourth constituent is an element that had been implicit in many other studies—including those of Margaret Hermann—but which Winter brought forward as a fundamental category that warranted separate and explicit recognition in the analysis of political leadership. This is the theme of motivation—i.e. the driving impulse towards objectives that energize activity and give an anticipatory focus to specific behaviours. Winter developed David McClelland's theory of three types of motivational need[50] and applied it to the realm of political leadership. Winter propounded the existence of three major social motives or dimensions of motivated behaviour—namely *achievement* (a concern for excellence); *affiliation*

[48] Margaret G. Hermann, 'Explaining Foreign Policy Behavior Using the Personal Characteristics of Political Leaders', *International Studies Quarterly*, 24(1) March 1980: 7–46; Margaret G. Hermann, 'Assessing the Personalities of Soviet Politburo Members', *Personality and Social Psychology Bulletin*, 6 (3) September 1980: 332–52; Margaret G. Hermann, 'Personality and Foreign Policy Making', in Donald Sylvan and Steve Chan (eds.), *Perceptions, Beliefs, and Foreign Policy Decision Making* (New York, NY: Praeger, 1984, pp. 53–80; Margaret G. Hermann and Charles F. Hermann, 'Who Makes Foreign Policy Decisions and How: An Empirical Inquiry', *International Studies Quarterly*, 33(3) June 1989: 361–87; Margaret G. Hermann, 'Leaders, Leadership, and Flexibility: Influences on Heads of Government as Negotiators and Mediators', *The Annals of the American Academy of Political and Social Science*, 542(1) 1995: 148–67; Margaret G. Hermann, and Joe D. Hagan, 'International Decision Making: Leadership Matters', *Foreign Policy*, 110 Spring 1998: 124–37.

[49] David G. Winter, *Personality: Analysis and Interpretation of Lives* (New York, NY: McGraw-Hill, 1996); David G. Winter, '"Toward a Science of Personality Psychology": David McClelland's Development of Empirically Derived TAT Measures', *History of Psychology*, 1(2) 1998: 130–53; David G. Winter and Nicole B. Barenbaum, 'History of Modern Personality Theory and Research', in Lawrence A. Pervin and Oliver P. John (eds.), *Handbook of Personality: Theory and Research*, 2nd edn. (New York, NY: Guilford Press, 1999), pp. 3–27.

[50] David C. McClelland, *Personality* (New York, NY: William Sloane, 1951); David C. McClelland, *The Achieving Society* (New York, NY: Van Nostrand, 1961); David C. McClelland, *Human Motivation* (New York, NY: Cambridge University Press, 1985).

Table 3.2 Brief characterization of achievement, affiliation, and power motives

Characteristic	Achievement	Affiliation	Power
Typical verbal images	Excellence, quality of performance, innovation	Warmth, friendship, unity	Impact on the behaviour or emotions of others, prestige
Associated actions	Moderate risks, use of information to modify performance, entrepreneurial success, dishonesty when necessary to reach goal	Cooperativeness and friendliness under safe conditions, defensiveness and even hostility under threat	Leadership and high morale of subordinates if high in sense of responsibility, profligate impulsivity if low in sense of responsibility
Negotiating style	Cooperative and 'rational'	Cooperative under safe conditions, defensive and hostile under threat	Exploitative, aggressive
Approach to negotiating partner	Cooperator	Either fellow worker or opportunist	Yielder, gambler, competitor, resister
Help sought from	Technical experts	Friends and similar others	Political 'experts'
Political psychological manifestations	Frustration	Peacemaking and arms limitation, but vulnerability to scandal	Charisma, war and aggression, independent foreign policy, rated greatness

Source: David G. Winter 'Presidential Psychology and Governing Styles: A Comparative Psychological Analysis of the 1992 Presidential Candidates', in Stanley A. Renshon (ed.), *The Clinton Presidency: Campaigning, Governing, and the Psychology of Leadership* (Boulder, CO: Westview, 1995), p. 116.

(a concern for good relations and unity); and *power* (a concern for having an effect on others). Motives are treated as implied processes which are revealed through word and deed depending on different circumstances. In Winter's model, the three motive forces are identified and assessed through the motive imagery used by individual leaders in their written materials, public addresses, and speeches. The scoring definitions that form the basis of Winter's assessment-at-a-distance methodology are summarized in Table 3.2.[51]

The differentiation of the three motives allows for the formation of a trichotomous basis of analysis in which a motivational profile can be generated for each individual. Leaders are not assigned exclusively to one of the three motivational categories. While each individual displays a mix of motives stretching across the

[51] David G. Winter, 'Measuring Personality at a Distance: Development of an Integrated System for Scoring Motives in Running Text', in Daniel J. Ozer, Joseph M. Healy, and Abigail J. Stewart (eds.), *Perspectives in Personality*, Volume 3: *Approaches to Understanding Lives* (London: Jessica Kingsley, 1991), pp. 59–89; David G. Winter, 'Content Analysis of Archival Data, Personal Documents, and Everyday Verbal Productions', in C. P. Smith (ed.), *Motivation and Personality: Handbook of Thematic Content Analysis* (New York, NY: Cambridge University Press 1992), pp. 110–25; D. G. Winter, O. P. John, A. J. Stewart, E. C. Klohnen, and L. E. Duncan, 'Traits and Motives: Toward an Integration of Two Traditions in Personality Research', *Psychological Review*, 105(2) April 1998: 230–50; David G. Winter 'Motivation and Political Leadership', in Linda O. Valenty and Ofer Feldman (eds.), *Political Leadership for the New Century: Personality and Behavior among American Leaders* (Westport, CT: Praeger, 2002), pp. 27–47.

three bands, a person will have an asymmetrical distribution in which one of the three registered motives will show a marginal preponderance over the others. Moreover, it is recognized that motives can be fluid and contingent in nature: 'In contrast to the consistency of traits, motives are variable. How a motive is expressed in behaviour will depend on many factors, such as obstacles and opportunities, the time since last satisfaction, the functional substitutability of different incentives for satisfying that motive, and conflicts and fusions with other motives.'[52]

What Winter and the school associated with this format can show is how the mix of motives, along with the other elements of personality related to traits, cognitive constructions, and social contexts, can provide a range of insights not just into the composition of personality variables but into the tensions and cross-currents that can affect individuals in the exercise of their leadership roles. Using his collection of personality profiles of all US presidents, Winter has been able to examine a variety of different types of external and internal strains, and to compare the cases across time. For example, it is possible for a leader with a high affiliation motivation to find that he or she does not possess a strong enough trait in extroversion to be successfully aligned with a motive that requires a sociable personality. Whereas presidents like Franklin Roosevelt and John Kennedy had a close congruence between trait and motive in this sphere, President Nixon did not, which is thought to have created a continuing source of strain for him.

More problematically, if a political leader has a high achievement motivation then the medium of politics can be a problem in its own right. With its arenas of opposition, challenges, and delays—together with the commensurate needs for compromise and limited progress—the theatre of politics will not always suit a president with the inflexible temperament, high performance standards, and need for personal control that distinguish an achievement-minded leader. Accordingly, such an individual may become withdrawn and resentful, and given to attempts to retrieve what is considered to be a compensatory degree of authoritarian control. Winter highlights the significance of the delicate balance between power motivation and achievement motivation within some individuals. The latter impulse can work to compromise the former to an extent where a leader no longer has the kind of assurance and confidence that emanates from a power-motivated politician. In Winter's view, the corrosive effects of political uncertainties and insufficient outcomes can lead achievement-minded leaders to react against the frustrations of politics in favour of rigid stances and extreme measures that may breach constitutional conventions, legal rules, or ethical norms. Winter cites the presidencies of Lyndon Johnson, Richard Nixon, and Jimmy Carter as keynote examples of leaders personally motivated by achievement but who could not adjust to the exigencies of contemporary politics and as a result became increasingly disillusioned with the presidential role.[53]

Winter's model provides a highly durable form of systematic leadership analysis that depends upon a fourfold conception of personality typing and a featured

[52] David G. Winter, 'Things I've Learned about Personality from Studying Political Leaders at a Distance', *Journal of Personality*, 73(3) June 2005: 567.

[53] It should be acknowledged that while power-motivated leaders have a family resemblance to Barber's 'active-positive' types, achievement-motivated leaders have a discernible resonance with Barber's 'active-negative' types.

emphasis upon the dynamics of individual motivation in relation to different contexts. Like Barber, Winter has a normative dimension which assigns those with a motivation towards power as having the most appropriate personality profile to suit the leadership role and therefore the most likely to succeed as presidents. Even though the model has remained largely unaltered for forty years, it continues to generate a host of personality studies that carry considerable explanatory weight in terms of diagnostics, prognoses, and predictive probabilities. By 2011, Winter was able to depict Barack Obama's profile as moving from a close cluster of motivations during the 2008 presidential campaign to a much wider distribution as president. In the White House, power motivation emerged as dominant with affiliation motivation a lowly third in ranking, and achievement motivation at a median point in between. Commenting on a discerned rise in the achievement category in motive imagery during the course of 2010, Winter offered the appropriate note of caution: 'Obama will enjoy being president (very high power and only average achievement); however, if his achievement motivation increases further, he may become frustrated by political conflict or the ebbing of popular support . . . Power-motivated leaders tend to enjoy politics as a "scrimmage," in which alliances and the balance of forces are constantly changing. In contrast, achievement-motivated leaders tend to complain that their good ideas go unappreciated.'[54]

CONTINUING PATHWAYS OF UNDERSTANDING

The interest in explanatory accounts and predictive trajectories based upon personality typing is also reflected in a renewal of interest in developmental psychology. For example, in a thirty-year survey based on the British Cohort Study, researchers have concluded that by the age of ten, children have acquired an enduring self-image which has a greater influence upon their life trajectories than academic distinction or social position. This research suggests that children whose sense of self-esteem is secure will have a higher than average chance of being successful in their chosen career pathways. Thus, it can be claimed that irrespective of a socially deprived background or a poor school record, individuals with high self-esteem at an early age can and do rise to positions of social and economic leadership. By the same token, it is not unusual for children who are high achievers at school and later at university, but who nevertheless retain a sense of low self-esteem, to have significant underperformance problems in their subsequent careers.[55]

---

[54] David G. Winter, 'Philosopher-King or Polarizing Politician? A Personality Profile of Barack Obama', *Political Psychology*, 32(6) December 2011: 1074.

[55] Leon Feinstein, *The Relative Economic Importance of Academic, Psychological and Behavioural Attributes Developed in Childhood* (London: Centre for Economic Performance/London School of Economics and Political Science, 2000). See also Richard B. Felson and Mary A. Zielinski, 'Children's Self-Esteem and Parental Support', *Journal of Marriage and Family*, 51(3) 1989: 727–35; Terri Apter, *The Confident Child: Raising Children to Believe in Themselves* (New York, NY: Bantam, 1998).

Such research opens up the question of how such resilient levels of self-esteem are formed at such an early age. Many of the answers are centred upon family structures and positions. Recently, particular interest has been shown in the distribution of perceived attention and affection amongst different children within the same family. The perception of parental favourites and the link from that distinction to childhood high self-esteem is a commonly reported dynamic and one that has some considerable basis in fact.[56] Another aspect of this presumptive ascription of status and roles is afforded by the dimension of birth-order within families. This has generated a rich vein of research that offers considerable interest to the study of leadership (Box 3.2).

Box 3.2 Birth order and character formation

From its early inception—most notably with the work of Sigmund Freud and Alfred Adler—the study of birth order has now become a major theme in evolutionary and developmental psychology. At its simplest, it examines the effects of birth order patterns and sibling structures upon the formation of personality and behaviour. From a set of foundational categories and descriptors, the analytical genre investigates the properties and effects of these sequences not just within family structures but more significantly upon the later lives of individuals. It centres on both (i) the attribution and weighing of relative advantages and disadvantages within bounded social contexts, and (ii) the way that siblings interact with and condition one another in their respective niche positions.

In summary form, the main characteristics that are commonly associated with different birth order positions are as follows:

Oldest sibling: responsible; assertive; intelligent; confident; dominant position; comfortable in existing structures; approval of authority; conservative outlook; preference for incremental change; cautious; risk averse.

Middle sibling: lacks attention of older and younger siblings; flexible; sociable; diplomatic skills in seeking compromises; tends to lack self-esteem and recognition.

Youngest sibling: creative; innovative; outspoken; challenging; impulsive; attention-seeking; open to new experiences; disposition to rebel against the status quo; adventure seeking; risk tolerant.

It is conceded that these categories along with their profiles of experiences, adjustments, and impulses are contingent upon a host of moderating factors (e.g. gender, temperament, class, physique, family size). Nevertheless, it is a widely held view that birth order data offer a key resource in the formulation of analytical agendas in a host of subject fields. One such area in which birth order effects have attracted increasing interest is the study of leadership and especially the reasons why some individuals appear to be more suited than others to such a role.

One commonly expressed conclusion is that a measure of correlation exists between the first-born category and both the occupancy of leadership positions and the prescribed traits often associated with leadership distinction (e.g. emotional maturity; balanced outlook; measured approach to problems and decisions). A number of studies show that there is a disproportionately high representation of firstborns in a range of leadership sectors. At the same time, it is also noteworthy that the strength of these correlations has been challenged on grounds usually related to counterclaims of biased evidence collection; flawed or inconsistent methodologies; and the presence of contradictory findings.

(*continued*)

---

[56] See Frank J. Sulloway, *Born to Rebel: Birth Order, Family Dynamics, and Creative Lives* (New York, NY: Pantheon, 1996).

Box 3.2 Continued

Notwithstanding these objections, the field continues to attract large-scale and intensive studies that serve to swell an already substantial birth order literature. At its most fundamental level, it can be said that early family experiences and sibling rivalries can be considered to be important influences upon personality but that influence cannot be reduced to a simple causal linkage into the spheres of leadership behaviour or success. It should also be noted that the genre can point simultaneously to different conclusions. A case in point is the way that firstborn characteristics will not always be consistent with the changing profiles of required leadership outlooks and skills. Contexts may shift in such a way as to make the temperaments and traits associated with the last born (i.e. innovative and flexible approach to problems; sceptical attitude to established structures and modes of operation) more suitable in changing and challenging times.

Sources: Robert B. Zajonc with G. Markus, 'Birth Order and Intellectual Development', *Psychological Review*, 82 1975: 74–88; Joan Newman and Alan Taylor, 'Family Training for Political Leadership: Birth Order of United States State Governors and Australian Prime Ministers', *Political Psychology*, 15(3) September 1994: 435–42; Frank J. Sulloway, *Born to Rebel: Birth Order, Family Dynamics, and Creative Lives* (New York, NY: Pantheon 1996); Richard L. Zweigenhaft and Jessica von Ammon, 'Birth Order and Civil Disobedience: A Test of Sulloway's "Born to Rebel" Hypothesis', *The Journal of Social Psychology*, 140(5) 2000: 624–7; Albert Somit, Alan Arwine, and Steven Peterson, *Birth Order and Political Behavior* (Lanham, MD: University Press of America, 2002); Rudy B. Andeweg and Steef B. Van Den Berg, 'Linking Birth Order to Political Leadership: The Impact of Parents or Sibling Interaction?', *Political Psychology*, 24(3) September 2003: 605–23; Del Jones, 'First-born kids become CEO material', *USA Today*, 4 September 2007. Accessed 17 July 2012 at: <www.usatoday.com/money/companies/management/2007-09-03-ceo-birth_N.htm>.

Investigations into these areas of formative influence lend weight to a number of inferences concerning the source of leadership generation. At the same time, they can also lead to very different and even conflicting conclusions. For example, it is generally accepted that leadership requires individuals who are necessarily extrovert in outlook and style. The working assumption is that leaders have to possess those characteristics which allow them to operate successfully in front of crowds, to be gregarious with staff and other politicos, and to be adept at the rigours of campaigning for policy agendas and electoral support. However, it is increasingly recognized that introverted individuals have certain advantages in the politics of leadership.[57]

Counter-intuitively, it is extroverts who in some cases are seen as self-centred liabilities in the way that they are believed to be drawn to those actions offering exciting, dramatic, and immediate pay-offs. Their rush to judgement can lead to serious political mistakes. Introverts on the other hand have the virtue of being methodical, focused, and careful in their approach to decisions—i.e. a preference for thinking through all the implications of different options. Moreover, it can be argued that introverts will be far better attuned to that other element of leadership which often goes unacknowledged—namely the ability to cope with the inevitable solitude of a leadership position. A positive construction of an introvert as leader has been ascribed to President Barack Obama. In contrast to his predecessor in the White House, President Obama is considered to be comparatively introverted in

[57] See Jennifer B. Kahnweiler, *The Introverted Leader: Building on Your Quiet Strength* (San Francisco, CA: Berrett-Koehler, 2009); Susan Cain, *Quiet: The Power of Introverts in a World That Can't Stop Talking* (New York, NY: Crown/Random House, 2012).

temperament and as such is seen to be operating an altogether different model of leadership. In February 2012, *TIME* magazine printed the following assessment:

> In fact, Americans may all be living under an introverted leader right now. Barack Obama isn't shy—no shy person survives a presidential campaign—but he shows tendencies toward introversion, including the love of solitude that helped him thrive as a writer. As a leader, Obama is more facilitator than dominator, and before he was a politician he was an academic—a line of work that probably has more introverts per capita than any other profession . . . [He] simply prefers to spend his limited free time with his family rather than at Washington parties. . . . That sets him apart from many of his predecessors, like the gregarious George W. Bush, whose bonhomie was one of his great selling points—to say nothing of Clinton, who had to be physically torn away from crowds. But if extroversion is great on the campaign trail, it doesn't always help in the business of governing. Both Clinton and Bush endangered their presidencies by engaging in what turned out to be graver risks than they might have imagined: one with an intern, the other in Iraq. An introvert like Obama is more inclined to think before he acts, and if anything, the President has been criticized as too risk averse.[58]

Another case of disputed causality and cross-cutting conclusions is provided by the commonly accepted correlation between leadership attainment and high self-esteem referred to above. While there may be many cases to support the linkage, a different interpretation can support a contrary impression of the conditioning processes governing the pathways to leadership acquisition. In sum, a long-term and embedded *lack* of self-esteem can motivate strategies of compensation and even transferred retribution. These impulses may have the effect of cultivating the kind of drive and commitment to secure a leadership position of dominance and power over others. Incidences exist where child abuse, familial rejection, and school bullying have provided the stimulus for victims of this kind of emotional trauma to restore their sense of self-esteem by striving for reconnection and compensation through the medium of political engagement.[59] On occasions, the severity of the initial suffering can generate extraordinary reactions in the shape of acute forms of insecurity and paranoia. These in turn can foster types of leadership activity that can only be described as extreme.[60] An illustrative case is provided by Jerrold M. Post's psychological profile of Saddam Hussein (Box 3.3).

Other studies seek to approach the subject of leadership more directly on its own specific terms as a political phenomenon and thereby one that requires a more aggregative and focused iteration of *political* psychology. These inquiries normally seek to incorporate a host of different dimensions which combine the formation and conditioning of individual character with designated situational

---

[58] Bryan Walsh, 'The Upside of Being an Introvert (And Why Extroverts Are Overrated)', *TIME*, 6 February 2012.

[59] Karen Robson, 'Peer Alienation: Predictors in Childhood and Outcomes in Adulthood', *Working Papers of the Institute for Social and Economic Research*, Paper 2003–21(Colchester: University of Essex, 2003); John Elliot, 'There's a bullied boy in every politician', *Sunday Times*, 10 August 2003.

[60] See the cases of Hitler and Stalin in Joachim C. Fest, *Hitler* (San Diego, CA: Harcourt, 1974), chs.1–3; John Toland, *Adolf Hitler: The Definitive Biography* (New York, NY: Doubleday, 1976), chs. 1, 2; Kershaw, *Hitler 1889–1936: Hubris*, chs. 1–3; Edvard Radzinsky, *Stalin: The First In-depth Biography Based on Explosive New Documents from Russia's Secret Archives* (New York, NY: Anchor Books, 1997), chs. 1–3; Robert Service, *Stalin: A Biography* (London: Pan, 2005), chs. 2–4; Simon Sebag Montefiore, *Young Stalin* (New York, NY: Vintage, 2008), chs. 1–7.

Box 3.3 Painful beginnings: Saddam Hussein and the 'wounded self'

Saddam Hussein was born in 1937 to a poor peasant family near Tikrit, some 100 miles north of Baghdad, in central-north Iraq. But the central lines of the development of Saddam Hussein's political personality were etched before he was born, for his father died of an 'internal disease' (probably cancer) during his mother's pregnancy with Saddam, and his 12-year-old brother died (of childhood cancer) a few months later, when Saddam's mother, Sabha, was in her eighth month of pregnancy. Destitute, Saddam's mother attempted suicide. A Jewish family saved her. Then she tried to abort herself of Saddam, but she was prevented from doing this by her same Jewish benefactors. After Saddam was born, on April 28, 1937, his mother did not wish to see him, strongly suggesting that she was suffering from a major depression. His care was relegated to Sabha's brother (his maternal uncle) Khayrallah Talfah Msallat in Tikrit, in whose home Saddam spent much of his early childhood. At age three Saddam was reunited with his mother, who in the interim had married a distant relative, Hajj Ibrahim Hasan. Hajj Ibrahim, his stepfather, reportedly was abusive psychologically and physically to young Saddam.

The first several years of life are crucial to the development of healthy self-esteem. The failure of the mother to nurture and bond with her infant son and the subsequent abuse at the hands of his stepfather would have profoundly wounded Saddam's emerging self-esteem, impairing his capacity for empathy with others, producing what has been identified as 'the wounded self'. One course in the face of such traumatizing experiences is to sink into despair, passivity, and hopelessness. But another is to etch a psychological template of compensatory grandiosity, as if to vow, 'Never again, never again shall I submit to superior force.' This was the developmental psychological path Saddam followed . . .

At age 20, inspired by Nasser, Saddam joined the Arab Ba'th Socialist Party in Iraq and quickly impressed party officials with his dedication. Known as a 'street thug', he willingly used violence in the service of the party, and was rewarded with rapid promotion . . . He has a flexible conscience: commitments and loyalty are matters of circumstance, and circumstances change. If an individual, or a nation, is perceived as an impediment or a threat, no matter how loyal in the past, that individual or nation will be eliminated violently without a backward glance, and the action will be justified by 'the exceptionalism of revolutionary needs'.

Source: Jerrold M. Post, *Leaders and Their Followers in a Dangerous World: The Psychology of Political Behavior* (Ithaca, NY: Cornell University Press, 2004), pp. 211–13.

---

categories that shape the dynamic between a politician and his or her social context. Such studies tend to be wider in scope and, thereby, dependent upon the more intuitive properties of aggregative analysis. This more expansive approach is reflected in a number of other key exponents of leadership analysis.

Bert Rockman, for example, posits the significance of a series of interlocking dimensions: namely *social environment*; *life experiences*; *stylistic traits*; *personality characteristics*; *attitudes*; *repertoire of skills/competences*; and *performance*. Each possesses a comparable status and each represents a nodal point in what is necessarily conceived as a highly mutable set of different variables that coexist within the leadership matrix.[61] Another integrative approach is offered by Dan

---

[61] Bert A. Rockman, *The Leadership Question: The Presidency and the American System* (New York, NY: Praeger, 1985).

McAdams who advocates the need to include five different dimensions of leadership analysis—i.e. (i) *personality*; (ii) *characteristic adaptations* (goals, motives, beliefs, strategies, mechanisms of defence, internalized object relations); (iii) *individual scenes and stories*; (iv) *biology*; and (v) *culture*.[62]

But it is the work of Stanley Renshon which is particularly illustrative of the broadening remit of leadership analysis in this sphere.[63] Renshon acknowledges the value of Barber's categories but believes that a core psychological component has been left out of the equation. This is the sphere of personal ambition which to Renshon is a major determinant of leadership because it relates to an individual's drive and capacity to achieve his or her own chosen purposes. In Renshon's scheme of analysis, character constitutes an integrated pattern of response to the sphere of ambition and to two other domains of individual experience. One relates to personal identity, self-esteem, and perception of competence (i.e. the 'identity sphere'). The other centres upon an individual's stance towards interpersonal connections (i.e. the 'relational sphere'). From these three sectors, it is possible to discern identifiable sets of stable psychological orientations on the part of individual leaders. These compound orientations emerge from the way that the three separate domains of character formation have come together within an individual's experience.

To Renshon, the individual's connections to these tripartite spheres 'represent one's approach to the most basic cornerstones of human experience and existence. They are the psychological foundations on which the superstructure of personality develops.'[64] As such, they amount to a critical conditioning agent in the conceptions of leaders in regard to their own sense of purpose and to their capacity for effective performance. For Renshon, 'character shapes performance but does not determine it. Character has a developmental history. The child shapes, but the adult is not synonymous with the child.'[65] As a consequence, while the development of character is an important part in the study of leadership personality, it is not confined to an individual's developmental history. Accordingly, it is both possible and necessary for personality analysis to include different approaches to psychological inquiry.

Many alternative points of access exist that locate significance in the psychology of the leader. Some give emphasis to what could be termed phenomenological aspects of outlooks and behaviour, while others centre more upon the interactional nature of the psychodynamics between the leader and other individuals

---

[62] Dan P. McAdams, *The Person: An Introduction to the Science of Personality Psychology*, 5th edn. (Hoboken, NJ: Wiley, 2009); Dan P. McAdams, *George W. Bush and the Redemptive Dream: A Psychological Portrait* (New York, NY: Oxford University Press, 2011).

[63] Stanley A. Renshon, *The Political Psychology of the Gulf War: Leaders, Publics and the Process of Conflict* (Pittsburgh, PA: University of Pittsburgh Press 1993); Renshon, *The Psychological Assessment of Presidential Candidates*; Stanley A. Renshon, *High Hopes: The Clinton Presidency and the Politics of Ambition* (New York, NY: Routledge, 1998); Stanley A. Renshon, *In His Father's Shadow: The Transformations of George W. Bush*, new edn. (New York, NY: Palgrave Macmillan, 2005), chs. 2, 3, 4; Stanley A. Renshon, *Barack Obama and the Politics of Redemption* (London: Routledge, 2011).

[64] Stanley A. Renshon, 'Character, Judgement, and Political Leadership: Promise, Problems, and Prospects of the Clinton Presidency', in Stanley A. Renshon (ed.), *The Clinton Presidency: Campaigning, Governing, and the Psychology of Leadership* (Boulder, CO: Westview Press, 1995), p. 62.

[65] Renshon, 'Character, Judgement, and Political Leadership, p. 62.

within the social and relational context of leadership. As social psychology forms an important element of the materials examined in Chapter 4, it is sufficient at this point to record its significance as a conditioning factor in the contingencies of leadership. More pertinent at this juncture is the need to acknowledge the contributions of cognitive psychology to the categories through which leaders are examined and assessed. Because this branch of psychology refers in the main to issues of mental stimulus and response, information processing, and problem-solving, it has had a place in analysing how different leaders adjust to the profusion of information and advice that gravitates to those in leadership pos-itions. While some leaders are able to retain a sense of strategic priority in the way they handle information, others become excessively embroiled in the myopic detail and multiple options of an overburdened agency of mediation between input and output.

Leaders will reveal, adopt, or learn methods by which they prefer to operate within such a congested environment. Whether or not an adopted style and the acquisition of a particular role can be said to be derived from an intuitively based cognitive coping mechanism or more from a conscious and purposeful form of self-management, leaders can be and have been distinguished through their different styles of leadership activity. As was noted in Chapter 2, individual leaders can be analytically assigned to different styles through the observation of their behaviour. With cognitive psychology, it is possible to speculate on the ways in which leadership styles can be derived from the personalized techniques and priorities of different sets of cognitive processes. It is for this reason that the term 'cognitive style' has now become a regular feature of leadership analysis.

One other aspect of being a leader that has a particular relevance to the dynamic between personality and the operational aspects of leadership structures is that of 'emotional intelligence'. This is a term that has become increasingly prominent in the business sector of leadership studies. It refers to the central significance that is now ascribed to the ability of leaders to channel their feelings and impulses into positive and constructive channels of behaviour. More specifically, it relates to the notion that because a leader's emotions can have a significant effect upon the performance of even the largest organizations it is vital that leaders remain emotionally stable in the wider interests of the structures for which they are responsible. It can be argued that this theme of emotional maturity and stability has been an implicit feature of those genres of political leadership studies that have always given emphasis to the personal and psychological components of leaders. Notwithstanding the debates concerning the provenance of the 'emotional intelli-gence' category as an analytical instrument, it is significant that the term has become increasingly evident in those studies that centre upon the attitudinal profiles of leaders.[66]

---

[66] The profile of 'emotional intelligence' and its value in the operation of leadership has been popularized by the work of Daniel Goleman. See Daniel Goleman, *Emotional Intelligence: Why It Can Matter More than IQ* (New York, NY: Bantam, 1995); Daniel Goleman, 'What Makes a Leader?', *Harvard Business Review*, November 1998; Daniel Goleman, Richard Boyatzis, and Annie McKee, *Primal Leadership: Realizing the Power of Emotional Intelligence* (Boston, MA: Harvard Business School Publishing, 2002); Roger Gill, *Theory and Practice of Leadership* (London: Sage, 2006), pp. 71–82.

This trend is reflected in Fred I. Greenstein's summative study of presidential leadership. In *The Presidential Difference: Leadership Style from FDR to George W. Bush*, this august figure in the field of political psychology examines the background, style, and conduct of every chief executive over the past seventy years. Greenstein employs six categories to rate the effectiveness of individual presidents: namely communication, organization, political skill, vision, cognitive style, and emotional intelligence. According to Greenstein, the premium property for any leader is 'what the German sociologist Max Weber called "the firm taming of the soul" and has come to be referred to as *emotional intelligence*—the president's ability to manage his emotions and turn them to constructive purposes, rather than being dominated by them and allowing them to diminish his leadership'.[67] In Greenstein's view, a leader's performance in all the other five categories will ultimately depend upon the extent to which that person is able to maintain control over their emotions and therefore able to make rational and non-compulsive decisions. A leader may possess many intellectual, cognitive, political, and rhetorical skills but without emotional stability these other talents will be compromised by mood swings, uncertain tempers, and symptoms of paranoid inflexibility. Greenstein's advice is succinct. 'Beware the presidential contender who lacks emotional intelligence.'[68] Without it a leader is unable to function: 'In its absence all else may turn to ashes.'[69]

The notion of emotional intelligence often leads back to the character-driven issue of temperament which is almost invariably regarded as a keynote factor in the provision and performance of leadership. Many would go further and claim that temperament is the most widely accessible and extensively discussed aspect of leadership assessment by public audiences and by political analysts. More often than not a leader's outlook and behaviour are interpreted in terms of what is perceived to be his or her temperament both as an inherent quality but equally as a property exposed by the demands of office. In this light, a person's qualification for a position of political leadership is routinely discussed according both to those aspects of temperament that are intentionally or unintentionally projected by the aspirant, and to the impressions of temperament that are received by those in non-leadership positions. Normally, a leader is judged by reference to certain high-value notions of temperament that are considered to be positive assets in a leadership situation. In liberal democracies, these notions of appropriate temperament usually include such categories as political skills, managerial competence, intelligence, adaptability, trustworthiness, strategic awareness, integrity, moral authority, effective communication and persuasion, a unifying presence, and an ability to accept responsibility. Implicit in these kinds of selected categories is the underlying theme of fitness conveyed both in respect to the general concept of fitness for leadership and in relation to the more specific notion of a fit between the person and a particular leadership office or role. Whether the issue is one of fitness or of fit, the categories used in a positive sense are also used in a negative framework in order to convey the impressions of poor leadership temperament

---

[67] Greenstein, *The Presidential Difference*, p. 6.

[68] Greenstein, *The Presidential* Difference, p. 223.

[69] Greenstein, *The Presidential Difference*, p. 223.

(e.g. political and managerial incompetence, remoteness, intransigence, lacking integrity, untrustworthy, unaccountable, poor communicator, lacking persuasive skills, unresponsive, evasive and divisive).

The position is complicated, however, by the change in attitudes towards what might be considered as the appropriate temperament depending upon the type of issue or situation with which a leader is confronted. For example, a sober, cautious, and inclusive style may be thought to be a measure of sound leadership in some contexts but not in others—especially where the presence of a crisis is discerned. Judgements over temperament will be further compounded by the presence of operational, traditional, and cultural variations across different political and social systems. Even liberal democracies experience periodic changes in the configuration of priorities assigned to different temperaments. A leader with a strong reputation for having the 'right' temperament can easily find that such a status is tenuous at best and volatile at worst. A leader's temperament can be a strong asset but by the same token it remains susceptible to the changing temperaments of that leader's public and professional constituencies. In effect, the category of temperament can cut both ways.

CONCLUSION

In the same way that the theme of leadership is almost invariably centred upon individual leaders and their claims to positions of leadership, so the leaders themselves evoke intense debate concerning the nature of their roles and identities as well as their relationships to wider social and political contexts. As the focal point of the subject narrows to that of the leaders themselves and their purpose in acquiring such levels of power and responsibility, so the picture becomes progressively more disputed and increasingly open to a widening set of contested perspectives. Far-reaching differences in the foundational priorities, the methodologies, and the levels of analysis associated with varied forms of psychological inquiry have already been noted. But these accounts represent only a part of what is a widening spectrum of research that continuously reaches out for fuller understandings of who leaders really are and why some individuals rise to leadership positions while others do not.

Other perspectives rely on different disciplines or analytical sub-genres for their insights and claims in respect to the attitudes, style, and general behaviour of leaders. One such study, for example, uses a combination of anthropology, primatology, and neurology in order to advance the proposition that leaders are essentially engaged in fulfilling a social role as head of the body politic—and in doing so they become entrapped in a series of socio-biological and psycho-biological processes which involve an increasing compulsion to strive for power. The analysis uses the higher-order primates as a point of cross-reference in order to make the claim that there are demonstrable parallels between human leadership behaviour and the world view of alpha males in a simian context. The conclusion reached is that the personality properties of leaders are moulded by a matrix of pre-human social impulses and biological drives. In essence, leaders become expressions of primitive instincts fuelled by glandular activity prompted by the most ancient parts of the brain as an intuitive pre-human response to competitive circumstances for dominance.[70]

The sheer range and virtuosity of these types of exposition on the subject of who leaders are bear witness not just to the enduring fascination of the subject but also to its complexity as a phenomenon. Inherent in these multiple perspectives and the debates prompted by them is the way that they lead to a renewed appreciation of the need to examine leadership in the round—i.e. to underline the central importance of the relational nature of leadership and in particular the way that leaders are only able to exert leadership through a medium that involves large numbers of individuals who do not have a leadership role. The study of leaders can distort the study of leadership by focusing on only one part of the equation. The attractiveness of leaders as a subject of analysis often means that the mutual dependency of leaders and followers is a factor that is marginalized and even neglected in the overall examination of the subject field.

Notwithstanding the progressive sophistication of analytical models and surveys centring upon the psychological origins and behavioural repertoires of individual leaders, the fact remains that leaders operate within a set of dependency relationships. When leadership is subjected to close scrutiny it becomes increasingly evident that the consumers of leadership constitute an indispensable feature of a dynamic that is inherently reciprocal in nature. Whether non-leaders are seen as a recipient audience or a participant crowd, it is they who in one way or another facilitate the provision and exercise of political leadership. It is they who experience the behaviour and actions of leaders. It is they who form opinions, make judgements, and embody attitude structures. While the present study has already given passing acknowledgement to the presence of this element in the leadership matrix, it is now necessary to move on to a more explicit examination of the other side of the leadership relationship.

---

[70] Arnold M. Ludwig, *King of the Mountain: The Nature of Political Leadership* (Lexington, KY: University Press of Kentucky, 2002).

4

Experiencing leadership: Factors in followership

'In the House of Commons your opponents are sitting opposite you on the opposition benches while your real enemies are behind you.'

A well-known Parliamentary dictum

'[T]he needs of the group carry it half-way to meet the leader, yet he too must fit in with it in his personal qualities.'

Sigmund Freud[1]

PREAMBLE

In the study of leadership, there exists a strong and arguably logical disposition towards a leader-centric approach to the subject. Notwithstanding the standard acknowledgement that leadership has an inherent connection to groups and publics that are considered to be non-leaders, the relational aspect of leadership can very often be overlooked. Because the focus of leadership is more often than not directed towards the motives, intentions, methods, and consequences of leaders, the natural tendency is for the other side of the equation to be reduced to an analogue of the active agency dimension of leadership. In this way, the nature of followers and followership can be taken as the precise reverse of what was described in the chapter on 'doing leadership'. Taking the cue of a leader as the initiator in a sequence of cause and effect, non-leaders can appear to be the passive receivers or consumers of leadership activity. They can be taken as simply the measure of a leader's influence in changing behaviour. They can also be seen as a subordinate layer in a hierarchical system of top-down domination, manipulation, and even coercion. In such circumstances, the position of the non-leader becomes little more than a register or an appendage of leadership action which is seen as emanating from the agency of an unmoved mover.

---

[1] Sigmund Freud, 'Group Psychology and the Analysis of the Ego' (1921), in James Strachey (ed.), *The Standard Edition of the Complete Psychological Works of Sigmund Freud, Volume 18 (1920–1922: Beyond the Pleasure Principle, Group Psychology and Other Works* (London: Hogarth Press/Institute of Psychoanalysis, 1955), p. 81.

This kind of derogation of the other participants in the leadership matrix led James MacGregor Burns to complain that an unnecessary division in the literature had emerged which had increasingly allowed the non-leadership sector to appear as a disengaged component of the phenomena surrounding the exercise of leadership.

> One of the most serious failures in the study of leadership has been the bifurcation between the literature on leadership and the literature on followership. The former deals with the heroic or demonic figures in history, usually through the medium of biography... The latter deals with audiences, the masses, the voters, the people, usually through the medium of studies of mass opinion or of elections... The leadership approach tends often unconsciously to be elitist; it projects heroic figures against drab, powerless masses. The followership approach tends to be populistic or anti-elitist in ideology.[2]

To Burns, the marginalization of the non-leadership participants in the process was a false dichotomy that amounted to an analytical disjunction which misrepresented the necessary and desirable dynamics of an active engagement between the two parties within a leadership structure. The contributions of Burns and others[3] helped to underline not only the operational significance and conditioning nature of followers, but also to give emphasis to the methodological, conceptual, and theoretical issues raised by the relationship between those with a leadership role and those who have to take that role into their own calculations and subsequent behaviour patterns.

It is one thing to acknowledge the importance of the non-leadership dimension as an important principle and as a necessary corrective to the leader-centred character of the subject area; it is quite another to establish how the field should be approached and what questions should be posed in relation to it. In many respects, the subject generates as many contentious issues as the other side of the equation. In addition to disputes over how 'followership' can be understood and under what conditions, there are controversies over different approaches and levels of analysis. If it is accepted that leadership is a property which is imparted and received, then it poses questions over how it is conveyed—as well as what it is that is being accepted and by whom. Given also the linkage between leaders and non-leaders, an issue also arises over the contingency relationships between the two elements, and the way that they engage in a process of mutual conditioning. In order to achieve some semblance of analytical order in this highly variable field, the intention is to proceed on the basis of three distinct dimensions of the relationship. Engaging with a set of differentiated areas of focus will enable the study to convey something of the complexity of the subject whilst delineating an orderly strategy of access.

---

[2] James MacGregor Burns, *Leadership* (New York, NY: Harper & Row, 1978), p. 3.

[3] See also Robert E. Kelley, *The Power of Followership: How to Create Leaders People Want to Follow and Followers Who Lead Themselves* (New York, NY: Doubleday-Currency, 1992); Ira Chaleff, *The Courageous Follower: Standing Up to and for Our Leaders*, 3rd edn. (San Francisco, CA: Berrett-Koehler, 2009); Barbara Kellerman, *Followership: How Followers Are Creating Change and Changing Leaders* (Boston, MA: Harvard Business School Press, 2008); Micha Popper, 'Toward a Theory of Followership', *Review of General Psychology*, 15(1) March 2011: 29–36; Nannerl O. Keohane, *Thinking about Leadership* (Princeton, NJ: Princeton University Press, 2010), ch. 2.

NEGOTIATING COMPLIANCE

The first dimension conceives the leader–follower connection from the perspective of a primarily contractual relationship based upon the material exchange of resources. In the same way that a leader may offer incentives in order to achieve the desired end of compliance from another party, so the latter will agree to support the leader on the basis of an accommodation of reciprocal interest and mutual benefit. This minimalist approach to followership has as its point of departure the presence of two actors who arrive at a transactional basis for action. A leader enters into negotiation with other participants who have resources of their own that can limit, curtail, and even veto a leader's preferred choices. In these circumstances, leaders have to have the required skills to secure their chosen objectives from others who possess the discretion not to follow the lead given to them. Leaders therefore have to expend political capital and concerted effort in order not merely to maximize their chances of ensuring a measure of compliance from others, but also to consolidate and sustain the security of their own leadership positions.

This perspective of political leadership offers an important and necessary corrective to those studies that either commence with the presumption of established leadership power, or proceed on the basis that leadership is wholly dependent upon a formal or constitutional investment of authority. Niccolò Machiavelli's celebrated exposition on the arts and crafts of political leadership underlined the importance of highly proficient and experienced individuals in leadership positions. Because politics was a highly volatile domain, leaders needed to have an innate or highly developed sense of how power could not only be secured but also maintained against a background of uncertainty and insecurity. In Machiavelli's world of power politics within the confines of a city state, leaders could never afford to stand apart from issues of political calculation, strategic control, and tactical advantage. On the contrary, Machiavelli gave particular emphasis to the central importance of maximizing both leadership power and follower compliance through the optimum distribution of rewards and benefits on the one hand, and threats and punishments on the other. To Machiavelli, an effective prince needed to know how to work the currencies of political exchange in order to acquire and retain sufficient support to act effectively as a ruler. Whether it was through fear, or appeasement, inducements or penalties, leaders had to have the political skills to sense the shifting tides of support and opposition, and to be sufficiently adaptive to changed conditions to negotiate a safe passage through the various pitfalls of leadership existence. In this reductionist scheme of political relations, followers only followed on the basis of calculated interest.[4]

A very similar analytical and normative logic was followed by Richard Neustadt, the celebrated scholar of the contemporary presidency in the United States. As has already been noted, Neustadt has been called the American Machiavelli because of his insistence on seeking to wrestle the study of the presidency away from the formalism of constitutional and legal provision which he regarded as a

---

[4] Niccolò Machiavelli, *The Prince*, translation and introduction by George Bull (Harmondsworth: Penguin, 1961), chs. 15–19.

distraction from the real source of power in such a leadership position—namely the central importance of political persuasion.[5] Even in such an institutionalized office with an array of executive powers, Neustadt's message is that the presidency cannot be understood unless it is accepted that it operates within a political environment. Successful presidents are those who comprehend their own situation. They understand that they operate in a system of shared and competing powers, which means that presidents have to negotiate with others to achieve any form of leverage. Leadership in these conditions amounts to the explicit acknowledgement that power is provisional in nature and as such the power to lead is dependent upon a continuing ability to use whatever positional or personal advantages a leader may have in order to reach accommodations with other political actors. In essence, Neustadt underlined the contingent character of political leadership—i.e. that leadership does not transcend politics but rather is firmly rooted within it. As a consequence, a leader's power should be conceived as one part of a continuous reciprocal relationship with others who operate inside the same context of political interdependency.

Like Machiavelli, Neustadt asserts that leadership is primarily a *behavioural characteristic*, related to the ability of an individual to exert influence within a politically resistant and even hostile environment. As such, a leader's level of influence has to be seen as a highly variable property dependent upon a host of different factors but specifically reliant on the leader's own skills, experience, and judgement in relating to other political actors. In this respect, the arts and crafts of political persuasion through the medium of negotiation and hard bargaining have a premium value. Neustadt placed this process of acquiring compliance at the centre point of his political realism. It gave emphasis to his view that because those who followed a presidential lead had the option of not complying with it, leaders had to be professional politicians with an intuitive sense of the mercurial nature of leadership and the requisite style to maximize whatever influence was possible in the circumstances. It is difficult to imagine Neustadt's faith in the skills of experienced political operatives being better exemplified than by the legendary techniques of President Lyndon Johnson (Box 4.1) who was renowned for his capacity to sense the potential for support and to ensure that he acquired it to maximum effect.[6]

It is a matter beyond dispute that techniques like those ascribed to an individual like Johnson can be a very effective form of leadership. By the same token, it is equally the case that for many people in many circumstances this is how leadership is experienced; it is how compliance is achieved and how followers are mobilized. Leaders will seek to maximize the impact of the limited resources they have at hand by way of offering rewards, favours, and incentives, or alternatively threatening the imposition of penalties of one kind or another. Likewise, those who are positioned on the other side of the relationship will have to take into account the need to calculate the relative costs and benefits of compliance or

---

[5] Richard E. Neustadt, *Presidential Power: The Politics of Leadership—With Reflections on Johnson and Nixon* (New York, NY: John Wiley, 1976).

[6] Rowland Evans and Robert Novak, *Lyndon B. Johnson: The Exercise of Power* (London: George Allen & Unwin, 1966), chs. 6–11; Robert A. Caro, *The Years of Lyndon Johnson, Vol. 3: Master of the Senate* (New York, NY: Vintage, 2002), Parts IV and V.

Box 4.1 Lyndon B. Johnson: The Treatment

The technique described below is drawn from Lyndon B. Johnson's legendary activities as Majority Leader in the US Senate. The same methods were in evidence during his time as President of the United States (1965–9).

The Treatment could last ten minutes or four hours. It came, enveloping its target, at the Johnson Ranch swimming pool, in one of Johnson's offices, in the Senate cloakroom, on the floor of the Senate itself—wherever Johnson might find a fellow Senator within his reach. Its tone could be supplication, accusation, cajolery, exuberance, scorn, tears, complaint, the hint of threat. It was all of these together. It ran the gamut of human emotions. Its velocity was breathtaking, and it was all in one direction. Interjections from the target were rare. Johnson anticipated them before they could be spoken. He moved in close, his face a scant millimeter from his target, his eyes widening and narrowing, his eyebrows rising and falling. From his pockets poured clippings, memos, statistics. Mimicry, humor, and genius of analogy made The Treatment an almost hypnotic experience and rendered the target stunned and helpless . . . The Treatment began immediately: a brilliant, capsule characterization of every Democratic Senator: his strengths and failings, where he fit [sic] into the political spectrum; how far he could be pushed, how far pulled; his hates; his loves. And who . . . must oversee all these prima donnas, put them to work, knot them together, know when to tickle this one's vanity, inquire of that one's health, remember this one's five o'clock nip of Scotch, that one's nagging wife? . . . Nobody but Lyndon Johnson.

Source: Rowland Evans and Robert Novak, *Lyndon B. Johnson: The Exercise of Power* (London: George Allen & Unwin, 1966), pp. 104–5.

---

non-compliance with the leadership. This interpretation of leadership activity posits the view that a leader has to have the skill to persuade others to give their support on the basis of a rational calculation of their self-interest—i.e. 'what he wants of them is what their own appraisal of their own responsibilities requires them to do in their own interest, not his'.[7]

The role of joint negotiation and mutual accommodation is an integral feature of the reciprocal nature of the connection that exists between leaders and non-leaders.[8] Nevertheless, despite the political traction and explanatory value that is widely afforded to this kind of dynamic, it does have its limitations. For example, this kind of leader–follower depiction is usually narrowly conceived in that it is customarily portrayed, or at least exemplified, as a small-scale encounter in which the principal parties operate in close proximity to one another in a bounded environment that allows for the kind of face-to-face encounters through which transactions can be negotiated.

In many respects, the portrayal of leadership in these circumstances has the appeal of minimalist realism in that it conveys leadership in terms of a material and contractual interaction between two quite separate parties. Its positivist and almost visceral inclination to perceive the experience of leadership as a set of ongoing terms and conditions—constructed as it is within a power relationship model of stimulus–response at close quarters—can lead to a very limited perspective of the leader–follower relationship. This is because it tends to marginalize and

---

[7] Neustadt, *Presidential Power*, p. 114.   [8] See Burns, *Leadership*, pp. 257–397.

even to out rule other influences and alternative leadership methods. While the techniques employed by a political maestro like Lyndon Johnson may be very effective in certain contexts, they are also considered to be one-dimensional and unsustainable in their operational and explanatory remit.[9]

This is not to say that the conception of tightly bounded interaction does not have considerable explanatory merits. Many elements of leadership and follower-ship are dependent upon the material immediacy of direct and interpersonal relationships in which specific synergies are developed to produce a mutually conditioned state of existence.[10] The transactional basis of such a perspective has not only contributed towards a necessary readjustment away from leader-centric analysis but has underlined the importance of leaders being constrained by the need to match their ambitions or agendas to their respective audiences. But in acknowledging the significance of the relational factor in leadership, this approach tends to confine its remit within very tight parameters. It does so by giving marked emphasis to the themes of bargaining and negotiation, as well as to the force of direct and conscious persuasion in the process of leadership traction. In this perspective, the experience of leadership is reduced to a matter of contractual accommodation based upon the costs and gains to be derived from a settlement. By giving so much weight to the tangible features of stimulus–response, the transactional construction of following a leader precludes other whole areas of the relationship without which the notion of followership cannot adequately be grasped.

LEADERSHIP AT THE SERVICE OF EXPECTATIONS

The linkage between leader and follower can be far more complex than may appear to be the case at first sight. Experiencing leadership can extend far beyond the characteristic properties of persuasion and exchange into other less tangible dimensions of compliance. Widening the remit raises questions and issues that allude to an altogether richer mix of mediums through which leadership can be felt. These may be more difficult to access analytically but nevertheless it is necessary for them to be taken into account in order to reach a fuller understand-ing of the different iterations and contingencies of leadership from the other side of the equation.

---

[9] For a critical response to the Neustadt model, see Peter W. Sperlich, 'Bargaining and Overload: An Essay on Presidential Power', in Aaron Wildavsky (ed.), *The Presidency* (Boston, MA: Little, Brown, 1969), pp. 168–92.

[10] See F. Dansereau, Jr., George Graen, and William J. Haga, 'A Vertical Dyad Linkage Approach to Leadership within Formal Organizations: A Longitudinal Investigation of the Role Making Process', *Organizational Behavior and Human Performance*, 13(1) 1975: 46–78; George B. Graen and J. F. Cashman, 'A Role Making Model of Leadership in Formal Organizations: A Developmental Approach', in J. G. Hunt and L. L. Larson (eds.), *Leadership Frontiers* (Kent, OH: Kent State University Press, 1975), pp. 143–65; George B. Graen and Mary Uhl-Bien, 'Relationship-Based Approach to Leadership: Development of Leader-Member Exchange (LMX) Theory of Leadership over 25 Years—Applying a Multi-Level Multi-Domain Perspective', *The Leadership Quarterly*, 6(2) Summer 1995: 219–47.

At the outset, it is important to note that, like most transactions, those that occur between a leader and a non-leader do not take place in a vacuum. On most occasions, the parties to such an exchange are not strangers to one another; neither do they proceed from a wholly flat or neutral basis devoid of all prior conditioning. On the contrary, it is likely that the two parties will possess some previous experience of one another that may well have a significant influence upon the character and content of any accommodation reached between them. This element of previous experience leads to an altogether more substantive dimension that relates to the way that the connection between leaders and non-leaders is initially framed not merely by the actors involved but by the accepted ways and means by which such arrangements are structured. These modes of exchange amount to a form of prior foundation to the notion of compliance and following a lead. Their provenance will vary across a range of different formative areas but they all have one aspect in common in respect to this field of interest— namely that they underline the multifaceted and multilayered nature of experiencing leadership in general and of comprehending responsiveness in particular.

One notable area of leadership resource and followership behaviour is the dimension that is very often disregarded and which was explicitly marginalized by those seeking to emphasize the transactional features of leadership. Despite being often dismissed as neither a necessary nor a sufficient condition of leadership, the formal arrangements of an institutionalized hierarchy remain a key facet in how people sense leadership and how they react to it. It is normal for leadership behaviour to be influenced by the requirements of formal roles and constitutional powers. In like manner, non-leading actors will also be shaped by the explicit and implicit expectations that surround an office of established authority. The origins and nature of such an authority—and with it the expected roles and obligations assigned to it—will vary according to both the specific context of the position and the generic culture of the respective polity. The reach of a leader's influence, therefore, may well depend upon how well he or she is able to co-opt a primary basis of legitimacy within a given political system.

If a leader is effective either in drawing upon a fixed field of authority, or in achieving a justifiable reconfiguration of that authority, then it increases the chances that the rank and file will respond to the leadership without the need for resources to be continually and routinely expended in the process of persuasion. This is not to say that leaders can rely upon the formal lines of executive command and control as if the political factor of personal and social persuasion were surplus to requirements. What does need to be grasped is that individuals can and do follow leaders not least because they represent an agreed form of governance that evokes an authoritative location of rightful and duly constituted position. This will not normally extend as far as ceding an exclusive and comprehensive right of command to a leader, nor an uncontested duty to obey on the part of other political actors. Nevertheless, it will amount to a *prima facie* basis for cooperation in a settled polity.

A leader can expect at least a modicum of compliance, therefore, on the basis of a pre-existing state of shared attachments to a common basis of authority. It may be to the nation or to the constitutional order or to some other established social value, but as long as leaders can successfully graft their own claims to influence upon a core source of authority then it is more likely that other actors will acknowledge the existence of a prior basis of leadership status. To this extent, followers will not always need to be persuaded by a leader into a particular course of action. They will often be prompted into movement by what the leadership represents to them, rather than by what it negotiates with them.

This theme of what might be termed predisposed followership opens up an array of dimensions related to a more voluntarist conception of leadership compliance. A notable example and one that is shared in most political contexts is the reaction to a defined crisis. When an organization feels that its core interests are under threat, it can very often precipitate a marked rise in solidarity that finds its focus with the leadership. A leader's position can suddenly and unexpectedly be enhanced by a surge in supportive sentiments in which previous differences are spontaneously set aside in a collective impulse to close ranks in the face of adversity.[11] In the same way that this type of integration is symbolized by an adherence to the leadership, so leaders in this kind of situation can rely upon an almost reflexive form of unsolicited followership. Such an episode may be short-lived in duration but it does underline the potential that leaders have for summoning up an extensive field of cooperation with little in the way of resources being expended in negotiations and persuasion. In these kinds of circumstances, non-leaders are conspicuously more receptive to the messages of leaders than is normally the case. Indeed, it is far from unusual for non-leaders to offer their support not on the merits of any expressed argument, but through an instinctive drive for a commonality of purpose signified through the singularity of leadership. Whether this pattern of behaviour is interpreted as depicting a suspension or a redefinition of the normal rules of engagement, the net effect is a shift in the customary parameters of the leader–follower relationship into an altogether more intuitive and harmonious convergence.

A supportive reaction of this kind can be attributed to a range of factors but two in particular are normally present. Both have a direct bearing on the theme of predisposed followership. The *first* draws upon what is primarily a protective impulse in which a leader is assigned the *de facto* responsibility for making decisions and taking action in the interests of a wider constituency that is dependent upon leadership action in exceptional conditions. The expectation laid upon the leaders by others may constitute an implicit or an explicit part of a leadership's brief. Whatever the arrangements, it is generally understood in these circumstances that a leader has an obligation to act as a trustee for others who have come to rely upon effective leadership for their own good.

The *second* factor is related to the first in that it relates to the way that leaders are regarded as having the capacity to respond to conditions, to make judgements, and to take appropriate action. It is not simply that leaders are expected to assert themselves in unusual circumstances but that they have the functional means—and with it the executive authority—to do so. It may be that such an authorized capacity is formally assigned to a leader in a crisis, but more often than not it is taken as read that the executive figure has inherent powers to react to a

---

[11] See John E. Mueller, *War, Presidents and Public Opinion* (New York, NY: Wiley, 1973); Marc J. Hetherington and Michael Nelson, 'Anatomy of a Rally Effect: George W. Bush and the War on Terrorism', *PS: Political Science and Politics*, 36(1) 2003: 37–42.

threatening turn of events. Either way, the executive authority ceded to a leadership on the basis of a largely blind trust bears witness to the way that non-leaders are prepared to become followers on the basis of a generalized impulse rather than a specified prospectus.

This kind of predisposed followership can be interpreted as having its foundations in such factors as the force of accepted custom, the logic of governance, or the mode of reflexive reactions to emergencies. Another element exists within this matrix but it is one that is often overlooked in the more positivist accounts of the leader–follower relationship. That element is emotion. As our inquiries into followership deepen, the analytical reach of emotion intrudes further into the subject area. Far from being displaced by the material gains and losses of leadership constructed around the medium of contractual exchange, the instincts and habits of emotionally charged linkages between leaders and non-leaders retain their status as strong conditioning agencies in the overall dynamics of followership. In response to the question of why it is that individuals willingly defer to a leader, therefore, many of the answers revolve around ties that are more grounded in emotionally charged outlooks and behaviours than they are in logical rationales.

THE PSYCHODYNAMICS OF EMPATHY

The psychology of intuitive compliance comes in many forms but they all tend to share the common feature that individuals can be so receptive to leadership cues that the relationship amounts less to a convergence of two positions and more to a register of an undifferentiated amalgam in which followers do not feel the need to be prompted into a supportive position. For example, a leader may represent a form of intrinsic gratification amongst those who have direct experience of the leadership in action. In such a context, an individual may view a leader's lead as an inherently positive experience that carries its own interior rewards on the part of the follower. A leader's positions and prescriptions can become progressively internalized by those who closely associate themselves with the leader and with what that leader represents. As a result, followers will tend to remain supportive in their behaviour irrespective of the leader's interest in, or attempts at, actively soliciting their compliance.

Another example of self-generated followership is provided by those who simply comply out of an impulse to be identified with a leader. This may be because of a leader's political position or social status. It may be born out of a belief that a particular leader shares an individual's beliefs, ideals, or aspirations, or because a leader is seen as symbolizing or signifying a set of impulses that have a natural—and arguably a primal—appeal to a follower. In many cases, an identity with a particular group committed to an agenda of group-based priorities will act as a catalyst for being highly receptive to the influence of a leadership which is perceived as being either explicitly sympathetic to the group's aims or implicitly tied to them by past and present attachments. An additional dimension to this notion of a deep and far-reaching connection to the leader is when an individual simply wishes for whatever reason to be similar to a leader that he or she admires.

Given an initial attachment on the basis of earnest affection, a non-leader can be drawn towards the leader's positions and values on the coat-tails of an emotional pull to the object of admiration. Similar to the other forms of largely self-induced followership mentioned above, the follower in this case may exhibit symptoms of a psychological dependency projected upon the authority figure of the leader in such a way that following becomes something of a compulsive activity—even 'an extreme passion for authority'.[12]

Some constituent elements of these depictions of followership have resonance with Max Weber's celebrated description of charismatic leadership in which an individual acquires a dominant position over others by virtue of possessing properties that are regarded as 'inaccessible to others and incompatible with the rules of thought and action that govern everyday life'.[13] In contrast to other forms of power relating to traditional or legal/rational rule structures, charismatic leaders are able to secure an exceptional status based upon an effective claim as an agency of providence with both a mission and a higher order of legitimacy.[14]

While it is true that the contemporary usage of Weber's term has often been overused and even trivialized, the notion of charismatic properties relating to leadership roles does give emphasis to the role of emotionally charged appeals and the dynamics of social psychology in explaining how it is that some followers internalize the position and status of a leader to such an extent that their compliant behaviour is wholly incommensurate with the active stimulus provided by the leader. Far from merely persisting in their supportive behaviour long after the leader may have ceased attempting to engage in exerting influence, these kinds of followers are notable for the way that their level of responsiveness can be quite out of synch with the cues provided by the leadership. Just as charismatic leaders tend to supersede and supplant the constraints of traditional and legal sources of authority in a process of transformation, so followers tend to act above and beyond any external call of duty. As long as such a leader can sustain a personal connection to a demonstrable mission, then others will follow through a faith which disables any compulsion to do otherwise. In such a situation, non-leaders do not become followers on the basis of choice or calculation. As Weber notes, a charismatic leader 'does not derive his "right" from their will, in the manner of an election. Rather, the reverse holds: it is the *duty* of those to whom he addresses his mission to recognize him as their charismatically qualified leader.'[15]

---

[12] See Sigmund Freud, *Group Psychology and the Analysis of the Ego*, trans. and ed. James Strachey (New York, NY: Liveright/Norton 1990), ch. 10.

[13] Quoted in Reinhard Bendix, *Max Weber: An Intellectual Portrait* (London: Methuen, 1966), p. 300.

[14] Edward A. Shils, 'Charisma, Order and Status', *American Sociological Review*, 30(2) 1965: 199–213; Ann Ruth Willner, *The Spellbinders: Charismatic Political Leadership* (New Haven, CT: Yale University Press, 1985); Jay A. Conger, *The Charismatic Leader: Behind the Mystique of Exceptional Leadership* (San Francisco, CA: Jossey-Bass, 1989); Douglas Madsen and Peter G. Snow, *The Charismatic Bond: Political Behavior in Times of Crisis* (Cambridge, MA: Harvard University Press, 1991).

[15] Max Weber, *From Max Weber: Essays in Sociology*, trans. and ed. H. H. Gerth and C. Wright Mills (London: Routledge, 1998), pp. 246–7.

Another conception of this kind of enhanced integration between leader and follower is provided by Howard Gardner in his study *Leading Minds*.[16] This influential exposition focuses upon the traction provided by the device of a shared narrative in the formation of a tightly constructed relationship between leaders and non-leaders. Using themes and techniques drawn from cognitive psychology, Gardner's analysis of gifted and effective leaders leads him to conclude that it is the penetrative properties of mental interaction between leaders and others which afford disproportionate influence to those leadership figures who can master the arts of this kind of communication. In essence, a successful leader is one who can create and own a defining narrative that not only makes sense to those he is appealing to as a leader, but more importantly shapes their thoughts, feelings, and behaviours along the lines laid down by the leader.

For a story to become a controlling narrative, it has to be effective in competing with other patterns of perception and in having the potential to become an enduring and adaptable mental representation. 'In a Darwinian sense, the "memes"—a culture's version of genes—called stories compete with one another for favor, and only the most robust stand a chance of gaining ascendancy.'[17] Gardner affirms that the stories which have the greatest capacity for generating a viable cohesion between leaders and followers relate to the theme of identity— namely narratives of particular origins, predicaments, and directions. A leader who is proficient in this kind of competitive trafficking of stories will find the required niche of an identity narrative which will 'make sense to audience members at [a] particular historical moment'.[18] The best leaders at devising and operating such conceptual landscapes are adept at placing themselves at the heart of their own depictions—i.e. they not only relate the story but serve to embody it and to affirm it in person. They possess the kind of leverage and security that come with the 'vantage point of power . . . [being] yoked to specific messages'.[19] The leaders cited by Gardner as exemplars of group identity management[20] are those who managed to place themselves at the heart of what were engineered to be cognitive and social partnerships. Both leaders and followers were, thereby, able to support, share in, and be part of the same story.[21]

This emphasis upon identity has become a common basis of analysis in leadership studies. The genre is a broad one that serves many applications but its main rationale is typified by the work of Haslam, Reicher, and Platow.[22] They have looked at followers as the litmus test of effective and creative leadership rather than as ciphers or subordinates in a one-sided process. The adhesion

---

[16] Howard Gardner, *Leading Minds: An Anatomy of Leadership* (London: HarperCollins, 1995).

[17] Gardner, *Leading Minds*, p. 14.

[18] Gardner, *Leading Minds*, p. 14.

[19] Gardner, *Leading Minds*, p. 16.

[20] They include Martin Luther King, Margaret Thatcher, Mahatma Gandhi, Jean Monnet, and Pope John XXIII.

[21] See also Nick Forster, Martin Cebis, Sol Majteles, Anurag Mathur, Roy Morgan, Janet Preuss, Vinod Tiwari, and Des Wilkinson, 'The Role of Story-Telling in Organizational Leadership', *Leadership & Organization Development Journal*, 20(1) 1999: 11–17; James Cuno, 'Telling Stories: Rhetoric and Leadership, a Case Study', *Leadership*, 1(2) June 2005: 205–13.

[22] S. Alexander Haslam, Stephen D. Reicher, and Michael J. Platow, *The New Psychology of Leadership: Identity, Influence and Power*, new edn. (New York, NY: Psychology Press, 2011).

between leaders and non-leaders is provided by the formative, summative, and operative properties of a joint social and group identity. A cultivated identity allows individuals to see themselves as a definable entity with an agenda, a purpose, and a shared impulse to strive for shared goals. An effective leader becomes so when followers are induced to regard themselves as having a group identity so that their interests and that of the group are believed to be one and the same. Leaders not only have to represent the identity but essentially have to live it with sufficient conviction that the group comes to believe that the leadership's traits and behaviour are in accord with the group's own sense of distinctiveness and legitimacy. While leaders are expected to interpret and shape the identity as an instrument of collective action, they are also bound by its parameters and by the need to ensure that the role of that identity remains relevant as a real, valued, and shared frame of reference. On this basis, Haslam, Reicher, and Platow conclude that 'leadership is essentially a process of social identity management— and hence that effective leadership is always *identity leadership*'.[23] Accordingly leadership necessarily entails an entrepreneurial role in evoking and embedding a common sense of joint existence in such a way that leaders can be interpreted as 'artists', 'impresarios', and 'engineers' of identity.[24]

Clearly, experiencing leadership is a far more complex phenomenon than the passive properties that are commonly assigned to it. The many that do not have access to a leadership position are far from being merely passive ciphers in an invariably top-down structure. Followers may well experience leadership in one sense, but that leadership will be conditioned not only by the rank and file imparting a need for leadership, but also by the active projection of their own group demands and identity—as well as their projected leadership ideals—upon the actual provision of leadership.[25] This dynamic can be especially strong amongst those elements that have close proximity to the centre of leadership. It can be argued that the experience of leadership is a positional variable that alters with the degree of distance from the leader's centre of operations. Leaders have different levels of operation and intensity with different constituencies and forms of dependency. In like manner, followers might be said to vary in their levels of interest, commitment, and attachment depending upon the basis of their relationship to the leader. Some of the patterns of predisposed followership mentioned above are often associated with those actors whose relationship with the leadership is nearer than most.

---

[23] Haslam, Reicher, and Platow, *The New Psychology of Leadership*, p. 197. See also S. Alexander Haslam and Michael J. Platow, 'The Link between Leadership and Followership: How Affirming Social Identity Translates Vision into Action', *Personality and Social Psychology Bulletin*, 27(11) November 2001: 1469–79; Stephen Reicher, S. Alexander Haslam, and Nick Hopkins, 'Social Identity and the Dynamics of Leadership: Leaders and Followers as Collaborative Agents in the Transformation of Social Reality', *The Leadership Quarterly*, 16(4) August 2005: 547–68.

[24] Haslam, Reicher, and Platow, *The New Psychology of Leadership*, ch. 7.

[25] Robin Martin and Olga Epitropaki, 'Role of Organizational Identification on Implicit Leadership Theories (ILTs), Transformational Leadership and Work Attitudes', *Group Processes & Intergroup Relations*, 4(3) July 2001: 3 247–62; Michael A. Hogg and Deborah J. Terry (eds.), *Social Identity Processes in Organizations* (New York, NY: Taylor & Francis, 2001); Michael A. Hogg and Daan van Knippenberg, 'Social Identity and Leadership Processes in Groups', in M. P. Zanna (ed.), *Advances in Experimental Social Psychology* (San Diego, CA: Academic Press, 2003), pp. 1–52; Michael A. Hogg, 'Social Identity and Leadership', in David M. Messick and Roderick M. Kramer (eds.), *The Psychology of Leadership: New Perspectives and Research* (Mahwah, NJ: Lawrence Erlbaum, 2005), pp. 53–80.

Weber's analysis of the way in which some leaderships can evoke an integrated and even holistic relationship between themselves and their followers continues to be insightful in this respect. In many respects, his observations prefigure many of the contemporary contributions of social and group psychology to the study of the operational formation and consolidation around the focal point of a leader. The work of Irving Janis and others on the communal integration around the senior decision-making levels within organizations is especially pertinent in this respect. This is because it illuminates the way that designated groups of followers can organize themselves around a leadership to the extent that they come to constitute a collective personality.[26] It was Janis in particular who popularized the usage of the term 'groupthink' to characterize the dynamics of this kind of intense brand of indigenous followership.

'Groupthink' is defined as the result of the interrelationship that develops between individuals within cohesive and durable groups. Such groups build up boundaries, norms, and conformity. In other words, Janis studies the way that individuals in a group context engage in behaviour which makes the group into a very tight and protective unit that becomes bound up with the esteem, investment, reputation, and interests of its individual members. In effect, the group assumes a collective entity. As it does so, it becomes ingrown and preoccupied with perpetuating its own subconscious drives to maintain its integrity as a collective force. According to Janis, the characteristic symptoms of groupthink can be specified as a syndrome of psychological pathways and organizational behaviour (Box 4.2). As well as specifying the onset of characteristic decisional processes, Janis also enumerates a set of clearly identified consequences. These include a dynamic that limits the range of alternative options and prevents the re-examination of both initial preferences adopted by the group and of those options that were initially rejected. It also leads to a selective bias towards information that supports the preferred policy; a reluctance to acquire information from outsiders with claims to specialist knowledge on the likely costs and losses of key decisions; and a general failure to consider potential negatives in the shape of unpredicted opposition and bureaucratic inertia as well as accidents and unintended consequences.

Janis's book was written as an explicit warning against the development and effects of 'groupthink'. The conclusion reached by him was that the *consensus-seeking tendency* of close-knit groups can cause them to make not only inferior decisions but also seriously flawed policy choices that have the potential to become outright policy failures, and even disasters.[27] The foundational premises and operational logic of Janis's model have been subjected to a considerable volume of critical complaint—usually either disputing the sequence of in-group formation and attitude acquisition or citing possible alternative processes in the production of myopic and risky outlooks (e.g. structural/organizational faults, framing effects, erroneous intelligence, information overloads, fatigue, deep

---

[26] Irving I. Janis, *Victims of Groupthink* (Boston, MA: Houghton-Mifflin, 1972); Irving I. Janis, *Groupthink: Psychological Studies of Policy Decisions and Fiascoes*, 2nd edn. (Boston, MA: Houghton-Mifflin, 1982).

[27] Janis, *Groupthink*, chs. 1, 2, 8, 10.

Box 4.2 The distinguishing processes and properties associated with the formation and maintenance of the 'groupthink' condition

---

1. The creation of an *illusion of invulnerability*. This is shared by most members or all members. It creates excessive optimism and encourages the taking of extreme risks.

2. The collective effort to *rationalize information*. This allows the group to discount warnings that might lead the members to reconsider their assumptions before recommitting themselves to past policy decisions.

3. An unquestioned belief in the group's *inherent morality*, allowing members to ignore the ethical or moral consequences of their actions.

4. The development of *stereotypes*. Adversaries become enemies who are construed as being either too evil to warrant genuine attempts at negotiation, or too weak or stupid to resist whatever attempts are made to defeat them.

5. The imposition of *conformity*. Direct pressure is exerted on any member who expresses strong arguments against any of the group's stereotypes, illusions, and commitments. Dissent is characterized as contrary to that which is expected from loyal members of the group.

6. The onset of *self-censorship*. Intolerance of deviations from the group consensus is progressively internalized. Members become inclined to minimize, to themselves, the importance of doubts and counterarguments.

7. The *shared illusion of unanimity*. As groupthink develops, the appearance of unanimity deepens as the majority view becomes a prevailing core assumption (via self-censorship and the onset of an assumption that silence denotes consent).

8. The emergence of self-appointed *'mindguards'*—i.e. members who protect the group from adverse information or judgement that might undermine their shared complacency about the effectiveness and/or morality of their decisions.

Sources: Irving L. Janis, *Groupthink*, 2nd edn. (Boston, MA: Wadsworth, 1982); Paul 't Hart, *Government: A Study of Small Groups and Policy Failure* (Baltimore, MD: Johns Hopkins University Press, 1994); Clark McCauley, 'The Nature of Social Influence in Groupthink: Compliance and Internalization', *Journal of Personality and Social Psychology*, 57(2) August 1989: 250–60.

---

prejudice, ignorance, panic, as well as risk taking and group polarization).[28] Other studies have sought to preserve the integrity of the original model by incorporating revisions and refinements to its explanatory scheme.[29]

---

[28] For a recent study of the attributed effects of groupthink processes in the transformation of US government attitudes towards Saddam Hussein's regime after 9/11, see Dina Badie, 'Groupthink, Iraq, and the War on Terror: Explaining US Policy Shift toward Iraq', *Foreign Policy Analysis*, 6(4) October 2010: 277–96.

[29] Glen Whyte, 'Groupthink Reconsidered', *The Academy of Management Review*, 14(1) January 1989: 40–56; R. J. W. Cline, 'Detecting Groupthink: Methods for Observing the Illusion of Unanimity', *Communication Quarterly*, 38(2) 1990: 112–26; Won-Woo Park, 'A Review of Research on Group-think', *Journal of Behavioral Decision Making*, 3(4) 1990: 229–45; Ramon J. Aldag and Sally R. Fuller, 'Beyond Fiasco: A Reappraisal of the Groupthink Phenomenon and a New Model of Group Decision Processes', *Psychological Bulletin*, 113(3) May 1993: 533–52; Mark Schafer and Scott Crichelow, 'Antecedents of Groupthink: A Quantitative Study', *Resolution*, 40(3), September 1996: 415–35; Glen Whyte, 'Recasting Janis's Groupthink Model: The Key Role of Collective Efficacy in Decision Fiascoes', *Organizational Behavior and Human Decision Processes*, 73(2/3) February/March 1998: 185–209; Roderick M. Kramer, 'Revisiting the Bay of Pigs and Vietnam Decisions 25 Years Later: How Well Has the Groupthink Hypothesis Stood the Test of Time?', *Organizational Behavior and Human Decision Processes*, 73(2/3) February 1998: 236–71; David Dryden Henningsen, Mary Lynn Miller

Notwithstanding its possible limitations, Janis's depiction of self-enveloping integration remains salient for the way that it throws into high relief a number of problematic issues surrounding the theme of leadership. For example, it might be argued that 'groupthink' may not be actually due to a leader's ability to motivate those that surround him or his immediate entourage. A group's sense of solidarity may have been formed prior to, and independent of, an individual's elevation to a leadership position, rather than as a result of the dynamics set in motion by the leadership. Moreover while it might be conceded that a form of 'groupthink' could coincide with a particular leadership, this need not necessarily be synonymous with customary meanings associated with deference and followership. Effective leaders are often adept at building and consolidating positive linkages between selected sets of subordinates through the use of tacit exchange agreements. This kind of organizational behaviour can serve to develop inner circles of trusted colleagues that are assigned special forms of access, influence, and responsibility in return for professional dedication and personal loyalty.[30] Many other cases of highly advanced forms of conformist behaviour can emerge from spontaneous processes of self-organization and mutual security, rather than through the directive medium of exerted leadership influence. Nevertheless, it is equally the case that many instances of behaviour that display a close correspondence to groupthink do have a connection to the particular pressures associated with the kind of intensive and enclosed subcultures that can arise in the vicinity of leadership organizations and which can generate forms of reliable yet dysfunctional followership.

The demands and strains associated with sustaining the status of a leadership and its related resources can and do lead to various forms of advanced and even extreme collective behaviour. The phenomenon of groupthink is perhaps the most marked and celebrated manifestation of the kind of empathetic solidarity and defensive cohesion that can evolve in the high-exposure conditions of visceral leadership politics. This is not to say that groupthink accounts for all the forms and variants of conditioned followership set within the operational logic of a leadership structure. These patterns may reveal different forms of leadership experience but they all tend to be distinguished by the same common factor of proximity to the leadership. While they may accurately depict many of the key dynamics of leader–follower relationships at close quarters, they do so by necessarily directing their attention on a limited sector of leadership-related activity. In essence, the experience of leadership that is analysed is usually situated within the exclusive inner circles of power. Given that the representative and corporate properties of a leadership can be extended into a surrounding retinue of senior levels of political allies, trusted associates, and dedicated staffers, it follows that the levels of intimate association with the leadership must decrease with the distance from that central zone of concentrated contact and fused identities. As such, it

---

Henningsen, Jennifer Eden, and Michael G. Cruz, 'Examining the Symptoms of Groupthink and Retrospective Sensemaking', *Small Group Research*, 37(1) February 2006: 36–64.

[30] For the classic description of what is often termed the Leader-Member Exchange Theory as well as a review of its theoretical development, see Dansereau *et al.*, 'A Vertical Dyad Linkage Approach to Leadership within Formal Organizations'; Graen and Cashman, 'A Role Making Model of Leadership in Formal Organizaitons'; Graen and Uhl-Bien, 'Relationship-Based Approach to Leadership'.

raises reasonable doubts over the extent to which the experiences of leadership—and the forms of followership—alter in relation to the widening constituency of a leader's reach.

RELATIONSHIPS AT A DISTANCE

It has been noted above that receiving leadership can come in many different forms and attach itself to a range of differing connections. Nevertheless, it is equally the case that the examples that are normally cited in this respect tend to dwell upon those frameworks in which the leader and the led have some close or regular relationship with one another. It is by focusing upon this often intimate connection that an analysis of the effects and conditions of leadership can be monitored more closely. While this can yield important insights, the tight focus of these studies will often lead to the screening out of other and arguably wider dimensions of leadership's social interrelationships. To concentrate solely upon the examination of leaders and those with whom they interact in a largely bounded environment risks drawing conclusions that are markedly unbalanced and even misleading. This is because of what such accounts leave out, or fail to develop in their analytical premises and categories. By concentrating upon the observable dynamics of the leaders and the led, there is a risk that the experience of leadership will become generalized on the basis of an immediate relationship between leaders and followers—as if those who comply do so as a result of a direct experience between themselves and the leadership.

In some ways, this construction fits into the idea that leadership is necessarily a reciprocal relationship between the leader and the led. In other ways, it risks being superficial, or at least one-dimensional, because in a complex mass society the individual citizen does not ordinarily have close contacts with the leadership. Such societies are multilayered with a profusion of structures and institutions that act as filtering intermediaries. These channel information, claims, demands, choices, concerns, interpretations, and beliefs etc. through a framework of governance. The leadership has to work through this system of intermediaries and constraints. It will seek to maximize whatever advantages it possesses—both to sustain its position and to develop its potential as a political force. More often than not, leaders have to operate in mass environments that are either suspicious, sceptical, and distracted, or else volatile, antagonistic, and negative. Both variants can be characterized as disconnected in one form or another. As such, it is a mistake to proceed on the basis that the public experience of leadership is necessarily comparable to those personal dynamics that are discernible between a leader and other political actors.

For example, earlier in this chapter reference was made to the way that leaders may secure compliance from others by framing choices designed to evoke decisions based upon the desire to receive rewards, or to avoid punishments. This may be so, but it raises questions over the degree to which this kind of direct relationship can be extended to an altogether different scale of operations. It raises very searching questions over whether the public can ever be a party to this kind of direct and interpersonal form of leadership pressure. Even if a general election, for example, could be accepted as an equivalent form of such a relationship, it is still difficult to conceive that members of the public calculate their voting behaviour on the basis of the transactional costs and benefits of their relationship with the leadership. Rational choice theory may claim that political consumers take market decisions on different policy programmes based upon likely gains and losses, but it is questionable whether this process can be convincingly portrayed as a choice between the rewards and punishments ensuing from a leader. Leaders in advanced democracies may well benefit from such choices, and may regard their party programmes as a leadership resource, but this is not the same as saying that voters are literally complying with a leader.

It would perhaps be more accurate to say that a leader has varied relationships with different constituencies and even different publics. The scope of his or her authority as a leader can often be represented as a series of concentric circles—ranging from the intense loyalty of a leader's immediate entourage to the more measured support drawn from various party, group, and organizational allegiances and thence outward to a state of almost suspended indifference or volatile fluctuation by elements of the general public. A leader's general outlook and strategic behaviour towards these different sectors will be calibrated according to the relative costs and benefits to be accrued from the allocation of leadership resources in the form of differentiated types and levels of engagement.[31] Likewise, the reactions to a leader will vary from the hard support of principled consent, ideological conviction, and forms of mutual interest and joint identity interest through to such soft support categories as acquiescence, tolerance, conditional allegiance, and variable interest down to a position of unreliable indifference. Hard support tends to foster commitment; soft support often merely condones the position of the leader until such time that a better leader can be found.

In effect, leaders can construct different leaderships for others to experience at different levels of consciousness and engagement. They can tap into the preferences, expectations, and aspirations of their audiences. They can also elicit responses based upon different attachments, motivations, and anxieties, in order to enhance their standing and to make appeals for support. It has already been noted that leaders will seek to create power bases or political constituencies by developing a variety of evocative linkages to established or emergent bases of authority ranging from political parties, social groupings, institutions, programmes, and ideologies to religious, class, ethnic, regional, and national categories of allegiance. Leaders will not only try to generate sets of powerful associations but will often seek to symbolize and even embody these attachments (e.g. appeals to the nation and enjoining public audiences to take action on behalf of the nation). In these circumstances, leaders can be said to be co-opting compliance from other sources. They are borrowing them for political effect. They may try to monopolize their appeal but it is difficult to claim that these factors are reducible to, or synonymous with, the leaders themselves. Even though a leader can assert

---

[31] A classic depiction of the spatial-political variation in sectors of support for a representative leader is provided by Richard F. Fenno's examination of the central significance of leadership style set within the layered landscapes of political allegiance. Richard F. Fenno, *Home Style* (Boston, MA: Little, Brown, 1973); Richard F. Fenno, 'U.S. House Members in Their Constituencies: An Exploration', *The American Political Science Review*, 71(3) September 1977: 883–917.

an equivalence with the national interest and claim access to the resources and prerogative powers of the state, such a leader usually has to rationalize these privileges in terms of acting as a trustee for the nation, the people, or the public interest.

In one sense, seeing compliance in these terms can suggest leadership without effort. In other words, a successful leader can be portrayed as 'free-riding' on party attachments, institutional norms, and traditional allegiances to nation, etc. On the other hand, a leader will be aware that (i) this is a deeply interdependent relationship requiring close attention and cultivation; and (ii) the claims to represent, embody, or articulate these entities will have to be continually negotiated through the intervening structures between citizen and leadership within which there will be competing assertions, interpretations, and challenges—not least the challenge of alternative leaders. In effect, leadership status becomes an unstable value that is contingent not just upon the strategies of competing leaders but on the way that incumbent and alternative leaders have to develop and maintain a convincing engagement with various structural, attitudinal, traditional, and other supports that will allow a leader to operate with a measure of social compliance.

While these processes of leadership conceptualization offer the prospect of a mutually dependent synergy of leaders and followers, they nevertheless have difficulty in reconciling the claims of a constitutive relationship at a generalized, and often abstract, level with the evident lack of a tangible connection between the two parties. In this most visceral of subject areas, the heavy presence of a material disconnect between leaders and their publics within the context of a mass society raises important issues over the precise way that those who experience leadership can have a formative influence upon its state of existence. This is particularly so in a context where the volume measures of civic detachment tend to rise commensurately with the physical and social distance from leadership elites.

At first sight, therefore, the notion of leadership and followership operating at a mass level to generate an observable dynamic of mutual dependence seems at variance with the operational realities of political engagement within the expanse of a social order. It is indeed the case that if this theme is approached from the perspectives drawn from those elites that have a close or proximate connection with leadership, then the likely outcome will be negative. Set against these benchmarks, the idea that a similar relationship might exist at several points removed from such a sphere of leadership does seem highly improbable. At the very least, it would appear in this light to be a notably tenuous and deeply problematic connection. Nevertheless, in giving due recognition to its limits, this is not the same as saying that leaders and their publics have little or no connection with one another—or that such a connection is devoid of political substance and significant consequences. The linkages may well have different properties. They may be elusive and even contentious in nature. But strands of mutual conditioning and interdependence, nonetheless, do exist between leaders and non-leaders at the sub-elite level. Moreover, they can on occasion make more of an impression upon leaderships than the closest of counsellors or the tightest of hierarchies.

These reciprocal linkages between leaders and non-leaders assume many forms and are dependent upon a range of shifting criteria. Subsequent aspects of this study will inevitably settle upon various conditioning aspects of this dynamic and bring to light the consequences that flow from its manifold character. It is not a realistic proposition to seek to encompass the full scope of these linkages. Nevertheless, some measure of their character can be grasped by giving some indication of the different forms of mutual conditioning that can occur at this level of engagement.

At one end of the spectrum of mutual conditioning are those exercises which actively attempt to elicit feedback from those who experience leadership. These take the form of assessments and judgements on what leadership is or should be, and how far those in leadership positions satisfy the requirements of their respective offices. The categories that are routinely employed by opinion pollsters and focus group operators to gauge leadership qualities are particularly significant in this respect. They are used both to elicit the properties of individual leaders that are most appealing to the public and to determine which evaluative criteria leaders need to be aware of, in order to maximize their chances of sustaining their approval levels or of securing a wider appeal.

Survey organizations use a variety of terms to evoke non-leader reactions towards leaders or potential leaders. These categories can relate to selected personality traits and behavioural characteristics that are deemed to be commonly significant to the requirements of leadership. Some prompts will be couched in the positive (e.g. 'in touch with people'). These require respondents to express their views over the extent to which a leader is seen as approximating to a particular value. At other times, a negative category is used (e.g. 'out of touch with people'). These kinds of cues invite respondents to engage more critically with the subject matter. Both types of category, however, are designed to elicit a measure of leader estimation by those who are not in a leadership position, and at the same time to refine the evaluative criteria of leadership itself. Notwithstanding the possible elements of tautology in such a process that mixes the empirical with the normative, the significance of these surveys is that over time they generate a selection of values associated with popular estimations of leadership.

What emerges on the basis of the generic expectations surrounding the personal and behavioural attributes of leadership is an extensive range of indicators relating to what can be considered to be a portfolio of requirements generally regarded as germane to the provision of leadership. The categories below give a representative sample of the themes that are repeatedly used on this basis in leadership surveys.[32] In addition to the category mentioned above (*in touch with ordinary people*) are the following widely cited attributes:

Well-informed	*Clever*
Intelligent	*Grasp of detail*
Sincere	*Sound judgement*
Likeable	*Friendly*
Appealing	*Down to earth*
Honest/ethical	*Knows own mind*
Says what he/she believes	*Can believe what he/she says*
Will get things done	*Competent*

[32] Drawn from survey categories from the following polling organizations: Gallup; Harris; Rasmussen Reports; Ivan Moore Research; YouGov; ICM; Ipsos MORI; NOP; Pew Research Center; Zogby International; and Populus.

Experienced	*Explains himself/herself effectively*
Compassionate	*Tough*
Hard-working	*Flexible*
Vision for future	*Ability to fulfil vision*
Understand problems	*Patriotic*
Trustworthy to do the right thing	*Good in crisis*
Leads unified organization	*Persuasive*
Presents good image for the country	*Strategic grasp*

Whilst these types of categories can be useful in building up a picture of public perceptions and evaluations of leadership, the usage of such indicators is not devoid of problems. For example, it is not always possible to discern whether leadership assessments are driven primarily by the behaviour and reputations of individual leaders in their own right, or by reference to some underlying standards of leadership against which contemporary claimants are being measured. In addition, each leadership category selected in surveys may well possess a singular value but this does not necessarily mean they can be aggregated together to achieve a form of generic coherence. Even correctly perceived traits can be logically inconsistent with one another (*compassionate/tough*; *knows own mind/ flexible*; *strategic grasp/grasp of detail*). Nevertheless, because these and other categories are almost invariably used in isolation from one another, it is generally the case that leadership criteria are bundled together with no clear organization of overall priorities or emphasis.

Another issue that can be raised in relation to these categories concerns the way that they can be context-dependent. In other words, the value given to an ascribed criterion of leadership may well be affected by a particular issue or crisis that was current at the time of the survey. The salience, for example, of having 'expertise in financial issues', or being 'strong on security measures' therefore may be accurate at the time of a particular survey but might not represent a settled level of leadership value at other times when agendas may have shifted to other areas of concern.

In spite of the sophistication of such analyses, they can neither determine the relationship between one attribute and another nor assign a higher leadership value to one set of characteristics over another. What these measures, and other simpler rankings, reveal is the volatile nature of the leadership market. This is shown not just in relation to public attitudes to changing leadership but also to shifting emphases attached to different attributes. The polls continually track leaders against a moving canvas—namely in respect to the public's estimation of their performance and in terms of their varying relationship to the public dis-course on political leadership.

This point goes to the heart of an underlying problem in that while leadership categories may act as benchmarks of good practice or normative value, they are nevertheless inherently changeable in accordance with altered conceptions of appropriate leadership. These variable priorities make the notion of an optimum fit between an individual leader and a leadership role into a highly elusive concept. And if this is the case with time, it is also relevant in respect to location. Different cultures will have differing sets of categories and priorities, depending on their specific historical experiences and social attitudes. In essence, just as there is no set universal rank ordering of key leadership components or characteristics, so there can be no finality to what is a continuous process of opinion formation.

Despite the ambiguities that are implicit in the selection and usage of leadership categories across different periods and in different systems, what remain clear are the ways in which they indicate the role of public expectations of leadership in shaping the operational contexts of what leaders do and how they approach the roles assigned to them. What can be described in one form or another as the contemporary market conditions of leadership within a system denotes the existence of a two-way process of mutual conditioning between leaders and non-leaders. Instead of the simplified depictions of organizational hierarchies that so often afflict the presentational logic of leadership positions, it is important to take account of the reciprocal connections between leaders and the expectations and traditions of their constituencies. These linkages stretch far beyond the formal arenas of explicit opinion exchange. They involve a richer and altogether more nuanced matrix of conditioned behaviour in which leadership actions and decisions are governed as much by the dynamics of anticipated reactions and mutual deterrence as by direct expressions of support and opposition.

LEADERS AND FOLLOWERS: APPROACHING EQUIVALENCE

At the other end of the spectrum of relational dynamics between leaders and those who experience leadership lies the more impenetrable but no less significant dimension of what can be described as the psychic and emotional factors involved in the reception of leaders by their audiences. These factors cover a broad expanse of responses and conditions that pertain to the productive interplay between leaders and non-leaders and which permit a degree of leadership authority that does not always appear to be commensurate with the contributory factors in its production. In other words, the power and authority of leaders cannot simply be reduced to the sum of their political or bargaining resources. In some instances, a condition of compliance can be the result of successive conditioning to a leadership that allows little or no space for any forms of political dissent or any alternative conceptions of governance. The systematization of intolerance and oppression can generate a type of reflexive conformity that is based upon the normalization of fear (Box 4.3).

But there are more complex forms of close followership which are dependent less upon syndromes of coercion and more upon the willing and often spontaneous impulse on the part of others to cede authority and power to those in leadership positions. Those experiencing leadership, therefore, can be in a position where they are in effect experiencing their own pre-existing needs and even demands for leadership—i.e. attending to their own drives to respond positively to those offering themselves as leadership figures. In this sense, leaders can be construed to be merely pushing against open doors, even to the point of not having to push at all.

Box 4.3 The equivalence of followership and silence

In many repressive regimes, what can appear as an equivalence of leadership and follower-ship is in reality a syndrome of compliance based upon a prolonged conditioning process of implied or actual threats leading to a compulsive form of silence on the part of a citizenry existing within a collapsed public space. This phenomenon of conditioned quiescence is captured in the following illustrations of populations held in a state of silence.

Chile under the Pinochet regime

I thought I knew Chile well, I had friends and acquaintances on the left and the right. Yet nothing had prepared me for the metamorphosis that the country went through in September 1973. People were absolutely silent, as though they had been struck dumb, cowed as much by a sense of failure as by the prevailing atmosphere of fear and repression. I travelled up and down the country, to find that there was in fact no resistance to speak of, certainly no civil war. Most people were exhausted by the previous three years of daily political struggle, and simply surrendered to the new regime.

Source: Richard Gott, 'Legacy of Terror', *New Statesman*, 15 September 2003.

Albania under the regime of Enver Hoxha (1941–85)

Since the Black Widow [Nexhmije Hoxha] and her husband had first come to power half a century earlier, their name had been indissolubly associated with Albania itself. Every-thing revolved around the quasi-sacred name of the Great Leader and his spouse. But this did not imply that it could be freely spoken. The regime founded by this remarkable couple was so concerned by its possible misuse that, to avoid it being profaned, they had even made its utterance unlawful except on special occasions or by authorized officials. Paradoxically, under the new government of Dr Sah Berisha the situation was unchanged but for the opposite reason. Political chaos and economic decline were now so rife that they were afraid the hated name might induce nostalgia. Or deference. So even in the new democratic Tirana it was still inadvisable to allow the name to pass your lips. Possibly forbidden. Certainly dangerous.

Source: Riccardo Orizio, *Talk of the Devil: Encounters with Seven Dictators* (London: Secker & Warburg, 2003), p. 94.

The nature of this kind of dynamic is complex and assumes a variety of forms operating at different levels of consciousness. At one level, it is possible to interpret the behavioural patterns of concurrence with leadership from the point of view of a reasonable form of cost–benefit calculation. It is possible to view those who condone the leadership over others as respondents who place value in the structure of such a relationship. It may be that they appreciate the functional logic of an organizational hierarchy, or that they approve the status of leaders as legitimate expressions or derivatives of an accepted authority, or that they defer to the executive roles and prerogatives of leadership in situations which are deemed to be threatening.

At another level, the processes of ceding power to and affirming the status of leaders can be couched in far more reflexive ways. For example, some of those who respond favourably to leaders will do so in an instinctive and impulsive manner because the appeal is primarily received in terms of an emotional reaction. It may be a question of who the leader is, or what that leader may signify, or what the basis of the leadership's project may be, or the issues that a leader chooses to emphasize, or the people surrounding the leadership. Whatever the reason, there are occasions when non-leaders are content to be designated as 'followers' because of the emotional ties that exist between themselves and a particular leadership. In effect, a follower would not regard the act of following to be the product of leadership exertion so much as a function of intrinsic gratification. Given the rewarding nature of the experience, it is possible to construe such a relationship as an internalized form of self-sustaining compliance that persists irrespective of a leader's attempts at influence or of a leader's available resources.

This theme of inner-directed compliance brings with it a further dimension that locates leadership even more emphatically within the realm of psychological stimulus and response. In the phenomenon of groupthink, the dynamics of cohesion and consolidation within small groupings were examined from the point of view of decision-making and control at the leadership level. Similar forms of intense interaction and mutual conditioning can also play a role at the level of those who are located at the other end of the leadership relationship. It would not be appropriate to claim that the intimate factors associated with groupthink can be precisely extended to the large numbers of a mass society. Nevertheless, it is possible to recognize the role of broad-based social psychology in the construction and maintenance of support bases for leadership. These social psychological categories can range from the contribution made by the forces of group identity and social allegiance in the cultivation of leadership to the way that the dynamics of social learning, 'social proof', 'social contagion', and even crowd dynamics can settle upon the agency of leadership.[33] High levels of imitative behaviour can even lead to concerns over the well-being of a polity. It is possible for the relationship between leaders and followers to become so closely fused that the two parties not only lose any clear lines of demarcation but risk entering into an intolerant and even extreme form of mutual need.

Some analysts would claim that the excesses which are often associated with extreme forms of leadership are due primarily to the zeal of those whose support for such leadership both allows for, and actively promotes, its extremes. Just as there is thought to be situational leadership, so it is suggested that in certain contexts a phenomenon of situational followership can be also be discerned which can in its own right be responsible for excessive forms of dominant behaviour over others. More often than not, this refers to those occasions when groups of individuals develop a pack or herd mentality that carries them forward into demeaning, harmful, and even destructive acts which under normal circumstances, and acting individually, the participants would not have contemplated.[34]

---

[33] See Steve Reicher, 'The Psychology of Crowd Dynamics', in Michael A. Hogg and Robin S. Tindale (eds.), *Blackwell Handbook of Social Psychology: Group Processes* (Oxford: Blackwell, 2001), pp. 182–208; Howard Rheingold, *Smart Mobs: The Next Social Revolution* (Cambridge, MA: Perseus, 2002); James Surowiecki, *The Wisdom of Crowds* (New York, NY: Anchor, 2004); Robert B. Cialdini and Noah J. Goldstein, 'Social Influence: Compliance and Conformity', *Annual Review of Psychology*, 55 2004: 591–621.

[34] Craig Haney, Curtis Banks, and Philip Zimbardo, 'A Study of Prisoners and Guards in a Simulated Prison', *Naval Research Review*, 30(9) 1973: 4–17; Craig Haney, Curtis Banks, and Philip Zimbardo, 'Interpersonal Dynamics in a Simulated Prison', *International Journal of Criminology and Penology*, 1 1973: 69–97; Philip Zimbardo, *The Lucifer Effect: How Good People Turn Evil* (London: Rider, 2009), chs. 1, 10–13.

Whether it is derived from the attribution of roles within a social hierarchy, or from the unmonitored and unrestrained forces of peer pressure, the net effect is interpreted to be one of unthinking and irrational behaviour set within a protective and inward-looking environment of intolerance, abuse, and contempt for those who are deemed to be inferior or hostile, or most likely both.

A deeper and more disquieting source of this kind of self-motivating collective action is assigned to the individual rather than from their interactions with one another. This locates the nature and extremes of followership within the sphere of individual dispositions. In other words, unscrupulous leaders do not have to rely upon the dynamics of group formations in order to service a repressive regime; they can depend upon an altogether more generic source of potential repression in what is claimed to be an innate psychological drive towards order and authority. Opinions vary over the basis of this alleged impulse for compliance that is discernible amongst what Gardner calls 'chronic followers'.[35]

Sigmund Freud, for example, speculated on the way that groups and individuals develop close dependency relationships with leaders—or rather with what leaders represent or suggest to those who follow them. Freud was intrigued by the attachment to leaders—even when a leader was seen to be weak or incompetent or despicable. For Freud, the motive force lay in the personality of the follower and specifically in the primal human need for care and protection that originates in a child's relationship with the father figure. Through the processes of what Freud termed 'transference', individuals perceive and react to leaders on the basis of deep-seated emotional needs drawn from their pasts.[36] At an unconscious level, Freud surmised that the emotional yearning for a dominant figure was projected on to, and transferred to, a leader as a representation of an ancient father figure. For some, religion offered a divine form of this projected desire, with God as the depicted father possessing full paternal authority. In like manner, earthly leaders become similarly invested with patriarchal properties through the compulsive need of their followers for submission to a form of forceful parental guidance.

What Freud describes as the 'thirst for obedience' by followers who actively seek domination in the manner of complicit children, was developed by others like Erich Fromm and Theodore Adorno. Fromm thought that the psychological states of individual existence are strongly influenced not just by the ego but by repressive social structures of one sort or another. The reaction against the imposition of the latter finds its expression in another person whose leadership offers a means by which individuals can achieve greater autonomy over life's forces than would otherwise be the case. Fromm's theory of the 'authoritarian character' refers to the 'tendency to surrender the independence of one's own individual ego, to merge it with someone or something outside oneself and thus gain a force that is absent from his own ego'.[37] In essence, one sort of unfreedom would be exchanged for a more preferable variant.

Adorno's work on the 'authoritarian personality' was primarily driven by the need to explain the appeal of fascist ideologies and the nature and determinants of

---

[35] Gardner, *Leading Minds*, pp. 34–5.

[36] Sigmund Freud, *Moses and Monotheism. The Standard Edition of the Complete Psychological Works of Sigmund Freud, Volume 18* (London: Hogarth Press, 1939), pp. 109–11.

[37] Erich Fromm, *Escape from Freedom* (New York, NY: Owl Books, 1994), pp. 140–76.

those personality types that were drawn to such ideas. The research examined the deep-lying trends in some personality types that made them highly susceptible to authoritarian messages. These predispositions included an entrenched sense of social hierarchy; a rigid attachment to rules; an intolerance of ambiguity; an inclination to think in rigid categories; a violent dislike of the unconventional; a compulsive identification with powerful figures; and a submissive and uncritical attitude towards leaders as idealized moral and coercive authorities.[38] The works of both Adorno and Fromm, as well as their many derivatives, suggest that authoritarian leaders may well find that they are pushing against an open door in their search for followers.

Whether the level of analysis operates in terms of an individual or a group frame of reference, and whether the emphasis lies primarily with dispositional or with situational factors, these insights do open up dimensions of followership that are entirely different from the more conventional depictions of a unidirectional construction based upon a leadership figure influencing others to engage in thoughts and actions that they were unlikely to adopt or perform of their own volition. Just as individuals can become subsumed within a social or group identity to the point of extremes, and just as some personalities in certain situations can be triggered to disclose their inner drives for compliance and submission, so leaders can become the beneficiaries of followers who have severe dependency needs that require the release of outlets. Leaders in this situation can become the incidental object of highly subjective forces.

CONCLUSION

It will be evident from the above discussion that the relationship between leaders and what are almost invariably referred to as 'followers' is not as simple and straightforward as the key terms would suggest. It might be argued that it leaves us with less than we started with at the outset. The initial position was that leaders and followers are clearly component parts of a power relationship that is inherent in the very subject matter of leadership. Given the common emphasis in many leadership studies on the need for leaders to maximize the potential for power that would not otherwise be available without their active intervention, the conventional conclusion is that non-leaders in general are consigned to the role of incidental concomitants of the processes of leadership. According to this logic, for every leader there needs to be an accompanying analogue of followers in just the same way that causes are deemed to be followed by effects—and stimuli lead ineluctably to responses.

On closer inspection, it becomes clear that this apparently simple symmetry is something of a chimera. The relationship is far more variable, provisional, and

---

[38] Theodor W. Adorno, Else Frenkel-Brunswik, Daniel Levinson, and Nevitt Sanford, *The Authoritarian Personality* (New York, NY: Harper & Row, 1950); Stanley Milgram, *Obedience to Authority: An Experimental View* (New York, NY: Harper & Row, 1974); William F. Stone, Gerda Lederer, and Richard Richard (eds.), *Strength and Weakness: The Authoritarian Personality Today* (New York, NY: Springer-Verlag, 1993).

multidimensional than appears to be the case at first sight. In fact, the term 'followers' emerges as a crude collective noun that is as distortive as it is capacious in its usage. Far from adhering to a clearly consistent pattern, followers encompass a diverse set of attachments positioned in different constituencies of support with differing levels of intensity. Soft support in some areas can contrast sharply with hard-core followership in others. Acquiring and sustaining followers can be a continual political challenge for some leaders; for others, the issue of support can seem akin to a form of inertial physics in that followers appear almost to self-generate and self-organize into a state of permissive acquiescence or voluntary control and, thereby, into an assured resource for the leadership. For James MacGregor Burns, leadership and followership are so closely 'intertwined and fluid' that they raise the question of whether and how it might be possible to 'distinguish conceptually between leaders and followers'[39] at all. With transformative leadership, it is not a case of where leadership might end and followership begins: 'persons initially labelled leaders or followers come to succeed each other, substitute for each other. "Leader" and "follower" roles become ephemeral, transient, and even indistinct.'[40] The proposition evokes the celebrated statement by a British prime minister: 'I must follow the people. Am I not their leader?'[41]

Whether or not the relationship between leaders and followers can be said to reach this level of converged identity, it is nevertheless the case that a resonance exists between the two categories. So much so in fact, that in some quarters the analytical categories used to organize the study of leaders are regarded as being equally applicable to the sector of followers. To be specific, just as leaders are assumed to reveal a distinctive leadership style, so according to some analysts logic dictates that their supporters necessarily possess an equivalent 'follower style'. Some studies even resort to the usage of familiar four-cell tables not in order to portray leadership categories but to map out different follower styles. Such analyses even tend to feature styles based on performance/task priorities and on relationship/integration values—thereby underlining the close resemblance to the standard typologies of leadership styles.[42]

Despite all these references to complementarity and mutually constitutive relationships, the distinction between leaders and followers remains a central and defining element in the study of political leadership. Some leaderships may well achieve a highly developed harmony of outlook and purpose, but such genuine unity is rare and even where it exists it is never permanent. Its very impermanence leads back to the conventional logic that describes leadership as a functioning *relationship* with those who are not leaders. The widely attributed corollary of possessing a capacity to lead—and with it an ability to fulfil the requirements of agency associated with leadership—remains one of a secure positional resource that implies a measure of control and even domination over others. But as we have seen, the compulsive rationale of this intuitive perception is

[39] James MacGregor Burns, *Transforming Leadership* (London: Atlantic, 2003), p. 171.

[40] Burns, *Transforming Leadership*, p. 185.

[41] Political epigram widely attributed to Prime Minister Benjamin Disraeli.

[42] For example, see Earl H. Potter III, William E Rosenbach, and Thane S. Pittman, 'Followers for the Times', in William E. Rosenbach and Robert L. Taylor (eds.), *Contemporary Issues in Leadership*, 5th edn. (Boulder, CO: Westview, 2001), pp. 163–86.

often at odds with an underlying dynamic that assigns a profound conditioning influence upon leadership relations. In other words, a secure positional resource is only secure if its security is negotiated into existence through others.

This more nuanced and intermediate perspective is relevant even in those regimes that have a reputation for being wholly leader-centric and authoritarian in nature. Totalitarian states have in the past gone to extreme lengths to enforce systematic and comprehensive subordination through coercive power and social indoctrination. But even with these regimes, it proved ultimately impossible to prevent the outbreak of dispute and dissent over any sustained period of time. In some of these extreme systems, the adopted policy has been that of instituting a dominant narrative portraying the leader's relationship with the masses as a symbiosis of identities. In Hannah Arendt's study of totalitarian systems, leaders are distinguished by their ability to metabolize themselves into the collective psyche of their peoples rather than simply through their techniques of material domination. In Hitler's Germany and Stalin's Soviet Union, totalitarianism 'discovered a means of dominating and terrorizing human beings from within'.[43] This allowed a process of convergence to ensue which eliminated the normal distance and distinction between rulers and the ruled:

> In substance, the totalitarian leader is nothing more nor less than the functionary of the masses he leads; he is not a power-hungry individual imposing a tyrannical and arbitrary will upon his subjects . . . [H]e depends just as much on the 'will' of the masses he embodies as the masses depend on him. Without him they would lack external representation and remain an amorphous horde; without the masses the leader is a nonentity.[44]

The radical effectiveness of such totalitarian regimes was based upon the leaders' ability to claim to be both the agency and the instrument of a transformative movement within an otherwise disordered and fractured socio-historical context. The disorientation, loneliness, and alienation of ordinary people permitted leaders to collapse the normal dynamics of the public sphere, and to offer themselves as the only workable and legitimate forms of replacement. But even in what were apparently impregnable regimes, these totalitarian movements ultimately overreached themselves with the consequence that their bases of followership rapidly eroded, leaving the leaders in an increasingly untenable position.

In the final analysis, therefore, a leadership is most effective when it is able to draw in supporters and maximize a followership to the point where the relationship between the two components becomes one of near equivalence. While this relationship can lead to a deeper understanding of the properties and contingencies of viable leadership, the dynamics of mutual dependence also work in reverse. In effect, the close reliance of leaders upon the foundational resources of their various forms of followership means that if the relationship is compromised, weakened, or damaged in some way, then the outcome is one that will be to the distinct disadvantage of the leaders. Far more often than not, leaders appear to be secure in their leadership positions. But even the most secure of leaders find that

---

[43] Hannah Arendt, *Totalitarianism: Part Three of The Origins of Totalitarianism* (San Diego, CA: Harvester/Harcourt, 1968), p. 23.

[44] Arendt, *Totalitarianism*, p. 23.

sooner or later the time and the conditions will arrive when the leader–follower relationship from which they previously benefited will operate against them. At this point, what may once have seemed an enduring leadership lapses instead into a pathology of decline. At no time are the bottom-up energies within the processes of leadership more evident than when they encounter the top-down impulses of leaders at bay. It is these occasions, when the leader–follower relationship is chronically disrupted, which serve to cast further light on the general anatomy of political leadership.

5

Losing it: Leadership as a life cycle

'For every action there is always an equal and opposite reaction.'

Isaac Newton's Third Law of Motion

'I really was catapulted overnight into a world of fairy tales, and then, in the years that followed, had to return to earth, the better to realize that fairy tales are merely a projection of human archetypes and that the world is not at all structured like a fairy tale... I was given no diplomatic immunity from that... long fall from a fairy-tale world onto the hard earth.'

Václav Havel[1]

PREAMBLE

It has already been noted that leadership is a relational concept. Its logic, as well as its appeal, rests upon a level of symmetry between a leader—or a focal point of leadership—and those who are not in such positions but who nevertheless allow, condone, or actively support the position, policies, and prerogatives of the leadership. As a consequence, the analytical and explanatory agendas surrounding the subject of leadership largely follow the themes and processes associated with the formation and maintenance of this central relationship. These agendas reflect a simple yet compulsive orientation in the examination of the phenomenon; namely that both the allure and the utility of leadership are drawn almost exclusively from the fact of its presence rather than from its absence. Leadership is inherently correlated with such positive categories as security and stability. Correspondingly, a lack of leadership is widely regarded not merely as an outright negative condition but also as a just cause for the establishment of its corrective antidote in the shape of new leadership. In this way, the study of leadership becomes naturally inclined towards what are considered to be the evident properties of its subject matter.

The net effect of this understandable bias is that the rationale of leadership becomes closely tied to notions of stability, settlement, direction, and order that are self-evidently oriented towards an effective establishment of a leadership-based hierarchy. In other words, the customary approach to the study of leadership is

---

[1] Václav Havel, translated from the Czech by Paul Wilson, 'A Farewell to Politics', *New York Review of Books*, 24 October 2002.

based upon the manifold conditions of leadership. On the other side of the equation, such adverse political conditions as disruption, instability, disorganization, and other forms of political strain become conspicuously associated with an asserted lack of leadership, which is habitually transposed into being both a symptom and a cause of an unsettled state of existence. Just as dysfunctional leadership relationships herald wider systemic problems, so the provision of leadership is generally interpreted as the source and agency of their solution.

This close correlation of the principles and practice of leadership with the virtues of an ordered polity tends to generate a halo effect around the subject area in two main senses. The first is that leadership is generally taken to be a positive good that should be encouraged and supported. And the second is that leadership is widely accepted to constitute a functional imperative to the effective operation of a political system. It is for these generic reasons that leaders are normally invested with the legitimacy, authority, and resources which are considered to be commensurate with the benefits to be accrued from their roles. The corollary of these processes is that the phenomenon of leaders and their positional strengths tend to marginalize the issue of their decline—practically to the point of preclusion. Almost everything about leadership is palpably geared to the justifiable significance of acquiring and maintaining the required levels of status and leverage. However, this compulsive attraction raises a host of questions in relation not just to the ways that leaders come to lose their authority and position, but also to how these falls from grace can be adequately explained within the context of a subject area that normally prioritizes the rise to, and usage of, leadership power. It is noteworthy that just as the passage to leadership offers a rich vein of analytical value, so the loss of leadership provides an equally revealing set of insights into the properties and dynamics of the field.

It has already been intimated above that there is a natural predisposition in the subject area towards the allure of leaders who are on the rise and leaders who are in the ascendancy. In many ways, the contextual logic of the phenomenon determines the orientation. So much so that it can be difficult to even conceive how such a resource-rich hierarchical position can be brought to an end. Given the scale of their remit and the functional value attached to their roles—as well as the proficiency of elites in devising measures of protective self-perpetuation—leaders are often depicted as dominant and durable fixtures. But by the same token, it is also evident that leaders fail. They disappear. They are replaced by other leaders. In the final analysis, leaders are exposed as temporary and mortal; their leaderships are abandoned and fade into the realm of memory. This may seem self-evident but it nevertheless cuts against the grain of much of what leadership is considered to be and how it is approached as a field of inquiry. What is now required in this study is the adoption of a different pathway to the normal tracks that gravitate towards new leaders and sustained leaderships. This approach will allow us to examine the pathologies that accompany leaders and to explain the processes of their demise.

In his novel *Anna Karenina*, Leo Tolstoy makes the following celebrated observation: 'Happy families are all alike; every unhappy family is unhappy in its own way.' This epigram carries some resonance with the phenomenon of collapsing leadership. While successful leaders are often interpreted as being comparable to one another in the security of their positions, so leaders in decline seem to occupy their own particular syndromes of dissolution. At the very least, it can be said that the processes of decline for any particular leader should not be seen simply in terms of an equal and opposite reaction to that individual's rise to prominence. The likelihood that a leader's fall can be construed as a mirror image reversal of the same processes responsible for its inception appears to be remote and unfeasible. But if it is the case that leaders tend to follow different courses towards their separate departures, then arriving at any broad conclusions evidently poses a number of difficulties. Nevertheless, it is possible to discern some key compositional and interpretive dimensions that can help in clarifying the often opaque chemistry of losing leadership.

KEEPING UP APPEARANCES

Perhaps the most overt example of leadership decline comes with the actual demise of the principal actor. As political leadership is generally constructed around a central figure of authority, the death of that figure throws into high relief the significance of leadership stability within any ordered realm of social existence. In one way, the death of a leader may be said to reduce the notion of leadership decline to its simplest, starkest, and most self-evident terms. In another way, it forcefully opens up the ramifications of losing a leader and the necessary adjustments that need to be made in the wake of what are usually highly unexpected events. The shock value attributed to the sudden disappearance of a leading political figure is almost invariably heightened by the dominant narrative that surrounds most leaderships; namely that leaders are projected as robustly fit and healthy individuals who are able to withstand the pressures of office and the strains of decision-making. By convention, the organizational provision of authority to a leader is implicitly reciprocated by the beneficiary's assurance of a basic physical capacity to fulfil the requirements of the position.[2]

When this contractual understanding is disrupted by illness or speculations of infirmity, then a leadership can quickly be undermined on the grounds of evident or supposed incapacity. It is not simply that the leader as an individual may be disabled by an illness; it is that the integrity of his or her own organization itself becomes compromised by what is assumed to be a leadership vacuum. This is one of the main reasons why leaders habitually conceal or even deny that they are suffering from any kind of health disorder which might cause consternation within their own organizations and outside in the public sphere. This kind of news management can take various forms. On some occasions, leaders may admit to a minor disorder in order to conceal a more serious affliction from attentive observers. The overriding priority is to maintain the appearance of a vigorous leader focused wholly on the issues that concern those that he or she is representing.

---

[2] See Rose McDermott, *Presidential Leadership, Illness, and Decision Making* (New York, NY: Cambridge University Press, 2008).

On other occasions, leaders will opt for a position of complete denial of any health issues that could cast doubt on their fitness for office. Such leaders will go to extreme lengths to retain the image of good health. They will rearrange their travel plans and work schedules in order to prevent having to disclose any medical issues to the public and to their political opponents. Arguably the most illustrative example of this kind of concealment was François Mitterrand who held the French presidency from 1981 to 1995. At the beginning of his tenure, Mitterrand had instituted a scheme of six-monthly disclosures on the health of the president. This declaration of transparency followed from the events surrounding the death of President Pompidou in 1974 after a two-year, and very private, battle with cancer that occurred in the middle of his presidential term of office. And yet in spite of an undertaking to give regular disclosures on the state of his own health, Mitterrand soon engaged in a concerted policy of concealment when his condition was diagnosed in November 1981—i.e. only six months into a seven-year term. Apart from the pressure that was placed upon his doctor to issue misleading public statements on his condition and to engage in secret courses of treatment over a period of eleven years, a series of countermeasures was put in place that ensured that his true condition was given the status of a state secret.

> The democratic influences, which had been part of his life in his rise to power, suddenly became optional; his party, the electorate and the human rights of French men and women became subordinated to one all-pervasive demand—the need to keep his illness secret ... Mitterrand's insistence on protecting the secrecy of his illness for 'raison d'état' led to the most massive invasion of privacy in French republican history. On Mitterrand's orders, an unauthorised team of gendarmes tapped the telephones of hundreds of French politicians, journalists, publishers and Parisian personalities. The President justified it on the grounds that he needed to know if any of them were preparing to divulge the details of his illness.[3]

Ultimately, Mitterrand's condition forced him to disclose the presence of an illness but only after he had devised a phased release of information designed to portray it as a recent condition. He survived through a second term of office that was punctuated by periods of incapacity and which has become the subject of retrospective speculation centring upon whether he should ever have been re-elected in 1988.[4]

In the context of political leadership, the impression of good health is a highly valued asset that has to be cultivated and projected as a strategic and tactical imperative. Whether it is Silvio Berlusconi opting for hair transplantation treatments allegedly associated with a high sexual appetite for young women, or Vladimir Putin's efforts to portray a machismo image through a succession of photo opportunities featuring a bare-chested prime minister swimming in icy rivers, riding on horseback, and tagging tigers and polar bears, the logic remains one of a compounded identity of physical, mental, and psychological fitness for office.

[3] David Owen, *In Sickness and in Power: Illness in Heads of Government during the Last 100 Years* (London: Methuen, 2009), p. 228.

[4] Following his death, Mitterrand's doctor gave an extended account of the deception surrounding the president's illness in a book entitled *The Great Secret*. However, the reach of censorship extended after death when a criminal court ordered Dr Claude Gubler's book to be withdrawn from sale on the grounds that it violated doctor–patient confidentiality. Dr Gubler was also issued with a suspended prison sentence and a Fr 300,000 fine.

By the same token, the physical and reputational features of a leadership can become a source of vulnerability and one that can be used as a device by which to arouse damaging speculation amongst opponents both at home and abroad. At the height of the Cold War, for example, the Central Intelligence Agency investigated several ways to undermine Fidel Castro's position as prime minister of Cuba. The project was to alter his appearance so that he could no longer portray himself as a vigorous revolutionary leader. One plan was to contaminate Castro's diving suit with fungus spores that would cause a disfiguring skin disease. Another was to insert thallium salts into the inner linings of his shoes. These salts would have had a powerful depilatory effect that would have denuded Castro of all his body hair—including his beard and eyebrows.[5]

While these plans were not in the end put into practice, a similar strategy of facial degradation was carried out in the Ukraine in 2004. Viktor Yushchenko was a key leader in the opposition coalition at a time of serious political unrest in the Ukraine. In the 2004 presidential election, Yushchenko faced a run-off ballot against the government-sponsored candidate Viktor Yanukovych. Although Yanukovych won the election, there were so many allegations of widespread electoral fraud that pressure arose for the result to be invalidated and for the ballot to be re-run. It was during this period of political crisis that Yushchenko was struck down with a serious illness that was conspicuously evident from his severely disfigured face. The issue surrounding the mysterious onset of the illness became a key element of Ukraine's 'Orange Revolution' that ultimately saw the electoral process repeated and Viktor Yushchenko securing the presidency in January 2005. Later it became clear that he had been poisoned by a powerful dioxin which led to dioxin levels in his blood which were registered as being over 6,000 times above normal. Those responsible for the plot have never been identified although suspicion continues to surround a group of senior Ukrainian officials with alleged connections to Russia.[6]

The emphasis upon portraying a vigorous constitution can lead those in leadership positions to adopt strategies that are designed to conceal features which might militate against the perception of good health. The devices for avoiding the disclosure of minor illnesses or accidents are seen as relatively normal and are rationalized on the basis of not needlessly arousing the concern of those outside the immediate leadership circle. What is far more noteworthy are the sometimes extraordinary lengths that some leaders will go to in order to convey the impression of individual normality. Anthony Eden provides a case in point.[7] He had a public image of a healthy, debonair, and self-assured statesman. In reality, he was a prime minister who experienced difficult health problems as a result of a failed gall bladder operation two years before securing the premiership.

---

[5] Fabian Escalante, *The Cuba Project: CIA Covert Operations 1959–62* (Melbourne: Ocean Press, 2004); Don Bohning, *The Castro Obsession: U.S. Covert Operations Against Cuba, 1959–1965* (Dulles, VA: Potomac, 2005), chs. 4–7.

[6] 'The Dioxin Poisoning of Victor Yushchenko: Need for Methods in Routine Analysis of Metabolites of the Poison TCDD', *Medical News*, 5 August 2009. Accessed 5 March 2012 at: <www.medicalnewstoday.com/articles/159819.php>. Timothy Garton Ash and Timothy Snyder, 'The Orange Revolution', *New York Review of Books*, 28 April 2005.

[7] Anthony Eden was prime minister from 7 April 1955 to 10 January 1957.

As a consequence, he was plagued with internal disorders that left him in often acute abdominal pain. This in turn prompted not only a constantly changing regime of medication but also an increased dependence upon a largely concealed array of morphine derivatives, barbiturates, and amphetamines which he used to counter the debilitating effects of the underlying illness.[8]

Ironically, Eden had succeeded Winston Churchill as prime minister who himself had been the subject of many rumours concerning his health while in office. During the Second World War, Churchill suffered a heart attack while visiting Franklin D. Roosevelt at the White House in December 1941. The US had just entered the war and Churchill's doctor thought it prudent not to release any details concerning the severity of the prime minister's illness. In the circumstances, Dr Charles Wilson, who later became Lord Moran, 'felt the effect of announcing that the PM had had a heart attack could only be disastrous'[9] to public morale. In December 1943, Churchill's extensive international travel schedule led to him suffering from a serious strain of pneumonia when visiting General Eisenhower in Tunisia. The seriousness of this bout of illness was also minimized at the time. In becoming prime minister relatively late in life and in wartime, Churchill had always sought to project himself as fit, energetic, and galvanized with the responsibilities of leadership. He was therefore highly sensitive to reports that might suggest the existence of problems concerning fitness for office.

After the war when he entered the opposition ranks, Churchill's fitness for office increasingly became an issue within his own party. Despite suffering a mild stroke on holiday in 1949, Churchill retained his position as Conservative Leader and regained the premiership in October 1951 at the age of 78. However, in June 1953, he suffered a more severe stroke in 10 Downing Street itself. Doctors at the scene initially feared for his life. Once again, the significance of his condition was kept out of the press and media[10] and therefore concealed from Parliament and the public. It was at this stage that he could have been, and arguably should have been, forced to make way for another leader but the main contenders (Anthony Eden, Harold Macmillan[11]) were themselves indisposed through illnesses which were publicly known. Churchill continued in office for another two years before resigning.[12]

An arguably more extreme example is provided by President John F. Kennedy (1961–3). He suffered from the ill effects of a succession of childhood illnesses as well as from a wartime injury to his back that left him with a long history of severe

---

[8] Following a series of episodes of jaundice and abdominal pain related to the presence of gallstones, Eden underwent an operation to remove his gallbladder. The surgical procedure, however, damaged the bile tract from the liver to the small intestine. The injury required four subsequent biliary tract operations. The prolonged effects were periods of post-operative disability, recurrent fevers, and a syndrome of fatigue related conditions. See David Carlton, *Anthony Eden: A Biography* (London: Allen Lane, 1981), pp. 11–28, 100–31; John W. Braasch, 'Anthony Eden's (Lord Avon) Biliary Tract Saga', *Annals of Surgery*, 238(5) November 2003: 772–5; Owen, *In Sickness and in Power*, pp. 109–40.

[9] Quoted in David Owen, 'Diseased, Demented, Depressed: Serious Illness in Heads of State', *QJM: An International Journal of Medicine*, 96(5) 2003: 332.

[10] A news blackout was agreed to by the 'press barons' Lord Beaverbrook, Lord Camrose, and Lord Bracken.

[11] Rab Butler was another contender but was always regarded as a very cautious individual who was temperamentally unsuited to a leadership challenge.

[12] Charles M. W. Wilson, *Winston Churchill: The Struggle for Survival 1940–1965* (London: Constable, 1966).

back pain from spinal compression fractures. He was also diagnosed as suffering from Addison's disease, colitis, various allergies, bowel disorders, osteoporosis, autoimmune disorders, as well as a range of skin, respiratory, and urinary-tract infections. Kennedy was hospitalized on more than thirty-five occasions in his life and was given the last rites three times. He had been admitted secretly to hospital on nine occasions during his rise to power in the mid 1950s. Despite this profusion of disorders, his public persona was one of a carefully cultivated image of a fit young man who was wholly equal to the task of being president. In order to reconcile the public perception of youthful vigour with the private debilitating reality of multiple conditions, Kennedy had to resort to orthopaedic supports and an extensive regime of drugs which by the time he became president amounted to between ten and twelve medications a day (Box 5.1).

In states where the media are subjected to a high level of political control, leaders can go much further in creating a public perception of good health and well-being. In the Soviet Union, for example, it was possible not only to present ageing leaders in ways that were reassuringly stable but also to prevent any news leaks or privately sourced information that contradicted the official line. All three leaders in the closing years of the communist regime—Leonid Brezhnev (1964–82), Yuri Andropov (1982–4), and Konstantin Chernenko (1984–5)— suffered from ill health and in all three cases the severity of their medical conditions was concealed up to and until their positions became critical.[13]

Box 5.1 Complex medical dependency: President John F. Kennedy

President Kennedy's regime of regular medication included the following for a series of complaints:

- Antispasmodics for his bowel (*Paregoric Lamodal Transatine*)
- Stimulants (*Ritalin* and thyroid hormone)
- Muscle relaxants (*Phenobarbital, Librium, Meprobomate*)
- Painkillers (*Codeine, Demerol, Methadone*)
- Oral cortisone
- Injected cortisone
- Testosterone
- Sleeping tablets (*Nembutal*)
- Local anaesthetics (*Novocaine, Procaine*)

This profusion of medications did not include those prescribed and administered by the celebrity doctor Max Jacobson. His secret visits to the White House usually resulted in the president being injected with an amphetamine-based compound which Dr Jacobson called a 'miracle tissue regenerator'.

Sources: Lawrence Altman and Todd S. Purdum, 'In J.F.K. File, Hidden Illness, Pain and Pills', *New York Times*, 17 November 2002; Robert Dallek, 'The Medical Ordeals of JFK', *The Atlantic Monthly*, December 2002; Robert Dallek, *An Unfinished Life: John F. Kennedy, 1917–1963* (Boston, MA: Little, Brown and Company, 2003), ch. 11; Rose McDermott, *Presidential Leadership, Illness, and Decision Making* (New York, NY: Cambridge University Press, 2008), ch. 5.

---

[13] Jerrold M. Post, *Leaders and their Followers in a Dangerous World: The Psychology of Political Behavior* (Ithaca, NY: Cornell University Press, 2004), pp. 87–90, 96–8; Georgi Arbatov, *The System:*

The most notorious case was that of Leonid Brezhnev. He had developed a cult of personality even when his health was in decline. During the last ten years of his leadership, Brezhnev had become overweight; he drank and smoked to excess; he suffered several strokes and was diagnosed with cerebral sclerosis which had left him with speech and mobility problems. He had been brought back from the brink of death on several occasions and doctors were in close attendance on a permanent basis. In order to preserve the appearance of normality both for the leader and the regime, elaborate arrangements were put in place to disguise the extent of Brezhnev's infirmity. These ranged from special lighting and camera angles for any televised coverage to the installation of railings and ramps to allow Brezhnev to be pushed or lifted up to public rostrums. Valery Boldin, who later became Mikhail Gorbachev's chief of staff, recalls the spectacle:

> It had become increasingly apparent that he was no longer capable of running the party or the country. At meetings of the Politburo ... he would stare with a vacant stare, seemingly unaware of his surroundings, the identity of those present, and the business they had come to discuss. More often than not he would read out a note prepared for him, by his assistants, printed in very large characters on a special typewriter. He often got so confused that he read the same sentences over and over again, and then looked round pathetically, as if acknowledging his helplessness.[14]

The official Communist Party line was always that Brezhnev was not seriously ill. In part this fiction was sustained because those who had received political patronage from him wished to see him continue in office at any cost. But it was also a systemic response—the party apparatus feared that concerns over his possible demise might fuel domestic turmoil and a leadership transition crisis. Either way, the true state of Brezhnev's health was largely concealed for the best part of ten years.[15]

A more recent example from an authoritarian state centred upon the health of the North Korean leader Kim Jong-il.[16] Since 2008, the North Korean authorities had become increasingly sensitive over his medical condition, not least because of fears that his demise might trigger a leadership succession crisis with far-reaching ramifications for regional and even global security. In August 2008, it was widely suspected that the leader had suffered a stroke. While the government and party apparatus presented their leader's health as a non-issue, intense international media speculation kept the spotlight on the leader's rate of public appearances and assessments of his condition. In 2009, reports emerged in South Korea claiming that Kim Jong-il was suffering from pancreatic cancer and that the leader's projected incapacitation would exacerbate the problem of succession and with it the regime's very survival. In order to minimize the effects of internal

An Insider's Life in Soviet Politics (New York, NY: Times Books, 1992), pp. 191–2, 198, 201–2, 207, 241, 245, 248–52, 260, 273–5, 281–93, 322; Yegor Ligachev, *Inside Gorbachev's Kremlin: The Memoirs of Yegor Ligachev* (Boulder, CO: Westview, 1996), pp. 18–39, 53–8, 65–7.

[14] Valery Boldin, *Ten Years That Shook the World: Gorbachev Era as Witnessed by His Chief of Staff* (New York, NY: Basic Books, 1994), p. 40.

[15] Jerrold M. Post and Robert S. Robins, *When Illness Strikes the Leader: The Dilemma of the Captive King* (New Haven, CT: Yale University Press, 1993), pp. 140–3.

[16] Bradley K. Martin, *Under the Loving Care of the Fatherly Leader* (New York, NY: Thomas Dunne, 2004); Michael Breen, *Kim Jong Il: North Korea's Dear Leader* (Hoboken, NJ: John Wiley, 2004); Jasper Becker, *Rogue Regime: Kim Jong Il and the Looming Threat of North Korea* (Oxford: Oxford University Press, 2005).

factionalism amongst the regime's multiple power centres, Kim Jong-il worked quickly to establish the acceptance of his youngest son as his successor. The leader died in December 2011—reportedly after becoming enraged over problems with a prestigious dam project. His son Kim Jong-un immediately assumed the position of Supreme Leader.

Even more recently, a health-based leadership crisis has occurred in Venezuela where the condition of President Hugo Chávez has become a live political issue. The president had to absent himself from the country in 2011 and 2012 in order to receive medical treatment in Cuba for an abscess that was not at first thought to be life-threatening. However, it became increasingly evident that his condition was sufficiently serious for him to require further operations which allowed his health to become a central topic of public and political speculation over an extended period covering 2010 to 2013. Because only general and non-specific information was released by his office, it generated a host of interpretive indicators as to the real condition of the president. In June 2011, President Chávez revealed that his treatment was for cancer but that he was confident of a full recovery. Accordingly, a month later he not only had to absent himself from the national celebrations marking the 200th anniversary of Venezuelan independence, but also had to postpone a meeting of Latin American and Caribbean heads of state that had been organized to coincide with the anniversary.

Following reports of a further three operations, four courses of chemotherapy, and more periods of extended absence, Chávez's position in 2011 and 2012 gave rise to an array of rumours, conspiracy theories, and diagnoses-at-a-distance surrounding his condition. The situation was exacerbated by the lack of information concerning the type and location of the cancer, its level of aggression, or the exact treatment being received. The resultant hiatus did not prevent the president's re-election in October 2012 but his inability to attend the inauguration in January 2013 sparked a political and constitutional dispute with opposition forces. The Supreme Court ruled that the president could continue his convalescence in Havana indefinitely and be sworn into office at a later date. Although the president quietly returned home in February 2013, he nevertheless remained in seclusion. The prolonged lack of resolution continued to pose a threat not just to the political stability of the country but also to the Venezuelan model of revolution.[17] A few weeks after coming back to Venezuela, the president's condition was finally disclosed as being critical. He died of a heart attack on 6 March 2013. The exact nature of the underlying cancer remained confidential. After fourteen years as president, no clear successor had been established.

Death of course may well be the natural outcome of chronic health problems. Leaders in this respect are no different from other individuals. However, what is noteworthy is that almost all leaders die as ex-leaders. The potential disruption caused by any sudden loss of leadership through ill health means that leaders are usually eased out of office well before they reach the point of disability. In fact it is expected that the key individuals and organizations surrounding and supporting a

---

[17] Eva Golinger, 'False Reporting on the Health of Venezuela's President Hugo Chávez', *Global Research*, 31 May 2012; William Neuman, 'Of Many Woes, One Man's Illness Threatens Venezuela's Revolution', *New York Times*, 12 December 2012; William Neuman, 'Chávez Returns to Venezuela, Trailing Doubts', *New York Times*, 18 February 2013.

leadership will prevail upon the stricken incumbent to surrender the position before the situation degenerates into a leadership crisis. Opinions, of course, may well vary amongst the different parties to a dispute of this kind. Such an impasse might in extreme cases lead to action approximating to a coup in which the reluctant leader is forcibly displaced very often on the stipulated grounds of poor health and failing faculties.

In other circumstances, more extreme measures may be taken. The ultimate form of an accelerated decline in health would in this case be a violent death either at the hands of a particular movement or faction, or else from a disaffected individual. As is noted below, the unscheduled demise of a political leader through assassination can have very serious consequences for any governing system in terms of political settlement, policy continuity, and social cohesion. It is for this reason that the lives of leaders are usually given an extraordinary degree of protection. This can embrace contributions from the armed services, intelligence agencies, police authorities, and special forces. But in a more immediate and personal sense, it also includes those measures and resources that are dedicated wholly to the protection of a leader and his or her family. These facilities can range from the use of decoys and doppelgangers to elite units focused wholly on the physical safety of the leadership—even to the extent of laying down their lives for the sake of protecting their charges.

The president of the United States, for example, is protected by the US Secret Service which is permanently assigned to assure his safety at all times. If he has to travel away from the White House, then in effect the White House goes with him. In effect the protection systems in place at the White House detach themselves from the headquarters and become mobile so that the president travels in what has been described as a security bubble. On foreign trips, the president's entourage will always include not merely Secret Service agents but armour-plated vehicles, home-sourced supplies of authorized food, water, and petrol, White House cooking staff, and communication systems to keep the president connected to Washington twenty-four hours a day. There is also a military ambulance, a mobile blood bank and surgical unit, as well as a heavily armoured presidential car, along with its own separate oxygen supply, that can offer a completely sealed interior to protect the president from a chemical attack.

The prodigious scale of these security measures serves to underline the central importance of an incumbent leader's health and personal safety. In protecting the leader and in minimizing the risk of conditions injurious to his or her health, the intention is to maximize the chances that a leader's decline will not only be attributable solely to political factors but will occur according to the established procedures for the transfer of power. In leadership politics, death has a sting which is felt throughout the body politic. The untimely deaths of Labour Party leaders Hugh Gaitskell (1963) and John Smith (1994), for example, had long-term implications for the direction and management of the party that stretched over very many years. The living deaths of stroke victims like Vladimir Lenin (USSR), Woodrow Wilson (US), and Ariel Sharon (Israel)[18] are arguably even more

---

[18] Vladimir Lenin suffered three strokes between May 1922 and March 1923. The second paralysed him and forced him to withdraw from active politics. The third was even more severe and he was

disruptive in effect because of the shadow that they cast over those who act in their place as alternative leaders but with only provisional and ambiguous authority.

All these cases relating to the health of leaders underline two significant aspects of leadership decline. The *first* is the way that leadership and its processes generate close conceptual and colloquial associations with categories related to fitness and viability. It is not merely that leadership is normally equated with individuals and thus by extension to the general condition of their health and well-being. It is more that leadership itself comes to be seen as a natural process in its own right. Because of the recurrent patterns of rising and falling, the notion of a life cycle becomes a dominant metaphor in assigning meaning and understanding to the dynamics of leadership.[19]

In effect, our approach to the subject of leadership becomes dependent upon direct analogies to the more visceral realities of life. Thus, declining leaderships are often diagnosed as tired, slow, and even chronic and sclerotic. Leadership comes to be seen as an ageing process in its own right. As a consequence, it is also commonly depicted as a mortal illness whose course has to run to the point of inevitable and unavoidable closure. Although some ex-leaders have managed to secure a return to high office, such cases of resurrection are few and far between.[20] In the main, the personal metaphor of decline becomes synonymous with the passage of political time and the prospect of irreversible departure. For example, when Anthony Eden was forced to resign as prime minister in the aftermath of the Suez crisis in 1956, the reasons given were based on his own state of ill health. But his physical condition exactly matched the political condition of his leadership. The two spheres had become interchangeable in meaning and effect. The only recourse for Conservative Party managers, therefore, was to allow Eden's chronic condition to take its course by easing him out of the premiership.

The *second* aspect is the importance attached to leaders both as individuals and as embodiments of a corporate entity in which the human properties of one become enfolded into the other. In this way, the perceived vitality of an

---

rendered mute and bedridden until his death in January 1924. Despite these handicaps, he remained in the leadership position within the Soviet Communist Party while others positioned themselves for the succession. In September 1919, President Woodrow Wilson suffered a serious stroke which left him paralysed on the left side and partially blind. Even though his incapacitation was successfully concealed from the public, the political agendas of his administration were badly compromised for the remaining seventeen months of his presidency. Ariel Sharon was another case of a leader incapacitated through a non-fatal stroke. Shortly after forming his new party Kadima in November 2005, Sharon suffered a major cerebral hemorrhage only two months before the elections to Israel's Knesset. Although Kadima won a plurality of seats, its leader could not assume the office of prime minister. Sharon remains in a persistent vegetative state.

[19] For an arresting exposition on the applicability of different stages of a life cycle in personality development applied to leadership, see Jerrold M. Post, 'The Seasons of a Leader's Life: Influences of the Life Cycle on Political Behavior', *Political Psychology*, 2(3/4) Autumn–Winter 1980: 35–49; Post, *Leaders and their Followers in a Dangerous World*, pp. 22–49.

[20] Noteworthy cases include Winston Churchill's return to the premiership in 1951 after a six-year period out of office; in 2009, Sheikh Hasina became the prime minister of Bangladesh for the second time after being out of office for eight years; and in 2008 Silvio Berlusconi resumed the position of prime minister of Italy following a two-year break from his previous period in that role (2001–6)—as he had briefly held the post for an eight-month period in 1994–5, his return to office in 2008 amounted to a second resumption.

organization can become endowed with the presented characteristics of that person with the highest profile and the most conspicuous role within it. The more visceral categories of the leader can enhance or disadvantage the wider body with whom the leader is associated. The dynamic becomes one of a circular metaphor in which public life, civil society, and even the state are increasingly assigned to categories associated with the degenerative characteristics of their chief representative. This process of mutual attribution has been evident for example in the recent cases of Saddam Hussein and Iraq, Silvio Berlusconi and Italy, Robert Mugabe and Zimbabwe, Hosni Mubarak and Egypt, and Muammar Gaddafi and Libya. When leaders begin to invest their sponsoring organizations with serious negatives, the response is normally that of irreversible decline. Occasionally, the process of detachment can be swift and dramatic. In this light, it is enormously suggestive that very few leaders die in office. It would be more accurate to say that very few leaders are allowed to die in office. Almost without exception, political death precedes natural death.

SEARCHING FOR STASIS

Even though generalized observations of leadership have generated comparisons to a life cycle, numerous leaders have sought to limit the utility of this metaphor and even to reverse the onset of any form of decrepitude. It is true that in some political contexts, a leader can experience a form of reincarnation, whereby after a period out of office, a political career is renewed to the point of being able to return to a position of leadership. However, almost all leaders have to proceed on the basis that there will only be one chance to reach the culmination of a political life and that whatever measures can be taken to extend it have to be taken in order to delay or to defer the processes of dissolution. The need to do so is no more pressing than in those regimes which are especially leader-centric in their sources and exercise of political authority. In contrast to those systems which are built upon, and experienced in, the processes of stable political transition, the arrangements associated with the more authoritarian character of the strong leader model carry with them implications relating to both short- and long-term sustainability. It would be no exaggeration to claim that many such regimes are specifically designed and powerfully geared to prevent any indication of decline. For the purposes of the analysis, it is important to take due note of these systems in which specific leaderships are embedded and maintained with the aim of establishing a permanent hierarchy and thereby foreclosing any references to inevitable decline.

These types of embedded leadership have many different roots but in the main they tend to be reduced to variations of two drivers—namely difficult pasts and insecure futures. Very often the leaderships of these more authoritarian states have had to wrest power and position from previous regimes or social orders that themselves had been highly resistant to challenge. It is for this reason that new leaderships in such contexts tend to be sensitive towards the issue of their own security. Concern for political stability tends to be reduced in many respects to an overriding priority being given to the continuity of the leader within the polity. When the operation, well-being, and even viability of the state become dependent upon the asserted centrality of its leadership, then it allows for an extraordinary level of resources to be channelled towards assuring the durability of its key object of value.

The concentration of material and social provision in this sphere can reach lavish proportions. It may take the form of palatial presidential buildings and high-profile capital projects, or symbolic representations and showpiece spectacles. It might come in the guise of constitutional manipulation and political 'management', or media-driven personality cults and cultivated mass-produced depictions of charisma. Another indicator may be the establishment of extensive infrastructures of domestic intelligence gathering, the secret surveillance of political opponents, and the entrenched political status of the internal security forces. Authoritarian regimes very often assume all these forms. Such is the intensity of the drive for stability that they are successively inclined to devise ever more intensive methods to extend their reach, and to protect their claims to legitimacy—thereby fostering greater guarantees for the leadership's security of tenure.

The cultivation of a supportive social conservatism—complemented almost invariably by a pervasive culture of coercive conformity—can and does offer extensive bases for leadership security. So much so in fact that it is often difficult to conceive of how such a leadership could ever become vulnerable to decline, or be considered as a victim of some process of inevitable ageing. On the contrary, in many cases the burden of analysis would seem to be heavily weighted towards discerning the possibility of any weaknesses existing in the evident durability of numerous leadership-centred regimes. Far from exhibiting signs of decline and weakness, these types of regime present themselves in the main as exemplars of consolidation in which organizational dynamics are explicitly geared towards sustainability and continuity. A nexus between a leader and a host system is formulated and propagated so that the well-being, functionality, and viability of a society—as well as the integrity and logic of its political system—come to be regarded as tightly bound to the interests and security of the leadership. It is this assertion of mutuality that not only justifies the extraordinary measures that are taken to preserve such leaderships but also explains the persistence of social norms which militate against dissent and calls for change. Such reticence can be seen as an entirely rational reaction in a system for which no credible alternative will have existed for many years.

In addition, it is quite normal for regimes like this to induce a generalized fear over any prospect of leadership disruption on the grounds that this would inevitably usher in a dysfunctional response throughout the social order. In part, this concern is promoted either implicitly or explicitly by the self-interest of those established in power. In part, it is also a consequence of the unease surrounding the prospect of leadership change when no settled system of transferring power exists and when the insecurities surrounding such disjunctions deepen with the passage of time. It is for this reason that many regimes foment states of anxiety over the dangers surrounding leadership strife in the event of any challenge to the established order of political status. When this concern is mixed with memories of past episodes of political instability and violent disorder associated with conditions prior to the establishment of a settled leadership, then the symbiosis of high insecurity and high leadership dependency is raised to even higher levels.

ASSASSINATION *IN EXTREMIS*

The strategic value of fear in respect to any projected disruption in the leadership of such regimes is given a further stimulus by the dramatic consequences that can be visited upon those states which have experienced a sudden leadership crisis. The assassination of a leader, for example, can precipitate profound strains in the social and political fabric—even to the point of generating civil strife and occasionally genocide.

In Lebanon, for example, a political assassination occurred in 2005 that was to have a series of major consequences for the country. Mr Rafic Al-Hariri and his entourage were killed by an explosion estimated to be the equivalent of 1000 kg of TNT. Mr Rafic Al-Hariri was a senior figure in Lebanese politics. He was a popular leader who had held the prime ministerial position on two occasions (1992–8, 2000–4). He had been closely associated with the cause of Lebanese independence, especially in respect to the call for Syrian forces to reduce their presence and influence within the country. Early reports indicated that the Syrian government had been involved in the assassination. Moreover, following Hariri's death there had been other bombings and assassinations against critics of Syria's position in Lebanese society and its governing arrangements.[21]

The popular reaction to these events led to what was termed the Cedar Revolution in which massive demonstrations against Syria's long-standing occupation of Lebanon not only prompted the withdrawal of Syrian forces and security services from the area but precipitated the collapse of the pro-Syrian government in Beirut. While these events had fostered a surge in demands for Lebanese national independence, they also disrupted the complex internal balances of a historically segmented social order. A year later (2005), Hezbollah paramilitary forces in Lebanon launched an attack on Israeli forces in the border region between Southern Lebanon and Israel. The effect was a thirty-four-day military conflict that included air strikes and artillery assaults as well as an air and naval blockade. Israel's view was that because Hezbollah was closely associated with Syria, it was acting as a proxy for Syria's strategy of undermining Israel's security. The result was an action that led to approximately 1,300 deaths, the displacement of approximately one million Lebanese and 300,000–500,000 Israelis, and severe damage to Lebanon's social and commercial infrastructure.

A better known and more notorious case of a political leader's untimely death setting in motion a succession of violent events came in 1994 when President Juvénal Habyarimana of the Republic of Rwanda was killed in a plane crash along with the president of the neighbouring state of Burundi. The incident, which occurred near the airport serving Rwanda's capital, Kigali, immediately became a flashpoint event within what had been a deteriorating situation of rising ethnic

---

[21] Kim Ghattas, 'Lebanon finds unity in street rallies', BBC News Report, 23 March 2005. Accessed 17 April 2012 at: <http://news.bbc.co.uk/1/hi/world/middle_east/4315223.stm>; Joshua Hammer, 'Getting Away With Murder?', *The Atlantic Magazine*, December 2008; Hazem Saghieh, 'Rafiq al-Hariri's murder: why do Lebanese blame Syria?', *Open Democracy*, 14 March 2011. Accessed 17 April 2012 at: <http://www.opendemocracy.net/conflict-middle_east_politics/article_2347.jsp>.

divisions in the region and within Rwanda in particular.[22] Since its independence in 1962, Rwanda had experienced severe inter-tribal problems between the minority Tutsi community which had enjoyed a privileged status under the old monarchical system and the majority Hutus who had been regarded in colonial times as an inferior race to the Tutsis on account of the latter's more European appearance. The post-independence period brought about a one-party regime that formally institutionalized the ethnic divide into a highly discriminatory system of quotas and exclusions which increasingly penalized the Tutsis and precipitated large-scale Tutsi migrations to such countries as Uganda, Congo, and Burundi.

Apart from creating serious refugee problems within neighbouring countries, the 'Tutsi diaspora' which has been estimated at between one and two million displaced people also created a backlash in the form of a rallying movement to secure a return to Tutsi homelands (i.e. Rwandan Patriotic Front). By 1990, the RPF was strong enough to organize a military incursion into Rwanda. During the early 1990s there had been international pressure for the Rwandan government to reform its policies and engage in a process of conflict resolution. However, at the same time there developed a deepening of divisions and a radicalization of political activity which witnessed anti-Tutsi political parties forming militias that openly sponsored extreme discrimination, incitement to violence, and even localized massacres. It was in this context that the presidents of two Hutu-based regimes lost their lives as their aircraft plunged into the grounds of the Rwandan presidential residence in what was quickly interpreted as an act of political assassination. The effect was immediate, dramatic, and unprecedented in its scale. Within three months, between 500,000 and one million Rwandans—mostly Tutsis—had been massacred, with a further 300,000 Tutsis fleeing into Uganda and Burundi. As much as 20 per cent of the population had been exterminated in a sustained campaign of brutal extermination.[23]

It is possible to argue in the case of political assassination that the death of a single person can never fully explain a train of events leading to civil disorder or even war. For example, it has remained commonplace in the numerous histories of the First World War to describe the assassination of Archduke Franz Ferdinand of Austria in Sarajevo (1914) as the spark that led to a global conflagration which claimed an estimated 37 million lives. However, it is equally the case that a singular act of violence could not conceivably have led to such an outcome if the necessary preconditions for war had not been established prior to the assassination. It is wholly right to point out the precariousness of propositions that seek to establish a unilinear chain of causality from one incident to a far more complex set of circumstances that are dependent upon a profusion of other

[22] Tiphaine Dickson, 'Rwanda's Deadliest Secret: Who Shot Down President Habyarimana's Plane?', *Global Research*, 24 November 2008. Accessed 10 March 2012 at: <http://www.globalresearch.ca/index.php?context=va&aid=11133>.

[23] Gerard Prunier, *The Rwanda Crisis: History of a Genocide* (New York, NY: Columbia University Press, 1995), ch. 7; Philip Gourevitch, *We Wish to Inform You that Tomorrow We Will Be Killed with Our Families: Stories From Rwanda* (New York, NY: Farrar, Straus & Giroux, 1998); Linda Melvern, *A People Betrayed: The Role of the West in Rwanda's Genocide* (London: Zed Books, 2000), ch. 12; Scott Straus, *The Order of Genocide: Race, Power, and War in Rwanda* (Ithaca, NY: Cornell University Press, 2006).

factors. In the case of Lebanon and Rwanda, it is clear that the assassinations and their aftermath occurred in a context of long-established enmities, conflictual social developments, polarized politics, and pre-planned contingency responses.

Nevertheless, it is equally important to underline the critical significance of an assassination in conditions of incipient crisis. Because political leaders occupy a particularly prominent and symbolically enriched public space, their violent removal can act not merely as a focus of concentrated outrage and disgust over the event itself, but also as an accelerant to much larger forces of communal distrust and social disintegration. While the role of prior conditions resting upon social forces and historical bases must be given full recognition, nonetheless it is the case that a leadership-related event of such high intensity as an assassination can provide both a seminal point of access into a complex matrix of political stress, and a catalyst for reconfiguring issues and releasing energies into the kinds of myopic and exclusionary mindsets which can foment chronic distrust, endemic polarization, and savage retribution. In essence, such events reaffirm the defining and signifying properties of leaders as highly usable political metaphors—both in life and in death.

THE FORCE OF CONTINUITY

The immensity of these kinds of episode provides a contextual basis to the efforts made in similar regimes to institutionalize their own narratives of leadership indispensability and to enhance the value of social continuity through the medium of a settled pattern of leadership. So central is this attribution of leadership to stability that it is not uncommon for leaders in systems that have either been formed under conditions of strain, or are considered to be actually or potentially fragile in nature, to propagate the notion that the optimum arrangement is for the leadership to ensure continuity by bequeathing the role to family members.

In Saudi Arabia, for example, the status and stability of the House of Saud have ensured that any leadership succession has been managed with a minimum of disruption. This is something of an achievement given that the country sits at the centre of a highly unstable geo-strategic region and that the royal family extends to over 7,000 members. In many other contexts, this mix might well have led to the presence of factions and succession crises. Nevertheless, the country has been distinguished by exceptionally untroubled transfers of power through a traditionally flexible order of patriarchal succession in which the line from King Abdul Aziz, who was instrumental in founding and unifying the nation in 1932, stretches through four other monarchs to the present-day King Abdullah bin Abdulaziz.[24]

A similar reliance upon blood lines in preventing conflict over leadership transitions has been visible in regimes that are very different from conventional monarchies. The Democratic People's Republic of Korea—otherwise known as North Korea—is arguably the last authentically totalitarian communist regime in existence and yet it has opted for a leadership cult of personality in which the polity

---

[24] Madawi Al-Rasheed, *A History of Saudi Arabia* (Cambridge: Cambridge University Press, 2001) chs. 3–5; James Wynbrandt, *A Brief History of Saudi Arabia*, 2nd edn. (New York, NY: Facts on File, 2010), chs. 9–11.

has become dependent upon an exclusive family connection for its leaders. Notwithstanding the fact that it is an avowedly communist state that abhors any semblance of class privilege, the leadership of Kim Il-sung (1948–94) and his descendants has become integral not only to the regime's security but also to the nation's entire identity. In 2010, it was disclosed that Kim Jong-un, the third and youngest son of Kim Jong-il who succeeded Kim Il-sung as supreme leader in 1994, had been assigned as the heir apparent on the grounds that he was closest in outlook and temperament to his father. In 2011, the leadership had secured the acceptance of the military, the ruling Workers' Party, and the regime's chief sponsor, China, of an eventual transfer of power to Kim Jong-un—thereby maximizing the chances that the personality cult begun by Kim Il-sung in 1948 and continued from 1994 by his son Kim Jong-il would be secured through a second process of hereditary succession.[25] Kim Jong-il died on 19 December 2011. The transfer of power was duly completed ten days later when Kim Jong-un was confirmed as the Supreme Leader and formally named as the 'Great Successor'.[26]

This kind of dynastic dependency is not limited to new, or undeveloped, or autocratic systems. In what is often termed the biggest democracy in the world, there has been a marked inclination to look to one political family in particular for its leaders. The Nehru-Feroze Gandhi family in India has been at the centre of national politics since the country's independence in 1947. It has not only acted as an anchorage point in the rise to power of the Indian National Congress Party but over the course of three generations has provided three prime ministers—i.e. Jawaharlal Nehru (1947–64), Nehru's daughter Indira Gandhi (1966–77, 1980–4), and her son Rajiv Gandhi (1984–9). The family tradition of prominent public service is currently being continued by Rajiv Gandhi's widow Sonia Gandhi who is currently President of the Congress Party. Even though the family's representation at the highest levels of Indian political life cannot be characterized as an unbroken line of prime ministerial succession, it is nonetheless noteworthy that in a system of open democratic choice the Nehru/Gandhi name continues to have an instinctive hold on the loyalties of so many voters. An embedded political family like this can offer a form of visceral continuity with the past. At the same time, it can impose costs not only in terms of adaptability and responsiveness but also in respect to the strains imposed on the family itself—as the assassinations of both Indira and Rajiv Gandhi will attest.[27]

It is evident that some leadership establishments seem to manage longevity with an impressive degree of success (Table 5.1). Many instances exist of leaders staying in power for extended periods of time. For example, President Omar Bongo led the government of the oil-rich state of Gabon in west central Africa from 1967

---

[25] See Ji You, 'Kim Jong-Il's and North Korea's succession crisis', *EAI Background Brief No. 429*, East Asian Institute, National University of Singapore, 5 February 2009; Jack Kim, 'North Korea leader Kim has pancreatic cancer: report', *Reuters*, 13 July 2009. Accessed 22 April 2012 at: <http://www.reuters.com/article/2009/07/13/us-korea-north-idUSTRE56C0EL20090713>; Ian Bremmer, 'Kim Jong Il's illness changes North Korean picture', *Foreign Policy*, 15 July 2009. Accessed 23 May 2012 at: Available at: <http://eurasia.foreignpolicy.com/posts/2009/07/15/kim_jong_ils_illness_changes_north_korean_picture>.

[26] 'Succession in North Korea: Grief and Fear', *The Economist*, 31 December 2011.

[27] Jad Adams, *The Dynasty: Nehru–Gandhi Story* (Harmondsworth: Penguin, 1997); Judith M. Brown, *Nehru: A Political Life* (New Haven, CT: Yale University Press, 2003); Katherine Frank, *Indira: The Life of Indira Nehru Gandhi* (London: HarperCollins, 2010).

Table 5.1 Longest-serving world leaders (excluding hereditary and monarchical office-holders). Census date 22 February 2011

Leader	Country	Date of leadership acquisition	Years in power	Total population (in millions)	Per cent knowing no other leader
Muammar al-Gaddafi[28]	Libya	1/9/1969	41	6.5	77
Ali Abdullah Saleh[29]	Yemen	18/7/1978	33	23.5	80
Teodoro O. N. Mbaso	Equatorial Guinea	3/8/1979	32	0.7	72
José E. dos Santos	Angola	10/9/1979	32	13.0	80
Robert G. Mugabe	Zimbabwe	18/4/1980	31	11.7	77
Ali Khamenei	Iran	2/10/1981	30	76.9	66
Paul Biya	Cameroon	6/11/1982	29	19.3	83
Hun Sen	Cambodia	14/1/1985	26	14.5	66
Yoweri Museveni	Uganda	26/1/1986	26	33.4	78
Islom Karimov	Uzbekistan	23/6/1989	22	27.7	50

Sources: Business Insider Inc.; International database; U.S. Census Bureau. Full dataset available at <http://www.businessinsider.com/longest-serving-leaders-2011-2#>.

until his death in 2009. President Bongo's forty-two-year period was eclipsed by Enver Hoxha whose dominant position as the leader of Albania stretched to forty-three years and six months from 1941 to 1985. Until recently, Colonel Gaddafi proceeded on the premise that his leadership of Libya would extend indefinitely beyond the landmarks of longevity set by Bongo and Hoxha. However, the Libyan Revolution of 2011 precipitated the end of his previously pre-eminent position which he had held since 1969 (i.e. forty-two years).

In some cases leadership continuity can be interpreted as a reflection of a settled political and social order that is embodied in the sustained appeal of the leadership. In other cases, the continued presence of leaders can be attributed to serious concerns over any form of leadership transfer and therefore to more forceful methods of political management. All too frequently, long-term security of tenure is established through patronage, intimidation, coercion, corruption, and the ruthless usage of state resources in the interests of the leadership cadres and the political classes which support them. Whether it is one-party states, or military dictatorships, or forms of dynastic governance, leaders can be conspicuously effective in devising schemes to defy the ageing process and to engage in exercises of successive renewal. And yet despite the extensive and elaborate efforts to halt time and to remain functionally effectively in power, these types of regime cannot be relied upon to sustain their own preferred configuration of the status quo. Notwithstanding the scale of their strategic advantages in controlling their own destiny, many of these regimes find that in the end even they cannot hold stasis in place and withstand the processes of disaggregation.

[28] In 2011 Libya descended into civil war. Opposition to the Gaddafi regime was organized around the National Transitional Council which received recognition by thirty countries as the legitimate government of Libya. Rebel militias eventually captured Gaddafi on 20 October 2011. Amid various contested accounts of the circumstances, he was killed on the same day as his capture.

[29] Saleh became leader of North Yemen in 1978 until 1990 when he assumed the position of president of the Republic of Yemen. On 27 February 2012, President Saleh stepped down after 33 years in power following months of protests which took the country to the brink of civil war. He was granted immunity from prosecution.

THE AUTOCRACY OF TIME

The common failure of even the most repressive leaderships in acquiring long-term immunity for themselves raises the issue of how such dominance can ever be lost when the likelihood of change in so many cases and on so many occasions has appeared to be so remote. Many reasons can be cited for the decline of an apparently immovable leadership. On a specific level, individual illness and disability may have a precipitating effect upon the capacity of a leadership to retain power. But as we have already noted, individual decline and even death may not necessarily detrimentally affect the continuity of a dynastic or family-based leadership. On a more generic level that embraces the linkage between the sphere of leadership and the systemic properties of the host regime, a leader's survival can be placed in jeopardy by the onset of a wider category of negative properties. For example, while a long-term leadership may initially have acquired a basis of authority and may have succeeded in maintaining its claims to rightful power for an extended period, there comes a time when the issue of leadership legitimacy will begin to reappear. Scepticism may be directed to the original sources of the leadership, or to the succeeding period of leadership activity.

Criticism of long-established leaderships will often take the form of negative comparisons. The reference point may be located in the past with comparisons being made between current conditions and those that existed, or were thought to exist, in a previous period before the inception of a particular leadership. The authority of a long-term leader can be eroded by those who challenge the leadership's framing of recent history and the construction of official narratives surrounding a country's progression from the past. While the established leadership will cite extenuating circumstances or mitigating factors in failing to deliver on historical promises, opponents will gradually cast doubt on the leadership's adherence to its own prospectus and on its integrity as a government in living up to the expectations that it had itself generated in the past.

Another key reference point that is commonly deployed in these situations is based upon some contemporary standard of assessment. It may be the status or performance of another country in the region, or a comparable nation in another region. It may be a moral principle or an ethical code that is believed to have been transgressed on an individual or systemic basis by the leadership's form of governance. Even a deeply dormant condition of political activity can finally be aroused from its torpor by the scale and persistence of accusations surrounding official corruption, nepotism, violence, and other forms of unethical behaviour. Such indictments can assist in activating another type of reference point. This relates more to a disjunction in temperaments between the leadership and those outside its sphere of self-interest. It is likely to reveal itself as a mercurial shift in public mood and an alteration in social attitudes leading to a generalized desire for change. In these contexts, the emergence of widespread scepticism can foster a culture of complaint and a readiness to depict the leadership not so much as an indispensable feature of social life but as a tired and moribund encumbrance.

The leaders of autocratic regimes will almost invariably seek to redress any disruption to the established order by casting doubt on the legitimacy of alternative agencies of leadership, and by reaffirming and renewing the claim of a symbiotic relationship between civic or national security on the one hand

and the value of leadership continuity on the other. Leaders will once again attempt to assert that the very absence of an established process of power transfer or of any recent experiences of leadership change amount to a significant deterrent against any departures from the norm. Given that the official framing of such leadership will have persistently invoked the theme of a political settlement, then any threat to that leadership will be couched as an attempt to undermine an entire political order—bringing with it a severe risk of social disintegration. Authoritarian leaderships always exploit these dimensions of high dependency and high security as deterrent devices against the onset of speculation over possible alternative arrangements.[30] These implicit warnings over any challenge to the mantras of mutual utility involving the leadership and its constituent social base will not always be effective. At this point, a leadership may well resort to more explicit and coercive methods of persuasion in order to extinguish the possibility of a political crisis becoming centred upon the issue of leadership. However, heavy-handed attempts to marginalize dissent or actually to crush opposition can lead to the very kind of challenge that autocratic leaderships so strenuously attempt to avoid.

When the reach and legitimacy of an autocratic leadership seriously come into question, this can lead to precisely the kind of disruption that established leaderships will have always warned against. In these circumstances, the more critical the challenge the more likely it is that a dynamic will develop in which the abnormality of change will not only become increasingly attractive but will also be deemed to be necessary. The decline may take the form of a gentle slide to the periphery. A previously dominant leadership may be declared to have failed in managing political expectations, or to have mismanaged the administration of a country. The indictment might be that of excessive leadership activity, or by contrast of insufficient attention to the leadership needs of a society. In the politics of authoritarian regimes, a key dynamic is often that of a leader's strategic relationship with the rest of the governing regime. In this type of ruling coalition, a leader's tenure may ultimately be dependent upon whether the concentration of power affords enough space for a competitive form of power-sharing between the leadership and those elites who regard themselves as co-partners in government. In the end, it is common for government insiders to ease a once dominant leadership out of office—usually through a process of non-institutional and non-constitutional accountability that facilitates an unscheduled transfer of power.[31]

Grounds for complaint in authoritarian states can range from poor economic management to foreign policy miscalculations; from issues of social development to incidents of civic and cultural disorder. Problems may be attributable to perceptions of drift and accusations of stasis as a negative property; or they can revolve around claims of leaders having become isolated through shifts in political

---

[30] Carl J. Friedrich and Zbigniew K. Brzezinski, *Totalitarian Dictatorship and Autocracy* (New York, NY: Praeger, 1962); Juan J. Linz, *Totalitarian and Authoritarian Regimes* (Boulder, CO: Lynne Rienner, 2000); Jennifer Gandhi, *Political Institutions under Dictatorship* (Cambridge: Cambridge University Press, 2008), chs. 1, 6; Erica Frantz and Natasha M. Ezrow, *Dictators and Dictatorships: Understanding Authoritarian Regimes and Their Leaders* (New York, NY: Continuum Publishing, 2011).

[31] See Milan W. Svolik, 'Power Sharing and Leadership Dynamics in Authoritarian Regimes', *American Journal of Political Science*, 53(2) April 1999: 477–94.

norms, geopolitical realities, and ideological orientations. A leadership that is seen as having become detached from a dominant belief system is particularly damaging to its prospects for continuation. A once successful leadership that may have originally caught a current of social attachment can find that tides turn into surges of disillusionment, fatigue, and disinterest. If Howard Gardner is correct in asserting that an effective leadership is built upon an ability to convey a definitive story of social and political purpose,[32] then any serious challenge will either subject that story to close critical scrutiny, or else co-opt it in a revised form so that the proprietorship of the narrative is transferred to a different form of stewardship. A leadership that allows this to occur is likely to have reached a chronic position.

While it is possible for a leadership-centred polity to evolve gradually into an altered state of political existence, it is more probable that the process of change will be far from a seamless transition. The interaction of a prolonged period of political suppression on the one hand and a regime increasingly resistant to demands for change on the other is more likely to provoke the dysfunctional and transformative effects that the leadership had worked so assiduously to prevent. The impasse of a leadership's resources being increasingly committed to preserving its legitimacy whilst confronted by rising evidence of its erosion usually draws to it a language of leadership pathology and chronic decline. It is in these conditions that the metaphors of fatigue, age, and infirmity become commonplace. In some cases, a leadership can still endure under unfavourable conditions. But even in these cases, the pall of long-term decline becomes more evident. In some circumstances, the ageing theme is suddenly accelerated into attributions of terminal disease, mortal illness, and very limited life expectancy. It is then that the underlying fragility of ostensibly authoritarian regimes is revealed.

Because such polities are organized and even designed around the indispensability of their leadership structures, the decline when it comes is commensurately more serious to the societies in question and more dangerous to the leaderships involved. It is serious because after deferring change for so long through neglect or suppression, the likelihood is that change will be extensive, sudden, and violent which for societies unused to any kind of substantive change will probably amount to a highly stressful transformative process and on occasions a full-blown adaptation crisis. This scenario will be dangerous to the established leadership not just because it will usually act as the focal point of newly emergent forms of protest and dissent, but will embody the object of an increasingly critical retrospection on a discredited past. In many ways, the old warnings that a change in leadership would be the harbinger of social disruption are seen to have a self-fulfilling property through the leadership's own previous resistance to change. In the end, many leaders pay a high price for their prolonged tenures in office. The speed and finality of a collapse of what had once seemed an impregnable regime headed by an irresistible leadership are graphically displayed by the violent demise of the Ceauşescu government in Romania in 1989 (Box 5.2).

More recently, a similar dynamic was dramatically illustrated by the plight of several leaders during the Arab Spring uprisings of 2010–11. Long-standing

---

[32] Howard Gardner, *Leading Minds: An Anatomy of Leadership* (London: HarperCollins, 1995).

Box 5.2 The sudden end of a lengthy and ostensibly secure leadership: President Nicolae Ceaușescu

Romania offers a prime example of a long-established regime that had been sustained by a concerted leadership cult and an extensive internal security apparatus but which was subjected to a violent overthrow by forces of resentment which had built up over years of political oppression, economic underdevelopment, and social dislocation. The communist government under Nicolae Ceaușescu had been in power since 1965 but in December 1989 it came under the same pressures for transformative change as many other Warsaw Pact countries. However, unlike their previous regional allies in the Eastern bloc, Romania experienced a violent seizure of power by an insurgent coalition named the National Salvation Front. Of all the 'revolutions' experienced in Eastern Europe at this time, only Romania witnessed the violent overthrow of its communist regime. The fate of the previously hard line and apparently immovable leadership of Nicolae Ceaușescu and his wife Elena is described below:

'The anti-Christ died. Oh, what wonderful news,' a Bucharest radio announcer exulted after the dramatic announcement that President Nicolae Ceaușescu and his wife Elena had been jointly executed by a firing squad. Confirmation of Monday's execution of the despised pair came yesterday, when Romanian television showed viewers two bodies crumpled beneath a bullet-shattered wall. A closeup revealed the fallen Ceaușescu, his eyes open, the right side of his head stained with blood that also spattered the stone wall. The other body was that of Elena, who had told her executioners: 'We want to die together, we do not want mercy,' before she was led out with her husband to be shot.

. . . The Ceaușescus were captured on Friday in a car about 60 miles from Bucharest, after attempting to flee in a helicopter that was forced to land, said Captain Mihai Lupoi, a member of the ruling National Salvation Front. The execution was carried out at 4pm local time by a three-man firing squad after a two-hour trial by military tribunal on Monday. Captain Lupoi said that he had seen full videotapes of the trial and execution. He recounted that as the couple were led out to their execution by the soldiers, Elena said to them: 'I was like a mother to you.' 'What sort of a mother were you, who killed our mothers?' one soldier replied.

The trial and execution took place in a secret military installation whose location would never be revealed for fear of sabotage by remnants of Ceaușescu's dreaded Securitate secret police, he said. The television film showed the couple being taken out of an armoured car and a doctor examining Ceaușescu. It then showed a lengthy scene of the two sitting in a room, possibly during their trial by the military tribunal which condemned them to death.

. . . The Ceaușescus had refused to collaborate with the tribunal, saying it had no authority over them, and had demanded to be tried by the Grand National Assembly (parliament) as the members of the tribunal were only ordinary citizens. 'You can shoot us if you like but we do not recognise you as a court,' Ceaușescu, 71, had said in his final hours. The couple had each been offered a defence lawyer but had refused. A military officer who asked not to be identified said that 300 soldiers had volunteered for the firing squad, but only three were chosen—an officer and two privates—by lottery, for the grisly task of avenging the years of increasing poverty and repression.

The Ceaușescus' last wish was to die together, the officer said. The Ceaușescu had rejected charges of causing the 'genocide' of more than 60,000 people during their 24 years in power, the provisional government announced. The couple were also accused of hiding more than $1 billion in foreign banks and having ruined the national economy and heritage.

Source: 'Television shows last hours of the "anti-Christ"', *Guardian*, 27 December 1989. Copyright Guardian News & Media Ltd 1989.

leaders and their repressive states were suddenly forced into positions of extreme insecurity. In January 2011, the president of Tunisia was forced into exile in Saudi Arabia following weeks of street protests against his regime. After twenty-four years as president, Zine El Abidine Ben Ali suffered the further indignity of being sentenced *in absentia* by Tunisian courts to thirty-five years' imprisonment on embezzlement, corruption, and drug-trafficking charges and thence to a further sentence of life imprisonment for inciting violence and murder. In January 2011, nationwide protests in Egypt led only a month later to the resignation of the previously entrenched presidency of Hosni Mubarak who had held the office since 1981. In August, Mubarak suffered the indignity of appearing in the same kind of caged dock that many of his opponents in the past had had to occupy in trials that often led to their deaths. The ailing 83-year-old leader was brought into court on a stretcher to face his accusers in a televised trial that was beamed around the Arab world. He was found guilty of charges relating to corruption, abuses of power, and the premeditated killing of peaceful protesters. He was sentenced to life imprisonment.[33]

In June 2011, the upsurge in violent street protests in Yemen reached the presidential palace when a bomb inflicted serious injuries on President Ali Abdullah Saleh. He was transferred to Saudi Arabia to receive treatment for shrapnel wounds, broken bones, smoke inhalation, internal bleeding, and extensive burns. He eventually returned home amidst further disorder in September 2011. His thirty-three-year rule ended when he was persuaded by international allies to step down from office in November 2011 thereby ending months of internal turmoil that had threatened to deteriorate into civil war. The year 2011 also marked the end of the regime in Libya that had been headed by Muammar Gaddafi since 1969. Beginning in February with protests against a regime that was widely regarded as based upon corruption and patronage, the situation rapidly deteriorated into open civil disorder and ultimately to a state of civil war. This provoked an international crisis that involved the United Nations which called for the regime's violent behaviour towards dissidents to be investigated by the International Criminal Court (ICC), and for the imposition of a no-fly zone to protect civilians from aerial attack. The latter was enforced by NATO which placed further pressure on President Gaddafi. During 2011 the major cities came under the control of the rebels' National Transitional Council (NTC). The manhunt for Gaddafi himself came to a brutal end outside one of his last remaining strongholds in October. After his convoy was attacked, the injured and blood-stained president was captured and amidst chaotic scenes was subsequently proclaimed dead either as a result of his injuries or from summary execution.

Looked at more generically, these kinds of unconventional transitions are not wholly untypical in repressive regimes. In one cross-national historical survey of leaders leaving office,[34] research organized at the University of Rochester in the

---

[33] The final outcome of the legal proceedings remains unresolved. In January 2013 an appeals court overturned Mubarak's life sentence and ordered a future retrial. Nevertheless, the ex-president remains in custody amidst varying reports concerning his physical and mental condition.

[34] Henk E. Goemans, Kristian S. Gleditsch, and Giacomo Chiozza, 'Introducing Archigos: A Dataset of Political Leaders'. Accessed 5 January 2012 at: <http://www.rochester.edu/college/faculty/hgoemans/ggc-text-jpr-v2.pdf>.

USA identified 549 leaders as having entered office through 'irregular means'—i.e. not in accordance with the 'prevailing rules, provisions, conventions and norms of the country'.[35] This category of entry is closely associated with the conditions of authoritarian leadership. Similarly, it is also the category which has a strong correlation with what are termed irregular exits from power. These irregular departures include the results of civil disorder, rebellions, military coups, power struggles, foreign intervention or threats of intervention, and assassinations. The Rochester study shows that of those leaders who experienced an 'irregular manner of exit', a very high proportion of them suffered personal privations following their periods in office; as many as 43 per cent of them were exiled, 18 per cent were imprisoned, and 20 per cent were killed.[36]

By focusing on those types of polity that amass resources for the purpose of sustaining the leadership in a condition of tenured perpetuity, it has been possible both to examine the measures taken in support of such an objective and to understand something of the dynamics that ultimately militate against their long-term effectiveness. Far from demonstrating how the reference point of an ageing process is inapplicable in such a regime, these cases show that the course of decline can only be delayed rather than stopped. Moreover, the way in which leaderships can be seen to age along with their hosts, and the way in which a particular leadership can come to depict a government and even an entire system in decline, is captured with vivid intensity in precisely these kinds of leader-centric polities.

Ironically, it is the systems with little experience of settled forms of leadership change that become most susceptible to the allure of leadership entrenchment with the result that the leaders and their governments become susceptible to being progressively eroded by virtue of their very longevity. The anxieties over sustaining the legitimacy of a political settlement, which may initially have led to an aversion towards any uncertainty at the highest reaches of government, has the effect of locking a system into a degenerative syndrome of leadership preservation. Ultimately, this can foster the kind of severe disruption that comes with the collapse of a leadership that has been artificially prolonged in an attempt to resist or retard the processes of any decline. If leadership in general can be understood as a condition shaped by its contextual situation, then it is evident that even in those cases where a leadership seeks to fashion and to dominate its own context, the outcome will in the end be one of an aggravated disjuncture, or in other words a situational death.

LEADERSHIP DECLINE IN A LIBERAL DEMOCRACY

We now turn to the processes of leadership decline that are more familiar in liberal democratic societies. In these polities, the position and security of political leadership have an altogether different pedigree which in most cases is manifested

---

[35] Goemans, Gleditsch, and Chiozza, 'Introducing Archigos', pp. 8–9.
[36] Goemans, Gleditsch, and Chiozza, 'Introducing Archigos', p. 31.

in a series of measures both to provide leaders but at the same time to constrain them. It may be through devices of popular consent and electoral sanction, or by way of representative institutions and party controls, or through constitutional and legal constraints, or else through systems of dispersed powers and pluralistic centres of political resource—or more usually by combinations of all these categories. The net effect is commonly one of ambiguity and contingency in which political leaders have to maximize their leverage through limited powers and to negotiate their agendas with other political actors that have alternative sources of political capital at their disposal. Therefore while a prime minister or president may occupy a strategic position within a political order this does not by any means always convert into an assured and effective capacity to pursue their objectives. On the contrary, the task of leadership within liberal democracies is one that is continually conditioned by the need to work within a political ecology that can be highly responsive to popular currents of opinion, to the deterrent effects of electoral processes, and to the constitutional challenges to executive authority.

This is not to claim that such offices have little or no leverage. On the contrary, they are accorded a proliferation of leadership roles and prerogatives related to their legal, representative, institutional, and political credentials—including some extremely sensitive and highly potent sources of executive control. Furthermore, they are normally expected to infuse their respective systems with a sense of direction, decisiveness, and coordination that would otherwise often be missing in arrangements that formally assign value to the virtues of reciprocal constraint operating through complex checks and balances. Nevertheless, it is equally the case that coexisting with the dispensations accorded to the positions of executive leadership are strong historical, cultural, and political anxieties over the possible dangers of such positions to the premises, principles, processes, and norms of liberal democratic governance. As such, leaders in liberal democracies have to be adept at operating within an area of ambivalence in which the utilitarian demand for leadership coexists with the traditional precepts of constitutional and democratic restraint. The net effect is one in which liberal democratic polities develop a functioning duality of attitudes—where 'leadership is a subject of enduring interest' not least because the 'political system seems designed to inhibit its exercise'.[37] Some would go further and claim that the 'constitutional tradition of balance does not require a theory of leadership. The processes of government are so widespread and participatory, and the institutions so permeable, that the idea of the people as sovereign, working through representative institutions, is sufficient.'[38]

A key constituent feature of these types of system therefore is one of continuing ambiguity over the principle and practice of political leadership. In one sense, leaders in established liberal democracies can draw upon strong foundations of precedent and process to substantiate their claims to political status. They have the additional benefit of a foundation of electoral legitimacy and representative

---

[37] Ryan J. Barilleaux and Mary E. Stuckey, 'Introduction', in Ryan J. Barilleaux and Mary E. Stuckey (eds.), *Leadership and the Bush Presidency* (New York, NY: Praeger, 1992), p. xv. See also Bert A. Rockman, *The Leadership Question: The Presidency and the American System* (New York, NY: Praeger, 1985), pp. 1–81.

[38] Erwin C. Hargrove, *The President as Leader: Appealing to the Better Angels of Our Nature* (Lawrence, KS: University Press of Kansas), p. 49.

authority—in many cases even to the point of being able to claim something of a personal mandate to pursue a leader-centred agenda. Even operating in the midst of different layers and compartments of political power, leaders in these systems have access to a variety of executive assets in the shape of privileges, immunities, and discretionary powers which are rationalized on the basis of functional necessity but also of what are usually cited as democratic credentials. While presidents and prime ministers operating within such a system will invariably ground their claims to a generic leadership authority on the basis of popular consent, they will at the same time seek to be as responsive as possible to contemporary currents of public opinion and to shifts in political allegiance. And it is this element of a conditional position shaped by the requirements of adjustment and adaptation which signifies the existence of an altogether different dimension in the position of democratic leaders.

The other side of the arrangement is not empowerment so much as an ever present potential for debility. What may be represented as a centripetal point of unity will in reality amount to something of a force field of centrifugal energies in which a leader persistently has to expend substantial political resources in an effort to limit their effects. The dynamics of provisional power and disputed authority are rooted in traditional liberal democratic fears of arbitrary government which are manifested not just in a reflexive scepticism of political hierarchies but in the constitutional emphasis upon bringing power to account. This outlook is epitomized in the binding authority of those legal, institutional, and political processes surrounding the replacement of one leader with another. It would be no exaggeration to state that the orderly and peaceful transfer of power has been widely regarded as the *sine qua non* of liberal politics. The highly problematic issue that plagues so many other regimes is seen in liberal democracies as one of its signature strengths. Indeed it is often taken to be a litmus test of the constitutional effectiveness and political benefits of liberal democracy.

An integral feature of this perspective upon politics is the presumptive operational principle that leadership is not a right or a privilege, and that it should not last for an indefinite period. Far from envisaging leadership as a static or progressive claim upon legitimacy, the liberal democratic tradition incorporates the prospect of routine delegitimation. In some systems, the terms of office are fixed in length and in number in order to underline the temporary nature of leadership tenure. In these structures, a president or prime minister will experience the political equivalent of infirmity and declining strength by simple virtue of a constitutional clock running down on their incumbency. While other leaders may not have to deal with the constraints of an allocated time frame for their specific office, they are nevertheless always aware that periodic elections will continue not only to shape their conduct in office but also keep the possibility of defeat always in prospect. The notion of a political clock in the parliamentary context may not be exactly the same as it is in the more precise timings of most presidential systems, but nonetheless they both share the same concerns over the processes of leadership erosion.

In both types of system, the cut and thrust of political competitiveness, combined with the difficulties of sustaining a functioning electoral coalition, make for a largely negative perspective on the subject of political time for most leaders. Far from being seen as exemplars of experience and durability, leaders in liberal democracies are generally placed in positions of increasing discomfort, scepticism, and disrespect born out of progressive overexposure, public fatigue, and political impatience. With the ever present availability of alternative leadership in democratic societies proffering the prospect of challenge and displacement and with the damaging weight of accountability ever more firmly attached to the established leadership, it is normal for incumbent leaders to be placed under increasing time pressures. They either manage to engage in exercises of temporary damage limitation that may prolong their political lives, or else suffer the ultimate indignity of being forced from office. Whether the final passage is depicted as one of party democracy, constitutional democracy, or electoral democracy, the outcome is normally conveyed as both the culmination of a process of decline and the simultaneous commencement of a newly conceived leadership. The effective and stable transfer of power from one leadership to another represents an affirmation of liberal democratic politics and a renewal of its ethos of leadership creation and leadership dissolution.

The issue of leaders and leadership, therefore, constitutes a highly problematic question at the heart of the liberal democratic ethos. The emergence of leaders through open competition represents one of the defining narratives of a democratic society in which social mobility on the basis of skill and merit can determine the selection of even the highest office-holders. A president or prime minister in these conditions can be represented as a refined distillation of the democratic process and, as a consequence, a person in possession of enhanced democratic credentials for government. By the same token, the principles that enable the establishment of political leadership on liberal democratic grounds also provide for its constraint. From the imposition of constitutional checks and balances through to a cultural scepticism of hierarchies and distinction, political leaders in these systems are given the task of continually squaring the circle—i.e. offering decisive leadership in support of a clear direction whilst working within the traditions, norms, and contingencies of democratic contestation and jurisdictional dispute. Many individuals have been highly proficient in balancing the different demands of leadership within a scenario that poses serious difficulties to the exercise of leadership. Others have found the problems to be prodigious and have effectively had their leaderships neutralized as a result. Ultimately, both categories of leader are united by a common experience whereby the system ensures either sooner or later that their contracts are not renewed.

THE CASE OF JOHN MAJOR

In order to give an impression of the complex nature of leadership in these conditions and, in the process, to provide an indication of the kind of dynamics which can be responsible for the erosion of leadership positions, this section presents a short illustrative example of a leader who had to endure a particularly exacting process of terminal decline. The case is that of John Major—UK prime minister from 1990 to 1997. He had succeeded the controversial Margaret Thatcher who herself had undergone the experience of a declining stock in resources, status, and respect during the late 1980s. In 1990, she was challenged for the Conservative Party leadership. Without having to stand against the prime minister, John Major emerged as her successor.

Initially John Major benefited from the transition. His premiership had answered two fundamental questions that had dominated British politics during the latter part of the 1980s. Major's emergence as party leader and prime minister had finally resolved the issues not merely of who would succeed the figure of Margaret Thatcher but also how the change would be made. The immediate contrast between the two leaders was at first favourable to the new entrant. Margaret Thatcher had been a conviction politician with a forceful, confrontational, and divisive style. John Major by contrast offered a welcome relief from the strident polarities of the Thatcher years in the shape of a far more emollient outlook that privileged the values of consultation, pragmatism, and consensus.[39] Because the negative properties of Thatcher had been dramatically discarded, Major was able to portray his premiership as a substantive change in style and yet at the same time one that imbued the succession with a conciliatory and unifying theme. As a consequence, both the Conservative Party and the Conservative government experienced something of a boost in the polls from the change of personnel. Major was left with the task of maintaining this immediate reaction and of ensuring that the broad Conservative ascendancy of the 1980s could be extended into the different political conditions of the 1990s.

In the event, John Major's honeymoon period was conspicuously short in duration. This is not to deny that the two Major administrations had a number of notable claims to success—including controlling inflation, reforming public services, instituting a Northern Ireland peace process, and negotiating various UK opt-outs and exemptions in the process of European integration. Most noteworthy was his unexpected victory in the 1992 general election which ensured a further five years of Conservative administration.[40] And yet despite these achievements, the lasting impression of the Major years was one of policy failures, economic recession, faction fighting, party splits, leadership challenges, attempted relaunches, and dysfunctional government. Although Major could claim ownership of a personal authority following the 1992 election, the conditions of his premiership did not materially improve his situation either within the party or the government. On the contrary, it subjected him to a position of persistent duress. It became increasingly evident that the key significance of his victory was the extent to which it had failed to resolve the difficulties surrounding his leadership. In many respects, the election campaign had merely suspended the problematic properties of his position and style. After the election, the initial doubts and restrained disquiet over John Major's premiership generated a debilitating process of corrosive complaint.

The early reservations in respect to the first administration acted merely as the precursor of his second administration which came to be characterized by an

---

[39] See Edward Pearce, *The Quiet Rise of John Major* (London: Weidenfeld & Nicolson, 1991); Brendan Evans, *Thatcherism and British Politics 1975-1999* (Stroud: Sutton, 1999); Dennis Kavanagh, *The Reordering of British Politics: Politics after Thatcher* (Oxford: Oxford University Press, 1997).
[40] David Butler and Dennis Kavanagh, *The British General Election of 1992* (Basingstoke: Macmillan, 1992); Susan Hogg and Jonathan Hill, *Too Close to Call: Power and Politics—John Major in No. 10* (London: Warner, 1996).

almost continuous crisis of leadership.[41] In retrospect, it became apparent that the problems that John Major confronted in the immediate post-Thatcher period represented a largely untapped potential for discord. The net effect was one in which Major's premiership became synonymous with an apparently unbreakable spiral of declining public confidence and intensifying divisions within the governing party. The administration was damaged by a series of assertive initiatives that were made under pressure and then followed either by retreats, or by public perceptions of retrenchment.

The most extreme example of the government's reputation for losing control of events came with the decision to suspend Britain's membership of the Exchange Rate Mechanism (ERM). In response to massive movements in the currency markets that culminated in Black Wednesday (16 September 1992), the government repeatedly raised interest rates and depleted its reserves in order to protect sterling. The emergency action had no effect and in the end the government was forced to accept the market was intent on devaluing the pound. The ERM had been the centrepiece of John Major's economic policy and the symbol of the government's claim that counter-inflation was its highest priority. The ignominious defeat was compounded by the subsequent need of the government to raise taxes and in doing so to break the central campaign commitment of the 1992 general election. The ERM fiasco destroyed the Conservatives' reputation for economic management, which had already been undermined by the deepest recession since the Second World War.[42]

If the collapse of Britain's membership of the ERM had initially been responsible for undermining the reputation of the government, it was followed by a series of events and developments that served to diminish the administration's authority even further. Major had to withstand a succession of debilitating conditions—from the enduring controversy over the future development of the European Union and of Britain's place within it through to multiple allegations of sleaze and declining standards in public life—and from a series of spectacular Conservative defeats in by-elections, local elections, and European elections to the continual speculations over the prospect of a leadership challenge.[43] Faced with these conditions, Major's premiership became an object lesson in the possibilities of political survival in the face of an openly degenerative process in which the power base of his position and that of his party had become progressively eroded. Within a year of his election triumph, Major's government was experiencing a huge 24 point deficit in relation to the Labour Party (i.e. 25 per cent to 49 per cent). This represented the second biggest lead recorded since Gallup began polling in 1937. During the same period MORI reported that Labour was outranking the Conservatives in thirteen out of the fourteen benchmarks of party image. These figures set the tone for the remainder of Major's premiership and pointed to only one conclusion: namely the prospect of impending electoral disaster.

---

[41] Anthony Seldon, *Major: A Political Life* (London: Phoenix, 1997); Hywel Williams, *Guilty Men: Conservative Decline and Fall 1992–1997* (London: Aurum, 1998); Michael Foley, *Tony Blair, John Major and a Conflict of Leadership* (Manchester: Manchester University Press, 2002), chs. 2, 3.

[42] Norman Lamont, *In Office* (London: Warner, 2000), pp. 191–298.

[43] Seldon, *Major: A Political Life*, ch. 33; Michael Heseltine, *Life in the Jungle: My Autobiography* (London: Hodder & Stoughton, 2000); Foley, *Tony Blair, John Major and a Conflict of Leadership*, ch. 6.

From this brief overview, it is clear that John Major suffered all the classic symptoms of a process of leadership decline within a parliamentary democracy. In answer to the following diagnostic questions, Major would have had to have answered in the affirmative:

- Was the party's image negative?
- Was the direction of policy confused?
- Was government disunity manifest?
- Was the party in organizational disarray?
- Were the party's finances depleted?
- Was the media and intellectual environment hostile?
- Was the public's perception of the economy critical?
- Had the government lost control of events?
- Had the administration failed to radiate a sense of governing competence?
- Was there widespread belief that it was 'time for a change'?
- Did the opposition party offer a credible alternative government?

The collective disarray surrounding the Conservative Party and the Major government found several expressions but the most conspicuous, and arguably the most damaging, was the concerted criticism of John Major himself. The multiple indictments tended to devolve upon the single dimension of prime ministerial leadership as the primary location of governmental image, competence, and accountability. In the same way that John Major had sought to personalize the electoral appeal of party and government in 1992, so the process was reversed in the long fractious aftermath of the election. Major became increasingly synonymous with the general deficiencies and failures of the Conservative Party, the administration, and the state of the British economy. From being a talisman of positives, Major's reputation rapidly degenerated into a defining symbol of drift, vacillation, and loss of purpose. For his part, Major was often reported as being depressed and occasionally disturbed by the unfolding of events. These reports only led to further speculation on the question of whether Major was temperamentally equipped for the position of prime minister.[44] As weak leadership became equated with personal weakness, John Major's premiership became identified with inevitable dissolution. This final stage of irreversible decline was completed on 1 May 1997 when Labour secured a landslide election victory.

The significance of John Major's troubled premiership is that it offers an object lesson in the processes of decline within a fully functioning liberal democracy. Despite his election victory and the presumption of a mandate, Major was beset at an early stage with a proliferation of difficult problems relating to the economy, Europe, and foreign policy at a time when his parliamentary majority was small, party cohesion was breaking down, and the Conservative ascendancy was coming under increasing pressure after four successive administrations. Given this context and his own diffident style of management, Major's claims to leadership were continually confronted by the deployed weight of an array of active countervailing

---

[44] For example, see Roy Jenkins, 'Major is not up to the job', *The Observer*, 18 October 1992; 'Is John Major up to the job?', *Sunday Telegraph*, 28 February 1993; 'Is he up to the job?', *Independent on Sunday*, 4 April 1993; William Rees-Mogg, 'Major fails the leadership test', *The Times*, 10 May 1993; Paul Routledge and Simon Hoggart, 'Major hits out at Cabinet', *The Observer*, 25 July 1993.

forces. Major was particularly unfortunate in that these forces were mobilized so early in his premiership and remained firmly fixed against his government over the duration of the parliament. The combination of high-exposure leadership coupled with a marked shift in public attitudes made for a very discomforting term of office which amounted to an unusually protracted and lingering political death. One of Major's predecessors in Number 10 suffered a comparable process of uncomfortable decline and painful departure from office. It elicited the following conclusion: 'Anthony Eden's political career was unusual in that it was wrecked by his achieving the highest office.'[45] The same epitaph became equally applicable to John Major in 1997.

Major's premiership underlined the extent to which the operation of political leadership in a liberal democracy like the UK is only ever feasible on the basis of a provisional licence. The toleration and even the temporary acceptance of effective leadership in a framework of multiple power centres, constitutional restraints, and extensive rights remains a highly contingent phenomenon that rests upon a complex set of circumstances. Leadership in this context is strongly conditioned by the operational requirements of coexistence within pluralist structures and traditions. In essence, the potential capacity for challenge is a permanent feature of such a system. A leader may successfully manage to suspend the normal dynamics of scepticism attached to the role but there will always come a time when the underlying reflexes of liberal resistance and democratic claims will begin to gravitate towards the presence of a particular leader. Even the most popular leaders find that their position and their legitimacy will come under assault. Sooner or later, like all leaders in such systems, they will find themselves pulled back into an altogether more tenuous position and in the end pushed out of office either by personal resignation, or by internal displacement, or through the operation of the electoral cycle.

CONCLUSION

The general issue of decline raises a host of questions over the place and status of leadership in any system of governance. It is possible to speculate on the comparability of the processes related to leadership displacement in different contexts and traditions of government. Notwithstanding such variations, it is evident that the status and traction of leadership are distinguished by their impermanence and by the way in which political leadership draws both specific and generic forms of accountability within its remit. Whether these properties can be enfolded into an iron law of entropy—in which all incidences of leadership order can be said to move ineluctably towards dispersal and disorder—is open to dispute. What is beyond debate is that political leadership is a phenomenon of interactive exchange. And that being the case, the onset of decline is marked by a relationship which breaks down on both sides. The wear and tear of leadership are often

---

[45] Ian Gilmour, 'Eden's paradise lost' (review of D. R. Thorpe, *Eden: The Life and Times of Anthony Eden, First Earl of Avon 1897–1977*), *Financial Times*, 15/16 March 2003.

portrayed by the more visible aspects of personal ageing on the part of the leader but a similar if less visible countenance operates on the led as well. Whatever measures are taken by leaders to retard any personal effects of ageing, the processes of an ageing political leadership are far less susceptible to restorative or cosmetic treatments. Just as new leaders are almost invariably associated with notions of revival and renewal, so established leaders have to withstand the downward pressures of the familiar and the prosaic that prefigure the demands for changed leadership.

New leaders generally make their case for change on the basis that the established leadership has lost touch with the people, with the issues, with events, and with the requirements of high office. There may also be accusations or inferences of abuses of power, usurpation, and poor judgement. When these critiques come to erode the levels of respect and tolerance that are normally assigned to the leadership, then opportunities open up for change. The scale of these opportunities will of course be conditioned by the nature of the polity in question. As has been noted above, the prospect of leadership change in authoritarian or traditionally inflexible regimes can induce severe strains which in many cases can lead to socially disruptive and even violent behaviour. Democracies are more accustomed to the derogatory aspects of political life which devolve with unerring accuracy upon a leadership whose time is always limited. In both cases, it is generally the case that what may originally have been characterized as a triumph of the public or national interest will have set the political clock running down in which the incoming leadership will have reaffirmed a life cycle that ensures a successive pattern of similar appeals to the *idea* of prospective leadership over the political *reality* of its exercise.

Part II

Contexts and Claims

6

The business of leadership: Cross-sector interplays

'Level 5 leaders channel their ego needs away from themselves and into the larger goal of building a great company. It's not that Level 5 leaders have no ego or self-interest. Indeed, they are incredibly ambitious—but *their ambition is first and foremost for the institution, not themselves.* The term *Level 5* refers to the highest level of executive capabilities.'

Jim Collins[1]

'IESE's Advanced Management Program (AMP) offers CEOs and general managers new learning experiences, fresh knowledge and the diverse perspectives necessary to enhance their leadership style. In the current climate, leaders who want their companies to advance have to be ready to confront new challenges. IESE's Advanced Management Program will allow you to identify new opportunities for you and your company. The program offers a practical approach and the chance to reflect on your leadership style though coaching and peer discussion of real life business scenarios.'

IESE Business School, University of Navarra: Promotional material

PREAMBLE

At a time when the normal parameters and credentials of political leadership have arguably become disorientated and, in many ways, diminished by the forces of globalization as well as fragmentation, leadership within the sphere of economic organization has seen a corresponding rise in significance, status, and relevance. Instead of the ambivalence which shapes so much of the speculation over the state of leadership within the explicitly political sphere, business models of organization assign a clear and unequivocal priority to the cultivation of leadership. Far from derogating the role of leadership as either a phenomenon belonging more appropriately to the world of politics, or as a temporary improvisation in the founding and establishment of an enterprise, the performance of leadership functions and the presence of leadership figures are seen as being essential

---

[1] Jim Collins, *Good to Great: Why Some Companies Make the Leap . . . and Others Don't* (London: Random House, 2001), p. 21.

requirements in the effective operation of business activity. In fact, leadership is now universally recognized as both an asset value and an economic factor of production in its own right.

Of the many alternative bases of leadership provision that now tend to crowd around the more conventional locations of political leadership, there can be little doubt that the most significant and most influential contemporary source lies within the sector of business organization. It is indisputable that no other sector sets such store in the value of leadership, and no other sector assigns so many resources and such lavish rewards to the establishment and promotion of leadership. It does so as a matter of course in recognition of the functional effectiveness that is assumed to inhere in the capacity of leaders to act as a counterweight to the deficiencies of any organization. At one level, the raised profile of business leadership has been a consequence of the recently established hegemony of neoliberal principles and norms which have created new spaces for economic hierarchies and enhanced forms of social legitimacy.

In this context, private sector organizations have shown what have been widely applauded capacities in responding to market conditions with speed and agility. Their skill in formulating strategic approaches to market-driven opportunities has been more than matched by the reputation of leaders in their role as expediters and facilitators of what is cited as an evolutionary process of transformative adaptation to a new epoch of social organization. As a consequence, business leaders and leadership have become recognized as market-driven resources in their own right—with all the kudos accorded to such a noted resource of pivotal value. So much so in fact that at a time when globalization has in many ways been instrumental in diminishing the reach of political leadership, it is the sector of business leadership which is now often cited as the main source of compensation in this sphere of social activity.

ORGANIZATION WITH A HUMAN FACE

In the world of business, there are no apologies for leadership. The only apologies in this respect are for a recognized lack of leadership. Leadership is privileged within business models for a host of different reasons. They can offer or at least indicate a sense of hierarchy within which a command structure and a clear direction can be established within an organization. The operational presumption is that leaders can infuse energy, innovation, and responsiveness into a business environment. According to this view, leaders provide an essential focus for coordination, planning, implementation, and accountability. Those with leadership skills are identified as the sources and drivers of a range of ascribed competences that are deemed essential for any business to fulfil its potential as an organizational force. It is on the leadership sector that businesses depend for strategists, enforcers, team builders, production maximizers, task-induced facilitators, and agents of conflict resolution and accommodation. The very range of ascribed functions reflects the high expectations that are commonly ascribed to contemporary leaders in order for them to fulfil their role specifications.

The paradigm that allocates such a pivotal value to leadership is one that also promotes a market outlook upon the recruitment, activity, and turnover of leaders. Large-scale industrial, commercial, and financial activities are regularly attributed to individual leaders who are personally reputed to having reassured, or alternatively having disturbed, the markets. Just as the markets scrutinize the appointments and track records of corporate executives, so productivity, profit-ability, and share values are widely assumed to be closely aligned to the quality of leadership within the enterprises under examination.

It might be thought that with progressive increases in organizational complex-ity there would be less significance attached to the role of individual leadership. Although the correlation between output or profits and the quality of manage-ment remains an inexact and disputed science, the belief that organizations can be sensitive to personal initiatives and that individuals can therefore be pivotal to business success still occupies a key position in business thinking and in the hierarchy of corporate values. Individual leaders are still seen as catalysts that can turn entire companies around, or else precipitate their decline and even collapse.[2] Even in an era of downsizing, outsourcing, and various forms of organizational 'flattening', there continue to be multiple claims relating to the central significance of leadership and to the need for leadership resources, training, and remuneration to be in line with the demands and stakes attendant upon the role of leadership within contemporary corporate culture.

Moreover, it can be argued that the responsibilities of business leaders are increasing rather than being marginalized through the processes of organizational segmentation and horizontal configuration. It is noteworthy that in 2003, *The Economist* reported that the 'leaders of large companies are increasingly in the public gaze'.

> A company's boss is now expected to take personal responsibility for its fortunes as never before. This is reflected not just in new corporate-governance rules, but also in the way that financial markets scrutinise the appointment of a new corporate boss and that companies feel they have to defend executive pay packages. Yet the task of the corporate leader has never been more demanding.[3]

---

[2] The pivotal significance attached to entrepreneurial and visionary individuals in building or sustaining large-scale corporate organizations is reflected in the prominence given to 'how I did it' autobiographies and related biographies in the genre of business books. See Lee Iacocca with William Novak, *Iacocca: An Autobiography* (New York, NY: Bantam, 1984); Ray Kroc with Robert Anderson, *Grinding It Out: The Making of McDonald's* (New York, NY: St. Martin's Press, 1990); Sam Walton with John Huey, *Made in America: My Story* (New York, NY: Bantam, 1993); David Packard, *The HP Way: How Bill Hewlett and I Built Our Company* (New York, NY: HarperBusiness, 1995); Daniel Gross and Editors of Forbes Magazine, *Forbes Greatest Business Stories of All Time: 20 Inspiring Tales of Entrepreneurs Who Changed the Way We Live and Do Business* (New York, NY: John Wiley, 1996); Howard Schultz and Dori J. Yang, *Pour Your Heart into It: How Starbucks Built a Company One Cup at a Time* (New York, NY: Hyperion, 1997); Stewart Lansley and Andy Forrester, *Top Man: How Philip Green Built His High Street Empire* (London: Aurum, 2005); Robert G. Hagstrom, *The Warren Buffett Way* (Hoboken, NJ: John Wiley, 2005); Walter Isaacson, *Steve Jobs: The Exclusive Biography* (London: Little, Brown, 2011); Bill Saporito and Auburn Hills, 'Power Steering: How the boss of Fiat and Chrysler is driving an auto-industry revival', *Time*, 19 December 2011; Walter Isaacson, *Steve Jobs: The Exclusive Biography* (London: Little, Brown, 2011); Richard L. Brandt, *One Click: Jeff Bezos and the Rise of Amazon.com* (London: Portfolio Penguin, 2011).

[3] *The Economist*, 'Tough at the top', 23 October 2003.

Apart from the numerous changes in corporate structures and processes, leaders are faced with a host of other problems: 'Layers of middle management have gone, so that more divisions report directly to the person at the top. The pace of innovation is quicker, new technologies have to be applied faster and product life cycles have become shorter.' As a consequence, 'for more and more businesses the abilities of a relatively small number of people are thought to be the key to success, and retaining and developing their talents are vital'.[4] This emphasis upon the value of corporate leadership is reflected in the rise to prominence of executive recruitment agencies that specialize in locating individuals either with proven records or with high achievement potential, and matching them to the requirements of senior-level appointments. The reputational prestige of these headhunters—as well as the high fees charged for their talent location and capture services—serve further to enhance the patina that attaches itself to the significance of leadership provision as an organizational and capital asset in its own right.[5]

One of the signature reasons that is cited for the attributed increase in the salience of business leadership is the scale and pace of new conditions which not only place a premium upon adaptive innovation but generate competitive demands for translating market opportunities into realizable organizational advances. The ramifications of an increasingly globalized market together with the commercial consequences of digital technology, high-speed connectivity, and multilevel platforms have resulted in an emphasis upon accelerated responsive and flexible solutions. Within this allegedly more protean context, it is leaders who are identified as both the instruments of change and the signifiers of the need for change. As a consequence of this equation, leaders have become almost invariably marked as the prime agency of strategic adaptation and as the most conspicuous manifestations of a paradigm shift away from settled pyramidal structures of organization towards more sensitive registers of new trends towards devolved systems of management.

The move away from command-and-control models of corporate governance has generated an entire sector of prescriptive and normative analysis related to leadership dependency in relation to what are considered to be new and complex conditions. This has injected a new stimulus into the classic debate over the difference between leadership and management. Discussions over the location and value of leadership within changing contexts usually occur against the backdrop of the extent to which leadership can be clearly distinguished from management. In spite of the fundamental shifts in organizational configuration and complexity during the era of globalization, outsourcing, and horizontal systems, a consensus remains in the business world that leadership remains conceptually and operationally distinguishable from management. The conventional categories used to support this proposition are given in Box 6.1.

---

[4] *The Economist*, 'Tough at the top', 23 October 2003.
[5] See Robert M. Melançon, *The Secrets of Executive Search: Professional Strategies for Managing Your Personal Job Search* (Hoboken, NJ: John Wiley, 2002); Claudio Fernández-Aráoz, *Great People Decisions: Why They Matter So Much, Why They are So Hard, and How You Can Master Them* (Hoboken, NJ: John Wiley, 2007).

Box 6.1 The management–leadership duality

The issue of whether and how leadership can be differentiated from management

---

MANAGEMENT	LEADERSHIP
Produces order and consistency	Produces change and movement
Planning/budgeting	Vision building/strategizing
Organizing/staffing	Aligning people/communicating

Source: Adapted from John P. Kotter, *A Force for Change: How Leadership Differs from Management* (New York, NY: Free Press, 1990).

The 'Management–Leadership Balance'

MANAGEMENT	LEADERSHIP
Systems, processes, technology	People—context and culture
Goals, standards, measurement	Preferred future, principles, purpose
Control	Commitment
Strategic planning	Strategic opportunism
Way of doing	Way of being
Directing	Serving
Responding and reacting	Initiating and originating
Continuous improvement of what is	Innovative breakthroughs to what could be

---

Source: Categories of differentiation widely cited in business and management literature.

Great leadership is a unique form of art, requiring both force and vision to an extraordinary degree...Management is one thing. Leadership is another. As Warren G. Bennis...puts it, 'Managers have as their goal to do things right. Leaders have as their goal to do the right thing.' Leadership is more than technique, though techniques are necessary. In a sense, management is prose; leadership is poetry...The manager thinks of today and tomorrow. The leader must think of the day after tomorrow. A manager represents a process. The leader represents a direction of history. Thus a manger with nothing to manage becomes nothing, but even out of power a leader still commands followers.

Source: Richard Nixon, *Leaders* (London: Sidgwick & Jackson, 1982), pp. 4–5.

The presence of internal and external environments that have become highly mutable and organizationally demanding is the basis of a new emphasis upon leadership as opposed to mere management. John Kotter is emblematic of the functional and cultural status that has been afforded to leaders in their ascribed role as an agency of adjustment and navigation through more challenging conditions. The way in which leadership has become unreservedly privileged over management within the field is well captured in one of the most cited empirical and normative pieces to appear in the *Harvard Business Review*. Under the title, 'What Leaders Really Do', Kotter lays out his generic claim that leadership is the organizational analogue of change. It is only by assigning a premium value to leaders that organizations can respond effectively to the challenges posed by the advent of major changes in the contemporary business environment.

Part of the reason it has become so important in recent years is that the business world has become more competitive and more volatile. Faster technological change, greater international competition, the deregulation of markets, overcapacity in capital-intensive industries, an unstable oil cartel, raiders with junk bonds, and the changing demographics of the work-force are among the many factors that have contributed to this shift. The net result is that doing what was done yesterday, or doing it 5% better, is no longer a formula for success. Major changes are more and more necessary to survive and compete effectively in this new environment. More change always demands more leadership.[6]

To Kotter, the dangerous syndrome for most corporations in the United States is that they are 'over-managed and under-led'.[7] Accordingly, the priority in any business organization is to create a 'leadership-centred culture'[8] that promotes the identification and training of leaders, and encourages the formation and communication of leadership visions of the future. If Kotter's anxieties over the state of corporate leadership were largely prompted by the conditions of the 1990s, it is reasonable to suppose that these concerns have deepened still further over time with the onset of a host of further conditioning influences upon the activities of leaders. These would include the introduction of more intrusive regulations of corporate governance including rigorous transparency and reporting requirements in order to safeguard shareholder rights and to acknowledge public interest claims in business practice. The altered business environment is also characterized by the growing number of stakeholders connected to public and private organizations; the increase in 'best practice' and other norm regimes; and the pressure of social advocacy and campaigning networks directed towards ethical issues of global justice, sustainable development, and corporate social responsibility.

The concerns and prescriptions of analysts like Kotter are emblematic of an entire genre of work on the issue of leadership and its place in business organization. This prodigious body of work reflects not only the functional value that is assigned to the contribution of leaders within their structural environments, but also the cultural emphasis that is laid upon leadership in affording both strategic direction and collective purpose to an enterprise. Even in the largest of organizations, leadership is regarded as a premium quality and one that needs to be harnessed, projected, and rewarded as an organizational imperative.

The importance that is accorded to the virtues of leadership is not confined to the highest levels of decision-making, but is by a process of extrapolation applied to every tier of management. If effective leadership at the top is seen as the *sine qua non* of effective corporate activity, then it is also the case that those further down the chain are encouraged to see their positions as roles requiring leadership skills within their own particular sections. As such, those occupying middle and lower levels of responsibility are expected to adopt leadership outlooks and to use leadership techniques to provide optimal

---

[6] John P. Kotter, 'What Leaders Really Do', in *Harvard Business Review on Leadership* (Boston, MA: Harvard Business Scholl Press, 1998), p. 40. See also John P. Kotter, *A Force for Change: How Leadership Differs from Management* (New York, NY: Free Press, 1990), chs. 1, 2.

[7] Kotter, 'What Leaders Really Do', p. 38.

[8] Kotter, 'What Leaders Really Do', p. 53.

outcomes within their areas of responsibility. It is for this reason that large organizations devote such extensive resources and give such priority to the recruitment, training, and development of what is almost universally characterized as leadership. The contemporary emphasis placed upon leadership has given rise to an entire organizational sector devoted to the study and delivery of leadership skills. These facilities vary in size and scope but they nevertheless share a common purpose in responding to demands for leadership credentials in a host of different areas of social life.[9]

In the business sector, the main source and the most conspicuous showcase of this culture of leadership is shared between on the one hand successful individual entrepreneurs who construct successful and durable organizations, and on the other leaders who inherit the commanding heights of established structures but who manage to make them responsive to their own personal agendas. In many respects, the two categories are not that dissimilar . An effective form of succession leadership will often involve attempts at replicating the pioneering initiatives of the foundational leadership in seeking to reconfigure or, in some instances, entirely to reconstruct an established organization in response to contemporary operating conditions. Modern corporate CEOs are hired, and in many cases fired, on the understanding that the right person in the right position can act as a catalyst upon the largest and most complex of impersonal bodies. At a minimum, a CEO and his or her management team are expected to maintain accepted standards of competence and to sustain an established market position for the company. Even within this minimalist specification, the presumption is one in which the leadership sector is assumed to have the potential for creating adverse conditions within a company—but is entrusted not to do so on the grounds of the proven credentials of individual background and personal judgement on the part of those selected for the job.

On a more dramatic scale, a CEO can be regarded as a saviour who is able to redeem a failing enterprise and who can turn a company around by the injection of a creative programme for change, along with the drive to secure the stated objectives. In this context, the depth and durability of the belief system in the instrumental agency of business leadership are revealed to their fullest extent. CEOs who have saved a business organization, or taken it to an entirely new level of prominence, have popularized the notion of a leader as an 'X-factor' or a 'magic bullet' that can restructure a corporation even to the point of giving it a new identity. These legendary exponents of high-profile leadership, along with the transformative narratives that they generate, exemplify the high level of leadership consciousness in even the most impersonal of contexts. They also underline the retained conviction in the significance of the possible synergies that can exist between an individual and an organization, which can not only enhance overall performance but also allow concealed potential to be unlocked and actualized.

---

[9] For example, see Leadership Foundation for Higher Education; Foundation for Church Leadership; Scottish Leadership Foundation; Health Foundation Leadership Programme; Clore Social Leadership Programme; Sports Leaders UK Foundation; Young Leaders Programme; London Leaders Programme.

This outlook is supported by the legendary narratives of individual corporate leaders who are deemed to have succeeded in their organizations juxtaposed with those leaders who are regarded as having failed in either the same companies or similar enterprises (Box 6.2).

Box 6.2 Winners and losers

Case #1 Ford and General Motors
Ford and General Motors were two car-making giants with similar profiles and pressures. In the mid 2000s, GM was thought to be in a better position. But with the hiring of an industry outsider, Alan Mulally, as CEO in 2009, it was Ford that went from strength to strength. As a result, Mulally achieved mythic status in the corporate and investment sectors. Meanwhile GM, which continued to engage in insider promotion practices, became bankrupt and needed an injection of $50 billion in public funds.

Case #2 General Electric and Westinghouse
General Electric and Westinghouse were comparable businesses that competed in the same diverse power generation and electric equipment markets. Over the course of the 1980s and 1990s, GE surged ahead under the leadership of CEO Jack Welch. By the end of the 1990s, Westinghouse had all but disappeared in name. GE on the other hand became a high-value industry leader. The main difference in fortunes has been widely attributed to the difference between the settled leadership of Welch in GE and a succession of lacklustre CEOs in Westinghouse.

Case #3 Citigroup
Sandy Weill was instrumental in building up what had been a small financial outfit in Baltimore into the massive international banking entity Citigroup. He was succeeded by Chuck Prince who had only limited banking experience. Prince became CEO in 2003 and chairman in 2006. But in 2007 he was forced to resign as a result of a sudden poor performance by the organization. Weil later apologized for what was seen as a misman-aged process of corporate succession which had nearly led to bankruptcy. At the same time, Weill's initial protégé, James Dimon, who had earlier been sacked by Citigroup, went on to head JP Morgan which outperformed Citigroup during the credit crunch crisis.

Case #4 Who comes next?
In the light of these kinds of cases, the management of leadership succession has become increasingly recognized as a major strand in strategic planning, organizational sustain-ability, and growth potential. Succession management involves the need to identify the internal potential, or the external location, of future leadership responsibilities in order for a business not only to retain its high-value assets and market position but also to ensure that it is alert to new pathways and alternative strategic directions. Particular problems arise when organizations become synonymous with those individuals who have built up a particular corporate identity, and an idiosyncratic leadership cult, centred upon their own entrepre-neurial achievements. Companies with iconic leaders can find it difficult to replace what is often regarded as the irreplaceable. Moreover companies that 'have an all-consuming "great man" at the top can go horribly wrong. Great men don't always know when to leave the stage or how to nurture superstar replacements.'[10] The internal problems incurred in dealing with charismatic chief executives and their iconic associations are further com-pounded by the external pressures placed upon their replacements in respect to market and investment anxieties. Even within the global parameters of the corporate world, therefore,

---

[10] Steven Rattner, 'The "great man" theory of business', *Financial Times*, 19 January 2011.

the security of individual leadership brands remains a crucial element in the public and institutional resource base of a company. This is both a fact and a concern that is occupying the attention of such companies as Apple, Berkshire Hathaway, and News Corporation as they face the present or imminent challenges of adjusting to life without their legendary founders—namely Steve Jobs, Warren Buffett, and Rupert Murdoch.

Sources: Stephen A. Miles and Nathan Bennett, 'Best Practices in Succession Planning', Forbes.com, 9 November 2007. Accessed 23 August 2012 at: <http://www.forbes.com/2007/11/07/succession-ceos-govern ance-lead-cx_sm_1107planning.html>; Francesco Guerrera and Jeremy Lemur, 'Executive anointments', *Financial Times*, 30/31 October 2010; Dean Fink, *The Succession Challenge: Building and Sustaining Leadership Capacity Through Succession Management* (London: Sage, 2010); Katrina Brooker, 'Citi's creator, alone with his regrets', *New York Times*, 2 January 2010; Anne Fisher, 'Apple's not alone in succession plan woes', *CNN Money*, 19 January 2011. Available at: <http://management.fortune.cnn.com/2011/01/19/who-will-be-your-company%e2%80%99s-next-ceo/>.

In an era when CEO figures occupy key positions in a celebrity culture geared to success and material affluence, and when a belief in the transformative power of individual corporate leaders has become established as a popular orthodoxy, the social currency of organizational leadership has in turn become more marked and more penetrating as a widely subscribed role model. For their part, economic leaders who acquire high-profile social status help to further the widespread conviction that just as individuals adjust to organizations, so structures can and do engage in processes of collective learning that are very often precipitated, motivated, and guided by leaders with personal visions and styles of their own. It is against this background of presumptive leadership significance and relative leader autonomy that business schools, corporate recruiters, market researchers, organization analysts, and media commentators point to the dependency of corporate structures upon leadership to provide the necessary means for adaptive change in an increasingly complex, competitive, and fluid business environment.

BUSINESS CULT OF LEADERSHIP

The value that is currently attributed to leadership in organizational development is reflected in the resources that are devoted to its active promotion within institutions. Extensive measures are put in place to ensure that an advanced awareness of the ascribed significance of leadership properties to organizational effectiveness is maintained as a central priority. Organizations are increasingly under pressure to demonstrate their capacity in maximizing leadership potential within their structures and in raising the profile of leadership skills within their portfolio of competences. It would be no exaggeration to assert that the demonstrable demands for, and expectations of, leadership have reached epidemic proportions within both private and public organizations. Whether it is project management, decision-making, team building, or problem solving, leadership is widely taken to be an indispensable element in the productive process.

Businesses not only have to demonstrate an ability to recruit leaders but also to provide the conditions and training opportunities to produce leadership qualities on a regular basis. Within business culture, the notion that leadership is a form of transferable knowledge has prompted the establishment of an entire industry geared to the analysis of leadership and to the enhancement of leadership skills. The importance attached to the need for individuals to be able successfully to demonstrate leadership behaviour and to fulfil leadership roles has now reached such a level that the once venerable distinction between leadership and management has increasingly been eroded by the sheer weight of managers who now wish to be designated as leaders.

This shift in values and aspirations has generated an entire industry directed towards the examination of leadership and the provision of leader-based skills. It has been responsible for a profusion of books, articles, journals, CDs, audio cassettes, webcasts, podcasts, DVDs, video channels, and specialist 'apps' on the subject area, as well as for a huge array of leadership institutes, academies, professional organizations, schools, courses, programmes, conferences, and seminars run by analysts, exponents, coaches, and even leadership gurus. The widening recognition of organizational leadership as a capital asset now represents a key intersection point between the education and business sectors. Barbara Kellerman notes that 'leadership development is without question what those within the academy as well as those without are much the most interested in—growing leaders, training leaders, teaching people how to lead'. Kellerman observes that business leadership has in effect become a business in its own right: 'The shared assumption is that leadership development is a legitimate undertaking—that people can and do learn how to lead, from those paid to teach them, which is why so many shell out so much to buy whatever it is the leadership industry has to sell.'[11]

Some indication of the scale of activity in this field and the volume of resources assigned to this area is reflected in the number of books on business leadership listed on the Amazon.com website. At the time of access, the number of publications in print was registered at 42,020.[12] A similar survey in the catalogue of the *Harvard Business Review* also revealed a noteworthy level of editorial emphasis on the significance, sources, locations, styles, and strategic and operational value of leadership. Apart from the fact that this key journal in the business field operates its subscriptions promotions almost exclusively through the access it offers to key articles on leadership and bound collections on the same subject, the *Review* supports a back catalogue of nearly 7,000 articles on leadership. Their scope and range—as well as their almost obsessive attention to the theme—can be gauged from a random selection of titles published since 2000 (Box 6.3).

Within the vast matrix of leadership-centred instruction, there exist some distinctive sub-categories. One is characterized by the presentation of role models and by the inference that it is possible to emulate their example. These can range from historical or even fictional and mythical figures to contemporary examples of

---

[11] Barbara Kellerman, *The End of Leadership* (New York, NY: HarperCollins, 2012), p. 161.
[12] Accessed 22 February 2013.

Box 6.3 Representative selection of article titles on the genre of leaders and leadership published in the *Harvard Business Review*

- ❖ HBR: 'Leadership That Gets Results' (2000)[13]
- ❖ HBR: 'Why Should Anyone Be Led by You?' (2000)[14]
- ❖ HBR: 'The Work of Leadership' (2001)[15]
- ❖ HBR: 'Primal Leadership: The Hidden Driver of Great Performance' (2001)[16]
- ❖ HBR: 'Crucibles of Leadership' (2002)[17]
- ❖ HBR: 'Developing Your Leadership Pipeline' (2003)[18]
- ❖ HBR: 'What Makes a Leader?' (2004)[19]
- ❖ HBR: 'Seven Transformations of Leadership' (2005)[20]
- ❖ HBR: 'Managing Authenticity: The Paradox of Great Leadership' (2005)[21]
- ❖ HBR: 'Discovering Your Authentic Leadership' (2007)[22]
- ❖ HBR: 'Building a Leadership Brand' (2007)[23]
- ❖ HBR: 'Women and the Labyrinth of Leadership' (2007)[24]
- ❖ HBR: 'In Praise of the Incomplete Leader' (2007)[25]
- ❖ HBR: 'Five Steps to Building Your Personal Leadership Brand' (2007)[26]
- ❖ HBR: 'Social Intelligence and the Biology of Leadership' (2008)[27]

---

individuals who have been responsible for the creation of a successful enterprise or the renovation of an established organization. The variety of sources together with the uniformity of the underlying parable can be illustrated by a selection of some keynote titles in the field:

---

[13] Daniel Goleman, 'Leadership That Gets Results', *Harvard Business Review*, March 2000.

[14] Rob Goffee and Gareth Jones, 'Why Should Anyone Be Led by You?', *Harvard Business Review*, September 2000.

[15] Ronald A. Heifetz and Donald L. Laurie, 'The Work of Leadership', *Harvard Business Review*, December 2001.

[16] Daniel Goleman, Richard Boyatzis, and Annie McKee, 'Primal Leadership: The Hidden Driver of Great Performance', *Harvard Business Review*, December 2001.

[17] Warren G. Bennis and Robert J. Thomas, 'Crucibles of Leadership', *Harvard Business Review*, September 2002.

[18] Jay Conger and Robert M. Fulmer, 'Developing Your Leadership Pipeline', *Harvard Business Review*, December 2003.

[19] Daniel Goleman, 'What Makes a Leader?', *Harvard Business Review*, January 2004.

[20] David Rooke and William R. Torbert, 'Seven Transformations of Leadership', *Harvard Business Review*, April 2005.

[21] Rob Goffee and Gareth Jones, 'Managing Authenticity: The Paradox of Great Leadership', *Harvard Business Review*, December 2005.

[22] William W. George, Peter Sims, Andrew N. McLean, David Mayer, and Diana Mayer, 'Discovering Your Authentic Leadership', *Harvard Business Review*, February 2007.

[23] Dave Ulrich and Norm Smallwood, 'Building a Leadership Brand', *Harvard Business Review*, July 2007.

[24] Alice H. Eagly and Linda L. Carli, 'Women and the Labyrinth of Leadership', *Harvard Business Review*, September 2007.

[25] Deborah Ancona, Thomas W. Malone, Wanda J. Orlikowski, and Peter M. Senge, 'In Praise of the Incomplete Leader', *Harvard Business Review*, February 2007.

[26] Dave Ulrich and Norm Smallwood, 'Five Steps to Building Your Personal Leadership Brand', *Harvard Business Review*, December 2007.

[27] Daniel Goleman and Richard Boyatzis, 'Social Intelligence and the Biology of Leadership', *Harvard Business Review*, September 2008.

- *Leadership Secrets of Attila the Hun*[28]
- *What Do Leaders Really Do? Getting Under the Skin of What Makes a Great Leader Tick*[29]
- *Awaken the Giant Within: How to Take Immediate Control of Your Mental, Emotional, Physical and Financial Life*[30]
- *The New Leaders: Transforming the Art of Leadership into the Science of Results*[31]
- *The 7 Habits of Highly Effective People: Powerful Lessons in Personal Change*[32]
- *Living Leadership: A Practical Guide for Ordinary Heroes*[33]

Another sub-category seeks not just to elicit practical insights from other genres but to draw upon their cultural status both as source and expressions of leadership legitimacy. The context can range from social and economic categories to more expansive and broadly conceived sources of inspiration. On occasion, the frame of reference can even stretch to the overtly religious as the basis for direct emulation:

- *Running with the Giants: What Old Testament Heroes Want You to Know About Life and Leadership*[34]
- *Moses on Management: 50 Leadership Lessons from the Greatest Manager of All Time*[35]
- *The Bible on Leadership: From Moses to Matthew—Management Lessons for Contemporary Leaders*[36]
- *Jesus, CEO: Using Ancient Wisdom for Visionary Leadership*[37]
- *Lead Like Jesus: Lessons from the Greatest Leadership Role Model of All Time*[38]
- *Leadership Lessons of Jesus: A Timeless Model for Today's Leaders*[39]
- *The Leader's Way: Business, Buddhism and Happiness in an Interconnected World*[40]

[28] Wess Roberts, *Leadership Secrets of Attila the Hun* (New York, NY: Time Warner Electronic Publishing, 1995).

[29] Jeff Grout and Liz Fisher, *What Do Leaders Really Do? Getting Under the Skin of What Makes a Great Leader Tick* (Chichester: Capstone, 2007).

[30] Anthony Robbins, *Awaken the Giant Within: How to Take Immediate Control of Your Mental, Emotional, Physical and Financial Life* (New York, NY: Free Press, 2003).

[31] Daniel Goleman, *The New Leaders: Transforming the Art of Leadership into the Science of Results* (London: Time Warner, 2003).

[32] Stephen R. Covey, *The 7 Habits of Highly Effective People: Powerful Lessons in Personal Change* (New York, NY: Free Press, 2004).

[33] George Binney, *Living Leadership: A Practical Guide for Ordinary Heroes*, 2nd edn. (London: Pearson Financial Times, 2009).

[34] John C. Maxwell, *Running with the Giants: What Old Testament Heroes Want You to Know About Life and Leadership* (New York, NY: Time Warner, 2002).

[35] David Baron and Lynette Padwa, *Moses on Management: 50 Leadership Lessons from the Greatest Manager of All Time* (New York, NY: Pocket Books, 1999).

[36] Lorin Woolfe, *The Bible on Leadership: From Moses to Matthew—Management Lessons for Contemporary Leaders* (New York, NY: AMACOM, 2002).

[37] Laurie B. Jones, *Jesus, CEO: Using Ancient Wisdom for Visionary Leadership* (New York, NY: Hyperion, 1995).

[38] Ken Blanchard and Phil Hodges, *Lead Like Jesus: Lessons from the Greatest Leadership Role Model of All Time* (Nashville, TN: Thomas Nelson, 2005).

[39] Bob Briner and Ray Pritchard, *Leadership Lessons of Jesus: A Timeless Model for Today's Leaders* (Nashville, TN: B&H Publishing, 2008).

[40] Dalai Lama and Laurens van den Muyzenberg, *The Leader's Way: Business, Buddhism and Happiness in an Interconnected World* (London: Nicholas Brealey Publishing, 2009).

A further strand in the leadership literature concentrates on the more practical issues of defining methods and skills, and offering instructive advice on how these might be attained by aspiring leaders, or by those in established leadership positions who wish to improve or adjust their positional performance. This didactic element has a direct appeal because it is based upon the premise that leadership can in many respects be learnt as a form of acquired competence. The notion that leaders can be *made* has a close resonance with the concept of leadership itself which offers the prospect of transformation from one state of existence to another. In this case, individuals are encouraged to transfigure themselves into positions where they can successfully claim to demonstrate leadership behaviour and to fulfil leadership roles.

The ways and means of developing organizational responses to the needs of leadership offer another strand to the genre. It is now an accepted part of a business portfolio that it should have processes in place to identify leadership skills, to establish the means by which to recruit and retain leaders, and to cultivate a leadership culture that will offer them the opportunity to deploy their capabilities. Whether it is called 'transition management', 'talent strategy', or 'high-level reconfiguration', the acquisition of leaders and the existence of 'strong leadership' are now considered to be key criteria in how companies are evaluated. For example, in the *Sunday Times* '100 Best Companies to Work For' survey, 'leadership' and 'my manager' are regarded as high-value categories. In 2007, the highest ranked in the leadership category was Denplan. The distinction was secured on the following grounds:

> One of the keys to success is strong leadership, for which Denplan wins one of our special awards. Workers have a great deal of faith in managing director Steve Gates (93%), think he runs the organisation on sound moral principles (89%) and are inspired by him (91%). His senior managers also get a vote of confidence from staff for their leadership (89%) and for listening to people (80%), all scores for which Denplan ranks first or second among all 100 best companies.[41]

Five years later, the emphasis laid upon the values of good leadership remained the same. The 2012 *Sunday Times* survey[42] demonstrated yet again that success in the leadership category was likely to have a close correlation with the overall rankings of companies in the study: 'Difficult times require strong leaders—and the evidence . . . shows a resurgence among businesses with the most dynamic and forceful personalities leading them.'[43]

Given the attention that is directed towards the provision and maintenance of leader positions, there can be little doubt as to the instrumental, strategic, and social value that is attached to effective leadership within business organizations. The controlling premise is that leaders can have a disproportionate effect even within very large organizations. In essence, it is understood that leaders can offer not merely an agency of organizational security but on occasions a catalyst to facilitate a paradigm shift in organizational behaviour.

---

[41] '100 Best Companies to Work For—2007', *Sunday Times*, 11 March 2007.
[42] '100 Best Companies to Work For—2012', *Sunday Times*, 2 March 2012.
[43] Alastair McCall, 'Their people know they are valued', *Sunday Times*, 2 March 2012.

CONTEXTS AND 'FIT'

All these different strands tend to revolve around a common underlying theme concerning the principal dynamic of leadership within organizations. This is centred upon the relationship between the source or provision of leadership and the context within which it has to operate. The definition and analysis of the nature and effect of leadership within an organizational setting are necessarily structured around the identification of factors that shape the emergence of leadership roles and condition their exercise. The reciprocal and interactive properties of exerting leadership within structures that invariably possess resources of their own for limiting the scope for external direction mean that leadership will always remain based upon context and contingency. As a consequence, the study of leaders and their roles tends to be organized around sets of criteria that attempt to incorporate and even to systematize the various permutations of located context and specified contingency. One particular sub-genre is represented by those studies that seek to use the roles, experiences, and insights drawn from a military environment and relate them to the conditions and resonances of the civilian sector. This is reflected in the recent prominence given to Sun Tzu's *The Art of War* in the business community and in other studies applying military strategy and combat leadership techniques to the management of non-military organizations.[44]

In seeking to reduce the inherent variability in the incidence of leadership provision, the organizing principles of these studies vary enormously. Different types or styles of leaders are examined in relation to different leadership roles and purposes—very often with the express objective of specifying a fit between a form of leadership and the requirements of a particular situation. Just as various brands and sources of leadership are distinguished, so different settings and levels are identified in order to improve our understanding of the dynamics of leadership possibilities. Given the profusion of different contingencies within which leadership is observed, and very often prescribed, a range of devices has been formulated to simplify the genealogy of leaders and leaderships. More often than not, these devices centre upon a duality of one kind or another. One of the most pervasive of these dualities concerns the spectrum that ranges between forceful and task-related leadership on the one hand, and consultative and consensus-based leadership on the other. Such a distinction raises the issue of which type of leadership might be more appropriate in any given situation, and how this might be determined to any degree of accuracy.

Other notable dualities include the distinctions between leadership engaged in small-scale or short-term objectives, and that which is geared to large-scale or

---

[44] See Sun-Tzu, *The Art of War*, ed. John Minford (New York, NY: Penguin, 2009); Gerald A. Michaelson and Steven Michaelson, *Sun Tzu—The Art of War for Managers: 50 Strategic Rules Updated for Today's Business* (Avon, MA: Adams Media, 2010); Mark R. McNeilly, *Sun Tzu and the Art of Business: Six Strategic Principles for Managers*, 2nd edn. (New York, NY: Oxford University Press, 2012). See also William G. Pagonis, 'Leadership in a Combat Zone', *Harvard Business Review*, December 2001: 107–16; Marilyn Darling, Charles Parry, and Joseph Moore, 'Learning in the thick of it', *Harvard Business Review*, July/August 2005: 84–92; Jeff Weiss *et al.*, *Leadership Lessons from the Military—HBR Spotlight Article Collection*, *Harvard Business Review*, November 2010, first published in the 'Idea Watch' section of the *Harvard Business Review* November 2010.

long-term and sustainable goals.[45] While some leaders may be categorized according to whether they are oriented towards either inclusive or exclusive outlooks, other leaderships can be divided between symbolic or substantive modes of appeal. The empirical and conceptual work of James MacGregor Burns in the field of leadership studies has been the source of another widely subscribed duality in the classification of business leadership. In this case, the ascribed polarity relates to the separate motive forces and modes of conduct associated with what Burns terms 'transactional leadership' compared to those associated with what he defines as 'transformative leadership'. In contrast to the former which sees the task of leadership as one in which a leader acts primarily as broker seeking a stable equilibrium between competing interests, transformative leaders aspire to maximize their resources in order to secure substantive and principled change—i.e. 'alterations in entire systems . . . alterations so comprehensive and pervasive . . . that new cultures and value systems take the place of the old'.[46]

Many other dualities can be cited ranging from the differences between leaderships located in hierarchical structures and those existing in flat delayered organizations, to the differences between leadership in crisis conditions and leadership exercised under more normal circumstances; and from the distinctions between insiders engaged in private and even secretive leadership to those that operate as outsiders with a more open and even confrontational style of leadership. In the study of leadership, even the methodologies tend to be organized along divergent pathways. While some analyses give emphasis to the traits, skills, or styles of individual leaders, others stress the explanatory utility of discrete contexts and situational factors. The overall effect of all these approaches and frameworks is one that not only bears witness to the significance attached to the provision of leadership within organizations but underlines the prodigious array of settings, levels, and contingencies within which leadership can be discerned and valued as an essential component of associational life.[47]

Given the importance that is assigned to the role of leadership within business organizations, and given the extent to which business values have permeated the wider social sphere in an era of neoliberal principles, it has become increasingly evident in many systems that business themes and methods have not only

---

[45] An excellent depiction of this duality is given in Gayle Avery and Harald Bergsteiner, *Honeybees and Locusts: The Business Case for Sustainable Leadership* (New York, NY: Routledge, 2011).

[46] James MacGregor Burns, *Transforming Leadership* (London: Atlantic, 2003), pp. 24–5.

[47] For a review of the various iterations of business and organizational leadership—including the contemporary resonances with post-heroic leadership, post-industrial leadership, and post-hierarchical leadership—see Joseph C. Rost, *Leadership for the 21st Century* (Westport, CT: Praeger, 1993); Ronald A. Heifetz and Donald L. Laurie, 'The Work of Leadership', *Harvard Business Review*, January/February 1997:124–34; Mary Uhl-Bien, 'Relational Leadership Theory: Exploring the Social Processes of Leadership and Organizing', *The Leadership Quarterly*, 17(6) December 2006: 654–76; David Woodward, 'Enterprise 2.0: Social Workers', *Director Magazine*, August 2008; Stephen Linstead, Liz Fulop, and Simon Lilley, *Management and Organization: A Critical Text*, 2nd edn. (Basingstoke: Palgrave Macmillan, 2009), ch. 10; Warren Bennis, *On Becoming a Leader* (New York, NY: Basic Books, 2009), chs. 2, 8; Richard Bolden, Beverley Hawkins, Jonathan Gosling, and Scott Taylor, *Exploring Leadership: Individual, Organizational and Societal Perspectives* (Oxford: Oxford University Press, 2011); Rachel E. Silverman, 'Who's the Boss? There Isn't One', *Wall Street Journal*, 19 June 2012; James M. Kouzes and Barry Z. Posner, *The Leadership Challenge: How to Make Extraordinary Things Happen in Organizations*, 5th edn. (San Francisco, CA: Jossey-Bass, 2012), chs. 8, 9.

penetrated the nature of political activity over the past twenty-five years, but have actively reaffirmed the centrality of leadership in politics. Notwithstanding the serial impulses towards deregulation, privatization, and a diminished state, political leaders and leadership in Western liberal societies have to a growing extent become part of a convergent culture in which the categories of business and politics are less susceptible to clear differentiation. It is in this way that the organization and framing of political life have come increasingly to be structured in terms of the extent to which individual leaders are projected and assessed in terms of a contextual fit in relation to those agendas and methods considered compatible with a competitive market.

THE MARKETING OF POLITICAL LEADERSHIP

Given the cultural impact of neoliberal precepts over the past quarter of a century, it would have been difficult for responsive types of political leadership to immunize themselves from such a major shift in attitudes and operational norms. As it is, political leaders and their organizations have tended if anything to embrace the new economic order and to assimilate its doctrines within the remit of their own leadership modes. This convergence into an increasingly standardized culture of explanatory doctrines and socio-economic priorities fed directly not only into the construction of political agendas and reform programmes but also into the more conventional areas of leadership activity and organization. The business-centred cult of professionalized leadership has continued to influence the way that political leaders perceive their social and political role and to shape their strategies in the acquisition and maintenance of their positions.

Probably the most conspicuous impact of business models and techniques upon the operation of leadership has come in the sphere of political marketing. Increasingly, professional specialists have been employed to devise, refine, and promote the branding of actual or potential leaders within what is conceived as a political market. In many advanced industrialized countries, the working assumption has become one of appealing to electorates that have become significantly more de-aligned in terms of party attachments and therefore more fluid, discriminating, and independent in respect to political choices. As a consequence, the operating rationale has in many cases become one of translating the concepts and techniques associated with market positioning in the business sector directly to the tasks of product identity, brand alignment, and active promotion in the political sphere.[48]

---

[48] Nicholas O'Shaughnessy and Stephan C. Henneberg, 'The Selling of the President 2004: A Marketing Perspective', *Journal of Public Affairs*, 7(3) August 2007: 249–88; Catherine Needham, 'Brand Leaders: Clinton, Blair and the Limitations of the Permanent Campaign', *Political Studies*, 53(2) June 2005: 343–61; Heather Savigny, 'Focus Groups and Political Marketing: Science and Democracy as Axiomatic?', *British Journal of Politics and International Relations*, 9(1) February 2007: 122–37; Robert P. Ormrod, 'Political Market Orientation and Its Commercial Cousin: Close Family or Distant Relatives?', *Journal of Political Marketing*, 6(2/3) 2007: 69–90; Heather Savigny, *The Problem of Political Marketing* (London: Continuum International, 2008); Viv Groskop, 'Brand Me!', *New Statesman*, 11 August 2008; Heather Savigny, 'Political Marketing', in Matthew Flinders, Andrew Gamble,

The devices used by political organizations to achieve a positive relationship between themselves and the configurations of the political market are many and diverse. They can include the adoption of sophisticated forms of market research, policy development, product presentation, news output, and electoral coordination. These in turn can involve the extensive usage of opinion polling companies, focus group intelligence sources, media relations specialists, and a host of various political consultants providing strategic and operational guidance on product design, projection, targeting, and impact. Within this environment, both the logic and the terminology are geared explicitly to the notion that different political organizations and leaders coexist in a competitive setting in which resources have to be devised and deployed to their optimal effect in order to claim and to retain the maximum market share of consumer confidence and attachment—at the direct expense of other participants.

The electoral impact attributed to what have become increasingly sophisticated and professionalized forms of political management has had the effect of creating an elite corps of strategists with portfolios of effective campaigns in policy design, message management, and marketing intelligence. These consultants can move seamlessly across from commercial to political sectors depending upon their market value to campaigns and other communication strategies. Their reputation for expert service delivery allows them to be regarded as essentially agents for hire in which political organizations are accepted in the same way as any other client. Within this field, the controlling premises are (i) that the technical and strategic skills which specialists have developed in a business setting are directly applicable to political contexts; and (ii) that because political markets are not seen as substantially different from their commercial counterparts they are by extension susceptible to the particular competences of business sector consultants. It is certainly the case that these kinds of provision are run on business lines in which specialist agencies offer their services to clients on a professional basis rather than on any particular attachment to the political 'product' in question. This can lead to individual or group specialists being hired for a variety of different forms of political intelligence gathering, marketing operations, or promotional exercises on behalf of separate clients.

Specialist agencies like the Sawyer Miller Group, Weber Shandwick Public Affairs, WPP, the Public Affairs Network, FM Consultants, and Bell Pottinger Public Affairs offer a range of bespoke services relating to programme and project management in the field of strategic communications and public relations. Their services range from campaign methods advice, media management, market monitoring, and public positioning to advocacy techniques, intelligence sourcing, profile branding, message development, events organization, contact facilitation, and the management of access to key personnel. The expertise developed through corporate clients, business groups, and trade associations are simply regarded as transferable skills that are equally applicable to political parties, candidate campaigns, government agencies, issue advocacy groups, and leadership organizations. These multiple sector and multiple client agencies are also adept at

Colin Hay, and Michael Kenny (eds.), *The Oxford Handbook of British Politics* (Oxford: Oxford University Press, 2009), pp. 798–817.

projecting their services outside their home bases and in essence acting as transnational operatives by servicing clients in other countries with different political systems and traditions.[49]

Such is the appeal of the market ethos and the remit of its influence that political marketing in many arenas has been transformed into an altogether more systematized alignment with the logic of consumer-driven models. Originally, political marketing used to be generally confined to issues of promoting and advertising an electorally marketable product based upon either a clear set of policies or a more traditional set of social attachments. More recently, marketing in this area has tended to progress towards a much more market-oriented business model. In this form of marketing, the emphasis is placed less on a fixed product or on its simple projection through advertising channels. The focus is more on responsiveness to changing consumer demands in order to maximize the chances of generating new bases of intuitive long-term loyalty. In the sector of political marketing, this model maps on to campaigns that seek to establish a continuing organic relationship between the producers and consumers—i.e. between policy-making organizations and those whose support they seek to attract.

In more advanced liberal democratic states with their generally more fluid electoral attachments, the trend has been away from the simplicity of earlier models of mobilizing the core vote or of pursuing a conventional sales campaign, and towards a market-sensitive operation based on in-depth intelligence and rapid reaction techniques. Darren Lilleker and Ralph Negrine describe the dynamic and the logic of a process that has seen consumer-based marketing techniques migrate into the political sphere:

> Just as commercial marketers are interested in discovering how to satisfy consumers' sophisticated needs, so too are political strategists, party managers and policy designers; and in order to fulfil those needs, it is vital to involve consumers in the design of the product, as well as the design of associated communication. As such ideas are institutionalised within an organisation's working practice, it begins to adopt a market-orientation toward all its activities.[50]

Jennifer Lees-Marshment agrees that political marketing has shifted away from previous models towards a more focused adoption of business techniques and concepts related to market intelligence, product design, and consumer satisfaction priorities. It is not that political parties and leaders have dismissed the earlier emphases upon the political product or the means by which it is sold. It is that these elements have been joined by, and in some cases superseded by, a drive towards a market-oriented operation that depends upon a continual engagement with supporters and voters.[51]

---

[49] See James Harding, *Alpha Dogs: The Americans Who Turned Political Spin into a Global Business* (New York, NY: Farrar, Straus & Giroux, 2008).

[50] Darren Lilleker and Ralph Negrine, 'Mapping a Market Orientation: Can We Detect Political Marketing Only Through the Lens of Hindsight?' in Philip J. Davies and Bruce I. Newman (eds.), *Winning Elections with Political Marketing* (Binghamton, NY: Haworth Press, 2006), pp. 33–4.

[51] Jennifer Lees-Marshment, *Political Marketing and British Political Parties: The Party's Just Begun* (Manchester: Manchester University Press, 2001), ch. 1; Jennifer Lees-Marshment, *The Political Marketing Revolution* (Manchester: Manchester University Press, 2004); Jennifer Lees-Marshment, *Political Marketing: Principles and Applications* (Abingdon: Routledge, 2009). See also Margaret

While there remains some debate over the full extent to which major parties and key campaigns have moved to this kind of operation, what is clear is the way that leaders have become central to this developing mode of marketing. In what is an increasingly complex operation of communication and outreach, it is leaders who not only provide the defining identity of the brand to be promoted, but also the focal point of responsibility for drawing together a team of specialists capable of devising and managing an ongoing bespoke engagement with the target audiences. Leaders in this environment are often judged as much by their record in identifying, assembling, and managing their own marketing strategies as by their positions on policy or their governing experience. The operational logic of engaging in such a political environment suggests far more than an analogy with business categories and practices. The resonances with market-oriented business models are very strong as the terms and techniques associated with this kind of linkage have seamlessly migrated to a political market. It is a matrix that has become increasingly segmented into ever more sophisticated units of analysis which in turn offer greater benefits to those who can both signify and organize those campaigns that can generate a competitive edge in a context of ever finer margins of calculated gain.

TWO CULTURES IN ONE?

Political marketing may be one of the most conspicuous business-related influences on the definition and projection of leadership in many systems but it is by no means the only one. The policy prescriptions and scale of values associated with what might be termed the enterprise culture represent another significant dimension in the political environment of contemporary leadership. Also noteworthy is the penetration of business vocabulary into the language of political exchange. This relates to the usage of key terms not merely as forms of rhetorical licence or as illustrative analogies but also as direct and immediate terms of political relevance. Whether it is the categorization of public services as social investment, or the extension of business-grounded markets into depictions of a social market, or the reconfiguration of political-civil relations into partnerships of providers on the one side and consumers and clients on the other, the neoliberal parameters of political legitimacy confer a conditioning influence upon both the terminology and character of leadership positioning. The predominance of the business and enterprise paradigm constitutes not just a conditioning influence upon the language and conduct of politics, but a medium within which political and business leaders share a common basis of social attachments and policy preferences.

Scammell, *Designer Politics: How Elections are Won* (London: Macmillan, 1995); Margaret Scammell, 'Political Marketing: Lessons for Political Science', *Political* Studies, 47(4) September 1999: 718–39; Philip Gould, *The Unfinished Revolution* (London: Little, Brown, 1998); Paul Baines and Richard Lynch, 'The Context, Content and Process of Political Marketing Strategy', *Journal of Political Marketing*, 4 (2/3) 2005: 1–18.

A particularly significant feature of this increased commonality is the rise in the number and scale of those occasions when business and political leaders meet and interact together in an atmosphere of comparable social standing and mutual interest. These exchanges take place in a variety of different forums. Some will take the form of private consultations while others will be part of an open and public gathering. Notwithstanding the specifics of the medium, the rationale is almost invariably one of projected or actual synergy between two sectors which through an increasingly active process of aggregation is becoming one of a common leadership identity. Under the transformative aegis of neoliberal and market imperatives, economic and political leaders have to a growing extent become part of a homogeneous culture of market managerialism. The deepening proximity of leaders from previously differentiated realms of activity has not simply been a sign of an improved state of coexistence but rather an indication of an assimilative development towards a largely unchallenged *de facto* convergence of hierarchies.

The net effect in many contemporary political systems is one in which CEOs and leading political figures not only increasingly come to occupy the same physical and cultural spaces, but signify the extent to which the business and political sectors are seen as genuinely overlapping spheres of activity, legitimacy, and purpose. As such, leaders become the primary means by which these different centres of activity are progressively drawn together in the complex matrices of multilevel and multi-sectoral governance. It is now commonplace for major issues to be discussed, debated, and appraised by business and political leaders either in public forums, or else in more restricted locations but nevertheless with some forms of wider access (e.g. World Economic Forum).

The mutual transposing of roles through a medium of leadership convergences also occurs within government itself. The onset of neoliberal principles in conjunction with the conditions of globalization and market-based states has led to a steady rise not just in the development of network-based arrangements of multilevel governance but also in the decreasing differentiation between the public and private spheres within society.[52] The net effect is that while traditional or formal hierarchies are seen to be experiencing a process of erosion, they are replaced by a more complex and mercurial matrix of economic and political elites that allow not just for greater volumes of exchange but for an increasing dissonance of clearly assigned contexts of leadership roles. These processes have been variously characterized as representing the privatization of the public sphere; or a form of new corporatism in which economic statecraft operates under the cover of apparent depoliticization; or a type of cultural hegemony that sanctions the marketization of everyday life as a self-evident aspect of an immutable natural order.[53] Whatever

---

[52] R. A. W. Rhodes, *Understanding Governance: Policy Networks, Governance, Reflexivity and Accountability* (Buckingham: Open University Press, 1997), chs. 2, 3; Stephen Goldsmith and William D. Eggers, *Governing by Network: The New Shape of the Public Sector* (Washington, DC: Brookings Institution, 2004).

[53] Will Hutton, *The State We're In: Why Britain Is in Crisis and How to Overcome It*, rev. edn. (London: Vintage, 1996); 'The New Establishment: A New Corporatism', *The Economist*, 12 August 1999; Peter Burnham, 'New Labour and the Politics of Depoliticisation', *British Journal of Politics & International Relations*, 3(2) June 2001: 127–49; Dan Coffey and Carole Thornley, *Globalization and Varieties of Capitalism: New Labour, Economic Policy and the Abject State* (Basingstoke: Palgrave

the interpretation, the net effect has been one in which business leaders have a wider remit to engage openly with government and enjoy strong legitimacy claims to being acknowledged as an integral part of its operation.

In the UK, for example, it is noteworthy that New Labour distanced itself from the Labour Party's traditions of socialist antagonism towards the capitalist model and sought to achieve a reconfiguration of social democracy along the lines of an enterprise culture and an infusion of wealth creation through deregulated markets. Business leaders were not merely tolerated but welcomed as an integral feature of New Labour's signature objective of modernization.[54] Tony Blair established a profusion of task forces and advisory groups to provide policy reviews and to prepare the ground for policy innovations. It has been estimated that in the first year of his premiership, approximately 350 business leaders were absorbed into the government's advisory structures. Moreover, Blair was quite prepared to privilege the need for business acumen and organizational experience over the claims of his elected MPs in the search for professional competence at high levels of government. Accordingly, private sector leaders like Sir David Simon, Sir David Sainsbury, and Gus Macdonald were given significant minister- ial responsibilities at the outset of Blair's premiership.

Ten years later, the culture of business expertise had become firmly embedded in Labour administrations with a regular injection of private sector leaders in advisory and ministerial roles as well as streams of consultancies, partnerships, and transfers. When Gordon Brown succeeded Blair as prime minister in 2007, one of his initiatives was to launch a scheme entitled a 'government of all the talents' which saw a new tranche of leaders from the commercial, financial, and industrial sectors enter government departments in senior positions. While the declared rationale had been to widen the talent pool available to government ministries, there was little doubt as to which pool of talent was identified as the primary source of prime ministerial interest.

Private sector skills and experience were considered to be premium value assets. Accordingly, major figures in this area received the call to transpose their leadership abilities to government without the normal qualifying requirements of a pre-existing seat in parliament, or even a semblance of a standard political apprenticeship.

Invitees included Sir Digby Jones who was appointed minister of state for trade and investment at the Department for Business and Enterprise. Jones had been Director General of the Confederation of British Industry (2001–6). When he was appointed he was acting as a senior adviser to such major concerns as Barclays Capital, Ford, Deloitte, and JCB. Other business figures who featured in Brown's administration were Paul Myners at the Treasury; Paul Drayson as minister of science; Stephen Carter as minister for communications, technology and broad- casting; and Sir Alan Sugar who was ennobled as a member of the House of Lords

Macmillan, 2009); Will Hutton, *Them And Us: Changing Britain—Why We Need a Fair Society* (London: Little, Brown, 2010), chs. 1, 2, 6, 7.

[54] Colin Hay, *The Political Economy of New Labour* (Manchester: Manchester University Press, 1999); 'The New Establishment: A New Corporatism', *The Economist*, 12 August 1999; David Osler, *Labour Party Plc: The Truth behind New Labour as a Party of Business* (Edinburgh: Mainstream Publishing, 2002); Stuart Hall, 'New Labour's Double-Shuffle', *Soundings*, 24, July 2003, pp. 10–24.

at the same time as becoming an adviser to the Brown administration on business enterprise.[55] The trend line of seconding notable figures from the private sector into government has continued under David Cameron's premiership—most notably with the businessman Lord Young becoming the new 'enterprise csar' in 2010 and the fashion and retail entrepreneur Mary Portas hired to conduct a review for the government into the future landscape of UK high streets.

This close relationship between business and politics at the leadership level should not be conceived in the simple terms of a convergence of sectors. It is a more nuanced development than that. It relies upon physical and professional proximity; an emergent comparability of role specifications; and the high value that is placed upon the functional element of leadership in setting and achieving objectives. Leaders in both sectors regularly frequent the same habitats of personal and social interaction. They are also the recipients of similar levels of status and responsibility which are attributed to their positions as sources of organizational competence, managerial reassurance, social guidance, and personal vision.

Their occupation of similar physical and cultural spaces, combined with their reputational resources for shaping agendas, exerting strategic influence, and assuming responsibility for organizational direction means that CEOs and political leaders increasingly generate synergies between one another that have considerable social consequences. Not the least of these is the growing dynamic of leaders migrating between what are ostensibly different organizational spheres and separate public roles. In doing so, they have the effect of dissolving the lines of differentiation that have normally characterized the relationship between them. The effects of this sociology of leadership interplay can be seen not just in the influence of business people and practices in government but also in the way that businesses adopt norms usually associated with the principles, procedures, and functions of representative government. The latter is evidenced by the adoption of codes of corporate governance, an emphasis upon transparency and due diligence, and the widespread subscription to the obligations of corporate social responsibility.

CONCLUSION

The proposition that business and politics operate in two quite distinct spheres is still a view which retains some validity. Differences do exist in terms of the formal bases of authority and in relation to many of their operational functions. Nevertheless, it is equally the case that the boundaries between the sectors have become increasingly indistinct as governments search for ever greater and faster ways to fulfil their obligations in the most efficient and cost-effective ways possible. Just as they have become more attentive to various market-driven initiatives, so they have assimilated numerous business and commercial practices in the organization of

---

[55] Richard Wray, 'Brown convenes economic "war cabinet" to help UK through credit crunch', *Guardian*, 3 October 2008; 'PM creates economic council', Civil Service Live Network, 3 October 2008. Accessed 27 July 2012 at: <http://network.civilservicelive.com/pg/pages/view/262545/pm-creates-economic-council>.

the public sector. Governments in many parts of the world are now expected to be comparable to the private sector in ensuring required objectives and targets are met through the establishment of incentive structures, devolved management, and increased agency autonomy.

The values of innovation, agility, efficiency, and delivery are no longer confined to the financial, industrial, and commercial spheres of activity. As we have observed, one of the most significant and conspicuous strands in this cultural convergence has been the conspicuous allusions to the indispensability of leaders in establishing strategic direction and organizational performance within their respective areas of responsibility. In both sectors, the positional predicaments and expectations of leaders and leadership have become part of an increasingly common code of organizational existence. This pertains to an altogether deeper level of proximity than the more conventional forms of corporatist interdependency between business and government that feature links ranging from subsidies, loans, and procurement contracts to 'revolving door' arrangements where senior government officials retire to corporate boardrooms. The more advanced types of proximity rely less on the incidence of transfers and more on a process of osmosis that reconfigures the difference to one of an ongoing continuum based upon comparable currencies of perspective, discourse, and social intercourse.

As we will see in Chapter 11, the consequences of this process of conflated identities and functional mergers can reach as far as the international level and the matrices of global governance. What is important to note at this point is that the ascribed roles and functions of leadership increasingly transcend boundaries—not least between business and politics. Leadership is a business in its own right in the corporate world but it is equally seen as a business-related function in the political sphere. Leaders and leadership are considered to be both the symbols and the agencies of a concerted drive towards improved problem recognition, more creative use of resources, higher levels of responsiveness, greater strategic awareness, better instruments of delivery, and the means by which to acquire optimum solutions. As leadership becomes more synonymous with 'can do' leaders operating in flexible and often unbounded conditions, so the behaviour and remit of these leaders are increasingly coming to be associated with a trend towards more fluid and interchangeable conceptions of the public and private elements of social existence.

7

Representation, communication, and the politics of 'leadership stretch'

'I am a man who belongs to no one and who belongs to everyone.'

President Charles de Gaulle[1]

'In recent months, in Moscow and in the regions, I sensed your understanding and support. Often, ordinary people said a few simple words to me which were very important to me. They said "We believe in you, we are counting on you. Do not betray us." ... My sacred duty is to bring together the Russian people, unite the people around clear tasks. We have one Fatherland, one people and a common future.'

President Vladimir Putin[2]

PREAMBLE

The relational element of leadership has become an almost commonplace observation in this investigation of the topic. What is far less clear is the nature of the composition and operation of these relationships. Chapter 5 alluded to this theme in its negative guise when leaderships falter and decline as a result of failing relationships between themselves and their constituencies. This chapter seeks to examine the key relationships that effective leaders not only depend upon but manage to exploit to their benefit. At the heart of the inquiry lie the themes of representation and communication. Leaderships are conspicuously reliant upon establishing a representational linkage between themselves and forms of social and cultural value. It is usually imperative for leaders to be highly attentive to the origins, sources, and usages of these connections. It is equally the case that they have to be able to cultivate these representational logics in the service of another form of relationship: namely the linkage between leaders and an expansive volume of non-leaders. An integral part of leadership entails the need to impart itself outwards to a receiving audience—whether they be subjects, citizens, co-participants, electorates, or publics. In essence, leadership status and authority have to be conveyed to others.

---

[1] Remarks at a presidential press conference, 19 May 1958.
[2] Excerpt from Vladimir Putin's Presidential Inauguration Speech, 7 May 2000. Accessed 27 October 2012 at: <http://archive.newsmax.com/articles/?a=2000/5/7/111609>.

When this is done effectively, it enhances the initial claims of rightful leadership. It is possible for a virtuous circle of relational symmetry to be completed at the point when the reactions to leadership choices and decisions become fused with a positive construction of the leadership's claims to representational legitimacy.

The subject area of representation and communication may be central to the study of leadership but it is also a complex and problematic field. It raises several conceptual and empirical questions that are central to any analysis of leaders and leadership. For example, whatever leadership may be conceived to be it will always be necessary for that property to be carried from one point to another in order for any conception of leadership to be complete. The act of leadership involves a process of transmission and reception. Whether this is seen as primarily a cause-and-effect relationship, or as an exchange mechanism, the functional status of any leadership is closely aligned to the requirement of conveyance. An intrinsic analogue of leadership, therefore, is at the same time something separate from it and yet also an obligation laid upon it. Leaders are expected to have consequences far removed from their immediate presence. In one respect, leaders are required to close the gap between themselves and those who are not in leadership positions. But in another way, they also have to retain the gap in order to preserve their status as leaders. The challenge of simultaneously fulfilling the necessary conditions of both detachment and attachment raises a number of demanding questions—not least the issue of what the gap is and how it is both cultivated and diminished.

Another highly problematic factor in this field centres upon the nature of the relationship between the source of a leader's authority and the substance of the decisions and choices made and subsequently disseminated by reference to that authority. In other words, there are many fine distinctions that exist between a leader's derivative authority based upon fulfilling a prescribed foundational position and a more idiosyncratic status based upon individual skills in making effective appeals and evoking designated responses. On occasions the latter can conflict with the more institutionalized character of the former. But it is far from being a clear dichotomy. Most successful leaders recognize that the two elements can be mutually advantageous and as a consequence work to fuse them together into a closer alliance. As they do so, the conflation poses a series of questions over which element may be serving the other. In centring the focus upon himself or herself, a leader may appear to be engaging in a personalized form of political appeal that might be interpreted as contrary to the more established or formal arrangements of leadership legitimacy. On the other hand, just such an appeal might also be claimed to be underwriting and reaffirming the original allocation of authority and ensuring that its reach remains intact. In essence, a leader as an effective communicator might be considered to be less of an iconoclast and more of a consolidator than his or her reputation might at first suggest. This difference in perspective can offer insights but it can also generate a host of interpretive challenges over what precisely is being set in motion.

These and other questions, together with the significance that can be attached to them, will become increasingly evident as the chapter progresses. What is important to note is that just as the exercise of leadership can generally be considered to be a highly dynamic subject, so the same can be said for its analysis. The character of the subject matter and the necessary manner of its observation are particularly applicable to this particular area of analysis which focuses on how leadership is conveyed; how its resources are related to its projection; and how its transmission can evoke responses.

REPRESENTATION

The claims and operationalization of leadership are usually heavily dependent upon some interpretation of a representative role undertaken by the individual leader. The position, status, and function of a leader almost invariably involve some aspect of representation both as an originating source of authority but also as a continuing theme of the day-to-day praxis of leadership within a political community. The functional logic of leadership can seem to be self-evidently based upon the idea of a singular and concentrated focal position of political standing that is only sustainable through some foundational claim to representation. And it is indeed the case that leaders normally assert that they have representational responsibilities towards some other feature, or features, of the political landscape. Representation in this context can appear to be a clear depiction of the relational character of leadership.

In one sense, representation and leadership can be seen to be two mutually inclusive concepts in which leaders are construed as both epitomizing the flow and force of representational arrangements, whilst clarifying the operational rationale of representation's logic of political transmission. In short, the unity of a singular leader can offer the prospect of a tangible expression of a unified conception of representation. However, this would be something of a false prospectus not least because representation is a concept that is one of the least susceptible to a unified definition. On the contrary, representation is not only associated with multiple and contested meanings, but is further distinguished by the concept's capacity to generate contradictory conclusions. As a consequence, numerous empirical and normative debates have arisen over the conditions, character, and purpose of representative claims and processes.[3]

The analyses of the nature and meaning of representation have produced a profusion of insights into what can be portrayed as a representative relationship. In the more formal constructions, representation tends to be regarded as something approximating to a one-to-one relationship between a principal party and an agency that has been authorized to act on behalf of the former. This enabling process can operate under a range of different conditions and expectations leading to a variety of types, bases, and levels of representation—along with their own specifications of responsiveness and accountability. In the more critical and revisionist studies of the subject, representation is recast less as a single strand and more as an aggregate process operating through the systemic properties of an organization. In her classic exposition on the subject, Hannah Pitkin underlined

---

[3] Samuel H. Beer, *Modern British Politics* (London: Faber and Faber, 1969); A. H. Birch, *Representation* (New York, NY: Praeger, 1972); Hanna Pitkin, *The Concept of Representation* (Berkeley, CA: University of California Press, 1972); Bernard Manin, *The Principles of Representative Government* (Cambridge: Cambridge University Press, 1997).

the plural and contingent nature of representation by analysing the way that different usages of the concept are invoked in political practice. The delineated variations between 'formalistic', 'symbolic', 'descriptive', and 'substantive' types of representation are considered by Pitkin to operate according to different premises. Furthermore, they have different corollaries in their patterns of usage and, as such, they generate quite separate criteria of evaluation and suggest notably different analytical agendas.[4]

The attribution and exercise of political leadership have close associations with the concepts and claims of representation. Political leaders often act as key reference points and illustrative cases in analyses on representation. Leadership issues not only draw upon debates on various themes of representation, but offer valuable points of access to complex issues surrounding the premises and operation of representative processes. However, while the foundations and claims of political leadership can have a connection with the conceptual and operational aspects of representation, the exact nature of that relationship is far from clear. It is evident that many properties associated with leadership have resonances with issues and themes rooted in representation. It can even be said that the nature of political leadership compels an active engagement with channels and devices that are representative in their origins and effect. Nevertheless, it is equally the case that the precise conjunction of these two themes remains highly mutable and at times quite unstable. The different ways in which political leaders can be dependent upon claims to representative legitimacy but also be in a position to shape and deploy those claims to their own advantage are integral parts of the creative repertoire of effective political leadership. Some illustrative aspects of this complex synergy will now be considered.

Just as political leadership suggests a focal centre of organizing power within a polity, so a monarchical structure of leadership provision can serve to exemplify not only the claims of such a systemic authority but also the expansive basis of its presumptions of representation. In this pre-modern sense, representation was, and still remains in many areas, a property based upon a religious or mystical claim to monarchical authority. A king or queen—emperor or empress—would justify their roles in terms of their ascribed roles as agents or instruments of a divine power. The logic of such a representative position supported a summative status that could be deployed as analogous to the absolute and transcendent position of a deity.

The imperial system in China, for example, conferred the title of 'Son of Heaven' upon the emperor. This incorporated the concept known as the 'mandate of heaven' which afforded the emperor a ruling position over everyone else in the world on the basis that imperial commands were representations of sacred authority. Another iteration of this kind of presumptive representation was visible in the reign of Louis XIV of France. A defining depiction of this absolutist monarchy was the Greek and Roman deity Apollo which was used to symbolize the reach and purpose of the king in terms of cosmic significance. In mythology, Apollo was the god of light and sun as well as truth. Louis portrayed himself as occupying an equivalent position in the realm of France. The 'Sun King' was

---

[4] Pitkin, *The Concept of Representation*.

depicted as the central point of the kingdom evoking not merely enlightenment and vitality but a symbolic axis around which the courts, nobles, and people revolved. Similar motifs of divinely inspired absolutism were used by the Russian czars. Enormous significance was given to the symbolic value of icons in respect to their representational force in which the depictions of religious subjects were intimately associated with the ascribed divinity of the czars. On occasions, the sacred and the political were literally combined with visual references to individual czars being included in the portraiture itself. Under the communist regime, the cultural traction of the icon tradition was simply appropriated by Soviet leaders for their own political purposes—thus establishing comparable personality cults through the ubiquitous usage of iconic portraits of Lenin and Stalin in both public and private spaces.

In both cases, the literal representation of the divine on earth was the defining instrument of the leadership positions and the grandeur of the jurisdictional remit that went with them. The term 'absolutism' was both a quantitative measure of their power and also a qualitative characterization of their power source. In this context, the singularity of God was necessarily conveyed on earth by the representative singularity of monarchy. The dynamic was circular in nature. Just as it was in the monarch's interest to promote popular attachments to the deity in question, so the claims of divinity in respect to monarchical power could be secured through the continued legitimacy of a world view towards the universe that placed God—or the gods—in direct contact with a temporal ruler.

One major difficulty with such a system was that the integrity of such an attributed chain of being with a divine presence at its apex could be compromised by more earthly disputes and counterclaims concerning the rightful place and proper conduct of a monarch. Monarchs had to ensure that they were always in a position to displace other claimants to the throne. They needed to remind their subjects of the authenticity of their regal position, the exceptional social value of their presence on the throne, and the disruption that could be caused by other attachments. Tradition and continuity could be very effective instruments in support of a monarch's regal claims because they offered a supplementary form of representational status.

But these properties could also be turned against their customary beneficiaries. Opponents of a particular monarch could contest the occupancy of the throne on representational grounds. It could be claimed that a king or queen had broken with the traditions of his or her forebears and therefore with the spirit of divine lineage. This could lead to a monarch resorting to a fundamentalist claim of divine representation confronting others asserting that the throne implied a representative obligation towards the evolved traditions and laws of the society—as well as the settled rights and privileges of other estates within the realm. In effect, a sovereign had to adjust to the idea of operating within a sovereign kingdom.[5]

---

[5] The clashes between these two forms of sovereign authority are epitomized in the jurisdictional and institutional disputes leading to the English Civil War (1642–9). For commentaries on the early seventeenth-century context in which claims of crown authority confronted settled patterns of legal tradition, common law precedent, and parliamentary practice, see John P. Kenyon, *The Stuart Constitution: Documents and Commentary* (Cambridge: Cambridge University Press, 1966); J. G. A. Pocock, *The Ancient Constitution and the Feudal Law: A Study of English Historical Thought in the Seventeenth*

Conflicts between these two realms were, and still remain, transformative in effect. They have led to many regal thrones either becoming progressively constrained into constitutional monarchies, or alternatively removed altogether in a revolutionary drive for representative modernization.

There remain many examples of retained royal houses in the world today. The successful ones still exercise powerful leadership roles based upon their positions in traditional social hierarchies and upon their ability to fuse their own status with strong narratives on security needs and national identities. In the main, the processes of modernity have led increasingly to legitimacy in political representation being afforded broader categories of participants as well as to more immediate and more secular bases of representational relationships. Sometimes these conceptions of representation are based upon a plurality of communities and interests. On other occasions, the emphasis is placed more on class attachments and mass parties. In the main, however, political representation has come to be intimately associated with the values, operations, and constructions of democracy. Whether representative government is seen as being a derivative or a direct expression of popular opinions and choices, the foundational and organizational logic of a democratic polity rests with the value assigned to the principle of responsiveness to a fully enfranchised public and, with it, the sanction of specified accountability for the record of governance. Within this flatter political landscape, the position and role of political leadership become more ambiguous and even anomalous.

Given democracy's association with such concepts as civic equality, self-rule, and popular consent, political leaders operating within a democratic framework are confronted with a series of problems related to the implications of distance, hierarchy, and power. Democracies can foster claims relating to the legitimacy of other political participants based upon their more proximate connections with the originating source of democratic authority. They are also known to regard the effective restrictions upon concentrations of power as the key credentials of an effective polity and the defining features of a just political order.[6] At first sight, political leadership would appear to be compromised by the democratic exigencies of modernity—including as they do references to due process, constitutional checks and balances, electoral deterrence, the rule of law, and a pluralistic distribution of political resources. Nevertheless, leadership has generally remained not merely a viable component of democratic governance but a valued instrument of its adaptability. Far from being a handicap, the theme of representation has in fact offered leaders an influential source of relief from the more exacting conditions of democratic levelling.

Century (New York, NY: Norton, 1967); Michael Foley, *The Silence of Constitutions: Gaps, 'Abeyances' and Political Temperament in the Maintenance of Government* (London: Routledge, 1989), pp. 15–34.

  [6] See Walter F. Murphy, 'Constitutions, Constitutionalism, and Democracy', in Douglas Greenberg, Stanley N. Katz, Melanie B. Oliviero, and Steven C. Wheatley (eds.), *Constitutionalism and Democracy: Transitions in the Contemporary World* (New York, NY: Oxford University Press, 1993), pp. 3–23; Cass Sunstein, 'Constitutions and Democracies', in Jon Elster and Rune Slagstad (eds.), *Constitutionalism and Democracy* (Cambridge: Cambridge University Press, 1988), pp. 327–53; David Held, *Models of Democracy* (Cambridge: Polity Press, 2006), chs. 3, 9; John Keane, *The Life and Death of Democracy* (London: Simon & Schuster, 2009), pp. 159–373.

Political leaders in democratic states have been highly adept at harnessing the potential of representational idioms to counteract the anti-elitist rationales of some democratic narratives. In some cases, leaders have been the beneficiaries of an impulse for historical or traditional continuities to be embodied by representational figures in government. Many modern states that categorize themselves as democracies are in fact states that have undergone a process of gradual or accelerated democratization in which key features of the state are reconfigured but which remain in existence—albeit under different organizing principles.[7] Democratic leaders have not usually relinquished an opportunity to occupy or co-opt the executive prerogatives of a previous order in the name of representative authenticity. Presidents and prime ministers habitually allude to their representative roles. They are cited as being representative of a governmental process that whatever its basis of authority has ultimately to produce a form of functional and operational government. Leaders are normally drawn to the Burkean interpretation of representation which privileges the contribution of reason, reflection, perspective, and judgement on the part of representatives over the claims of uninformed and unreflective preferences or opinions of those who are more inclined to give priority to their immediate interests rather than to the national or public interest.[8]

Another linkage to the representative ethos comes in the form of the electoral process itself which while facilitating the provision of multiple representatives and sub-system leaders also carries with it the logic of an aggregated structure of representation from which prime ministers and presidents emerge. It is even the case that electoral systems are widely evaluated from the perspective of the extent to which they can generate effective governance in the shape of an administration represented by a clearly identifiable leadership to which is attributed a direct representational connection to a wider social or national entity. In France, for example, if no candidate in a presidential election secures more than 50 per cent of the vote, there follows a run-off election between the top two candidates. The outcome of the ensuing election will always assure the winner of receiving over 50 per cent of the vote, thereby allowing the successful candidate to claim a representative position within a national constituency. The United States has another device that translates the popular vote into a medium which almost without exception produces a definitive winner with substantive claims to electoral legitimacy (Box 7.1).

Other democratic systems find different ways of constructing leadership hierarchies from notionally non-hierarchical materials. Sometimes it is a case of organizationally facilitating the emergence of strong leadership positions from the aggregative effect of complex patterns of minor elections. At other times, leadership legitimacy is afforded by electoral devices that amplify winning

---

[7] Arend Lijphart, *Patterns of Democracy: Government Forms and Performance in Thirty-Six Countries* (New Haven, CT: Yale University Press, 1999); Held, *Models of Democracy*, chs. 5–10.

[8] Edmund Burke, 'Speech to the Electors of Bristol' (1774), in *Works*, Vol. 2, 95; Melissa S. Williams, 'Burkean "Descriptions" and Political Representation: A Reappraisal', *Canadian Journal of Political Science*, 29(1) March 1996: 23–45; Pitkin, *The Concept of Representation*, pp. 168–90; Samuel H. Beer, 'The Representation of Interests in British Government: Historical Background', *American Political Science Review*, 51(3) September 1957: 613–50.

Box 7.1 Representational grade inflation

The mediating role of the US Electoral College in expanding margins of victory

The United States has another device that translates the popular vote into a medium which almost without exception produces a definitive winner with substantive claims to electoral legitimacy. In this system, presidential elections are determined by the Electoral College in which a successful candidate has to secure a majority of 'electors' from each of the fifty states plus the District of Columbia (DC). The distribution of the current 538 members of the College is determined by the current combined number of seats in the US Congress allocated to each state. Given that the Electoral College is only very loosely based upon population density, and that the College votes are assigned to candidates on a winner-takes-all block basis within each state,* the final result is normally skewed to enlarge the winning margin of that candidate who secures more of the popular vote than the other contenders.

The system, however, can lead to gross distortions. On three occasions (i.e. presidential elections of 1876, 1888, and 2000), the Electoral College winner did not even secure a plurality of the national popular vote. On the whole, however, the system normally converts a marginal victory into a decisive outcome generating the finality and unity required for a key national office.

Selected examples:

- The 1980 Presidential Election:
  o Ronald Reagan won 50.8 per cent of the popular vote but secured 90.9 per cent of the Electoral College vote—i.e. *a positive distortion rate of 40.1 per cent.*

- The 1992 Presidential Election:
  o Bill Clinton won 43.0 per cent of the popular vote and yet secured 68.8 per cent of the Electoral College vote—i.e. *a positive distortion rate of 25.8 per cent.*

- The 2008 Presidential Election:
  o Barack Obama won 52.9 per cent of the popular vote but secured 67.8 per cent of the Electoral College vote—i.e. *a positive distortion rate of 14.9 per cent.*

---

* Two states (Nebraska and Maine) have recently changed their rules to allow for a more proportional distribution of the electors allocated to their respective states.

---

margins in order to create a representational effect that may be quite dispropor-tionate to the actual levels of support gained by the winning candidates. Either way, the intentional effect is to maximize the chances of producing an unambigu-ous leadership outcome that will give the winners considerable opportunities to offer themselves as unifying representatives of the public or nation at large. It is evident from the conduct of even advanced democracies that leadership positions are regarded as a high-value resource that must be secured through necessarily representative processes. While the democratic principle may be one of forming governments from the bottom up, it is important to note that the operative direction is still up, and that it is the representative assets of leaders within such a system which mark out the elevation.

The usage of representative processes by leaders can be instrumental in clarify-ing the political positions of respective leaders and in affording ways of organizing government structures in accordance with leadership interests. But this is not the same as saying that the precise relationship between political leadership and representation is itself clarified in the habitual claims of the former upon the latter. On the contrary, it can be argued that, in their pursuit of representational legitimacy, political leaders have very often confused and even compromised the theme rather than simplifying it within a political setting. A particularly problematic area, for example, centres upon the terms and conditions of representational claims in such a leadership context. Given that a person in a representative position necessarily represents something other than the individual representative, then the issue with political leaders relates to what is being claimed and on behalf of whom. A leader may speak and act for others under the aegis of a representational authority but in assuming such a role it raises issues of when and how such a position is legitimized. It also calls into question the point at which this authority is exceeded and how this jurisdictional line can be determined and acted upon in terms of practical politics.

Such issues give rise to others such as whether representation should be seen as a process of transference from one entity to another, or whether it is more accurate to see leadership as a way in which representation becomes something of a convergence, or a fusion, of categories and identities in which the rulers and the ruled become conflated together. Many leaders can and do define themselves—and operate—on the basis that they amount to an equivalence of that which they deem to represent or to embody. While some leaders will allude to themselves and their position as a derivative of the represented, others will develop the linkage into a much more organic relationship in which a leader and a public are interpreted as a mutually constituted unity that is exclusive and self-contained in nature. This has been the strategy of those leaders who have relied upon plebiscites and referenda as instruments of governance working thorough orchestrated appeals to popular legitimacy. In this representational scheme, an attributed source of authority can become merged into material and spiritual claims of leadership—and through it into a reconfigured form of authoritarian government by apparent consent. The rise of the Nazi regime in Germany, for example, was marked by the pivotal use of plebiscites to ratify the centralization of power in the figure of Adolf Hitler as the supreme representation of the German nation.[9]

Many other leaders have followed similar lines of authoritarian presumption. They have promoted their own status to inflated levels of representational value in order to consolidate and to extend their discretionary powers, and to establish one-party states along with the full panoply of repressive measures. Sustained references to their substantive and symbolic representation of nations, classes, ethnic identities, religious affiliations, and varieties of social and historical destinies have served the corporatist ambitions of innumerable political leaders. In general their purpose has been to construct an array of representational narratives in order to generate an aura of transcendent and unifying political leadership very often to compensate for the weaknesses either of their own political positions or the political stability of the systems in which they operate. The usage of representational

---

[9] The most notable use of this device was August 1934 when a Nazi-dominated plebiscite produced a massive demonstration of popular assent. Over 38 million Germans—i.e. 90.4 per cent of those voting—supported the proposition that Hitler should amalgamate the offices of Reich President and Reich Chancellor—thereby allowing him to command the full power of the state and in the process allow him to claim the completion of the Nazi revolution and the inception of a thousand-year Reich.

claims in the transfiguration of both themselves and their regimes has led many leaders to acquire forms of political settlement based on their ability to replace normal politics with an overarching medium of leadership centrality.

Ostensibly, political leadership in liberal democratic systems operates within altogether different environments. Apart from the fact that the liberal democratic ethos of responsive yet also limited and accountable government militates against the availability and usage of those measures of political control that are available to leaders in authoritarian regimes, the claims and remit of democratic leadership are continually mediated through forms of representation. The most conspicuous element in this framework of dependency is the electoral process which according to the logic of popular consent legitimizes the consequent government for a limited timescale until the next election. The issues surrounding the formation of leadership positions and the authority of the individuals occupying them are in many respects thought to be resolved through the grand organizational device of a controlling election.

In a formal sense, this may be true but it tends to overlook the large tracts of political time and space between elections when leaders can quickly become beleaguered by the challenges of an open and pluralistic environment in which political resources are widely distributed. In these cases, leaders cannot rest on the representational laurels of an election victory. Government invariably concerns the need to form alliances and to reach settlements with other centres of actual or potential power. Far from relying on electoral authority, a leader will have to supplement that authority and seek to extend its reach in order to secure any chance of achieving a form of effective governance. Even in liberal democracies, political leaders are dependent upon their skills and ingenuity in developing the meaning and currency of their claims to representation. In fact, it would be more accurate to state that leaderships in such systems have to be particularly mindful of the need for constant outreach and, thereby, for effective political communication.

COMMUNICATION

At a minimum, leadership always involves some element of communication. Even in terms solely of representation, leaders have to be able to convey what is being represented and how that representation is channelled through the leadership. The importance of communication to the function of leadership underlines the way that the value and leverage of representational authority are dependent upon a continuing process of assertion and corroboration. Notwithstanding the nominated basis of representation, a leader cannot afford to rely upon an abstract declaration of such a distinction or upon a singular event at a particular point in time. Leadership and what it represents have to have lasting value to achieve any effect. In order to protect its prominent status and to optimize its sphere of influence, a leadership has to ensure that its position is widely understood and recognized by those with whom a representational association is advanced. This means that leaders have to engage in ways both to achieve a heightened social consciousness of their rationale, and to sustain a durable connection between themselves and the subject of their representational narrative. In effect, leaders not only claim to represent a particular entity, but have to re-present themselves back to these particular sources of foundational origin. Both dimensions of this relationship require cultivated and persistent forms of communication.[10]

Leaderships that function within authoritarian systems—as well as authoritarian leaders that operate within weak and unstable systems—have devised a variety of ways by which to project their position upon their respective publics. Many of these techniques would be recognized by those tasked with projecting the status of monarchies and emperors in the past. Leadership is presented as a multiple signifier through which a leader is habitually identified with a series of positive associations and subconscious connections. This type of cognitive engineering can take the form of a visual and representational suggestion in which a leadership becomes linked to items of public consumption. It may be a leader's image ubiquitously displayed on public buildings, on government materials, or even upon banknotes and stamps. The propagation of a leadership's identity can be more indirect but no less insidious by recourse to associational devices. In these polities, the projection of prestige public projects, civil engineering schemes, and items of advanced military hardware can be used to convey a host of subtextual messages concerning the ascribed source and meaning of such conspicuous objects of material stature. In some regimes, the reliance upon subtextual messages can give way to far more explicit devices of representational association in which leaders are overtly conjoined to objects of cultural and civic value (Box 7.2).

Very often these implied representations will be combined with another narrative designed to give further validation to a leadership's purposive rationale. Leaders will use these opportunities to link the presence of high-stature materials to the evocation of a national history and of a theme of national renewal, facilitated by an ostensibly patriotic leadership. Leaders and their respective movements commonly assign to themselves the role of representing the nation and with it the responsibility of defining and fulfilling its historic objectives.

When the focus is turned towards political frameworks that are less controlled and authoritarian in their organizational logic, then the position of leaders is more limited in scope because of the relative paucity of communication resources available to any one centre of power in open societies. Political leaders not only have to contend with the political, institutional, and constitutional constraints that have already been alluded to, but also to engage with a greater array of competing power centres with political resources of their own. In these circumstances, political leaders have traditionally resorted to the written word and especially to the spoken word. The arts and crafts of rhetoric and oratory have long had a close association with effective leadership. Those individuals who have a particular facility with language and the ways it can be used to support political arguments and to articulate positions in a persuasive manner often find that they have a fast track to political prominence. Likewise, politicians who suffer from a lack of confidence with the substance and techniques of vocal appeal usually

---

[10] For a general overview of these themes, see W. Lance Bennett and Robert M. Entman (eds.), *Mediated Politics: Communication in the Future of Democracy* (Cambridge: Cambridge University Press, 2001); James Stanyer, *Modern Political Communication: Mediated Politics in Uncertain Times* (Cambridge: Polity Press, 2007); Karen Sanders, *Communicating Politics in the Twenty-First Century* (Basingstoke: Palgrave Macmillan, 2009).

Box 7.2 Leadership and the high politics of public symbolism and monumental depiction

Saparmurat Niyazov (1940–2006): President of Turkmenistan
Following the fall of the Soviet Union, the leader of the newly independent republic of Turkmenistan replaced the cult of Soviet leadership with one centred upon himself. This formed the basis of a highly authoritarian system of arbitrary executive edicts—ranging from the banning of both ballet and opera to the construction of man-made desert lakes and cypress forests as well as a pyramid 130 feet high. More insidious were the projects designed to reflect his self-designated status as 'Leader of all Turkmen'. These included the renaming of schools, airports, and other public facilities after himself and his immediate family; the ubiquitous presence of his portrait in all public spaces; and the enforced usage of his book *Ruhnama* as the official guide to the spiritual nourishment of the nation—making it the central point of reference for Turkmenistan's entire educational system. In addition to the construction of the Spirit of Turkmenbashi, the largest mosque in Central Asia, Niyazov's other most conspicuous project was a series of gold-plated statues around the country, thereby affording a continuously idealized representation of the leader in Turkmen society. Most notable is the one positioned in the capital city and which revolves on its plinth to allow the statue to reflect the sun during the course of the day.

Félix Houphouët-Boigny (1905–93): President of the Ivory Coast
President Houphouët-Boigny decided to make the place of his birth into the new capital of the Ivory Coast. Despite being located in a remote area of the interior, the town of Yamoussoukro became the incongruous beneficiary of a project that included universities, hotels, boarding schools, parklands, an eighteen-hole golf course, a large airport, a system of eight-lane boulevards, and a presidential palace. The centrepiece, however, was the construction of the largest church in the world. Over a four-year period (1985–9), the Basilica of Our Lady of Peace was built to imitate, but also to surpass, St Peter's Basilica in the Vatican City. The finished project is a colossal structure of imported Italian marble with 7,000 individually air-conditioned seats, standing room for an additional 11,000 worshippers, and a marble plaza outside that can accommodate crowds of 200,000 people. In addition, there is an adjoining mansion that by presidential decree is reserved exclusively for the pope. President Houphouët-Boigny hoped that the Basilica would serve as a place of pilgrimage for Africa's Catholics. But the overriding reason for its construction was to achieve a monumental form of prestigious leadership projection and self-memorialization—an intention made evident by the president's commission of a stained-glass window of his image to be placed beside a gallery of stained glass of Jesus and the apostles.

Saddam Hussein
In order to give an enhanced public expression of his regime, Saddam Hussein commissioned an immense range of palaces, museums, memorials, ceremonial avenues, galleries, and libraries. The intention was to arouse a heightened consciousness of Iraq's ancient history and to combine it with a concerted linkage to the country's immediate past and more especially to the historical significance of Saddam's leadership. Arguably the most arresting example of this adopted symbolism was the construction of The Arc of Triumph, or the Swords of Qādisiyyah, in Baghdad. Completed in 1989, the bronze structure consisted of two triumphal arches each formed by a pair of hands carrying swords that crossed in the middle of an arc formation. Each of the four swords was 140 feet in length and weighed twenty-four tons and met at a height of 140 feet. The structure was conceived as an affirmation of the regime's claim of victory in the Iran–Iraq War. Saddam not only devised the original plan but was the model for the hands and forearms holding the swords. The symbolic fusion of the leader with his depiction of history was completed by the inclusion of metals from the guns and tanks of Iraqi soldiers killed in the war. The immense structure became not only a landmark feature of the Baghdad skyline but a signature representation of the regime itself—and one whose propaganda value was confirmed by the priority given to its capture by coalition forces in the 2003 invasion of Iraq.

experience notable disadvantages in creating the right medium for connecting to public audiences.

Leadership normally involves the need to generate shared meanings, perceptions, and assurances through the strategic use of discourse and the logic of argumentation calibrated to particular contexts. The communicative power of many leaders in public and organizational spheres is usually seen as a personal resource that is necessarily confined to an individual's special skills in argument and presentation. But it is worth noting that the techniques of rhetoric and oratory have a long history stretching back to Greek and Roman times, and that noted contemporary exponents in the craft of speech-making have either consciously or unconsciously drawn from these classical designs of advocacy.[11] The evocative subtleties and emotive rhythms of Barack Obama's speeches are especially noteworthy in this respect (Box 7.3).

Box 7.3 Public oratory and rhetorical register: The case of President Barack Obama

---

Barack Obama's rise to power has been widely cited as signifying a revival in the arts of speech-making and in the place of public oratory in civic life. It has led to a renewed interest in the general techniques of rhetoric and the ways in which an accomplished practitioner can succeed in invoking a persuasive and often emotive hold upon an audience for the purposes of securing the intended response. The appeal of Obama's speeches has been attributed to the ways in which he has, either consciously or subconsciously, drawn on classic speech patterns and key communication tropes in order to generate the desired political effect within a public sphere.

One illustration has been Obama's reliance upon the usage of the *tricolon*, *anaphora*, and *epiphora* devices for dramatic effect. A *tricolon* denotes a series of three words, phrases, or clauses that are juxtaposed to produce a rhythmic pattern. In his Inaugural Address in 2009, the president employed no fewer than twenty-two tricolons. For example:

> I stand here today humbled by the task before us, grateful for the trust you have bestowed, mindful of the sacrifices borne by our ancestors. . . . our security emanates from the justness of our cause, the force of our example, the tempering qualities of humility and restraint.
>
> Presidential inaugural address, 20 January 2009

An *anaphora* refers to the technique of creating a sequence by giving emphasis to the same word or phrase at the beginning of each element within the series. An *epiphora* works in the same way but with the repeated component placed at the end of each element. Obama has proved himself especially adept at using both these rhetorical techniques.

Examples:

> You know, *they said* this day would never come. *They said* our sights were set too high. *They said* this country was too divided, too disillusioned to ever come together around a common purpose. But on this January night, at this defining moment in history, you have done what the cynics said we couldn't do.
>
> Speech following victory in the Iowa Caucuses, 3 January 2008

---

[11] See George A. Kennedy, *A New History of Classical Rhetoric* (Princeton, NJ: Princeton University Press, 1994); Richard Leo Enos, *Roman Rhetoric: Revolution and the Greek Influence* (West Lafayette, IN: Parlor Press, 2008); James D. Williams, *An Introduction to Classical Rhetoric: Essential Readings* (Chichester: Wiley-Blackwell, 2009).

Don't tell me we can't change. Yes, we can. Yes, we can change. Yes, we can heal this nation. Yes, we can seize our future.
Speech following victory in the South Carolina primary election, 26 January 2008

In his election night speech in 2008, Obama finished a series of six sections with the phrase 'yes, we can'. The final element used a tricolon as the preamble to the last climactic call of the epiphora:

This is our time—to put our people back to work and open doors of opportunity for our kids; to restore prosperity and promote the cause of peace; to reclaim the American dream and reaffirm that fundamental truth—that out of many, we are one; that while we breathe, we hope, and where we are met with cynicism and doubt, and those who tell us that we can't, we will respond with that timeless creed that sums up the spirit of a people: yes, we can.
Presidential election victory speech, 4 November 2008

Two other devices used by Obama also demonstrate the articulated inheritance of classical rhetorical technique. One is the *praeteritio* which is a device for drawing attention to a subject by giving the impression of not raising it. Under the guise of not needing to enumerate a point or a set of observations, the speaker in fact draws attention to the very information that he or she is purporting to exclude.

Tonight, we gather to affirm the greatness of our nation—not because of the height of our skyscrapers, or the power of our military, or the size of our economy. Our pride is based on a very simple premise, summed up in a declaration made over two hundred years ago.
Keynote address at the Democratic National Convention, 27 July 2004

He has also drawn from the Ciceronian tradition in the rhetorical practice of juxtaposing contrasting words or ideas (i.e. *antithesis*), but doing so in a way that wins an audience's favour or sympathy through a form of self-effacement and apparent humility (i.e. *captatio benevolentiæ*). Thus:

I realize that I am not the likeliest candidate for this office. I don't fit the typical pedigree, and I haven't spent my career in the halls of Washington. But I stand before you tonight because all across America something is stirring. What the nay-sayers don't understand is that this election has never been about me. It's been about you.
Acceptance speech for the Democratic Party nomination, 28 August 2008

In cultures that afford a high priority to the freedoms of opinion and expression and to the rights of a free press, leaders usually have to negotiate their way to acquiring access to the channels of mass communication. Apart from the constant presence of alternative and aspiring leaders seeking to attract public attention in order to enhance their claims to representational credentials, incumbent leaders almost invariably have to be attentive to the organizational demands, editorial priorities, audience dynamics, and market disciplines of what are for the most part privately owned concerns. Where the communication channels are sourced from public funds, then even here—or rather especially here—the principles of independence from political control and of fair, free, impartial, and balanced political coverage are usually culturally embedded as primary values. Moreover, both publicly and privately run media organizations in liberal democracies have strong traditions of independence and marked professional incentives to resist forms of external manipulation and undue political influence.

In this continuing struggle for leverage, leaders have to negotiate a passage through the various channels of public communication—each one of which has its own set of priorities, filters, and gate-keeping strategies. In seeking to maximize their opportunities for news and media coverage, leaders have had to employ a range of devices designed both to arouse public awareness of their positions and to accommodate the interests of those operating the media outlets. These techniques can include press conferences, speeches, addresses, interviews, briefings, and advanced notice of decisions, plans, and objectives. Special access to public and ceremonial occasions are also used to ensure media coverage and through it the required linkage between leaderships and national audiences.

The increased importance that is attached to the need for leaders and their organizations to achieve a sustainable functioning relationship between politicians, voters, journalists, advocacy groups, media outfits, and communication institutions has prompted a sharp rise in the resources directed to the professional management of information flows and communication strategies. Leaders have to ensure that their political assets as public figures are not only made as secure as possible but also maximized to optimum levels through a productive engagement with the main sources of opinion formation.

Political parties and other sponsoring groups now expect leaders to be adept at cultivating the media, thereby ensuring the maximum extent of beneficial coverage relating to the competence, unity, and coherence of their respective organizations. Given the strategic primacy assigned to communications in these sophisticated political operations, leaders have to have the ability to engage effectively in what is a compulsive process of reflexive positioning set within an increasingly complex media environment. Leaders are now judged not just on their ability to create policy programmes and to manage political colleagues but by their capacity to devise and operate effective schemes of strategic outreach, promotional communication, message dissemination, and political marketing, as well as methods of securing favourable media coverage through the usage of 'spin doctors' or 'sultans of spin'.[12]

While the job specifications of leaders in advanced democracies are now strongly oriented towards presentational skills, media understanding, and even news management, the reciprocal elements of the relationship should not be overlooked. Leaders are not limited to a stimulus–response dynamic in projecting

---

[12] See Nicholas Jones, *Sultans of Spin: The Media and the New Labour Government* (London: Victor Gollancz, 1999); Howard Kurtz, *Spin Cycle: How the White House and the Media Manipulate the News* (New York, NY: Touchstone, 1998); Bob Franklin, 'The Hand of History: New Labour, News Management and Governance', in Steve Ludlam and Martin J. Smith (eds.), *New Labour in Government* (Basingstoke: Macmillan, 2001), pp. 130–44; Frank Esser, Carsten Reinemann, and David Fan, 'Spin Doctoring in British and German Election Campaigns: How the Press is Being Confronted with a New Quality of Political PR', *European Journal of Communication*, 15(2) June 2000: 209–39; Frank Esser, Carsten Reinemann, and David Fan, 'Spin Doctors in the United States, Great Britain, and Germany: Metacommunication about Media Manipulation', *The International Journal of Press/Politics*, 6(1) January 2001: 16–45; David L. Swanson, 'Political News in the Changing Environment of Political Journalism', in Philippe J. Maarek and Gadi Wolfsfeld (eds.), *Political Communication in a New Era: A Cross-National Perspective* (London: Routledge, 2003), pp. 11–31; Lance Price, *Spin Doctor's Diary: Inside Number 10 with New Labour* (London: Hodder & Stoughton, 2005); Richard Heffernan, 'The Prime Minister and the News Media: Political Communication as a Leadership Resource', *Parliamentary Affairs*, 59(4) October 2006: 582–98.

themselves into media outlets. They are assisted by the professional and market-based incentives of the media channels themselves. Just as leaders gravitate towards these communication networks, so the latter are in many ways dependent upon leaders for the focus of their news gathering and analysis.

The basis of the connection is one of mutual interest. The media need to report the news, but at the same time they need news to report. Political leaders are in a unique position to satisfy both requirements. They feed the demands for events, incidents, controversy, competition, comment, and pictures that allow leaders to remain as central subjects for the public gaze. Media organizations are drawn to leaders, and to the issues surrounding leadership provision and assessment, in the formation of news agendas and news cycles. Leaders for their part have a similar dependency relationship with the media. News outlets can provide leaders with information, assessment, and advice on the state of public opinion. From the same sources, leaders receive information about issues and conflicts inside their own organization, the progress or otherwise of policy proposals, and the condition of their political status. More especially, they provide a channel of communication through which leaders can convey their own construction of events and their own interpretation of the issues and problems requiring political action.[13]

As in all forms of interdependence, the relationship between leaders and the media does not always function smoothly. When the interplay deteriorates, the effect can be highly dysfunctional. While leaders go to great lengths to optimize the relationship, there will always be limits to the productivity of such a linkage. In fact, some analysts would claim that deterioration is practically assured and that a cyclical pattern is discernible as leadership relations with the media turn from largely positive to largely negative with the passage of time.[14] Whether the causes are structural or incidental, the effect on the position of leaders can be very serious. The substance, agenda, and tone of information provided by the news services will not only influence the professional standing of a leader, but can affect his or her public status and political capital as well a leadership's reputation for professional, managerial, and administrative competence. This being the case, when the media's disposition becomes more critical then the whole process can work in reverse—very much to the detriment of the leader in question. Adverse news coverage can reflect and subsequently reinforce a downward cycle of economic performance or a trend in public opinion. The media will often respond to these contextual shifts and accordingly alter the terms of their reporting in such a way as to promote and reaffirm the change.

It is during these times of strained relations that political leaders will complain about the role and behaviour of the media in society and in particular their position in the framework of political engagement and transmission. These are

---

[13] Lori C. Han, *Governing From Center Stage: White House Communication Strategies During the Television Age of Politics* (Cresskill, NJ: Hampton Press, 2001); Heffernan, 'The Prime Minister and the News Media'; Raymond Kuhn, 'Media Management' in Anthony Seldon (ed.), *Blair's Britain, 1997–2007* (Cambridge: Cambridge University Press, 2007), pp. 123–42; Stephen J. Farnsworth, *Spinner in Chief: How Presidents Sell Their Policies and Themselves* (Boulder, CO: Paradigm, 2009).

[14] Michael B. Grossman and Martha J. Kumar, *Portraying the President: The White House and the News Media* (Baltimore, MD: Johns Hopkins University Press, 1980); Kurtz, *Spin Cycle*; Kuhn, 'Media Management'.

the occasions when leaders resort to counterarguments against what they regard as the prominence and privileges of the media. The case made is usually constructed around the claims of representation and the rights of communication. Leaders assert that it is they who have submitted themselves to the electoral process and who have secured their position on the basis of political consent. The leaders of majority parties are responsible for formally constituting a government. Moreover, it is they who remain directly accountable to the public in subsequent elections. Given the process by which democratic governments are formed, leaders can find serious objections to the way that media organizations occupy an intermediary and filtering position between government and the citizenry.

Just as leaders will resent the resources that have to be deployed towards facilitating their message to the wider public, so they will struggle to accept the proposition that a free press is a neutral form of mass communication. On the contrary, leaders normally become convinced that the media inevitably distort the news—and especially the news concerning the evaluation of leaders and their agendas. One charge is that news organizations have an excessive interest in personalities, conflicts, and divisions in the selection criteria of newsworthy themes. This propensity means political news becomes habitually refracted through the lens of leadership behaviour, performances, motives, and evaluations. While this can be beneficial to leaders, it can also be highly critical and persistent in nature—prompting the principals to complain that such saturated coverage not only has a corrosive effect on their political status but lays the groundwork for narratives of leadership pathology.[15]

Another issue relates to the media's positional power. To leaders struggling to establish and to secure a set of political objectives, the media can disrupt the process. From a leader's perspective, the media will appear as if their position permits them effectively to shape the political agenda and to frame the discussion of issues along lines that may well be at variance with those preferred by political leaders. A further complaint revolves around the treatment of leaders as public commodities. Modern leaders find that their public and personal lives are continuously subjected to intense and even invasive scrutiny. In their drive to fill not merely news pages but also a plethora of commentaries, op-eds, social interest features, and lifestyle supplements, media organizations are accused by leaders of diverting public attention away from the prescribed agendas of elected politicians.[16] These complaints pertaining to structural bias, personal privacy, and the control of public exposure are closely connected to a more generic problem that goes to the heart of the disputed relationship.

---

[15] For the close relationship between an insurgent media and a deterioration in the processes of political communication and public trust, see Theodore Draper, *A Very Thin Line: The Iran-Contra Affairs* (London: Chapmans, 1991); Stanley I. Kutler, *Wars of Watergate: The Last Crisis of Richard Nixon* (New York, NY: Norton, 1992); Fred Emery, *Watergate: The Corruption of American Politics and the Fall of Richard Nixon* (New York, NY: Touchstone, 1995); Lawrence E. Walsh, *Firewall: Iran-Contra Conspiracy and Cover-up* (New York, NY: Norton, 1998); Robert Busby, *Defending the American Presidency: Clinton and the Lewinsky Scandal* (Basingstoke: Palgrave Macmillan, 2001); Jeffrey M. Togman, Robert E. Denton and Rachel L. Holloway, *Images, Scandal, and Communication Strategies of the Clinton Presidency* (Westport, CT: Praeger, 2003).

[16] Stanyer, *Modern Political Communication*, ch. 3.

The issue in question is one of authority within a functioning democracy. Because of the importance of public attitudes and opinion formation within such systems, political leaders are intensely sensitive over how they and their policies are presented to mass audiences. In the face of the media's referral to the rights of a free press and free expression, leaders often claim that those who control the means of public communication operate outside the frameworks of political consent, responsibility, and accountability. Moreover, it is not uncommon for leaders to claim that editors, proprietors, journalists, and commentators have assumed the prerogative of imposing themselves as a separate and alternative representational process between the government and the governed. It is now a common assumption that the media have in some way become incorporated into the machinery of government. Timothy Cook observes that 'not only is the news a "coproduction" of the news media and government, but policy today is likewise the result of collaboration and conflict among newspersons, officials, and other political actors'.[17]

This being the case, leaders will almost invariably reach the conclusion at some point in their term of office that the media are in open competition with the electoral and representative processes of governance. Many would go further and claim that the media—either intentionally or unintentionally—compromise the results of public choice made through democratic elections. As a consequence, it is not unusual for frustrated political leaders to raise the issue of political and social legitimacy in respect to the position and behaviour of the media. Accordingly, news organizations are commonly criticized for allegedly usurping the role of elected public officials not just through their control of access to the channels of public communication, but by the way that they can interpose their own editorial priorities and interpretive modes upon political news and analysis.

Media organizations can strongly influence the capacity of leaders to manage their parties, their political partners, and their electoral strategies. The difficulty of engaging effectively with constitutional and institutional structures and processes—as well as with policy communities, professional organizations, and other political constituencies—means that leaders will often cite media outlets as a major determinant of their acute predicament. Problems of government can become equated with the problematic challenge of dealing with the channels of communication. Faced with the combination of complex governmental demands and media that are normally disposed towards critical analysis, along with the attendant corrosive effects upon a leadership's professional reputation and public prestige, leaders will often resort to a fundamentalist position—namely accusing the media of exercising 'power without responsibility' and of undermining a government's constitutional responsibility and practical ability to govern.

Faced with accusations of dubious legitimacy and of acting imperiously within a democracy, media representatives offer a spirited defence based upon principled reference points comparable to those used by their opponents. Those speaking on behalf of the media claim that their intermediary position is not only a legitimate component of democratic governance but provides an essential

---

[17] Timothy E. Cook, *Governing with the News: The News Media as a Political Institution* (Chicago, IL: University of Chicago Press, 1998), p. 3.

service in ensuring that the gap between the government and the governed does not become too wide during those periods between elections. The argument is made that news organizations do not instigate or shape opinion so much as reflect and report it. Furthermore, it can be claimed that in an era which has witnessed the relative decline of legislatures and legislative oversight, it is the media which have performed a vital role in calling governments to account and in making leaderships more responsive to public demands. Far from acting as a rogue element in the political processes, the media can be seen as a necessary *de facto* constitutional check upon the presumptions of executive power and upon its sophisticated manipulation of government information by leaders in the service of their own interests. The charges and countercharges result in an impasse which can be rationalized as a form of creative tension but which can also act as a stimulus for leaders to devise more imaginative ways by which to assert their claims to representative and communicative primacy.

LEADERSHIP DIRECT

Given the scale of the constraints that are perceived to exist within the organization and operation of media-controlled lines of communication in liberal and democratic societies, leaders in these systems have been highly active in attempting to reverse what they see as a detrimental imbalance of power. Their counteroffensives have taken many forms. On the one hand, there have been strategies to devise independent means by which to monitor and track the state of public opinion rather than to rely upon media organizations as primary conduits of popular attitudes or to defer to them in the formative exchanges of political information. On the other hand, leaders have adopted more active measures to penetrate the public's consciousness and to attract more focused attention to their own messages and to their own sets of priorities. The combination of these and other communication strands have been geared not merely to improving the transmission lines and information flows between leaders and the public, but also to reducing the effect of the more conventional mediation processes. The overall design is categorized as 'public leadership' or as 'going public'.

The dynamics, processes, and significance of public leadership are probably best conveyed through the example of recent developments in the US presidency. The holder of this office is assigned a pivotal position of leadership within the system of government. Howard Gardner's injunction that leaders should establish meaningful narratives[18] resonates in the conventional descriptions of the presidency. Mary Stuckey offers the following job description for the chief executive's role in the US government: 'The President has become the nation's chief storyteller, its interpreter-in-chief. He tells us stories about ourselves, and in doing so he tells us what sort of people we are, how we are constituted as a community. We

---

[18] Howard Gardner, *Leading Minds: An Anatomy of Leadership* (London: HarperCollins, 1995).

take from him not only our policies but our national self-identity.'[19] But while presidents may have this expansive role, they also have to operate in a system of limited powers and constitutional constraints. This means that the presidential voice and stories told through it may not always be heard. On the contrary, it is often more likely that a president's narratives will be drowned out by the profusion of alternative political narratives on the part of others in the crowded power centres of US government.

This being the case, presidents have increasingly sought to compensate for their weaknesses in Washington by appealing directly to the public for political support. For modern American presidents, 'going public' relates to both the impulse and the requirement of contemporary presidents to enhance their political status and increase their political leverage by cultivating a direct relationship between the institution of the presidency and the concerns of a wider public constituency. The limited and conditional nature of presidential authority is thereby supplemented by strategies that are designed to maximize a leader's outreach and, in doing so, to diversify a president's political base and bargaining resources. Just as presidents exploit the individuality of the office to project themselves as the focal embodiments of popular concern and the public interest, so through the same process they are able to enhance their claims to representational legitimacy and to communicative priority. The controlling logic of this form of public leadership is a process of 'disintermediation' in which the leader attempts to marginalize or even displace the claims of other representative agencies to speak or act on behalf of the wider public or national interest.

Political scientists such as Jeffrey Tulis, Elvin Lim, and Samuel Kernell have been in the forefront of monitoring shifts in this sector of presidential development. Tulis discerns a conspicuous disjunction between presidential communications in the nineteenth century and those in the twentieth century. Earlier presidents had been reticent in their usage of oral communications. But since the presidencies of Theodore Roosevelt and Woodrow Wilson, 'popular or mass rhetoric has become a principal tool of presidential governance . . . Today it is taken for granted that presidents have a *duty* constantly to defend themselves publicly, to promote policy initiatives nationwide, and to inspire the population.'[20] Accordingly presidents have grown highly adept at rhetorical devices 'designed to manipulate popular passions rather than to engage citizens in political debate'.[21]

For Tulis, the problem is one of sheer volume of presidential communications and the way that these devices of mobilization are often equated with effective

---

[19] Mary E. Stuckey, *The President as Interpreter-in Chief* (Chatham, NJ: Chatham House, 1991), p. 1.

[20] Jeffrey K. Tulis, *The Rhetorical Presidency* (Princeton, NJ: Princeton University Press, 1987), p. 4. See also Ryan Lee Teten, 'The Evolution of the Rhetorical Presidency and Getting Past the Traditional/Modern Divide', *Presidential Studies Quarterly*, 38 2008: 308–14. Especially noteworthy is the special edition of the *Critical Review* in 2007 focusing on 'The Rhetorical Presidency After Twenty Years'. See John J. DiIulio, Jr., 'The Hyper-Rhetorical Presidency', *Critical Review*, 19(2–3) 2007: 315–24; Jeffrey K. Tulis, 'The Rhetorical Presidency in Retrospect', *Critical Review*, 19(2–3) 2007: 481–500. For an analysis of a similar phenomenon in the British system, see Richard Toye, 'The Rhetorical Premiership: A New Perspective on Prime Ministerial Power Since 1945', *Parliamentary History*, 30(2) June 2011: 175–92.

[21] Tulis, *The Rhetorical Presidency*, p. 188.

governance. Elvin Lim's critique is based more on the quality of presidential communications which he claims has declined over the course of the twentieth century. In an analysis that incorporates extensive interviews with presidential speechwriters and statistical surveys of sentence lengths and targeted reading levels, Lim concludes that the language, substance, and logic of presidential communications have become progressively oversimplified to the point of being simplistic. His case is one of an attitude of anti-intellectualism on the part of presidents and their communication teams. The focus upon distractive platitudes, emotional appeals, and rudimentary knowledge at the expense of conveying the complexity and multi-causality of real world issues has in Lim's view debased not just the standards of presidential communications but also the general levels of discourse in the public sphere.[22]

To Samuel Kernell, the usage of rhetoric is part of a much wider portfolio of techniques in personal projection and public outreach. Contemporary presidents now have no alternative other than to compete in the mass marketing of the self. They are compelled to publicize themselves in order to maintain their political visibility as leaders and, thereby, their influence over other Washington decision-makers. Through public appearances, televised addresses, photo opportunities, presidential conferences, political trips, visual spectacles, etc., presidents now engage in an unremitting strategy of personal projection in what is already a media-saturated environment. In this way, presidents further enhance the centrality of the office in American politics and generate a personal identity in the country at large, which can help to obviate the traditional need for political negotiation and accommodation within Washington. The failure to engage in a strategy of directly cultivating a public constituency is now seen as tantamount to inviting popular complaints over distance, disconnection, and elitism. Presidential authority has to be continually supplemented by palpable exertions in outreach and by the constant application to the task of extending and diversifying the leader's political base and bargaining resources.[23]

Just as presidents seek to circumvent other institutional and organizational intermediaries in their desire to develop a visceral rapport with the public, so they also develop a language and a role centred upon giving expression to popular causes and private impulses. Presidents are able to exploit their appeal to news organizations to create events and even public spectacles in order to exert a marked gravitational force upon the generation of news cycles and the agendas of political commentary and analysis.[24] The scale and depth of this trend have been so marked that it is generally regarded as one of the most significant changes in the formation and operation of political leadership in the US over the last thirty

---

[22] Elvin T. Lim, *The Anti-Intellectual Presidency: The Decline of Presidential Rhetoric from George Washington to George W. Bush* (New York, NY: Oxford University Press, 2008).

[23] Samuel Kernell, *Going Public: New Strategies of Presidential Leadership*, 4th edn. (Washington, DC: Congressional Quarterly Press, 2007).

[24] See George C. Edwards III, *The Public Presidency: The Pursuit of Popular Support* (New York, NY: St. Martin's Press, 1983); George C. Edwards III, 'George Bush and the Public Presidency: The Politics of Inclusion', in Colin Campbell and Bert A. Rockman (eds.), *The Bush Presidency: First Appraisals* (Chatham, NJ: Chatham House, 1991), pp. 129–54; George C. Edwards III, 'Frustration and Folly: Bill Clinton and the Public Presidency', in Campbell and Rockman (eds.), *The Clinton Presidency: First Appraisals*, pp. 234–61; Kernell, *Going Public*.

years. It has reached the point where 'contemporary presidents have the capacity to reach the public in ways that could not have been imagined by earlier presidents, and they have consciously formed their strategies for governing to exploit that capacity'.[25] The availability of the means to engage in individual outreach through the mass media, together with the generated imperatives to cultivate public links and maintain the conspicuous pre-eminence of national audiences, has shifted the priorities, objectives, and strategies of the contemporary presidency to a point where the office is commonly referred to as the 'public presidency'. For modern incumbents, the issue of leadership as public outreach has simply become a *sine qua non* of the presidency: 'Presidents can no longer choose whether to engage in public leadership, only what form that leadership will take.'[26]

The influence of this kind of leadership projection has been confined neither to the presidency nor to the United States.[27] Leaders in other systems have also experienced similar drives to expand their portfolios of outreach and in doing so to change the normal contexts of leadership activity. Despite operating in a different institutional and constitutional environment, British political leaders, for example, have increasingly become responsive to very similar political calculations concerning strategy and outreach. Their contemporary roles demand that they project themselves into the public sphere not merely as representatives of their respective organizations but as expressions of wider notions of social consciousness and cultural identity. In effect, prime ministers are expected to have an ability to connect visibly and even intimately with individual concerns and national moods. In doing so, they are required to demonstrate the responsiveness of governing processes, to reveal an understanding of populist impulses, and to affirm their personal accessibility to the wider public. This leads to prime ministers having to be adept at embedding themselves in the national consciousness, ensuring a high level of news management skills, mastering techniques of popular communication, and associating themselves directly with such themes as the public interest, 'the people', and the nation.

Like their counterparts in the United States, British premiers have come to recognize the imperative nature of effective and continuous public outreach in the construction and maintenance of their political authority. The impulse to publicize leadership not only drives the strategies of political parties, but dominates their political calculations, their strategic planning, and their agenda-setting priorities. In the same way that one leader's failure to maintain a positive projection to the public can undermine a party's authority, so another leader's success in establishing an effective public outreach can enhance a party's appeal and electoral potential. Parties openly confront each other on the leadership issue. Leaders not

---

[25] James Pfiffner, *The Modern Presidency* (New York, NY: St Martin's Press, 1994), p. 36.

[26] Stuckey, *The President as Interpreter-in Chief*, p. 2.

[27] For example see Douglas B. Harris, 'The Rise of the Public Speakership', *Political Science Quarterly*, 113(2) Summer 1998: 193–212; Franca Roncarolo, 'Campaigning and Governing: An Analysis of Berlusconi's Rhetorical Leadership', *Modern Italy*, 10(1) 2005: 75–93; Cristina Marcano and Alberto B. Tyszka, *Hugo Chávez: The Definitive Biography of Venezuela's Controversial President*, trans. Kristina Cordero (New York, NY: Random House, 2007), ch. 13; Rory Carroll, 'Government by TV: Chávez sets 8-hour record', *Guardian*, 25 September 2007; James Stanyer, *Intimate Politics: Publicity, Privacy and the Personal Lives of Politicians in Media Saturated Democracies* (Cambridge: Polity Press, 2012).

only dominate the media's coverage of party and electoral politics, they constitute the defining feature of an entrenched public preoccupation with the properties, values, and roles of leadership. Just as the vocabulary of political description and explanation is dominated by references to leaders and leadership, so the merits and demerits of individual leaders are continually analysed and tracked by polls, surveys, and commentaries in what can be described as the political institutionalization of public opinion research.

Because the capacity to provide leadership is widely accepted as a key criterion of governing, the alternative prospectuses of leadership have come to dominate the medium and the terminology of political exchange. Within this context, the possession of a public identity on the part of a leader has become a political resource in its own right. Party leaders have to be able to command public attention, in order to maintain the confidence of their respective parties in a medium of political exchange that is increasingly dominated by leadership figures making claims in public and on behalf of the public. The net effect is that of 'leadership stretch', in which party leaders become progressively differentiated from their organizational bases in terms of media attention, public recognition, and political identity.[28] Just as their roles and resources become enhanced in response to the requirements of their positions, so they have to cultivate an expansive portfolio of public and political engagement. Closely related to the theme of the public projection of leadership is the increased personalization of both the requirement and provision of leadership. In this context, political leadership is not only embodied by individual leaders, it is promoted by the claims, status, and personas of leaders in direct competition with one another over the attributes of party and national leadership. The heightened emphasis upon the focal significance of individuality amongst leaders coincides with a trend towards the depiction of politics through leadership figures.

In many democracies party leaders have risen to, and been propelled into, positions of greater prominence with the result that points of distinction between different parties have become notably personalized in nature. Increasingly, the public consumption of politics is geared not just towards what are construed to be the constitutive elements of leadership but also towards the relative merits of different leaders in respect to these designated components. The rising volume of opinion polls on leadership and its constituent attributes, together with the public prominence given to their results, reflect the rise of publicly perceived and assessed 'leadership attributes' as separate and substantive categories of political evaluation. Members of the public are regularly asked to assess and to rate the personal qualities of their actual and potential leaders on the assumption that the public's appraisal of selected components of personality is central to the estimation, and ultimately the reality, of contemporary political leadership. The collective result is that the perceived properties of individual leaders in many systems now constitute an entire currency of political evaluation and a discourse of political differentiation.[29] It can

---

[28] Michael Foley, *The Rise of British Presidency* (Manchester: Manchester University Press, 1993), pp. 120–48; Michael Foley, *The British Presidency: Tony Blair and the Politics of Public Leadership* (Manchester: Manchester University Press, 2000), pp. 116–45.
[29] Anthony Mughan, *Media and the Presidentialization of Parliamentary Elections* (Basingstoke: Palgrave Macmillan, 2000), pp. 22–76; Ludger Helms, *Presidents, Prime Ministers and Chancellors*

even allow leaders to develop identities that are portrayed as separate and distinct from those of the governments that they purportedly lead.

The case for the enhanced prominence of leaders through the processes of 'disintermediation' has usually been based upon references to the themes of representation, responsiveness, and political legitimacy. But these assertions do not go unchallenged. It is these very principles that provide the basis for the critiques that come in the wake of this form of leadership activity. For example, it can be asserted that leaders engaged in this strategy of unmediated contact devote disproportionate resources to the task of maximizing their influence upon media outlets at the expense of other political relationships and responsibilities. The emphasis on media management has seen the rise of new hierarchies within government organizations. Individuals and agencies specializing in media relations have not only been given priority access to leadership circles but have been afforded considerable power and prestige within the senior levels of decision-making.

In the United States, for example, the presidency's Office of Communications has become an elite institution because it is responsible for providing not only a news service and information source to media channels both inside and outside Washington, but also for coordinating information flows across the entire executive branch.[30] It lies at the centre of a rolling exercise in daily news management that is geared towards the optimum construction and dissemination of news. The ability to penetrate public perceptions through the use of well-timed, coherent, and targeted messages—together with an effective choreography of public appearances—is now considered the *sine qua non* of presidential leadership. The emphasis that is placed upon a continuing engagement with the public generates complaints that this kind of leadership, and the way it relies upon sophisticated techniques of outreach, has the effect of marginalizing other governing priorities or even of reducing them to functions of media relations. So much so in fact that it can be said to have led to a synergy that privileges media management elites within leadership structures as it simultaneously enhances the political status of media actors and organizations.[31]

Executive Leadership in Western Democracies (Basingstoke: Palgrave Macmillan, 2005); Thomas Poguntke and Paul Webb (eds.), *The Presidentialization of Politics: A Comparative Study of Modern Democracies* (Oxford: Oxford University Press, 2005); Ludger Helms, 'Governing in the Media Age: The Impact of the Mass Media on Executive Leadership in Contemporary Democracies', *Government and Opposition*, 43(1) Winter 2008: 26–54.

[30] John A. Maltese, *Spin Control: The White House Office of Communications and the Management of Presidential News*, 2nd edn. (Chapel Hill, NC: University of North Carolina Press, 1994); Kurtz, *Spin Cycle*; Timothy E. Cook and Lyn Ragsdale, 'The Presidency and the Press: Negotiating Newsworthiness at the White House', in Michael Nelson (ed.), *The Presidency and the Political System*, 5th edn. (Washington, DC: Congressional Quarterly Press, 1999), pp. 297–330; John A. Maltese, 'The Media and the Presidency', in Mark J. Rozell (ed.), *An Introduction to Media and Politics* (Lanham, MD: Rowman & Littlefield, 2003), pp. 1–24; Martha J. Kumar, *Managing the President's Message: The White House Communications Operation* (Baltimore, MD: Johns Hopkins University Press, 2007).

[31] For a representative overview of the UK and US contexts, see Dick Morris, *Behind the Oval Office: Winning the Presidency in the Nineties* (New York, NY: Random House, 1997); Philip Gould, *The Unfinished Revolution: How the Modernisers Saved the Labour Party* (London: Little, Brown, 1998); Jones, *Sultans of Spin*; Kathryn Dunn Tenpas, *Presidents as Candidates: Inside the White House for the Presidential Campaign* (New York, NY: Routledge, 2003); Jennifer Lees-Marshment, *Political Marketing and British Political Parties* (Manchester: Manchester University Press, 2005), chs. 5, 6;

Another critique is that exponents of public leadership very often try to circum-vent more established centres of news reports and analysis altogether. One device that was popularized in the 1930s by President Franklin Roosevelt in the US and prime minister Stanley Baldwin in the UK was the usage of personal radio broadcasts directly into the homes of the electorate. These not only allowed leading politicians to influence the framing of issues and positions but afforded them the opportunity of developing a transmission channel that was independent from the more conven-tional centres of opinion formation. Radio was followed by television and more recently by the Internet and a whole swathe of digitally based communication platforms that offer another layer of leader-to-citizen pathways. The implications of this resource of information provision and audience access to the politics of leadership presentation and positioning will be considered later in the study.[32] What is important to note at this point is that leaders have exploited a profusion of media forms and techniques in order to take their message directly to those audiences whose attention they require for political purposes. The objection is that these activities can be seen as methods by which leaders seek to bypass knowledge-able, experienced, and authoritative networks of political communication and as-sessment that can act as valuable informal checks within a pluralistic democracy.

A further concern is raised over the extent to which the manner of 'going public' leads not merely to the bypassing of the more conventional forms of political reporting and news gathering but to deliberate attempts to transcend the standard notions of political understanding and choice on the part of the citizen consumer. Given the imperative need for leaders to penetrate the con-sciousness of the public audience in an increasingly segmented media environ-ment and given the centrality of television in the field of political communications, an issue arises over the way that messages are transmitted and received by those to whom they are directed. To a growing extent, the techniques of public leadership are being questioned on the grounds that far from informing the citizens so that they are able to make reasoned choices, the use of the mass media and television in particular militates against the use of rational argument in favour of a sensory distraction from complex issues.

Bruce Miroff, for example, has concluded that presidents in the US have increas-ingly derogated the substance of leadership into a derivative of public spectacle in which actions are meaningful 'not for what they achieve but for what they signify'.[33] Spectacles and television both feed off passive audiences. The combination allows public attention to be focused upon a central character engaged in an emblematic action that is designed to appeal to the senses of the onlookers, rather than to their reason. According to this perspective, television is instrumental in shaping the

Price, *Spin Doctor's Diary*; Kumar, *Managing the President's Message*. For an indication of the international dimension of political marketing, see James Harding, *Alpha Dogs: The Americans Who Turned Political Spin into a Global Business* (New York, NY: Farrar, Straus & Giroux, 2008).

  [32] See Chapter 11.

  [33] Bruce Miroff, 'The Presidency and the Public: Leadership as Spectacle', in Michael Nelson (ed.), *The Presidency and the Political System*, 2nd edn (Washington, DC: Congressional Quarterly, 1988), p. 272. See also Murray Edelman, *Constructing the Political Spectacle* (Chicago, IL: University of Chicago Press, 1988); Michael Schudson, 'Politics as Cultural Practice', *Political Communication*, 18 (4) October 2001: 421–31.

categories of popular political judgement in accordance with television's own properties as a communications medium. This encourages people to think not only that they can adjudicate between different candidates, but that they can do so on the basis of the visual impressions conveyed through television.

In a trend that has been discerned in other systems, the increased reliance upon television has changed the form and substance of political communication and with it the nature of political deliberation. The sober reflection of professional reputations and policy ideas supposedly gives way to personal immediacy, accessibility, and subliminal associations which in the contextual pressures of public leadership can be said to exert an increasingly disproportionate influence on the perceptual approaches to the issue of leadership itself. It has now become increasingly common for presidents and other leaders to combine spectacle and rhetoric so that the visual setting becomes choreographed to support, complement, and deepen the messages of a speech. Indeed the mix has generated complaints that the visual element has increasingly become the dominant constituent.

Kathleen Jamieson takes note of the way that imagery in general and television in particular evoke a particular set of cognitive repertoires which it is claimed have come to inhabit the projection, reception, and consumption of political leadership in media-rich environments.[34] Jamieson points out that because 'television is a visual medium whose natural grammar is associative, a person adept at visualizing claims in dramatic capsules will be able to use television to short-circuit the audience's demand that those claims be dignified with evidence'.[35] In the 1980s, President Ronald Reagan was especially adept at giving strategic emphasis to the visual dimensions of political communication. The Reagan White House went to great lengths to fine-tune the visual context of his public appearances and routinely to favour camera crews over reporters in respect to media access.[36] This strategy led to a host of complaints that it was tantamount to a process of distraction and displacement which in essence deflected the audience's critical faculties through an all-encompassing experience of artful exchange that allegedly rewarded impressionistic style over material political substance. In Jamieson's view, the 'moving synoptic moment . . . replaced the eloquent speech'[37] of reason, analysis, and argument. Notwithstanding the critiques of a style in which the sober reflection of legislative agendas and policy ideas was said to have given way to personal immediacy and symbolic appeals, many of the techniques deployed by the Reagan team have regularly been imitated by subsequent leaders (Box 7.4).

Perhaps the most serious critique concerning the processes and techniques of going public is their effect upon governance and arguably upon the value of leadership itself. It is possible to view this construction of leadership as a way

---

[34] Kathleen H. Jamieson, *Eloquence in an Electronic Age: The Transformation of Political Speechmaking* (Oxford: Oxford University Press, 1988).

[35] Jamieson, *Eloquence in an Electronic Age*, p. 13.

[36] See Anthony R. Dolan, 'Four Little Words', *Wall Street Journal*, 8 November 2009. See also President Reagan's Address at the Ceremony Commemorating the 40th Anniversary of the Normandy Invasion, D-day at Point-du-Hoc, 6 June 1984. Accessed 27 November 2011 at: <http://www.youtube.com/watch?v=eEIqdcHbc8I>; President Reagan's remarks on East–West relations at the Brandenburg Gate in West Berlin, Germany, 12 June 1987. Accessed 20 November 2011 at: <www.youtube.com/watch?v=5MDFX-dNtsM&feature=relmfu>.

[37] Jamieson, *Eloquence in an Electronic Age*, p. 117.

Box 7.4 David Cameron: The launch of the Conservative Party election campaign at the outset of the 2010 general election

---

David Cameron had already made a reputation for the strategic staging of policy statements and positioning events in the previous four and a half years between his election as leader of the Conservative Party and the start of the general election in April 2010.

On 6 April, Cameron addressed party workers in an open-air event on the banks of the Thames. The visual context was one of political renewal in which the Conservative Party, revitalized by its new leadership, would be able to displace what was depicted as an old and discredited administration lodged in the institutions of power. In order to convey that message, Cameron spoke to the assembled party loyalists in a rousing call for change that positioned the leader against a backdrop of a mobilized insurgency framed by the Houses of Parliament on the opposite bank of the river.

See 'David Cameron: The most important election for a generation', *Guardian*, 6 April 2010.

Available at: http://www.guardian.co.uk/uk/video/2010/apr/06/conservatives-david-cameron>.

A week later saw David Cameron launch the Conservative Party manifesto—not inside a purpose-built media arena but at a press conference located at the well-known London landmark of Battersea power station. Although the structure and surrounding area had already been designated for redevelopment, Cameron used the derelict site both to portray a sense of economic stagnation and to illustrate his trademark theme of a 'broken society'. Cameron ensured that the parallels were drawn. He underlined that the power station was a building 'in need of regeneration in a country in need of regeneration'.

The previous evening, a giant illuminated image of David Cameron had been projected onto the walls of the power station in a publicity event that bore a close resemblance to the classic Wonderbra marketing campaign in 1994. The product on this occasion was not underwear. It was an invitation for citizens to join the next Conservative government that offered a 'new kind of politics and a new kind of country'.

See 'Tories launch power-to-the-people manifesto', *Sky News*, 13 April 2010.

Available at: <http://news.sky.com/home/politics/article/15600327>.

---

of diminishing the status and role of other intermediary entities within the political process. The various ways of promoting the principle of disintermediation may allow a leader more discretionary licence in marginalizing other political participants and even other political institutions, but this relative independence from competing intermediaries can create concerns over the nature and direction of this form of direct connection between a leadership and its public.

One objection emphasizes the possible or actual deleterious effects upon the normal processes of political participation, consultation, and accountability. The argument here is that the strategic and tactical imperatives of the public leadership mode foster a condition known as the 'permanent campaign'[38] which is often

---

[38] Sidney Blumenthal, *The Permanent Campaign*, rev. edn. (New York, NY: Simon & Schuster, 1982); Norman J. Ornstein and Thomas E. Mann (eds.), *The Permanent Campaign and Its Future* (Washington. DC: The American Enterprise Institute for Public Policy Research/ Brookings Institution, 2000); George C. Edwards III, 'Campaigning is Not Governing: Bill Clinton's Rhetorical Presidency', in Colin Campbell and Bert A. Rockman (eds.), *The Clinton Legacy* (New York, NY: Chatham House Publishers/Seven Bridges Press, 2000), pp. 33–47; Corey Cook, 'The Contemporary Presidency: The Permanence of the "Permanent Campaign": George W. Bush's Public Presidency', *Presidential Studies Quarterly*, 32(4) 2002: 753–64; George C. Edwards III, *Governing by Campaigning: The Politics of the Bush Presidency*, 2nd edn. (New York, NY: Longman, 2007).

regarded as antithetical to the requirements of good governance or to the principles of a constitutional order. The phenomenon of permanent campaigning either between competing claimants to public leadership, or in support of one overriding exponent of 'going public', can therefore be viewed as endangering the normal interplay of democratic politics in favour of a *de facto* substitute in the form of an enhanced leadership operating according to a self-defined construction of national democracy. In this way the fusion of leadership and representation can appear to point in two quite separate directions. Leaders can utilize the authority derived from their representative status in order to establish a legitimized programme of governance. On the other hand, leaders can opt to cultivate a close and continuing engagement with their representative base which can displace governing responsibilities in favour of an order of priorities that privileges responsiveness but also caution and lack of direction.

A variant of this concern refers to the way that public leadership methods can cultivate excessive responsiveness to popular moods and to the appeasement of unmediated expressions of public opinion. Enriched levels of political communication based on a high-profile relationship between leadership and public can be consistent with volatile forms of populist politics along with its attendant spasms of instability, uncertainty, and even intolerance. According to this perspective, the impulse to engage in a style of permanent campaigning is based upon a need to subordinate policy and governing responsibilities to the maintenance of public support and the need for leaders to remain within the parameters of current popular opinion. Far from offering a leading sense of direction, this kind of public leadership appears to be shaped, presented, and projected by a continual process of market testing and message engineering dominated by teams of political advisers, media consultants, market strategists, focus groups, and pubic relations experts. 'Going public' under this guise is less about its usage as an instrument of programmatic agenda construction and more as a device for maintaining leadership penetration in audience profiles. Ironically, the increasingly sophisticated techniques of leadership projection and rapid responsiveness to themes of popular concern, in what is an already a crowded media context, have the effect of contributing further to the very diversification of political communication and to the segmentation of governance that challenge the positional resources of leaders in advanced mediated democracies.[39]

CONCLUSION

The issue of leadership and its relationship to representation and communication is one that is open to various interpretations and prescriptions. Given the numerous theories and constructions of representation—as well as the variety of ways of communicating its claims and implications within the realm of practical politics—the position of political leaders is normally one of constant negotiation. In terms

---

[39] See Jay G. Blumler and Dennis Kavanagh, 'The Third Age of Political Communication: Influences and Features', *Political Communication*, 16(3) 1999: 209–30.

of the precise nature of the relationship, it is often difficult to determine who or what is being represented, how it is operationalized, and to what purpose. It is evident, for example, that just as political communication cannot always be conceived as a one-way process, so representational processes can be reversed with some leaders intent upon acting as a mirror image of their audiences by effectively re-presenting their opinions and positions back to them in the guise of populist leadership. Locating leadership within such a spectrum of representation and communication, therefore, will largely define the nature of a leader's style and the type of narrative which is attached to the task and purposes of an adopted leadership role.

As a consequence, the degree to which a leadership remains politically feasible will be dependent upon its capacity to deploy its representational and communication resources to good effect. A failure to do so, or an inability to prevent the depletion of such resources, will usually expose the vulnerability of a leader and with it increase the likelihood of a leadership's deterioration in favour of another with a different portfolio of representational claims and communication strategies. It is this element of contingency, disconnection, and vulnerability within what is almost invariably an implicitly or explicitly competitive environment of contested leadership claims that makes leaders so concerned over their position in respect to those whom they claim to represent. It is for this reason that many of them increasingly turn to private organizations with specialist competences that are not based upon party or political attachments. This form of professionalized ancillary assistance constitutes a growing force in the field. More than that, it opens up an entire dimension of leadership studies which has become conspicuously germane to the construction, viability, and even ethos of contemporary political leadership. It is this phenomenon and its repercussions that form the basis of the next chapter.

8

Women leaders: A case of problematic parameters

According to a Rasmussen Poll in 2005, 72% of Americans said they would be willing to vote for a woman for president, but only 49% thought their family, friends and co-workers would vote for a woman candidate.

Rasmussen Poll, April 2005

'For men who have spent all of their life engaged in the conquest of power, seeing a woman overtaking them is viscerally unbearable.'

Ségolène Royal[1]

PREAMBLE

Women leaders in politics have been and remain an unusual phenomenon. Even in modern democracies with clearly articulated commitments to equal opportunities and heightened awareness of feminist issues, female leaders are something of a rarity. This is not to deny that advances have been made by women in this domain. However, it is still the case that female political leaders continue to be very much out of the ordinary and to an extent that makes them still outstanding in the sense of being conspicuously at variance with a norm that becomes more evidently dominant through the reference point of the largely absent category of women in leadership positions.

This disjunction raises a number of important questions about the relationship between gender on the one hand and leadership sources and personnel on the other. Given that women make up over half the pool of available human resources, the dearth of female leaders opens up a host of issues concerning not just the recruitment of leaders but also the study of political leadership in general. The lack of proportionality in the incidence of women leaders opens up themes concerning the level and location of bias and other forms of restriction in the channels of elevation to leadership positions. The distribution patterns of women at these levels throw light on the conditioning effects of social forces, historical traditions,

---

[1] Ségolène Royal quoted in Matthew Campbell, 'Royal: I'll end the French malaise', *Sunday Times*, 19 November 2006.

and cultural attitudes towards both the access channels to leadership and the nature of its constructed meaning and legitimacy within a political order.

ON THE POLITICAL MARGINS

The presence of women in positions of political leadership is not a neutral phenomenon. It is not so much a theme as a cause for comment and controversy. Females at the apex of political hierarchies are still regarded as conspicuous in their own right—not primarily as office-holders but as women who have achieved the ultimate distinction in what is an otherwise male-dominated environment. Women who have acquired the rank of a leader are normally seen as individuals who are distinguished by an extraordinary level of achievement that in turn is translated into a personal narrative and status that are widely deemed to amount to an exceptional set of circumstances. In essence, the connection between women and leadership continues to provoke particular forms of ambivalence. These are distinguished by a series of confusing and even paradoxical outlooks coexisting with one another around a theme that lends itself to multiple prejudices on what constitutes the appropriate place of women in respect to the sources and exercise of leadership.[2]

The continued existence of what remains in many quarters an enduring scepticism towards the idea of women acting as leaders manifests itself in a variety of ways that indicate different forms of prejudgement and discrimination. At its most negative level, the bias against women in this field feeds off a more generalized antipathy towards the entire gender that simply extends itself compulsively to nearly all walks of life. In terms of leadership, this misogynistic outlook tends to settle upon critiques that view women as either a damaging source of distraction to leaders or as manipulative agencies behind the throne who allegedly exercise power not just without responsibility but more often than not with neither reason nor judgement. Lady Macbeth, and the way that she was depicted by Shakespeare,[3] has proved to be the classic cautionary tale of the destructive effects of a scheming woman at the centre of power. Through the act of inciting her husband to follow ambition and seize the Scottish crown through an act of regicide, the

---

[2] Hannah R. Bowles and Kathleen L. McGinn, 'Claiming Authority: Negotiating Challenges for Women Leaders', in David M. Messick and Roderick M. Kramer (eds.), *The Psychology of Leadership: New Perspectives and Research* (Mahwah, NJ: Lawrence Erlbaum, 2005), pp. 191–208; Patricia L. Sykes, 'The Gendered Nature of Leadership Analysis: Lessons from Women Leaders as Executives in Anglo-American Systems', in Joseph Masciulli, Mikhail A. Molchanov, and W. Andy Knight (eds.), *The Ashgate Research Companion to Political Leadership* (Farnham: Ashgate, 2009), pp. 219–39; Jennifer L. Lawless and Richard L. Fox, *It Still Takes a Candidate: Why Women Don't Run for Office* (New York, NY: Cambridge University Press, 2010); Robin J. Ely and Deborah L. Rhode, 'Women and Leadership: Defining the Challenges', in Nitin Nohria and Rakesh Khurana (eds.), *Handbook of Leadership Theory and Practice: A Harvard Business School Centennial Colloquium* (Boston, MA: Harvard Business Publishing, 2010), pp. 377–410; Alice H. Eagly and Linda L. Carli, 'Gender and Leadership', in Alan Bryman, David Collinson, Keith Grint, Brad Jackson, and Mary Uhl Bien (eds.), *The Sage Handbook of Leadership* (London: Sage Publications, 2011), pp. 269–85.

[3] William Shakespeare, *Macbeth* (London: Heinemann Educational, 1968).

character of Lady Macbeth has become a metaphor for vicarious and manipulative ambition behind the throne. It is a name whose notoriety as a readily available caricature continues to haunt the wives of senior politicians in their quest to establish a role for themselves without inciting accusations of improper and illegitimate influence.

This kind of absolutist negativism is of course directed with particular force to those women who actually aspire to be leaders in their own right, or who have actually achieved leadership status. The same prejudice against women in positions of proximity to power is simply extended to those who have by one means or another succeeded in climbing to the senior ranks of political status. This reactionary standpoint is often joined by more calibrated views that are not as extreme but which have much the same effect in respect to material and attitudinal conclusions. One variant is based on the view that the traditional purpose of a social order has been and remains the protection of the vulnerable which is a category epitomized by women. This perspective is deemed to be historically sanctioned through custom, practice, and in many cases by religious doctrine.

Because women have been regarded as possessing different social natures and separate social roles to those of men, their political and legal rights in many social contexts have not been denied so much as cast as largely irrelevant to the effective conduct of a secure and orderly society. In many cultures, the subordination of women to a largely enclosed domestic context of patriarchal hierarchy has had a self-perpetuating effect in which women are still commonly conceived as requiring protection not only from politics but also from the complexities and calculations as well as the dangers and vulgarities of the public realm.[4] This outlook was common in the West during the nineteenth century when women were thought to be entitled to protection from what was viewed as an exceptionally male preserve. While this view has diminished, remnants of it remain with varied references or subtexts implicitly relating either to a presumptive lack of aptitude on the part of women in this field, or to a generic need to prioritize male characteristics in politics as a matter of natural history, biological composition, and social cohesion.

A less traditional but no less oppressive source of discrimination comes in the form of what is presented as an empirical conclusion drawn from the incidence and location of leadership in society. In what is often cited as a form of social realism, the claim is that leadership is an intrinsically male-oriented activity. In the same way that leadership functions are closely aligned to notions of domination, so it is that the subject area is permeated not just with male characteristics but with the prevailing physical presence of male individuals. To the extent that women are absent from the ranks of leadership, so it is that further weight is added to the initial presumption of a revealed dynamic which naturally privileges men in such an area.

The circularity of this position is completed by the way that women come to be categorized as a negative descriptor of leadership properties. Just as women conspicuously fail to acquire the leadership positions in ratio to their numbers,

---

[4] For an illuminating reflection on the heavily circumscribed role of women in the nineteenth century's political and public spheres—and on the corresponding need for liberal reform to secure women's rights—see John Stuart Mill's 1869 essay on the *Subjection of Women*. John Stuart Mill, *On Liberty and the Subjection of Women* (London: Penguin, 2006), pp. 131–244.

so the logic of this position determines that the reason lies in a fundamental gender difference that relates to behaviour, aptitude, and temperament. The conditioning effect of this view is strong because it possesses a self-perpetuating and self-validating logic. It takes the lack of women in leadership positions and converts what is a factual observation into both a functional argument and a normative principle to be followed on the basis of a utilitarian prescription for leadership as a necessarily male domain in which males naturally excel.[5]

The roots of this attitudinal predisposition are so deep-set within the fabric of most societies that they are difficult even to explain with any degree of causal precision—let alone to redirect them into a wholly different trajectory. Amanda Sinclair has been particularly insightful in demonstrating the way that a complex amalgam of factors linked to history, culture, politics, language, gender, and knowledge production exert behavioural and psychological pressures against the entry of women into leadership positions. Because of the way that leadership is presented and prescribed in social arrangements as a set of preferred and even essential characteristics depicted through male figures, women have found themselves confronted by practices based upon cultural assumptions that are circular in their logic and exclusionary in their effects. In essence, women are unfavourably differentiated from men in the context of leadership. Sinclair describes the distinction as one that is maintained by an array of unconscious processes and societal archetypes which generate highly durable patterns of gender-inscribed notions of what leadership is and who leaders should be. As a consequence, women who aspire to leadership positions do not simply have to contend with overt forms of bias but also with less tangible types of preselection that limit women's access to leadership spaces and confine them to an outlier status in the competition for leadership credibility.[6] It is because of the culturally conditioning forces operating at the centre of what is categorized as a social construction of leadership which prompts Sinclair to assert that 'leadership doesn't speak to women in the way it does to many men'.[7]

Even in societies that classify themselves as attached to liberal and modern norms, enduring senses of gender difference remain in existence. Notwithstanding the adopted discourses of discrimination denial, cultural biases persist—albeit in more nuanced and subtle forms. These still draw on the old reflexive drives against women but they are portrayed in a far more measured manner. One example of this kind of unfavourable treatment is illustrated by those cases where women have either acquired positions of leadership or are thought to have considerable influence over a leader. There may be no explicit critique of a woman in this position. On the contrary, the legal right and social appropriateness of women in leadership positions may be advanced as a matter of principle.

---

[5] See Alice H. Eagly and Steven J. Karau, 'Role Congruity Theory of Prejudice toward Female Leaders', *Psychological Review*, 109(3) 2002: 573–98; Alice H. Eagly and Linda L. Carli, *Through the Labyrinth: The Truth About How Women Become Leaders* (Boston, MA: Harvard Business School Press, 2007), chs. 2, 3, 6, 7.

[6] Amanda Sinclair, *Doing Leadership Differently: Gender, Power, and Sexuality in a Changing Business Culture* (Melbourne: Melbourne University Publishing, 1998); Amanda Sinclair, *Leadership for the Disillusioned: Moving Beyond Myths and Heroes to Leading That Liberates* (Crow's Nest, NSW: Allen & Unwin, 2007), chs. 6, 8.

[7] Sinclair, *Doing Leadership Differently*, p. vii.

Nevertheless, the actual occupancy can be treated in a way that diminishes the achievement. Instead of focusing on the substantive qualities of an individual woman, or on the general themes of equity, access, and inclusion, it is not uncommon for advances of this kind to be trivialized as bizarre diversions from the norm. The subtext is that of a curiosity which again underlines the exceptional nature of the elevation.

The sources of a woman's rise to power and the circumstances surrounding it are usually closely examined with the clear intention of casting doubt not only on the independence of the office-holder but also on her authenticity as a leader in her own right. In giving emphasis to the unorthodox nature of a woman in such a position, news organizations and journalists can all too easily fall prey to the more customary approaches and styles reserved for the analysis of women for mass public consumption. The newsworthiness of women leaders often takes the form of adopting either implicitly or overtly sexist categories of analysis that relate to physical appearance, personal deportment, dress sense, hair style, and accessories selection as well as a host of lifestyle indicators. Some of this treatment may well come from a simple lack of experience in selecting alternative forms of commentary and assessment that are more appropriately distinct from the sensory and superficial modes that characterize so much of the public projection of women in the media. Another base of this impoverished and often patronizing coverage comes simply from an inertial drift towards the standard categories of gender bias which are unreflectively extended to embrace the implied notoriety of women in such a high-profile and high-exposure position.

This is not to imply that the visual and symbolic accoutrements of personal identity are insignificant in the presentation of male candidates for leadership. It is that with women leaders, the physical aspects of appearance and performance are thought to acquire a much higher degree of salience which can privilege style over substance. So much so that it is suggested that women who aspire to, or hold, leadership positions exemplify a process by which 'the body' becomes a device through which gendered constructions of leadership become highly salient. The presentation of physical features, mannerisms, stance, clothing, and vocal delivery, together with such framing aspects as backgrounds, settings, and staging, underline the extent to which leadership is a performance designed to stimulate responses that are often visceral, sensual, and subliminal in nature. Sinclair, for example, draws particular attention to the importance of 'bodies and bodily performances' and the way these are represented and received in 'the construction of leadership personae'. She continues: 'The bodies of men and women . . . are often represented differently, activating unconscious processes and societal archetypes that reinforce or undermine authority, power and leadership capital.'[8] Women are considered to be at a defining disadvantage because in the competition to establish a leadership identity and to acquire leadership resources women have to engage in a public representation of bodies that almost invariably acts as a site for negative differentiation.[9]

[8] Amanda Sinclair, 'Bodies and Identities in Constructing Leadership Capital', in Paul 't Hart and John Uhr (eds.), *Public Leadership: Perspectives and Practices* (Canberra: ANU E Press, 2008), p. 84.
[9] For example, see Caroline Heldman, Susan J. Carroll, and Stephanie Olson, '"She Brought Only a Skirt": Print Media Coverage of Elizabeth Dole's Bid for the Republican Presidential Nomination',

The physical dimensions of male leaders appear to operate within a wide threshold of cultural tolerance—even to the extent where their physical characteristics are often regarded as being practically invisible.[10] While male leaders are normally represented in formal suits with little or no exposure of non-facial skin, women have no resort to such an established dress code with the result that the subsequent variation in presentation can evoke an unpredictable diversity of interpretive constructions even within the same audience. Women are commonly constrained to highlight a more expansive degree of bodily exposure with its connotations of a pronounced sexually based identity. Men on the other hand normally convey a more masculinist imagery of bodily concealment that suggests intellectual power, a seriousness of purpose, and a dedication of the mind over emotional sources of distraction. As a result, women are left to negotiate their way through a far more volatile range of consumption drives that can respond impulsively to what are considered to be cues by women to be seen as set apart on the grounds of bodily defined identities. In these conditions, otherness can be equated with idiosyncrasy, eccentricity, oddness, precocity, superficiality, frailty, or simply indiscipline. As such, female leaders can serve not only to reify gendered stereotypes, but also to disorientate the normal evaluative faculties of audiences more accustomed to male depictions of leadership roles. The net effect can be one either of incitement to conventionally sexist responses, or of bemused distraction that allows a more random set of reactions that are often construed to preclude a fair and balanced assessment of leadership credentials.

Two examples illustrate the predicament. For the 2007 French presidential election, the Socialist Party nominated Ségolène Royal as its candidate. Royal was not only a serious contender for national office but was also the first woman to be nominated by a major party in France. However, the allure of physical appeal became a constant subject of political comment, prompting a concern as to whether she was 'just an elegant vase in which voters were busily arranging the flowers of their dreams'.[11] The issue of her physical attraction became a distraction in its own right. This was typified by the fact the most abiding image of her campaign was a private photograph of her on a beach in a bikini. In a different vein, Sarah Palin, the Republican vice-presidential candidate in the 2008 US presidential election was the first woman to be selected by her party on a national ticket. Palin was subjected to sustained allegations relating to a dysfunctional family, her low intelligence, her ingrown attitudes, and her political inexperience.[12] The most memorable photograph of her campaign was that of Palin and her son 'field-dressing'[13] the bloodied carcass of a 900 lb moose that she had shot dead. It may well have been an attempt to demonstrate masculine virtues amidst

Political Communication, 22(3) 2005: 315–35; Caroline Heldman and Lisa Wade, 'Sexualizing Sarah Palin: The Social and Political Context of the Sexual Objectification of Female Candidates', *Sex Roles*, 65(3–4) August 2011: 156–64.

[10] See Amanda Sinclair, 'Body Possibilities in Leadership', *Leadership*, 1(4) November 2005: 387–406.

[11] John Thornhill, 'Liberté, égalité, feminité', Financial Times, 21/22 October 2006.

[12] See Matthew Continetti, *The Persecution of Sarah Palin: How the Elite Media Tried to Bring Down a Rising Star* (New York, NY: Sentinel HC, 2009).

[13] 'Field dressing' includes cleaning, bleeding, and some initial butchery.

an otherwise heavy media emphasis upon her as a sexualized object[14] but it was widely acclaimed to be proof positive of a misplaced episode of role confusion derived from her redneck backwardness. Both candidates lost their elections.

A slightly less negative posture but one that still betrays a prejudicial outlook is when a woman is regarded as an acceptable candidate for leadership but only on certain quite specific grounds and in particular circumstances. A woman might be considered as a suitable leader in order to fulfil what may be considered to be an idiosyncratic set of requirements. For example, there is something of a tradition whereby the wives of members of the US Congress can be asked to take over legislative responsibilities on the occasion of the unexpected death of their husbands.[15] Solowiej and Brunell claim that this 'widow effect' can be regarded as 'the single most important historical method' by which women have entered Congress and that as a result this form of political recruitment has over time 'changed the fundamental make-up of both chambers of the U.S. Congress'.[16]

The rationale of such a preferment is usually defended on utilitarian grounds as an interim arrangement to allow time for the party involved to identify suitable candidates and to complete the process of selection in preparation for the next scheduled election. In acting as a temporary replacement, a widow in this position is seen more as a leadership solution rather than a leadership problem. However, the solution is a heavily qualified one insofar as the cause of female access to leadership is concerned. In such circumstances, the widow is accepted as a convenient adjunct to her late husband and as a non-controversial instrument to an exercise in power management. In effect, she is accepted in the short term on the understanding that she would be unacceptable in the long term. Women in these predicaments become figures of political memorialization whose only political and representative authority is derived from their late husbands rather than from any individual claim to merit or standing. They are acceptable as women in a leadership context but only insofar as they offer to facilitate a transition to another set of arrangements in which they will play no further part.

Two other types of occasion when women are favoured as leadership material to meet specific political requirements are worthy of note. The first relates to those circumstances when a female member of a political family is seen as the best available opportunity for a party or an organization to ensure either its continuity in power, or its potential for regaining power. Probably the best illustrative case of this kind of dynastic strategizing has been that provided by the Nehru/Gandhi political family which was discussed in Chapter 5. The other form of accelerated female promotion in this category occurs when a wife or partner of a leader enters the reckoning as a possible replacement or as a future successor. The favourable outcome of a cost–benefit calculation regarding a female candidate in these

---

[14] Nathan A. Heflick and Jamie L. Goldenberg, 'Objectifying Sarah Palin: Evidence that Objectification Causes Women to be Perceived as Less Competent and Less Fully Human', *Journal of Experimental Social Psychology*, 45(3) May 2009: 598–601.

[15] See Diane D. Kincaid, 'Over His Dead Body: A Positive Perspective on Widows in the U.S Congress', *Western Political Quarterly*, 31(1) March 1978: 96–104; Lisa Solowiej and Thomas L. Brunell, 'The Entrance of Women to the U.S. Congress: The Widow Effect', *Political Research Quarterly*, 56(3) September 2003: 283–92.

[16] Solowiej and Brunell, 'The Entrance of Women to the U.S. Congress: The Widow Effect', p. 283.

circumstances may be based upon an already achieved high recognition factor, or on a perceived political apprenticeship having been served under the aegis of a male spouse; or alternatively as a means by which to evade constitutional or legal limitations on the tenure of a presidential or prime ministerial office (Box 8.1).

Box 8.1 Women leaders and the issue of family connection: Four cases

Family connections #1: Cristina Fernández Kirchner
Cristina Fernández Kirchner rose to prominence as the wife of Néstor Kirchner who became a popular and influential president of Argentina in 2003. Cristina Kirchner had been a senior partner in the law firm set up by her future husband before he became Governor of Santa Cruz—a position from which he campaigned for the presidency. His wife combined the role of First Lady with her position as a representative in the National Congress. Despite leading a successful administration, Néstor Kirchner successfully groomed his wife to succeed him after only one term of office. In 2007, Cristina Kirchner became the first woman to be elected president in the country's history. Amidst rumours that her husband occupied the position of a parallel president who set the agendas and made the key decisions in the government, Cristina built up her own following in the Peronist tradition of Argentinian politics by cultivating a suggested identity with the iconic figure of Eva Peron. At the same time, it became increasingly clear that Néstor Kirchner was intent upon returning to the presidency in 2011. This led to widespread speculation that the Kirchners were devising a way around the constitutional prohibition on any individual serving more than two *successive* terms as president. It was thought that they were planning to extend their presence in the presidential office to a succession of alternating four-year terms. While this strategy was nullified by the unexpected death of Néstor Kirchner in 2010, it nevertheless led to Cristina Kirchner offering herself as a candidate for the 2011 presidential election. She was re-elected by a landslide margin with 54 per cent of the popular vote. The second-place candidate secured just 17 per cent.

Family connections #2: Hillary Clinton
While it is true that Hillary Clinton had been an influential lawyer and a political activist at the state level, she first emerged on to the national stage through her husband's prominence as president of the United States (1993–2001). Her conception of the First Lady's role was conspicuously at variance with the historical norm in that she was regarded as a major political figure within the Clinton administration. In addition to having an office in the premium West Wing of the White House, Hillary had considerable influence in appointments and policy decisions. Her political skills and status were underlined by her taking the lead in the organization and promotion of the Clinton administration's priority policy initiative in health care. Although this plan did not receive Congressional support, it did underline her strategic role at the highest levels of government—so much so that it was widely seen to amount to an informal system of 'co-presidencies'. When her husband was constitutionally required to leave the presidential office after two terms, Hillary was increasingly able to carve out a political career in her own right. She won a seat in the US Senate in 2000 and was re-elected in 2008. During this period, she built up her own political base and was a long-term favourite to become the Democratic Party's presidential candidate in 2008. While narrowly losing out for the nomination, she nevertheless secured the prestigious position of Secretary of State in the Obama administration—a position which has kept her in the public eye and with it the potential for securing her party's nomination for the 2016 presidential election.

Family connections #3: Yingluck Shinawatra
Yingluck Shinawatra is the younger sister of Thaksin Shinawatra who was prime minister of Thailand for five years until he was ousted from office in 2006. He had not only become

the first prime minister to serve out a full term of office but had won re-election in a landslide victory in 2005. However, he was displaced by a military junta in 2006 and while he returned to power in the post-coup elections of 2008 he was once again manoeuvred out of position when he was accused of financial irregularities and sentenced to two years' imprisonment while he was out of the country. Despite his self-imposed exile, Mr Shinawatra has remained a major force in Thai politics. Apart from controlling the main opposition Pheu Thai Party, he has been a central figure in the United Front for Democracy against Dictatorship which is a highly organized protest movement known colloquially as the 'Red Shirts' owing to their dress code in street demonstrations. In Thaksin's absence, Yingluck—who Mr Shinawatra has described as his 'clone'—became the leader of the Pheu Thai Party. Despite having virtually no political experience, Ms Shinawatra managed to infuse new energy into the party by reaffirming its populist credentials and consolidating its traditional support base amongst the rural poor. In the 2011 general election, she ran an accomplished campaign which combined charismatic appeal with a conciliatory posture towards opponents in what has become an increasingly polarized society. The outcome was an emphatic electoral victory with Yingluck becoming Thailand's first female prime minister and the country's youngest premier for over 60 years.

Family connections #4: Park Geun-hye

In securing victory in the 2012 presidential election, Park Geun-hye became the first female leader in South Korea's history. However, her passage to the presidential Blue House was less of a new experience for her than at first it may have appeared. This is because Park Geun-hye is the daughter of Park Chung-hee who was president from 1961 to 1979. Born in 1952, Park Geun-hye had not only been a resident of the Blue House for much of the 1960s and 1970s, but had served as the *de facto* First Lady after her mother was killed in an assassination attempt on her father in 1974. Although President Park Chung-hee is widely credited with being the chief architect of South Korea's model of economic development, President Park Chung-hee was also regarded as a highly autocratic figure who was responsible for an array of human rights abuses.

In 1979, he was assassinated by the Director of the Korean Central Intelligence Agency. In her 2012 campaign, the president's daughter pledged to retain her father's conservative base but also to modernize it by confronting the social problems associated with the high level of economic inequality and with the power of the South Korea's *chaebol* conglomerates. Despite the symbolic force of being the country's first female president, commentators remain doubtful whether Park Geun-hye's return to the presidential mansion will result in a transformation of attitudes towards gender equality as South Korea is distinguished as having the highest median male–female pay differentials in the OECD.

Whatever the rationale, the female element still tends to be couched in the mould of an option of convenience and accordingly as a derivative of the initial male leader. The sequential pattern is invariably that of a woman following on from the male counterpart and as such it is often described as a device through which the 'senior partner' acquires a *de facto* extension of tenure.

Perhaps the most insidious form of gendered exclusion is that which is portrayed as inclusion. This often assumes the form of a liberal attachment to the principles of equal rights and non-discrimination but one that is not translated into political practice where leadership positions are concerned. It is as if the declaration of open access is conjoined to a state of denial in which those who are apparently certain in their adoption of women's rights as a guiding axiom neither implement them in practice nor recognize the disjunction between norms and practice. On the contrary, the likelihood is that the reasons for engaging in forms of biased selection against women leaders are rationalized not on the basis of any inherent prejudice on the part of those closely involved in planning or organizing the recruitment processes but on the basis of the attitudes and positions of others in the wider public. Any responsibility for discrimination is thereby transposed to the requirements of political strategizing in which the weaknesses and liabilities of candidates for public office have to be assessed and acted upon.

Adherents of equal access in such circumstances might claim that while they were genuine in their views, they necessarily had to be guided by the behavioural responses and political attitudes of others in the wider political process. Of course, it is equally plausible that such a position can be conceived as revealing a nominal or conditional attachment to women's rights which is more symbolic than substantive in nature and one that involves little actual conviction in the area of women's advancement to positions of leadership. Either way, the outcomes are broadly similar to the consequences of the more uninhibited suspicions of, and explicit antagonisms against, women aspiring to positions of political leadership.

INROADS AND ACQUISITIONS

These varied strands of absolute and qualified prejudice can be seen as having a cumulative effect which maintains women in the position of high-risk options for leadership. While it is true that women in many systems and situations are still regarded more as *potential* leadership material rather than as *actual* contenders, it is also the case that gender barriers have diminished over recent times. Increasingly, there are signs that general social and cultural movements towards greater accessibility for women entering into the top flight of organizations have reached the sphere of political leadership. Notwithstanding the continued presence of scepticism and resistance, another aspect to the issue of women and leadership has been opening up. It has raised the issue of whether the conditioning forces of gendered discrimination are in the process of being overcome.

This more positive perspective is based upon the claim that as women have made increasing strides into senior positions in the professions and in the commercial field, the barriers against women progressing into positions of political leadership are no longer as insurmountable as they once were. The main argument in favour of this viewpoint is the rising incidence of women both as serious aspirants to leadership and as individuals who have actually acquired the status of senior political leadership. In mid 2011,[17] there were female presidents in Argentina, Brazil, Costa Rica, Finland, India, Ireland, Kosovo, Kyrgyzstan, Liberia, Lithuania, San Marino, and Switzerland. In addition, women held prime ministerial positions in Australia, Bangladesh, Croatia, Germany, Iceland, Mali, Peru, Slovakia, and Trinidad and Tobago and in the self-governing territories of

---

[17] Data drawn form Worldwide Guide to Women in Leadership. Accessed 17 February 2012 at: <http://www.guide2womenleaders.com>.

Bermuda, Sint Maarten, and the Åland Islands.[18] In addition to the recorded number of women in high leadership positions, the geographical and cultural spread of these advances is equally worthy of note—including as they do states in Europe, Latin America, Asia, Africa, and the Caribbean.

It must also be acknowledged that the women in these powerful and emblematic offices should not be seen as necessarily a kind of token and isolated presence in what are otherwise male-dominated systems. They often signify a more cumulative process of female representation in the senior ranks of political and governmental responsibility. The Worldwide Guide to Women in Leadership is the main organization that records and measures the incidence of women in leadership positions on a global basis. According to its figures, women have increasingly acquired positions of responsibility in the sector of party organizations and in the ranks of ministerial positions. In the former, women have featured in the senior cadres of 161 party systems around the world during the first eleven years of the twenty-first century.[19] In the latter, the number of governing units whose governments have included female ministers stands at 342.[20]

Of course, these kinds of indices can mask great variations in depth and distribution (Figure 8.1). Denmark, for example, has a very rich tradition of female representation in party and ministerial structures. Since the Second World War, forty-nine women have reached senior positions in Danish political parties,[21] while the number of female ministers in Denmark is recorded as sixty-three.[22] By contrast, 2009 marked the year that Monaco and Saudi Arabia acquired their very first female ministers—making these states the last ones in global politics to include a woman in their ministerial systems.[23] Notwithstanding the uneven profile of female incidence in such leadership positions, it is nevertheless noteworthy that the trend towards female representation at these levels has become a worldwide phenomenon and one in which there is clear evidence of a rising trajectory of incidence. This can be discerned in the following comparison. The number of women who achieved a position of vice-president or deputy leader of government within their states during the period between 1900 and 1989 has been recorded as forty-four.[24] By contrast the

---

[18] It is noteworthy that the number of female presidents had increased from 9 (2009) to 12 (July 2011) in less than two years. Likewise, the number of female prime ministers also increased from 7 to 12 over the same period.

[19] Data drawn from 'Woman Party Leaders', Worldwide Guide to Women in Leadership. Accessed 17 February 2012 at: <http://www.guide2womenleaders.com/woman_party_leaders.htm>.

[20] Data drawn from 'Female Ministers by Country', Worldwide Guide to Women in Leadership. Accessed 18 February 2012 at: <http://www.guide2womenleaders.com/female_ministers_by_country. html>. It should be noted that in this dataset, the category of 'country' included self-governing and non-self-governing dependencies as well as various territories and protectorates.

[21] Data drawn from 'Danish Female Party Leaders—and Holders of other High Party Offices'. Accessed 27 February 2012 at: <http://www.guide2womenleaders.com/Danmark_Party_List.htm>.

[22] Data drawn from 'Danish Female Ministers', Worldwide Guide to Women in Leadership. Accessed 27 February 2012 at: <http://www.guide2womenleaders.com/Danmark_List.htm>.

[23] Saudi Arabia 2009—Deputy Minister of Education for Women's Affairs, Norah al-Faiz; Monaco 2009—Government Councillor of Finance and Economy, Sophie Thevenoux.

[24] Data drawn from 'Woman Vice Premier Ministers and Deputy Chiefs of Government 1920–1990', Worldwide Guide to Women in Leadership. Accessed 27 February 2012 at: <http:// www.guide2womenleaders.com/Vice_Premiers1920.htm>.

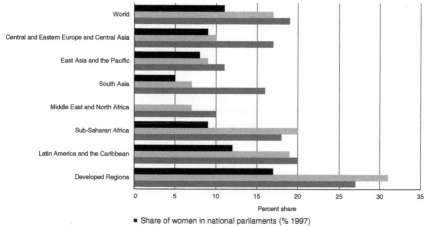

Figure 8.1. Women's advances in parliamentary seats and ministerial positions: World and regional rates

Source: United Nations/UN Women, *Progress of the World's Women 2011–2012: In Pursuit of Justice*, pp. 122–6. Available at: <http://progress.unwomen.org/pdfs/EN-Report-Progress.pdf>.

number of women acquiring the same position over the 1990–9 period was seventy-six.[25] The levels rose again to 108 between 2000 and 2009.[26]

Whether these shifts can be attributed to a triumph of feminism, to a pragmatic use of a social resource, to the recognition of a representational value, or to a liberalization of opportunities, the effect can be presented as signifying a marked penetration by women into the higher reaches of political power. A number of cases can be cited to give a more specific and tangible property to what are often portrayed as long-term trend lines. Scandinavia offers a profusion of examples of the extent to which women have entered the ranks of political leadership. For example, from 1990 to 2011, women had held ministerial positions on sixty-nine occasions in Denmark and on seventy-one occasions in Finland, while the incidence of female ministers in Sweden registered reached the figure of eighty-four.[27]

Far from being atypical members of their governments, women ministers have at times even reached the point of achieving parity with their male counterparts. In Sweden and Finland, there have actually been occasions when women ministers were preponderant within their respective governments. These senior layers of

---

[25] Data drawn from 'Woman Vice Premier Ministers and Deputy Chiefs of Government 1990–1999', Worldwide Guide to Women in Leadership. Accessed 27 February 2012 at: <http://www.guide2womenleaders.com/Vice_Premiers1990.htm>.

[26] Data drawn from 'Woman Vice Premier Ministers and Deputy Chiefs of Government From 2000', Worldwide Guide to Women in Leadership. Accessed 27 February 2012 at <http://www.guide2womenleaders.com/Vice_Premiers2000.htm>.

[27] Data drawn from 'The Situation of Female Membership of Governments', Worldwide Guide to Women in Leadership. Accessed 27 February 2012 at <www.guide2womenleaders.com/situation_in_2011.htm>.

female politicos can and have led to women achieving the top jobs. In Norway, as early as 1981, Dr Gro Harlem Brundtland became Norway's first woman prime minister. Moreover she went on to lead two further administrations (1986–9, 1990–6) amounting to over ten years in office. In 2003, Finland witnessed the extraordinary concurrence of two firsts in female leadership when the country's first female president, Tarja Halonen, was joined by Finland's first female prime minister, Anneli Jäätteenmäki. While these conspicuous female incursions into the highest reaches of their governments have been impressive, it is important to note that they have been made within a region renowned for its long-standing political norms and legal strictures on behalf of gender equality.

Arguably, more significant indicators of progress lie elsewhere. Latin America has a reputation for social conservatism but even in this region there have some conspicuous advances in the political appeal of female leaders. In 2006, Michelle Bachelet became the first woman to be elected president of Chile. In fact, she was also the first woman to become president of any Latin American state who was not the wife or widow of a previous head of state or political leader.[28] After being both health and defence minister in the government of President Ricardo Lagos, Ms Bachelet led a centre–left coalition to secure 53.5 per cent of the vote in the presidential election. In a society renowned for its hierarchical attitudes, Catholic values, and macho sentiments, President Bachelet was a highly active president. She introduced a series of social and economic reforms—including some high-profile measures related to gender issues and women's rights (e.g. increased numbers of free crèches, new flexible working guidelines, and equal pay initiatives). She also declared her intention to close the gap between the rich and poor, and to press for improvements in the position of indigenous people within Chilean society.

It is noteworthy that one of President Bachelet's key presidential priorities was to facilitate increased female representation in the highest reaches of government. With this in mind, one of her first acts as president was to honour a campaign promise to operate with a cabinet that was gender balanced—i.e. an unprecedented equality of composition between male and female ministers. She even extended the principle of parity through to other senior layers of the central and regional administrations. Far from being an accidental or fortuitous political figure, President Bachelet had a personal authority of her own. She consolidated her position during the course of her presidency to such an extent that at the end of her term of office she had an approval rating of 81 per cent. Michelle Bachelet was a political heavyweight whose hold on the Chilean presidency only came to an end in 2010 because of a constitutional provision limiting presidents to one term of office. Her skill in holding a centre–left coalition together was underlined by the failure of her male successor to retain the coalition's hold on the electorate and to take advantage of a leftward trend in the region at the time.[29]

---

[28] Three other women have won presidential elections in South America (Janet Jagan of Guyana, Mireya Moscoso of Panama, and Violeta Chamorro of Nicaragua), but Bachelet was the first to win a seat without first becoming known through a husband's prominence. Maria Estela Isabel Martinez de Peron was her husband's vice-president in Argentina before her accession to the presidency after his death.

[29] Jennifer Ross, 'Michelle Bachelet', Canadian International Council/*International Journal*, 61(3) Summer 2006: 724–33; Alexei Barrionuevo, 'Chilean president rides high as term ends', *New York Times*, 28 October 2009; Gwynn Thomas, 'Michelle Bachelet's Liderazgo Femenino (Feminine Leadership)', *International Feminist Journal of Politics*, 13(1) 2011: 63–82.

Another case which challenges the view that women leaders may be more suited to quieter times and settled social orders is provided in Bangladesh. In what can be described as a relatively new state with a fragile democracy that has witnessed periods of military dictatorship and martial law set against a background of political volatility, social unrest, and numerous power struggles, two women have effectively dominated Bangladeshi politics from its first democratic elections in 1991. In that year, the leader of the Bangladesh Nationalist Party (BNP), Begum Khaleda Zia, became the country's first woman prime minister. Even more noteworthy was that her main political rival was also a woman—namely Sheikh Hasina Wajed, the leader of the Awami League. Although both leaders had worked together to force an end to Bangladesh's second period of military rule in 1991, they quickly developed a highly competitive attitude towards coalition building and political leverage.

So successful were they in the political arts of traction that they became sufficiently dominant to establish a *de facto* system of alternating female leaderships that continues to the present day. Prime Minister Khaleda Zia therefore was succeeded by Bangladesh's second female premier Hasina Wajed who served from 1996–2001only to be replaced by her former rival with a second term of office (2001–6). After a constitutional hiatus during 2007–8, the elections in December 2008 produced a clear victory for the Awami League and the return of Khaleda Zia as prime minister in January 2009. Her term of office is not scheduled to end until 2014. This means the personal rivalry of these two women will have dominated the politics and elite leadership of the seventh largest country in the world for nearly a quarter of a century. The 'Two Begums' as they are called have together not only organized a sustainable two-party system between themselves but have established in effect two political dynasties which are bound to condition the future course of an emergent democracy of over 155 million people.[30]

It is possible therefore to refer to a broad spectrum of female gains in leadership positions around the political world. Women have made inroads into five out of the top seven most populous states (India, Indonesia, Brazil, Pakistan, Bangladesh). They have been as successful in small states (e.g. Iceland, Lithuania) and developing states (e.g. Trinidad and Tobago, Liberia), as they have in advanced industrialized countries like Germany and Australia. Some systems have a remarkable record in female recruitment at the highest level. Apart from being the first country to have an elected prime minister in the figure of Sirimavo Bandaranaike,[31] Sri Lanka can also claim the distinction of being the first nation

---

[30] Aminul Islam, 'The Predicament of Democratic Consolidation in Bangladesh', *Bangladesh e-Journal of Sociology* 3(2) July 2006: 4–31. Accessed 22 February 2012 at: <http://www.bangladeshsociology.org/BEJS-%20Final%20Issue%203.2.pdf>; 'Everybody but the politicians is happy', *The Economist*, 8 February 2007; Anand Kumar, 'Will "Battling Begums" of Bangladesh Come to a Compromise?', South Asia Analysis Group, Paper No. 2860, 26 September 2008. Accessed 20 February 2012 at: <http://www.southasiaanalysis.org/%5Cpapers29%5Cpaper2860.html>; Kamal Uddin Ahmed, 'Women and Politics in Bangladesh', in Kazuki Iwanaga (ed.), *Women's Political Participation and Representation in Asia: Obstacles and Challenges* (Copenhagen: Nordic Institute of Asian Studies, 2008), pp. 276–96.

[31] Her first tenure in office as prime minister was 21 July 1960–27 March 1965.

to possess a female prime minister and a female president at the same time.[32] In 1994, Sri Lanka marked another first in the field: namely the first time a female prime minister directly succeeded another female prime minister.[33] Perhaps most noteworthy of recent developments has been the case of Switzerland. This is a country that until very recently had a reputation for conservative social attitudes in which women traditionally had a secondary status in public life. It was only in 1971 that women had been granted full voting rights in national elections. And yet in September 2010, it became the fifth country in the world to have a female majority government as a consequence of the election of Simonetta Sommaruga as the fourth woman in the seven-member-strong Federal Council.

These and other cases offer material reasons for speculating on the extent to which the barriers to women in senior political positions are no longer insuperable in nature—or at least not as insuperable as they once were. They show that while difficulties and constraints may remain, they can be overcome to allow women to progress to the highest positions of leadership. Such advances raise questions not just over the durability of gender prejudice and discrimination in this sector, but also over the meaning that can be assigned to these achievements, and over the extent to which they amount to a conclusive and even triumphant shift against previous negative contexts and outlooks.

Comparative research across Anglo-American systems points to a mixed picture of variable and contingent advances that are not always indicative of substantive change. For example, while there has been a steady growth in the incidence of female ministers in many advanced systems, they have commonly been assigned to posts that have traditionally been associated with gendered attributes (e.g. education, health, welfare) which in many cases are considered to be of peripheral concern especially in the neoliberal epoch of fiscal and social conservatism. Moreover, as the organizational trend in many of these parliamentary systems is towards a centralization of prime ministerial power, female ministers have often found themselves marginalized into roles of descriptive and symbolic representation as the masculinist character of executive leadership has become intensified.[34]

A broader remit of global research reveals an even more variable underside to the headline figures of women's advancement into the elite stratum of political leadership. Farida Jalalzaia analyses the conditions under which women gain access to senior positions and how these processes are shaped by the nature of the posts or the opportunities that afford access to women.[35] In stable systems, women can be seen securing important executive positions but these are mostly

---

[32] Sirimavo Bandaranaike's third term of office as prime minister (14 November 1994–10 August 2000) coincided with the tenure of President Chandrika Kumaratunga (12 November 1994–19 November 2005) for a period of nearly ten years.

[33] Prime Minister Chandrika Kumaratunga (19 August 1994–12 November 1994) was succeeded by Sirimavo Bandaranaike on 14 November 1994.

[34] Patricia Lee Sykes, 'Incomplete Empowerment: Female Cabinet Ministers in Anglo-American Systems', in John Kane, Haig Patapan, and Paul 't Hart (eds.), *Dispersed Democratic Leadership: Origins, Dynamics, and Implications* (Oxford: Oxford University Press, 2011), pp. 37–58.

[35] See Farida Jalalzaia, 'Women Rule: Shattering the Executive Glass Ceiling', *Politics & Gender*, 4(2) June 2008: 205–31; Farida Jalalzai and Mona L. Krook, 'Beyond Hillary and Benazir: Women's Political Leadership Worldwide', *International Political Science Review*, 31(1) January 2010: 5–21.

confined to roles that involve some measure of power sharing as is the case in dual executive structures—i.e. 'women are more likely to be executives when their powers are relatively few and generally constrained'.[36] As a result, women 'serve more often in systems where executive authority is more dispersed, as opposed to in those with more unified executive structures. Furthermore, in most of these cases, women tend to be placed in positions of weaker authority.'[37]

Furthermore, although advanced and stable systems are seen as making female leadership more institutionally and ideologically probable, Jalalzaia shows that this equation does not always hold true. On the contrary, female leaders can emerge from highly unstable regimes with low levels of institutionalization and gender equality. In these cases, women leaders can be accepted on the basis of their links to elite or familial groupings with strong bases of social power and patronage—especially so during periods of regime instability and political transition. The conclusion is at best ambiguous: just as 'gender equality is neither a sufficient nor a necessary condition for shattering the executive glass ceiling . . . [so] a country with a woman leader does not signify the end of gender discrimination'.[38]

SCALING THE HEIGHTS OF ORGANIZATION

While there have been clearly documented forms of advance for women in various leadership sectors, it is possible to place a different and more critical construction upon these developments, and to claim that their significance may be far less than might at first appear. This perspective views the presence of women in high-profile leadership positions as essentially a distraction from the continuation of attitudes and processes that still operate in ways to disadvantage women in reaching the highest levels of organizational governance. Rather than showcasing a new accessibility of women to leadership posts, the publicity that accompanies the recruitment of any woman to the leadership of a political party or a government serves to underline the way that such a distinction is still treated as something out of the ordinary.

In spite of being nominally received in terms of leadership material, a female leader continues to generate forms of notoriety and controversy that suggest an attitude which is far from meritocratic in spirit or neutral in outlook. The prominence that is invariably afforded to any leader as a matter of course is given an additional edge when that person is of a gender which is not normally associated with leadership categories. In effect, the accession of a female leader is at one and the same time both an advance in terms of liberal norms of equal opportunity but also a marker for the maintenance of a more prejudicial outlook that gives women leaders something of a rarity value worthy of note.

The substance of this critique comes in the form of different analytical and evaluative constituents. The business sector provides an illustrative focus of the

---

[36] Jalalzaia, 'Women Rule: Shattering the Executive Glass Ceiling', p. 228.

[37] Jalalzai and Krook, 'Beyond Hillary and Benazir: Women's Political Leadership Worldwide', p. 12.

[38] Jalalzaia, 'Women Rule: Shattering the Executive Glass Ceiling', p. 229.

way that ambivalent attitudes towards women leaders can translate into significant aggregate disparities. One key indicator is that which centres on the issue of commensurate levels of gender presence. Far from acting as a conditioning agency for social, cultural, and political change, corporate hierarchies are susceptible to those social dynamics which operate to reinforce or at least to stabilize pre-existing attitudes. It is the case that the number of women in senior management positions in top companies has risen and continues to rise. This is reflected in the increasing prominence given to Forbes's inclusion of a 'Women in Power' category in its yearly assemblages of rank-ordered charts of influence and resources. In the 2010 Forbes *List of Women in Power*, businesswomen accounted for the largest subgroup with 39 per cent of the total.[39] However, when set against the broader category of *The World's Most Powerful People*, then the picture changes to a minimal female presence (i.e. four out sixty-eight cited individuals—5.9 per cent).[40]

Notwithstanding the various gains achieved by women in the higher reaches of organizations, there remains a marked disjunction between incidence and proportionality. Female representation both in the boardroom and at the CEO level is still far below the rates of male representation in the higher reaches of corporate hierarchies. Apart from the Nordic countries, the proportion of company directors in Europe that are female is on average 9 per cent. It should be pointed out that variations exist within the parameters of this average figure. In 2010, the levels of female presence in the boardrooms of Britain and the Netherlands were registered at 13.5 per cent and 15.8 per cent respectively. These countries have a better record than for example France (11.9 per cent), Ireland (8.9 per cent), Italy (3.9 per cent), and Portugal (3.4 per cent).[41] Nevertheless, when these rates of female representation are compared with the proportions of women in both the population and the labour force, then even the levels achieved by the Netherlands and the UK pale into relative insignificance.

The position is further aggravated by the rising trajectory of women in education, skills, qualifications, and economic activity. Numerous surveys have revealed a steady trend towards females outperforming males. In the UK, for example, three out of every five recent graduates are women.[42] This has come to reflect a generational condition in schools where boys now persistently lag behind girls in educational attainment.[43] In the United States, women not only have a predominant position in securing undergraduate degrees (57 per cent) but this is also

---

[39] Forbes, 'The World's 100 Most Powerful Women 2010'. Accessed 20 October 2011 at: <http://www.forbes.com/wealth/power-women/list>.

[40] Forbes, 'The World's Most Powerful People 2010'. Accessed 20 October 2011 at: <http://www.forbes.com/wealth/powerful-people/list>.

[41] Figures from European Professional Women's Network, 'EPWN Board Women Monitor 2010, 4th edn.' Accessed 5 March 2012 at: <http://www.europeanpwn.net/files/europeanpwn_boardmonitor_2010.pdf>.

[42] Higher Education Statistics Agency, 'Qualifications obtained by students on HE courses at HEIs in the UK by mode of study, domicile, gender and level of qualification obtained 2005/06 to 2009/10 (1)'. Accessed 20 February 2012 at: <http://www.hesa.ac.uk/dox/pressOffice/sfr153/SFR153_table_5.pdf>.

[43] See Office for Standards in Education, 'Boys' achievement in secondary schools', July 2003 HMI 1659. Accessed 20 February 2012 at: <http://www.ofsted.gov.uk/resources/boys-achievement-secondary-schools>.

extended to master's degrees (59 per cent).[44] And yet, these advances are not reflected in the upper echelons of key organizations. For example, while women account for 47 per cent of all law degrees in the US, the proportion of law partnerships held by females remains rooted at 17 per cent. A similar pattern holds for MBAs and the lack of proportionate conversion into American board-rooms.[45] According to the 2010 Catalyst Census of the Fortune 500 Companies,[46] women held only 15.7 per cent of board seats. Over one in ten companies had no women directors at all (i.e. 12.1 per cent of companies) and the rate at which women had acquired the elite status of boardroom chairs remained rooted at around the 2.5 per cent mark. Because the share of female leaders in the board-room had barely increased over the previous five years, the study concluded that female advance in this area remained flat.[47] Results from this and other 2010 Catalyst Census surveys have been similarly pessimistic:

- In 2010, women held only 14.4 per cent of executive officer positions.
- In 2010, women executive officers held only 7.6 per cent of the top earner positions.
- In 2009, more than two-thirds of companies had at least one woman executive officer; this number did not change in 2010. The same held true for companies with no women executive officers.
- Over a quarter (27.4 per cent) of companies had no women executive officers.
- Out of the five hundred leading corporations in the Fortune 500 group there were only thirteen female CEOs (i.e. 3.0 per cent). Even when the pool is extended to cover the next group of companies—*Fortune* 500–1001—the incidence rate remains almost exactly the same with fourteen women CEOs.[48]

These figures provide a salutary reminder of the existence of a marked gender gap in the business world. Even though this sector of society has a reputation for being a highly responsive and pragmatic register of available skills, it appears to be conspicuously resistant to the pool of female talent on offer.

It is evident that even in advanced liberal societies, a gender gap remains a persistent fact of economic life. Set against rising trends of female success in education to the point where women outrank men in many categories of

[44] 'The triumph of feminism', *The Economist*, 13 September 2008.

[45] See Peter G. Northouse, *Leadership: Theory and Practice*, 4th edn. (Thousand Oaks, CA: Sage, 2007), pp. 270–1.

[46] The Fortune 500 Companies refers to *Fortune* magazine's yearly list of the largest corporations in the United States.

[47] Catalyst Inc, '2010 Catalyst Census of the Fortune 500 Companies'. Accessed 6 December 2011 at: <http://www.catalyst.org/press-release/181/latest-catalyst-census-shows-women-still-not-scaling-the-corporate-ladder-in-2010-new-study-indicates-clue-to-reversing-trend>.

[48] Catalyst Inc, '2010 Catalyst Census of the Fortune 500 Companies: Women CEOs of the Fortune 1000'. Accessed 6 December 2011 at: <http://www.catalyst.org/publication/322/women-ceos-of-the-fortune-1000>; Catalyst Inc, '2010 Catalyst Census of the Fortune 500 Companies: Women Board Directors1000'. Accessed 6 December 2011 at: <http://www.catalyst.org/file/413/2010_us_census_women_board_directors_final.pdf>; Catalyst Inc, '2010 Catalyst Census of the Fortune 500 Companies: Women Executive Officers and Top Earners'. Accessed 6 December 2011 at: <http://www.catalyst.org/file/412/2010_us_census_women_executive_officers_and_top_earners_final.pdf>.

achievement, it is clear that for the most part there has not been a commensurate step change in the position of women reaching key leadership positions in organizations and institutions. This disjunction underlines a depth of resistance that sustains an intractable unresponsiveness to demographic and social shifts not only in the composition of the labour force but also in its profile of skills. The phenomenon of leadership disenfranchisement of women is often referred to as the 'glass ceiling' because of the apparent way in which female promotion is blocked by practices and conventions that are not readily discernible in terms of organizational policies and formal processes.[49] Some of the more evident dynamics that are routinely ascribed to the 'glass ceiling' are enumerated in Box 8.2.

Box 8.2 Factors commonly ascribed to the existence of a 'glass ceiling'

- Historical structures and corporate hierarchies have developed as largely male domains with macho operational and managerial cultures.
- Disproportionate responsibility of women for child rearing and domestic tasks.
- Truncated employment experience due to maternity leave and childcare.
- Problems of work re-entry at that same place and pace as prior to a period of leave.
- Fewer developmental opportunities due to male-dominated networks, differential training regimes, and less committed mentoring arrangements.
- With fewer female role models, women have restricted access to key career resources in the form of advisory contacts, informal apprenticeships, and collegial support.
- Conscious or unconscious bias against women as long-term managerial investments.
- Women gravitate to, or are assigned to, managerial sections that are considered to be marginal and less visible (e.g. human resources) than the pathways to elite leadership positions.
- Prejudicial attitudes towards what are characterized as female attitudes, behaviours, and traits.
- Gendered perspectives of what defines effective leadership and what types of individual and behavioural styles can fulfil the role.
- Women considered to be less competitive, less ambitious, and less inclined to engage in political game-playing.
- Senior male elites—either consciously or subconsciously—tend to reproduce and perpetuate familiar patterns of stratification.

Sources: Nic Paton, 'Why Women are Doomed to Failure', *Management Issues*, 18 July 2007. Available at: <http://www.management-issues.com/2007/7/18/research/why-women-are-doomed-to-failure.asp>; Peninah Thomson and Jacey Graham with Tom Lloyd, *A Woman's Place is in the Boardroom: The Roadmap* (Basingstoke: Palgrave Macmillan, 2008).

---

[49] See Linda Wirth, *Breaking Through the Glass Ceiling: Women in Management*, 2nd edn. (Geneva: International Labour Office, 2001); Janet Holmes, *Gendered Talk at Work: Constructing Gender Identity Through Workplace Discourse* (Oxford: Blackwell, 2006); Institute of Leadership & Management, 'Majority of women say glass ceiling is still a barrier to top jobs', 21 February 2011. Accessed 16 November 2011 at: <http://www.i-l-m.com/research-and-comment/9515.aspx>. It should be noted that while the ceiling analogy is the predominant descriptive device, it is not the only analogy that is used in this context. See Eagly and Carli, *Through the Labyrinth*.

However, the impediments to women's mobility in this sphere are not solely limited to these kinds of general biases, in-house practices, and career structures. There are other sources and forms of prejudicial behaviour that operate at a deeper level of consciousness which also help to explain both the difficulties that women experience in reaching leadership levels and the way that these restrictions can become self-perpetuating in their operation. This process is exemplified in the way that women tend to gravitate to less prominent organizational positions in response to established conventions of what constitutes leadership material and what are believed to be female attributes. Studies suggest that women will often adopt two types of behaviour in such circumstances. Many will adapt to dominant conceptions of appropriate female roles on the basis of a rational calculation of how individual benefits can be maximized and career or social costs can be minimized. Others will simply exclude themselves from leadership track opportunities because they have come to evaluative themselves instinctively on the basis of an organizational culture whose criteria for leadership have a gender bias against women. These subtle dynamics of engineered de-selection operate through internalized forms of psychological conditioning and processes of socialization.[50] In deferring to these allegedly standard categories of female traits and roles, women help to sustain themselves in a cyclical process of exclusion. In many organizations, women who do not conform to this kind of intuitive stereotyping are regarded either as disruptive mavericks or else as incongruously masculine in nature.

Given the durability and self-sustaining character of these institutional, social, and cultural restraints, it is alleged that the proposition of a glass ceiling is a proven dynamic which permits organizations to give nominal support to the principle of equal opportunity whilst operationally discriminating against women in leadership recruitment. The United States has a notable reputation for identifying equality of opportunity as a core social value and for giving priority to the promotion of women's rights. And yet, despite the increased consciousness and sensitivity ascribed to this area of economic and social life, women struggle to break through to the senior leadership tiers in the workplace. A similar pattern exists in Britain. Here the UK Equality and Human Rights Commission (EHRC)—whose aim is to reduce inequality, eliminate discrimination, and promote human rights—has made particular use of two devices to underline the extent of sexual discrimination in elite positions across a range of institutional, governmental, and non-governmental organizations. One is that of drawing attention to the 'missing' women leaders in British society and the other is the projected time frames to reach equality on the current rate of progress. In 2008, the EHRC estimated that 5,600 women leaders were missing from the 31,000 top positions of power in Britain. The estimated time for women to achieve equity within the boardrooms of the FTSE 100 companies was seventy-three years—up from the sixty-five-year estimate in the 2007 report.[51]

---

[50] For an elegant examination of the way that gender differences in the leadership sector are engineered through socialization and cultural expectations, see Nannerl O. Keohane, *Thinking about Leadership* (Princeton, NJ: Princeton University Press, 2010), ch. 4.

[51] Equality and Human Rights Commission, *Sex and Power Report 2008*. Accessed 13 January 2012 at: <http://www.equalityhumanrights.com/uploaded_files/sex_and_power_2008_pdf,pp3–11>.

The scale of the problems pertaining to the gender gap in business leadership has in some quarters prompted radical action aimed at an accelerated shift in attitudes and practices. In 2003, the Norwegian government passed legislation to force companies to change the gender composition of their boards in line with the levels of women in the workforce. The target quota was set at a figure of 40 per cent by the year 2008. Given that the level of women in Norwegian boardrooms in 2002 was 6 per cent, the law was seen as a major corporate and public policy experiment. Nevertheless, in 2009 the 40 per cent level was not only reached but surpassed. Although other Nordic countries have not resorted to legislation, they have been influenced by the Norwegian model and in the case of Sweden by the threat of legislation. The result is that the region easily heads the international tables of women holding positions of elite leadership in the business sector—with Sweden at 27 per cent, Finland at 20 per cent, and Norway in the prime position at 44 per cent. Other countries like the US (15 per cent), France (15 per cent), Germany (13 per cent), the UK (12 per cent), and Spain (10 per cent) demonstrate a clear deficit in comparison. Nevertheless, the Norwegian example has created significant interest elsewhere with Spain recommending a 40 per cent target by 2015 and France committed to achieving the same quota of boardroom seats by 2016.[52] In similar vein, the European Commission announced in 2011 that it was drawing up proposals for a voluntary code[53] to achieve the same benchmark minimum of 40 per cent representation across the European Union.

The active intervention of states through techniques of affirmative action, prescriptive measures, and legal coercion underlines the continuing difficulties of opening up leadership positions in the business sphere. There are increasing signs that business culture is becoming less resistant to the correlation of women and leadership. It is true that this adaptability is often couched in utilitarian terms by reference to tapping wider pools of talent, strengthening claims to corporate social responsibility, and alleging linkages between female representation and company performance.[54] Nevertheless, some advances have been made in breaking the spiral of workplace prejudice and internalized self-discrimination. The extent to which equity may be possible in the high-stakes and ultra-competitive world of corporate leadership remains an open question. It is also one that will be conditioned by the position and performance of women in the even more testing and exposed field of political leadership.

[52] See Richard Milne, 'Skirting the boards', *Financial Times*, 15 June 2009; Susan Vinnicomb, Ruth Sealy, Jacey Graham, and Elena Doldor, 'The Female FTSE Board Report 2010: Opening up the Appointment Process', Cranfield School of Management, International Centre for Women Leaders. Accessed 13 January 2012 at: <http://www.som.cranfield.ac.uk/som/dinamic-content/news/docu ments/FemaleFTSEReport2010.pdf>; McKinsey & Company, 2010 Women Matter Report, *Women at the Top of Corporations: Making it Happen*. Accessed 15 January 2012 at: <http://www.mckinsey. com/locations/paris/home/womenmatter.asp>; 'Still lonely at the top', *The Economist*, 23 July 2011.

[53] The quota policy was declared to be voluntary in the first instance but with the threat of being made compulsory if the voluntary arrangement proved to be ineffective.

[54] See Alice H. Eagly, 'Female Leadership Advantage and Disadvantage: Resolving the Contradictions', *Psychology of Women Quarterly*, 31(1) March 2007: 1–12; McKinsey & Company, 2010 Women Matter Report, *Women at the Top of Corporations: Making it Happen*; Barry Wade, 'Women directors "hounding" CEOs into falling profitability', *Management Issues*, 7 August 2009. Accessed 23 January 2012 at: <http://www.management-issues.com/2009/8/7/research/women-dir ectors-hounding-ceos-into-falling-profitability.asp>.

WOMEN LEADERS AND THE PUBLIC GAZE

In many respects, the record and position of women in the field of political leadership bear a close resemblance to the experience of their counterparts in the business sector. Like the private sector, there is a marked disparity between the rising incidence of women in leadership positions and the proportions of posts accorded to female contenders or applicants. For example, it is true that the number of women members in the US Congress has risen from eighteen in 1980 to forty-seven in 2010.[55] However, even with this increase, the number of female representatives accounted for only 8.8 per cent of the main representative institution in the United States. The same point can be made in relation to the cases mentioned earlier concerning the rising incidence of women holding high political office. In one sense the count of twenty-four prime ministers and presidents in 2011 can signify a diminishing resistance to women holding positions of political leadership. However, when this figure is compared to the total number of member states of the United Nations (193), then the strike rate is conspicuously poor—i.e. one in eight.[56]

Even where women have had notable success in gaining substantial access to the senior ranks of government, it is often the case that conversion to the most senior levels has not followed on from these advances. As was noted above, Denmark has an outstanding track record of female representation at the ministerial level. And yet, in spite of the extensive presence of women in government, and in spite of an evident cultural acceptance of a non-gendered approach to political recruitment, no woman has ever secured the premiership in Denmark. In a state where there is a history of comparable levels of representation between men and women, it is significant that the latter have remained wholly unrepresented in respect to the top position.

While the sphere of political leadership reveals similar patterns of recruitment and promotion to the business sector, the conclusions that can be drawn from the two profiles are not quite the same. Noteworthy differences of emphasis and intensity point to a mixed assessment of the social and cultural place of women as political leaders. As has been noted above, women have made some remarkable gains in this field and have shown themselves to be as adept at leadership skills as any of their male counterparts. Nevertheless, they are still regarded as newsworthy items primarily because of their gender. This can carry positive connotations in that each woman who becomes a leader is either contributing towards a cultural initiation into female leadership, or else is helping to consolidate an acceptance of women in such positions, following on possibly from a previous pioneering figure. The relative rarity value of a female political leader, though, can generate more ambivalent responses concerning women at such levels of power, influence, and visibility. The very conspicuousness of a woman in this most exposed of positions can evoke sets of

---

[55] House of Representatives, Office of Art and Archives/Office of the Historian, 'Women in Congress, Women Representatives and Senators by Congress, 1917–Present'. Accessed 3 March 2012 at: <http://womenincongress.house.gov/historical-data/representatives-senators-by-congress.html?congress=111>.

[56] To be strictly accurate, the incidence rate is 1 in 9. This is because out of the 24 recorded prime ministers and presidents in 2011, three came from self-governing territories rather than from sovereign nation states.

highly gendered reactions which can cast serious doubts on the current levels of assimilation and even the likelihood of a neutrality of attitudes in the future.

Political leaders are expected to attract publicity and to dominate news agendas. While women leaders have the advantage of claiming the mantle of the unorthodox and the new, they have the disadvantage of being placed in a position of compounded scrutiny in which they are judged in terms of more criteria than their male counterparts. Female politicians occupy a public space where they are closely observed in terms of how they appear and behave in what is an evidently male-dominated environment. In becoming political leaders, women can exploit the highly symbolic value of their achievement in that their accession to such positions can be portrayed as a marker for wider social advances and for greater representation of minorities and excluded groups. But enhanced symbolism can cut both ways. If women leaders are self-defined and portrayed as pioneers because of their gender, then this very exceptionalism can arouse precisely the gendered responses that such leaderships are often characterized as having negated.

One aspect of this reaction is the way that established attitudes surrounding the whole character of leadership as a functional process can receive a renewed stimulus that reaffirms women leaders in a less than favourable light solely on the basis of their gender. In placing themselves in stark juxtaposition to the normality of male occupancy, women in leadership positions can through their very presence prompt impulsive and ill-considered reactions based on gender stereotypes. Even amongst those who may claim to support women's rights—or who may genuinely believe in the principle of women rising to the heights of political power—it can be difficult to ascertain whether those claims and convictions are translated into actual choices. What often concerns political strategists is not just the difficulties of negotiating the passage between the generic and the specific, but calculating the manner and level of possible resistance to an individual female aspirant to leadership.

In the United States, for example, polls show that there is strong general support for the idea of a woman becoming president. But when the question is switched to the prospect of a particular female candidate the picture can change. The discrepancy, of course, can be due to a host of factors relating to party allegiance, policy positions, and perceptions of competence. However, the issue of gender is relevant. Pollsters allude to a 'gender gap' phenomenon which sees female candidates regularly attract significantly more support from women than from men. Relative male resistance shown towards a female candidate, therefore, can become compounded by the relatively gendered nature and scale of support given to such a candidate. These dynamics were evident in the 2008 presidential election when Hillary Clinton encountered severe difficulties in translating the general approval given to the prospect of a female candidate into a sustainable campaign that was able to convert an early lead in the polls into a viable candidacy for national office.[57]

---

[57] See 'Mind the Gender Gap', *New York Times*, 18 January 2008; Patricia Lee Sykes 'Gender in the 2008 Presidential Election: Two Types of Time Collide', *PS: Political Science & Politics*, October 2008: 761–4; Diana B. Carlin and Kelly L. Winfrey, 'Have You Come a Long Way, Baby? Hillary Clinton, Sarah Palin, and Sexism in 2008 Campaign Coverage', *Communication Studies*, 60(4) September–October (2009): 326–43; Erika Falk, *Women for President: Media Bias in Nine Campaigns*, 2nd edn.

A particular source of anxiety is the fear that a woman in such a position will trigger an unpredictable and even volatile set of reactions based upon cognitive reflexes and subconscious instincts. The very symbolic properties of a woman in such a publicly projected role of central significance can summon up responses based less upon rational judgement and more on instinctive and often derogatory generalizations. Placing a woman in a publicly exposed position within what is almost invariably a masculinized context can easily generate forms of fast-track cognitive processing in which information about classes or groups of individuals is accelerated along pathways that assign characteristics and assessments of individuals according to generically based presuppositions. The risk with the prospect of a woman leader is that these processes will be subversive in effect as the audience will be drawn to the central focus of difference. In doing so, it will encourage a heightened awareness of how a woman can be seen to be inherently controversial in such a location of overt power.

While this reaction can foster doubt and even scepticism, another response develops the theme of leadership qualification in a more explicit and defined manner. This relates to the common preconception that because political leadership is so commonly associated with men, so there must be an inverse relationship between leadership roles and women. A degree of proof is provided by the paucity of women leaders in what is a large sample of states in the world. But the argument does not depend merely upon a statistical measure of incidence. More compelling is the assertion that female traits are simply less applicable, and therefore less appropriate, than male traits to the task of leadership. On grounds that mirror the points of resistance that have afflicted the business world, the classic depiction of female traits (e.g. nurturing concern for others, communal spirit, inclusive impulse, emotional intelligence, interpersonal skills, team values, supportive style), compared to male traits (e.g. assertiveness, confidence, self-promotion, ambition, independence, decisiveness, rationality)[58] have had the same traction in the political world—namely to pose the question of whether women are behaviourally and psychologically suited to leadership—in effect whether a woman can lead. In raising the very question, much of the damage is already done because it implies doubt and thereby risk which in high political office are particularly corrosive properties.

The prejudicial consequences of this kind of stimulus–response mode are similar to the more sexist impulses noted above. Nevertheless, the arguments are couched in a more analytical language based upon the identification of essentialist differences between men and women. While this view draws upon

(Urbana, IL: University of Illinois Press, 2010), chs. 7, 8; Regina G. Lawrence and Melody Rose, *Hillary Clinton's Race for the White House: Gender Politics and the Media on the Campaign Trail* (Boulder, CO: Lynne Rienner, 2010), pp. 73–108; Pew Research Center/Andrew Kohut, 'Are Americans Ready to Elect a Female President?' 9 May 2007. Accessed 24 January 2012 at: <http://pewresearch.org/pubs/474/female-president>.

[58] For classic reviews of the processes of gender stereotyping within organizations, see Kay Deaux and Mary Kite, 'Gender Stereotypes', in Florence L. Denmark and Michele A. Paludi (eds.), *Psychology of Women: A Handbook of Issues and Theories* (Westport, CT: Greenwood Press, 1993), pp. 107–39; Madeline E. Heilman, 'Description and Prescription: How Gender Stereotypes Prevent Women's Ascent Up the Organizational Ladder', *Journal of Social Issues*, 57(4) 2001: 657–74; Gary N. Powell and Laura M. Graves, *Women and Men in Management*, 3rd edn. (Thousand Oaks, CA: Sage, 2003).

both traditional observations and evidence-based claims relating to attitudes and temperaments as well as psychological composition and behavioural patterning, its logic depends upon an alleged operational correlation between certain kinds of traits and the attributed requirements of leadership. Women are necessarily disadvantaged in this equation because of the way it self-perpetuates an emulative model of leadership which privileges traits that are viewed as intrinsically male. The gendered manner in which leadership characteristics and stereotypes can be established in this way as an apparently neutral, objective, and independent variable has a specific effect—namely that women encounter a host of problems in adapting to what is for them a norm which is incongruous with the traits and roles that are culturally ascribed to them as women. The presence of this traditionally dominant model often means that women who aspire to senior leadership positions are discomforted into a choice between the need to imitate masculinist approaches and styles, or to risk trying to resist and reconfigure leadership stereotypes into alternative leadership constructions.[59]

A genre of recent research in this field of gender and differential capability has centred not so much upon societal stereotyping and conditioning but on the anatomical and physiological analysis of the differences between male and female brain functions. Various claims have been made concerning what are cited as innate structural and processing forms of observable distinction. The basic thrust is that modern techniques of neurological investigation can be used to suggest significant generic characteristics in the brains of men and women and that these differences are used to demonstrate the existence of biological and systemic explanations of psychological behaviour. The implication is that brain structures and processes are gendered in such a way that males and females are hardwired with different perspectives, propensities, and aptitudes which help to account for the distribution of social roles and status.[60] These forms of research and interpretation, of course, have prompted severe criticism from those claiming that neuroscience is being manipulated in order to revive types of prejudice and condescension relating to women's position in the social order.[61] As a consequence, these claims and counterclaims have a particular resonance with the issues surrounding the theme of women acquiring the level of social standing and political power associated with political leadership. For many, the deployment of highly advanced techniques of brain scanning risks giving renewed weight

[59] Patricia Lee Sykes, 'Women Leaders and Executive Politics Engendering Change in Anglo-American Nations'. Papers on Parliament No. 49, August 2008, pp. 11–23. Accessed 10 February 2013 at: <http://www.aph.gov.au/About_Parliament/Senate/Research_and_Education/pops/pop49/womenleadersengenderingchange>; Sykes, 'The Gendered Nature of Leadership Analysis'; Sykes, 'Incomplete Empowerment: Female Cabinet Ministers in Anglo-American Systems'. See also Michael A. Genovese (ed.), *Women as National Leaders: The Political Performance of Women as Heads of Government* (Newbury Park, CA: Sage, 1993); Sinclair, 'Body Possibilities in Leadership'; Blema S. Steinberg, *Women in Power: The Personalities and Leadership Styles of Indira Gandhi, Golda Meir, and Margaret Thatcher* (Montreal: McGill-Queen's University Press, 2008).

[60] Simon Baron-Cohen, *The Essential Difference* (London: Penguin, 2004); Louann Brizendine, *The Female Brain* (London: Bantam, 2007); Hannah Hoag, 'Brains Apart: The Real Difference between the Sexes', *New Scientist*, 16 July 2008, pp. 28–31.

[61] Lise Eliot, *Pink Brain, Blue Brain: How Small Differences Grow into Troublesome Gaps—And What We Can Do About it* (Oxford: Oneworld Publications, 2010); Cordelia Fine, *Delusions of Gender: The Real Science Behind Sex Differences* (London: Icon, 2010).

either to traditional gendered forms of stereotyping, or to those socio-biological propositions that necessarily equate leadership with the primal and essentialist archetypes of male domination.[62]

A third source of negative reaction towards the assertion or prescription of women in positions of political leadership is rooted in a more overtly political objection to such a development. The objection here is one of suspicion towards the symbolic meaning and substantive effect of what can be portrayed as an explicitly feminist political agenda in which the individual aspirant or incumbent is conceived to be the mere superstructure of a much deeper programme of social transformation. The disquiet is not confined simply to the gender of the leader in question. It is what such a figure can suggest or be made to represent to an ambivalent or distrustful public. Opposition to female campaigns for leadership can use gender not merely to create doubt over a candidate's credentials but also to open up an associative subtext that centres on an implied relationship between the unconventionality of women political leaders and an ascribed feminist world view that embraces a profusion of social and economic issues. It is because this world view is usually—though not invariably—deemed to be liberal, progressive, or even radical in nature that women who aspire to, or who hold, leadership positions have to be highly conscious that as a matter of course they carry a great deal of political baggage in the eyes of their various audiences.

Women in these positions of high exposure and symbolic intensity already generate a higher level of interpretive licence than is the normally the case with their male counterparts. In many circumstances, the evident attraction and sheer spectacle of a woman in this position stimulate a public gaze of free association whose reflexive properties can ramify into a profusion of key areas of concern. It is the way that the image of a woman running for high office can act as an accelerant of subliminal connections that makes such candidacies politically problematic. In this way a leader's gender can act as a catalyst for arousing controversial issues and divisive agendas. Because of this representational facility, a female aspirant for office can constitute a provocative wedge issue in its own right. This can relate to a variety of explicit and implicit reference points ranging from presumptions of hard policy preferences to cross-cultural pressures relating to the attributed significance of women in such positions of high exposure. For many female aspirants to leadership responsibilities, their campaigns for office have often had less to do with the normal demands of political competition and more with dealing with the cultural and attitudinal hinterland of their gender.[63]

These kinds of leadership experiences on the part of leading women underline the extent to which the three kinds of negative reaction mentioned above can still afflict the campaigns and administrations of female political leaders. Notwithstanding the progress that has been made in this area, it is evident that the enduring effects of cultural scepticism and even outright sexist hostility continue to constitute a challenge to the assimilation of women into senior levels of society.

---

[62] For example, see Arnold M. Ludwig, *King of the Mountain: The Nature of Political Leadership* (Lexington, KY: University Press of Kentucky, 2002), ch. 2.

[63] See Rainbow Murray (ed.), *Cracking the Highest Glass Ceiling: A Global Comparison of Women's Campaigns for Executive Office* (Santa Barbara, CA: Praeger/ABC-CLIO, 2010); Heflick and Goldenberg, 'Objectifying Sarah Palin'.

It is often remarked that the equation of leadership with the male gender has a self-perpetuating set of properties—not least because of the sheer preponderance of leadership analyses conducted by males studying a subject field that is predominantly male. The same can be said of the current rarity value of women leaders in the way that a profile of low incidence tends to reproduce itself. Just as women leaders are perceived as being exceptional in one way or another, so their very infrequency generates not only an aura of controversy and high exposure but also inflated expectations of political difference and change. To this extent, women leaders can often be seen as operating under different rules to their male counterparts. It is suggested, for example, that the tolerance thresholds on the part of the public for female leaders are lower than they are for men. In effect, they are not thought to receive the same benefit of any doubt and as such are not given many second chances. The pollster Peter Kellner of YouGov puts the point graphically: 'They are like a dog with one life rather than a cat with nine lives.'[64]

A related dimension to this difficulty is the way that the ascribed exceptionalism of female leaders can become equated with an expectation that female leaders have necessarily to be exceptional women. The inference may be a logical conclusion drawn from the narratives of barriers being overcome by pioneering women in male-dominated environments. Nevertheless, the supposition raises the bar for many women who are deterred by this implicit equivalence with being some kind of extraordinary political presence. The other side of this equation is the possibility that some women might aspire to leadership positions in order to demonstrate that it can be done and to create inroads for others to follow. The issue raised here is another version of the classic leadership critique of those individuals who are primarily driven to acquire key leadership positions as ends in themselves—and in doing so are exposed as having little in the way of other objectives to be secured.

CONCLUSION

The relationship between women and the issue of leadership recruitment and provision is clearly a problematic issue that touches upon a range of historical, cultural, traditional, psychological, and operational dimensions. It has been noted that the correlations between leadership roles and personal traits have supported a strongly gendered set of generic conclusions about the suitability of women for these positions. Evidently there have been exceptions to what is taken to be 'the rule'. But because these are seen as exceptions they have tended to strengthen the conditioning processes against regarding women leaders as being located fully within the parameters of normality. It remains the case that even in advanced liberal democracies, where women are formally assigned equal rights, these are made more contingent in specific cases of occupational tasks. In many instances, positions of political leadership still languish in this gender-sensitive zone of asserted practical realism. As a consequence, the issue of women and leadership is sustained as an open question. Just as the level of congruence can be viewed as

[64] Quoted in Sarah Baxter, 'Will women rule the world?', *Sunday Times*, 4 February 2007.

indeterminate and unproven, so the relationship between the two categories is suspended through the assignment of what are in effect progressively higher standards of verification.

An open verdict on such an issue is a deferred verdict which is why it is difficult to foresee a position of gendered equivalence arising within the current structures and paradigms of leadership selection. When these considerations are taken into account, it makes pessimistic projections of female entry into positions of political leadership more understandable. The UK's Equality and Human Rights Commission, for example, has estimated that under current rates of progress it will take around 200 years for women to achieve equal representation in parliament.[65] Nevertheless, there are grounds for more measured assessments that take into account the reciprocal nature of female leadership and social context. The relationship is often conceived to be a unidimensional and unidirectional pathway of influence that leads to a firmly embedded outlook of gender bias. But this perspective can not only ignore the conditioning effect of women leaders over time but fail to recognize the way that changing social attitudes can be manifested by the emergence of female elite figures.

The trend lines of women in leadership positions may not satisfy the strict criteria of equal opportunity, but they are nonetheless indicative of a shift against seeing such figures as outliers or peculiarities. On the contrary, there are signs that the male-centred claims of functional realism in this field may be losing their traction and that an altered paradigm of realism is in the process of emerging in response to different situational requirements. On an increasing scale, business models now acknowledge the functional effectiveness of those more inclusive, unifying, and emotionally intelligent forms of leadership that have in the past been commonly associated with female characteristics. This more expansive outlook has given greater credence to the proposition that there may even be a 'female advantage'[66] within the arts and crafts of leadership.[67] These signs of a cultural turn have also coincided with the onset of revisionist assessments of the nature and influence of gendered stereotyping within adaptive organizations—so much so that it can be claimed that gender is no longer a reliable indication of an individual's leadership style.[68] Changes in social outlook have also been increasingly reflected in the numerous high-profile features specializing in the rising impact of women in key sectors in society. Appearing under such titles as 'Women

---

[65] Equality and Human Rights Commission, *Sex and Power Report 2008*. Accessed 13 February 2012 at: <http://www.equalityhumanrights.com/uploaded_files/sex_and_power_2008_pdf>, p. 4.

[66] Marloes L. Van Engen, Rien Van der Leeden, and Tineke M. Willemsen, 'Gender, Context and Leadership Styles: A Field Study', *Journal of Occupational and Organisational Psychology*, 74(5) December 2001: 581–98; Alice H. Eagly and Linda L. Carli, 'The Female Leadership Advantage: An Evaluation of the Evidence', *Leadership Quarterly*, 14(6) December 2003: 807–34.

[67] It is noteworthy that such an advantage can sometimes be derived from the attribution of female stereotyped traits as a counterweight to the more conventional depictions of political behaviour. See Sebastián Valenzuela and Teresa Correa, 'Press Coverage and Public Opinion on Women Candidates: The Case of Chile's Michelle Bachelet', *International Communication Gazette*, 71(3) April 2009: 203–23.

[68] Robert P. Vecchio, 'In Search of Gender Advantage', *The Leadership Quarterly*, 13(6) December 2002: 643–71; Robert P. Vecchio, 'Leadership and Gender Advantage', *The Leadership Quarterly*, 14(6) December 2003: 835–50.

of the Decade', 'The Top 50 Women in World Business 2010', 'The Power Sex', and 'Women who Want to Run the World', their prominence in mainstream media outlets not only signifies the rising incidence of women in elite positions but also serves as an educative reinforcement of a progressive conditioning of attitudes away from gendered presumptions surrounding the issue of leadership provision.[69]

As indicated in this chapter, the pattern of female migration into positions of leadership has increasingly been extended to the political domain. To a growing extent, the prejudicial and self-perpetuating tautologies that used to dominate discussions of the relationship between women and political leadership have begun to diminish in the face of rising numbers of female leaders. The appearance of women contesting and securing leadership positions has assisted in eroding the binary suppositions of gender in this area of public life. The notion of political leadership being confined to male characteristics had always involved two forms of essentialism—namely an essentialist view of leadership mixed with an equally essentialist view of women as being inherently unsuitable and ill-equipped for such a role. In many ways, the two categories reached a point where they became defined as being incompatible with one another. The emergence of altered conditions and outlooks has had the effect of undermining both these essentialisms at the same time. Far from being regarded as fundamentally out of synch with leadership responsibilities, women have increasingly come to be seen as viable candidates for political office. It has even been claimed that contemporary forms of political organization are becoming increasingly suggestive of a correlation between leadership skills and female traits in what might be termed a post-heroic era.

The significance of such claims will be examined at a later point. Before doing so, it is necessary to open up another dimension of leadership studies. Like the issue of women leaders, it is similarly invoked as the source of challenging questions concerning the operation and contingencies of leadership. It is also heavily cited as a sphere of decision-making that is traditionally and uniquely masculine in the demands made upon leaders. By the same token, it is also a context which has increasingly been claimed as having a particular contemporary congruence with female outlooks, styles, and competences. That dimension is the highly interdependent and elusive context of the international sphere.

---

[69] For example, see 'Women of the Decade', *Financial Times*, 11/12 December 2010; '100 Most Inspiring Women', *Guardian*, 8 March 2011; 'The Top 50 Women in World Business 2010', *Financial Times*, 16 November 2010; Forbes, 'The World's 100 Most Powerful Women 2010'. Accessed 17 March 2012 at: http://www.forbes.com/wealth/power-women/list. Also note regular front cover features entitled 'Women and Leadership' in *Newsweek*—for example, 20 October 2008; 21 September 2009; 19 April 2010; 6 September 2010; Beth Kowitt and Rupali Arora, 'The 50 Most Powerful Women', *TIME*, 28 November 2011; 'Women of 2011', *Financial Times*, 10/11 December 2011; 'The Top 50 Women in World Business 2011', *Financial Times*, 10/11 December 2011.

Part III

Outside the Box

9

Leaders abroad: The promise of abnormal politics

'[T]he good of the society requires that several things should be left to the discretion of him that has the executive power. For the legislators not being able to foresee, and provide by laws for, all that may be useful to the community, the executor of the laws, having the power in his hands, has by the common law of nature a right, to make use of it for the good of the society in many cases where the municipal law has given no direction ... [N]ay, 'tis fit that the laws themselves should in some cases give way to the executive power, or rather to this fundamental law of nature and government ... This power to act according to discretion for the public good, without, the prescription of the law, and sometimes even against it, is that which is called prerogative.'

John Locke[1]

'In the modern presidency, every chief executive, sooner or later, no matter what his background or predilection, is drawn to a particular concern with foreign affairs. It is not just that foreign questions are often more interesting or offer presidents more scope for personal manoeuvre and decision; it is above all that the issues are more fateful.'

Arthur M. Schlesinger, Jr.[2]

PREAMBLE

Principles and concepts of leadership exist in many situations but the context in which the capacity for leadership usually receives its strongest endorsement is when leaders have to engage with actions, interests, systems, and other leaders beyond the water's edge. It is when political leaders have to take on the mantle of corporate representation and to promote their countries' interests abroad that their inherent utility and fundamental rationale become more marked. Whether it is seen as a consequence of organizational logic, or of a historical development, or of political prudence, the provision of leadership positions within societies does have a very close connection with the driving force of outside pressures.

---

[1] John Locke, 'The Second Treatise of Government', in David Wootton (ed.), *Political Writings* (London: Penguin, 1993), p. 344.
[2] Arthur M. Schlesinger, Jr., *A Thousand Days: John F. Kennedy in the White House* (London: Mayflower-Dell, 1967), p. 351.

The exalted status of leaders within their respective political structures gives material form to both the stimulus and the response of external world. So much so in fact that leadership is often taken to be not merely a device by which to facilitate foreign policy choices, but the very signature of a system's effective adaptation to its own wider environment. The activity of a leader in this sphere is doubly relational in nature, in that he or she has to combine the normal relationships of the indigenous political environment with those that lie beyond the jurisdictional sphere of conventional autonomy. In examining the origins and sources, as well as the pressures and claims, connected to this field of political behaviour, it will be possible to arrive at a clearer understanding not just of what the exercise of leadership can explain about the nature of this dimension, but also what the international sphere can tell us about the wider functions and remits of contemporary political leadership.

The purpose of the first section in this chapter is to give an introduction to the place of leaders in the traditional field of foreign policymaking before going on in subsequent chapters to consider some of the wider and more problematic issues raised by the substance of the international medium and by the assignments of possible meanings and locations related to the theme of international leadership. The following analysis is divided into three component parts that are designed to offer an aggregative approach to the main contours of leadership development within this area.

COMMANDING HEIGHTS

The first stimulus is that of formal responsibility. Political leaders usually have a defined basis of authority in respect to the engagement of the state with other states, and thereby with other leaders. The level and clarity of this assigned responsibility will vary considerably across different systems but it is commonplace for prime ministers and presidents to have access to executive powers that may not be ostensibly congruent with either the foundational principles of their systems of governance or with the ascribed logic of their operational processes. This type of exceptionalism is particularly conspicuous in those polities that purport to be heavily dependent upon rules-based governance and constitutionally specified powers. In these cases, the basis for the exercise of such powers is usually surrounded with a degree of strategic ambiguity. As we will be examining in the next section, the prerogatives of executive leadership are deemed on some occasions to lie within the normal frameworks of legal and constitutional provision. At other times, these discretionary powers are interpreted as extraordinary provisions that are located above and beyond the standard processes. This *de facto* position is simply attributed to the unique and abnormal responsibilities of those who have access to such authority.

The accumulation of positional resources on the part of leaders is not limited to the transfer of executive powers. The usage and legitimacy of such powers are in large part dependent upon the extent to which leaders can perform the role of a unifying point of focus for the polity as a whole. Far from this being an exclusively legal-constitutional construct, leaders almost invariably claim an altogether more transcendent form of responsibility in this international sphere. This relates to a presumptive responsibility on the part of political leaders to give material form to a national voice and a national capability in the pursuit of the national interest. Service to the nation's welfare comes in many different forms but the common theme is one where an obligation to act on behalf of the nation and its interests is assumed to exist. Such an obligation is taken to be paramount over party, personal, or even moral objections. In essence, this reflexive convention depicts leadership as both a reflection and an embodiment of a structure sufficiently unified to facilitate effective leadership activity—especially in respect to intensifying social attachments, underlining a collective identity, and mobilizing support for concerted action in the pursuit of common objectives.

The extent to which leaders can utilize, consolidate, and extend their executive powers will often depend upon their skill in refining and projecting this role of national trustee. Many prime ministers and presidents have attempted to exploit the mobilizing properties of national ideals to arouse public support for their domestic policies and programmes. The most resourceful in this regard are those who are especially skilled in combining their own identities as national archetypes with the symbolic properties of national office in order to fuse policy prescriptions with portrayals of an authentic national spirit. If this kind of identity mobilization on the part of leaders is possible in domestic policy, then the potential for infusing it into the field of foreign policy is markedly greater.

Given the projected presence of the leader in a nation's consciousness, and given the direct linkages that are customarily drawn between leadership narratives and concepts of the national interest and common purpose, the potential of leaders to cultivate intimate associations between themselves and a deep responsibility for their respective nation states is considerable. It is a potential that in very many instances is more than fulfilled. The demands of international engagement become compounded with the proffered role of leaders as focal points of national reference and social solidarity. The consequence is the emergence of a dynamic that increasingly draws formal and informal responsibilities for foreign policy into the orbit of leadership contextualization. The usage that leaders customarily make of national values, traditions, and associations in the projection of policy in the domestic field is further intensified, refined, and projected when the medium is expanded to international relations. It is in this sphere that leaders make a particular virtue not merely of accepting responsibility for foreign policy but of claiming responsibility for its direction and conduct.

For example, the priority attached to the United States president as chief executive officer and primary locus of government responsibilities in the broad field of foreign policy and national security is exemplified in the way that periodically the entire focus of the US's relationship with the world becomes defined by the establishment of a presidential doctrine. Such a device denotes the declaration and acceptance of a reconfiguration, or a rearticulation, of defining principles and priorities that become a recognized point of reference in respect to the US's general orientation towards the international sphere. The phenomenon of presidential doctrines represents a convergence between the pre-eminence of the US as a world power and the primacy of the presidency's status in shaping the rationales of its foreign policy. While presidential doctrines do not have the force of law, they nevertheless possess considerable traction in the way that they can set the tone, direction, and objectives of the country's relationship with the rest of the world. This does not mean that every president has to be responsible for a doctrine or that a president necessarily has to create a self-conscious imprint upon foreign policy. But it does mean that occasionally a president will deem it right to invoke the special executive properties of the office to respond to a shift in world conditions, or to a new threat to national security, in order to prescribe a strategic readjustment to its stance as an international power. Under these conditions, just as the declared or interpreted doctrine comes to characterize the posture of the United States, so the doctrine itself comes to define the presidency of its author (Box 9.1).

Box 9.1 Presidential doctrines

Examples:
  Truman Doctrine

In response to the increasing threat of communist subversion in Greece and Turkey following the Second World War, President Truman advocated a programme of military and economic assistance as a preventative measure. In a keynote speech on 12 March 1947, the president underlined the strategic need to 'support free peoples who are resisting attempted subjugation by armed minorities or by outside pressures'. This declaration became the defining mantra of the United States' Cold War posture towards what was seen as the inherently expansionary nature of world communism as well as the Soviet Union's projected sphere of global influence. What became known as the Truman Doctrine established the main principles of the US policy of communist containment for over forty years.

  Carter Doctrine

While President Carter had initially embedded human rights and international law as the conditioning principles of US foreign policy, these were later displaced by more immediate concerns to US security—in particular the fear that the Soviet Union was seeking to enhance its strategic position in the Persian Gulf. In January 1980, the president called political and public attention to what he described as a 'grave threat to the free movement of Middle East oil'. He stated that any 'attempt by any outside force to gain control of the Persian Gulf region' would henceforth be regarded 'as an assault on the vital interests of the United States of America' and that such an assault would be 'repelled by any means necessary, including military force'. The Carter Doctrine amounted to a clear and direct response to what had become recognized as an emergent threat with a region that represented a high security risk.

  Reagan Doctrine

The Reagan Doctrine referred to a shift from a position of presumptive containment to one of challenging the belief that communist gains were to be considered as irreversible and therefore necessarily to be assimilated as pragmatic adjustments to the global order. During the 1980s, the Reagan administration proceeded on the basis that communist regimes could be construed as transient entities that might be emancipated by way of US support of indigenous forces challenging what were thought to be non-democratic governments. A case in point was provided by the provision of military and financial support to the Contra guerrilla fighters in Nicaragua. At the same time, the administration engaged in a vast increase in military capital projects and technological research which has since been cited as exerting such severe stress upon the Soviet Union that it was instrumental in the end of the Cold War and in the subsequent break-up of the USSR.

Bush Doctrine

It is disputed whether the Bush Doctrine is really a single coherent posture or a set of different and only partially related positions. In essence, the term represents the character of the response to the terrorist attacks on the US on 11 September 2001. The Bush administration duly recognized that global terrorism had fundamentally altered the international security environment to such an extent that it required a set of new principles of engagement. The logic of this kind of asymmetrical warfare led to the declarations (i) that no distinction would be made between terrorists and the states that harboured them; (ii) that the US would pursue all terrorists and terrorist organizations with global reach; and (iii) that the US possessed the right to act pre-emptively in the exercise of national self-defence. As a consequence of these principles, the Bush Doctrine became central to the 'global war on terror' and its many corollaries in the conduct of international relations.

Sources: Special Issue: 'Presidential Doctrines', *Presidential Studies Quarterly*, 36(1) March 2006: 1–88; Heiko Meiertöns, *The Doctrines of US Security Policy: An Evaluation under International Law* (Cambridge: Cambridge University Press, 2010), chs. 3, 4.

National leaders either know, or come quickly to comprehend, that foreign policy is the arena in which their reputations for leadership will be closely examined. It is no exaggeration to assert that there exists a substantive association between the role of national leader and the medium in which states interact with one another. The scale of the privileges assigned to leaders in foreign policymaking and international engagement are matched by the extent to which leaders and their leadership credentials are tested in this specialist field. Leaders have to meet high expectations of satisfactory performance in reaching accommodations with other leaders and in maximizing the strategic advantages to be accrued from international relations. In this diplomatic role, a leader has a responsibility not just to represent the nation state but to provide a defining expression of that state's sovereign autonomy. Just as the powers invested in a leader are given their most explicit rationale in this context, so leaders themselves are acutely conscious that foreign policy affords them considerable scope for discretionary authority and high-profile distinction.

However, the responsibility that is assigned to leaders in this environment is not solely reducible to the exercise of power. Leaders have to be aware of the responsibility they have in maintaining the customs and conventions of international diplomacy, in acquiring the arts and skills of conducting negotiations, and in ensuring that agreements and understandings are honoured. As part of their remit in this sphere, leaders are assigned a set of further responsibilities which can be far more onerous than the formalistic or ceremonial duties. A leader is expected to possess and to use negotiating skills; to establish and maintain lines of communication; to grasp the interconnections between different factors and issues; to build relationships and optimize what can be derived from them; to read subtle signals and act accordingly; to exploit negotiating opportunities when they are presented; to sense the parameters of mutual interests and common purposes; to know when and how to be cooperative but also to be confrontational when the situation requires it; to trace the ramifications of positions and make choices based upon political calculations; and to have the capacity to communicate positions and decisions to others in a judicious and convincing manner. These skills amount in effect to a responsibility related to the requirements of statecraft.

Such responsibilities far surpass the general competences related to such factors as specialist team building, background knowledge, technical expertise, and policy assessment. In this environment of multiple centres, diplomatic cross-currents, different leading players and incomplete information, a leader is expected to combine political intuition and persuasion with social awareness and sound judgement. Leaders are expected to understand the codes and customs of international subtleties and nuances. They have to comprehend the sensitive nature of coalition building and the delicacy required for preserving alliances in conditions of strain. In effect, they have to have what is termed 'contextual intelligence': namely 'an intuitive diagnostic skill that helps a leader to align tactics with objectives to create smart strategies in varying situations'.[3] An awareness of context in this sense relates to an ability to grasp the complexity of a host of interdependent factors and issue linkages as well as to take numerous sets of actors and positional layers into account. It also includes a level of political skill that allows a leader to interpret and manipulate situations in order to acquire a mediating and negotiating role that will optimize the support for particular policy choices.[4]

The challenge confronting a national leader in such a multidimensional matrix is particularly well captured in those high-profile international encounters that are known as 'summit meetings'. These encounters can catch the spirit of high leadership responsibility in ways that few other occasions can match. Summits not only place a premium upon the skills and perspicacity of a leader but do so in a pressurized environment which usually involves a high-risk combination of power politics, public scrutiny, and alternative futures. It can be argued that summit meetings embody the extended logic of national leadership in the way that the major responsibility for pivotal decision-making at the international level inevitably devolves upon that office which has the major claim to the legitimacy of national representation. That being so, attempts at resolving interstate rivalries have often occurred through the specific medium of leadership figures. As a consequence, summit meetings have traditionally operated on the premise of a conjunction of great issues and conspicuous leadership status in which the international order becomes susceptible to the chemistry of individuals who share a developed sense of advanced responsibility.[5]

---

[3] Joseph S. Nye, Jr., *The Powers to Lead* (New York, NY: Oxford University Press, 2008), p. 87.

[4] Margaret G. Hermann, 'Explaining Foreign Policy Behavior Using the Personal Characteristics of Political Leaders', *International Studies Quarterly*, 24(1) March 1980: 7–46; Margaret G. Hermann, 'The Role of Leaders and Leadership in the Making of American Foreign Policy', in Charles W. Kegley, Jr. and Eugene R. Wittkopf (eds.), *The Domestic Sources of American Foreign Policy* (New York, NY: St Martin's Press, 1988), pp. 266–84; Margaret G. Hermann, 'Leaders, Leadership, and Flexibility: Influences on Heads of Government as Negotiators and Mediators', *The Annals of the American Academy of Political and Social Science*, 542(1) November 1995: 148–67; Margaret G. Hermann and Joe D. Hagan, 'International Decision Making: Leadership Matters', *Foreign Policy*, 110 Spring 1998: 124–37; Andrea Grove, *Political Leadership in Foreign Policy: Manipulating Support across Borders: Manipulating Support from the Outside In and the Inside Out* (Basingstoke: Palgrave Macmillan, 2007).

[5] For example, see William B. Quandt, *Camp David: Peacemaking and Politics* (Washington, DC: Brookings Institution, 1986); David Naveh, Paul Hare, and Ilan Pelet, *Camp David, 1978: International Negotiations as Drama* (Boulder, CO: Lynne Rienner, 1989); James E. Goodby, *At the Borderline of Armageddon: How American Presidents Managed the Atom Bomb* (Lanham, MD: Rowman & Littlefield, 2006); Sidney D. Drell and George P. Shultz, *Implications of the Reykjavik Summit on Its Twentieth Anniversary: Conference Report* (Palo Alto, CA: Hoover Institution Press, 2007); S. M. Plokhy, *Yalta: The Price of Peace* (New York, NY: Viking Penguin, 2010).

In his historical survey of summit meetings, David Reynolds identifies a set of factors that were instrumental in creating the conditions in which international summits emerged as a mid to late twentieth-century phenomenon.[6] They include the onset of air travel, the increased public provision of visual mass media in the form of newsreels and television, the invention of weapons of mass destruction, and the emergence of the United States as a global power. These contextual factors acted as a stimulus for individual leaders to take upon themselves the task of working for international peace and security.

The tensions related to the Cold War's ideological and geopolitical divisions offered the prospect of a greatly enhanced sense of leader-centred responsibility for acting on behalf of a greatly expanded constituency in the cause of constructive coexistence. In effect, leaders were drawn to the area on the basis of a premise that personal relationships between one another could have direct diplomatic benefits. Key principal figures could work to break through obstructions, correct misunderstandings, ameliorate tensions, and even engage in transforming initiatives. Summits offered the advantage of direct and even visceral contact: 'Face to face across the conference table, statesmen can sense each other's needs and objectives in a way that no amount of letters, phonecalls and emails can deliver.'[7] As Reynolds notes, summitry amounts to a 'dialogue between states, conducted at the highest level'.[8]

It is also worth noting that in what is widely seen as a supreme test of character in an environment of dramatic intensity and international attention, the attraction of a summit to leaders is not entirely devoid of self-regarding considerations. On the other hand, it is acknowledged that private ambition can serve a public good. In this respect, leaders have been able to use summits to combine individual advancement with the maintenance of international equilibrium. On occasion, summits have even led to a qualitative shift to a new set of conditions and to the opening up of new areas of dialogue. By the same token, summits are far from risk-free environments. There can be many possible pitfalls in terms of preparations, negotiating positions, political circumstances, and implementation. But the prize objectives have usually been sufficient to drive the participants onwards towards what for many remains an onerous compulsion. This is because 'for all its complexities, international summitry remains essentially a human drama'. It is 'about skilled and self-assured men who meet in order to understand and manipulate each other. They have taken huge risks to get to the negotiating table and they operate under immense stresses—political, physical and psychological—that expose deeper flaws.'[9] Although the margins between success and failure are always tight, the prospect of the former usually prevails over the risks of the latter.

The history of these leader-centred events shows that summits can be effective under the right contextual conditions and with the appropriate motivations. By the same token, they also carry the risk of damaging failures. It is probable that many more could be designated as ambiguous in their effect. What is far less open to question is the evident decline of bilateral summits in the post-Cold

[6] David Reynolds, *Summits: Six Meetings that Shaped the Twentieth Century* (London: Penguin, 2008).
[7] Reynolds, *Summits*, p. 393.   [8] Reynolds, *Summits*, p. 7.   [9] Reynolds, *Summits*, p. 10.

War era. These classical encounters have in large measure been superseded by the altogether more regularized and prosaic instruments of multilateral engagement related to global governance. This is not to say that leaders have forsaken their claims to a special role in international affairs. It is still normal for most leaders to take it upon themselves to combine their own sense of individual purpose with that of a higher vocation to the national interest on the one hand and an attraction to the international stage on the other.

Even though the issues may not have the same frisson as the rivalry between two nuclear superpowers, and although the agendas of many international institutions and events may be dominated by the more technical aspects of multilateral incrementalism, the international sphere continues to draw leaders into its ambit. It may be the case that much of this leader-associated activity has become normalized and even routinized but as we will see in the next chapter and in other parts of this study, leaders still have opportunities to expand the international scope of their individual and collective responsibilities and to advocate substantive policy changes as legitimate expressions of leadership obligation.

EXIGENCIES OF NEED

The second factor to take into account is that of need. Foreign policy is not just a question of leaders accepting an obligation or taking responsibility for fulfilling an expected role. Political leaders are seen as the necessary concomitants of a process of international engagement that has its own dynamics and imperatives. For a political system, the demands of the international sphere are almost invariably construed as a matter of stimulus–response. The political structure of a state has to be able to respond to the conditions of the international environment in the terms with which those conditions present themselves. While the principle of state sovereignty offers a political and legal foundation to a claim of basic security, it gives no guarantees of safety or autonomy in a context that is commonly equated with the ascribed meaning of anarchy—i.e. an environment composed of formally equal sovereign states with no principles of formal hierarchical organization, no sense of automatic harmony, and no centralized legal authority.[10] Within the logic of this perspective, states have to find ways of adapting to what is a highly competitive environment in which nations habitually struggle with one another to preserve and advance their interests.

Most political systems experience problems with the necessary requirements of international participation and foreign policymaking.[11] Even in those

[10] For a classic statement of this perspective, see Kenneth N. Waltz, *Man, the State, and War* (New York, NY: Columbia University Press, 1954) chs. 6, 7.

[11] See Steven W. Hook, *Comparative Foreign Policy: Adaptation Strategies of the Great and Emerging Powers* (Upper Saddle River, NJ: Prentice Hall, 2001); Ryan Beasley, Juliet Kaarbo, Jeffrey S. Lantis, and Michael T. Snarr, *Foreign Policy in Comparative Perspective: Domestic and International Influences on State Behavior* (Washington, DC: CQ Press, 2002); Christopher Hill, *The Changing Politics of Foreign Policy* (Basingstoke: Palgrave Macmillan, 2002); Valerie M. Hudson, *Foreign Policy Analysis: Classic and Contemporary Theory* (Lanham, MD: Rowman & Littlefield, 2006); Steve Smith,

authoritarian regimes which do not have a strong adherence to the rule of law and the principles of due process, tensions can exist in matching the inherent properties of an external realm to their own sets of priorities. More often than not, the rationales of foreign threats and security challenges are used to rationalize further extensions of state power. The customary logic of this shift is one of a centralization of resources around the figure of a leader who is increasingly portrayed as a vital defender of national security within a hostile environment. In these types of polity, the concentration of executive force in response to outside challenges can be seen as an accentuation of the same patterns of governance as those devised for the rigours of internal security.

In other less restrictive polities, the processes of adaptation towards the external world generate more severe challenges to their traditional, foundational, or operational criteria of political legitimacy. This is particularly so in liberal democracies where the strains between the principles of procedural and limited government on the one hand, and the priority demands of defence and foreign policy on the other, can be manifestly acute. Liberal democracies have usually found the adjustment to the exigencies of security to be highly problematic.[12] They have experienced difficulties in retaining a degree of exceptionalism in relation to other regimes.

> Even leaders who generally do not have the authority to commit the resources of their governments without consulting with others can act like predominant leaders under certain conditions. When such leaders have an intense interest in foreign affairs or a particular substantive foreign policy issue or find themselves in the midst of an international crisis, they can assume more authority than is ascribed to their positions … [I]n international crises there is a strong tendency for a contraction of authority to the highest levels of government which, even in democracies, decreases usual institutional and normative restraints and increases leaders' decision latitude while at the same time encouraging them to act on their perceptions of the national interest and their images of the public's preferences.[13]

Two main reasons are usually advanced to explain the particular predicament of liberal democracy in this policy terrain. First, given the strong likelihood that liberal democracies will experience the greatest threats from states that are not liberal democracies, and given that such states do not conform to, or recognize the validity of, liberal democratic norms and principles, a liberal democratic state has to devise ways to respond to such an illiberal and undemocratic context. Second, although the alleged anarchy and dangers of the international context may be ameliorated by various international agreements and organizations, the influence of any one state upon such networks will be marginal. Therefore, a single state cannot rely wholly upon the solution of supranational structures to serve and protect its domestic interests.

Amelia Hadfield, and Tim Dunne (eds.), *Foreign Policy: Theories, Actors, Cases* (Oxford: Oxford University Press, 2008).

[12] For an authoritative overview of these problematic properties and the internal strains and conceptual binaries that they generate, see John Kane and Haig Patapan, *The Democratic Leader: How Democracy Defines, Empowers, and Limits its Leaders* (Oxford: Oxford University Press, 2012).

[13] Margaret G. Hermann, Thomas Preston, Baghat Korany, and Timothy M. Shaw, 'Who Leads Matters: The Effects of Powerful Individuals', *International Studies Review*, 3(2) Summer 2001: 85–6.

As a consequence, liberal democracies are confronted by the need to operate within, and to respond to, this wider environment which in many ways is neither liberal nor democratic. In fact, it can often be interpreted as amounting to a wholly unpredictable, lawless, and dangerous arena of alien activity. The prevailing solution to this problem for liberal democracies has been to entrust political leaders with an executive authority that provides them with discretionary powers that will allow the state sufficient latitude to make the appropriate responses to the wider world of international politics.

These powers are not expressly reducible to law or to the normal processes of governmental conduct. Their status is implicitly *extra-constitutional* in nature as they can be interpreted as necessarily transcending a juridical order for the sake of an alternative set of needs in a priority area—i.e. the higher purpose of a national interest. The net effect is that these executive powers override conventional political and legal processes. They outweigh and outrank other powers and institutions in this sphere of policymaking. As such, the condoned powers of executive authority possess a curiously ambiguous status. The powers that leaders possess to preserve the liberal democratic norms and traditions of their own systems can stretch to the point of having a licence to act outside those selfsame conditioning constraints. Thus, in comparison with other more specific powers, these executive powers are differently rooted, differently resourced, differently treated, and differently applied.[14]

The inherent ambiguity of these leadership arrangements is as deliberate as it is functional in effect. Imprecision and tautology in such a dimension serve the statist element of a liberal democratic system of government. In sum, the exceptional properties of executive authority even in a liberal democracy are dictated by the nature of the challenges that confront the individual state. What may be considered to be an abnormal degree of authority exercised by individual leaders in the field of foreign policy and national security can be regarded as a logical correlate of what is perceived to be a set of abnormal and even alien conditions. The appropriateness of the extreme reaction is thus rationalized by the extremity of the perceived threat.

The imperative nature of this systemic response to a declared need has posed very difficult questions to both theorists and practitioners of liberal democratic politics. Various attempts have been made to rationalize the powers possessed and exercised by leaders of ostensibly liberal democracies. For example, one method of legitimating executive discretion in this area has been to match the stimulus of international realism with a response of *de facto* constitutional realism. This usually takes the form of an implicit or explicit acknowledgement that certain powers must

---

[14] See William Banks and Alejandro D. Carrio, 'Presidential Systems in Stress: Emergency Powers in Argentina and the United States', *Michigan Journal of International Law*, 15 Fall 1993: 1–76; D. L. Keir and F. H. Lawson, *Cases in Constitutional Law*, 6th edn. (Oxford: Clarendon Press, 1979), ch. 2; Michael Foley, *The Silence of Constitutions: Gaps, 'Abeyances' and Political Temperament in the Maintenance of Government* (London: Routledge, 1989) chs. 3, 4; Mark Tushnet, 'Emergencies and the Idea of Constitutionalism', in Mark Tushnet (ed.), *The Constitution in Wartime: Beyond Alarmism and Complacency* (Durham, NC: Duke University Press, 2005), pp. 39–54; Oren Gross and Fionnuala Ní Aoláin, *Law in Times of Crisis: Emergency Powers in Theory and Practice* (Cambridge: Cambridge University Press, 2006); Eric A. Posner and Adrian Vermeule, *The Executive Unbound: After the Madisonian Republic* (New York, NY: Oxford University Press, 2011).

be deemed to be inherent in the provision of an executive authority.[15] Even if such powers are not actually specified in a constitutional settlement, they often receive authorization through a process of precedent and convention. These executive powers therefore can be claimed to be intuitive in character and revealed through usage.

Another way of grounding discretionary powers within such a polity is to cite the organizing rationale of the constitutional arrangements, which in most cases operate on the premise that governmental authority ensues from the various processes of democratic and representative consent. As a result, even the operation of an executive prerogative can be formally enfolded into the logos of a system that is assumed to satisfy the criteria of a liberal democracy. In other words, the discretionary powers in the field of international affairs and security can be couched as necessarily a derivative of the overarching logic of the constitutional order—i.e. executive actions and decisions can be assumed to have been validated in one way or another through the matrix of representative institutions. This may be expressed through the medium of active consent. Alternatively, it can be presented as a positive outcome inferred from the absence of a negative position—i.e. the legitimacy of a leadership's executive powers can be assumed from the acquiescence of an elected representative assembly.

The lack of resistance, objections, or counterclaims can be used, and has on many occasions been used, to infer a condition of implicit consent to the need for executive initiative to meet the needs of the international system. A more robust interpretation of this strategic silence is to equate it with a *de facto* partial suspension of constitutional arrangements. While it would not usually be described in such stark terms, the urgency ascribed to the need for freedom of governmental action can be tantamount to an admission that normal processes have been temporarily superseded in order to facilitate a different kind of policy-making framework. Of course, there may be caveats to such a reconfiguration. It may be taken as read, for example, that a change on this scale represents an emergency device. This may mean that final decisions concerning the legitimacy of any actions taken during the emergency will in essence be deferred to a later occasion. Emergency measures therefore may be permitted in the heat of a crisis but whether they will be accepted on a permanent basis may rest upon the outcomes of a period of reflection during which more settled opinions and sober constitutional judgements may prevail. In effect, the checks and balances of a constitutional order can be revived through the operation of time as a functioning constraint in its own right.

But perhaps the most authentic way of rationalizing the operation of a leadership's executive role in the area of security and foreign policy is to assert that no

---

[15] Even in an advanced and sophisticated constitutional order like that of the US—with its deep cultural attachments to the rule of law and the principle of a clear distribution of institutional powers— there is nonetheless a recognition of the presence, utility, and legitimacy of presumptive executive powers implicitly situated within the textual base of the US constitution and cultivated by processes of custom, practice, precedent, and interpretive tradition. See Louis Fisher, 'Presidential Inherent Power: The "Sole Organ" Doctrine', *Presidential Studies Quarterly*, 37(1) March 2007: 139–52; Louis Fisher, 'The Unitary Executive and Inherent Executive Power', *Journal of Constitutional Law*, 12(2) 2010: 569–91; Mark J. Rozell, *Executive Privilege: Presidential Power, Secrecy, and Accountability*, 3rd edn. (Lawrence, KS: University Press of Kansas, 2010).

wholly satisfactory rationale exists that can square a legal order and the principles of liberal democracy with the privileges and immunities of an executive leader operating in an anarchical environment. It is not simply that leaders are afforded a special licence to react to a known prospectus of defined threats. The function of an executive in this field is to operate as a sensory register of the largely unseen undercurrents of international politics, and to react accordingly as an agency of prediction, initiative, prevention, and rapid response. The capacity to exercise this kind of advanced competence and finely weighted judgement is highly dependent upon specialist resources, confidential information, tight circles of decision-makers, and a division of political labour based upon trust rather than on legal sanction or demonstrable consent.[16] The more effective a leader becomes in this characteristically executive role, the more difficult it is to reconcile the position with the very principles of government that the leadership is dedicated to preserving. The net effect is that of a continuing tension between need and law; between security and due process; between executive responsibility and political account-ability; and between unified executive direction and the claims to a self-regulating equilibrium of pluralistic forces. It is perhaps better to conceptualize this tension not as an aberrant condition but as an operationally viable—if logically unsatisfactory—dualism in which an assumed or declared need becomes a conditioning adjunct to the processes of liberal democracy.

The dynamics of a dualism like this are revealed by the way that the declared imperatives of need are deployed to amend the interior relationships between the institutions of even the most self-conscious of constitutional orders. The United States, for example, has a long tradition of constitutional sovereignty and of an independent judiciary with the authority to judge cases by reference to a pre-existing fundamental law. Nowhere are the power and responsibility of judicial review more acute than in the US Supreme Court which has the final authority to interpret the meaning of the US constitution. Despite the fact that the Court's main remit is to preserve the structural and purposive integrity of the United States constitution and in particular its basic rationale of limiting the powers of government, the Court has occasionally taken upon itself the task of effectively revising the constitution to take account of the exigencies of international relations.

In the landmark decision of *United States* v. *Curtiss-Wright Export Corpor-ation*,[17] the Court engaged in an extravagant piece of constitutional jurisprudence in order to establish a marked distinction between domestic and international

---

[16] See Loch Johnson, *America's Secret Power: The CIA in a Democratic Society* (New York, NY: Oxford University Press, 1991); Christopher Andrew, *For the President's Eyes Only: Secret Intelligence and the American Presidency from Washington to Bush* (London: HarperCollins, 1996); Rhodri Jeffreys-Jones, *The CIA and American Democracy*, 2nd edn. (New Haven, CT: Yale University Press, 1998); Karl F. Inderfurth and Loch Johnson (eds.), *Fateful Decisions: Inside the National Security Council* (New York, NY: Oxford University Press, 2004).

[17] *United States* v. *Curtiss-Wright Export Corp.*, 299 U.S. 304 (1936). The case has provoked consider-able controversy among constitutional scholars and legal practitioners. See Charles A. Lofgren, 'United States v. Curtiss-Wright Export Corporation: An Historical Reassessment', *Yale Law Journal*, 83(1) November 1973: 1–32; Michael D. Ramsey, 'The Myth of Extraconstitutional Foreign Affairs Power', *William and Mary Law Review*, 42(2) 2000: 379–446; Saikrishna B. Prakash and Michael D. Ramsey, 'The Executive Power over Foreign Affairs', *Yale Law Journal*, 11(2) November 2001: 236–356; especially 238–49.

affairs, and therefore between the powers of the presidency in these two different spheres. Far from acting to restrain executive power, the Court posited the existence of an unprecedented level of inherent executive authority in the conduct of foreign relations. The implicit nature of that authority had been driven to the surface by force of circumstances—namely the rise of international tensions in the 1930s and the emergence of the United States as a world economic power with global interests.

The Court explicitly drew attention to the contextual shifts in the international system and, thereby, to the prerogative right of the president to react to them. As a consequence, the president was afforded 'a degree of discretion and freedom from statutory restriction which would not be admissible were domestic affairs alone involved'.[18] The Court referred to the presidency's own circumstances and conditions as a chief executive—including intelligence briefings, private information, specialist resources, diplomatic linkages, and decision-making capacity. As a consequence, the Court concluded that the president possessed a 'very delicate plenary and exclusive power . . . as the sole organ of the federal government in the field of international relations'.[19] In effect, the intrusive dangers posed by the outside world necessarily created the momentum for conferring an expansive legitimacy upon the executive office. So much so, that one commentator writing nearly seventy years after the decision was prompted to remark that the Court's adoption of what was a 'statist conception of sovereignty' had in essence 'anthropomorphized the national government in the person of the president'.[20]

It is true that the Court has not always deferred to this conception of statist centralism in the light of a controlling international context.[21] However, in the main the Supreme Court and other parts of the judiciary, as well as the Congress, have been notably reticent to challenge the remit of executive privilege in this area. In fact with the onset of the Cold War, the traction of declared and implicit need upon institutional and legal frameworks became even more intense. Either implicitly or explicitly, the fabric of the United States' constitutional order became progressively oriented towards the need to respond to the heightened security threats posed by nuclear weapons and other forms of technological competition in combination with the requirements for emergency planning, military preparedness, and a range of sophisticated structures of decision-making, intelligence assessment, and crisis management. As Cold War doctrines and postures became embedded in the matrix of social and political imperatives, references to a necessary form of 'presidential government' founded on the executive

---

[18] *United States* v. *Curtiss-Wright Export Corp.*, 299 U.S. 304 (1936) 320.

[19] *United States* v. *Curtiss-Wright Export Corp.*, 299 U.S. 304 (1936) 320.

[20] Mark E. Brandon, 'War and the American Constitutional Order', in Tushnet (ed.), *The Constitution in Wartime*, p. 36.

[21] The most notable case of the Court's resistance to extend the presidency's inherent executive powers came in *Youngstown Sheet and Tube Company* v. *Sawyer*, 343 US 579 (1952). Against the background of a possible strike by the United Steelworkers of America union, President Truman had taken emergency action to seize American steel mills in order to ensure the continuity of steel production during the Korean War. The Court declared that the president did not have the authority to take such unilateral action as the power to nationalize such assets lay with the legislative authority of Congress.

prerogatives of foreign policy assumed the status of a logical extension to the perceived international threat to American security.[22]

So ingrained had the prerogative of need become during the Cold War that it was widely considered to have ushered into the American republic not merely a 'military–industrial complex' but a 'national security state' in which the chief patron and main beneficiary were the presidential office and its presumptive role of demand-led executive leadership.[23] From an initial basis rooted in the formal powers assigned to the commander-in-chief, the presidential office was at the centre of a developmental process that increasingly projected the military core of emergency powers into the conduct of foreign policy and even into many aspects of domestic policy. That transforming impulse towards externally driven demands would become equally evident in the 'war on terror' which occasioned an intrusive set of domestic imperatives and even an alleged 'militarization' of American society guided by fearful security prognoses, authoritative claims of implicit executive powers, and declarations of an absence of strategic alternatives.[24]

The driving logic has generally been one of enforced adaptation in which the virtue of responsiveness through the agency of executive leadership facilitates what is considered to be an appropriate redistribution of internal power. This often results in clear projections of a necessary presidential pre-eminence born out of a conception of executive authority as an analogue to the realpolitik imperatives of the international sphere. But at the same time, it is also the case that a residuum of a constitutional order in this field remains and with it a continuing potential for tension between constitutional principles and international realpolitik. As a consequence, there persists in the words of one noted jurist a 'zone of twilight' that can be played out between concurrent authorities in which 'any actual test of power is likely to depend on the imperatives of events and contemporary imponderables'.[25]

The example of the United States is particularly revealing in the way it has sought to reconcile the principles and norms of constitutional restraint with the demands for exceptionalism in the field of foreign policy and national security. The US has served to exemplify both the issues raised by the international context and also the devices by which context, principle, and pragmatism mutually condition one another. The familiar phenomenon of high-profile liberal democracies investing their leaders with the rights to operate outside their own system's

---

[22] James M. Burns, *Presidential Government: The Crucible of Leadership* (Boston, MA: Houghton Mifflin, 1963).

[23] Louis Fisher, *Presidential War Power* (Lawrence, KS: University Press of Kansas, 1995), chs. 5–8; Louis Henkin, *Foreign Affairs and the United States Constitution*, 2nd edn. (Oxford: Oxford University Press, 1997); Harold H. Koh, *The National Security Constitution: Sharing Power After the Iran-Contra Affair* (New Haven, CT: Yale University Press, 1990), chs. 3, 5, 6; Rozell, *Executive Privilege*; John Yoo, *The Powers of War and Peace: The Constitution and Foreign Affairs After 9/11* (Chicago, IL: University of Chicago Press, 2005).

[24] Eyal Ben-Ari, 'The Military and Militarization in the United States', *American Ethnologist*, 31(3) August 2004: 340–8; Andrew J. Bacevich, *The New American Militarism: How Americans Are Seduced by War* (New York, NY: Oxford University Press, 2006); Roger Stahl, *Militainment, Inc.: War, Media, and Popular Culture* (New York, NY: Routledge, 2010).

[25] Justice Robert Jackson, concurring opinion in the US Supreme Court case *Youngstown Sheet & Tube Co.* v. *Sawyer* 343 U.S. 579, 637.

professed codes and processes amounts to a standing reminder of the lengths to which a liberal democracy will go in order to meet the perceived threat of international danger. The norms of legitimacy, representation, law, consent, and accountability are central to the ethos and identity of a liberal democracy. Nevertheless, the way in which political leaders are afforded such licensed exemptions from these principles is a measure of the importance that is attached to a system's ability to adapt in the face of overriding need. Political leaders are the prime manifestations and chief beneficiaries of this dualism. For their part, leaders have to show that they have the compulsion to use these powers to serve the needs of the nation.

THE ALLURE OF THE FOREIGN

The third factor is one that can be termed leadership choice. Very many leaders actively choose to become involved in foreign affairs and even to place foreign policy at the heart of their leaderships. To put the matter more forcefully, it is possible to discern a pattern in which political leaders develop an inclination towards the sphere of international relations that in turn becomes something of a definite preference. It is almost part of the accepted life cycle of leaders that after entering office on the basis of a mainly domestic claim to leadership, they tend to gravitate over time towards a role on the grander stage of foreign policy. This type of progression may not be a universal one, but the trend line is sufficiently evident to allude to it as a significant factor which is worthy of examination.

The term 'choice' is possibly one that might arouse some initial reservations, especially in the light of the two drivers described in the previous sections. There will clearly be some element of interaction between individual preferences and the conditioning factors of need and responsibility. What is noteworthy is the *transition* that is often made by leaders from a primary concern with domestic issues to a more active engagement with foreign affairs during the course of their incumbencies. It is this apparent shift in priorities, which is widely attributed to personal considerations on the part of leaders, that prompts a profusion of explanations that might account for the change of approach and for the related claims of inner-directed leadership choice.

One of the chief reasons cited for this migration of leadership interest is that foreign affairs offer a degree of executive discretion that is largely missing in domestic politics where more often than not even popular leaders are confronted by multiple constraints drawn from political, institutional, and procedural considerations as well as value conflicts, aroused partisanship, and constitutional sanctions. In such a context, foreign policy can act as an antidote to the frustrations and disappointments generated by the lack of achievement and negative publicity accompanying leadership action in domestic politics. Foreign affairs by contrast can appear to offer some relief from the more visceral and entrenched political interplays on the home front.

On a more positive note, it is possible that a leader who has been sufficiently successful in the domestic context will begin to look further afield for fresh challenges. It may be that a leader has already established a political agenda or even secured a roster of priority policies. This might allow a leader to engage in a process of renewal by a widening of horizons and even by an extension of the selfsame domestic agendas to an international constituency. Sometimes this move into foreign affairs might be justified in order to complete a domestic programme. At other times a similar manoeuvre might have a preventative purpose in that an excursion into bilateral or multilateral arrangements may be deemed necessary in order to ensure that a programme is not compromised by actions taken abroad.

The international arena can offer a form of graduation from the often more mundane routines of domestic politics. It is possible that foreign policy may act as an antidote to the disappointments engendered by the lack of achievement, the negative publicity, and the apparently intractable problems associated with domestic politics. With a domestic strategy and position achieved, a leader will increasingly be able to leave subordinates to attend to the day-to-day tasks and the detailed administration of a domestic programme. Foreign affairs can provide the prospect of achieving something new and exciting—even possibly a place in history. With experienced department heads and civil servants taking up the slack at home, a leader will have the time and space to work on fashioning a presence on the international stage. President Richard Nixon summed up the differential in the following blunt terms: 'I've always thought this country could run itself domestically without a President. All you need is a competent Cabinet to run the country at home. You need a President for foreign policy; no Secretary of State is really important; the President makes foreign policy.'[26]

President Nixon's remark is suggestive of a particularly conspicuous strand in the study of presidential leadership. It centres upon the commonly expressed proposition that there exists what amounts to a functional differentiation in the roles and responsibilities that are assigned to presidents between the foreign policy field and the domestic policy sector. In sum, this posits the coexistence of two entirely distinct and separate spheres of policy formulation which in turn supports the idea of a systemic governing response in the form of essentially two *de facto* parallel presidencies set within the parameters of a single institutional entity.[27] The 'two presidency' thesis not only rests upon the notion of a clear bifurcation of policy domains but serves to reinforce the depiction of a duality by virtue of the presidency's close affiliation with the requirements of foreign policy. The standard portrayal of the 'two presidencies' model contrasts the chief executive's range of discretionary powers and range of political autonomy in the sphere of foreign policy with the more limited resources and constricted powers of a presidency operating in the domestic arena.

This dualistic approach to policy domains is now very much associated with the zero-sum mindsets and security anxieties of the Cold War. While foreign policy became characterized by the unifying drives of presidential primacy, domestic affairs were associated with the decentralization of the Congress and

---

[26] Quoted in Rowland Evans and Robert D. Novak, Jr., *Nixon in the White House: The Frustration of Power* (New York, NY: Vintage, 1972), p. 11.

[27] For the classic articulation of this position, see Aaron Wildavsky, 'The Two Presidencies', *Transaction*, December 1966, pp. 7–14.

its representation of society's multiple interests and cleavages. A key element of the thesis was the way that foreign policy was not considered to be part of the normal run of political pluralism. The more general pattern of social and political pluralism was considered to be displaced or suspended either by the force of an active consensus, or by a passive deference to the technical expertise required for the complexities and dangers of international power politics. While the concept of two concurrent presidencies was subjected to some close scrutiny and successive forms of marginal revision,[28] the general profile of two spheres of policymaking requiring different systemic responses became not only an explanatory norm during the Cold War, but also a popular analogue of the conflict itself.

After the Cold War, the position radically changed as foreign policy was opened up to the challenges of an altered ecology in terms of issues, players, and attitudes. Patterns of policymaking became less settled as the distinctions between the foreign and domestic spheres eroded away under the pressures of globalization, complex security problems, and the proliferation of new internal and external players along with the marked growth of transnational activities, communication channels, and 'intermestic issues'. As a consequence, the two-presidencies thesis was subjected to renewed critical assault which largely reduced it to the status of a Cold War remnant in terms of both a retrospective and a contemporary critique.

Far from operating on the basis of relative autonomy, presidents are now considered to be part of a multidimensional matrix of interlocking dependency relationships set in a context of increasingly specialist resources and embedded power centres engaging in a continual process of bureaucratic politics and positional competition. And yet, notwithstanding the many complaints concerning its formulaic perspective and misplaced realism, the idea of an exceptional domain of policy that is separate from the rest, and which has a distinctive appeal requiring particular leadership skills, continues to have a recognizable resonance in contemporary politics. The attraction of foreign policy and the international stage remains a strong gravitational field in the sphere of leadership politics and one that even those least inclined towards its multiple layers find themselves unable to resist. In many respects, the draw towards the dimensions of the international becomes almost part of a political leader's process of developmental adjustment to the exigencies of office (Box 9.2).

In the light of this retained imagery of an exclusive sphere of policymaking and executive scope, many leaders show signs of having opted to move towards a fuller engagement with foreign affairs, in order to derive some relief from the customary syndrome that tends to afflict the holders of leadership positions at one time or another—namely that of a declining trajectory in popularity. The phenomenon of what is often termed decaying support relates to the processes of leadership fatigue on the part of a rising number of public and private constituencies as

---

[28] See Donald A. Peppers, 'The "Two Presidencies" Eight Years Later', in Aaron Wildavsky (ed.), *Perspectives on the Presidency* (Boston, MA: Little, Brown, 1975), pp. 462–71; Lee Sigelman, 'A Reassessment of the Two Presidencies Thesis', *The Journal of Politics*, 41(4) November 1979: 1195–205; J. E. Cohen, 'A Historical Reassessment of Wildavsky's "Two Presidencies" Thesis', *Social Science Quarterly*, 63(3) September 1982: 549–55. For a general overview, see Steven A. Shull (ed.), *The Two Presidencies: A Quarter Century Assessment* (Chicago, IL: Nelson-Hall, 1991).

Box 9.2 The allure of the international: The case of Tony Blair

---

When Tony Blair entered Downing Street, he had very little grounding or experience in issues relating to international politics. His general level of knowledge and understanding of foreign policy was widely considered to be exceptionally poor for an incoming prime minister. Before securing the premiership, he had 'not served on any parliamentary committee on foreign affairs' and apart from one exception was 'not known to have made a single significant speech on global issues'. He had 'a typical middle-class knowledge of France and Italy. But overall he was not particularly well-travelled. In his decade in parliament before becoming a party leader he had not signed a single parliamentary motion on the Kurds, the first Gulf War in 1991 or the disintegration of Yugoslavia. He had travelled light.'[29]

Although Blair had transferred Jonathan Powell from the Foreign Office to the post of Downing Street Chief of Staff, Powell found it difficult to establish foreign policy issues as priority items on the prime minister's agenda or even to reserve diary time for meetings related to international matters. Blair's view was that an incoming prime minister necessarily had to concentrate upon domestic issues in order to secure an election victory and a legitimizing mandate for government. The format of Cabinet meetings reflected the direction of priority: 'The weekly Thursday gatherings were short and to the point. Rarely did they venture away from the domestic agenda.'[30] Later on in his premiership, Blair became almost wholly preoccupied with foreign policy issues and international crises. He followed a course that is well-travelled in Washington, DC and other capitals—i.e. a democratic leader graduating to an increasing engagement with foreign policy concerns from an initial and almost exclusive base of conspicuously domestic attachments. Blair himself reflected upon the transition in his autobiography: 'The 1997 campaign was fought almost exclusively on a domestic policy basis. If you had told me on that bright May morning as I first went blinking into Downing Street that during my time in office I would commit Britain to fight four wars, I would have been bewildered and horrified.'[31]

The relative silence that had once characterized the prime minister's relationship with international affairs now shifted to a different kind of silence—one that was more associated with the prerogatives of executive privacy and concentrated responsibility. Cabinet sessions remained mostly assigned to domestic items and rarely deviated into the prime ministerial preserve of international relations. On those occasions when Cabinet meetings included a foreign policy matter, the format is described in one account as a brief presentation 'followed by a few cursory and polite questions and a reminder from Blair for everyone around the table to adhere to "the line"'.[32] According to this source, members of the Cabinet 'could not recall in-depth discussions about Europe, the Middle East, Saddam or the Balkans—or anything at all, in fact'.[33] One Cabinet minister is quoted as claiming that at 'no stage over those first four years did we have a single Cabinet discussion about the principles or conduct of foreign policy'.[34]

In the political and biographical accounts of the Blair years, it is evident that the prime minister became enthused by the palpable intensity and high stakes of international politics. He was increasingly drawn both to the immediacy and focus of crisis situations and to the possibilities of transformative leadership action in pursuit of key interests and fundamental values. One account notes the way that in periods of international conflict when Blair had to deal directly with the military and a clear chain of command up to the

---

[29] John Kampfner, *Blair's Wars* (London: Free Press, 2003), p. 8.
[30] Kampfner, *Blair's Wars*, p. 14.
[31] Tony Blair, *A Journey* (London: Hutchinson, 2010), p. 224.
[32] Kampfner, *Blair's Wars*, p. 14.
[33] Kampfner, *Blair's Wars*, p. 14.   [34] Kampfner, *Blair's Wars*, p. 14.

prime minister, 'the sense of burden was mixed with a curious excitement'.[35] The conflict in Kosovo not only conspicuously energized the prime minister, but did so in such a way as to raise a question over the perceived differential between his foreign policy persona and that which seemed to afflict him in the field of domestic policy:

> The war had a profound effect on Blair. The initial despair... gave way to a determination and self-assurance that would endure... [T]he prime minister's resilience in the face of adversity and the impact he had made on the international stage conferred on him an aura, overturning for a time at least, the perception of him as a politician tossed to and fro in the winds of public opinion. Yet the missionary zeal remained a puzzle: why was a leader so cautious at home so willing to take risks abroad? Part of the answer lay in the very nature of military action, the way it puts power directly in the hands of the prime minister... More importantly, though, the Kosovo conflict matched his gifts as a politician with his moral purpose.[36]

Another account notes that Blair's early success in the Kosovo encounter led him to acquire 'an increasingly large appetite for the global arena which would prove to have huge significance for what came next'.[37] The contrast between his international and domestic roles became ever more pronounced: 'Abroad he was free of the chafing shackles imposed on him at home by his power-sharing agreement with Gordon Brown. The world stage gave Blair a sensation of high drama, great adventure and clarity of moral purpose that he didn't feel when grappling with the duller graft of grinding out domestic reform.'[38] In sum, 'Blair believed that he had located an international calling for his premiership.'[39]

From an initial position as a primarily domestic politician engaged in a specific political project to make his party into an electable alternative, Blair underwent a remarkable shift that saw him become heavily involved in major international issues and themes during what was considered to be an epoch-changing period in global politics. In many respects, these concerns were forced upon him but it is equally clear that Blair responded to them with conviction and even zeal—not least because the international sphere offered an elemental excitement as well as a sense of moral purpose and political urgency that appealed to his conception of leadership responsibility. Even in an era when differences between foreign and domestic policy domains were allegedly in a state of dissolution, Blair experienced the sensation of having moved into a different political dimension when he became personally involved in a series of foreign policy issues. With echoes of the two-presidencies thesis, the prime minister gave every indication of having moved into a quite different political landscape and one that afforded him a marked dispensation from the normal profile of constraints. It was as if the international domain was literally a different world and as such afforded the possibility of a different leadership identity—arguably even a different person in a leadership role.

the initial novelty of a leader fades into the familiarity of an extended officeholder. Whatever the precise cause, or combination of causes, for the effect may be, the trend line of approval for most leaders is generally one of decline. Political leaders will become aware that particular events can occasionally diminish the eroding forces of time and allow a leader the possibility to lay claim to some form

[35] Philip Stephens, *Tony Blair: The Price of Leadership* (London: Politico's, 2004), p. 218.
[36] Stephens, *Tony Blair*, p. 232.
[37] Andrew Rawnsley, *The End of the Party: The Rise and Fall of New Labour* (London: Penguin, 2010), p. 7.
[38] Rawnsley, *The End of the Party*, pp. 7–8. [39] Rawnsley, *The End of the Party*, p. 42.

of renewal. Events like an international crisis or a major foreign policy commitment can help to galvanize a nation around the representational and symbolic assets of a unifying leadership. At such junctures, political leaders who are usually already well attuned to the 'two-level games'[40] associated with the entanglements of the domestic and international dimensions will often seek to take advantage of an opportunity to use the foreign sector to alter the perceptions of their governments and to re-energize their leadership standings.

A recent example of such a strategy was provided by the French President, Nicolas Sarkozy, who in the long run-up to the 2012 presidential election found himself in need of a personal rebranding exercise. In May 2011, Sarkozy's poll figures had slumped to levels lower than that of any of his presidential predecessors a year ahead of a re-election campaign. While the president's engagements in domestic policy streams seemed to arouse more rather than less political discontent, his main opportunity for repositioning and relaunching his presidency necessarily came in the field of foreign policy which was not only a sector traditionally and constitutionally assigned as a presidential preserve but also one that was central to France's national identity as an independent world power.

Previous presidents had used this field to enhance their domestic standing. However, Sarkozy's reputation in the field of diplomacy and foreign policy had not been particularly distinguished. In February 2011, a group of French diplomats had publicly criticized the president for diminishing France's international standing through what they claimed was his amateurish and impulsive engagement with foreign affairs which had resulted from the way he ignored the advice of his ambassadors and failed to develop a firm grasp of the fundamentals of international politics. In their view, the result was one of disarray and marginalization: 'Africa escapes us, the Mediterranean snubs us, China has crushed us and Washington ignores us!'[41] France had even initially supported the Tunisian and Egyptian regimes in the face of the popular uprisings for democracy in 2011.

Against this background, President Sarkozy surged into a feverish exercise of foreign policy activism which included military action in Côte d'Ivoire, air strikes and logistical support for the revolution against the Gaddafi regime in Libya, new initiatives to resolve the issue surrounding Iran's nuclear ambitions, bold agendas for the reform of the world's financial architecture during France's presidency of the G8 and G20 in 2011, and a concerted recasting of French foreign policy into a more assertive and emancipatory set of priorities. President Sarkozy's efforts to reconfigure himself as a war leader and international statesman were instrumental in arresting the slide in his polling figures and in exposing the foreign policy inexperience of his main rival, François Hollande. Nevertheless, in spite of his 'artful grasp of how to turn a diplomatic action into a personal triumph',[42] his

---

[40] The classic statement on this phenomenon of 'two-level games' is provided by Robert D. Putnam, 'Diplomacy and Domestic Politics: The Logic of Two-Level Games', *International Organization*, 42(3) Summer 1988: 427–60.

[41] Quoted in Angelique Chrisafis, 'Nicolas Sarkozy's foreign policies denounced by rebel diplomats', *Guardian*, 23 February 2011.

[42] 'Super Nicolas, saviour of the universe', *The Economist*, 27 May 2010.

efforts in this sphere were in the end not enough to prevent his defeat in the 2012 presidential election.

Where the action is geared to emergency conditions and to the deployment—or possible deployment—of military forces, the beneficial consequences for leaders can be significantly enhanced. Customarily, such emergencies evoke a popular and patriotic response with public opinion not merely 'rallying around the flag' but rallying around the political leader taking decisions for the nation. In such circumstances, the authority and value of a leader's executive command are underlined with dramatic emphasis. The 'rally round the flag' effect is strongly featured in studies of the US presidency.[43] Presidents are recognized as being both the chief instigators and the primary embodiments of such an effect. Events like military interventions, major diplomatic initiatives, and actions relating to international tension, therefore, tend to be conveyed and explained to the nation through the medium of the presidency. Even on those occasions when the presidential office itself may be regarded as having been partly responsible for a crisis, or when an action has led to a set of unintended negative consequences, a president can under most circumstances still expect to gain a boost to their poll ratings.

While the projection of crisis-driven national leadership onto the centre stage has an obvious appeal to presidents, its utility is generally considered to be limited in scope. This is because these sudden surges of support are usually short-lived and are not necessarily the harbingers of long-term consolidated shifts in public sentiment. In effect, the call to close ranks in a show of bipartisanship, social cohesion, and national unity is the equivalent of a temporary suspension of politics rather than a durable condition. Nevertheless a spike in the polls—albeit short-lived—can be a significant stimulus to presidents and other national leaders to gravitate towards the distracting zone of external priorities.

An additional factor in the progressive turn towards foreign policy is commonly thought to be due to the way leaders come to appreciate their own acquired competence in the area. Leaders develop a specialized knowledge of international relations, disputes, issues, intelligence reports, diplomacy, as well as the strengths and weaknesses of other leaders. With experience come confidence and a perceived sureness of touch. And the more experienced leaders become, the more they come to place a higher value upon their own roles and insights. When this is combined with the increased camaraderie of elites in regular contact with one another through international organizations and alliances, the effect can become one of enhanced attraction through shared experiences and the comparable positional circumstances as leaders.

As noted above, the usage of 'choice' as a category of explanation opens up a number of questions concerning the extent to which leaders actually select foreign policy engagements or are led into them under the guise of choice. Very few would

---

[43] John E. Mueller, *War, Presidents, and Public Opinion* (New York, NY: John Wiley, 1973); Marc J. Hetherington and Michael Nelson, 'Anatomy of a Rally Effect: George W. Bush and the War on Terrorism', *PS: Political Science and Politics*, 36(1) January 2003: 37–42; John E. Mueller, 'The Iraq Syndrome', *Foreign Affairs*, 84(6) November/December 2005: 44–54.

assert the existence of a wholly free choice in these matters, and in a recognized emergency the position undertaken by leaders is normally conveyed as an imperative without the distraction of differing options. While the position and role of a leader may be those of agency, this cannot be equated with autonomy. However, it is also important to note that leadership skills can often extend to the effective construction of an architecture of choice—and one to which a leader can subsequently claim to be subjected in the consideration of policy. As such, a leader can present a decision as one of executive choice made from a set of options on the basis of responsible leadership.

Alternatively, a leader may present a decision on the basis of a presented conception of no choice—embracing an urgent and necessary response to conditions. But even in this case, it is the leader who interprets the conditions as a crisis and who configures them as a case for extraordinary or even emergency action. Either consciously or unconsciously, a leader can be said to choose a course of action in terms of either an explicit choice, or as a response construed on the basis of a claimed absence of available alternatives. On both counts, it is fair to say that the sphere of foreign policy tends to underscore and even to dramatize these dynamics of leadership choice.

CONCLUSION

It has been noted that the transition from domestic policy to international affairs is a complex field of analysis that embraces aspects of demands, obligations, and choices. The individual components and the relationships between them are open to shifting interpretations concerning their respective influence and effect. One very significant consideration is worth noting at this point. Notwithstanding the various reasons why individual leaders may be drawn to the international sphere, it is customary to conclude that this field has generally been regarded as constituting a stimulus to leadership power and authority. It is commonplace for a positive relationship to be cited between this area of policy and the progressive enhancement of leadership resources in the form of institutional positioning, administrative structures, budgetary priorities, and discretionary powers. Nevertheless, it is equally important to note that international relations can be a volatile field within which to operate. Foreign policy may possess elements of glamour and possible kudos but it is also a high-risk environment in which success is far from assured.

A close engagement with an international issue can lead to serious costs for individual leaders not just in terms of specific failures but in the way that a personal association with a particular foreign policy can alter both the terms of the political debate and the shape of political agendas across the spectrum of public policy. Leaders with a conspicuous attachment to a foreign policy can find that their international ventures have a detrimental effect upon their domestic programmes and on their overall political positions within their immediate constituencies. The effects of a foreign policy therefore can be experienced back home—sometimes with very damaging effects. For example, a foreign policy can become a matter of heightened political controversy in its own right. In these circumstances, a leader may well struggle to regain the kind of control over the terms of the issue that he or she may initially have had at the outset of the policy. Moreover, these difficulties can become a debilitating legacy passed on to a leader's successors.

Foreign policy controversies can also lead to more generic challenges over the style and processes of governance. These can take the form of backlashes against executive privileges, accusations of abuse of power, and indictments relating to public trust and political judgement. Even successful foreign policy presidents and prime ministers can suffer for their evident competence in the international arena by those who will claim that the very success of such leaders is proof positive of their inattention to domestic responsibilities and even to their relative disregard for the national interest of their respective states.

The fate of Winston Churchill in suffering electoral defeat following the end of the Second World War has proved to be a salutary reminder of the fragility of reputation even for a successful war leader. A similar fate was visited upon President George H. W. Bush who, after a mobilizing a highly successful international coalition to remove Saddam Hussein's forces from Kuwait in 1991, was defeated in the 1992 presidential election by Bill Clinton whose campaign tagline was 'It's the Economy, Stupid'. Another case of a foreign–domestic disjunction was that of Mikhail Gorbachev. During the mid and late 1980s, Gorbachev achieved recognition as a visionary statesman and transforming leader within the sphere of international relations. During the same period, however, he acquired a progressively negative standing within the Soviet Union itself. Since that time, Gorbachev has remained an international political celebrity whose decisions are widely regarded as heralding the end of the Cold War. Inside contemporary Russia, however, his status is one that has remained enduringly low.

In examining the appeal of international engagement to leaders, it is evident that much of the analysis proceeds on the basis of a binary construction of different fields of policy and action. The relationship of leaders to the international arena is one that is conventionally conceptualized in terms of two separate spheres of politics—each with its own set of conditions and its own particular modes of operation. Traditionally, the controlling premise has been that political leadership originates with what is usually deemed to be the primary and originating location of the state. When individual leaders connect with the international sphere, they are usually portrayed as crossing over into an altogether different context. Some might argue that this environment is a secondary or derivative matrix. An opposing position would claim that the international field has a co-equal standing in political substance. Either way, leaders entering into the international field are normally seen as being involved literally in a form of movement—transferring from the domestic to the more exotic arena of *foreign* policy.

As a consequence, the notion of international leadership more often than not has been limited by this sense of priority and sequencing. Many notions of international leadership, therefore, have been confined to these extensions of personal statesmanship onto a larger stage. It is true that certain leaders do attempt in effect to internationalize their leaderships by transferring them to a different medium. But this kind of shift still constitutes a narrowly construed and simplistic conception of the possibilities surrounding the notion of international leadership. The decision on the part of leaders to go abroad is certainly an important element in the relationship between leadership and the international sphere but it is only part of a much larger, more demanding, and more problematic set of dimensions concerning the possible meanings, sources, and iterations of international leadership.

10

International leadership: Dealing with a contextual conundrum

'Excellencies, we have come to a fork in the road. This may be a moment no less decisive than 1945 itself, when the United Nations was founded. At that time, a group of far-sighted leaders, led and inspired by President Franklin D. Roosevelt, were determined to make the second half of the twentieth century different from the first half. They saw that the human race had only one world to live in, and that unless it managed its affairs prudently, all human beings may perish.'

UN Secretary-General Kofi Annan[1]

'The American author F. Scott Fitzgerald is famously known for his remark that: "The test of a first-rate intelligence is the ability to hold two opposing ideas in mind at the same time and still retain the ability to function." Nixon and Mao went well beyond this and dazzled us all with their ability to not only hold two opposing ideas in mind, but to do it on a big stage, in real time, in front of a worldwide audience, without a safety net below them. High risk, to be sure, but it worked. This was leadership at its finest moment, and, as Nixon himself put it, the result was: "this was the week that changed the world!"'

Bill Fischer[2]

PREAMBLE

It has already been noted that political leadership is a notoriously elusive and variable construct. It is susceptible to an intricate diversity of different interpretations and categories of associational life. This variability is particularly conspicuous when the focus is changed to the international sphere. The breadth of scope that is embraced in this domain offers new perspectives into the contingencies and forms of leadership but at the same time it also generates fresh challenges in the

---

[1] Kofi Annan, UN Secretary-General, Address to the General Assembly, New York, 23 September 2003.

[2] Bill Fischer reflecting upon the fortieth anniversary of the meeting between President Richard Nixon and Mao Zedong—the founder of the People's Republic of China. Bill Fischer, 'Nixon and Mao: When Leadership Changed the Game', *Forbes*, 13 March 2012. Accessed 1 November 2012 at: <www.forbes.com/sites/billfischer/2012/03/13/nixon-and-mao-when-leadership-changed-the-game/.>

selection of analytical approaches towards such a different context to those that normally condition the study of leadership. The significance of the territorial dimension has tended to divide the examination of political leadership into two distinctive but wholly unequal parts.

The main mode of approach which this study has largely concerned itself with up to now approaches the subject through the conventional lens of leadership centred within state and sub-state units. This traditional approach focuses upon the study of leaders in their immediate locations where analysis is directed primarily towards the individual traits, styles, and actions of leaders embedded in their own indigenous political contexts. Leadership in an international context on the other hand is usually construed in more diffuse and abstract terms relating to general themes of stability, security, and equilibrium. Leaders operating in an international environment are normally seen as diminished figures coexisting with other leaders to the point where the sources and exercise of leadership become highly imprecise. In effect, leaders are seen as engaging—or trying to engage—in a structure with minimal foundations and a lack of operational substance. The complexity and conditionality of such a context mean that leadership is usually conceived as possessing an exceptionally mercurial existence set as it is in within an exceptionally opaque political realm. It is for this reason that political analysts, like political participants themselves, tend to retreat to the more familiar confines of the state and sub-state levels where the exercise and study of leadership have greater clarity.

The aim of this chapter is to reverse the customary process of retrenchment and to examine both the conditions and occasions where some form of leadership may be said to be either already in existence or to have the potential to emerge at this level. Given the scale of global change and the challenges that arise from it, demands are generated for international leadership in order to secure the appropriate means of adjustment in an era of accelerated transformation. Calls for directive international action in the face of severe and chronic issues requiring coordinated responses are often accompanied by persistent complaints of a leadership deficit as both an explanation of the problem and a prescriptive solution to it. The disjunction between demand-led calls for leadership and the response-led critiques over its shortfall throws into high relief the problematic aspects related to the formation and operation of leadership in this sphere. In order to proceed with an inquiry into this particular context of leadership therefore, it is essential first to examine some of the key conceptual and analytical issues that are generated by references to leadership in such a complex area.

THE INTERNATIONAL AS CONTEXT

Leadership is widely cited as a variable concept, yet it is also assumed that the conditions and parameters surrounding the operation of different leaderships will retain a discernible correspondence to one another. Against this background, it might be thought that the presence, practice, and ascribed meaning of leadership at the international level would be a relatively straightforward exercise in giving established observational criteria a wider remit. Given the adaptive and even transcendent properties of leadership within social organizations, it would seem more than likely that leadership at an international level would not only assume a recognizable presence but would be capable of being understood by conventional instruments of leadership analysis. However, what is known as the international sphere is an altogether different entity to those matrices which have fostered our conventional understanding of leadership. Because the international context has little in the way of an originating source of political settlement that would afford structure and legitimacy to a claim of leadership location, the existence and operation of any form of leadership are normally disputed in principle and constrained in practice.

The lack of an immediately recognizable and established reference point also means that another customary approach to the subject field comes under strain. Under normal conditions, the operation and study of leadership are influenced by the situation in which leaders attempt to generate and exert some measure of direction. But in this case, there is considerable doubt over the nature and boundaries of what could be termed the international situation. Indeed, it is difficult to define with any precision how such a situation might be categorized and how a leader might adapt to the requirements of leadership in such a fluid and elusive set of conditions.

As we have already observed in a profusion of different settings, political leadership is varied in basis, style, and operation. Accordingly, its analysis has had to be similarly adaptable to different contexts. This has had the effect of creating an analytical tension that reflects the disjunctions within the exercise of leadership itself. Such a tension relates to the difficulties of establishing a clarity of focus on the subject—namely the issue of whether leadership refers to variations to a singular and static concept with a number of fixed descriptive categories, or whether leadership is necessarily mutable and adaptive in nature and, therefore, requiring different forms in differing sets of circumstances. In this spectrum, the realm of international politics would appear to occupy the furthest end of the variability pole. As such, it is difficult not only to arrive at a guiding definition of leadership in this context, but also to establish any sense of a fit between an individual agency and the specifications of a leadership role.

Another problematic area relates to the way that however the international sphere is defined, it embraces a world of multiple hierarchies that sits uneasily with the concept of a unifying sense of leadership and all the derivatives that are normally associated with the establishment of a leadership structure. While it is possible to view leadership under these conditions as a set or coalition of different leaderships, it nevertheless raises issues over the meaning of leadership in such a segmented context where a bewildering proliferation of different forms of power constantly connect and intersect with one another.[3] It may be the case that the provision of leadership in these conditions is plausible and possible. It may equally be the case that such a device offers some form of functional utility on leadership grounds but only by transcending—and even confounding—the more conventional criteria of leadership identification.

A further difficulty in acquiring any kind of access to this subject is the issue of how leadership resources are to be conceptualized in what is an expansive yet also limited field of activity. Apart from the problems associated with the types of

---

[3] For a representative overview of the theoretical ecology of this complex matrix, see Michael Barnett and Raymond Duvall (eds.), *Power in Global Governance* (Cambridge: Cambridge University Press, 2005).

political reach and jurisdictional authority that are at the disposal of a leadership in the international sphere, there are major conceptual challenges in defining the nature and contingency of any leadership platform as well as the pathways that lead both towards it and away from it. If it is accepted that leadership is a relational arrangement, then in this context demanding questions will be fostered concerning the identity of the followers and both the connections to, and consequences for, an ascribed location of leadership activity. In similar vein, another troublesome aspect of this relational model of leadership generates issues of accountability—namely whether a claimant to international leadership can be said to be accountable and if so what might such an actor at the international level be answerable for, and to whom.

The study of international relations continues to be largely based upon the foundational axiom that the autonomy of sovereign states is coexistent with an absence of an overarching international polity. As a consequence, a condition of anarchy in the sense of a lack of a collective sovereignty has been the defining property of the international system. This not only means that states are customarily conceived as compulsively self-preserving and power-seeking agencies but that they also inhabit a sphere that is not reducible to the categories and dynamics which are commonly associated with the political arrangements at the domestic level of individual states. The international order therefore is seen to be different not simply because of its scale. A long-established premise of analysis in this area asserts that the subject of international relations is qualitatively different to the internal processes of its constituent state units—i.e. that the behaviour of states is more affected by system-level considerations than by domestic or unit-level factors.[4] Far from being conceived as an extension of domestic structures and dynamics, this construction of the international sphere posits the existence of a transcendent structure that significantly shapes the relationships, motivations, and strategies of the individual units of state sovereignty.

It is for this reason that international relations specialists have tended to marginalize the significance of individual leaders and decision-makers within the international sphere. Given the emphasis upon system structures in explaining the pattern of international events, the branch of the IR discipline that examines the relationships between foreign policy and the internal dynamics of individual states has generally been regarded as a peripheral sub-genre. Many would go further and claim that because foreign policy analysis is too closely aligned to such actor-specific and agency-based categories as the perceptions, actions, and reactions of individual states and leaders set within particular institutional and political contexts, the 'subject matter of foreign policy belongs naturally to the empirical domain of public policy rather than of international relations'.[5]

---

[4] For the classic statement of this structural realist or neorealist position in which the international is conceptualized as a self-contained form of realism, see Kenneth Waltz, *Theory of International Politics* (New York, NY: McGraw-Hill, 1979). See also John J. Mearsheimer, *The Tragedy of Great Power Politics* (New York, NY: Norton, 2003).

[5] For an incisive review of the claims and counterclaims concerning the place of foreign policy analysis within the domain of international relations, see Walter Carlsnaes, 'Foreign Policy', in Walter Carlsnaes, Thomas Risse, and Beth A. Simmons (eds.), *Handbook of International Relations* (London: Sage, 2002), pp. 331–49.

Some strands of international relations have speculated on the viability of a paradigm shift in which the 'domestic analogy'[6] might change from the status of a perceived fallacy to that of a viable proposition in which interstate relations could be regarded as susceptible to the same form of institutional control as that between individuals and groups within states.[7] This kind of outlook finds encouragement in a more holistic conception of an international society of states that has the potential to generate a productive juxtaposition between sovereign entities and the cultivation of common interests through the growth of international rules, norms, ideas, values, and institutions.[8] Notwithstanding the various iterations of these positions, the main emphasis and conditioning feature of international relations remain rooted in the conviction that the international and domestic spheres remain highly differentiated from each other and that the international political system amounts to an independent dimension with its own autonomous imperatives and processes.

The logical corollary of this position is that there will be fundamental constraints on any attempt to view forms of international leadership as extrapolations of the prevalent organizing principles of the nation state. In other words, the study of international leadership cannot proceed on the assumption that leadership modes can simply be scaled up in a linear progression in accordance with a higher level of political activity. The study of international leadership therefore has to take account of this substantive difference in dimensions. In other words, given that international relations constitutes a different political and analytical context, any study of leadership at this level has to speculate not just on the degree of difference that is present but on how this difference impacts upon leadership provision and how its effects can be discerned. It also raises the intriguing prospect that the international sphere may disclose alternative conceptions and constructions of the leadership role.

PLURAL APPROACHES

From the difficulties noted above, it is evident that the international sphere brings with it an additional dimension to the challenges of elucidating the contextual nature of leadership. At the outset, it is evident that in moving to the international sector, the understanding of leadership becomes far more plural in character. The complex and contested character of the subject field becomes even more so with the shift in levels. In many respects, it can be claimed to be far more contentious and even more elusive within this territorial and analytical sphere.

[6] See Hedley Bull, 'Society and Anarchy in International Relations', in Herbert Butterfield and Martin Wight (eds.), *Diplomatic Investigations* (London: Allen & Unwin, 1966), pp. 35–50.

[7] See Hidemi Suganami, *The Domestic Analogy and World Order Proposals* (Cambridge: Cambridge University Press, 1989).

[8] See Tim Dunne, *Inventing International Society: A History of the English School* (Basingstoke: Macmillan, 1998); Andrew Linklater and Hidemi Suganami, *The English School of International Relations: A Contemporary Reassessment* (Cambridge: Cambridge University Press, 2006); Andrew Hurrell, *On Global Order: Power, Values, and the Constitution of International Society* (Oxford: Oxford University Press, 2007).

In Chapter 9, it was acknowledged that an integral component of political leadership relates to the need or the impulse of leaders to go abroad in order to promote their political agendas as well as their leadership credentials. The term 'international leadership', however, denotes something quite different to national leaders interacting with one another or having an overseas dimension to their domestic leaderships. Similarly, while the themes associated with leadership often carry connotations of a power differential or the exertion of force, exercises in international leadership usually have connotations with rather different properties. The inference is one that is more ill-defined yet also something that carries a legitimacy which is distinctive in relation to more conventional leaderships.

In its most positive form, international leadership suggests a collection of means and ends that are inclusive, collective, beneficial, and enlightened. It suggests a basis for the pursuit of public goods and collective security that can stretch across different states and cultures. This kind of leadership offers the prospect of an escape from state-centred politics towards a more productive interplay of human and social dynamics. However, international leadership, or the term 'international leadership', is not always used in this manner. There are many different iterations of international leadership and equally many different situations that give rise to the term being employed. In numerous instances its usage denotes a variety of conditions and actions that are altogether more minimalist and less positive than the grander visions which commonly adorn the term.

International leadership may be a commonplace term which is habitually used in political language and which is a staple element in the statement of positions and aspirations. Nevertheless, it is also one that covers a profusion of different dimensions and conceptions of leadership. Far from constituting a spectrum upon which instances of international leadership can be located upon a single scale, it is more accurate to conceive the term as a descriptive assemblage of different species or variants of leadership-based arrangements. As a consequence, it is necessary to proceed with caution. Instead of embarking on an attempt to establish the generic parameters of this expression of leadership, it is necessary to adopt a reverse strategy of identifying modes and practices of leadership that might go some way to ascertaining the scope of the subject area and to recognizing the plurality of its different forms.

At a minimal level of conceptualization, international leadership might be said to relate to the evident incidence of political leadership structures and processes that are present across the globe, irrespective of cultures, societies, or levels of development. In this way, the provision and exercise of political leadership can be seen as a universal phenomenon that constitutes a unifying link or medium of understanding between nations and states. The common experience of possessing forms of leadership which are comparable—to a greater or lesser degree—with one another affords the basis at least of a representational coexistence of different entities.

A slightly less minimalist expression of international leadership would conceive it more in terms of consequences rather than of potentialities. Domestic leaders, for example, who make domestic decisions on domestic grounds but whose decisions have repercussions abroad can be described as engaging in forms of leadership behaviour that have numerous and varied consequences outside their territorial bases. The effects of their choices may be incidental but they neverthe-less have an impact on other states and societies. The leaders involved may be utterly unaware of, or wholly indifferent to, the ramifications of their policy choices upon other peoples. Nevertheless, they are leaders and their leadership decisions may well have a sufficient range of ripple effects at a distance to constitute a claim of transnational or international remit.

A more customary perspective on the subject gives prominence to those actions by leaders who intend to create effects abroad in a conscious and deliberate manner. The linkage here to something that could be described as an international form of leadership is conceived in terms of a much more direct relationship between cause and effect. The familiar aspect of national leaders operating in a context external to their own sovereign bases usually comes within this category. Leaders may voluntarily choose to engage in foreign affairs or they may be compelled to do so for the sake of the national interest. They may be mainly concerned with maximizing national self-interest on a short-term basis, or they may have longer-term aims. Whatever their motives or designs, they can be considered as actors who are consciously participating in politics at an inter-national level with specific purposes in mind. The standard conception of leader-ship at the international level is precisely this interplay of actors operating through a state-centred medium. It includes leaders of strong or highly influential states with an established international reach and with expansive agendas of policy preferences. It also includes the representatives of states with fewer resources but with a concerted drive to acquire as much negotiating leverage as possible in international forums. This matrix of international leadership will embrace not only the leaders of global and regional hegemons whose every move has wide repercussions for others, but also lesser players who are directly involved in actions and choices geared to creating or maintaining alliances, or to furthering regional integration and other forms of pooling sovereignty for the benefits of collective security.[9]

A less familiar but no less significant meaning ascribed to the term of inter-national leadership relates to leaders who have developed what are in effect international constituencies. An example of this genre would be leaders of internal liberation movements whose purpose is to lay down a systemic challenge to an existing form of government that is claimed to be illegitimate in relation to key international criteria of good governance and human rights (e.g. Nelson Mande-la's international campaign against the apartheid regime in South Africa;[10] Aung San Suu Kyi's struggle for transformative change in Burma in which she has become a powerful international symbol for peaceful resistance against an

---

[9] Charles A. Kupchan and Clifford A. Kupchan 'The Promise of Collective Security', *International Security*, 20(1) Summer 1995: 52–61; Inis L. Claude, *Swords into Plowshares: The Problems and Process of International Organization*, 4th edn. (New York, NY: McGraw-Hill, 1984); Barry Buzan and Ole Wæver, *Regions and Powers: The Structure of International Security* (Cambridge: Cambridge University Press, 2003).

[10] See Nelson Mandela, *Long Walk To Freedom: The Autobiography of Nelson Mandela* (London: Abacus, 1995); Anthony Sampson, *Mandela: The Authorised Biography* (London: HarperCollins, 2000); Martin Meredith, *Mandela: A Biography* (London: Simon & Schuster, 2010).

oppressive state[11]). Many such leaders work assiduously to generate a supportive body of opinion outside their own countries. Although leaders who adopt this kind of emancipatory role are often marginalized in their own countries through imprisonment or exile, they nevertheless strive to create a high public outreach that can extend to sympathizers abroad.

Other cases of this strategy of generating an international appeal in the interests of an individual state can include those leaders who work to attract the support of international organizations and agencies either to promote the formation of a new state or to maintain the security of a beleaguered state. Possibly the best example of both these types of leadership situations is provided by the dispute between the Palestinians and the Israelis over the allocation of territory and governance. In this case, international constituencies are mobilized on both sides. Palestinian leaders such as Yasser Arafat and Mahmoud Abbas have both headed aspirational movements whose aim is the formation of a state.[12] Similarly, Israeli leaders summon up international public opinion in the cause of improving the security of a precariously positioned state. The international in these kinds of case refers to a frame of reference through which individual leaders can appeal either to some sense of an international community, or more simply to another state or set of states for political support.

A more recent case of a state or states cultivating international constituencies is the various social and political movements characterized as the 'Arab spring'. In this context, it is not so much that domestic leaders have co-opted the support of regional powers or intergovernmental alliances or individual states. It is more that the complex processes of post-revolutionary settlements in Tunisia, Egypt, Yemen, and Libya—together with the turmoil of ongoing insurgencies in Syria and Bahrain—and the international interest generated as a result have had the joint effect of both supporting individual leaders and also undermining the foundations of local leadership resources and authority. Hussein Agha and Robert Malley offer a succinct observation of the resultant dynamic as they observed it in 2012:

> In Tunisia, Egypt, Yemen, Libya, Syria, and Bahrain, no unifying figure of stature has emerged with the capacity to shape a new path. There is scant leadership.... More often than not, legitimacy is bestowed from abroad: the West provides respectability and exposure; Gulf Arab states supply resources and support; international organizations offer validity and succour. Those in charge often lack the strength that comes from a clear and loyal domestic constituency; they need foreign approval and so they must be cautious, adjust their positions to what outsiders accept.[13]

They conclude by pointing out that these contemporary types of transformation in what has become a more interdependent global order constitute a step change

---

[11] See Aung San Suu Kyi, *The Voice of Hope* (New York, NY: Rider, 2008); Justin Wintle, *Perfect Hostage* (London: Arrow, 2007); Hannah Beech, 'Aung San Suu Kyi: Burma's First Lady of Freedom', *TIME*, 29 December 2010.

[12] See Barry Rubin and Judith Colp Rubin, *Yasir Arafat: A Political Biography* (New York, NY: Oxford University Press, 2005); Efraim Karsh, *Arafat's War: The Man and His Battle for Israeli Conquest* (New York, NY: Grove, 2004); Nigel Parsons, *The Politics of the Palestinian Authority: From Oslo to Al-Aqsa* (New York, NY: Routledge/Taylor & Francis 2005), chs. 7, 8.

[13] Hussein Agha and Robert Malley, 'This Is Not a Revolution', *New York Review of Books*, 8 November 2012.

from many past experiences of radical political reformation: 'Past revolutionary leaders were not driven by such considerations. For better or for worse, they were stubbornly independent and took pride in rebuffing foreign interference.'[14]

The mainstream conception of international relations gives emphasis to power politics and from that to notions of international leadership in terms of the drive towards some kind of competitive advantage. But a different conception of the international dimension gives weight to it as a medium of cultural exchange which can incorporate constituencies of transnational and transcendent value. It is possible for individual leaders to draw on other countries, societies, and value systems in order to enhance their own messages, identities, or agendas. In doing so, they can widen their appeal and challenge the isolation they often encounter within their own domestic contexts. During the Cold War, many Third World leaders became adept at fusing their own leadership claims and stakes with those of the 'West' or the 'Eastern bloc'. However, this process of merging identities across state borders should not necessarily be cast in terms of a one-way transition from the developing world to the developed world. Just as a radical leader like Malcolm X in the 1960s sought to foster a common racial, religious, and colonial consciousness between black communities in the United States and societies in Third World countries,[15] so many leaders of newly emergent states have striven to cast off their imperial pasts in favour of a cultural reattachment to what are portrayed as pre-colonial states of existence.

A variant of this cultural focus is afforded by those leaders who specialize in disseminating messages that transcend different states and societies—and arguably carry weight across different time periods. These leaders can be heads of government or have ambitions to be so. On the other hand, they may be leaders whose appeal arises primarily from the doctrines that they espouse or from the movements with which they are associated. Such leaders engage in advocacy on an international level. But they do more than this. The most effective exponents of this activity manage to combine their individual or organizational identity with the content of the transmitted message so that one becomes indistinguishable from the other. The transcendent properties of such an appeal are usually grounded in a message or agenda that claims to be rooted in universal values. It may be couched in terms of universal ethics or international justice, or a reaffirmation of the democratic ethos, or the obligations to human rights. Actors operating in this kind of dimension may be religious leaders like the pope, or those occupying elite positions of international organizations such as the Secretary-General of the United Nations, or NGO activists, or even lone voices supporting a particular ethos of social harmony or global justice (e.g. the Dalai Lama, Liu Xiaobo). They can also include mainstream state leaders who adopt transformative agendas calling for normative shifts in the international order. Despite the variety in causes and personnel, one feature remains constant. This is the strong emphasis upon ideational and attitudinal change working through leaders engaged in a medium of symbolic politics, ethical injunctions, and a language of common appeal.

[14] Agha and Malley, 'This Is Not a Revolution'.
[15] Malcolm X, *The Autobiography of Malcolm X* (London: Penguin, 2001); Manning Marable, *Malcolm X: A Life of Reinvention* (London: Allen Lane, 2011).

INTERNATIONAL LEADERSHIP AS GLOBAL HEGEMON

By reputation, the most widely cited contender for the function of international leadership has been the United States. For over fifty years, the United States has been regarded as an organizational force in the construction of an international order of mutual security and economic interdependence. Following the Second World War, it took the lead in the formation of key international organizations that were designed to create an institutional architecture of global governance that would foster conditions of peaceful and productive coexistence between states. In the twenty-first century, the United States has acquired the status not merely of a superpower but that of a dominant global hegemon whose pre-eminence is felt in every sphere of industrial, commercial, financial, and technological activity around the world.[16]

In the first decade of the new century, the US military surpassed the size of the next ten national forces combined. The Pentagon's budget for technological research and development dwarfed that of any other power centre. Its capability in force projection was equally immense with between 700 and 800 overseas military bases straddling a host of strategic and energy-sensitive areas in over sixty countries.[17] In addition to the unprecedented magnitude of its hard power, the US is also distinguished by its resources of soft power relating to cultural prestige, normative presence, and the global reach of its lifestyle patterns.[18] The scale and intensity of the United States' international influence have led to imperial terms of reference being appropriated to describe its contemporary position in the global order.[19] Given the position of the US in the world economy, its role in the liberalization of markets and capital transfers, its status in the institutions of global governance, and its status as a cultural hegemon, the US possesses the kind of credentials that might be associated with the responsibilities of international leadership.

On the other hand, the pre-eminence of the United States has also attracted a more negative construction of its international position. Critics point less to its leadership role and more to what is deemed to be the pernicious pursuit of its own self-interest. While the United States characterizes itself as a national embodiment of liberal democratic ideas, it is widely criticized on precisely the grounds on which it assumes excellence. The core element of anti-Americanism in this respect

---

[16] Walter LaFeber, *The American Age: United States Foreign Policy at Home and Abroad 1750 to the Present*, 2nd edn. (New York, NY: Norton, 1989), chs. 14–17; Stephen Ambrose and Douglas Brinkley, *Rise to Globalism*, 8th edn. (New York, NY: Penguin, 1997); Richard Saull, 'American Foreign Policy during the Cold War', in Michael Cox and Doug Stokes (eds.), *US Foreign Policy* (Oxford: Oxford University Press, 2008), pp. 63–87.

[17] Jules Dufour, 'The Worldwide Network of US Military Bases: The Global Deployment of US Military Personnel', *Global Research*, 1 July 2007. Accessed 3 May 2012 at: <www.globalresearch.ca/index.php?context=va&aid=5564.>

[18] See Joseph S. Nye, *Soft Power: The Means to Success in World Politics* (New York, NY: Public Affairs, 2004); Michael Cox and Inderjeet Parmar (eds.), *Soft Power and US Foreign Policy: Theoretical, Historical and Contemporary Perspectives* (Abingdon: Routledge, 2010).

[19] Geir Lundestad, *The American 'Empire' and Other Studies of US Foreign Policy in Comparative Perspective* (Oxford: Oxford University Press, 1990); Niall Ferguson, *Colossus: The Price of America's Empire* (New York, NY: Penguin, 2004); Chalmers Johnson, *Nemesis: The Last Days of the American Republic* (New York, NY: Henry Holt, 2006).

centres upon the critique that the United States fails to fulfil its own prospectus of high principles. It is charged with exerting national sovereignty in order to undermine the self-determination of other nations and that it employs liberal democratic norms as a device by which to widen its influence over other societies and economies. The United States commonly attracts claims of double standards and hypocrisy. They range from America's record of military interventions and counterinsurgency programmes to the manipulation of markets and elections, and even the overthrow of hostile governments. Punitive expeditions, bombing campaigns, and covert operations are cited as evidence of the lengths that America will go to in order to ensure that regional and international stability are privileged over transformative political change. Its hostility to radical social revolutions has led the United States not only to support local oligarchies and authoritarian regimes but also to destabilize nationalist movements and political movements that threaten to disrupt settled alliances.[20] While these forms of realpolitik may have been defensible during the Cold War, they have become far more problematic in the aftermath of the terrorist attacks of 9/11 and the subsequent military actions in Afghanistan and Pakistan.

The current position is that while the United States has continued to claim a presumptive position of international leadership, its equation of military, economic, technological, and cultural power with international influence and legitimacy is under increasing strain. Just as its conception of an intrinsic leadership role sourced from a historical and providential exceptionalism has less traction as a guiding rationale of international politics, so the normative vision of America's political and economic model is no longer accepted as a necessarily universal template for social development. Virulent strands of anti-Americanism have arisen from what is seen as the excessive projection of American power, the militarization of US diplomacy, the marginalization of allies, and the prevalence of a unilateral coercive force in the name of an emancipating *Pax Americana*.

The excesses associated with the American responses to asymmetrical warfare, terrorist activities, and religious extremism—combined with its military action in Iraq—have served to alienate public opinion abroad. Moreover, the emergency responses to what have been construed as existential threats have created a regime of homeland security that has arguably compromised the United States' own principles of constitutional democracy.[21] The polarizing consequences of these actions have exerted severe strain on the meaning and operation of American leadership. Some complain that the United States has shown too little leadership in the difficult transition to a new post-Cold War world and that its policies and

[20] Walter LaFeber, *Inevitable Revolutions: The United States in Central America*, 2nd edn. (New York, NY: Norton, 1993); William Blum, *Rogue State: A Guide to the World's Only Superpower* (London: Zed, 2001); Eric Hobsbawm, *On Empire: America, War, and Global Supremacy* (New York, NY: Pantheon, 2008).

[21] Louis Fisher, 'Deciding on War Against Iraq: Institutional Failures', *Political Science Quarterly*, 118(3) Fall 2003: 389–410; John Mueller, *Overblown: How Politicians and the Terrorism Industry Inflate National Security Threats, and Why We Believe Them* (New York, NY: Free Press, 2006); Joseph Margulies, *Guantanamo and the Abuse of Presidential Power* (New York, NY: Simon & Schuster, 2006); Chalmers Johnson, *Nemesis: The Last Days of the American Republic* (New York, NY: Henry Holt, 2006); Donald F. Kettl, *System Under Stress: Homeland Security and American Politics*, 2nd edn. (Washington, DC: CQ Press, 2007).

actions have in effect undermined its claims to a position of transcendent moral leadership. Others assert that America has demonstrated to excess the wrong kind of leadership both in its attachment to nationalistic and unipolar pretensions and in its misplaced confidence that American power and influence are irresistible and therefore immune to challenge.

The case of the United States raises a host of issues over the potentiality and actuality of leadership in and across the contemporary world. Some aspects of America's status as a leader for others to follow, or at least to emulate, are closely related to the material nature of its power resources. Given the interdependency of an increasingly integrated global economy, almost any action undertaken by the US could be conceived as an exercise in international influence that might be construed as being synonymous with leadership. Another view would differentiate types of power with types of leadership. While military or economic power might be related to notions of leadership within those particular fields, other forms of influence connected to cultural, moral, or ideational forces can be advanced as separate types of leadership-induced cause and effect within the international sphere. By the same token, some would advance the proposition that the two fields are in reality linked to, and conditioned by, one another.

This being so, it is argued that because the United States faces significant challenges in adjusting to new currents within the global order, it in effect disorientates and disrupts the international system as a whole in the process of adaptation to a new plural and multilayered environment. The issue of America's position and role in the world continues to generate confusion both inside and outside the United States. Conceptions of the nation's future position and role within the international order vary between that of an enduring global hegemon—albeit under altered conditions—and that of an international presence in marked decline as a result of the unsustainable costs of maintaining its position and responsibilities in a multipolar and 'post-American world'.[22] Notwithstanding its assertions of a historical and moral responsibility for global leadership, therefore, its capacity to clarify the specifications of leadership in such a context remains less than assured.

INTERNATIONAL LEADERSHIP AS AN INTERNATIONAL ORGANIZATION

Another way of conceptualizing international leadership is to focus upon the organization that was specifically designed to possess a set of transcendent properties and obligations that would allow nation states to operate as a collective device for the mutual benefit of its constituent parts. The United Nations is not only the biggest but also the most ambitious and prestigious of these institutions. It has a wide and expansive remit which includes responsibilities in the fields of

---

[22] Joseph Nye, *The Paradox of American Power: Why the World's Superpower Can't Go It Alone* (New York, NY: Oxford University Press, 2003); Fareed Zakaria, *The Post-American World* (New York, NY: Penguin, 2008); Robert Kagan, *The Return of History and the End of Dreams* (New York, NY: Alfred A. Knopf, 2008).

international law, economic development, social advancement, human rights, and international peace and security. Furthermore, the UN has the status of being the premier embodiment of an internationally based impulse for humankind to rise above conflict and the 'scourge of war'[23] and instead to work towards a more enlightened world order in which human freedoms would be enlarged and enriched. The high ideals and foundational logic of the institution have always implied a leadership role of international dimensions. The guiding ethos of its inception after the Second World War and the high principles of its investiture through the UN Charter (1945), the Statute of the International Court of Justice (1945), and the Universal Declaration of Human Rights (1948) have infused the United Nations with an aura of anticipated political, legal, and moral leadership on a world scale.[24] The scale of the role, however, has served to underline the challenges of the institution's own structural and operational ambiguities.

The difficulties associated with the UN's leadership function have often been attributed to the particular historical context of the institution's inception: namely the way that the Permanent Members of the Security Council reflected the configuration of the international system following the Second World War. The consequences of what was a fixed representational bias towards the Allied powers within the UN was further exacerbated by the onset of the Cold War and the subsequent polarities between East and West over various world issues. As a consequence, the UN had little room for manoeuvre within a largely intractable context of competing spheres of interest between the two superpowers. The decline of the Soviet bloc revived interest in the UN's ability to generate substantive international agendas for the post-Cold War world and the institution responded with a series of new initiatives relating to humanitarian intervention, global justice, education, gender equality, maternal health, child mortality, chronic disease, environmental protection, and climate change.[25]

The advent of these new expansive agendas, however, has prompted a familiar reaction in the shape of criticisms that focus on the disparity between the UN's purposive and principled rationales on the one hand and its ability to secure outputs commensurate with its stated objectives on the other. During the 1990s, criticism of the institution's record in the face of serious challenges became commonplace. Conspicuous policy failures in Somalia, Rwanda, and Bosnia, for example, were ascribed to the UN's inability to react effectively to humanitarian disasters. More recently, the attacks on the organization have taken the now standard critiques of the 1990s and combined them not just with renewed indictments against the institution's decision-making in response to violations of international human rights norms and its own genocide convention (e.g. Darfur) but also with serious allegations of criminal mismanagement and corruption (e.g. 'oil for food' scandal)

---

[23] Preamble of the Charter of the United Nations (1945).

[24] Paul Kennedy, *The Parliament of Man: The United Nations and the Quest for World Government* (London: Penguin, 2007), pp. 24–47.

[25] See Newton Bowles, *The Diplomacy of Hope: The United Nations Since the Cold War* (London: I. B. Tauris, 2004), chs. 5–14; Thomas G. Weiss, David P. Forsythe, Roger A. Coate and Kelly-Kate Pease, *The United Nations and Changing World Politics*, 6th edn. (Boulder, CO: Westview, 2009), chs. 3, 4, 7; Karen A. Mingst and Margaret P. Karns, *The United Nations in the 21st Century*, 4th edn. (Boulder, CO: Westview, 2011), chs. 4–6.

as well as charges of rape and sexual abuse on the part of UN military personnel (e.g. peacekeepers located in the Democratic Republic of Congo).[26]

These and other complaints have led to regular claims of the UN itself being an institution that is no longer fit for purpose. It is no exaggeration to assert that a discourse of chronic failure, structural incapacity, and procedural immobilism attaches itself to the UN very quickly in response to what are normally depicted as urgent issues and even crises in international politics. The difficulties and frustrations surrounding efforts to acquire resolutions to pressing security problems are easily transmuted into critiques of the UN that the institution has lost its authority, its legitimacy, its public trust, and its sense of purpose and identity. In some quarters it is described as nothing more than a brokerage centre for diplomatic positioning and an anachronistic expression of a post-war world that has been supplanted by new global realities. The UN is accused of repeatedly failing to confront the issue of forced migrations, mass atrocities, and genocide. The organizational equivocation over such a basic responsibility towards peace and security has led to charges of evasion and appeasement on a scale amounting to nothing less than a 'complicity with evil'.[27]

It is true that many qualifications and caveats are normally included in these indictments. By far the most significant is the recognition that the UN remains an organization based on the individual sovereignty of its member states. This means that its resources and freedom of action are constrained not merely by its own rules and processes but by the coalitions of self-interest drawn from its constituent units in general and the power politics that revolve around the Security Council's permanent members and their allies in particular. Even when the UN's many merits and achievements are taken into account, these are almost invariably deployed as qualifications to the headline categories relating to an alleged pathology of organizational decline and a failure to deliver on the ideals invested in its formation. Instead of fulfilling the agendas of those seeking transformative action, the UN is depicted as a victim of its own positional predicament in which the organization necessarily underwrites the transactional behaviours of member states and as a consequence becomes entangled in multilateral and multilayered blame games.

What is highly noteworthy in these reviews is the way that leadership is so often cited as a key factor both in the diagnoses of the UN and likewise in the character of the presented solutions. Even in the face of not only the most intractable and complex problems but also the acknowledged nature of the organization's endemic weaknesses, the thrust of those arguments pressing for remedial action settle with repeated alacrity upon the absent property of leadership. It is ironic in such circumstances that an institution which was formed to provide some semblance of collective leadership on an international scale—and whose anatomy is

---

[26] Kenneth Cain, Heidi Postlewait, and Andrew Thomson, *Emergency Sex: And Other Desperate Measures* (New York, NY: Hyperion, 2004); Paul Volcker, Jeffrey A. Meyer, and Mark G. Califano, *Good Intentions Corrupted: The Oil for Food Scandal and the Threat to the U.N.* (New York, NY: Public Affairs, 2006); Brian Urquhart, 'The UN Oil-for-Food Program: Who Is Guilty?', *New York Review of Books*, 9 February 2006.

[27] Adam Lebor, '*Complicity with Evil': The United Nations in the Age of Modern Genocide* (New Haven, CT: Yale University Press, 2008).

dominated by the multiple leaderships of member states acting in a sovereign capacity—should have its structural and operational difficulties reduced to an alleged lack of leadership. Therefore, far from regarding institutional leadership as a marginal value within a context that is already replete with leadership claims, reformers normally regard enhanced leadership as the indispensable *sine qua non* of any attempt by the organization to rise to the challenge of renewal or reinvention.

Just as leadership aversion and leadership failure are habitually cited as controlling conditions in the UN, so it is that reflexive calls for leadership provision offer the most usable and adaptable response to an otherwise overwhelming set of multiple defects. Not for the first time in this study, the term 'leadership' becomes both a descriptive explanation of a set of complex phenomena, as well as the primary means by which an ascribed malfunction is to be corrected. In this case, the interrelationship of analysis, explanation, and prescription is particularly marked. In the same way that generic leadership failure is commonly selected as a pivotal and enduring condition, so leadership is almost invariably chosen as the catalyst, the rationale, and the agency for facilitating the required transformative change to the institution. And more often than not, this emphasis upon leadership devolves upon the position of the UN Secretary-General. Whilst the Secretary-General is in many ways the most obvious recipient of such a mantle within the organization, the post is also renowned for the ambiguity of purpose and role that has traditionally surrounded it. At one level, the formal position is that of a 'chief administrative officer'[28] and this is reflected in the Secretary-General's managerial responsibilities for the UN Secretariat which consists of over 8,000 personnel from around 170 countries.[29] But at another level, the Secretary-Generalship carries with it an aura of expectation and potential that is often seen as transcending the administrative specifications of the role. The Secretary-General's position can and does offer the prospect of focus for the leadership requirements and demands of the wider institution. Nevertheless, at the same time, it also epitomizes the problematic nature and contested character of a leadership function located in such a complex and often disaggregated structure of governance.

The position of UN Secretary-General is one that carries great international prestige but it is also one which in effect offers a microcosm of the problems of the organization as a whole. In effect, the office-holder has to operate at the centre of a host of intersections that constitute the operational context within which the Secretary-General has to discover what leadership functions are possible and how to activate or develop them. A Secretary-General has to be able to negotiate passages between the pressures of the institution's cumbersome structures and the needs of various short- and long-term responsibilities; between the scale of global problems and the limited resources at the disposal of the UN; between the rights of individual nation states and the interests and goodwill of the major powers; and between the pressures both for reform and institutional action on the one hand and the organizational realities of veto points, consensus building, and the need for equity and fairness on the other.

[28] Chapter XV, Article 97, Charter of the United Nations.
[29] Thant Myint-U and Amy Scott, *The UN Secretariat: A Brief History* (Boulder, CO: Lynne Rienner, 2007).

A Secretary-General has to satisfy expectations of responding to complex issues whilst maintaining the conventions of neutrality and even-handedness in a consensus-based institution. Moral and visionary leadership may be a positive prospectus that all parties might endorse in the abstract, but the driving imperative is that a Secretary-General has to operate in an environment of multiple diplomatic accommodations. By the same token, while the UN can appeal to the spirit of an international community and an accompanying cosmopolitan and multilateral ethos, the operational reality is that of a membership-based organization based upon a reflexive set of state interests and non-negotiable claims to sovereignty.[30]

The difficulties of establishing an authoritative and enduring space in such a crowded, disputed, and changing environment amount to a formidable array of constraints that condition not only the role that a Secretary-General can aspire to but also the degree to which the office-holders can fulfil their own conceptions of the position. It is generally conceded that a Secretary-General has a degree of licence to explore and to develop the potentialities of the office. It is also acknowledged that a Secretary-General has discretion to adapt the position in the light of changing circumstances and organizational demands and in doing so to facilitate the institution's own adjustment to new conditions. However, it is also widely conceded that the position is heavily circumscribed by political and structural constraints; that it has no satisfactory settlement or developmental trajectory attached to it; that there is no agreed sense of an appropriate 'fit' between required credentials and experiences on the part of candidates and the nature of the position itself; and that while it remains a persistent repository of hope and expectation, it also continues to be a perennial object of controversy and complaint.

Each of the nine Secretaries-General has had different styles, different conceptions of the role, and different ways of adjusting to the situational demands. These have given some basis for comparative analysis and evaluation.[31] But the common thread which unites them all is the deep disjunction between the prodigious expectations of international leadership that are conferred upon the office, and the political, institutional, and organizational resources that fail to be assigned to the task, the office, or the individual incumbent. The idea of a leader, of course, often incorporates the notion of a personal drive and an acquired licence to expand the remit of the office. And in the case of the UN, it is evident that the nature of the discourse and the logic of the analytical attention given to it do lead to conclusions of individual culpability in which institutional failings are transposed to a single agency. Blame becomes part of what is an ever tightening tautology of definitions surrounding diagnosis, prognosis, and necessary treatment. The issue of the institution's own independence becomes fused with an ongoing controversy over the Secretary-General's position in which the office comes to exemplify not so much an extension or an encapsulation of the UN's institutional

---

[30] Simon Chesterman (ed.), *Secretary or General? The UN Secretary-General in World Politics* (Cambridge: Cambridge University Press, 2007).

[31] Kent J. Kille, *From Manager to Visionary: The Secretary-General of the United Nations* (New York, NY: Palgrave Macmillan, 2007). See also Kent J. Kille and Roger M. Scully, 'Executive Heads and the Role of Intergovernmental Organizations: Expansionist Leadership in the United Nations and the European Union', *Political Psychology*, 24(1) March 2003: 175–98.

autonomy as an unsatisfactory substitute for it. The resultant ambiguity can generate highly volatile shifts in the leadership status of a Secretary-General.

Kofi Annan, for example, became a world figure of high international stature in his first term as Secretary-General. This was capped in 2001 when he and the UN were jointly awarded the Nobel Peace Prize. But his second term became mired in various scandals and ascribed failures that culminated in a severe loss of international standing both for him and the institution. The predicament of a Secretary-General was revealed with brutal clarity at the close of Annan's tenure of office. The tenor of the critiques and the character of the challenges facing such a leadership position can be captured by some of the chapter titles in James Traub's authoritative study of the period: *'The Security Council fiddles while Darfur burns'*; *'Oil-for-Food: The nightmare'*; *'The black hole of Kinshasa'*; *'They're laughing at us in Khartoum'*; *'The gentle king and his court'*; and *'Nice guys get crushed'.*[32] So wide is the gap between formal leadership and real traction that the appointment of a new Secretary-General in 2007 was marked in many quarters by a widespread sense of scepticism and even sympathy for Kofi Anan's successor Ban Ki-moon. *Newsweek's* treatment of this international news story typified what has become a commonplace outlook on the position. The headline on the front cover story summed up the new Secretary-General's prospects in succinct terms: *'Why This Man Will Fail: The New U.N. Chief Embarks on Mission Impossible'.*[33] These kinds of indictment offer a parable of the way that leadership is simultaneously demanded and rejected as a predominant duality of attitudes. The prospect or concept of leadership remains an attractive catch-all solution to a vast range of institutional problems. Nevertheless, it is the very complexity of its structures, combined with the controlling logic of its representational composition, which ensures for the most part that effective decisive leadership is precluded as a matter of course.

INTERNATIONAL LEADERSHIP AS AN ORGANIZATIONAL GROUP

It has often been noted that many of the UN's derivative organizations (e.g. IAEA, IMF, UNESCO, UNHCR, WFP, WTO, WHO[34]) have managed to achieve a higher reputation than the source institution because of their ability to develop a focused, sustained, and responsive grasp of specified problem areas and their associated policy regimes. A similar logic holds in the emergence of a host of intergovernmental formations that have come into existence outside the UN's parameters. These bodies are designed to promote a range of consultative and cooperative initiatives. The most conspicuous of these relatively new claimants to

[32] James Traub, *The Best Intentions: Kofi Annan and the UN in the Era of American World Power* (New York, NY: Picador, 2007).

[33] *Newsweek*, 5 March 2007.

[34] Listed acronyms denote the following: International Atomic Energy Agency; International Monetary Fund; United Nations Educational, Scientific, and Cultural Organization; United Nations High Commissioner for Refugees; World Food Programme; World Trade Organization; World Health Organization.

international leadership is the Group of 8 based upon the world's main industrialized national economies.

In some respects, the G8 cannot be described as a *bona fide* international
organization in that it has neither an administrative headquarters with a permanent secretariat, nor a clearly defined method of setting agendas on the basis of an
inclusive form of representation. Nevertheless, it can be said to possess leadership
credentials within the international arena. These claims can be based upon the
system of regular ministerial meetings that the G8 maintains in an expansive
portfolio of subject areas (e.g. finance, trade, justice, security, the environment,
agriculture, labour, and foreign affairs). The organization is also noted for its
series of yearly high-profile summits when the heads of state and government
gather to consult with one another on global issues and to identify areas of
cooperation on key objectives, new agendas, and priorities for collaborative
action.[35] The G8 is often characterized as a discussion forum to promote constructive dialogue and mutual understanding between member states. Nevertheless, it can be a particularly effective device in those areas in which there is a
marked commonality of interest and experience (e.g. pooling information on
terrorist threats; judicial and police cooperation in areas of criminal activity
such as illegal immigration, money laundering, drug trafficking, and cyber
crime) and a potential for creating cooperative arrangements (e.g. G8 Global
Partnership's work on nuclear non-proliferation and disarmament).

From this immediate standpoint, it is possible to view an organization like the
G8 as an incremental but nevertheless cumulative development in transnational
governance. Its widening remit has helped to increase the momentum for other
more specific intergovernmental enterprises such as the G20 organization. The
G20 alludes to the regular meetings of finance ministers and central bank governors from the twenty largest elements in the global economy. Its origins lay in
the G8 meetings which used to embrace the agendas of international economic
consultation and cooperation but which were increasingly seen as inadequate both
because of the rising demands for detailed financial overview and because of the
growth of emerging economies outside the normal remit of the G8.

While the G8 was initially able to incorporate the G20 strand within its
portfolio, it was finally agreed in 2008 that the G20 would become the main
arena of economic cooperation amongst the wealthy nations. In many respects,
the G20 represents the institutional response to the forces of globalization and to
the liberalization of trade and capital flows across borders and with it the
increased risk of domestic economic and financial imbalances creating shocks
across an increasingly integrated system of international markets. The G20 has
sought to provide a level of cooperative, precautionary, and even regulatory
activity to a system that has demonstrated a capacity for serious instability and
rapid contagion. Its agendas have included the abuses of financial systems, the

---

[35] Risto Erkki Juhani Penttilä, *The Role of the G8 in International Peace and Security* (Adelphi Paper
355) (London: International Institute for Strategic Studies, 2003); Thomas J. Volgy, *The G8, the United
Nations, and Conflict Prevention* (Aldershot: Ashgate, 2003); Nicholas Bayne, *Staying Together: The G8
Summit Confronts the 21st Century* (Aldershot: Ashgate, 2005); Hugo Dobson, *Group of 7/8* (Abing-
don: Routledge, 2007); G8 Information Centre, G8 Research Group, Munk School of Global Affairs,
University of Toronto. Accessed 10 May 2012 at: <www.g8.utoronto.ca/.>

governance of domestic financial markets, the organization of regional economic integration, and the challenges posed by demographic change and natural resource security. The 2009 G20 summit gave graphic illustration of the organization's utility in drawing support for an emergency package of measures in response to what was a major recessionary disruption in the operation of global financial and commercial markets.[36]

It is the G8 with its close association with the constituent national leaderships of the day, however, which attracts international coverage and captures public attention. Its imagery of leading decision-makers in close proximity to one another directly engaging global issues conveys the impression of a structure urgently responding to the drive for solutions—or at least to partial remedies—in response to complex problems. On occasions, the G8 can give the impression of an agency facilitating substantive changes in the distribution of attention, priorities, and resources by the major forces in the world's economies. The 2005 G8 summit at Gleneagles, for example, was marked by a campaign to address the issue of global poverty and in particular the levels of inequality in many developing countries. The meeting marked the culmination of a high-exposure campaign by reform groups and African governments to restructure debt burdens and to increase aid. The summit produced some landmark outcomes in the field of debt cancellation and prospective financial relief to some of the world's most highly indebted countries.[37] By regularizing the inclusion of five 'emerging market' countries (i.e. South Africa, China, India, Brazil, and Mexico) into the summit's negotiation processes, the G8 also demonstrated a more inclusive and widening remit of agenda formation. While the decisions taken by the G8 + 5 were far from being radical enough for many campaigners in terms of the scale and speed of the proposed remedies, the summit nevertheless demonstrated a developing capacity to respond to severe and complex problems related to global justice.

A different and far more sceptical perspective asserts that the G8 and other similar groupings are more concerned with promoting the immediate interests of the member states and with protecting their position in the current global order. Serious global problems are said to be merely managed through the protective objectives of the members' transactional activities rather than through any serious intention to engage in transformative agendas. The critiques can reach the level of ascribing direct accountability to the G8 not only for the way it is alleged to sustain global inequality through its dominant economic paradigm but also for what is depicted as its less than positive contribution to global problems related to financial instability, restrictive trade practices, social and civic dislocation, and

---

[36] See Peter I. Hajnal, *The G8 System and the G20: Evolution, Role and Documentation* (Aldershot: Ashgate, 2007). See also G20 Information Centre, G20 Research Group, *The Group of Twenty: A History* (Munk School of Global Affairs, University of Toronto, 2008). Accessed 10 May 2012 at: <http://www.g20.utoronto.ca/docs/g20history.pdf>.

[37] Nicholas Bayne, 'G8 Summit: Generating the Gleneagles Effect', *The World Today*, 61(6), May 2005; Kate Nash, 'Global Citizenship as Show Business: The Cultural Politics of Make Poverty History', *Media, Culture & Society*, 30(2) 2008: 167–81; Nicolas Sirea, *Make Poverty History: Political Communication in Action* (Basingstoke: Palgrave Macmillan, 2009); Graham Harrison, 'The Africanization of Poverty: A Retrospective on "Make Poverty History"', *African Affairs*, 109(436) 2010: 391–408; Materials on the Make Poverty History campaign. Accessed 3 May 2012 at: <http://www.makepovertyhistory.org/2005/index.shtml>.

even climate change.[38] It is commonly depicted as a device by which a neoliberal hegemony of concentrated wealth and corporate power sustains a form of 'global apartheid'[39] by managing the international economy in such a way as to ensure a widening disparity between an elite of affluent nations and the mass of impoverished states.

The G8's own highly substantive and symbolic association with the stated advances of globalization bring in its wake robust forms of attention from anti-globalization advocacy groups and protest movements that focus upon G8 summits in particular for maximum impact. G8 summits now generate high levels of international media attention as well as considerable interest group activity. They can be the venue of large public events ranging from festivals and concerts to mass demonstrations—both peaceful (e.g. Edinburgh 2005) and violent (e.g. Genoa 2001). In 2005, suicide bombers in London disrupted the Gleneagles summit in 2005 at a distance. The attacks by radical Islamists had been timed to coincide with the summit in order to achieve the maximum propaganda effect.

International organizations like the G8 have been criticized for the nature and exclusivity of their operations. Their claims of representativeness have been seen as resting upon primarily material indicators relating to their global shares of gross domestic product, military expenditures, trade, and industrial, commercial, and financial assets. The legitimacy of the G8 has also been called into question because of the way that the increasing infrastructure of assistance through preliminary meetings of ministers and officials has 'added to the sense that a system of rule may be emerging in and around the annual summit of leaders'.[40] Notwithstanding the complaints over the role and ambition of an organization like the G8, its organizational template has nevertheless been imitated by those countries which have most reason to be aggrieved over the state of international management.

The Group of 77 provides an equivalent focus for a large collection of developing countries which now runs to 130 member states. Its aims have been to maximize the negotiating position of such countries at the UN and other international forums. It too has summit meetings and a structure of policy sectors in which ministers seek joint approaches and coordinated action on selected issues.[41] The G77's institutional development has even led to the formation of another assemblage of countries in the shape of a Group of 24. This is a derivative subgroup specializing in representing the developing nations in the technically challenging and politically contested area of development finance and international monetary

[38] Gill Hubbard and David Miller (eds.), *Arguments Against G8* (London: Pluto, 2005). See also varied reports and literatures from organizations like the Center for Global Development and the World Development Movement.

[39] The phrase was first used by the South African President Thabo Mbeki in his address during the Welcoming Ceremony for the World Summit on Sustainable Development (WSSD) at the Sandton Convention Centre in Johannesburg on 26 August 2002. See '[Anti-Caplitalist] Mbeki Slams "Global Apartheid" at Pre-Summit Gala'. Accessed 12 April 2012 at: <http://www.freerepublic.com/focus/f-news/739392/posts>.

[40] Anthony Payne, *The Global Politics of Unequal Development* (Basingstoke: Palgrave Macmillan, 2005), p. 106.

[41] Karl P. Sauvant, *The Group of 77: Evolution, Structure, Organization* (New York, NY: Oceana Publications, 1981); Keisuke Iidaal, 'Third World Solidarity: The Group of 77 in the UN General Assembly', *International Organization*, 42(2) March 1988: 375–95; Payne, *The Global Politics of Unequal Development*, pp. 227–42.

arrangements.[42] In essence, such groupings are attempts to challenge those notions of international leadership most closely associated with the high-profile coalitions of major interests like the G8 and G20, and to offer a different conception of an international organization in which representation is based more on population levels and where priorities are oriented towards the categories of need and global fairness.

INTERNATIONAL LEADERSHIP AS NON-STATE ADVOCACY

The post-Cold War world has become increasingly identified as a location of interpenetrating spheres public and private of activity. The latter includes a wide variety of different agencies that have developed claims of authoritative recognition.[43] Arguably one of the most significant sources of such emergent centres of international activity, and one that offers the prospect of alternative sources of leadership provision, has been the rise to prominence of non-state actors that specialize in policy advocacy. This category is almost invariably equated with non-governmental organizations (NGOs)[44] which have grown in scale and intensity to such an extent that they have come to acquire not only a political status in their own right but also a reputation for constituting a specific sector in the matrix of global political exchange. Far from having merely an ancillary or marginal role, NGOs now play a prominent role in the processes of opinion formation, agenda construction, and global governance. It is no exaggeration to assert that NGOs have achieved a stature whereby they are able to challenge the previously exclusive rights assigned to the traditional architecture of international organizations and even on occasion to dispute the sovereignty claims on the part of national states.

Of course, the range of these non-state actors varies enormously in terms of size, stature, and access. While some are small with limited resources and leverage, others have become virtually institutionalized in the way that they have been practically

---

[42] Its full title is the Intergovernmental Group of Twenty-Four on International Monetary Affairs and Development. Its main mission is to pool resources and expertise in issues elating to development and monetary policy—especially as it relates to those areas within the purview of the IMF. It also seeks to ensure developing countries have appropriate levels of representation and participation in negotiations concerning the reform of the international monetary system. Apart from its formal meetings, the G24 sponsors workshops and supports a host of specialist publications—including books, research publications, policy briefs, and discussion papers. For example, see David Woodward, 'Democratizing the IMF', G-24 Policy Brief No. 2; Nancy Alexander, 'The World Bank's Scorecard for Rating Performance of its Recipient Governments', G-24 Policy Brief No. 34; C. P. Chandrasekhar and Jayati Ghosh, 'Fiscal Policy and Global Growth', G-24 Policy Brief No. 59; Kevin P. Gallagher, 'Regulating Global Capital Flows for Development', G-24 Policy Brief No. 76; and Jomo Kwame Sundaram, *Reforming the International Financial System for Development* (New York, NY: Columbia University Press, 2011).

[43] Rodney Bruce Hall and Thomas J. Biersteker (eds.), *The Emergence of Private Authority in Global Governance* (Cambridge: Cambridge University Press, 2002).

[44] The term non-governmental organization is often regarded as being synonymous with the term civil society organization (CSO). While it is the case that very many NGOs are in effect CSOs, 'non-governmental organization' remains a more generic expression that can include a much broader mix of organizations than that in the sector of civil society organization.

incorporated into the governing structures of a number of international organizations. The UN, for example, established the practice of giving selected NGOs the status of formal accreditation to attend specific meetings and conferences. This has led to a stream of affiliations and partnerships between civil society NGOs and both member states and the UN Secretariat. NGOs have become increasingly important in a range of activities 'including information dissemination, awareness raising, development education, policy advocacy, joint operational projects, and providing technical expertise and collaborating with UN agencies, programmes and funds'.[45] The scale of non-governmental organization activity in this sphere of international governance is reflected in the rising trajectory of NGO participation in the UN's showpiece gatherings such as its world or global summits.[46] For example, 2,400 NGO representatives attended the 1992 UN Conference on Environment and Development. Ten years later, the UN World Summit on Sustainable Development (aka Earth Summit II) included over 6,000 accredited NGOs.[47]

Non-governmental organizations can perform a prodigious variety of roles and functions. They can focus attention upon the short- and long-term impacts of current developments, and can pressurize governments and organizations to respond to identified problems. NGOs are especially effective in mobilizing opinion in support of changes in economic practices, social attitudes, and policy regimes. By informing and shaping the substance of debates on international issues, NGOs are often able to play a key role in the ordering of priorities at governmental and intergovernmental levels.[48] Within the international sphere, such organizations can not only engage directly with governments and multilateral bodies but form alliances with one another in order to enlarge their influence both within the arenas of policy formulation and outside in the wider spheres of public debate and political discourse. For many alliances, it is the latter context that offers the optimum degree of traction—especially for those sectors that are felt to be marginalized in terms of their access to centres of power.

The opportunities to shape opinion and agendas have led to the formation of 'transnational advocacy networks'. These consist of individuals and groups who form cross-border affiliations, communication hubs, and stakeholder partnerships which can operate to call attention to selected issues and problems that are perceived to occupy an inappropriately low priority status within the normal

[45] United Nations Non-Governmental Liaison Service, 'UN–NGO Relations'. Accessed 22 May 2012 at: <http://www.unsystem.org/ngls/ngorelations.htm>.

[46] Mario Pianta, 'UN World Summits and Civil Society: The State of the Art', Civil Society and Social Movements Programme Paper Number 18 (Geneva: United Nations Research Institute for Social Development, 2005); Kleber Ghimere, 'The United Nations World Summits and Civil Society Activism: Grasping the Centrality of National Dynamics' *European Journal of International Relations*, 17(1) March 2011: 75–95.

[47] Michael Schechter, *United Nations Global Conferences* (New York, NY: Routledge, 2005), chs. 5, 6; Britta Sadoun, *Political Space for Non-Governmental Organizations in United Nations World Summit Processes*, Civil Society and Social Movements Programme Paper Number 29 (Geneva: United Nations Research Institute for Social Development, 2007); Carl Death, *Governing Sustainable Development: Partnerships, Protests and Power at the World Summit* (Abingdon: Routledge, 2010), chs. 5–7.

[48] Kim Reiman, 'A View from the Top: International Politics, Norms and the Worldwide Growth of NGOs', *International Studies Quarterly*, 50(1) 2006: 45–67; David J. Armstrong, Valeria Bello, Julie Gilson, and Debora Spini (eds.), *Civil Society and International Governance: The Role of Non-State Actors in the EU, Africa, Asia and Middle East* (London: Routledge, 2010).

parameters of international agendas. As such, many of these networks are concerned with issues related to the themes of human rights, consumer rights, women's rights, environmental issues, and international peace. The skilled use of political and social resources—combined with the generation of knowledge exchange and policy expertise working through multiple platforms of communication—have allowed many networks to infuse the normal contexts of global governance with an enhanced sense of civil society ideas and values; an increased awareness of discourse as an instrument of power; and a greater attentiveness to the themes of transparency, compliance, and accountability.[49]

The effectiveness of the NGO sector is closely related to its responsiveness and adaptability which in turn are dependent on its internal biodiversity. Different NGOs have different objectives, agendas, strategies, and methods. There are NGOs that have a very wide remit. They engage in areas of macro policy on a variety of different levels of social, economic, and governmental action. Organizations like Greenpeace, Amnesty International, and Human Rights Watch, for example, operate on an international scale. In monitoring the activity of a host of different private and public actors and in relating their behaviour to various international rules, norms, and conventions, such organizations are able to act not only as a channel of accountability but also as a contextual and conditioning influence on the formation of policy by states and international organizations.

Other NGOs have a sharper focus in that their advocacy usually concerns either a particular campaign that is centred upon a specific defining event or process, or alternatively the characteristics of a single issue and its direct derivatives. An illustrative case of an event-focused NGO campaign was the Make Poverty History movement in 2005. During this period, a grand international coalition of NGOs was mobilized specifically to use the G8 summit in order to raise public consciousness of the developing world's debt burden and to pressurize the G8 nations to reform the global trading system and to meet their obligations to the UN's Millennium Development Goals. The way in which NGOs can act as a driving force in the alleviation of a specified problem, and in doing so exemplify the possibilities of performing several leadership functions, can be grasped by the international campaign to secure international action against the uncontrolled proliferation of landmines (Box 10.1).

It is possible to assign considerable importance to NGOs for the way that they can generate alternative *de facto* systems of representation and participation. Because many NGOs cultivate the themes of citizenship politics and global civic society, they are able to foster a discourse in which extra-state or transnational forms of advocacy can claim to possess a strong leadership component that combines robust criticism of current governing arrangements with a vision of a more enlightened, progressive, democratic, and just international order. These types of organization have particularly benefited from the political space

---

[49] Margaret E. Keck and Kathryn Sikkink, *Activists Beyond Borders: Advocacy Networks in International Politics* (Ithaca, NY: Cornell University Press, 1998); Peter Evans, 'Fighting Marginalization with Transnational Networks: Counter-Hegemonic Globalization', *Contemporary Sociology*, 29 (2000): 230–41; Robert Rohrschneider and Russell J. Dalton, 'A Global Network? Transnational Cooperation among Environmental Groups', *The Journal of Politics*, 64 (2002): 510–33; Death, *Governing Sustainable Development*, chs. 3–5.

Box 10.1 The International Campaign to Ban Landmines

In the post-Cold War period, opportunities arose for the recognition of new security issues and agendas. One of the most significant of these controversies was the increasing attention given to the extensive stocks of anti-personnel landmines by most of the world's armies; the extensive scale of deployment in sensitive regions; and the short- and long-term effects upon local populations in war zones. As reports on the catastrophic consequences for human and economic life streamed in from humanitarian agencies in Africa, Latin America, Asia, the Balkans, and the Middle East, a broad-based movement began to raise public consciousness over the ethics and legitimacy of such weapons that could not only indiscriminately kill and maim civilians many years after their deployment but also represented a deterrent to refugees returning to their lands from previous experiences of displacement.

At a time when concepts of human security were becoming more salient and when there was an increased emphasis upon civil society participation in the formation of international agendas, a network of local, regional, and international NGOs arose to challenge the stockpiling and usage of landmines. Ultimately, this collection of human rights organizations, children's groups, development organizations, refugee organizations, medical and humanitarian relief groups formed an umbrella organization united in its campaign to achieve a worldwide ban on landmines. The International Campaign to Ban Landmines (ICBL) grew into a coalition of over 1,200 organizations operating in 80 countries.

The organizational élan of the NGO sector was complemented by the pressure exerted by several small and middle level powers of which Canada emerged as the catalyst to take the campaign forcefully into the diplomatic sphere. What became known as the 'Ottawa Process' was a daring challenge to the international community. At a strategizing review meeting for the pro-ban supporters in October1996, the Canadian government proposed that the supporting NGOs and countries should work towards a position that would witness within a year the signing of a formal treaty outlawing the usage of landmines. At the time, the policy was seen as a high-risk venture both in the way that it sought to force a complex issue at a pace unheard of in international negotiations and in seeking to depart from conventional diplomatic channels and consensus based procedures. Nevertheless, the adoption of this fast track treaty process led in December 1997 to a ceremony in Ottawa which witnessed the agreement of over 120 countries to the Anti-Personnel Mine Ban Convention, or what has become known as the 'Ottawa Treaty'. The achievement was underlined by the award of the 1997 Nobel Peace Prize to the ICBL and its leader Jody Williams, for their success in mobilizing a multilevel response to a serious human security issue and one that fostered speculation about the possible emergence of a viable form of global civil society.

Sources: Kenneth R. Rutherford, *Disarming States: The International Movement to Ban Landmines* (Santa Barbara, CA: Praeger, 2011); Jody Williams, 1997 Nobel Peace Laureate, 'The International Campaign to Ban Landmines—A Model for Disarmament Initiatives?', Nobelprize.org. Accessed 21 January 2012 at: <http://www.nobelprize.org/nobel_prizes/peace/laureates/1997/article.html>.

Isabelle Daoust, 'Canada's Role in the Ottawa Process', Speech at the Canadian Council on International Law 20 October 2007. Accessed 11 May 2010 at: <http://www.redcross.ca/main.asp?id=024621>.

that has opened up as a result of the end of the Cold War. The displacement of the bipolar rigidities of superpower competition now allows for a more contested global politics in which NGOs regularly offer themselves as legitimate agencies of scrutiny, dissent, resistance, and reform.

In the contemporary context of an international society of states, NGOs are often in the position of redefining and performing viable leadership roles in situations where it can be argued that leadership resources and activity would otherwise be minimal. Such organizations can be highly adept at claiming alternative loci of legitimacy. They do so through their positioning on sensitive global issues, and through their common recourse to juxtaposing the scale and seriousness of endemic problems with strong inferences that state actors are unable or unwilling to address to take corrective action. In providing separate channels of grievance and advocacy, and in offering different frameworks for collaborative action, NGOs generate alternative reference points for *de facto* governance in the wider public interest and arguably in the pursuance of a vision of global justice.

Their ethos is commonly depicted as being geared to direct action to alleviate suffering, improve conditions, increase security, and prevent conflict. In doing so, NGOs have often assumed—or been ascribed—a representational role with references to enhancing democracy, promoting human rights, and underlining the obligations that governments have towards their own peoples. The pervasive presence of NGOs in many areas, combined with their often strident declarations of principles and their cultivated linkages to various international organizations and funding networks, have occasionally prompted complaints over their intrusiveness and alleged cultural bias. However, such critiques are in part a reflection of the way that NGOs have effectively adopted the rhetoric of leadership and especially the motif of a leadership deficit in international development as a device for mobilizing pressure and resources in the cause of transformative change.

INTERNATIONAL LEADERSHIP: BROKERS

Instances of leadership in the international sphere can often come down to occasions when a particular agency acts as a point of contact in disputes between two or more parties. The presence of an active intermediary operating as a communication channel can facilitate forms of engagement and exchange where there might otherwise be none. Traditionally, this mediating function has normally been conducted through the prerogatives and protocols assigned to foreign ministries and their respective diplomatic services. While the skills of diplomacy have often been deployed in the cause of peace and reconciliation between sovereign nations, diplomacy has generally had a reputation for being governed primarily by the need to protect individual national interests and to maximize each state's independence, security, and integrity.[50] The instrumental value of diplomacy in maximizing a state's freedom of manoeuvre and in maintaining a prudent cost–benefit perspective of international relations has many benefits but it can cultivate a spirit of prudence to the level of caution in taking unnecessary risks in depleting political resources in the pursuit of objectives that may not be calculated to be attainable without excessive costs.

The major powers in particular have traditionally erred on the side of such caution mainly because they have not been inclined to use their substantial diplomatic resources in causes designed to alter the balance of an international system

---

[50] See Henry Kissinger, *Diplomacy* (New York, NY: Simon & Schuster, 1994); Paul Gordon Lauren, Gordon A. Craig, and Alexander L. George, *Force and Statecraft: Diplomatic Challenges of Our Time*, 4th edn. (New York, NY: Oxford University Press, 2007); Sir Ivor Roberts (ed.), *Satow's Diplomatic Practice*, 6th edn. (New York, NY: Oxford University Press, 2009), chs. 1, 2, 6, 8, 9, 29.

that privileges their interests. During the Cold War when much of the world was fixed in a bipolar pattern of superpower spheres of influence, diplomatic room for communications and discretionary action between and across different blocs was very limited. After the Cold War, the possibilities for intermediary activity rapidly expanded to take account of a more fluid international order and a more plural view of diplomatic status. Apart from the fact that diplomacy became less confined to the communication and negotiation between states, it was also evident that diplomatic functions were becoming increasingly diversified as well as being supplemented by new operational participants in the process of international mediation.[51] The activities of international organizations and NGOs in this field have already been acknowledged. But an equally noteworthy addition to this field and one that can serve to exemplify the facilitative effect of a broker in this kind of environment is provided by particular individual states which could not be said to be major powers but which have nevertheless acquired a reputation for acting as proactive intermediaries in the international order.

The significance of Canada as a centre for mobilizing civic and international action in support of a treaty on the banning of landmines has already been noted. But other countries have also been active in using their positions to advance international agendas and especially to promote communication and dialogue between adversaries in highly volatile conditions. Norway, for example, has developed an international reputation as an intermediary experienced in the processes of conflict resolution and peace building. Norwegian diplomats have been involved in several processes of high-level mediation in some of the world's most serious trouble spots (e.g. Middle East, Sudan, Sri Lanka). Its notable interventions as a peace brokering agency include (i) the process leading to the 1993 Oslo Peace Accords between Israel and the Palestine Liberation Organization;[52] and (ii) the 2002 ceasefire agreement between the Government of Sri Lanka and the Liberation Tamil Tigers of Eelam (LTTE).[53]

Norway has been able to exploit several positional and cultural characteristics that have given it an advantage in building trust and leverage as a facilitator. For example, it is a relatively small country with no traditions of colonialism or military conquest. Moreover, it has no geostrategic interests or designs. It is also significant that it has a strong resource base through a very high level of national per capita income. This not only gives it a measure of independence from other power centres, but permits it to substantiate its identity as a pacific country through its ability to finance an array of foreign aid programmes, peace missions,

---

[51] See Geoffrey Pigman, *Contemporary Diplomacy* (Cambridge: Polity Press, 2010), chs. 2, 5, 6, 7, 8, 11.

[52] J. Moolakkattu, 'Peace Facilitation by Small States: Norway in Sri Lanka', *Cooperation and Conflict*, 40(4) 2005: 385–402; K. Höglund and I. Svensson, 'Mediating between Tigers and Lions: Norwegian Peace Diplomacy in Sri Lanka's Civil War', *Contemporary South Asia*, 17(2) 2009: 175–91; Gunnar Sørbø, Jonathan Goodhand, Bart Klem, Ada Elisabeth Nissen, and Hilde Selbervik, *Pawns of Peace: Evaluation of Norwegian Peace Efforts in Sri Lanka, 1997–2009*, Norad (Norwegian Agency for Development Cooperation), Norad Evaluation Department, Report 5/2011, September 2011.

[53] Uri Savir, *The Process:1,100 Days That Changed the Middle East* (New York, NY: Random House, 1998), chs. 2, 3; Hilde H. Waage, *Peacemaking is a Risky Business: Norway's Role in the Peace Process in the Middle East, 1993–96*, Peace Research Institute Oslo (PRIO) Report 1, 2004; Hilde H. Waage, 'Norway's Role in the Middle East Peace Talks: Between a Small State and a Weak Belligerent', *Journal of Palestine Studies*, 34(4) 2005: 6–24.

and international monitoring activities. It should also be noted that Scandinavia as a whole has strong credentials in the usage of alternative models of international engagement that give priority to developing communication networks and regimes of social trust in the conduct of foreign policy.

Canada and Norway are examples of what are often termed 'middle powers'. Many of the these middle-ranking powers have an approach to international

---

Box 10.2 An emergent middle-ranking power: Turkey

Over recent years, Turkey has actively positioned itself not just as a source of stability within its region but as a geostrategic and cross-cultural bridge between the West and the East—a role that has demonstrated its ability to be a NATO member and an ally of the United States while at the same time maintaining close relationships with its Islamic neighbours and a supportive posture towards the Palestinian people and their predicament. Turkey's economic success, coupled with an ability to combine an attachment to Islamic culture with a market economy, and a secular state, has increasingly led the country to portray itself as an exceptional focal point of emulation. Since 2002 when the Justice and Development Party (AKP) under Recep Erdoğan came to power, Turkey's foreign policy has developed into a signature element of national identity in what is widely cited as a concerted strategy to become a model for other societies within its region and beyond.

Set against a historical background of enmity between Turks and many other peoples (e.g. Greeks, Russians, Iranians, Arabs), Turkey has set out to reconfigure itself within a more flexible and multipolar global order. Under what is termed its 'zero problems with neighbours' policy, the Erdoğan government has taken concerted action to improve relations with its near neighbours and beyond (e.g. Greece, Bulgaria, Ukraine, Russia, Georgia, Iraq, Iran, Azerbaijan). It has sought to reduce some of the tensions evoked by the long-established and highly emotive issues surrounding Cyprus and Armenia. Furthermore, with the vision of a progressive foreign policy and an international role in mind, the Turkish government has over the course of 2010–11 established no fewer than twenty-seven new embassies—three in Latin America, three in Asia and most notably twenty-one in Africa.

The project of a 'New Turkey', however, has not been welcomed in all quarters. While the Turkish system is widely seen as a positive regional model of modernity and has been cited as a major source of inspiration in the social movements associated with the insurgencies of the 'Arab Spring', the country's ambitions have raised a number of concerns. For example, Turkish foreign policy activism can evoke fears of a revival of Ottoman imperialism over Arab and Kurdish populations; any form of regional primacy on the part of Turkey also runs the risk of provoking various sectarian, religious, and economic divisions within the region; and its deteriorating relationships with Syria and Israel are likely to provoke opposition from Iran and Egypt both of which have their own claims to regional leadership. Notwithstanding these possible limitations, it can be concluded that Turkey has made great strides in transforming its image from that of a largely passive and neutral entity to one of a dynamic economic and cultural force that has become adept at opening up borders, creating lines of communication, establishing the bases for mediation in regional conflicts, and offering a distinct locus of leadership and engagement in an otherwise unstable region.

Sources: Bill Park, *Modern Turkey: People, State and Foreign Policy in a Globalised World* (Abingdon: Routledge 2012), chs. 7–9; Owen Matthews, 'The Erdogan Doctrine', *Newsweek*, 12 September 2011; Steven A. Cook, 'Erdogan's Middle Eastern Victory Lap', *Foreign Affairs*, 15 September 2011. Accessed 3 May 2012 at: <http://www.foreignaffairs.com/articles/68269/steven-a-cook/erdogans-middle-eastern-victory-lap>; Tony Barber, 'Foreign relations: Policy struggles to keep up with rush of events', *Financial Times*, 21 November 2011; Bobby Ghosh, 'Erdogan's Way', *TIME*, 28 November 2011; Daniel Dombey, 'Turkish diplomacy: An attentive neighbour', *Financial Times*, 26 February 2012.

relations which is marked less by an impulse for strategic advantage and regional domination and more by a desire to acquire distinct diplomatic identities, niche positions, and mediating roles in support of multilateral or collective solutions to global problems (Box 10.2).

Their commitment to international peace and stability through outreach, mediation, coalition-building, and conflict resolution can allow some of the powers to acquire a disproportionate significance in relation to their size.

In effect, because middle-ranking powers experience neither the pressures of great powers nor the constraints of lesser powers, they are in a position not only to offer themselves as intermediaries and facilitators in disputes, but also to take up leadership roles in the more general cultivation of attitudinal and behavioural norms in international arenas. As a consequence, these middle-ranking powers are often cited as fulfilling the role of 'norm entrepreneurs' in the conditioning processes of social forces surrounding the emergence and adoption of norms of engagement within global politics.[54] It would be an exaggeration to claim that the reduction of tensions, or the settlement of disputes, or the promotion of norms can be solely attributable to such individual agencies. In an international system of increasing complexity with diplomatic influences that can include international organizations, NGOs, multimedia platforms, academic institutions, and corporate bodies, single states cannot expect to dominate such a plural matrix. Nevertheless, it is possible to acknowledge the contribution made by certain influential state actors at particular times in undertaking a leadership role by deploying their resources, services, and status in bringing adversaries together in attempts to maximize the opportunities for peaceful reconciliation.

SEGMENTED AND AGGREGATIVE LEADERSHIP

It is evident from the above sections that the claims to leadership within the international sphere can be as extensive as the number and variety of modes and locations within what is a highly segmented field of political activity. It might be inferred from these individual examinations that each form of engagement exists within its own closed or limited context with little connection to other levels, dimensions, or processes of agenda formation and policy selection. It is true that these agencies are often motivated to operate on their own volition in large part because of a perceived absence of movement elsewhere to expedite action in accordance with the specified preferences of those with particular sets of policy, procedural, or structural priorities. This outlook is itself reflective of the multi-dimensional character of the international context and the way it facilitates such a diversity of leadership types.

[54] Tracey H. Slagter, 'International "Norm Entrepreneurs": A Role for Middle Powers?' Paper presented at the annual meeting of the International Studies Association, Le Centre Sheraton Hotel, Montreal, Quebec, Canada, 17 March 2004. Accessed 4 June 2010 at: <http://citation.allacademic.com//meta/p_mla_apa_research_citation/0/7/3/1/6/pages73163/p73163-1.php>; Christine Ingebritsen, 'Norm Entrepreneurs: Scandinavia's Role in World Politics'. Accessed 6 February 2012 at: <http://cac.sagepub.com/cgi/reprint/37/1/11>.

However, it is important to note that segmentation cannot always be equated with diffusion and inaction. On occasions, the pattern of separate parts can assume the shape and dynamics of an assemblage of leadership nodes. When this occurs, it is possible to observe a convergence of different types of leadership activity operating either at the same time, or in a successive sequence, or in compounded form of both formations. In many respects, the challenge of establishing and securing agendas in such a heavily fragmented system will necessarily be dependent upon attracting support from other sectors and levels in a form of implicit, or explicit, process of aggregation. Such an aggregative exercise involving so many different actors with different claims to leadership contributions is well illustrated in the case of the emergence of the 'responsibility to protect' doctrine as an internationally agreed rule of conduct for the behaviour of states towards their own peoples.

During the 1990s, a trend emerged that witnessed a rise in the number and ferocity of armed conflicts within states. So much so in fact that internal conflict had displaced the more traditional mode of interstate warfare as the main source of large-scale violence and high levels of civilian casualties. The appalling death tolls resulting from the conflicts in such countries as Cambodia, Rwanda, Bosnia, Kosovo, East Timor, and Darfur were widely construed as representing serious failures on the part of the international community in preventing such overt forms of disorder and mass atrocities. These incidents prompted activists in the international sphere to formulate some form of response that might impose preventative measures against future outbreaks of destructive violence within state borders.

The most obvious source of such an initiative was the UN but it was an international organization that worked through intergovernmental processes resting upon the principle of state sovereignty. Nevertheless, in 1999 and 2000 Kofi Annan used his position as the UN Secretary-General to highlight the need for a careful scrutiny of the problem and for imaginative solutions in squaring the norm of state sovereignty with the imperative to prevent both state agencies and non-state actors operating within states from engaging in mass violations of human rights. Other strands of opinion formation centred upon individual states like Canada which was instrumental in setting up a consortium of international experts in the field—namely the International Commission on Intervention and State Sovereignty. The ICISS sponsored a large-scale consultative exercise that gathered representations from governments, intergovernmental organizations, regional bodies, NGOs, think tanks, and universities. Its report entitled *The Responsibility to Protect* (2001)[55] had considerable influence on the process of agenda formation. Further reports from the UN High-Level Panel on Threats, Challenges, and Change (2004), and from the UN Secretary-General on his programme *In Larger Freedom* (2005)[56] increased the momentum towards a

---

[55] International Commission on Intervention and State Sovereignty, *The Responsibility to Protect, Report of the International Commission on Intervention and State Sovereignty* (Ottawa: International Development Research Centre, 2001).

[56] United Nations, *A More Secure World: Our Shared Responsibility*: Report of the High-Level Panel on Threats, Challenges and Change, 2004. Kofi Annan, Report of the Secretary-General, *In Larger Freedom: Towards Development, Security and Human Rights for All*, A/59/2005, 21 March 2005. Accessed 3 June 2012 at: <http://www.un.org/largerfreedom/contents.htm>.

recommendation that member states should endorse the principle of a responsibility to protect their peoples as an integral part of their governing remits.

The pivotal moment came in 2005 when the UN World Summit witnessed the formal culmination of a process in which the international community confronted the challenging issue of a state's obligation to its citizens in respect to their own human security. In addressing the issue of states that prosecute or permit mass atrocities against their own peoples, the heads of state at the summit endorsed the principle of a responsibility to 'protect its populations from genocide, war crimes, ethnic cleansing and crimes against humanity.' The agreement further states that this responsibility not only entailed the 'prevention of such crimes...through appropriate and necessary means', but also recognized the international community's own responsibility to take collective action where and when 'national authorities are manifestly failing to protect their populations'.[57]

Even though the declaration of this 'Responsibility to Protect' (R2P) principle was not as comprehensive as many of its supporters had hoped for, and even though it left a great many questions relating to its operation unanswered, the acceptance of R2P represented a radical reconceptualization of the principle of state sovereignty—i.e. the very principle that has traditionally underpinned the status and legitimacy of the primary elements in the international order. In explicitly recognizing the state as the primary locus of responsibility for the protection of its citizens, it established the corollary of a derivative responsibility assigned to the international community in those cases where states are considered to have absolved themselves from their primary protective responsibilities to their populations.

The establishment of the R2P principle has been widely cited as a case of innovative leadership within the international sphere. What it reveals is a complexity of attribution in which forms of leadership were demonstrated in a number of different contexts—but which together produced a positive cumulative outcome. The participants included the active advocacy on the part of individual political leaders like Tony Blair who championed new conceptions of international security obligations to prevent mass atrocity crimes. But they also included the contributions of 'norm entrepreneurs' like Francis M. Deng (Secretary-General's Special Representative for Internally Displaced Persons 1992–2004) who championed the direct linkage between sovereignty and responsibility within the UN secretariat.

Other pivotal individuals engaged in shifting mindsets and changing agendas included Gareth Evans (President and CEO of the International Crisis Group), as well as UN Secretary-General Kofi Annan whose supportive posture and enabling approval lent considerable weight to R2P's inception and development as an emergent norm. The cast of leadership nodes can also be assigned to those individual states whose active support made significant contributions to maintaining the pressure for reform (e.g. Canada, Switzerland, Sweden, and Ghana). Additionally, a role of organizational leadership can be ascribed to various NGOs, regional organizations, and other intergovernmental bodies—most notably to the International Commission on Intervention and State Sovereignty (co-chaired by Gareth Evans)

---

[57] United Nations General Assembly, 'UN World Summit 2005: Outcome Document', 16 September 2005, Sections 138–9.

whose report in 2001 added considerable diplomatic momentum to R2P's final emergence as an agreed principle by the UN World Summit in 2005 and by the UN Security Council in 2006. Through a cumulative process involving a variety of leadership activities and leadership claims, the international community succeeded in building upon a set of pre-existing international obligations relating to civil, political, social, economic, and cultural rights, in order to establish a significant conditionality to the principles of state sovereignty and territorial security.[58]

CONCLUSION

It is clear that while leadership represents a common and even habitual feature of the debates surrounding the conduct of international politics, the meanings attached to the concept and practice of leadership in such a context remain highly uncertain. In terms of strict political logic, it might be asserted that leadership in this sphere remains something of a chimera because of the absence of a recognizable, durable, and settled polity at international level. But as has been noted above, inferences and claims of leadership functions being performed by different agencies and actors abound in the analysis of international politics. Some of this can be regarded as a simple extrapolation from the parameters of conventional political leadership—rooted as these have been in domestic locations of political authority and activity. In a period of increased global interdependency, it is possible to speculate that established notions of leadership would always migrate into wider spheres of political operation. Yet while the references to leadership on the part of participants and analysts alike may have grown in response to shifting environments, they have at the same time lost some of their previous precision in terms of clarity and settled understanding. What has been lost in definition, however, has been more than compensated for by a broadening of horizons in relation to the variation of leadership activities as well as to the adaptive processes that can be attached to notions of leadership formation and operation.

In examining the expansive properties of the international dimension, it becomes possible to arrive at improved insights into the various contingencies, thresholds, and nuances that are linked to the emergence of leadership in complex and contested situations. In such contexts it is evident that, even at a minimal level, notions of leadership are used as a cognitive device which provides observers and participants with a method of navigating their way around the intricacies of international affairs and global governance. Leaders have always been used as symbolic entities in order to represent the interplay of states and to mark ways by which they relate to one another. The explanatory repertoire of leadership is now expected to absorb a far larger and more demanding volume of developments

---

[58] Francis M. Deng, Sadikiel Kimaro, Terrence Lyons, Donald Rothchild, and I. William Zartman, *Sovereignty as Responsibility: Conflict Management in Africa* (Washington, DC: Brookings Institution, 1996); Gareth Evans and Mohamed Sahnoun, 'The Responsibility to Protect', *Foreign Affairs*, November/December 2002; Gareth Evans, *The Responsibility to Protect: Ending Mass Atrocity Crimes Once and for All* (Washington, DC: Brookings Institution, 2008); see also Alex J. Bellamy, *Responsibility to Protect: The Global Effort to End Mass Atrocities* (Cambridge: Polity Press, 2009).

between and across different states as well as a host of transnational mediums that further disrupt the more traditional delineation of political exchange.

The adjustments made in response to these new conditions have opened up the study of leadership to new points of access and to enriched sets of agendas. Nevertheless, in revealing an adaptive virtuosity in the way that leadership can be depicted within an international setting, the reliance upon leadership-related modes of inquiry and explanation can still raise significant issues in terms of scale, scope, reach, and effect. For example, despite the fact that international problems arouse demands for leadership activity and even though manifold forms of leadership in this sphere have materialized, it is nevertheless the case that there remain powerful constraints on the development of a broad-based leadership capacity set within the largely narrow confines of state-centric units. Moreover, while the demands—and even the expectations—for international leadership may intensify in accordance with the perceived lack of leadership emanating from other sources, the very notion of a form of supranational leadership can seem an implausible organizational response to a problem posed by endemic resource limitations.

Notwithstanding the presence of extensive global issues coexisting with confining leadership capacities, the reflexive impulse to discern or to invent forms of leadership agency in a world that can often appear to be devoid of effective governance remains a potent instrument of political reconfiguration. This does not mean that the concept and operation of political leadership can be endlessly manipulated into a manifold device to satisfy all contingencies. But it does mean that the international realm is highly productive not only in revealing how much is invested in leadership as an instrumental, purposive, and explanatory political force, but also in disclosing the emergent variability and innovative potential of leadership claims to position and legitimacy in highly mutable conditions of political formation and organizational management.

Part IV

Horizons

11

New iterations and expansion joints

'Leaders are often sensitive to various dimensions of power, good at identifying its sources and using it... Effective leadership varies by the degree of
formality or informality of the setting and the public or private nature of the
enterprise.'

Nannerl O. Keohane[1]

'Understanding context is crucial for effective leadership.'

Joseph S. Nye, Jr.[2]

PREAMBLE

The interaction between the formation and exercise of leadership on the one hand
and the contextual conditions within which leaders have to operate on the other
has been a recurrent theme of this study. Another important dimension has been
the evident association of leadership activities with various forms of change. In
effect, leaders cannot be equated with static political universes. On the contrary,
they both signify the existence of altered environments and act as agents of change
through the substantive and symbolic resources of their own positions, choices,
and programmes. While 'great leaders' are said to be able to change the political
weather, it is more normal for leaders to have to adapt to a plurality of micro-
climates and in doing so to establish an ongoing process of adjustment and
accommodation in a highly mutable set of circumstances.

This chapter seeks to outline some of the more significant recent changes to
which leaders have had to adjust in their efforts to preserve the integrity and
leverage of their positions. Some of these contextual shifts can be seen as generating certain positional advantages and resource benefits that can be exploited by
leaders in their competition for political status. Other changes concern the
identification of trends and developments that condition and even constrain
leadership activity. These will often require leaders to be skilful not only in
negotiating effective adjustments to altered circumstances but also in defining
their roles and purposes in accordance with newly dominant contingencies. While

---

[1] Nannerl O. Keohane, *Thinking about Leadership* (Princeton, NJ: Princeton University Press,
2010), 27,35.

[2] Joseph S. Nye, Jr., *The Powers to Lead* (New York, NY: Oxford University Press, 2008), p. 90.

leaders are normally and necessarily adept at registering the existence of change, so they are also agents of new trajectories which on both counts make them time and case sensitive to new directions in the complex matrices of political leadership.

REACHING OUT

As we noted in Chapter 7, political leaders have increasingly had to broaden and deepen their bases of support in order to sustain their positions and defend their claims to legitimacy. In many systems, leaders have to transcend previous divisions, core constituencies, and plural power centres by aligning themselves to a more generalized form of appeal. To a growing extent, prime ministers, presidents, and opposition leaders have to engage in enhanced types of public outreach and have to define their leaderships explicitly in terms of expressions of public, national, or cultural identities.

Leaders are now expected to break out of the immediate confines of their own immediate organizations. They do so in order not only to provide a conspicuously identifiable figure within a political environment that is increasingly devoid of reliable anchorage points of firm attachment but also to devise and implement marketing campaigns that have to be responsive to the fluid character of shifting public concerns and issue profiles. Apart from being necessarily adept at the methods and arts of effective communication, leaders have to be able to reduce both the physical and social space between themselves and the citizenry. In effect, they are expected to have an ability to project themselves viscerally into the public sphere and to create compelling associations between their leadership claims and the popular concerns, anxieties, and agendas of their respective audiences.

Even a religious leader like the pope now has to be able to demonstrate an effective engagement with the modern requirements of public outreach. After a series of poorly handled pronouncements and ill-advised decisions, Pope Benedict XVI was criticized for being personally too remote and thereby poor in the field of communication. This prompted the Vatican to inaugurate not only a new portal aggregating information from the Vatican's various print, radio, and television media outlets but also the launch of a YouTube channel, a Facebook page, an iPhone app and a Twitter feed to enhance the pope's evangelizing ministry.[3] Even if they are established in office, therefore, modern leaders have to work assiduously to sustain the same kind of proximity to their supporters that they originally achieved during their rise to power. The defining strategy is always one of leadership security. Leaders have to ensure not only that they maximize their political base but that they prevent, or at least work to minimize, the displacement of public attention towards alternative leaders with separate agendas.

Players in the field of modern leadership politics now have access to an array of devices that can be used to project leaders to wide audiences, and to deepen and

---

[3] John Follain, 'Cardinals turn on Pope invisible', *Sunday Times*, 22 February 2009; Urvi Nopany, 'iPope: the Vatican and technology', *Daily Telegraph*, 29 June 2011; Nick Squires, 'Pope Benedict XVI to have his own personal Twitter account', *Daily Telegraph*, 27 February 2012.

refine the connection between leadership messages and currents of public opinion. These range from the adoption of sophisticated forms of news management, market research, and policy presentation to the more physical strategies of ensuring optimum leadership exposure on as many platforms as possible. More recently, leaders have had opportunities to enlarge their portfolios of professionalized communication with the advent of new strategies to exploit the outreach potential of soft format television outlets; local and regional news contacts; lifestyle and ethnic publications; focus group opinion testing; and the adoption of 'town meetings' and 'road shows' in which leaders engage directly with public audiences.

These devices have been used to supplement, and in some cases to supersede, the more conventional strategies of 'disintermediation' whereby leaders seek to circumvent those power centres that lie between them and their target audiences. In the past, radio and television have given leaders the opportunity of short-circuiting the intermediary roles of both the press and print journalism, and the published outputs of party organizations, in favour of a more open access regime of direct contact with the vehicles of mass public consumption. By optimizing the level of communicative resources in this way, leaders have been able not only to broaden their political appeal and increase their negotiating positions, but also to maximize the possibility of ensuring that it is *their* interpretations of issues and events, *their* definitions of current problems, and *their* policy agendas which have a greater chance of determining the shape of public discourse and political debate.

More recently, another form of communication has given leaders the opportunity of extending the logic of circumvention to a new level of sophistication. The onset of digital technology in political communications has already been cited as having far-reaching implications for the relationship between leaders and non-leaders. In a dimension that collapses time and space, and which offers expansive outreach with collapsing costs, leaders can generate highly advanced forms of interconnection with mass audiences that are not dependent upon traditional broadcast networks. Moreover, they can do so in such a way that the linkages become more interactive and organic in operation. Instead of the more conventional mass media outlets in which messages are targeted to the public in a top-down and largely undifferentiated way, the usage of cyberspace media allows leaders to build sophisticated networks in which individuals become less passive recipients of information and more participants in what is conceived as a joint enterprise of knowledge exchange and interactive processes. As leaders now have access to technologies that give them communication capacities that are comparable to major broadcasters, they are able to create strategies that are aimed at closing the gap between leaders and the public by increasingly resorting to methods that bypass or marginalize the more conventional routes of 'going public'.

It was the election campaign of President Barack Obama in 2008 that underlined the potential of these new media channels in the field of political communication. In that election, the Obama theme of 'change' was both mobilized and symbolized by a highly innovative electoral strategy that exploited a raft of devices designed to optimize direct leader–citizen connections through electronic and digital networks. The Obama organization was highly adept at email marketing techniques and at the formation of sophisticated databanks, but it was its usage of Web 2.0 facilities in forming volunteer and fundraising networks at ground level that set it apart as a pioneering operation. In addition to exploiting the organizing potential of such social network sites as MySpace and Facebook, Obama's own website my.barackobama.com became a networking hub in its own right that facilitated the creation of volunteer activist and affinity groups together with linked blogs, voter signups, digital forums, and online fundraising. These experiments in extensive and intensive public outreach were supplemented by Obama's open adoption of YouTube as a key media instrument. In channelling his speeches in their entirety through YouTube, he could circumvent the editorial control of network and local broadcasters that normally reduced speeches to a short news clip. Moreover, in doing so he strengthened his presence on the YouTube website and with it his recognition factor amongst the more youthful audiences that had higher incidences of connection to such open-source Web-based communications.

From the data-generating properties of his campaign website to the personal information gathered at mass rallies, and from the usage of blogs to the employment of viral marketing techniques, the Obama team was able to take political campaigning to a new level of audience cultivation, information exchange, collaborative enterprise, and popular advocacy. The scale of the enterprise can be gauged by the fact that my.barackobama.com recruited 13.5 million supporters and raised $500 million from 2 million individual donors. The Obama organization's development of social networks and email address books facilitated the formation of an online support network of over 16,000 groups. Obama himself accrued over 1.5 million 'friends' on MySpace and Facebook, and amassed over 45,000 followers on Twitter. These considerable electoral resources were then transferred to the White House where Obama sought to continue equivalent levels of public connectedness in government. For example, his team transformed the White House website in order to make use of new media platforms—allowing citizens to read the latest presidential blog postings and discussion boards, as well as to sign up for email news updates.[4]

This is not to say that Obama dispensed with the more conventional forms of 'going public'. In order to garner support for his key policies (e.g. economic stimulus, Afghanistan), the president not only deployed such customary techniques as presidential addresses, network appeals, and live prime time television press conferences but even extended this repertoire by instituting and hosting a television debate on the specific issue of health care. What was noteworthy was the way that the Obama team combined the resources of these channels with the opportunities afforded by the Web 2.0 instruments that had been refined during his election campaign. Included in these was the establishment of virtual town hall meetings in which President Obama would take questions from online participants who had used the White House website both to submit questions and to vote for the questions that should be put to the president.

---

[4] See Claire C. Miller, 'How Obama's Internet Campaign Changed Politics', *New York Times*, 7 November 2008; Ryan Moede, 'Digital Marketing Lessons from the Obama Campaign', *Viget/Advance: A Strategy and Marketing Blog*, 13 November 2008. Accessed 28 September 2012 at: <http://viget.com/advance/digital-marketing-lessons-from-the-obama-campaign>; John Allen Hendricks and Robert E. Denton, Jr. (eds.), *Communicator-in-Chief: How Barack Obama Used New Media Technology to Win the White House* (Lanham, MD: Lexington Books, 2010).

A variation of this device was instituted in January 2010 following the president's State of the Union Address when YouTube organized an exercise in which the public submitted questions and voted on the selection of those questions to be put to the president in an exclusive YouTube interview in the White House. Another way that the Obama team attempted to retain its conversation with the public through the interactive and collaborative ethos of Web 2.0 was through the extension of the my.barackobama.com website from a purely campaigning instrument into a mobilizing arm of the presidency and its agenda for change. The objective was to maintain the scope and energy of the grassroots movement that supported the Obama candidacy and to project its themes of social interconnectedness and community action into the processes of government.[5] The continuing engagement with the evolving technologies of political communication paved the way for Obama's 2012 re-election campaign which raised the profile of data harvesting, online targeting, interactive marketing, social media tracking, precision messaging, and Internet advertising to new levels of sophistication.[6]

The achievements of the Obama team in demonstrating the effectiveness of new technologies in the advancement and refinement of outreach strategies have become a point of reference for many subsequent campaigns in other countries. In their attempt to emulate the Obama phenomenon, leaders and leadership aspirants alike have sought to use similar methods to achieve comparable levels of public position and political leverage in support of similar narratives of sustained accessibility, proximity, and engagement. While the trend towards the high-level adoption of these forms of political communication may offer alternative resource bases for contemporary leaders, it is important to note that they can carry significant risks. Their usage can exacerbate the problems noted earlier in respect to the representational and reputational costs of public leadership strategies (Chapter 7). In addition to the more normal risks of isolation and detachment that come from extending leadership claims disproportionately and repeatedly through the medium of public projection and civil purpose, the adoption of these new platforms can set in motion equally innovative forms of counterclaim and opposition. In effect, the political usage of multiple platforms of the digital media and especially the Web 2.0 channels of online interaction can act as double-edged instruments of political communication.

The sheer volume and plurality of these outlets mean that public leadership messages can never achieve the position of a dominant narrative. On the contrary, the exploitation of these devices will almost certainly ensure that they will be used as political countermeasures by other contenders for the mantle of public

---

[5] For example, upon accessing the Obama website dedicated to the theme of Organizing for America the individual is encouraged to become an active part of a process of renewal. 'Join Millions of Americans Calling for Change Using Our Online Tools. Find an event near you. Join a local organizing group. Get trained on community organizing.' The message is one of citizen action in partnership with President Obama: 'When you create an account on My.BarackObama.com, you're joining the online community of organizers who helped elect President Obama and now are working to bring real change on critical issues, including healthcare, education and energy reform.' Accessed 28 September 2012 at: <http://my.barackobama.com/page/content/newenergysplash/>.

[6] Richard McGregor, 'Obama 2012 machine logs updates as race gears up', *Financial Times*, 10/11 December 2011; T. W. Farnham, 'Obama has aggressive Internet strategy to woo supporters', *Washington Post*, 6 April 2012.

leadership. Even as early as the 2008 presidential election, the Obama team found that its techniques were being imitated—albeit belatedly—by other contenders. The stream of anti-Obama interactive websites, however, turned into a torrent of online dissenting collaboration after the election when opponents sought to apply these new techniques to the task of opposing the administration's policy agendas. The severity of the blowback has underlined the political importance of the contemporary battleground over public leadership. It illustrates the volatile nature of a strategy that relies not only upon a highly sensitized responsiveness to currents of popular opinion but also upon establishing priority claims to leadership legitimacy in a process of ongoing disputation that is now as evident between elections as it is during the campaigns for office.

THE HYPE OF HYPER-PERSONALITY

Another aspect of leadership activity that has recently experienced a rise to prominence is the way that individual personality has increasingly become central to the presentation and understanding of leadership roles. Of course, leaders who make their own personas into a recognized public resource and who work to equate effective leadership with assertive personal power are not new. History is replete with examples of rulers who have fused their own identities with contemporary sources of legitimacy and sovereign power. Comparable conjunctions have remained evident in world politics during the modern era. Whether it is the inflated leadership claims of autocrats in weak states, or the 'cults of personality' associated with communist regimes, or the continuing traction of monarchies, many political systems have retained, and on occasion even revived, a close interdependency between personal authority and statecraft on the one hand, and political order and national security on the other. What is more notable than these residual or outlier cases are those instances where complex modern political systems have become increasingly susceptible to ascribing marked significance to the individual features of those who hold key political offices. This trend has been discernible in those positions that have historically and constitutionally afforded incumbents with considerable personal discretion. But it is equally important to acknowledge the movement towards a greater personalization of leadership attention and depiction that has been experienced in those systems traditionally less disposed to such themes and devices of differentiation.

In essence, the factors discussed in Chapter 7 relating to the emergence of a more personalized depiction of leadership even within liberal democracies have risen exponentially over the recent past and in many instances have reached a level where they have had a transformative effect on host institutions. To a growing extent, the credentials claimed by leaders themselves together with meanings and roles assigned to leadership have become centred upon the individuality of the respective leaders. In one sense, this is a function of the unifying messages relating to the public and national interest that leaders are drawn to as a dominant rationale of appeal. Grand themes of cohesion necessitate a single figure and lone voice for authenticity. In another sense, leaders are pulled into these positions of conspicuous recognition not only by the drivers of media priorities, agenda construction, and organizational branding but also by cultural shifts in the conduct and consumption patterns of contemporary politics. Just as leaders increasingly resort to individual appeals and campaigns that seek to tap into holistic notions of community, so the construction and presentation of politics become ever more geared to the personal abilities and reputations of leaders. What this means in practice is that leaders not only have to engage in a competitive process with one another but have to survive and even flourish within an equally competitive communications environment. Modern leaders, therefore, have to shape their individual purposes and priorities both to the techniques and outlets available, and also to the strategic need to convey personal themes and attributes as leadership virtues.

The cumulative effect of these developments has been that leaders are expected to be not merely public transmission points for their parties or governments but to be highly visible political personalities in their own right. It is not enough to be the public face of an administration or organization. Increasingly, prime ministers and presidents now have to project themselves actively and consistently as individuals engaging in personalized leadership. This is reflected in the growing practice by leaders of referring to an individual programme or manifesto that will guide their followers in the pursuit and exercise of power.

For example, it is becoming increasingly commonplace for political leaders— including those operating in parliamentary democracies—to possess and to convey an individual sense of vision for their respective parties and for their respective nation states as a whole. Such a vision is seen as important in creating a brand image that will lend coherence to an individual's claim to leadership. It is now no longer sufficient for prime ministers merely to arouse interest in a political agenda. They have to ensure that the agenda bears the personal stamp of the premier. The personalized nature of a leader's political vision is usually underlined by the way that it is declared to be sourced from the individual's unique background and formative experiences. Just as personal origins can support a leader's claim to the right to propound a public vision, so the leader's lifetime influences and accomplishments are extrapolated into a personified essence of the vision itself.

In many systems, leaders are now expected not merely to provide a tangible representation of their party's collective nature, but to offer a singular and integrated image of a driving rationale for government. Whereas political leadership might have been regarded in the past more as an institutionalized position held by a person, it is increasingly the case that leadership is characterized by, and then made dependent upon, the idiosyncratic properties of the leader. It is noteworthy that even in those systems that are traditionally based on party government, cabinet authority, and collective responsibility, the holders of leadership positions, as well as those who seek to displace them, now habitually speak in the first person rather than in the more collegiate argot that used to characterize the traditions of discourse within these systems.[7] As party identities, brand

---

[7] See Michael Foley, *The Rise of the British Presidency* (Manchester: Manchester University Press, 1993); Michael Foley, *The British Presidency: Tony Blair and the Politics of Public Leadership* (Manchester: Manchester University Press, 2000); Michael Foley, 'The Presidential Dynamics of Leadership Decline in Contemporary British Politics: The Illustrative Case of Tony Blair', *Contemporary Politics*, 14(1) March 2008: 52–69.

alignments, programmes, and manifestos become increasingly bound up with the penetration of leaders upon the consciousness of their respective publics so personal promotion rises to new levels of political significance. It is now regarded as simply prudent for a UK prime minister like David Cameron, for example, to operate a leadership blog and video diary (Webcameron[8]) recounting the premier's activities, visits, speeches, policy positions, and articles along with clips, photos, and external links. The strategic imperative of being able to find the right voice and the nuanced language to engage effectively with the currency of personal credos and visions now goes far in determining the success or failure of many modern leaderships.

In this environment, political leaders have to be able to inhabit and exploit what has become a 24/7 multi-platform media environment that is renowned for the speed and mutability of its agendas as well as its capacity to generate and facilitate increasingly segmented audiences. The demands of this media landscape have implications not just for leaders' own spheres of privacy but also for the way that politics is mediated in advanced industrial societies.[9] Leaders have to be skilled in the various arts of modern communication connected to what is also an increasingly visual culture in which the representational and symbolic elements of individual leadership figures have to be conveyed with sustained professionalism and attention to detail. This means that leaders have to carve out a public identity both for themselves and for their organizations in which their personal distinctiveness and individual claims to leadership qualities can be correlated to notions of fitness for governing responsibilities. The impetus to establish leadership attributes as substantive categories of political evaluation has fostered a competitive matrix in which high exposure and calculated self-disclosure have become conventional aspects of a leadership environment in which the private is central both to the portrayal of politics and to an understanding of public actions. The cultivated proximity of both spheres can even open up expansive social, historical, and moral landscapes to the remit of leadership roles and responsibilities.

One noteworthy example of the enlargement of leadership portfolios has come with the rising incidence of political leaders taking on the role of giving expression to social, cultural, or national statements of contrition. The reasons for such public apologies are normally to mark the recognition of historical episodes of repression, past abuses of human rights, gross miscarriages of justice, and elements of complicity in forms of extreme violence. In acknowledging the reasons for the existence of long-standing grievances and in articulating an understanding of the painful and damaging consequences for those involved, a leader's act of sorrow is normally motivated by the desire to reach some form of closure on the painful experiences of the past. Significantly, these exercises in apology are made by political leaders who endeavour to enfold such collective sentiments within their remits of representational value. Accordingly, they are not only made on behalf of the public but in the perceived interests of the public. Examples of such open declarations of belated recognition and responsibility are presented in Box 11.1.

---

[8] The website address is: <http://www.conservatives.com/video/webcameron.aspx>

[9] See James Stanyer, *Intimate Politics: Publicity, Privacy and the Personal Lives of Politicians in Media Saturated Democracies* (Cambridge: Polity Press, 2012).

Box 11.1 Selected apologies by national leaders

June 1997	UK Prime Minister Tony Blair expresses regret for English indifference to the Irish people during the Potato Famine of the 1840s.
March 1998	US President Bill Clinton acknowledges that the international community had to share responsibility for the inaction that allowed the Rwandan genocide (April–July 1994) to unfold.
October 1998	Japan's Prime Minister Keizo Obuchi expresses 'deep remorse' and extends a 'heartfelt apology' for Japanese behaviour in Korea during the colonial occupation and the Second World War.
March 1999	US President Bill Clinton recognizes that US involvement in the widespread repression during the Guatemalan war was wrong.
April 2000	Belgian Prime Minister Guy Verhofstadt apologizes to the Rwandan people for his country's attitude during the 1994 genocide.
February 2005	UK Prime Minister Tony Blair apologizes for the miscarriages of justice related to the 'Guildford Four' and the 'Maguire Seven'.
November 2006	UK Prime Minister Tony Blair expresses deep sorrow for Britain's historical role in the slave trade.
February 2008	Australia's Prime Minister Kevin Rudd apologizes for the past indignity and degradation inflicted upon the country's indigenous peoples.
March 2010	French President Nicolas Sarkozy admits to serious errors of judgement at the time of the Rwandan genocide.
June 2010	UK Prime Minister David Cameron condemns the 'Bloody Sunday' killings by British forces (30 January 1972) and makes a formal apology to the grieving families.
September 2012	UK Prime Minister David Cameron states his profound sorrow for the police actions at the time and the concerted campaign of official misrepresentation and cover-ups subsequent to the Hillsborough disaster (15 April 1989).

These exercises in public candour and remorse have provoked several criticisms. Questions have been raised over the sincerity and authenticity attached to such apologies; over whether they are morally suspect gestures or genuine 'speech acts'; over the political motives informing them; over the types of ritual and the levels of equivocation that accompany them; and over the extent to which they amount to an acknowledgement of liabilities and the need for remedial action. Other complaints concern whether such apologies can contribute towards a sense of reconciliation and closure as part of a process of transitional justice. On a more sceptical level, these apologetic statements can be considered to be low-risk–low-cost gestures that do not in themselves clear a moral debt or absolve past wrongdoing, and which cannot secure forgiveness on the part of the victims.[10]

---

[10] For a general discussion on the role of political apologies, see: Sandra Harris, Karen Grainger, and Louise Mullany, 'The pragmatics of political apologies', *Discourse Society*, 17(6) November 2006: 715–37; Melissa Nobles, *The Politics of Official Apologies* (New York, NY: Cambridge University Press, 2008); Zohar Kampf and Nava Löwenheim, 'Rituals of Apology in the Global Arena', *Security Dialogue*, 43(1) February 2012: 43–60; Janna Thompson, 'Is Political Apology a Sorry Affair?', *Social Legal Studies*, 21(2) June 2012: 215–25.

In the more specific terms of leadership analysis, however, what these episodes show is the way that leaders not only feel the need to engage in such public acts of moral declaration, but also believe that they occupy the kind of space that allows them the licence to assume a position of saying sorry on behalf of a nation or state. The fusion of public remorse and private action in the figure of leaders engaged in such displays of trenchant responsibility, informed conscience, and recovered memories are indicative of the high-exposure symbolic politics that surrounds modern leadership. It also illustrates the expansive properties of 'disintermediation' which are no longer limited to a purely spatial dimension but are shown to extend to one in which a leader can straddle the distant past with the contingencies of the present.

Situated in such a context, it is necessarily the case that in the same way that leaders promote themselves as *sui generis* political actors, so their public audiences are encouraged to conceive the categories of leadership in intrinsically personal terms. Opinion polls regularly pose questions designed to elicit responses on how members of the public assess and rate the personal qualities of individual leaders on the assumption that the public's appraisal of selected components of personality is central to the estimation, and ultimately the reality, of contemporary political leadership. By the same token, the thought processes, individual positions, and personal priorities of a leader become key components in the political process which, in turn, generates further demands for personal revelation and for in-depth psychological analyses. In such an inquisitive context that finds its focus in individuals, the physical health, emotional intelligence, and mental fitness of leaders are to a growing extent openly discussed as valid instruments of political insight and speculation. Leaders' parentage and origins, their childhood and formative experiences, their diets, tastes, and pastimes, together with their wives and children, are all regarded as suitable subjects for exposure and assessment. In being so, they all help to convey the notion that leadership is an inherently personal resource that must be consumed in like manner.

This style of politics offers several benefits for leaders. For example, it can foster devices that offer considerable security of position. This is not only because the normally lengthy, expensive, and disruptive process of selection deters leadership changes, but also because a leader is now increasingly seen as a major asset whose value must be protected and sustained. High-exposure personal leadership also gives incumbents major advantages in eclipsing possible rivals and in maximizing political attention and public presence in terms of the individual properties of such a position. The natural appeal of leadership figures in the construction of media agendas also means that leaders often have the initiative in defining their own idiosyncratic brand and in positioning themselves in respect to key issue areas. In their efforts to promote a supportive discourse surrounding their positions, leaders can exploit the processes of personalization in order to maximize the opportunity of creating a favourable correlation between themselves and valued leadership attributes. The usage of these various devices on the part of leadership teams to create approximate personal constituencies has resulted in the generation of new resources, strategies, incentives, and bases of authority for many leadership incumbents.

INDIVIDUALIZED BLOWBACK

The exponential shift towards the personalization of leadership has undoubtedly been a source of strength for many leaders. However, as we have noted before in the relational nature of leadership, what can be a resource can also act as a limitation. The high-profile focus upon a single individual, for example, always carries the risk of overexposure, public fatigue, and an increased probability of critical scrutiny. Apart from the almost inevitable erosion of authority and the debilitating nature of leadership responsibilities upon the individual concerned, the passage of time can generate speculation over an individual's fitness for such a personalized office. Each case of personalized leadership within a system carries the potential to generate the very levels of volatility which leaderships are normally intent upon preventing at all costs—knowing the damage that can occur to a previously successful and apparently durable leadership. As the terminology of political debate becomes ever more permeated by individual narratives and claims of leadership—and as the state of political parties, their programmes, reputations, and fitness for office are refracted through the lens of leadership figures—political challenge and calls for change more often than not find their sharpest expression in calls for changes in the leadership.

In such a context, leaders often find themselves trapped by the political game to which they are a party. An individual who has been successful in acquiring a leadership position will often proceed on the assumption that he or she has a particular affinity with, and a responsibility towards, a presumptive constituency that transcends and outweighs those of other political figures. This attachment to the concept of an idiosyncratic relationship with key sources of legitimacy, combined with an associated emphasis upon a leadership vision for a sense of defined purpose, means that a leader can become very vulnerable to sudden shifts in evaluative categories of leadership. Leaders who were once secure in their juxtaposition to the configuration of public attitudes and popular opinions can quickly find themselves exposed to a negative disconnect when preferences change in favour of a different notion of a leader's role or an altered conception of the right temperament for a leadership position. The sales pitch of contemporary leadership is necessarily geared towards declarations of unique individual qualities and towards establishing a consolidated authenticity of a distinctive political personality. This being so, it becomes very difficult for leaders to dissociate themselves either from the expansive remits of leadership campaigns or from the heavily personalized assertions and visions of generic government performance.

Exercises in enhanced personalization, therefore, can bring significant benefits to political leaders but at the same time these strategies can pose a considerable risk both to the leaders and to those who sponsor them or who are dependent upon them. The case of Gordon Brown's premiership is highly illustrative of the way that an individual leader can come to signify the nature of a governmental and organizational impasse, and the way that the flows of political stature and credit can be reversed in a context of heightened personalization.

Gordon Brown had served a long apprenticeship for the position that he had always wanted and had spent his political career preparing for—namely Leader of the Labour Party and Prime Minister. Tony Blair had beaten him to the party leadership in 1994 and thence to the premiership in 1997. Following an increasingly strained period as Chancellor of the Exchequer and heir apparent to Blair, he finally succeeded in securing the twin prize in June 2007. In many respects, Brown was well suited to such a prospectus. Despite being one of the founders of the modernizing New Labour movement, Brown was more in the mould of a traditional party politician with a firm attachment to traditional Labour values and disciplines along with an instinctive loyalty to the core constituencies of party strength and to the conventional forms of party management. At the same time, Brown realized that notwithstanding his inclinations towards the more tribal aspects of party leadership, he nevertheless had to engage with those modern features and techniques of leadership that his predecessor had done so much to establish as the prevailing norm. Herein lay the source of the serious personal and political strain that rapidly became evident during his ill-fated premiership.

On many grounds, Gordon Brown had the right credentials for a prime minister. He was a formidable political figure with extensive ministerial experience. He had a reputation as a master strategist and had acquired a dominant position within his own party. He was widely regarded as an individual with considerable personal integrity along with specialist expertise in several demanding policy fields—most notably in the crucially important sphere of financial management. After ten years as the 'Iron Chancellor', he seemed uniquely qualified to succeed Tony Blair. However, within a short period of time it became evident that his premiership was under extraordinary duress. It is true that Brown not only had to confront the effects of public fatigue with a government that had been in office for over a decade but also had to contend with the worst financial crisis since the 1930s. However, what became painfully apparent was the way that the new prime minister was unable to adjust to the demands and pressures of what had become the normal context of high-profile personalized leadership.

Gordon Brown was sufficiently astute to know that in modern British politics, a leader's capacity to establish direct personal connections to a broad public constituency had become an integral element in the job specifications of a prime minister. He was also well aware of the individual resources and benefits to be accrued from such a model in the form of alternative political resources and bases of authority. In spite of his partisan inclinations, Brown recognized the need to portray himself as an inclusive national leader who could operate as a unifying presence and as an instrument through which his party could continue to depict itself as a 'big tent' that could appeal to a broad coalition of interests. In preparing himself for the premiership, therefore, Brown and his team had gone to considerable lengths to follow the precedents of high-profile leadership. Even though he had sought in the past to differentiate himself in a variety of encoded ways from his predecessor, Brown now had little alternative other than to subscribe to the model of leadership which Blair had mastered for so many years.

At the outset of his administration, Brown had to distance himself implicitly from Blair whilst at the same time explicitly demonstrating that he could emulate him in the strategic imperatives of high-exposure leadership. Accordingly, the transition from Blair to Brown was marked by an array of measures designed to create an impression of a new administration that was authentically rooted in the individual credentials of Gordon Brown for the position of prime minister. Brown sought to differentiate himself from the discredited aspects of the Blair administration through a range of positions ranging from a personal manifesto for greater social justice and a constitutional reform agenda through to a principled renunciation of 'spin' and other forms of unacceptable media management. He made repeated disclosures about his formative experiences and how these were central to his own guiding convictions and core values. The campaign of person- alized public outreach was epitomized by the publication of Brown's own book on personal and political courage.[11] Yet notwithstanding these efforts at acclimatiz- ing himself to the visceral demands of contemporary leadership, the new prime minister quickly found that he was at the centre of an adaptation crisis—namely his own difficulties in adjusting to what was an entirely alien regime of high- exposure politics.

As the defining focal point of the new administration, Brown looked increas- ingly ill at ease with the persistent monitoring of his performances in a variety of conspicuous dimensions relating to leadership assessment and evaluation. Where he had tried to personalize his appeal and to create a new brand identity for the party, his deficiencies were revealed. Given that the New Labour project had always made a virtue of strong leadership and transcendent appeal set within a context of trust building, political marketing, and public outreach, Brown's antidote to the deficiencies of Blair's leadership had been based upon portraying himself as *not* being his predecessor. The problem was that the critical criteria by which Brown was being examined as a prime ministerial performer were mainly those that had been set during the Blair ascendancy. Brown's deficiencies in this area of high political value resonated across the range of prime ministerial functions and had a depressive effect upon his attempts to establish his own policy agendas and political positions.

The situation was exacerbated by a general deterioration in the economic and political landscape following his accession to the premiership. Complex issues began to be framed and presented as being reducible to Brown's personal failings. The new prime minister became embroiled in a succession of crises that touched upon practically every aspect of social life. Severe political and administrative difficulties became compounded with slumps in the government's public and professional standings which in turn fused with electoral shocks, political scan- dals, and allegations of chronic deficiencies in the organizational integrity of central government. As a result, Brown's premiership became disfigured by crises of instability, disorganization, and disillusion. The dynamics of high-profile public leadership which had benefited Blair for much of his tenure as prime minister now reversed themselves to the detriment of Brown. The decline in the reputation of his government and the party was dramatic and found its chief expression in the figure of Brown himself who was increasingly portrayed as an allegedly ill-equipped prime minister and an individual without the aptitude for a leader- ship role in an increasingly complex and demanding political environment.[12]

---

[11] Gordon Brown, *Courage: Eight Portraits* (London: Bloomsbury, 2007).

[12] See Colin Hughes (ed.), *What Went Wrong, Gordon Brown?* (London: Guardian Books, 2010); Anthony Seldon and Guy Lodge, *Brown at 10* (London: Biteback, 2010) chs. 7–9; Steve Richards, *Whatever it Takes: The Real Story of Gordon Brown and New Labour* (London: Fourth Estate, 2010), chs. 10–14.

Brown began to be seriously criticized for lacking a clear set of defining positions; for an alleged predisposition towards centralized control and limited consultation; and for an overdependence upon narrow sources of advice. He was further accused of a lack of strategic focus and guiding vision as well as becoming increasingly reliant upon media relations and news management to compensate for his government's deficiencies. Brown could claim several policy successes—especially in the field of financial management in the aftermath of the 2008 credit crisis—but these were not able to arrest his slide in the polls. In the face of increasing disquiet among backbenchers and party managers set against rumours of splits and revolts within the Cabinet, urgent calls for a leadership election arose after only one year of the Brown premiership. Although the prime minister made repeated efforts to relaunch his premiership and to re-engage with the electorate through such devices as 'cabinet road-shows', Number 10 petitions, YouTube policy announcements, Flickr photostreams and other PM-to-citizen direct channels (e.g. Number 10 website), it made little impact on the prevailing view that Brown had no effective public voice or any politically usable connection with the electorate. Andrew Rawnsley observed that 'it was not just his enemies but also his erstwhile admirers who pointed to the Prime Minister's paucity of communication skills'. In private, he may have been able to present himself as a more rounded individual but in public he was a 'constipated performer who found it beyond him to display any emotional range to the voters'.[13]

The more he tried to engage in these forms of outreach, the more he had to face criticism concerning his psychological condition, personal aptitude, individual trustworthiness, and managerial competence. The rapidity of his decline illustrated the degree of investment in and dependence upon the presence of an effective communicator in such a leadership role. Accordingly, Brown was dismissed in many quarters as a political liability on the grounds that he was distant, out of touch, and devoid of effective outreach. A profile in June 2009 summed up the mood and the judgement that accompanied it: 'Brown is a prime minister so beleaguered, so unpopular and seemingly exhausted, so apparently luckless and unsuited to the job, that he attracts general ridicule and even pity. Parliamentary sketchwriters and political bloggers describe him as a baited bear, a human car crash, painful to watch. News of his humiliations travels the world.'[14]

Long before Brown presided over a substantial defeat for his party in the 2010 general election, his administration was widely regarded as being in a chronic condition and already existing in the shadow of an alternative government-in-waiting. While his premiership was beset by a number of long-term issues and generic problems for which he could not be blamed, their potential for producing negative effects nevertheless became focused on the beleaguered figure of Gordon Brown—a prime minister whose attempts at opening up alternative dimensions through personal communication had the opposite effect of routing culpability directly back to the occupant of Number 10. What might have offered an escape channel became instead a tightening trap as Brown was revealed as

[13] Andrew Rawnsley, *The End of the Party: The Rise and Fall of New Labour* (London: Penguin, 2010), pp. 535–6.

[14] Andy Beckett, 'So what happened?', *Guardian*, 3 June 2009.

having a lack of congruence with a leadership model that had its own particular incentive structures, behavioural codes, embedded logics, and operational disciplines.[15] In effect, he became locked into a degenerative process of leadership decline that acted as an accelerant to the processes of associative culpability and personalized accountability. Brown's conspicuous problems with the style and repertoire of his leadership fomented an altogether richer form of pathology than that which could be attributed solely to the effects of contemporary economic, international, and social issues.

Gordon Brown's ill-starred premiership is not the only example of this dynamic in which a leader's personalized campaigns of self-promoting publicity generate their own critiques of leadership behaviour. Just as leadership resources allow or compel individual leaders to metamorphose into public commodities, they open themselves up to an almost continuous level of media intrusion and minute analysis into every facet of their personal and political lives. As leaders like President Nicolas Sarkozy (France), Prime Minister Silvio Berlusconi (Italy), and President Jacob Zuma (South Africa) have recently discovered, the enhanced methods of personal projection and public accessibility have led to new vulnerabilities and the onset of complex political risks. They typify the way that leaders become judged by the near unsustainable standards of accessibility, responsiveness, and responsibility that they themselves were instrumental in setting for themselves. In this environment, positive and appealing associations can quickly turn to a syndrome of negative linkages as personal attributes and revelations become increasingly exposed to public scrutiny and used to draw political implications from generalized impressions of individual behaviour.

CROWDED LEADERSHIP CONTEXT

It has already been noted that many forms of modern political leadership require its practitioners to exert themselves in reaching out and engaging viscerally with audiences in the public square. We have seen how leaders have increasingly sought to use sophisticated means both to position themselves in alignment with emergent profiles of public opinion, and to tap alternative sources of political leverage in order to widen their appeal. The competition between different leaders in capturing and holding public attention has generated an ever widening panoply of techniques and strategies in the field of political communication and marketing. This process of intensification between and amongst leaders has created a tight competitive context in which gains are almost invariably marginal and temporary in nature. While it is true that the complex political interplay between leaders evokes a self-limiting dynamic upon its participants, it is equally the case that political leaders are now confronted by an increasingly varied range of phenomena which is having the effect of making their habitats even more

---

[15] Michael Foley, 'Gordon Brown and the Role of Compounded Crisis in the Pathology of Leadership Decline', *British Politics*, 4(4) December 2009: 498–513.

congested. As a consequence, the lines and boundaries of leadership competition are becoming less precise and thereby less amenable to political management.

One major contributory factor in this increasing contextual dissonance has been the generic trend on the part of political actors to become associated, either implicitly or explicitly, with the attitudes, ethos, and language of the business sector. The recently enhanced status of neoliberal principles, with its mantras of market dynamics and organizational efficiencies, has been highly attractive to political leaders in many systems of government. Material presented in Chapter 6 alluded to the high levels of exchange relating to ideas, practices, and personnel between the two sectors of government and business. In some cases, these cross-migrations have become so prominent that they have led to speculation over the existence of a process of convergence. These claims have often been overstated. It is probably more accurate to conceive the relationship as a process of mutual adjustment between different spheres of activity that largely retain their separate rationales, identities, purposes, and modes of operation. Nevertheless, the increased proximity of these spheres does exert a degree of observational disruption on the subject area of societal leadership. And it is this emergence of a perceptual pluralism related to the usages and location of leadership which is arguably the more significant aspect of any notion of a politics–business conflation.

In this light, the different pathways and practices of leadership portrayed in the spheres of business and politics suggest another major factor in the crowded space within which contemporary leaders operate. The inference here is one of an altogether more substantive change that can best be described as a cultural shift towards who and what can be assigned to a leadership status within society at large. What is becoming increasingly noticeable is the presentation of a diversity of leadership spheres within the remit of public attention. This trend is particularly well conveyed in those publications that feature yearly rankings of the power and influence in society. Sometimes these listings are confined to internal national estimates. Others endeavour to offer international measures of esteem. What is common to both is the way that leadership is used as a common denominator which allows comparisons to occur across different spheres of activity.

While it is true that some listings attempt to make distinctions through the use of subdivided categories, they nevertheless tend to have similar cognitive effects to those that do not. This is mainly because of two factors inherent in such exercises. First, it is common for the cited sub-categories to receive little or no explanation for their formation as separate scales of status. And secondly, whatever grounds exist for these types of nominal differentiation, the fact remains that the overriding logic of such exercises is rooted in the depiction of degrees of prominence which more often than not are subsumed within a common cognitive frame of reference—namely leadership. In effect, these exercises serve both to illustrate the processes of osmosis that occur between different forms of societal leadership, and to strengthen the trend towards perceiving leadership as an expansive, capacious, and even promiscuous property that extends across a profusion of different contexts.

The Forbes organization, for example, generates a host of yearly listings that include the top ranked leading companies, CEOs, entrepreneurs, prominent celebrities, and varieties of rich lists across different regions and nations. Apart from the identification of a huge variety of successful individuals and organizations to whom and to which such terms as 'leading', 'leaders', and 'leadership' are habitually attached, this proliferation of lists is often reduced to a central compendium of the *World's Most Powerful People*. The signature characteristic of this ranking exercise is emphatically that of leadership. Equally apparent is the explicit mixing of political, industrial, financial, media, religious, and international governance leaders in the same scale of measurement. In the 2012 list, for example, prime ministers and presidents are strongly featured with President Barack Obama, President Hu Jintao, Prime Minister Vladimir Putin, and Chancellor Angela Merkel accounting for the top four positions. However, it is also the case that these political figures were joined in the top thirty by amongst others the CEOs of Wal-Mart and General Electric, the Chairman of News Corporation, the Co-Chair of the Bill & Melinda Gates Foundation, the Founder and Chairman of Facebook, the Co-founder of Google, and Pope Benedict XVI.[16] Other examples of such intermixed rank orders are presented in Box 11.2.

Of course the measurements of status and influence that form the basis of these exercises are highly disputable. But the inexact nature of the subject matter is not

---

Box 11.2 Leadership lists

TIME magazine has a long-established yearly list of the world's most influential people. It used to break them down into subcategories. For example, in 2004, the subdivisions were labelled as follows:

Leaders and Revolutionaries
Builders and Titans
Artists and Entertainers
Scientists and Thinkers
Heroes and Icons

By 2011, however, these subdivisions had been abandoned in favour of a generic top one hundred figures. As they were no longer placed in any rank order, it meant that individuals with widely differing sources of influence could be positioned adjacent to one another in the essay-based format of the feature. Thus in 2011 the economist Joseph Stiglitz is placed on the same page as comedienne Amy Poehler. Similar conjunctions present Angela Merkel with Angry Birds gamester Peter Vestabacka; US Vice-President Joe Biden with tennis star Kim Clijsters; David Cameron with actress Mia Wasikowska; pop star Sting with school reformer Michelle Rhee; and Barack Obama alongside footballer Lionel Messi.

Even though *Newsweek* prefers to concentrate on women leaders, the format is the same. In its 2011 feature on the '150 Women who shake the world', the rationale is explicitly plural in nature: 'They are heads of state and heads of household. Angry protesters in the city square and sly iconoclasts in remote villages. With a fiery new energy, women are building schools. Starting businesses. Fighting corruption. Harnessing new technologies and breaking down old prejudices.' Accordingly, women from various backgrounds and diverse claims to distinction are intermixed with one another.

Sources: 'The TIME 100: The A-list of the world's most influential people', *TIME*, 26 April 2004; 'The World's Most Influential People: The TIME 100', *TIME*, 2 May 2011; '150 Women who shake the world', *Newsweek*, 14 March 2011.

---

[16] Forbes, 'The World's Most Powerful People: 2012'. Accessed 11 October 2012 at: <http://www.forbes.com/powerful-people/list/>

the point. The real significance for this study is the way that leaders across different sectors of political, economic, and social life are literally juxtaposed with one another in text and pictures. It is not merely that different leadership categories are presented in proximity to one another through the design of the listings. It is that even when there are nominal attempts to differentiate these notables by reference to separate streams of activity, the selected categories tend to break down in usage—especially through the incidence of cross-over cases. More importantly, these exercises show how separate domains are routinely transcended by references to leadership as the primary and common value of distinction. This in turn provides a further stimulus towards a generally more reductive approach to leadership as a phenomenon. Ironically, what is presented as a set of vertical lists often turns into an agency for horizontal cross-references and even for presumptions of convergent properties.

The depiction of political leaders intermixed with leaders from other contexts may be thought to be a mainly presentational phenomenon and therefore one that lacks substantive weight in the world of political action. However, these portrayals are not as superficial as they may at first appear. Increasingly, certain roles that were once considered to be the traditional preserve of political leaders are being subjected to pressures by other agencies that are not directly rooted in what has normally been conceived as the political realm. It would be an overstatement to claim that these incursions are tantamount to direct or concerted challenges to the authority and legitimacy of political leaders. Nevertheless they do demonstrate the levels at which political leaders have to exist and operate within plural leadership environments. The direction and complexity of these kinds of interface can be illustrated by the growing overlap between the zones of political leadership and spheres of popular culture.

Political leaders in the past have often sought to associate themselves with emergent centres of popular attraction and political leverage. Whatever relationship may be said to exist, however, has almost invariably been one in which the leadership has retained not only a clearly identifiable status of legal and political hierarchy, but a position in which any association is conducted on his or her own terms. More recently, however, that degree of distinction and autonomy has become more open to question. It is not simply that leadership holders and aspirants are increasingly expected to act as public commodities and to exploit the full range of marketing techniques and presentational platforms. Nor can the dynamic be reduced to the leaders having to implant themselves—as well as their physical states and emotional conditions together with their families—within the public realm. Nor is it purely a matter of leaders resorting to appearances on 'soft format' television and radio shows, or of being suffused into lifestyle preoccupations, or generally being enfolded into a continuous process of populist imperatives and celebrity hype. What is arguably more noteworthy is the other side of the dynamic—namely the way that the movement of political leaders into popular culture has been reciprocated by the transition of non-political figures into areas normally regarded as the preserve of political action.

Two particular examples will serve to illustrate the force of these migratory flows. The *first* is the increasing incidence of what has been termed 'celebrity activism' or 'celebrity diplomacy' in which individuals with very high public profiles seek to use their prominence in order not just to raise popular awareness of political and even international issues, but in many cases to engage directly with decision-makers at the highest levels of government and within key arenas of international governance. The operative term in this development is celebrity. This is because many A-list figures from the world of show business have sought to lend the resources of public attention and appeal at their disposal to support various social and international causes. They do so in such a way that they can generate the kind of focused interest which can generate pressures on centres of policymaking and disrupt the normal processes of opinion and agenda formation.

The list of celebrities who have worked to establish close association with key issues continues to grow apace. They include:

Angelina Jolie	refugees/internal displacement; child welfare in conflict zones
Richard Gere	HIV/AIDS research; Tibetan independence
George Clooney	raising awareness of humanitarian crisis in Darfur
Leonardo DiCaprio	global warming
Robert Redford	Iraq War
Annie Lennox	Africa—HIV/AIDS work with women and children
Matt Damon	Africa—water hygiene
Adam Yauch (MCA Rap)	Tibetan independence; victims of 9/11
Jerry Hall	sustainable fish stocks
Greta Scacchi	sustainable fish stocks
Brad Pitt	World Food Foundation; Human Rights Watch; ONE campaign
Ben Affleck	raising awareness of humanitarian crisis in Congo
Alicia Keys	AIDS orphans in Africa; medicines for HIV children
Sean Penn	disaster relief in Haiti
Bob Geldof	famine relief; AIDS projects; fair trade; Third World debt; African issues; Make Poverty History campaign; UN Millennium Goals; ONE campaign
Bono (U2)	Amnesty International; extreme poverty; children in conflict zones; AIDS projects; fair trade; Third World debt; Make Poverty History campaign; UN Millennium Goals; ONE campaign; DATA organization[17]

The conspicuous incidence of these issue–personality partnerships can no longer be dismissed as peripheral curiosities. On the contrary, they have come to assume a notable presence in the management of many international issues. A recent study of the phenomenon alludes to a step change in the impact of celebrities upon those advocacy networks that characterize so many issue frameworks in international politics. Their experience in the fields of old and new media outlets, their ability to generate wide media coverage, and the global reach of their personal marketing and product promotion have all contributed towards a ready convergence of celebrities with the fields of transnational advocacy and public diplomacy.[18]

---

[17] DATA is the acronym for the multinational non-government organization Debt, AIDS, Trade, Africa.

[18] ONE Campaign is a grassroots advocacy and campaigning organization committed to combating extreme poverty and preventable disease. It merged with DATA in 2008.

It is claimed that 'these efforts to glamorise foreign policy are actually affecting what governments do and say'. In an article suggestively entitled 'Foreign Policy Goes Glam', Daniel Drezner goes on to assert that the 'power of soft news has given star entertainers additional leverage to advance their causes'. As a consequence, '[t]heir ability to raise issues to the top of the global agenda is growing'.[19] It is fair to say that within such conspicuous declarations of concern, there are some who are more committed than others. Moreover, it is also the case that there is not only great variation in the types of issue which receive celebrity sponsorship, but also considerable difficulty in assigning any reliable measure of comparable effectiveness across these widely divergent forms of activity. Nonetheless, it is evident that these activities by celebrities outside their normal habitats have had enough of an influence upon the normal processes of public information, political representation, and diplomatic conduct to evoke strong critiques of what is often cited as their interference.

The complaints vary from charges that this kind of superstar lobbying is inherently distractive and disruptive to the traditional processes of international diplomacy through to critiques that celebrity advocacy is invariably a narrow-based form of divisive propaganda that is usually focused on specific issues rather than on the more systemic and multidimensional nature of complex problems. To the extent that it is successful, 'celebrity diplomacy' is questioned in many circles not only for the way that its activities lack legal, sovereign, or electoral legitimacy, but also because these celebrity efforts are claimed to over-simplify the highly problematic issues surrounding economic development and cultural intervention.[20] Others disagree and assert that these kinds of high-profile interventions offer an injection of populist and democratic impulses into otherwise enclosed worlds of intergovernmental negotiations and opaque forms of decision-making. It is possible to argue that these forms of public advocacy can provide a necessary counterweight to what is arguably the elite-centred composition of global governance.

It is the sustained commitment, the organizational professionalism, and the acquired political experience of such individuals which lead some apologists to go as far as stating that the celebrity presence in these elevated circles can allow the formation of a valuable diplomatic symbiosis: 'Their ability to gain extended face-time with prominent national leaders is unprecedented . . . The largely untrained background, and mega-personality of celebrity diplomats, at first sight appears incompatible with traditional diplomacy, and yet it is validating it and bringing it into the modern age. The attraction is two-way: in celebrities, world leaders find a populist recognition and legitimacy they are unable to cultivate on their own; while celebrities find access to the world's powers helps advance their activist

---

[19] See Daniel Drezner, 'Foreign Policy Goes Glam', *The National Interest*, November/December 2007; Andrew F. Cooper, *Celebrity Diplomacy* (Herndon, VA: Paradigm, 2008); Paul 't Hart and Karen Tindall, 'Leadership by the Famous: Celebrity as Political Capital', in John Kane, Haig Patapan, and Paul 't Hart (eds.), *Dispersed Democratic Leadership: Origins, Dynamics, and Implications* (Oxford: Oxford University Press, 2009), pp. 255–78; John Avlon. 'A 21st-Century Statesman', *Newsweek*, 28 February 2011.

[20] See Heribert Dieter and Rajiv Kumar, 'The Downside of Celebrity Diplomacy: The Neglected Complexity of Development', *Global Governance*, 14(3) 2008: 259–64. See also James Panton, 'Pop goes politics', *The World Today*, June 2007.

agendas.'[21] Whether or not this can be equated with a new type of diplomacy is open to question. What seems beyond dispute is that this kind of activism has made sufficient inroads into what used to be a largely secluded area of statecraft to indicate the presence of a more complex set of international networks which can afford access, presence, and influence to those non-political actors who are able to take advantage of the new conditions.

The *second* example that illustrates the more congested environment within which political leaders now have to operate is provided by the onset of a form of philanthropy that moves beyond the transfer of resources to the point of asserted responsibility in schemes of activity that are tantamount to a condition of shared governance and therefore of joint leadership. This kind of development is exemplified by those individuals who use their access to great wealth in order not merely to promote selected causes but to do so on such a scale and with such an intensity that they effectively become integrated into the governing arrangements associated with the issue area concerned. In some circumstances, these benefactors can effectively generate entire agendas of activity in such a way that they not only offer a marked stimulus to established fields of inquiry or intervention, but provide the catalyst to the formation of new dimensions of issue advocacy, organizational responsiveness, and even global governance. The best known and most noteworthy example of this migration of leadership functions is the rise to prominence of the Bill & Melinda Gates Foundation (see Box 11.3).

A quite different but nonetheless equally revealing development comes in the shape of another multimillionaire seeking to change agendas through the agency of directed wealth. After making a large fortune as a mobile communications entrepreneur with interests in numerous African countries, Mo Ibrahim established a foundation designed to improve the standards of governance in sub-Saharan Africa. The defining ethos of the Mo Ibrahim Foundation is founded upon the proposition that the central issue in the profusion of social and economic problems afflicting Africa is one of political leadership. In particular, it is the imperative need to transform the culture of leadership to one that is driven by the interests and welfare of the peoples to which they owe their allegiance and to whom they are responsible as trustees.

The emphasis upon the value and utility of leadership that is not driven by corruption or sectionalism is underlined by the Foundation's work in two areas of activity. The first is the establishment of a sophisticated monitoring framework that assesses the record of each government in the region in respect to 84 criteria related to indicators of good governance. These criteria are grouped under four main categories of measurement—namely (i) Safety and Rule of Law; (ii) Participation and Human Rights; (iii) Sustainable Economic Opportunity; and (iv) Human Development. The Ibrahim Index aims not only to be Africa's leading assessment of governance on a year-by-year basis, but also a device by which citizens can assess the performance of their own governments in terms of public goods and services, human rights, security, and a host of other forms of development. By constructing and publicizing such a barometer, the Foundation attempts to lay the groundwork for

---

[21] Andrew Cooper quoted in Paul Vallely, 'From A-lister to aid worker: Does celebrity diplomacy really work?', *The Independent*, 17 January 2009.

Box 11.3 The Bill & Melinda Gates Foundation

Since its formation in 1999, the Bill & Melinda Gates Foundation has risen to become one of the major sources of developmental and educational assistance in the world. The Foundation's endowment assets of over $37 billion make its resource base larger than the GDP of each of over 90 countries. It sustains over a thousand staff and supports a myriad of partnerships and projects in over a hundred countries. The main rationale of the Foundation is one of self-improvement through giving people the initial resources to lift themselves out of hunger, low education, and extreme poverty. Its resources and ambition allow it to have a global reach not only in terms of the scale of its activities but also in respect to the diversity of its operations.

Thus, the Foundation's activities include a range of educational programmes in the US alongside an extensive range of health and development initiatives with a 'potential for high-impact, sustainable solutions that can reach hundreds of millions of people'[22] around the world. The latter includes research and development in the areas of (i) crop management and agricultural yields; (ii) the prevention and control of infectious diseases (e.g. enteric and diarrhoeal disorders, HIV/AIDs, malaria, pneumonia, tuberculosis); (iii) the development and integration of health programmes covering water, sanitation, hygiene, family planning, nutrition, maternal, neonatal, and child health, tobacco control ,and vaccine-preventable diseases; and (iv) the provision of financial services for the poor as well as facilities for emergency relief in areas of sudden and extreme hardship.

The sheer magnitude of the Foundation's impact in so many areas together with the high-profile status of its three trustees (Bill and Melinda Gates and Warren Buffet) and its 'philanthrocapitalism' and partnership-based modes of operation have propelled it into an active presence in numerous centres of policymaking circles from individual governments to international development and finance organizations as well as institutions of global governance (e.g. World Health Organization, UNICEF, G20).

Sources: Bill & Melinda Gates Foundation; 'The birth of philanthrocapitalism', *The Economist*, 23 February 2006; Andy Beckett, 'Inside the Bill and Melinda Gates Foundation', *Guardian*, 12 July 2010; Matthew Bishop and Michael Green, *Philanthrocapitalism: How Giving Can Save the World* (London: A & C Black, 2010), ch. 4.

---

improving levels of social provision and economic progress by distributing information which will allow sub-Saharan governments and public institutions—and especially leaders—to be held to account for their actions.[23]

The other signature aspect of the Foundation has been the creation of an exceptional prize for African leadership. The Mo Ibrahim Prize for Achievement in African Leadership is awarded to a leader whose record in office demonstrates a proven dedication to the needs of the people, a process of governance that is beyond reproach, and a leadership style which seeks to surmount the challenges of development. The first winner in 2007 was the former President of Mozambique Joaquim Chissano. The selection committee drew on the Ibrahim Index of African Governance for information on the relationship between leadership and records of governance. The choice was announced by the Chair of the Prize Committee, Kofi Annan, at a grand gathering of London's African diplomatic community, civil society representatives, and media representatives. Annan referred to the

---

[22] Bill & Melinda Gates Foundation, Global Development Program, 'Programs and partnerships'. Accessed 10 October 2012 at: <http://www.gatesfoundation.org/global-development/Pages/overview.aspx>.

[23] See Mo Ibrahim Foundation, 2011 Ibrahim Index of African Governance: Summary, October 2011. Accessed 20 September 2012 at: <http://www.moibrahimfoundation.org/en/media/get/20111003_ENG2011-IIAG-SummaryReport-sml.pdf>

progress made in such fields as poverty, health, infrastructure, and economic development during President Chissano's tenure of office. He went on to underline the importance of the linkage: 'the Prize celebrates more than just good governance. It celebrates leadership. The ability to formulate a vision and to convince others of that vision; and the skill of giving courage to society to accept difficult changes in order to make possible a longer term aspiration for a better, fairer future.'[24]

The significance that is attributed by the Foundation to this nexus between leadership and governance is made even more emphatic by the sheer scale of the prize itself—i.e. US$5 million over ten years and US$200,000 annually for life thereafter, as well as up to US$200,000 a year for ten years for those public interest activities and good causes espoused by the winner.[25] The clear intention of what is cited as the largest annually awarded prize in the world is both to institute a high personal reward for sound leadership, and at the same time to convey the symbolic value and substantive utility of leadership as a transformative force for good governance. In sum, it represents a significant attempt on the part of a business leader to implicate himself and his resources in an expansive agenda to incentivize broad scale reform through the agency of accredited and accountable political leadership.

LEADERSHIP CLUBS AND ASSOCIATIONS

Another category of rising inter-leadership activity comes in the form of particular associational activities in which leaders from different sectors are drawn together under the auspices of various sponsoring organizations. These entities are almost invariably committed to exploratory and innovative forms of exchange between and amongst those operating at high levels of social, economic, and political influence. The basic rationale of these gatherings is one of leaders separated from their customary formal and official contexts, and placed in close proximity to one another in order not merely to socialize together as fellow leaders but to interact with one another on a collegiate basis to discuss common issues and shared perspectives. In cultivating forms of direct and even intimate contact in a shared forum, the objective is mainly that of encouraging a process of mutual understanding between leaders from different sectors of society—and through this exchange an improved awareness of different viewpoints, new developments, common problems, and emergent opportunities for responsive initiatives. At one level, these forms of leadership associations can be seen as devices that perform an

---

[24] Mo Ibrahim Foundation, Press Release, 'Joaquim Chissano wins the largest prize in the world', 22 October 2007. Accessed 20 September 2012 at: <http://www.moibrahimfoundation.org/en/media/get/20091014_mo-ibrahim-prize-press-release.pdf>. See also Mo Ibrahim Foundation, Inaugural Ibrahim Prize for Achievement in African Leadership 2007, 26 November 2007. Accessed 20 September 2012 at: <http://www.moibrahimfoundation.org/en/media/get/20091014_alex-brochure-2007.pdf>

[25] In 2008, the Mo Ibrahim Foundation Prize was awarded to President Festus Mogae (Botswana). No prizes were awarded in 2009 and 2010. The third winner was President Pedro Pires (Cape Verde) in 2011 and the fourth winner in 2012 was Archbishop Desmond Tutu.

important integrationist function in opening up lines of communication, breaking down barriers, widening the information base for senior decision-makers, and facilitating cooperation in resolving complex problems that require coordination across different socio-economic sectors and national jurisdictions. Cast in a different light, they can be viewed as an extrapolation of leadership privilege that affords a medium in which the mutual attraction of elites is unimpeded and where leaders can engage in forms of mutual advantage pursued on the basis of privacy and exclusivity.

The variation in the views evoked by the existence of these organizations is matched by the diversity in their foundational origins, organizational logic, and styles of operation. For example, some of the earliest examples of these leadership consortia acquired reputations for being highly secretive organizations that have aroused suspicion and resentment in many quarters. The Bilderberg Group is a case in point. Formed in 1954, the organization was dedicated to countering Cold War strains between Western Europe and North America. In its quest to create a more consolidated Atlanticist outlook in approaching common problems and developing a closer understanding of mutual interests, the Bilderberg Group initiated meetings for an array of invited leaders that sympathized with this viewpoint. Although the Cold War has ended, the rationale of the Group is declared to be stronger than ever. According to the organization, there are now 'more, not fewer, common problems—from trade to jobs, from monetary policy to investment, from ecological challenges to the task of promoting international security'.[26] The interdependency of the two regions has increased exponentially with the rise of the global economy. As a result, the Group's perspective remains that of sustaining 'the concept of a European–American forum'[27] and of cultivating a close dialogue between the two regions in times that are conceived as critical to the Atlanticist project.

The Bilderberg Group remains controversial essentially because of its culture of secrecy and its process of elite agenda building that transcends notions of electoral choice and national sovereignty.[28] For its part, the organization claims that its meetings of approximately 120 participants are arranged in accordance with its published procedures and that its aim is to create nothing other than a 'broad cross-section of leading citizens' who can meet as 'small, flexible, informal and off-the-record international forum in which different viewpoints can be expressed and mutual understanding enhanced'. The official line is that the privacy of the meetings is to facilitate open and free discussions among the participants. In spite of the efforts made to reassure the various publics with which it is associated, the Group has continued to attract notoriety. Suspicions are aroused over the fact that it has no official existence. Although the names of the participants are now published, the meetings remain thoroughly opaque: resolutions are neither proposed nor accepted; votes are not taken; communiqués are not given; and policy

[26] Bilderberg, 'Bilderberg meetings: brief history'. Accessed 10 October 2012 at: <http://www.bilderbergmeetings.org/index.php>.

[27] 'Bilderberg meetings: brief history'.

[28] See James P. Tucker, *Jim Tucker's Bilderberg Diary: One Reporter's 25-Year Battle to Shine the Light on the World Shadow Government* (Washington, DC: American Free Press, 2005); Daniel Estulin, *The True Story of the Bilderberg Group*, 2nd edn. (Walterville, OR: Trine Day, 2009).

statements are not issued. The stature of those invited gives cause for further concern as it is thought unlikely in many quarters that prime ministers, senior government officials, boardroom chairs, corporation CEOs, ambassadors, mayors, trade representatives, financial experts, university leaders, and royal personages would allow their limited time to be given to nothing more than a discussion group.

The Trilateral Commission is another associative arrangement of leaders which often attracts unfavourable comment because like the Bilderberg Group it is a largely private body that has a distinct set of objectives based upon the development of an ongoing interaction between elites.[29] Unlike the Bilderberg Group which has always emphasized Atlanticist issues, the Trilateral Commission was formed to include a third sphere of reputedly common interest, communication, and cooperative action. In order to widen the basis of collaboration amongst Western economies and to enhance the early diagnoses of problems within the international economy, Japan was included as an equal partner to North America and Western Europe in the trilateral organization. Later the trilateral aspect was widened to include the Pacific Asia region. Similarly to the Bilderberg Group, the central feature of the Trilateral Commission is its annual plenary meeting which is attended by approximately 390 invited guests. The stated objective is to collect together 'distinguished leaders in business, banking and finance, media, academia, non-profit causes, labor unions, and other non-governmental organisations' in order to 'generate the will to respond in common to the opportunities and challenges that we confront and to assume the responsibilities that we face'.[30]

The sense of self-designated obligation on the part of the Commission in sponsoring 'a policy-oriented discussion group composed of members of high stature'[31] is underlined by the organization's emphasis upon the importance of responding to the rise of global interdependence by recognizing how it cuts across traditional delineations of national sovereignty. As a consequence, the organization asserts the need for 'new and more intensive forms of international cooperation' that will secure the benefits of globalization and foster conditions that 'counteract economic and political nationalism'.[32] Although the Commission has attempted to diminish its reputation for secrecy by publishing the reports of its various task forces, it remains an essentially private forum for the prescriptive designation of public and national policy. Like the Bilderberg Group, it bases its claims for legitimacy upon the functional and technocratic credentials of the leaders to whom it issues invitations.

---

[29] See Holly Sklar (ed.), *Trilateralism: The Trilateral Commission and Elite Planning for World Management* (Boston: South End Press, 1980); Stephen Gill, *American Hegemony and the Trilateral Commission*. Cambridge Studies in International Relations (Cambridge: Cambridge University Press, 1991); Andrew G. Marshall, 'The Political Economy of World Government', in Michel Chossudovsky and Andrew G. Marshall (eds.), *Global Economic Crisis: The Great Depression of the XXI Century* (Montreal: Global Research Publishers, 2010, pp. 262–301.

[30] Trilateral Commission, 'Who are the members of the Commission?' Accessed 7 October 2012 at: <http://www.trilateral.org/go.cfm?do=Page.View&pid=9>.

[31] Trilateral Commission, 'What are the goals of the Trilateral Commission?' Accessed 7 October 2012 at: <http://www.trilateral.org/go.cfm?do=Page.View&pid=9>.

[32] Trilateral Commission, 'What are the goals of the Trilateral Commission?'

The private nature of such organizations as the Bilderberg Group and the Trilateral Commission creates a number of misgivings over personnel, motivations, and process. It arouses concerns over the extent to which they cultivate not merely a sense of presumptive privilege and access but also a dynamic of subtextual unity that fosters the creation of specific agendas at the direct expense of other issue priorities. The working style of these kinds of leadership associations also makes them vulnerable to generalized inferences of improper influence and to charges of dubious legitimacy. More serious complaints make reference to their alleged role in the operation of international conspiracies. The Bilderberg Group and the Trilateral Commission are frequently cited as primary examples of the existence of conspiratorial forces at work within modern industrialized societies.[33]

The febrile character of a community that is preoccupied with the espousal of conspiracy theories means that intensity often displaces clarity in identifying the political persuasion of these bodies. Both groups have been denounced as left-wing front organizations through which corporate interests, central bankers, elitist intellectuals, interlocking bureaucracies, and other internationalist forces are working to impose a global agenda of centralized world government with collectivist programmes of social, economic, and financial control. At the same time that these indictments of a semi-communist ethos of power concentration are being made, the two leadership groups are also given prominence in the claims of a conspiracy on behalf of right-wing forces. In this guise, the Bilderberg Group and the Trilateral Commission are accused of promoting a 'new world order' of free market ideologies, global capitalism, transnational corporate power, military coercion, and a plutocratic 'superclass' over and above the principles of national sovereignty, regional autonomy, and democratic self-government. In both cases, it is clear how such associations might give rise to this kind of extreme speculation. The mystique that invariably surrounds the properties of leadership and secrecy is multiplied when leaders congregate together in an enclosed setting in order to share and to consolidate their own conceptions of cumulative leadership prerogative.

A much larger and far less secretive leadership association is the World Economic Forum (WEF). Its basis is explicitly business-centred and its organizing principle is that of promoting an expansive view of the global economy in a wholly positive light that fuses together the benefits of both economic and social development. The scale of the WEF is extensive with representatives from the top 1,000 companies as well as 200 smaller businesses. In addition there is a host of general affiliates, strategic partners, and regional bodies. Its governing ethos is expressed through its motto—'entrepreneurship in the global public interest'.[34] In this light, the WEF is pledged to generate global communities that will energize new forms of organization to 'improve the state of the world'. According to this outlook, because the world has become more complex and more fragile at one and the same time, the overriding imperative is now to recognize that challenges are global in nature and therefore 'cannot be met by governments, business or civil society

[33] For example, see Jim Marrs, *Rule by Secrecy* (New York, NY: HarperCollins, 2000); Mark Rich, *Hidden Evil* (Morrisville, NC: Lulu Enterprises, 2009).

[34] World Economic Forum, Annual Report 2005/06, 'Our mission and values'. Accessed 15 October 2012 at: <https://members.weforum.org/pdf/AnnualReport/2006/mission.htm>.

alone'.[35] The role of a body like the WEF is not only to highlight the nature of this governance gap but also to make a major contribution in filling it by cultivating a process of substantive and creative interaction between key specialists in the new context.

The WEF's agency of choice in the formation of a can-do global community of problem-solvers is that of business, political, intellectual, and social leaders who are seen as having the drive, insight, and specialist knowledge to transcend traditional attachments in the furtherance of a new international order of increased affluence and technological progress. The principle and practice of leaders from different sectors and communities interacting across various boundaries and divisions to generate new synergies of mobilization are evident from the priority statements and mission objectives of the organization. For example:

The World Economic Forum is the foremost global community of business, political, intellectual and other leaders of society who are committed to improving the state of the world. The Forum is an independent, not-for-profit organisation that brings these leaders together to work on projects that improve people's lives.[36]

The World Economic Forum brings together leaders in business, politics and society for reflection and connection to generate ideas and proposals, bridging countries and cultures to address the issues affecting our world. We also bring the very best minds and experts to provide the necessary insight to allow leaders to make decisions that can bring about change for the better.[37]

[T]he Forum regularly convenes business leaders and leaders from other key sectors of society to discuss, debate and address the major issues confronting humanity[38] ... Our members are influential, talented and powerful people. Many are also innovative and inspiring individuals who challenge conventional thinking and are committed to making the world a better place.[39]

Nothing exemplifies this ecumenical vision of multiple leadership more graphically than the WEF's annual meeting at Davos in Switzerland. It is a vast gathering of business and political leaders who convene together to see and be seen interacting with one another and engaging in a variety of arenas in which established and emergent issues are discussed.[40]

Although the level of public access is limited to a set of open forums in which civil society organizations are offered participatory opportunities, it is nevertheless regarded as far more inclusive and pluralistic than those leadership-based discussion boards that approximate more to the Bilderberg Group and the Trilateral Commission. It is not merely that the Davos meeting is a much bigger

---

[35] World Economic Forum, Annual Report 2005/06, 'Our mission and values'.

[36] World Economic Forum, 'Frequently asked questions: What is the World Economic Forum?' Accessed 15 October 2012 at: <http://www.weforum.org/faq>

[37] World Economic Forum, 'Frequently asked questions: 'What does the World Economic Forum do?' Accessed 15 October 2012 at: <http://www.weforum.org/faq>

[38] World Economic Forum, 'Frequently asked questions: Is the World Economic Forum just a private club for the rich and the powerful?' Accessed 15 October 2012 at: <http://www.weforum.org/faq>

[39] World Economic Forum, 'Frequently asked questions: Who are the World Economic Forum's members and partners?' Accessed 15 October 2012 at: <http://www.weforum.org/faq>

[40] See Geoffrey Allen Pigman, *The World Economic Forum: A Multi-Stakeholder Approach to Global Governance* (Abingdon: Routledge, 2007); The World Economic Forum, *A Partner in Shaping History: The First 40 Years 1971–2010* (Cologny/Geneva: World Economic Forum, 2009).

event with 2,500 participants from over ninety countries or that it regularly attracts a profusion of heads of state and government leaders. It is also seen as being responsive both to the regional shifts in the global economy[41] and to the emergence of new elites and therefore of new sources of international leadership (e.g. information technology, electronics, new media). Furthermore, it should be acknowledged that the Davos event receives intensive coverage from the international media and that it facilitates participation through social network and weblog sites. It is also worth noting that the WEF organization cultivates links with a range of bodies drawn from the arts, academia, and religious establishments, as well as sponsoring its own cluster of designated communities related to policy issues, cultural developments, and global exchanges.

Notwithstanding its asserted merits, the WEF is often criticized for being narrowly based in terms of perspective and direction. It is widely seen as an advocacy instrument for the integration of the global economy through open markets, tax cuts, deregulation, and the promotion of international trade and investment. The 'Davos consensus' and 'Davos man' can be equated with the celebrity aspects of a global elite and with its displays of wealth, ambition, and self-assurance situated within a particular conception of an international order combined with a dominant English-speaking global culture.[42] Nevertheless, the WEF can also be seen as something of a model for facilitating a high level of interaction between leaders from different sectors of society.

Whether it is seen as a successful pooling of resources, or as a gravitational force of mutual attraction, or as a common point of appeal, the WEF has demonstrated both the potential and the utility of such a deliberately designed arena for leader-to-leader exchanges. Its mediating properties and its transformative mission are reflected in the Forum's Global Leadership Programme which is explicitly dedicated to eroding the barriers between different leadership contexts and to fostering the 'next generation of world leaders; well-rounded professionals who feel equally at home in the public and private sectors'.[43] This is an ideal but it is also regarded as a functional response to the shifting contours of an increasingly complex social and economic order: 'As the world becomes increasingly more interconnected, the once well-defined line between these two sectors continues to blur, making it difficult for any one organisation to act effectively in isolation. To succeed in such an environment, organisations—both private and public—must often align numerous stakeholders so as to most efficiently approach problems, develop strategies and capitalise on opportunities.'[44] Seen in this light, Davos becomes less of an exception to normal politics and more a sign of times to come.

Different though these three examples may be, they typify a wider phenomenon in which leaders of various dispositions and contexts are drawn to one another as

---

[41] In 2010, it was reported that the number of attendees from the BRIC countries—namely Brazil, Russia, India, and China had more than doubled since 2005. See <http://oecdinsights.org/2010/01/27/the-road-to-davos>.

[42] See David Rothkopf, *Superclass: How the Rich Ruined our World* (London: Abacus, 2008), pp. 3–20, 265–76; Nick Paumgarten, 'Magic Mountain: What happens at Davos?', *The New Yorker*, 5 March 2012.

[43] World Economic Forum, 'Global leadership fellows: Developing tomorrow's leaders'. Accessed 20 May 2012 at: <http://www.weforum.org/global-leadership-fellows>

[44] World Economic Forum, 'Global leadership fellows: Developing tomorrow's leaders'.

embodiments of a common condition. The precise nature of this impulse for association differs from leader to leader. For some, it offers an outlet for the need to share information, insights, and perspectives. For others, it provides an instrumental device by which agendas can be pursued and problems can be reduced. For most, attendance at these elite gatherings is driven by an anxiety not to be excluded from them. The pulling power of other leaders cannot be lightly dismissed in this dynamic. This is because these leadership associations generate a self-referential and self-reinforcing symbiosis that not only operates to affirm the value and utility of leadership but creates an exponential rush among individual leaders to enhance their leadership credentials through the agency of other leaders whom they regard as their peers.

The attraction of what might be termed leadership clubs is reflected by the rise in their numbers, variety, and significance. These organizations are designed and largely operate to diminish the barriers between separate sectors of society and between different expressions of sovereign authority at the state, regional, and sub-state levels. While it would be an exaggeration to claim that they offer the prospect of an alternative form of social or global governance, they are nevertheless instrumental not only in facilitating synergies between leaders who would not otherwise have much contact with one another, but also in cultivating leaders as a kind of 'practitioner community' engaged in knowledge exchange, opinion formation, and agenda setting.

POST-LEADERSHIP CAREERS

To a growing extent, leaders who have left office have managed to maintain a presence in the contemporary matrix of leadership activities. Of course, most leaders have found withdrawing from positions of power to be a very difficult process of adjustment. Apart from having to cede authority to another figure, many leaders have claimed that the experience, insights, and connections that they had acquired over their years in office were a resource that needed greater recognition and utilization. In addition, the very process of relinquishing leadership has often had the effect of clarifying priority agendas and giving focus—albeit belatedly—to a defined sense of purpose. For the most part, these valedictory sentiments tend to be ignored as leaders who have left office do not have the platforms upon which to advance their claims to continuing relevance. The common resort for ex-leaders is to concentrate upon seeking to explain and justify their actions in office, and to work upon establishing a positive construction of their political legacies.

Increasingly, many ex-leaders have found that their activities are no longer confined merely to memoirs or other forms of retrospective political commentary. Neither are they limited to the role of engaging in non-political functions or social formalities. Instead, they are able to take advantage of a proliferation of new outlets that enable them to engage not just with current political issues but also with those leadership associations that have been described above. Former leaders are regular invitees to many of these gatherings where many continue to be regarded as high-profile A-list figures who serve to enhance the credentials and legitimacy of the organizations that invite them. But the trend amongst ex-leaders towards sustained visibility and to continued access to other leaders, as well as to conspicuous associations with key issues, goes well beyond being participants in other people's forums.

For example, ex-presidents like Jimmy Carter and Bill Clinton have formed well-established foundations that have given their figureheads considerable leverage in maintaining a public presence and in promoting particular causes. The Carter Center is a not-for-profit, non-governmental organization that has a partnership with Emory University in Atlanta. In 2011 the Center had net assets worth $463 million and a yearly income in excess of $84 million.[45] The Center has established a reputation for a variety of activities related to human rights, public health, and the promotion of good governance and peace. It has engaged in programmes and missions in over seventy countries ranging from peace building and the alleviation of debilitating diseases (e.g. malaria, lymphatic filariasis, Guinea worm disease) to election monitoring and the treatment of mental illness. The public and international profile of the former president has served to give particular prominence to its activities. This is evidenced in the selected sample from the Center's log for 2009 (see Box 11.4).

The William J. Clinton Foundation was founded in 2001 in order to carry forward the vision of the former president in respect to various global issues. The operational ethos is one of cultivating partnerships between governments, businesses, NGOs, and private citizens that in turn will generate productive collaborations which will achieve clearly discernible and sustainable improvements in a variety of priority areas (e.g. economic empowerment, education, environment and energy, health systems, and nutrition). The rationale of the Foundation is, in the words of one of its own key statements, that of using the ex-president's position and skills 'to identify and take action on global problems [that] he could uniquely influence through his experience as a global leader and public servant'.[46] Bill Clinton's post-presidential activities in raising funds for a host of humanitarian causes and in fostering a profusion of local, regional, and international networks have made the Foundation into one of the most rapidly growing NGOs in existence. Its size and reach can be gauged by its organization into several 'Initiatives'. These include specific programmes committed to reaching innovative and collaborative solutions in such areas as climate change, HIV/AIDS and malaria, childhood obesity, economic opportunity, and sustainable development in Africa and Latin America.[47]

But by far the most prominent element of the Foundation is the Clinton Global Initiative (CGI). Its showpiece event is an annual four-day meeting that draws a host of political leaders, heads of state, major CEOs, Nobel Prize laureates, leading philanthropists, NGO directors, and celebrities together in what has become widely known as an occasion comparable in purpose to Davos. Like the World Economic Form, the prevailing principle is one of promoting the benefits of globalization through the integration of leadership activities in business, commerce, government, and civil society. Unlike the WEF, however, the CGI meeting

---

[45] Carter Center, Financial Record for the Fiscal Year 2010–11. Accessed 20 August 2012 at: <http://www.cartercenter.org/resources/pdfs/about/carter-center-990-2010.pdf>

[46] Clinton Foundation, *Clinton Foundation Annual Report 2009*, p. 3.

[47] The Foundation's efforts in several of its key priority areas are described in Bill Clinton, *Giving: How Each of Us Can Change the World* (New York, NY: Alfred A. Knopf, 2007).

Box 11.4 Selections from the 2009 personal log of former US President Jimmy Carter

---

10–16 January: Former US President Jimmy Carter travels to China to commemorate the 30th anniversary of normalizing diplomatic relations with Deng Xiaoping and to expand the Carter Center's working relations with government ministries.

22 April: Health officials from 11 African countries honour former US President Jimmy Carter and the Carter Center for 'pioneering contributions to eradicating neglected tropical diseases in Africa' with an award presented in Washington, DC.

27 April–4 May: Former US President Jimmy Carter visits Ecuador, Peru, Bolivia, and Brazil to assess Carter Center projects, participate in a regional conference on the right of access to information, and meet with officials to discuss regional themes of importance following the Summit of the Americas.

8–17 June: Former US President Jimmy Carter visits Syria, Israel, West Bank, and Gaza following the Carter Center's observation of the 7 June Lebanese elections. As part of his ongoing efforts to promote constructive dialogue in the region, Carter held meetings with representatives of all parties to the Israeli–Arab conflict during his visit.

20 August: The Carter Center reaches an agreement with Sudan's Government of National Unity, the National Elections Commission, and the Government of Southern Sudan to observe the electoral process leading to anticipated presidential elections in 2010.

8 October: Former US President Jimmy Carter and a Carter Center staff delegation travel to Hispaniola to encourage international support for the elimination of malaria and lymphatic filariasis from the Caribbean. Haiti and the Dominican Republic launch a bi-national plan to eliminate the diseases as part of a Carter Center-sponsored pilot project.

18–30 October: Former US President Jimmy Carter travels to Saudi Arabia, Kuwait, Qatar, Dubai, Oman, Egypt, Jordan, and Turkey to discuss Carter Center programmes, including ongoing efforts to advance peace between Israel and its neighbours.

6 December: A Carter Center delegation of 18 observers from seven countries finds Bolivia's general election generally peaceful, notes that the new biometric registry (voter list) at polling stations served its intended purposes, and recommends Bolivian society and the National Electoral Court (CNE) continue to consolidate credibility in their institutions.

Source: The Carter Center.

---

is much smaller and more focused upon both celebrating the achievements of its activities, and ensuring that participants commit themselves either to organize initiatives for good causes or to pledge donations. According to the Foundation, CGI's members have made more than 1,700 Commitments to Action valued at $57 billion, which have already improved more than 200 million lives in over 170 countries. Although these figures cannot be fully verified, they do indicate a significant degree of global network activity that is routed through an organization embedded in the name and reputation of a former president long since out of office.

Similar forms of leadership networking and philanthropic campaigning channelled through and mediated by highly visible ex-leaders are now not uncommon in the schedules of global elites or in the processes of media attention and opinion formation. Mikhail Gorbachev is a case in point. After serving as General Secretary of the Communist Party of the Soviet Union, he along with Jim Garrison founded the State of the World Forum. This was designed to create a network of leaders and a centre for leadership that together could respond to the challenges of a new world order. The mission statement explicitly endorses the principle of 'cross-sectoral leadership'[48] as an effective strategy in confronting global challenges. The organizational principle is by now a familiar one—i.e. 'convening highly diverse sectors from around the world and a wide spectrum of disciplines, including Heads of State, Nobel Laureates, social analysts, grassroots activists, business executives, scientists, policy-makers, senior military officers, politicians, spiritual leaders, artists, academicians, and many others' in order to recognise the existence of a 'unique transitional moment in history'.[49]

In his home country, Gorbachev has also established a more personal organization committed to researching into major issues with a special focus on Russia. The Gorbachev Foundation is more a think tank based upon a cooperative network between universities, foundations, government bodies, and NGOs which draws together research materials that are then disseminated to centres of government around the world. Nevertheless, its research work is complemented by Mikhail Gorbachev himself who continues to make numerous international appearances in publicizing the Foundation's work on the problems of globalization, international security, poverty, and the environment. The Gorbachev name is used not only to add weight to Foundation's role as an independent think tank in Russia and a sponsor of Russian civil society, but also to promote a positive historical interpretation of Gorbachev's signature policy of Perestroika in modern Russia.[50]

These living monuments to past leaderships are no longer uncommon features of national and international political life. After twelve years in office as the President of France (1995–2007), Jacques Chirac was unable to draw back from public life. As a consequence, a new formation entered the ecology of ex-leadership organizations. The Fondation Chirac asserts such a body is needed in order to facilitate effective responses to urgent global problems—namely clean water and sanitation; health care; deforestation and desertification; conflict prevention; and the protection of cultural diversity. Another example of the genus is provided by Tony Blair. He resigned as UK premier in 2007 but far from melting into retirement, he was not only appointed as Middle East envoy working on behalf of the US, Russia, the UN, and the EU, but formed the Tony Blair Faith Foundation to promote respect and understanding between and amongst different world religions. The Foundation is formally dedicated to using the 'full power of modern communications'[51] to cultivate a greater appreciation of the positive value of faith within different societies. As part of its remit to 'ensure that the positive relationship between faith and globalisation becomes the dominant one in the 21st Century',[52] the Foundation has given particular priority to multi-faith social action programmes focusing on health and global

---

[48] State of the World Forum, 'Overview'. Accessed 22 October 2012 at: <http://www.worldforum.org/overview.htm>

[49] State of the World Forum, 'Overview'.

[50] The Foundation is also known as the International Foundation for Socio-Economic and Political Studies.

[51] The Office of Tony Blair, 'What we do'. Accessed 28 September 2012 at: <http://www.tonyblairoffice.org/pages/what-we-do2/>.

[52] Tony Blair Faith Foundation, 'Tony Blair in Reforma', 5 October 2012. Accessed 28 September 2012 at: <http://www.tonyblairfaithfoundation.org/news/2012/10/05>.

poverty. This is but one of many ventures established by the ex-premier. Other charitable organizations associated with the Blair brand include the Tony Blair Sports Foundation and the Cherie Blair Africa Foundation. In addition, Tony Blair has used his experience and contacts to develop an extensive portfolio of investment and consultancy services (e.g. Tony Blair Associates, Windrush Ventures, Firerush Ventures) that together employ over one hundred people engaged in using the Blair brand to develop a multi-million-pound network of business and strategic advice.[53]

No account of ex-leader activities would be complete without reference to what is probably the most conspicuous example of this phenomenon. After serving as President of South Africa for five years (1994–9), Nelson Mandela has not only maintained his presence on the national and international stage but has arguably increased it through an array of interventions, appearances, and outlets that have served to heighten his value as both a symbolic and material agency for a stream of different causes. The Mandela name has become almost a multiplex franchise in the way that it is invoked by innumerable organizations which have actively sought to establish an association with the person and the legend. Just as Mandela himself has cultivated a prodigious number of connections with social and human rights organizations, so these bodies have benefited from the status and authority of the Mandela brand. In addition to being an advocate for various charitable and philanthropic campaigns (e.g. Make Poverty History Movement; the ONE Campaign; SOS Children's Villages), he has sponsored his own signature establishments through the operation of the Nelson Mandela Foundation (NMF).

The Foundation, through its Centre of Memory and Dialogue, is formally tasked with promoting justice within societies by reference to the vision, values, work, and leadership style of Mandela and his historical record in conflict resolution. The operational premise is one of example and emulation: 'South Africa occupies a unique space in Africa and globally as an example of a country that emerged from the morass of deeply rooted racial, cultural and political divides—primarily because of timely dialogue between all its stakeholders.'[54] The NMF is therefore committed to sustaining an awareness of both the South African experience and Mandela's own contribution to peace by offering a 'non-partisan platform for public discourse on important social issues'[55] that will facilitate sound policy decisions and a just society.

> Drawing on the rich traditions of transformative dialogue, problem-solving and social renewal that made possible South Africa's remarkable transition, we hope to facilitate greater understanding and awareness about the problems faced by people particularly in South Africa and Africa, and the possible solutions available to them.[56]

In preserving the memory and legacy of Nelson Mandela, the Foundation has developed an extensive range of events, initiatives, services, facilities, and

---

[53] Isabel Oakeshott and Richard Kerbaj, 'Blair Tower: home for a global empire', *The Sunday Times*, 29 April 2012.

[54] Nelson Mandela Centre of Memory, 'About Dialogue for Justice'. Accessed 28 September 2012 at: <http://www.nelsonmandela.org/content/page/about-the-dialogue-programme>.

[55] Nelson Mandela Centre of Memory, 'About Dialogue for Justice'.

[56] Nelson Mandela Centre of Memory, 'About Dialogue for Justice'.

programmes—as well as several partner organizations[57]—that are all geared to appeal to African constituencies but also more generally to a global audience. In many respects, the NMF is both a charitable and a political organization. It engages in philanthropic work but it also supports Mandela's reputation as a global citizen with a large remit to engage in various issues within international society.

Possibly the most revealing development in this field of ex-leader role invention comes in the shape of another derivative of the Nelson Mandela organization. Appropriately, it is called the Global Elders. It was originally conceived as an idea to take the model of independent elders at the local level of many traditional societies, and expand it to the level of the 'global village'. After receiving the active support of Mandela, the group was formally launched in 2007 with a declaration that a designated task force of twelve ex-leaders would collaborate with one another to promote the peaceful resolution of conflicts and an effective response to global issues. The leaders in question were as follows:

- Martti Ahtisaari, former Finnish President, Nobel Peace Prize laureate
- Kofi Annan, former Secretary-General of the United Nations, Nobel Peace Prize laureate
- Ela Bhatt, founder of the Self-Employed Women's Association of India (SEWA)
- Lakhdar Brahimi, former Foreign Minister of Algeria and former United Nations envoy
- Gro Harlem Brundtland, former Norwegian Prime Minister
- Fernando Henrique Cardoso, former Brazilian President
- Jimmy Carter, former United States President, Nobel Peace Prize laureate
- Graça Machel, former Minister of Education Mozambique, President of the Foundation for Community Development, wife of Nelson Mandela
- Mary Robinson, former Irish President and former United Nations High Commissioner for Human Rights
- Desmond Tutu (Chair), former Archbishop of Cape Town, former Chair of South Africa's Truth and Reconciliation Commission, Nobel Peace Prize laureate

The group is characterized as a set of leaders who are able to focus upon the relief of human suffering and the protection of human rights because of their position of having in-depth experience but who are now 'free from political, economic and military pressures'.[58] Their self-assigned role as global citizens and their association with the concepts and norms of the international community form the basis of their claim that they amount to an unrivalled network of leadership resources.

> The Elders do not hold public office and have no political or legislative power. Because they are not bound by the interests of any single nation, government or institution,

---

[57] The Nelson Mandela Institute for Education and Rural Development; Nelson Mandela Children's Fund; Schools for Africa; Mandela Rhodes Foundation; and the 46664 organization.
[58] The Elders Foundation, 'Mission statement'. Accessed 17 May 2012 at: <http://theelders.org/elders>.

they are free to speak boldly and with whomever they choose on any issue, and to take any action that they believe is right.[59]

As such, their aim is to draw attention to humanitarian crises and to exert influence in a more rapid and penetrative way than would be the case if they were left to the more conventional channels of governance.[60]

Critics assert that a cooperative of elder statespersons on these lines risks not merely being a distraction to the normal processes of diplomacy and high-level decision-making, but carries the potential of being a disruptive influence upon sensitive negotiations. Others question the basis of their legitimacy and the nature of their accountability. Nevertheless, the Elders can be rationalized on the basis of the inadequacy of current forms of global governance in dealing effectively with complex emergencies, and on the grounds that as figures with leadership experience they have a duty to share their insights with others and to provide those leadership properties of energy and direction in circumstances where they discern a functional need for them. Their views on representation are consequently summarized on the following lines: 'The Elders amplify the voices of those who work hard to be heard, challenge injustice, stimulate dialogue and debate and help others to work for positive change in their societies.'[61] In terms of the foregoing analysis of ex-leaders, the Elders can perhaps best be categorized as the logical extension of those opportunities, outlets, and drives that now allow leaders to prolong their lives in leadership beyond previously drawn limits.

In sum, the motivations surrounding the formation and operation of these enterprises are probably mixed. For some, they are simply a means by which leaders out of time secure some form of a political afterlife and a measure of sustained personal prominence and social meaning. For others, such devices may afford an opportunity by which past mistakes or sins of omission might at least be partially corrected. In doing so, personal reputations might be redeemed and more favourable places in history be established.

Another common sub-theme in these organizations is the value attributed to experience gained through leadership itself. Integral to this outlook is the notion that holding a leadership position has an educative effective on the office-holder who essentially undergoes a process of transformation as a consequence of the experience. Apart from achieving a fuller understanding of the political constraints placed upon leadership, individual leaders come to realize that they had neither the time nor the resources to follow up on all the issues that they might have done and possibly should have done—or even to have recognized the existence of some issues whose subsequent importance should have made them a priority concern at an earlier point. As leaders near the end of their time in office, they often acquire not only a better grasp of strategic perspectives but also a keener sense of lost opportunities. With this realization comes the impulse to pursue agendas out of office on the basis of a heightened awareness of urgent problems, a studied appreciation of the complexities of interconnected issues, and

---

[59] The Elders Foundation, 'Mission statement'.

[60] Among the many crisis spots that have attracted the attention of the Elders are Cyprus, Gaza, Sudan, Zimbabwe, and Burma/Myanmar.

[61] The Elders Foundation, 'Mission statement'.

a renewed sense of personal responsibility. This syndrome of sustained engagement that can transcend the formalities of office-holding is well captured by the headline quote from President Jacques Chirac explaining the reasons for the Fondation Chirac's commitment to peace: 'A statesman's responsibilities do not end with his term of office. Above and beyond political commitments, there remains an individual's duty to fight for that which he believes to be right.' He continues: 'Today's major question concerns the world we will leave behind for future generations. It is also because this involves the future of the French people and their children that I wish to take on my full responsibility in this fight. I wish to remain fully mobilised in the thick of the fray on their behalf.'[62]

Whatever the true nature of their motivations may be, what is certain is that with the onset of new media communication devices as well as the contemporary shifts towards civil society organizations and network forms of governance, ex-leaders now have far more opportunities to retain a public presence and to remain politically engaged than used to be the case. It is not simply that they are experienced in the various formats of advocacy, projection, and opinion formation. It is that they have both extensive experience in the techniques of positioning within the complex ecology of modern leadership politics, and an understanding of their own value as a marketable brand in the competitive dynamics of public communications. Their high public profiles and assured recognition factors allow them to use their own personas as a visible resource even after leaving office. Some of their number may secure a passage to more enduring significance by opting for positions in the growing field of global governance. But many others will attempt to remain in that sphere of leadership and inter-leadership activity to which they had become habituated in office—and by doing so they further strengthen the gravitational forces that draw political engagement and participation into fields of leadership-centred movement.

THE LONG ARM OF ACCOUNTABILITY

Inherent in the normal processes of leadership activity are those devices that impose some element of accountability upon the office-holder. These usually take the form of political and institutional checks and balances which usually ensure that a leadership figure is in some way constrained in the usage of power either by the activities of bodies with concurrent political authority, or through the imposition of legal restraint, or alternatively by the threat of electoral sanctions or other forms of removal. Such devices usually exert some measure of conditionality upon the exercise of leadership. If leaders are not always constrained by the actual operation of political limitations, then their political calculations are usually influenced by the threat of future sanctions laid upon their both themselves and their supporting organizations. In contemporary circumstances, it is possible to speculate on the extent to which the principles of leadership responsibility and accountability have

---

[62] Fondation Chirac, 'Reasons for our commitment: pursuing my commitment to peace'. Accessed 7 October 2012 at: <http://www.fondationchirac.eu/en/foundation/reasons-for-commitment/>.

actually been enhanced with the onset of a more inquiring and unregulated media presence working on the basis of 24/7 news cycles, and with the emergence of NGOs that specialize in monitoring and investigating the behaviour of leaders and their governments. Nevertheless, it may equally be claimed that leaders still retain a significant capacity to evade responsibility for many of their decisions and do so for what are very often the most serious actions undertaken by, or on behalf of, their administrations. Ironically, it is precisely these extreme cases of governing misbehaviour—for which recognition and redress are most urgently required—that are often made conspicuous for their very lack of accountability.

The kind of actions which have aroused most controversy in this respect are those cases where power has not only been misused with impunity but where the perpetrators of these excesses have been allowed to escape any form of punishment or even reprimand. There have been historical occasions when international opinion has been formally mobilized to ensure that specified war leaders were not absolved from the legal or moral responsibility of their decisions.[63] However, the generic issue of accountability on a more sustainable basis has until recently never been satisfactorily addressed. With the rising incidence of violent intra-state conflicts following the end of the Cold War and with an increased recognition that the more traditional instruments and institutions of diplomacy were no longer adequate in such circumstances, a movement towards a concerted international response to gross violations of humanitarian conduct was instigated during the 1990s.

The outcome was the Rome Treaty of 1998 which instituted the formation of a permanent court to hear cases relating to the most serious issues of international concern and international humanitarian law—namely genocide, crimes against humanity, and war crimes. The International Criminal Court (ICC) built upon the precedents of various special and international tribunals of the United Nations but unlike them the new court was designed to be both a permanent institution and one with a status independent of the UN. Its brief is in essence to extend the principle of accountability to those very areas which up to then had been particularly associated with its denial.[64]

The ICC has a mandate to bring to justice those who are responsible for incidents of mass murder and other atrocities. As the Rome Statute makes clear, the Court focuses upon issues of individual criminal responsibility and therefore with those who commit, order, or solicit a crime within the jurisdiction of the ICC. The role and behaviour of military commanders have an evident significance

---

[63] Most notably the war crimes trials following the First World War under the terms of the Versailles Treaty. Forty-five indicted individuals were tried by the German Supreme Court in Leipzig in 1921. The Leipzig trial acted as a precedent for cases citing serious violations of international law by the Axis powers in the Second World War. The Nuremberg war crimes trials were held between 1945 and 1949. They featured senior figures in the Nazi leadership on various counts including indictments related to (i) the participation in a common plan or conspiracy for the accomplishment of crime against peace; (ii) planning, initiating, and waging wars of aggression and other crime against peace; (iii) war crimes; and (iv) crimes against humanity. Other war crimes trials followed the end of the Second World War as a result of actions undertaken by the Empire of Japan in the Asian theatre. The most prominent of these was the trial of twenty-five indicted Class A war criminals. These cases were heard by the International Military Tribunal for the Far East in 1946.

[64] Marlies Glasius, *The International Criminal Court: A Global Civil Society Achievement* (Abingdon: Routledge, 2006); William A. Schabas, *An Introduction to the International Criminal Court*, 4th edn. (Cambridge: Cambridge University Press, 2011).

in shaping the lines of responsibility in such circumstances as genocide and crimes against humanity but as the Statute declares, criminal responsibility extends both downwards to the decision-making of local subordinates and more especially upwards to the highest levels of authority within a state or government. Article 27 directs its attention to the position of leaders under the section entitled *Irrelevance of official capacity*.

1. This Statute shall apply equally to all persons without any distinction based on official capacity. *In particular, official capacity as a Head of State or Government, a member of a Government or parliament, an elected representative or a government official shall in no case exempt a person from criminal responsibility* under this Statute, nor shall it, in and of itself, constitute a ground for reduction of sentence.

2. Immunities or special procedural rules which may attach to the official capacity of a person, whether under national or international law, shall not bar the Court from exercising its jurisdiction over such a person.[65]

Its status as a permanent institution located in The Hague places the ICC at the centre of what can now be regarded as a process of accountability instead of the ad hoc and temporary devices of special tribunals. Moreover, the emphasis upon individual responsibility gives the Court an underlying logic of following the trails of culpability to those in positions of leadership. In effect, it places at risk of prosecution those leaders who may be deemed to have instigated or directed the commission of serious crimes; or to have colluded in their prosecution; or at least to have had opportunities of preventing them or of arranging their cessation while they were being committed. Herein lies the significance of the ICC in respect to the legal and political responsibilities of leadership.

Apart from the way that the Court infringes upon the doctrines of sovereignty and state autonomy as well as upon the more pragmatic traditions of international diplomacy, the ICC represents a frontal assault upon the many sources and types of executive immunity which have normally protected heads of government in the performance of their official duties. In addition to the immunities granted to them *within* their home jurisdictions, government leaders have traditionally been protected from prosecution when they are outside their home states either through the customary protocols relating to their official duties, or through the operation of legal immunities relieving them of any individual liabilities within the jurisdiction of foreign courts. But as the International Criminal Court develops its investigatory and prosecutorial remit, these once entrenched defences are increasingly coming under legal and political challenge in the face of pressures derived from international humanitarian law, human rights norms, and the turn towards more collective doctrines of international security. The Court has also benefited from the case law precedents that have emerged from the procedures and judgements of those special tribunals into war crimes and crimes against humanity that were set up before the ratification of the Rome Treaty.[66] Of particular note in this

---

[65] Rome Statute of the International Criminal Court, 'Article 27: Irrelevance of official capacity'. Accessed 14 October 2012 at: <http://untreaty.un.org/cod/icc/statute/romefra.htm>.

[66] William A. Schabas, *The UN International Criminal Tribunals: The Former Yugoslavia, Rwanda and Sierra Leone* (Cambridge: Cambridge University Press, 2006) chs. 4–8.

context has been the indictment and conviction of Charles Taylor in the Special Court for Sierra Leone. This established the principle that a serving head of state could be indicted, extradited, and prosecuted under the auspices of international war crimes jurisprudence (Box 11.5).

The ICC has incurred a number of criticisms relating both to its limitations and its powers. For example, concerns have been raised over its position as a court of

---

Box 11.5 The case of Charles Taylor, president of Liberia

After years of civil war, Charles Taylor finally became president of Liberia in 1997. While president, he was accused of aiding and abetting the Revolutionary United Front (RUF) in its rebellion against the government of the neighbouring state of Sierra Leone. When the civil war in Sierra Leone (1989–2002) came to an end the United Nations and the government of Sierra Leone signed an agreement establishing the Special Court for Sierra Leone (SCSL). After being indicted in 2003 for war crimes, crimes against humanity, and other serious violations of international law, Taylor resigned the presidency and accepted the offer of a safe haven in Nigeria. In 2006 he was extradited back to Liberia and thence transported to The Hague where the SCSL had been relocated for security purposes. He faced 11 charges in connection with his alleged role in Sierra Leone's vicious civil war and in particular with his support for RUF rebel forces which had been responsible for widespread atrocities (e.g. murder, rape, enslavement, the mass amputation of limbs, and the recruitment of child soldiers). In addition to the allegations of using 'blood diamonds' from Liberia to finance the RUF, Taylor was accused of advising rebel commanders in their offensives and urging them to capture diamond production centres in Sierra Leone.

Taylor's defence was that he had never been to Sierra Leone during the period 1991–2002 and that he had tried to negotiate various peace settlements at the time. But prosecutors demonstrated that he had conspired with the Sierra Leonean rebel groups and had supplied them with arms and communications equipment. In April 2012, Taylor was found guilty of eleven counts of war crimes and crimes against humanity. This decision made the former Liberian president the first head of state to have been convicted of crimes against humanity by an international criminal court since the Second World War. It was a landmark case for another reason. Although the Court had rejected the prosecution's case that Taylor had engaged in a joint criminal enterprise with rebel groups in which it could be assumed that he was a *de facto* part of the command structure, it had in fact established a new precedent in war crimes jurisprudence that will have serious implications for any future heads of states who come before such a tribunal. This established that even if a direct connection or joint enterprise between a head of state and the enactment of serious crimes cannot be proved, the very role of a head of state involves an obligation to use power to promote peace and stability. A failure to do so amounted in the Court's view to the presence of an aggravating factor that merited a comparable level of punishment to that of the main perpetrators of the crimes. This view was reflected in the same sentence of fifty years' imprisonment which had been reserved for the rebel commanders who directed the killing.

The Charles Taylor case underlined the principle that a serving head of state is no longer immune from prosecution. The later indictments by the International Criminal Court of Sudan's President Omar al-Bashir and former Ivory Coast leader Laurent Gbagbo are testaments to the significance of the Taylor precedent.

Sources: Colin M. Waugh, *Charles Taylor and Liberia: Ambition and Atrocity in Africa's Lone Star State* (London: Zed Books, 2011). Materials on the indictments; summary of the charges; prosecution and defence briefs; the judgement and sentencing outcomes drawn from The Special Court for Sierra Leone, Cases: *The Prosecutor v. Charles Ghankay Taylor*.

Accessed 15 September 2012 at: <http://www.sc-sl.org/CASES/ProsecutorvsCharlesTaylor/tabid/107/Default. aspx>.

last resort and its dependency upon the principle of 'complementarity' with the court systems of the signatory states.[67] Other issues have centred upon the processes of arrest and extradition, the length and development of trial procedures, and the discretionary powers of the Court Prosecutor. There have been additional questions concerning the Court's independence from the UN Security Council, the meanings of 'crimes against humanity', and the issue of whether the Court's actions might serve to exacerbate tensions and increase the prospects of further violence on the ground. More sweeping complaints have focused on the nature of the Court's international role and its jurisdictional priorities—i.e. that it allegedly represents a highly politicized enterprise among Western states to legitimize a post-Cold War interventionist impulse to exert good governance and human rights agendas upon those regimes that they consider to be in need of improvement. This is evidenced by the fact that of the thirteen leaders to have been indicted during the first eight years of the ICC's operation, all of them have emanated from five selected regions in Africa—namely, Uganda, the Democratic Republic of Congo, the Central African Republic, Darfur, and Kenya. Most notable is the warrant issued in 2010 for the arrest of Omar Hassan Ahmad al-Bashir, the sitting president of Sudan.

Notwithstanding these various reservations and critiques, it is nevertheless the case that the ICC amounts to a landmark both in the development of international standards of governing responsibilities, and in the assignment of political and legal accountability between and across national borders. The Court's actions in indicting past and serving leaders have been concurrent with two other developments. First is the increased usage of the legal doctrine of 'universal jurisdiction'[68] within national jurisdictions; and second are the substantive changes in the indigenous rules on immunity within states themselves.[69] In sum, they mean that leaders who were once thought to be safe from prosecution in the exercise of their duties can no longer take it for granted that they will remain free from charges of criminal responsibility fot their actions as leaders. The prospect of final accountability is underlined by the ICC Statute which affirms that time will afford no escape for any errant leader. Article 29 states explicitly that the 'crimes within the jurisdiction of the Court shall not be subject to any statute of limitations'.[70]

These international and domestic developments have generated the mutual formation of a medium of accountability which is highly dynamic—shaped and informed as it is by several strands of legal doctrine, institutional formation, and

---

[67] The doctrine or principle of 'complementarity' means that the ICC functions in co-partnership with national courts. This means that the Court can only exercise its jurisdiction when a national court is unable or unwilling to investigate allegations of serious crimes or to prosecute those responsible. The intention of the ICC is in not to replace the authority of national courts, but to act as a fail-safe when other courts fail to engage effectively with charges of genocide, crimes against humanity, and war crimes.

[68] The principle of 'universal jurisdiction' confers the right of domestic courts to have cases concerning genocide, torture, and crimes against humanity brought before them irrespective of any linkages between perpetrators, victims, or the locations of the criminal behaviour. The legal basis of 'universal jurisdiction' and the scope of its applicability are disputed.

[69] States are always able to change the conditions of immunity reserved to their own leaders. Increasingly, states have engaged in domestic prosecutions of their own past leaders.

[70] Rome Statute of the International Criminal Court, 'Article 29: Irrelevance of official capacity'. Accessed 14 October 2012 at: <http://untreaty.un.org/cod/icc/statute/romefra.htm>.

political innovation. It points to a convergence of agencies and movements directed towards the recognition of the principle of individual criminal culpability being assigned to leaders for the consequences of their actions and decisions in office. The effects of these multiple and interactive shifts in the development of accountability mean that leaders have become increasingly concerned over the future legal ramifications of their behaviour in office. An institution like the ICC was of course formed with a deterrent effect in mind so that those considering the commission of crimes against humanity would hold back if they knew that they might be brought to justice at a later point. In the main, it was thought that the chief targets of such an initiative were likely to be precisely those kinds of regime that were thought to be historically susceptible to disorder, tyranny, repression, corruption, atrocities, and all the other distinguishing characteristics of dysfunctional, weak, and collapsing states mired in intra-state conflict and human rights abuses.

However, the logics of identifying flows of accountability do not necessarily point in one direction. On the contrary, some established Western figures—many of whom would self-identify as natural subscribers to the rationale of the ICC—find that they themselves are now the subject of concerted campaigns to have their status as leaders used as the basis of proposed criminal prosecutions. Tony Blair is a case in point. His own administration had been instrumental in the establishment of the ICC and he had made the theme of international society and its humanitarian responsibilities a key part of his modernization project. And yet, the former prime minister now has to contend with a campaign of international lawyers and NGO activists[71] who are seeking his indictment under the Rome Statute in connection with allegations of war crimes relating to the conflict in Iraq since 2003. While the chances of Blair being subjected to trial at the ICC are currently minimal, the way that the Court's process can frame and organize political grievances around the issue of leadership criminalization can generate what is in essence not only a threat of future legal sanction but also a measure of *de facto* current accountability through the damaging reconfiguration of a political career in which a reputation and a legacy are compromised through the force of suspicion.

AFTERWORD

This chapter, along with the preceding ten chapters, has given renewed emphasis to the reactive nature of leaders and leadership in relation to the mutable contexts within which they are situated. The varied nature of the different sections bears

---

[71] The campaign is dedicated to 'giving a voice to those who believe the Iraq invasion of 2003 by the UK & the Allies was illegal'. The campaign is centred on a petition calling for the former prime minister to be arrested, indicted, and prosecuted for war crimes. See <http://tonyblair.org>, accessed 10 October 2012. See also materials presented by the Blair War Crimes Foundation: <http://blairfoundation. wordpress.com/>, accessed 10 October 2012. The various calls for Blair to be arrested have led to several attempts to make citizen arrests both in the UK and abroad. See <http://www.arrestblair.org/war-crimes-reports>, accessed 10 October 2012.

witness to the multidimensional character of the subject field and the way it can foster a proliferation of approaches, drives, narratives, constructions, and interpretive possibilities. The sheer diversity of iterations, applications, and contingencies leads almost necessarily towards issues concerning the extent to which it is possible to arrive at anything approximating to some discernible core meanings or defining categories amongst the multiple relativities that normally inhabit the area. The final chapter is intended to step back from the immediacy of the subject's proliferation of manifestations and attachments, and to offer instead some grounds for a perspective upon the character of its remit. It does not purport to provide a systematic antidote to the prevailing view of leadership as a mercurial and elusive property—nor does it pretend to offer a taxonomy of leaders set against an immutable analytical framework. Its ambition is governed by a more simple, albeit a deceptively simple, prospectus—namely to pose the question of what kind of subject political leadership may be and what kinds of challenge it invariably arouses. Leadership may well be a highly elusive subject but it is necessary now to examine the scale and properties of that elusiveness, and to fathom how those indistinct features are accommodated within a political setting.

12

Coming to terms with political leadership

'I want to ask you for forgiveness, because many of our hopes have not come
true, because what we thought would be easy turned out to be painfully
difficult. I ask to forgive me for not fulfilling some hopes of those people
who believed that we would be able to jump from the grey, stagnating,
totalitarian past into a bright, rich and civilized future in one go. I myself
believed in this. But it could not be done in one fell swoop. In some respects
I was too naïve.'

Boris Yeltsin[1]

PREAMBLE

Political leaders and leadership can always be relied upon to capture the attention
of the onlooker—whether they be bystanders, followers, or analysts. The level of
interest shown in the subject is a reflection of its compulsive appeal but at the
same time its sheer attractiveness generates intriguing challenges in attempting to
bring some coherence to understanding both its intrinsic properties and its
ramifications in the wider political realm. It remains a highly elusive subject. On
the one hand, it is an apparently accessible set of palpable phenomena. The stark
immediacy of leaders offers the initial prospect at least of a clearly demarcated
field of inquiry. And yet, this prima facie clarity is invariably lost in the processes
of closer investigation. Leaders struggle to acquire positions in the very foreground of public and private spheres, and yet individually and collectively they
ensure that any essential or generic features of the subject stay firmly in a highly
obscure background.

The present study has been conditioned throughout by this tension. But in the
course of the analysis it has become increasingly evident that it is a deep-seated
fracture line that has widespread implications for the practice and study of
political leadership. In many respects, the analysis has been concerned with
discovering and examining not just the countervailing forces that deter or inhibit
the study of leadership, but also those influences that distract analysis and
orientate it down certain specified pathways. In effect, the difficulties associated
with studying political leadership reveal an essential and significant dimension of

---

[1] Extract from Boris Yeltsin's resignation statement, 31 December 1999.

the subject itself. Closer inspection routinely discloses the immediate presence of a disjunction that inheres in the area of leadership production and consumption and which underlines much of the particular complexity of the field.

On one side is the supposition that the sector of leadership offers a readily available and highly digestible expression of concentrated political activity. Just as so much appears to depend on leaders within the political realm, so it is that our understanding of everyday politics seems to rely upon key leadership figures that mediate between areas of complex policy and organizational management on the one hand, and the broader constituencies of public observation on the other. The conspicuous positions and formal roles of leaders lend justificatory weight to the intrinsic nature of their assigned functions in providing a clearly demarcated set of navigation instruments by which others are able to acquire some semblance of cognitive grasp in respect to the political landscape.

It is a customary part of almost any political system that leaders offer an abbreviated and simplifying channel of direct, or more usually highly indirect, political engagement. Leadership not only offers the appearance of a singular source of agency but provides a unifying concept of political meaning. In essence, the evoked centrality of leadership provides a channel through which politics is conducted and understood. A prodigious amount of political activity and commentary is repeatedly oriented towards sustaining the notion of leaders as central points of anchorage in political orders which in nearly every other respect are increasingly multidimensional in their conceptual and operational formations. Leaders still offer a comfortable affective familiarity for their audiences. They provide a recognizable solidity and sense of actual political proximity. They give physical form to unifying and controlling themes. They provide defining narratives that mix social and historical authenticity with their own positions. And their self-consciously articulated exercises of self-reference allow them to operate as signifiers for a broad spectrum of cultural attachments.

By the same token, just as a leader can be an affirming agency of political mobilization, so he or she can also constitute the rallying point of dissent, resistance, and even revolutionary rejection. In both cases, leaders act as both symbolic and substantive entities that always succeed in investing politics with a visceral property drawn from their own personal and positional existence. In this guise, leaders give a raw existential presence to politics. If it is correct that leadership is a relational concept, then leaders lend weight to the perspective that the relationship is a manifestly tangible one based upon the evocation of leaders as clearly discernible entities in the political universe.

The other side of the disjunction offers an altogether different depiction of the subject. Leaders and leadership may offer the prospect of a unity of focus and a central point of political reference, but that initial promise is rarely fulfilled when it comes to the task of analysis. Far from constituting a clear framework of inquiry, the subject is notorious for its inability to settle into anything approaching a fixed set of thematic guidelines. Instead it ramifies into a proliferation of often particularistic sub-fields and discrete points of individual analysis. The sphere of leadership analysis is nothing short of vast, in both scale and complexity. Its relational properties mean that leadership is always subject to a prodigious array of different contexts and contingencies; varied situations and narratives; and a diversity of motives and intentions as well as activities and outcomes. The subject field of political leadership lends itself promiscuously to a host of different constructions, iterations, and interpretive possibilities. In doing so, it generates significant challenges in seeking to clarify and understand the main points at issue in any serious engagement with its multidimensional character.

One aspect of this explanatory challenge is the need to recognize and even partially to accommodate the magnitude of the subject matter. Apart from the evident profusion of leaders in both contemporary and historical settings—each with their own problems, agendas, and constraints—there is always an accompanying retinue of commentaries, analyses, and biographically centred studies that root any leadership within a differentiated political habitat. In the main, both leaders and leadership analysts suffer from the very centrality that leaders devise for their own political advantage. In making their own personas so central to the way that politics is conducted and understood, leaders are routinely portrayed as conspicuously unique in nature and therefore prodigious in their numerous variations. This means that leaders attract stylized forms of accountability which serve further to underwrite their idiosyncratic roles in the manner of their decline and in the processes of their replacement. Individual leaders may fail, decline, and disappear but their places are always taken by others who begin a fresh set of narratives related to the ascribed uniqueness of each new mix of personnel and contexts.

Another aspect of the challenge in clarifying the subject matter of leaders and leadership is related to the issue of volume and incidence but is directed more to the dissonance created by the varied approaches to that which is perceived to require explanation in this area of endeavour. Leadership as a generic term is a variable and compound expression that can attach itself to many different categories. Political leadership is no different to any other in this respect. In point of fact, it can be argued that it has an exceptional facility for attracting multiple sets of roles and meanings across a wide range of social existence. It is no exaggeration to claim that political leadership possesses something of a 'catch-all' character in the way that so many issues, attributes, and developments are channelled through the medium of leadership. There is hardly a subject in contemporary politics that does not have a connection—or is not permitted to have an association—with the theme of political leadership.

Moreover, the adhesive properties of leadership are not confined to political actors and participants. Political analysis is also affected by the plural nature of the subject. Leaders and leadership have a prismatic effect on their observers and the methodologies adopted by them. The subject draws attention to itself but at the same time it also disperses the attention given to it by accommodating a profusion of different analytical pathways. As an object of scrutiny, it becomes refracted through a kaleidoscope of alternative approaches and perceptual repertoires. As leadership loses its initial simplicity through its multiple attachments and its magnetizing effect on theories and practices of explanation, so it becomes progressively more mercurial and contested in nature.

The high political value given to leadership's attributed singularity of purpose and position does not translate into anything approaching clarity in terms of analysis. If leadership indicates a particular distribution of power and responsibility, then that profile is far from being replicated in the distribution of its explanations. The net effect is one in which the centripetal associations of leadership coexist with the centrifugal energies attached to its multiple accounts. Leadership becomes highly valued and devalued at one and the same time. In so many ways, the near universal incidence of leaders and the avowed necessity for leadership as a political value in its own right have made the categories of the subject area so ubiquitous that it becomes difficult to acquire a settled or coherent means for apprehending its multilayered nature.

On the basis of its scale and complexity, therefore, leadership is at best a field of political activity that imparts both the impression of clarity and an underlying capacity to confound the issue of its own meaning and practice. It offers an easily acquired familiarity and an intuitive surface outline of political landscapes, while also opening up deep seams and fault lines in the geological underpinnings of political explanation. Its position at the intersections of numerous substantive and analytical issues is matched by a capacity to generate its own plurality of intersections. The field of leadership places at the feet of any foolhardy observer a host of searching questions and testing puzzles—not the least of them the issue of the kind of subject it may be; the type of analysis that is best suited to its dimensions and dynamics; and whether it is a subject that can be defined and confined for the purposes of close examination.

The main objective of this study has been to confer some semblance of order on what is an otherwise dissonant and increasingly fractionated object of compulsive inquiry. The aim has been to locate the key constituent elements of the field and to examine them in relation both to one another and to the main theme of political leadership with the intention of clarifying the underlying logic and dynamics of a field that all too often becomes submerged in the particularistic properties either of individual leaders or of discrete derivatives of various analytical strategies and traditions. In attempting to establish a close connection with the more immediate political activity of leadership, the study has sought to arrive at a more substantive, but also more nuanced, representation of the defining parameters of what it is to be a leader within an explicitly political context. The adopted approach has not been one of working inductively towards anything approaching a grand theory or even to a more advanced level of generalization or unifying abstraction. Instead, it has assumed what might be argued to be a more realistic prospectus—namely the configuration of the main features of the subject field, the disclosure of emergent patterns and trends, and the examination of those generic issues that have claims of possessing a close lineage to the themes and contexts of political leadership.

While it is true that the study has been one of eliciting some semblance of coherence from an outwardly cluttered and discordant area of inquiry, the foregoing analysis has not proceeded on the basis of reaching for some systematic or foundational anchorage by which to exert a simplifying and arguably artificial order upon an intrinsically expansive arena of political activity. On the contrary, in exploring whatever approximate order may be possible within the constraints and diversions of the subject field itself, the operation of inquiry into so many different dimensions of leadership has allowed the study to acquire a greater awareness of the depth of some of the more challenging components in this kind of enterprise. Far from seeking a foreclosure on the more contested aspects inherent in the field, the exploration has in fact fostered a heightened sense of the ecology of problematic properties that condition the practice and study of political leadership. This being the case, it would be appropriate at this stage to bring into sharper focus some of these tensions that have been discerned during the course of the survey and which remain at the heart of the subject under review. Drawn as they are from a close and extended engagement with the components and processes of political leadership as a distinct field of relational activity, it is now time to turn our attention to those demanding points of tension which have arisen as a consequence of this extended study.

A FRACTURED LANDSCAPE

It is neither appropriate nor desirable to attempt to engage in a comprehensive exercise in problematizing the interior nature and external ramifications of political leadership in its various manifestations. What is suitable at this point is to use the momentum of the previous eleven chapters to take stock of the tensions that always arise in reaching for an understanding of political leadership. The objective here is to allow our previous inquiries to inform a discussion over the sources and identity of the problematic properties that continue to attach themselves to the subject and to generate significant barriers to acquiring an overall grasp of the subject matter. Through the study's previous engagement with key elements of the leadership sector, it is now possible to renew our acquaintance with some of the more enduring disjunctions that inhabit this sphere—and in doing so to re-examine their reach and implications from a different vantage point. At the same time, it will afford an opportunity to explore the way that changing conditions and emergent trends can reveal different facets of established issues as well as disclosing the existence of new analytical and interpretive controversies.

Disjuncture #1: Individual/structure

One commonly ascribed feature of a leader is that of an extension of a political system which both facilitates and authorizes a leader's position. The role and meaning of such a positional resource can be viewed as an outward signature, or visible representation, or even a characterizing embodiment of an empowering political structure within which the leader is situated and from which influence and power are drawn. Whether a leader is seen as the structure's highest expression, or merely as a concomitant feature of its organization, the meaning of such a prominent element carries the inference that the leadership is a derivative of something apart from itself, and other than itself. In this sense, a leader can be depicted as acting in accordance with a purely functional and formal remit in which the leadership is valued as a device operating within a network of institutional, legal, and constitutional constraints. These matrices may well vary from highly sophisticated arrangements to relatively underdeveloped schemes of governance. Notwithstanding these variations, leaders can in many ways be understood as holding a position that is not merely compatible with an underlying structure of government but is incorporated within it and even reducible to it.

At the same time, an altogether different characteristic is also used to distinguish leaders from other political actors. Instead of being seen as subsumed within a controlling structure, leaders are commonly recognized as possessing intrinsic and idiosyncratic responsibilities that allow for a more activist role to be taken within government. This may come in the form of creating agendas, devising policy programmes, mobilizing support for initiatives, and taking responsibility for a broad range of governmental functions. Far from being confined to a passive implementation role, contemporary leaders are often regarded as being the only source of the vitality, coherence, and direction required for effective government. In providing the catalyst for governing efficiency, leaders are explicitly or implicitly invested with special *de facto* powers that either stretch the *de jure* frameworks of due process or transcend them altogether through reference to extraordinary responsibilities and executive authority. Nowhere is this recourse to leadership-centred authority more evident than in the field of foreign and security policy. Where the contexts are designated as national emergencies, existential threats, or international crises, many political leaders consider it to be part of their responsibilities to claim the licence to circumvent, ignore, and even suspend normal legal and institutional arrangements. While these may constitute extreme cases of executive discretion, they nevertheless typify an overall continuum that often privileges individual leaders over the terms and processes of their structural accommodation.

Summary: These tensions foster a deep ambivalence over the primary value of leadership—i.e. between on the one hand leaders limited and directed by structural imperatives, and on the other leaders who take it upon themselves to compromise the integrity of their political processes in the service of an agenda that is defined by the leadership itself as serving a set of higher purposes.

Disjuncture #2: Agency/dependency

Leaders are commonly judged against the benchmark of great leadership which is equated with leaders who maximize their influence to an extent that substantiates the impression of control, autonomy, and self-possession. While most leaders do not achieve the mantle of greatness, they do become associated with the notion of political agency as both an empirical fact and a normative principle. It is accepted that leaders operate within an environment that includes other actors and participants. Nevertheless, it is equally the case that a leadership role encompasses the view that it has a significant instrumental capacity to move others towards a preferred set of objectives. Leaders may be stabilizers or innovators, but either way it is assumed that they provide a conscious presence that confers a causal force that acts upon their respective contexts. In their ability to set matters in motion, leaders can be viewed as creating effects that otherwise would not occur. Because leadership is conceived as a driving agency in this way, a form of what might be termed 'double instrumentalism' characterizes much of the discussion surrounding the role. Owing to the priority given to leadership as a means to an end, political arrangements themselves become oriented to what needs to occur in order secure a leadership capacity and thereby a primary source of political agency.

To the extent that leaders do possess the kind of autonomous initiative and motivating stimulus that inform a position of political causality, then they can also expect this status to be conditioned by the exigencies of political circumstances. In effect, this means that for every claim of agency, there is a counterclaim of dependency. Each leadership will experience its own particular profile of dependency relationships stretching across different dimensions relating to sources of political support, the timing of events, the interaction of issues, and types of authority invoked. Just as leaders may find that choices are drawn towards the leadership level, so they will also be aware that their position can become equated with being a register of forces over which they have little control. The cause-and-effect relationship therefore is far from being as unilinear and unidirectional as it is often portrayed to be. On many occasions, leaders are placed in a position of being reactive agents who need to demonstrate political receptiveness and responsiveness in order to retain their effectiveness in the leadership role. Leadership positions therefore can become immersed in multiple stimuli, numerous cross-pressures, and severe cognitive dissonance. In this context, leaderships can become overloaded and overstretched to the point where leaders come to perceive themselves more as victims than controllers. It is not merely that many leaders suffer from stress-related forms of ill health or that they are often observed as victims of an unsustainably intense work environment. It is that leadership itself can be viewed as an intrinsically disorientating condition.

Summary: The duality therefore is one in which leaders can be conceptualized as (i) functioning at the head of a putative chain of command with jurisdictional authority to act in the role of an 'unmoved mover'; and (ii) operating within a political context that both conditions and contests the operation of that position to the extent of making the claim to agency a highly qualified and contingent one.

Disjuncture #3: Continuity/discontinuity

There is a strong expectation that leaders offer a foundational element to the conduct of politics and governance. Leadership is commonly equated not only with the provision of organizational and managerial competence but also with the visible basis of settlement and order within a polity. To a significant extent, leaders offer a form of continuity in their adherence to the acquired social traditions and political processes associated with allocation of leadership roles, and in the way that they can suggest a sense of linear succession in which development can be construed as an evolutionary adjustment to conditions. Leadership in this guise is interpreted as a process of accumulation in which position, power, and authority are inherited by beneficiaries who fulfil their role in ways that retain its stabilizing influence at the centre of political activity. This does not mean that leaders are expected to refrain from invoking changes, or that leadership can only be understood as a form of reassuring stasis. However, it does suppose that leadership can be institutionalized to the extent that, notwithstanding the nature of contemporary political conditions or the incidence of past shifts in leadership personnel, a leader at any particular time can be said to represent a cumulative expression of political experience and operational continuity.

Set against this perspective is one that conceives leadership as a temporary state of settlement that offers some respite from the fissiparous tendencies of normal political exchange. These periods of leadership may be short or relatively extended in length but whatever their duration, they ultimately all become marked by the same processes of disaggregation and entropy. Just as leaders can be depicted as the centrepiece of a set of centripetal forces, so they can also be seen in terms of the polar opposite—namely the representative of a host of centrifugal forces. What is significant is that these two conditions are closely related to one another because of the way that one condition almost invariably succeeds the other. Moreover, they are usually observable within the confines of each leadership experience. Just as new leaders are usually ushered into office with the patina of fresh claims to settlement—and are given the initial benefit of any doubt—so established leaders will feel the reverse thrust of such a dynamic. However strong their credentials may be upon entering office, leaders will generally find that their earlier resources will be eroded in an ineluctable process of declining influence and depleted authority. The earlier personification of solidity will give way to a form of individual dissolution which in some systems may lead to serious forms of political disarray. In other more stable systems, transfers of power at the leadership level offer conjunctions—albeit temporarily—of both systemic continuity and leader-centred discontinuity. In both cases, new leadership is recognized as a preferred solution in the form of another turn of what is a cyclical process.

Summary: The provision and exercise of leadership marks a tension between what is deemed to be a systemic requirement of a functioning political order on the one hand and the disaggregated properties of a leadership in power on the other. Leadership changes can offer an affirmation of continuities but also elements of discontinuity that arguably become more prominent with the passage of time and the onset of pathological distances between a leadership and its point of inception.

Disjuncture #4: Rationality/mystique

In many instances, the notion of political leadership conjures up references to modernity in the sense that in developed complex social orders leaders occupy what are commonly termed the commanding heights of organizational power. These systems are formally designed to operate according to principles of organizational rationality based upon a division of specialist labour within formal hierarchies in which information flows up to the appropriate level of competence for decision-making. Because a leader is positioned at the apex of this pyramidal framework, then it can be concluded as a matter of principle and practice that he or she benefits from having access to the best available information as well as the optimum level of high calibre analysis and sophisticated assessment for the purposes of decision-making and policy formulation. A leader in such a position also serves to embody the idea of advanced functionality in giving weight to the impression that government possesses mechanistic properties of organization, rationality, and reliability. Leadership in such a positivist context can evoke a view that these types of organization can not only be led but are necessarily led through the force of their own operational logic which privileges the production of measured responses in line with clearly delineated processes based upon substantive, direct, and precisely defined authority.

The extent to which the positional resources of leadership can be equated with rational organization and clarity of operation is widely disputed. Far from suggesting the comprehensive presence of a materially based logic, leadership is widely conceived in terms of indeterminacy and even irrationality. In order to capture the essence of leaders and leadership, it is often claimed that it is necessary to have recourse to the influences of emotion, imagination, and mystique. The Weberian category of charismatic authority still exerts a strong conditioning effect upon the study and understanding of the subject area. But the imprecision of the field is not confined to the cited properties of individual exceptionalism that are normally attached to the theme of charisma. The appeal of leaders and the traction achieved through leadership can be extended to those factors related more to the pull of collective identity, transcendent appeal, suggestive instinct, and political symbolism. Leaders habitually engage in appeals not just to various sources of social and cultural identity, but also to traditional, intuitive, and allegedly pre-modern types of temperament. The same processes also work in reverse in the way that the subjects and themes related to identity production and psychological attachment become themselves signifiers of leadership—thereby closing the circle that makes the nature and operation of leadership so multifaceted and elusive. For many observers, locating leadership within this far less precise, more fluid, and conspicuously sensuous scenery means that both its meaning and its function are arguably related more to symbolism than to anything else.

Summary: While leaders and leadership are often portrayed as belonging to an ordered hierarchy based upon rational organization and positivist principles, they are also seen as being intimately related to, and dependent upon, resources drawn from and conveyed through a medium that transcends the one-dimensional configuration of a calculable set of interactions located within a structured hierarchy.

Disjuncture #5: Connection/disconnection

Leadership's relational property is usually exemplified by a leader's connection to those who are prepared to act as followers. More often than not this is conceived in terms of an active and continuing engagement with the wider public in such a way as to embed the leadership in a process that can link its own positions with ideas of public choice, political representation, and even a social contract. Leaders have become increasingly adept at giving physical and rhetorical form to the practice of leadership positioned within the public sphere and acting on behalf of a wider public interest. Leaders have become more skilled at invoking the claim that they are uniquely located to give (substantive or symbolic) expression to popular aspirations and anxieties. In like manner, they are able to sustain the impression that they have an intuitive proximity to a wide base of consent and outside support which can foster the proposition that their connectedness amounts to an extension of democracy. In these ways, leaders can promote themselves not only as the recipients of public trust and understanding but as the point of fusion between a form of public participation and a position of direct responsiveness and consensus values in service to the wider public interest.

The obverse side of this arguably simplistic yet often compulsive perspective is one that opens up the operational nature of the relational side of leaders and the sector of non-leaders. Far from being a clearly defined form of exchange, it can be argued that there is a very wide spectrum of 'followership'—stretching from the highly informed and engaged to those who are uninformed and disengaged. Given that the larger cohorts are usually positioned at the latter end of the scale, leaders have the potential to shape the formation of public opinion upon issues even to the point of suggesting that the leadership can be entrusted to act not so much on behalf of the public but in its place. In this respect, leaders are not representational ciphers. They do not always strive to achieve connection with, or to embody, the public. Instead they work to define and operationalize the public in what can be interpreted as a form of democratic disconnect. Although leaders are normally very skilful both at cultivating the theme of a linkage between individual and mass politics, and at propagating the image that they are one of the people, the logic of their assumed role generally points towards the presumption of difference and the actuality of distance—with all the potential for later discord and reaction that that would imply.

Summary: The practitioners and analysts of leadership constantly have to negotiate between two coexisting conditions and preconceptions that characterize the subject—namely leaders need to connect to others in order to become and to remain leaders. At the same time, they also have to retain a sense of strategic distinctiveness and to preserve their claims to political exceptionalism. In attending to the former, leaders can jeopardize their rationale and status as leadership figures; emphasizing the latter incurs equally serious risks. As a consequence, leaders have to be associated both with representational and responsive modes of activity on the one side, and with their polar opposites of idiosyncratic difference and appropriate disconnection on the other.

The above points of tension and disjuncture are key components in the practice, consumption, and study of leadership. It is not an exhaustive list but it is one that captures the essence of a subject area that has an exceptional facility for generating fault lines and for demanding a capability for working amidst them for those who wish to engage with the sector. It has been argued that while the field is one of different dimensions and intersections, it is nevertheless capable of an inner coherence not least because of the very preconceptions of leadership that such a field of inquiry accommodates and propagates as a central principle. And it may well be true that some leaders are able to achieve a measure of partial resolution to a number of these contentious issues for a limited time—or at least to realign some of these disjunctions into positions approaching a degree of consistency for a while. However, for the most part, the leadership field remains a cluttered landscape heavily marked with contested dimensions, cross-cutting cleavages, ramifying properties, divergent approaches, interpretive disputes, entrenched binaries, and enduringly resistant tautologies. It is the scale of this complexity that characterizes the leadership matrix which proffers a particularly resonant and deeply penetrative outlook upon the subject. Moreover, it might be said to both condition and drive many, if not most, of the fracture lines referred to above.

Despite the fact that political leadership has such a strong resonance with notions of agency, order, and direction, and notwithstanding its primary logic of attributable responsibility for a profusion of political phenomena, it is nevertheless the case that the subject field remains remarkably resistant to being reduced to a set of determinable properties. Political leadership is an activity that may be experienced both extensively and intensively on a grand scale but questions persist over the extent to which experience is matched by understanding. While political leaders may be in touching distance of broad swathes of society, the essential meaning that can be attached to their position and activity remains largely beyond our grasp. In like manner, political leadership can act as an explanatory device in numerous instances covering a range of diverse phenomena, but when it comes to the phenomenon of leadership itself then explanatory strategies appear to be far less serviceable and reliable. Herein lies the main paradox of *any* leadership study.

Basic ideas surrounding the theme of leaders and leadership are generally highly accessible with an intuitive appeal that makes for an easy familiarity with the apparent logic of their position. The material reality of leaders combined with their high-exposure profiles is suggestive of an apparently defined subject field but on closer inspection the composition of the sector and its effects are both highly complex and analytically confounding. Just as leadership as an objective reality all too often turns into a chimera, so the study of leadership is almost invariably transposed into the segmented and multilayered assemblages of leadership studies. It can be argued that this is the optimum way by which leadership can be examined. It has fostered a voluminous literature on individual leaders and groups of selected leaders. By examining them in relation to their particular contexts, it is possible to give substantive accounts of their idiosyncratic forms of leadership and even to combine some of these into a framework of types of leadership. In leadership studies, the classic methodology has literally been one of following the leaders.

While this approach has generated a prodigious amount of material on the lives and times of leaders, it tends to divert attention from wider issues and deeper patterns of leadership activity and leadership consumption. In this way, the profusion of such cameos—either singly or in combination with one another—still evokes the impression of a disjuncture between the scale of analysis and its reach. Even when other approaches and methodologies are brought into the analytical mix, the outcome is still one of a subject that is inherently incomplete and which is arguably not even compatible with a convincing or reliable form of explanation. The present study has attempted to convey the richness of the field while seeking to bring some order to the overall analysis of leadership. At the same time, the materials and debates presented in the course of this review have underlined the sources, nature, and potency of the limitations that characterize the subject's reputation for partial explanation and holistic inexplicability. What is required at this point is not so much a renewed search for a way out of the problem but a more considered way of coming to terms with its elusive and distractive properties.

In essence, the realism that is so often associated with the exercise of political leadership needs to be translated into its analytical and evaluative equivalent. However painful the conclusion may be, if there is one feature of the political leadership field that is common to all circumstances it is that the subject occasions a high level of dispute concerning its basic components, dynamics, meaning, and purpose. As we have observed, the subject has no agreed point of departure or accepted frame of reference that is generally applicable across the spectrum of leadership cases. The subject field is confirmed as a multidimensional entity with a marked capacity for preventing any settled consensus on the most appropriate units and levels of analysis or on the optimum bases and categories of explanation. An important part of any study of leadership is therefore one of conveying the extraordinary richness of its thematic and operational properties whilst seeking to secure some measure of an organizational and analytical overview on what is an intrinsically variable set of political activities.

But an equally important part of such an excursion into this demanding and perplexing terrain is not merely to acknowledge the reality of its complexity but to underline the value of its multiple properties. This aspect is normally overlooked or peremptorily dismissed in leadership studies. The subject's opaque and confounding nature is almost invariably taken as both the foundational basis and guiding rationale for successive attempts at eliciting or imposing some generalized principles of operation. The problem with this normalized approach to the field is that it can screen out a significant and valuable dimension central to how leadership functions within political societies. Controversies and disputes over leaders and leadership pose major issues over the ways by which, and the degree to which, the subject can be reduced to an analytical understanding. However, there are other forms of understanding which leadership issues can facilitate and draw out into the political realm. In this way, differing perspectives over the usage and value of leaders and their leadership roles can offer insights into expansive areas of political life. In other words, the contested nature of the subject field should not necessarily be interpreted in negative terms. Instead of demarcating the constraints and limits upon the acquisition of understanding, the mercurial elements of the leadership issue can make a very positive contribution to reaching a more rounded comprehension of the subject's idiosyncratic character.

Notwithstanding its status as a compound and variable descriptor of multiple phenomena, the extensive usage of the references and terminology surrounding leadership serves several purposes in the conduct of politics. These relate less to the functionally overt and material services provided by leadership resources and more to the way that leaders and leadership politics can generate a host of different facilities which possess an equal and arguably even greater utility than those features and responsibilities which are conventionally ascribed to their positions. A number of illustrative examples might be cited but it is appropriate to allude to *four* in particular that are especially representative of the wider contributions made by this sector of political activity. These will now be considered in the next four sections.

LEADERSHIP AS A FORM OF POLITICAL GRAMMAR

For a subject renowned for its lack of constancy or foundational integrity, the issues generated by, and expressed through, the themes of leadership nevertheless make it a highly adaptable set of categories which can be readily grasped, absorbed, and disputed among a wide section of any political community. Separate publics, or parts of publics, may have attachments to individual leaders but in developing these connections they are equally likely to foster a common experience of political exchange based upon the net effects of an enduring and competitive interplay between different claims to leadership. While the reporting and analysis of leadership politics have an inherent bias towards the atomized and mutually exclusive nature of each leader's idiosyncratic strengths and weaknesses, the overall effect is one of a cumulative orientation towards various categories of leadership as a medium of common usage and engagement. It is not so much the separate attachments and claims of the leaders themselves which are significant here. It is the way that these different forms of advocacy combine to create a strong subtext of understanding in respect to how politics becomes conceived as an operational medium with an underlying dependency upon a range of leader-centred characteristics.

In the same way that leaders are able to prompt a range of responses from their audiences, constituencies, or organizations so that they are able to acquire further resources by which to extend or consolidate their bases, so issues, choices, demands, anxieties, and a gamut of other impulses necessarily come to be framed by recourse to constructions of leadership roles and records. Successful leaders are shown to be adept at assimilating and re-representing common sentiments, attitudes, and positions either on substantive grounds or through symbolic expressions of common identity. As they do so, these accomplished leaders provide the stimulus to others to imitate their strategies of success. The gravitational force of accumulated and compacted precedents amounts to a compulsive frame of reference through which political understandings are arrived at and sustained as both a conscious and subconscious *modus operandi*.

According to this perspective, the politics of leadership becomes associated with more than the political positions of leaders. It is about the way that the issues surrounding leadership within a polity can generate and signify the existence of what can be portrayed as a reflexive community—i.e. one that is sufficiently well equipped to engage with political issues through a medium that relies on categories drawn directly, but also indirectly and even obliquely, from a leadership matrix that is as much intuitive in nature as it is a calculable device. The dissonant features relating to the kind of fault lines and dualities alluded to above can now be viewed in a different light. In effect, they can be interpreted as a measure of a community that is able not just to withstand their disparate forces, but to adjust to them and to work with and through them, in order to achieve a form of sustainable equilibrium. While it can be claimed that the perceptual apparatus afforded by leadership politics raises the consciousness of the manifold fractures inherent in the logics and operation of leadership, so it can be argued that this selfsame awareness and experience of the challenging elements of the subject field can also foster various processes of adaptation.

Under closer examination, the difficulties of arriving at anything approaching definitive positions or final answers to the puzzles and paradoxes of leadership nonetheless provide the backdrop to a whole range of acquired skills and experiences in accommodating the disjunctions while engaging in extensive forms of political discourse centring upon leadership issues. In other words, leadership does not just offer a location—or at least the prospect—of an instrumental capacity within a political system. The positional properties of leadership and the political themes that arise in their wake can provide the basis of what might be termed a perceptual instrumentality that guides and shapes the constructions of leaders and leadership within their own contextual frameworks. This means that the many unresolved tensions within the subject field are more often than not either select- ively marginalized or generically transcended in the cause of facilitating a workable form of political exchange in which leadership remains centrally significant but not to the point of extending its problematic aspects to the point of stasis.

Instead of being captives of a multiple impasse of insoluble problems and confounding questions, leadership issues can inform and give structure to the formation and interaction of political attachments. The multifaceted character of leadership politics can operate in ways that allow for the formation of a medium through which political communications can operate, and adjustments to demanding issues and realities can be facilitated. Far from always generating negative polarities, the pull of leader-centred constructions of attachment, under- standing, and activity often cultivate pathways that lead to the development of those kinds of habitual and sophisticated attitudes that may be conditioned by the complexities of leadership issues but which are not confined to them. On the contrary, they are able to devise the means to work alongside the perplexity of the subject's scope for incoherence in ways that offer the potential for drawing upon the implicit energies of leadership without always being drawn into the deep controversies of their extended logics.

Whatever else leaders may do, they are remarkably adept at providing key points of cognitive reference by which non-leaders can navigate their way through the com- plexities of political life. For all the reasons mentioned above in previous chapters, leaders are compulsive attention-seekers who, through the exploitation of their high- profile presence within their respective political contexts, manage to impose them- selves upon the perceptual processes of those who are actual or nominal followers. In doing so, leaders can literally shape not just their immediate political worlds but also the psychological equivalent of those who experience high levels of exposure to the public presence of leadership. Leaders offer the appearance of understandings and explanations. They propagate defining narratives and memorable associations. More- over, they do so through political theatre, spectacle, and symbolism. By cultivating these myriad resonances, leaders can come to exert a strong organizational influence upon the political moods and calculations of more ordinary citizens.

These landmarks can be negative as well as positive in nature. But irrespective of the dispositions they arouse one way or another, what is significant is the way that leaders, and disputes over leadership, can form a distinctive and highly suggestive political hinterland which offers an identifiable cast list of major players, a summary depiction of key issues, and an accessible device by which problems and solutions can be readily conceptualized. Just as leaders, and the interplay between leaders, can serve to depict political successes and failures as well as popular anxieties and grievances, so they can also offer an attractive metaphor of wider political under- standings and easily usable summations of accountability.

The intuitive appeal of leadership politics and its capacity to superimpose an organizational and cognitive pattern upon multidimensional phenomena can be critiqued for displacing complexity with stylized over-simplicity. It is possible to argue that in facilitating a form of political comprehension, leadership politics fosters high levels of reliance and even conditions of overdependency in the public consumption of politics. The complaint can be extended to the point of claiming that this kind of representational projection of political meaning may be equated to a condition of denial. This is because it can convey a false sense of leader-centred autonomy within crowded contexts as well as an ingrown distortion of the processes of political exchange and problem resolution. It is even possible to speculate on the extent to which such a dependency is tantamount to a syndrome of passivity and disconnection. This condition might be said to allow non-leaders to be satisfied with their positions comfortably at a distance from the need to give close consideration to making complex choices and decisions. In allowing their attention to become focused upon leaders and their interaction with one another, non-leaders become susceptible to assigning causality and responsibility for extensive phenomena to individual leadership failures—thereby prompting remedial action in the form of calls for alternative leadership. High dependency therefore becomes succeeded at some point by an equally proficient process of displacement that facilitates the rapid transfer of dependency to another leader.

However, such criticisms are themselves far from measured. They fail to account for the way that leadership politics possesses an appeal which is not merely reducible to affective or emotional categories but has a rational and organizational basis as well. It is an entirely defensible proposition that in an epoch of deepening globalization, ramifying transnational issues, proliferating forms of multilevel governance, increasingly complex security environments, and ever more obscure lines of responsibility and accountability, it is not unreasonable for non-leaders to appreciate the utility of leadership politics in reducing the costs of political observation, understanding, contestation, and engagement. It is true that the usage of such a medium can, in some contexts, go too far and become the hallmarks of a marginalized public whose cultivated capacity for voyeurism can support elements of leadership cult behaviour. But in very many other instances, the tracking of leadership activities and behaviour, placed in conjunction with the agendas of other leaders and the prospect of alternative sources of leadership, denotes the existence of a political society that is highly sensitized to the densely packed meanings that can be assigned to leaders operating within an explicitly political space.

The conditioning effect of jointly experiencing, interpreting, and disputing leadership positions, skills, and traits can provide the basis of a functioning political process that is marked as much by argument and dissent as it is by the kind of integrative effects derived from habituated processes of leadership gains and losses. Coming to terms with political leadership, therefore, usually denotes far more than a resigned adjustment to a one-way transmission of meaning. Far from being a concomitant of an insensitive system of political control reliant upon promoting myopic self-absorption and self-isolating passivity, the medium of leadership claims can denote the existence of a very agile political and social community with its own communications, conventions, norms, idioms, impulses, and subtleties of insight aligned to leadership watchfulness and assessment. It can be argued that this concatenation of leadership-related derivatives effectively amounts to a grammar of political understanding. For many, it constitutes the only grammar by which the political world can be comprehended. In this way, it becomes evident that the issues and controversies surrounding leadership serve to operate as a form of political agency in their own right.

LEADERSHIP AS A REGISTER OF POLITICAL ETHICS

Another way in which the positional resources of leadership can indicate categories of inquiry and interpretation is in the field of public and political ethics. Leaders are intimately associated with the themes of agency but these relationships are not confined to matters of material cause and effect. They extend to the point of being a medium for a wide range of ethical concerns raised by governmental action, policy choices, and decision-making processes. Just as a leader can signify a party or a government or even a state, so it is that he or she can also become the tangible expression of those principles that are at stake in the conduct of public life. In effect, leaders can on the one hand provide signature representations of the belief systems in operation within their particular contexts. On the other hand, they can also offer a point of challenge to those belief systems—either directly or surreptitiously. In these cases, leaders can become not so much the authoritative location of agreed principles, as the individual incitements and focal stimuli to ethically based concerns and disputes.

It is possible to go further and to postulate that leaders are especially qualified to draw moral categories and arguments into the political sphere. Most leaders seek to establish their legitimacy and to sustain their support through some reference to overarching principles of right that command widespread cultural assent. By the same token, the erosion of leadership is normally accompanied by a marked strain in the linkage between a leader's positional status and the normative foundations of that position. Leaders therefore have to be adept at maintaining acceptable levels of congruence between themselves and current iterations of what is acceptable political behaviour. Similarly, those who wish to challenge a government or a regime normally target the leadership and especially its ethical standards of conduct. They do so not merely because the leadership can be held responsible for certain claims of improper or corrupt or violent behaviour, but because leadership itself can be transmuted into a medium of heightened moral drama.

As a consequence of these dynamics, it is necessary to recognize that leaders and leadership can be highly effective instruments for the raising of consciousness in respect to the ethical dimensions within, and about, politics.[2] It is not merely that leaders attempt to appropriate fundamental principles within their prospectuses for power—or that they seek to summon up morally enriched issues to serve for their own purposes. It is that leaders place themselves in positions where they themselves become the means of translating issues into morally contentious realms of dispute. In other words, the ethically charged capital of leadership can rebound on itself to leave leaders as the unwitting objects of claims and counterclaims infused with a strong moral component. Thus, while leadership politics is

---

[2] See Max Weber, 'Politics as a Vocation', in Max Weber, *From Max Weber: Essays in Sociology*, trans. and ed. H. H. Gerth and C. Wright Mills (London: Routledge, 1998) pp. 77–128; Joanne B. Ciulla (ed.), *Ethics, the Heart of Leadership* (Westport, CT: Praeger, 1998); David Runciman, 'The Politics of Good Intentions', *London Review of Books*, 8 May 2003; Joanne B. Ciulla, Terry L. Price, and Susan E. Murphy (eds.), *The Quest for Moral Leaders: Essays on Leadership Ethics* (Cheltenham: Edward Elgar, 2006); Terry L. Price, *Leadership Ethics: An Introduction* (New York, NY: Cambridge University Press, 2008); John Mearsheimer, *Why Leaders Lie* (New York, NY: Oxford University Press, 2011); Robert A. Caro, *The Passage of Power* (London: Bodley Head, 2012).

able to ramify into multiple devices of moral consideration, the nature and meaning of ethical principles can turn into corollaries of leadership positions and interpretations.

Leaders and leadership are widely accepted as having a distinct utility within a polity. This functional dimension is more often than not equated with a set of roles which are largely assumed to be related to purposive organization, direction, and decision. What is usually overlooked is the way that the leadership sector can create space for the consideration of political ethics. Because leaders can make ethical issues into highly accessible and sharply defined forms of contention through the force of their own agency, it means that major themes connected to principled differences over moral principle are given a tangible existence. Through their personal, symbolic, representative, and educative credentials, leaders are able to depict themselves, and to be depicted by others, as especially central in the projection of what is seen as morally commendable or morally unacceptable. Coming to terms with leadership therefore is as much to do with reaching an ethical accommodation with its roles and presumptions as it is with an adjustment to its more material and substantive features. Accordingly, the practice and study of political leadership have always evoked a strong normative dimension stretching from classical antiquity to James M. Burns's conception of leadership as a moral partnership embedded in value hierarchies, and Nannerl O. Keohane's advocacy of morally informed prudence and good judgement as key leadership priorities.[3]

In the same way that leadership has a necessarily relational basis with those who are non-leaders, so it is equally the case that the subject area is conditioned by an open-ended set of processes in which leadership is routinely positioned between different ethical claims regarding the distribution and usage of power within society and even between different societies. Many political disputes involving fundamental principles are attributed to leadership issues and accordingly are converted to the medium of arguments over the rights and wrongs of various forms of leadership roles and actions. The spread of highly problematic issues that invariably characterize the analysis of political leadership is itself a consequence of the way that major normative divisions are both projected onto, and exemplified through, different constructions of the conditions and priorities of leadership. Major compositional and philosophical questions relating to the organization and operation of governance are not merely refracted through the lens of leadership politics, but are viscerally embedded in the sector and in the way that the subject is approached. Just as ethically framed arguments become attached to different conceptions of leadership, so leaders themselves offer the prospect of living and breathing expressions of the interplay between alternative conjunctions of principle.

It is necessarily part of their remit that leaders have to negotiate their way through highly contested forms of moral judgement. They occupy a densely packed moral universe in which the personal and the political are habitually enfolded into expressions of each other. Leaders straddle the many interpretive

---

[3] James MacGregor Burns, *Leadership* (New York, NY: Harper & Row, 1979), especially chs. 2, 6, and 16; Nannerl O. Keohane, *Thinking about Leadership* (Princeton, NJ: Princeton University Press, 2010), ch. 6.

and ethical disjunctions pertaining to those deeply contentious questions that characterize the exercise and analysis of leadership. Each leader's way of finding an individual and political passage through these disputed contexts will involve positions and actions that are susceptible to ethical scrutiny. To this extent, any leader's solutions to the perceived requirements and purposes of the role will generate moral issues of one type or another. They may be based upon concepts of personal morality in respect to the individual motives informing a leader's agenda or to the adopted methods for achieving it. On the other hand, they may be prompted by questions of political morality relating to the legitimacy of a leader's positional resources and access to power.

In this way, the instrumental character of leadership roles routinely extends to the sphere of moral judgement where the perceived behavioural and ethical composition of individual leaders can be translated into forms of understanding and engagement with altogether broader issues relating to political systems, historical inheritances, and government performances. More often than not the specifically personal element is used as the preferred instrument of leverage. This can facilitate a proliferation of arguments concerning the moral integrity of individual leaders and the relationship between this category of the appraisal and incidence of successful or failed leaderships. On the other hand, this emphasis on the personal dimension can lead to an altogether different perspective—namely the way that an individual is able to adjust to another schema of moral responsibility. This revolves around the extent to which the realism required within the sphere of political leadership constitutes a separate dimension of moral meaning and obligation that transcends conventional standards of ethical behaviour or traditional benchmarks of political idealism. Some leaders may be objectionable on personal grounds, but may nevertheless be highly gifted in political instincts and thereby markedly productive in political achievements. Others may rank highly in terms of individual integrity but do not have the insights and skills to operate successfully within a political setting. What may be designated 'good' or 'bad' in these circumstances will always lack precision in the changeable value judgements that pertain to individual leaders and notions of effective leadership within such a volatile context of opinion formation.

It is not without significance in this respect that a number of recent US presidents, for example, have experienced serious shifts in public attitudes against their administrations and policy agendas on the grounds of accusations of individual failings in the proper conduct of their positions. Their positions were undermined by crises fomented by ethically grounded critiques of their personal integrity. The damage inflicted upon the Nixon administration through the Watergate crisis, the Reagan administration through the Iran-Contra revelations, and the Clinton administration through the Whitewater and Monica Lewinsky investigations were all attributable to a heightening of the moral temperature surrounding their presidencies on the part of various political elites and large segments of the American public.[4] Those pressing for censure did so mainly on

[4] Theodore Draper, *A Very Thin Line: The Iran-Contra Affairs* (New York, NY: Hill & Wang, 1991); Fred Emery, *Watergate: The Corruption of American Politics and the Fall of Richard Nixon* (New York, NY: Touchstone, 1994; Lawrence E. Walsh, *Firewall: Iran-Contra Conspiracy and Cover-up* (New York, NY: Norton, 1998); Richard A. Posner, *An Affair of State: The Investigation, Impeachment, and Trial of*

ethical grounds that centred upon alleged abuses of power and claims of a proven unfitness for office. Presidential defence teams complained that the various scandals were politically motivated devices in which ethical arguments had been manipulated to facilitate an altogether wider assault upon presidential priorities and programmes. In the world of leadership politics, both positions carry weight because together they illustrate the ways in which an ethical dimension can transform personal and political considerations into interchangeable categories.

It is evident that the potential for ethically based controversy in this area is extensive. It ranges across a broad base of fundamental questions concerning the organization and conduct of politics, and its relationship with the sources and identity of cultural values. The spread of issue areas includes the ways in which, and the conditions under which, political leadership can be both empowered and simultaneously constrained within comprehensible and acceptable boundaries. It also embraces those issues that arise from the appropriateness of means and ends in the exercise of political leadership, and whether or not there is a moral distinction between the two categories. Additionally noteworthy in this perennial array of value-based fault lines is the extent to which leadership is—or can ever be—reducible to legal and constitutional frameworks of specified powers.

Even in advanced societies with embedded attachments to the principle of the rule of law, political leaders are at one and the same time expected to be both products of a legal order and also exceptions to the rule in their recourse to prerogative rights, discretionary powers, and transcendent obligations to varieties of a higher law. The contexts and conditionalities associated with this binary configuration are responsible for a profusion of ethical disputes surrounding the nature of the relationship between frameworks of virtue ethics and cultural values on the one side and the justifications for a leadership ethos of exceptionalism in respect to the customary or categorical demands of morality on the other side. Disputes over the place or rightness of moral relativism, or moral exceptionalism, in respect to the roles and behaviour of political leaders can generate severe disruption in the conventional patterns of political exchange and assessment.

The underlying ethical strains that can often accompany the presence of leadership within polities are of course particularly apparent in liberal democratic systems. The defining logic of liberal democracies lays emphasis upon the operational resolution of the cross-currents arising from liberalism and democracy. In practice, this means that markedly different principles are politically managed into a state of functional coexistence. The same is true in the dimension of democratic leadership where its viability is dependent upon a continual form of negotiation not just between different political interests and policy agendas, but also between variable constructions of the role of leadership within a democratic order. As a consequence, political arguments can become conflated with more systemic interpretations leading to compounded disputes centring upon (i) the rights and wrongs of power being assigned to leadership; (ii) the appropriate balance between the ideals and practicalities of leadership; and (iii) the ethical costs and gains accruing from hierarchical decisiveness on the one hand and dependent responsiveness on the other.

In one sense, leaders in these systems are both empowered and constrained on the same basis of democratic authority. As such, leadership can be construed as dependent upon electoral consent and institutional cooperation. The positional status of a leader, therefore, becomes conceptualized as part of a wider constitutional process that assigns primacy to the law-making body leaving the executive with the responsibility for implementation. In another sense, a democratic ethos can impose a genuinely contested set of dynamics that allow for leadership exemptions from the law as well as for programmatic agendas being initiated through executive resources. Leaders in this context have very variable and highly contingent claims to democratic authenticity that depend a great deal on being able to align their actions, and to mobilize opinion, in accordance with key indicators of political and cultural resonance.

As a consequence, democratic leaders have to be adept not only at navigating their way through the tensions implicit within the values and logics of liberal democracy but also in understanding the reach and potential of different ethical domains connected to the status of leadership within such a contested context. These different ethical constituencies are reflected in the dual prescriptions commonly advanced by theorists of democratic leadership who invariably assert the need for leaders to be both politically proficient and morally sound—i.e. to be worthy of public trust by managing to combine the arts and crafts of power with a driving sense of cultural and intellectual leadership fused with a defining moral purpose.[5]

In essence, democratic leadership involves a continual exercise in squaring the circle. Leaders are expected to lead but at the same time to be cognizant of democratic values; to be a representation of a moral community; and to possess the credentials of a 'democratic personality'. Such leaders are expected to have an intuitive grasp of the fundamental ambivalence that characterizes their position— i.e. they have to possess the skills to negotiate their way through the various priority disputes and principled disjunctions that democratic leadership entails. In sum, they have to devise their own hybrid formats which allow them to perform leadership functions while retaining a defensible alignment with the norms of democratic legitimacy.[6]

While other more explicitly hierarchical regimes foster clearer moral reactions drawn from what are usually more polarized contexts, liberal democracies experience considerable difficulties in reconciling the status of leadership with the foundational norms of a system whose emphasis lies in notions of self-government or at

---

[5] This is a common theme in many of the standard commentaries on the subject of political leadership. For example, see Burns, *Leadership*; Erwin C. Hargrove, *The President as Leader: Appealing to the Better Angels of Our Nature* (Lawrence, KS: University Press of Kansas, 1998).

[6] A significant recent strand of inquiry conflates democratic theorization with forms of leadership elitism in advanced democracies that can be said to possess credentials of legitimate representation. Examples of this thesis of 'leader democracy' include András Körösényi, 'Political Representation in Leader Democracy', *Government and Opposition*, 40(3), Summer 2005: 358–78; Jan Pakulski and John Higley, 'Towards Leader Democracy?' in John Uhr and Paul 't Hart (eds.), *Public Leadership: Perspectives and Practices* (Canberra: ANU E Press, 2008), pp. 45–54; Jan Pakulski and András Körösényi, *Toward Leader Democracy* (London: Anthem Press, 2012).

least representative and limited authority. These difficulties, however, help to reveal the depth and scale of the ethical problems in accommodating the roles and exigencies of leadership properties in such a conceptually flat organizational structure. The adopted solutions almost invariably come down to interpretive and evaluative exercises centred upon the current state of the personal–political nexus. These solutions are always partial and temporary. Nevertheless, what they show is a reliance upon individual leaders in devising ways in which the ethical dilemmas relating to leadership and its place within a political order can reach a form of uneasy resolution.

In many ways, the appeal and the traction afforded by the identification of types of leadership attributes (e.g. traits, styles, skills, situational themes, and personality categories) are rooted as much in ethical as in functional judgements. All the different units of analysis examined during the course of this study have distinct ethical undercurrents. Whether it is the individual properties ascribed to effective leadership, or the designated normative social purposes associated with particular forms of leadership, the net effect is one of leaders offering forms of assessment not just in relation to themselves but also to the wider realms of political meaning and engagement. Because political leaders present themselves and are depicted as junction points between the spheres of individual behaviour and political activity, they not only become highly susceptible to being regarded as compounded emblems of private and public morality but disclose our own susceptibilities in relating to the political world through this mutually constituted process. In this way, it is apparent that in coming to terms with political leadership, we underline a dependency upon the interplay of leaders and the disputes over leadership to allow us to come to terms with the more demanding character and more complex intricacies of a far wider political universe.

LEADERSHIP AS A FORMATIVE CATEGORY

The concept and practice of political leadership tend to suggest the location of a fixed point of influence or a discernible centre of direction from which far less precise and calculable effects are attributed to what is taken to be an identified agency. The open-ended nature of leadership has created a bias towards understanding it largely as a form of inverse explanation in which leadership phenomena are explained in terms of a regression from a present state of existence to a past set of conditions. In the case of political leaders, this retrospective predisposition normally leads to a heavy emphasis upon psychological drives, background influences, and formative experiences as well as on the historical and contemporary conditioning of political contexts. But it is important to reiterate the point that time flows both ways insofar as leadership is concerned. Leaders not only set themselves the task of formulating programmes of prospective policies to cover the short-, mid-, and long-term requirements of their respective social and economic orders, they are normally expected to mobilize sufficient political support to ensure that they are brought to fruition. In effect, leaders seek to guide their publics or peoples towards some semblance of a designated future.

It is this element of embodying an instrumental influence in summoning up a purposive process of political construction that gives leadership its reputation as a promissory force for controlled futures. It is also the main reason why the practice of leadership is normally distinguished by the spectres of failure. Intentions are rarely translated into anything resembling their original designs. On the contrary, unanticipated reactions, unintended consequences, unforeseen miscalculations, and unexpected turns of events, combined with all the other imponderable variables connected to the exigencies of power, mean that leadership experiences are almost invariably marked by narratives of digression from initial plans and programmes. In sum, the operational realities of leadership are normally accompanied by what can be summarized as the negation of leadership. This feature of leadership always provokes a strong impression of a disjunction at the heart of the subject.

The concept of political leadership infers the existence of an anchorage or reference point set within an otherwise unstable and volatile world of competing political interests, arguments, and claims. Leaders offer the prospect not just of a static property at the centre of a vortex of political contestation, but one that infers the presence of an active central agency of palpable political direction. At one stroke, leaders invoke a conception of the political world as one of calculable and controlling cause and effect, while at the same time persuasively insisting that they occupy key strategic positions within this environment. And yet in the very act of playing out such a role within such a context, leaders are revealed to be as much a set of dependent variables as locations of independent force. These harsh realities of political leadership can and do generate considerable turmoil in the provision and understanding of the phenomenon. In the case of its supply, the mutability and instability of the political world offer their own solutions in the form of alternative leaders and renewed claims to directional agency. Calls for different leadership can displace memories of leadership failures and, thereby, maintain the cycle of restorative optimism in leaders with fresh agendas. These prescriptive exercises will in all probability arouse expectations that cannot be satisfied and will in the end be shown to have exceeded the productive capacity of political realities—thus generating further complaints of a leadership deficit and with them opportunities for other leaders to rework the accustomed solutions to the deficiency.

But in the category of explanation, the position is one of a continual process of readjustment in the face of accumulating evidence of the serial mismatches between leadership expectations and realities; between promises and delivery; between overload and under-capacity; between positional focus and political dissonance; and between purposive clarity and the obfuscation of complexity. The cumulative effect has very often been one of strategic retreat in the face of the subject's multidimensional factors. The manifold cognitive, analytical, and methodological difficulties of engaging with such a variable subject commonly lead to a notably pessimistic reaction. One aspect of this response is the acknowledgement that because political leadership embraces so many different situational factors, no sensible meaning of the field can be adequately secured—except in relation to individual accounts of particular leaderships. This brand of sub-optimization usually adopts the more familiar form of backward projection in the search for causal relationships linking a particular style or decision with a prior set of conditioning factors.

Another variant of this response is to concede that there are simply too many possible units and levels of analysis with which to contend and that even with the adoption of various types of multilayer approaches, the subject fades away under the pressure of close scrutiny. In other words, the study of leadership becomes a receptor for such an array of different pathways straddling so many conceptual and operational disjunctions that the defining theme of a necessary connection between input and output becomes increasingly less secure. As a consequence, the analysis of leadership can devolve into an admission that the subject field is not susceptible to any precisely identifiable parameters. Just as there can appear to be no settled departure point, so there is little prospect of any agreement on an ascribed destination.

While the difficulties of engaging with such a subject can lead to this kind of fatalism and retreat, they can conversely also open up the prospect of a deeper understanding of the contingent, contextual, and developmental properties of leadership roles and actions in formation. Coming to terms with leadership can be extended to an enhanced awareness that the phenomenon is far from always being reducible—conceptually or empirically—to the familiar categories of de-marcated cause and effect, or to the conventional binaries of leader–follower dynamics. Adjusting to leadership therefore involves being attentive to its capacity to evolve into less apparent and less conventional iterations. It means being aware both of innovative claims to leadership in less familiar contexts and of emergent spaces where the effects of leadership might be said to be present. There will be many conditions and situations where these more nuanced and elusive forms of leadership experience may be glimpsed, but arguably the area that offers the richest potential for an expansive spectrum of observational and interpretive possibilities into these leadership-related formations is provided by currents within the international dimension.

The examination of the international dimension in Chapter 10 alluded to the problematic nature of attaching conventional leadership roles to contexts that are at variance with conditions normally associated with leadership profiles drawn from political structures based upon state-centric sources and traditions. The international context largely serves to highlight the fact that no polity in the usual sense of the term currently exists at this level and as a consequence no original or legitimating point of reference is present that might afford a founda-tional basis to the development of a transcendent leadership function. Given the lack of any settled hierarchical organization across different sovereign states and thereby the absence of a functioning polity on the lines of a conventional state, it is difficult to conceive of the feasibility of normal leadership structures within such a decentralized array of multiple structures, competing interests, and differentiated identities. On the other hand, the earlier survey also pointed out that the inter-national sphere is not devoid of developments that can support claims of nascent or rudimentary elements of transnational and even international leadership. Whether these attributions relate to figures or agencies connected to international organizations, to forms of global governance, to regional bodies, or to bilateral formations, there nevertheless remains an instinctive attachment to the more standard criteria in seeking to understand the nature of these strands of purported leadership activity.

It is necessary to approach the issue of leadership in this sphere with an altogether more open-handed and experiential sense of the leadership possibilities existing in what are complex and dissonant frameworks of political engagement. Just because the international environment does not lend itself to the more structured and formalized substructures of leadership activity, this does not necessarily equate to an intrinsically chronic condition of degraded or deficient forms of leadership capacity. On the contrary, it is by looking carefully at this sphere that it becomes possible to sense a medium that affords the kind of political space which allows for the emergence of conceptually expansive types of leadership incorporating versatile premises, perspectives, and assessments.

It is true that these kinds of cases can disrupt the more conventional configurations of leadership formation. Because of this, they can sometimes be regarded either as idiosyncratic outliers or else as approximations to leadership but not to the extent where they can be categorized as authentic types. But even though they may disturb the normal patterns of leadership location, identity, and operation, such cases do have an instructive value of their own. They demonstrate the way that in a conceptual and behavioural sense, the subject field of leadership possesses a transformative capacity that extends to an ability to reinvent itself in response to both the exigencies of political interplay and the interpretive constructions of leadership itself.

In such a generative context, even the international sphere can offer an object lesson into the way that some political matrices can be identified as possessing implicit leadership properties in areas not routinely considered to be correlates of such functional attributes. The differences in context also seem to underline the highly variable nature of the relationships between leadership structures, situations, and activities. In short, this often protean sphere of political interaction can disclose the presence of emanations of leadership that are sourced and located through the kind of mutable, opaque, and provisional processes which are not normally associated with the provision of leadership roles. In some respects, such leadership can be seen as almost experimental and counter-intuitive in the manner of its construction and operation. But it would be more accurate to see these leadership forms as representative of a more general set of negotiable possibilities accruing to what can be discerned not so much as a closed system of specified variables, as an open, versatile, and inclusive system of circumstantial stimulus and response.

LEADERSHIP AS A MEDIUM OF NEGOTIATION

At the very outset of this study, it was made clear that the field of political leadership was one beset with a number of initial difficulties concerning the variable nature of the subject and the disputed means by which it might be approached as an object of analysis and evaluation. During the course of the subsequent review, the problematic aspects have emerged as being both formidable and durable. Far from disclosing ways in which the area might be reduced to a simpler and more coherent scheme of activity, the study has in effect demonstrated the extent to which political leadership is related to a far more complex and disputed set of phenomena than its reputation might imply at first sight. Because it embraces so many themes, issues, and contingent properties, the subject is strongly resistant to clear lines of categorization and explanation. Nevertheless, despite its mercurial reputation, the concept and activity of political leadership continue not only to occupy a pivotal position in a host of defining issues concerning the fundamental character of politics, but also to provide the focal point of numerous empirical, conceptual, and normative disjunctions in the landscapes of political depiction and exchange. This has the effect of converting the subject into more of a signature arena of inquiry that draws contested political themes to the surface in a way that gives political leadership a quite different representational contribution to the ones which are more normally associated with the role.

Leadership engagement can refer to the interplay of different leaders and potential leaders with one another. It can also refer to the interrelationships between leaders and their various constituencies and audiences. But it is equally important to note a different kind of engagement which has been an underlying theme of this study. This is the way that leaders almost always succeed in activating a host of core themes and discourses that seem instinctively to accompany the presence and operation of political leadership. The principal parties do not have to make any effort in doing so. They neither have to exert any form of conscious will to create the effect, nor even to be aware of the dynamics that invariably generate these forms of reflexive consequence. Whether they want to or not—or realize it or not—political leaders are highly adept at summoning up and reinforcing entire repertoires of reactions that are as durable and repetitive as they are normally contradictory in nature. Just as leaders engage in a tangible and directly observable sense, so they also act as signifiers for, or portals into, a form of engagement with a substrata of more generic political meanings—namely a proliferation of divergent, and often polarizing, responses which persistently recur in those normative, evaluative, and interpretive contexts that customarily surround the presence of leadership.

In this way, political leaders should not be seen as operating on a merely superficial level of political engagement, or on a simplistic basis of material cause and effect. Whether singly or in combination with one another, political leaders not only evoke strong feelings but do so in ways that continually revive old debates, recurrent controversies, and compulsive dualities. Disputes relating to leadership activity always seem to conform to similar profiles of reflexive arrangements. The regularity of these reactive profiles strongly suggests the existence of a set of deeply embedded cognitive and interpretive devices through which leadership activities are comprehended, framed, and judged. Leaders appear to act as catalysts or accelerants in the way that they precipitate reactions which at one level employ familiar categories of leader-centred attribution but which at another level extends them into more generalized categories of delineation in political positioning.

The process operates along the following lines. Political leaders generally prompt the formation of opinions and assessments that are closely related to the properties, characteristics, and styles that leaders are widely expected to possess in some measure or another. These features can be conceived as generally positive components that in the main evoke consent and approval from non-leaders. It is recognized that each element will have a wide interpretive base allowing for a considerable degree of tolerance in respect to the way that different leaders will possess—or will be seen to possess—different levels of an approved category of leadership attributes. Nevertheless, given the dynamic and reactive environment within which leaders have to operate, any assignments to these categories can become highly contingent upon shifts in political conditions and opinions. When changes adversely affect a leader, he or she will increasingly find that the evaluative framework has widened out in such a way that it accommodates far less favourable interpretations of that leader's perceived position in relation to the criteria in question.

For example, it is generally thought that a leader should be suitably reactive in their political conduct. This being so, successful leaders find that they are able to position themselves along a continuum within the current range of acceptability in respect to this category of activity. In other words, a leader has to work to achieve an alignment within the contemporary condition of evaluative licence given to that criterion of assessment. When a leader falls outside that zone of tolerance in respect to a perceived form of behaviour, the positive constructions assigned to the previous position within the favourable section of the reactive spectrum are reconfigured into a negative attribution. Opinions begin to deteriorate as the leader is portrayed as having drifted into one or other extreme iteration of what had previously been considered to be a moderate composition or an acceptable compromise. In this way, a leader would find that in opting for, or being seen to choose, an unbalanced posture—or simply being effectively characterized as occupying a position beyond the outer limits of tolerance—he or she was being characterized as a polarizing presence and one whose leadership credentials were being seriously questioned. This process can be shown schematically (Table 12.1).

In this selected category, a leader may feel entitled to a measure of approval for satisfying expectations of leadership in which reactive qualities are commonly thought to be a positive characteristic for such a position. The conventional run of leadership politics is normally premised on the need for leaders to keep within these bounds of positive attribution. In effect, leaders always have to be aware of being caricatured—both literally and figuratively—in such a way that the shades and nuances of their behavioural profiles are displaced by the stark primary colours of exaggerated depictions. The problem for leaders is that they find it difficult to keep within the range of optimal positioning along what is a movable spectrum of opinion and assessment.

This challenge is made more exacting by the mutable nature of these inner zones. The intensity or durability of political conflict that often attaches itself to leadership issues can lead to significant adjustments not just in the demarcation of approved leadership traits but more significantly in the way that leaders can become reassigned nearer to one or other end of a particular evaluative polarity.

Table 12.1 Leadership behaviour spectrum: Negative polarities and the positive mid-point in respect to reactivity

Leadership trait		
Zone of tolerance/intolerance		
Negative of minimalism	Positive construction	Negative of excess
⟵		⟶
unresponsive	reactive	indiscriminate register

In the volatile and highly prescriptive world of leadership reputations, leaders have to devote enormous resources simply to addressing these forms of positional management. The extensive efforts at public outreach, personal projection, and media presence bear witness to the importance that is attached to the need to maintain a satisfactory location in such a judgemental spectrum as the one alluded to.

Retaining or developing reputational assets along one spectrum is difficult enough for any leader. However, the problem for leaders is that they are confronted by a profusion of different continua across which they are inevitably assigned to an assessed position. This is the case whether or not they make any effort to influence the attribution of their position along any one of these continua. As in the example above, leaders have to be cognizant of how they are perceived and how they can avoid being made the subject of processes which move them towards negative constructions of their leadership credentials. The issue is one of multiplication. Just as leaders seek attention of one kind or another, so it is that they receive the kind of close and sustained scrutiny which feeds into the formation of an expansive portfolio of judgemental criteria. Moreover, because leaders themselves necessarily promote an ongoing discourse of leadership properties and the reducibility of so many political issues to matters of leadership, they actively support and sponsor the very processes of categorization which create so many problems in the leadership sector. In effect, leaders themselves help to propagate both the establishment of the value-laden categories by which they are assessed, as well as the highly subjective processes by which their actions and behaviour are given either positive or negative constructions.

The scale of the political and managerial challenges confronting leaders in having to attend to their reputational assets across such a wide range of criteria can be gauged by the representation shown in Table 12.2.

It is manifestly clear that leaders cannot expect any combination of such continua to be aligned with one another so that a position on one scale will be replicated in the other assessment measures. On the contrary, it will be rare for any two of these categories to be sufficiently similar to ensure an exact repetition of placements on the part of a particular leader. What is clear is that leaders are faced with a dissonant array of interrelated yet separate categories of judgement that demand extensive efforts on the part of leaders to achieve an appealing and effective spread of positive combinations across as many of these domains as possible. A leader may attempt to offset a negative estimation in one area by cultivating a positive assessment in another but there can be no assurance that such a strategy will be effective. Apart from the fact that behavioural or character-centred reputations can be difficult to modify once they are formed, there is the additional difficulty of negotiating with multiple criteria which are susceptible to rapid accelerations in salience, and which can cut across and interact with one another.

Set against this irregular and mutable kind of grid, political leaders become hybrid figures seeking to calibrate their positions along several notably contingent axes at the same time. Their efforts in optimizing their reputational profiles in this way serve only to heighten the salience afforded to these forms of appraisal. What is already seen as an intensive and often burdensome process of cultivated leadership portrayal is in turn repeatedly stimulated by the extraordinary attention devoted to attempts at what may be compared to squaring so many circles at the same time.

Table 12.2 Leadership behaviour spectra: Negative polarities and positive mid-points in respect to multiple characteristics

Positive leadership traits		
Zones of tolerance		
Negative of minimalism	Positive construction	Negative of excess
⟵		⟶
unresponsive	reactive	indiscriminate register
introversion/inhibition	confident	arrogant/pompous
indecisive	decisive	rash/unmeasured
aggressive/abrasive	tough	ineffectual/weak
out of touch	in touch	compliant/cipher role
poor in a crisis	good in a crisis	makes everything into a crisis
self-effacement	ambition	self-aggrandizement
tactical preoccupation	strategic grasp	fixation with first principles
inflexible	pragmatic	shapeless flexibility
impassive/remote	calmness under pressure	febrile/excitable/volatile
untrustworthy	honest/trustworthy	disabling rectitude
social detachment	empathy	servile/sycophantic
poor rapport	communication	slickness over substance
inattentiveness to detail	managerial competence	micromanagement
inexperience/ingénue	experience	displacement of learning
limited comprehension	understands problems	immersed in problems
minimal discussion	consultative	defers to others' judgement
myopic/means over ends	vision	grandeur/ends over means
lethargy	energy	hyperactivity
pessimistic realism	optimism	unrealistic euphoria
inflexible	adaptability	malleable/events-driven
static/narrow-minded	expansiveness	deficiency in core principles
unsound judgement	good judgement	unsound judgement
marginal influence	power fused with authority	arbitrary behaviour

These tensions of attribution resonate through the texture of political leadership. Some may undergo temporary lapses in prominence but their abatement is always reversed at some point. The attitudinal patterns that are widely evoked by political leaders do not just transcend individual contexts; they commonly transcend strict logic in the characteristic way that binary positions on leadership are usually held on a simultaneous basis by the same respondents. Sometimes, these dual attachments are reconfigured into a kind of symbiotic blend; at other times their inherent tensions are simply held in a workable form of abeyance. For the most part, however, they are held in a state of uneasy coexistence. This condition generates a continual engagement by leaders to ensure that the internal balances are weighted in their favour, and that non-leaders are not able to switch attention to other instinctive pathways which carry a greater likelihood of being to the detriment of incumbent leaders.

While individual leaderships are normally presented, conceived, and received as palpably idiosyncratic phenomena that necessarily follow their own contextually contingent courses, it is evident that they function within certain predisposed categories of intuitive understanding and assessment. Political leaders invariably seek to offer a sense of new beginnings with fresh agendas and innovative programmes, but at the same time they have to operate within a framework of mutable and even volatile attitudes that not only condition the exercise of leadership but largely determine the nature of the complaints and critiques that are directed towards it. In sum, political leaders continually have to negotiate their presence within what is in effect an ongoing process of leadership politicization.

By repeatedly positioning and repositioning themselves in this context, leaders do not just engage with other leaders and non-leaders but effectively mediate between themselves and this more durable substratum of instinctive, yet also volatile, pairings of reflective categories. In this way, leaders work within the alignments of an affective complex of multiple twin tracks and in habitually doing so are instrumental in its continuation as a set of compulsive reference points. Political leaders—as well as potential or alternative leaders, and including non-leaders and political audiences—are all acutely aware of the interpretive and evaluative baseline of dualisms that lie at the heart of leadership production and consumption. They quickly come to appreciate the way that this stream of evaluative binaries operates not just as a mediating channel between leaders and their political and public constituencies, but also as a point of common reference in which both leaders and non-leaders make continual adjustments in response to the contemporary conditions of this generic register of leadership criteria.

These dynamics reaffirm the way that leaders have to work within contexts of observation and judgement which are only marginally of their own choosing. In seeking to optimize their positions in relation to these highly reactive frameworks of attitudinal conditioning, leaders not only have to be acutely aware of the various reflexive currents at work in respect to their positions, but have to be sufficiently skilled at working with them in order to protect and to sustain their claims to leadership status. In examining how leadership works at these levels of political activity, therefore, it is necessary to take full account not just of the situational relationships between leaders and others, but also between leaders and the potential and actual effects of the cross-cutting spectra that are always present at the gates. In this way, leaders who are often cited as necessarily having a central role in the mediation between their own positions and the interests of others have a second intermediary assignment—namely that between their own positions and their hybridized relationships with what is a highly unstable tangle of attitudinal strands rooted in the theme of leadership. In this way, coming to terms with political leadership is always rooted in a joint process between leaders, non-leaders, and a medium of signature criteria that is sustained by the stimulus of common engagement and mutual consent.

SLICES AND ANGLES OF LEADERSHIP WATCHING

From all that has been presented during the course of this study, it is evident that political leadership is a subject area that attracts an array of attributed meanings and modes of inquiry. A characteristic of the field lies precisely in its capacity to incorporate so many themes and issues within what is ostensibly a single frame of reference. The reality, of course, is that of a plurality of coexisting dimensions rather than any settled condition of an integrated whole. Far from being a determinate subject that imitates the apparent logic of leadership itself, the area of political leadership is one that is more approximate to a ganglion of interconnected strands and conditional relationships. Increasing the number of leaderships subjected to examination more often than not simply compounds the complex nature of the phenomenon. By the same token, narrowing the focus to achieve a closer engagement with a specific leadership or set of leaderships does not necessarily contribute to our understanding of the extent to which the subject possesses generic properties or core reference points.

As a consequence, the subject becomes one that is noted for its apparent form but also its evident indeterminacy. It is associated with the notion of commanding heights but at the same time it is heavily dependent upon the conditioning lowlands that surround it. Any disjunctions are entirely at one with a subject that is distinguished by contradictions and paradoxes, by the normal and the exceptional, by the substantive and the symbolic, and by the material and the mystique. While individual leaders usually possess discernible identities, the concept and practice of leadership do not afford clear definitions. In fact, it is largely because leaders so often have their own idiosyncratic appeal and even an allure that is peculiar to them alone that attempts to assign them to more generic categories pose considerable challenges. The position is made more acute by the fact that leaders attract exceptional levels of close attention and, with it, an intensified process of continuing interpretation and assessment which is necessarily an issue of political contestation. Leadership reputations therefore are almost always in a state of flux—either contemporaneously or historically, and usually both.

At the same time, the subject area is continually contorted by the repeated presence of themes that almost invariably divide opinion and occasion numerous priority disputes concerning not merely the perceived nature and prescribed roles of leadership set against the performance of particular leaders, but also the way that the latter can inform and condition the composition and applicability of the former. In many respects, the dissonance that characterizes the properties that are assigned to political leadership is a product of what is poured into the subject by the profusion of inputs that are drawn to it. The standard effect is that of an endlessly negotiable exercise in positioning in which leaders attempt to influence, or to adapt to, a succession of issues that have, by one means or another, leadership-related components. Many of these can centre specifically upon the particular behavioural and political profile of an individual leader. But at times, a leader's performance or reputation can become folded into a deeper set of issues that summons up one or more of a range of perennial disjunctions that normally have a subterranean existence within polities but which when they are effectively evoked can generate fundamental turmoil within the sphere of leadership politics. This is because they open up the dialectics that are normally subdued through the operation of practical politics.

Many of these unresolved and arguably insoluble tensions have made their presence felt in this study. Coming to terms with political leadership, therefore, is necessarily associated with devising ways of assimilating the existence of deep fracture lines within the domain. For example, while leaders can be seen as the products and beneficiaries of a process of institutionalization, they can also have claims to a legitimacy based on the need to transcend established legal and procedural frameworks in order to make adaptive responses to changing conditions and provide the stimulus to necessary forms of renewal. By the same token, political leadership can be viewed as a focal point of stability and unity, but also as an embodiment of the mutability, contingency, and conflictual tenor of political exchange. In similar vein, while the leadership position is commonly portrayed as a top-down construction both in conceptual and practical terms, it is also rationalized as a bottom-up arrangement in which the principle of representation is seen to reach its culminating point in the finality of a process of power transfer. But even where representation is concerned, no agreement exists over the directional logic of leadership. Political leaders can be seen as representative of a contractual arrangement between a state and its citizenry—or at least a large enough section of the public to satisfy the requirements of consent. Other conceptualizations of leadership, however, can give emphasis to more transcendent categories of representation that draw more upon the traditions of historical consciousness, the narratives of identity, and the prerogatives of exceptionalism.

Leadership therefore occupies a congested and discordant political space. Nothing contributes more to the contested intensity of the field than the competing interpretations and prescriptive claims surrounding the theme of leadership itself. As such, it is not just leaders who can suffer from conflicts over its prescribed roles and functions. The entire theme of leadership also suffers from several identity issues. Leadership therefore is a political resource that can be highly valued and devalued at the same time. Positive expectations are often accompanied by negative estimations of likely or actual effects. Leaders are expected to be attached to those they lead, but at other times the prescribed ethos becomes one of detachment. Accordingly, leaders can be conceived as the litmus test of a functioning pluralistic political order with embedded checks and balances. On other occasions, they can be encouraged not to engage in a re-representation of normal politics but to step outside the sphere of normality in order to secure solutions to problems. In another dimension, ideals and purposive plans can be swiftly followed by bouts of political scepticism and even cynicism couched as necessary realism. The overall effect is one of high-profile entities coexisting within a network of highly provisional contexts which ensures that leadership always remains at the centre of an extraordinary conflation of political intersections.

The multiple effects of this complexity are reflected in the difficulties posed to those who try and explain the phenomenon. We have noted the profound challenges involved in reducing the subject area to something approaching manageable proportions. In the characteristic manner of the subject itself, analysis is invariably shaped by context, contingency, and interpretive purpose. It is not merely that leadership is politicized on a continuous basis with the result that it becomes a highly mutable point of reference. It is that the subject continues to carry implications of a clarifying agency and, thereby, the prospect of a discernible state of existence with core meanings and an identifiable essence. The tension between these two perspectives continues to afflict analytical strategies in the field. While leaders routinely assume the role of acting as agents of political exposition and explanation, the subject area is less assured of how the process might be satisfactorily reversed. This leaves significant questions always hanging in the air: namely who will explain the explainers and how might it be done?

The present study is a register of the many difficulties of resolving these questions. But it is also testament to the appeal of the subject and the way that its allure draws so many to its ambit. The problem is usually not a lack of explanatory commitment so much as a proliferation of explanations drawing on an array of different analytical priorities and disciplinary frameworks. On some occasions, leadership is assumed to be an entity that is dependent upon various selected categories. At other times, it is leadership which is taken to be the base unit that inheres within every area of analysis. As a consequence, the examination of leadership can be pursued on the one hand as an essentially deductive exercise, yet it can equally be claimed that leadership necessarily involves an inductively conditioned form of inquiry. Another aspect of this strategic dissonance is evident in the disputes within leadership studies between those that give emphasis to what are claimed to be the constituent ingredients and individual characteristics of a causal agency, and those which focus on the latter half of the cause–effect relationship in the form of leadership outputs, decisions, and choices.

A further analytical dimension pivots around the extent to which leadership is the authentic central focus of study, or whether its explanatory usage serves more of an instrumental purpose in introducing other areas of political activity to closer scrutiny. The study of leadership can be used as a rationalizing device in its own right but it can also offer an access point to a range of other subject fields. In addition, leadership brings to the surface controversies over the sources of political authority and the conditions of legitimacy. As such, the field becomes highly susceptible to strains between its substantive and symbolic iterations. It is also distinguished by the way that normative dimensions can become closely associated with operational aspects of leadership behaviour. Leadership draws into its orbit an array of ethical issues that are related both to the nature and effect of political decisions, and to the foundational and constitutional status of the position itself along with its connections to issues related to the morality of power. In this way, strong interrelationships develop between explanatory techniques and prescriptive principles. In terms of an overall perspective, it is evident that the subject area of leaders and leadership always succeeds in ramifying into a richly diverse ecology of sub-themes, derivative issues, and approaches that fuel an abiding interest in its modes of operation and in its meanings as a political phenomenon.

THE SEARCH FOR MEANING

Leaders and leadership are not subjects therefore that lack the impulse of inquiry. On the contrary, the field is one that continues to hold adherents in its thrall with the result that there is never a prospect of a shortage of studies into the subject. In many respects, this becomes a problem in its own right. The prodigious number of publications on leadership reaffirms and adds to the dissonance surrounding the category and underlines both its myriad forms and elusive character. It is an entirely defensible position to conclude that the sector is a highly absorbent, mutable, and suggestive medium of political meaning which facilitates an immense reach and range of different phenomena and in doing so highlights the inherent puzzles, paradoxes, and unresolved tensions that inhabit such a contested theme. It is possible to go further and arrive at the proposition that leadership may well be a subject that simply generates more questions than it can ever answer.

Given the positional and political ambiguities that surround the presence and pathologies of leadership; given the innumerable contexts and situations within which leadership exists; given the formidable cognitive challenges entailed in engaging with the theme as well as the variety of interpretive and methodological devices used to examine it; and given the fact that all leaders are necessarily hybridized and contingency-based entities—it is entirely reasonable to suppose that no sensible or reliable meaning of political leadership is really plausible. In spite of, or arguably because of, the extensive literature on leaders, the disputed and mercurial features of leadership remain firmly in place. They support, and are supported by, the central anomaly that while the study of leadership is inherently leader centred—and while the field has an apparently definite basis in the material form of leaders—the subject of leadership itself is nevertheless conspicuously indistinct and even formless in nature. Just as the principle of leadership is one that is difficult to fully rationalize so its operation continues to impose severe limits in bringing it within the remit of analytical understanding.

The overall effect can be one of political and explanatory confusion in which leadership proceeds from an ostensibly immediate base to that of an endlessly mutable construct incorporating ramifying hosts of exigencies, relativities, and conditionalities. Whilst it is entirely appropriate to attempt to identify as many key variables as possible and to factor them into summative forms of analysis, such efforts more often than not generate both new iterations of established problematic issues as well as fresh challenges in assigning appropriate weightings to such dimensions as environmental contexts, cultural constraints, and the myriad processes of political negotiation. Studies of leadership operate on so many levels and engage in such a spread of thematic strands that the subject field quickly loses definition. The imprecision and impermanence surrounding this sphere of inquiry give weight to the proposition that while leadership is always closely related to specific situations, the prospect of identifying and defining a common or archetypal core situation remains a highly elusive enterprise. Arguably, it constitutes an unreachable form of generalization. And this being the case, the corollary that follows is that the subject area of leadership has no clearly delineated parameters. Just as it attracts multiple approaches with their distinctive formats and priorities, so it is equally the case that it emerges as a necessarily unbounded object of curiosity.

Confronted with the severity of its analytical challenges, the field of political leadership almost always gravitates back towards one of two responses. The first is what can be regarded as the subject's visceral heartland—namely the study of individual leaders set within their distinctive contexts and largely confined to the focus of derivative themes and issues. The second is what might be termed an anthologizing process in which leadership becomes heavily segmented into discrete sub-units at which point a host of different disciplines, approaches, and methodologies become engaged in unpacking the subject in accordance with their own selective frames of reference. The consequence of both responses is one in which the varied forms of engagement come to imitate and even to exemplify the manifest diversity of the subject. In this way, the examination of political leadership becomes locked into a dynamic which ensures that while the scale of attention towards the subject continues unabated and the volume of various studies—be they biographical, comparative, or aggregative in nature—continues to rise, the overall effect can be viewed as one of diminishing returns. Far from reducing the dissonance surrounding the subject, it is possible to speculate that the sheer profusion of vertical and horizontal slices into the field results in a rising rather than a declining trajectory of disarray.

When this proliferation of idiosyncratic or particularistic materials is combined with other explicitly sceptical perspectives, the outcome can cast the field of political leadership into an even more uncertain light. The view that political leadership possesses a recurrent pattern of rise and decline, for example, infers the existence of a merely cyclical process in which no single leadership has any lasting meaning and exists only as a transient form set within a larger scheme of historical repetition. Another perspective generates doubt over the significance and even the substantive reality of leadership within a polity. This view confines leaders and leadership to the superstructure of social and political arrangements which translates into assigning the subject to nothing other than a peripheral status in the structural architecture of organizational life. In reducing leadership to a merely epiphenomenal expression of deeper social forces, this conception not only marginalizes its status, legitimacy, and agency but also transforms its role from an active to a passive category as well as displacing its purposive and directional element to that of a signifier or symptomatic indicator of a wider political sphere.

A similarly sceptical outlook is provided by that form of analysis that gives emphasis to the situational context of leadership. The thrust of this empirical position also informs a normative injunction that points to the adaptive imperatives of acquiring and retaining whatever power might accrue to a leader. By extending this principle to its logical conclusion, the role and behaviour of leaders can be interpreted as merely appendages to or expressions of their respective environmental circumstances. Leadership in this context can be diminished to the point of being such a malleable vehicle of adaptation that it loses any real sense of an independent existence. Another source of lost identity is afforded by the view that the interrelationship between leaders and non-leaders is so close that they become in effect indistinguishable from one another. While leaders and followers initially seem to occupy different domains, closer inspection can suggest such a degree of dependency between the two categories that the gap between them can be considered closed to the point of equivalence. Leaders and followers can thereby be depicted as joint partners in a mutually constitutive process of fused significance.

When these analytical reservations are combined with the content and tone of many of the references to the state of political leadership in the contemporary world, puzzlement and confusion can change to outright scepticism and even cynicism. The meaning and operation of leadership become squeezed under the weight of the disparities between the scale of global problems and the inadequacies of political responses. Whether it is the organizational complexity of global governance on an international level, or the increasingly multilevel nature of government structures on a domestic level, individual political leaders are often interpreted as marginal figures who constantly have to reconcile a culture of high expectations with a low capacity for achievement. The situation is arguably further exacerbated by the prevailing traction of a neoliberal consensus which has arguably circumscribed the role of political leadership in accordance with the reduced sphere of the state within a market economy. The same orthodoxy has also largely discounted alternative systems of thought. Accordingly, the onset of what is widely cited as a post-ideological age has in its turn denied to leaders the kind of platforms through which they used to be able to create clear identities and mobilize integrated support.

As a consequence of these types of factors, the place of political leadership can be construed as being in the main an anomaly and even an anachronism. Furthermore, the analytical problems and political ambiguities surrounding the theme can give rise to the proposition of a *de facto* generic decline in leadership. It is possible to go further and to claim that the positions, responsibilities, and significance that have traditionally been associated with the phenomenon of political leadership are irrevocably set on a course of entropy. According to this perspective, just as it is increasingly possible to view leaders as the remnants of a simpler but bygone political age, so followers can be conceived as the manifestation of a set of nostalgic attachments born out of either a residual recourse to the mystique of leadership, or a form of political infantilism that assigns value to leadership's comforting assets of familiarity, dependency, and simplicity.

The implication of these controlling developments and critical insights is one in which an understanding of political leadership per se follows the same pathological course which is routinely evident in the decline of individual leaders. Instead of being an antidote to complex and demanding problems, contemporary leadership becomes incorporated into the same chronically intractable syndrome. Through this lens, leadership as an autonomous force and transformative agency amounts to nothing more than a modern chimera. The political realism which is so often associated with the field of leadership is in effect transmuted into a tough-minded recognition that while the idea of leadership is habitually cited, the basic reality is one of intrinsic limits, frustrated ambitions, lost opportunities, debilitating cross-pressures, unfulfilled expectations, and unresolved disjunctions. Leadership may often be described as more than the sum of its parts. However, cast in this context, it never reaches such a summative state of existence. Increasingly, it is perceived to be so intractably and enduringly in particulate form that it cannot be reduced to a unified concept worthy of the name.

LEADERSHIP AS A STATE OF MIND

After such an extended review of the conditions and dynamics of both the exercise and analysis of political leadership, it would be disingenuous to pretend that the subject does not present a set of formidable challenges in respect to reaching a fuller understanding of its meanings and deployments. A key element of this study's controlling logic has in fact been to document many of the enduring disjunctions that inhabit this sphere—and in doing so to examine their reach and implications from a variety of different perspectives. In doing so, it has afforded the opportunity to explore the way that changing conditions and emergent trends can open up different facets of established cognate problems as well as disclosing the existence of new analytical and interpretive controversies. While the results of these analytical excursions can certainly be complex, disaggregated, and cross-cutting in nature, these segmented perspectives should not be taken as a justification for abandoning the field in favour of an advanced state of scepticism. Neither is it appropriate for these multiple lines of inquiry to be conflated with claims of a material erosion in leadership's political significance to suggest a joint pathology of an irreversible process towards decreasing relevance. Far from signifying a transformative appraisal of analytical and political realities, indictments couched as a putative decline of leadership are themselves instructive as to why the appeal and traction of leadership remain as strong as they are even in advanced systems of contemporary politics.

Indeed, the complaints over the insufficiency of leadership provision and leadership understanding constitute an essential feature of the way that the issues surrounding the subject area serve to exemplify its strengths as a defining point of various cognitive, interpretive, and evaluative schemes of political action and reaction. The proposition that we are experiencing a *de facto* contraction of leadership is particularly apposite in this respect as it discloses so many of the underlying themes and reflexive logics that characterize the political milieu of the subject.

In the first instance, it is commonplace for the leadership dimension to become an essential component in the diagnostic construction of what are deemed to be political failures of one type or another. The issue of political leadership has been repeatedly shown to be not just a recurrent explanatory device by which to identify reasons for negative developments but a near universal schema of posited cause and effect—and with it an intrinsic remedy by which imbalances and disorders can be corrected. The stimulus–response character of this leadership equation animates a compelling logic that translates complex and multifaceted political issues into the familiar and highly adaptable matrix of competing leadership categories. Similarly, leadership politics is equally highly adept at extrapolating the positions and records of particular leaders, or potential leaders, into the sphere of more generic and systemic political themes. The combined effect is one of a compulsive calculus in which the conditioned reflexes associated with the prominence and agency of leaders operating in an environment of ingrained pathways of perception and interpretation serve to maintain the persuasiveness of a necessary nexus between manifold political conditions and the specificity of leadership operations. In essence, multidimensional issues become transmuted into the single-strand devices of leadership-centred problems and solutions.

Following on from these habitual processes of analytical definition is the significance of their sustained persuasiveness even in the face of developments which should ostensibly cast doubt on their respective authenticity as usable assemblages of premises and conclusions. It is a perfectly plausible proposition to advance the view that because the linkages between leadership provision and activity have become notably more complex—and thereby far less susceptible to clear operational pathways between behaviour and outcome—so the previous depictions of leadership agency and responsibility might be said to have become proportionately more compromised in terms of their explanatory appeal and political leverage.

Many developments can be cited that have served to introduce a much greater level of dissonance into what it had previously been possible to portray as a more settled construction of causal relations. These discordant shifts in the architectural and operational frameworks of leadership politics have been acknowledged and examined in several parts of this study. They include the emergence of increasingly fractured polities; the onset of multilevel governance models; the evolution of regional, international, and global frameworks of governance; the rise of cross-cultural influences, transnational bureaucracies, and globalized market imperatives; the deepening interaction between international networks of business elites and broad-scale policy communities; the rising trajectory of regulatory, legal, and constitutional rule-making; the increased remit and sophistication of international jurisprudence; the weakening of political attachments and affiliations in a post-ideological age; and the declining influence of such notions as national sovereignty, political autonomy, and full decision-making authority. And yet notwithstanding the scale of these changes and their myriad effects on the standard formats of political leadership operation, they have had significantly little impact upon the usage and leverage of those accounts of political cause and effect that place leadership at the centre of their explanatory thrust.

Far from leaders becoming acknowledged as intrinsically problematic entities performing ever less precise roles in increasingly disjointed landscapes, they have nevertheless remained central agents in the processes of contemporary political understanding and especially in the public assignment of primary responsibilities and prescriptive solutions. Instead of any discernible movement towards an acceptance of a major cognitive disjunction or long-standing attribution error, there remains a conspicuous attachment to the familiar pathways of political observation and argumentation. Just as demanding issues remain eminently accessible to themes of leadership deficiencies, so solutions continue to be couched in terms of readjustments in respect to leadership personnel or positioning. The continuing appeal of these linear sequences of political explanation reflects something of our own dependency or predisposition towards this kind of perceptual device. The attraction may be derived from its apparent explanatory elegance in defining issues in terms that can be resolved through recourse to a language based upon a rational requirement to restore a condition of equilibrium. On the other hand, the draw to follow these well-worn tracks of political assessment may be due less to rational calculation and more to an instinctive faith in the authenticity ascribed to a sequence of defined action and reaction which intuitively makes sense of key political phenomena. Either way, it is readily apparent that there continues to be a very noteworthy dependency upon the personnel, categories, and themes of leadership in the political engagement with increasingly complex issues and in the construction of what are deemed to be appropriate forms of political response.

These attachments to what is a particular type of political conceptualization become so embedded in the mindsets of political actors and audiences that they can appear to be a self-evident expression of political realities. In this way, what might arguably be described as a form of exceptional, and even anomalous, dependency upon a remarkably stable scheme of diagnostics acquires the status of a thoroughly conventional and even commonsensical approach to the political world. The repeated deployment of these analytical devices further enhances their salience to the point where they can appear to assume the status of a set of organizational and evaluative principles of first resort. Incumbent leaders as well as their challengers for leadership honours have been the major beneficiaries of this medium of political exchange. But they have been far from passive recipients of such a bequest. On the contrary, they have been and remain highly active agents in the protection and promotion of these trails of popular explication. It has been in their direct interest to operate as custodians of what is a particular mode of thinking about politics and the public sphere. In successively advancing the political salience of those analytical and normative categories associated with leadership provision, individual leaders serve not only their own individual and immediate objectives but also a wider generic purpose in sustaining the narratives of leadership-centred perspectives.

Competitors for leadership necessarily have to be highly attentive to the advantages to be accrued by drawing explicitly upon the various themes and access points connected to what amounts to reflexive medium of ascribed leadership value. In doing so, they are engaging in a recurrent cycle of reinforcement by which the claims and counterclaims relating to leadership qualification are continually rehearsed and revisited in different guises and contexts. While the myriad positions may appear to be discordant in tone and substance, they nevertheless acquire a coherent focus around the central theme of leadership significance. Just as leaders continually press home their advocacy campaigns by expressly adopting a succession of leadership-centred themes, so the related infrastructures of news coverage, political communication, media analysis, and opinion formation create a form of joint enterprise through which the cultural investment in leadership categories receives a further impetus of consolidation.

However, leaders cannot, and do not, simply rely on pre-existing traditions and practices to sustain the prominence and force of these valuable terms of reference. Their existence is one governed by a persistent drive for public recognition, professional prominence, and political relevance. That being so, leaders take every opportunity to explore innovative forms of engagement and to establish different nuances of leadership functionality. As we have noted during the course of this study, those in leadership positions and those with leadership aspirations are compulsively driven to enhance their claims to distinction. They have to be alert to changing trends; to respond to new techniques; to take up different issues and agenda profiles; to adapt to emergent forms of communication; to strike new chords of public concern; and to renew the rationales of responsiveness and representation.

For example, political leaders in many of the more advanced states have recently sought to compensate for the high levels of public distrust and cynicism by offering themselves as a *de facto* counterweight. This often takes the form of leaders deliberately seeking to distance themselves from their own party organizations, and even from their own governments, in an attempt to create a more differentiated location of legitimacy for themselves. Other leaders have employed a range of alternative devices by which to embellish and refine their claims to substantive and symbolic centrality. These include engaging in populist campaigns of public connectedness; opting for a format of permanent campaigning; adopting social networking and digital marketing technologies; making conspicuous personal interventions in micro policy areas; and experimenting in the political themes and methods of 'anti-politics'. At times, political leaders can appear to offer themselves as a form of social capital in the way that they seek to embody various iterations of a public ethos in the face of selected aspects of modernity. While these strategies have often served to enhance the power bases of individual leaders, they are arguably more significant in the pioneering way they have increased the scope and penetration of leadership-centred points of reference within the public domain.

As leaders exploit both established and emergent modes of political attention, so the narratives and purposes of leadership continue to insinuate themselves into the deeper recesses of social consciousness. The successive flows of cultural reinforcement surrounding this dynamic approximate to the closing of a circle in which the professed social significance of leaders' roles meets the habituated impulses of a public dependency on the explanatory and summative medium of political leadership. As leaders rise and fall, and as they invent and reinvent themselves in a continuing form of renewal, so the broader conceptual and interpretive mindsets become increasingly conditioned to the pervasive presence of leadership politics both as an immediate social phenomenon and as a framework of wider political meaning and significance.

The present study has served to illustrate the cumulative effects of these drivers and of the extent to which they constitute a clearly discernible dimension of political activity and understanding. Seen in this light, leaders are the physical expressions of a host of generative processes and as such they not only create political spaces but serve to occupy them in a range of different guises serving varied purposes and performing multiple roles. A conspicuous outcome of the foregoing analysis has been the disclosure of an extraordinary biodiversity in leadership forms and activities. The variety is very far removed from the more conventional depictions of political leadership. Instead of narrow constructions of hierarchal organization or formulaic depictions of powers, responsibilities, and protocols, what has emerged is an altogether wider and richer repository of capabilities, expectations, usages, and themes assigned to the leadership role in contemporary politics.

From our inquiries it is possible to discern leaders as emblematic figures who encapsulate complex realities and who offer a range of services for their audiences in a complex and crowded world. Leaders can demarcate boundaries and mark political time. They provide a means of navigation through demanding terrains of comprehension, explanation, and choice. They summon up themes of identity and purpose, and embody notions of representation, direction, and causation. In offering an alluring way of understanding a multiplicity of environments, leaders repeatedly revive and disseminate the theme of political autonomy as a realizable principle in a mass society and a globalized order. In the same way that leaders serve to animate political activity, so they condition the consumers of politics to assimilate the idea that politics can be transmitted and received through a medium of leadership exchange.

On very many counts, therefore, it would appear to be self-evident that the stock of leadership remains high and that our dependency upon leaders and their multifunctional roles continues to be as palpable as ever. And yet, the issue of its sustainability and even its contemporary relevance still haunts the subject area. References to the compound failures of leadership and to an alleged 'end of leadership'[7] are never far from the constructions of contemporary discourse or from the processes of opinion formation. These contrarian positions and the resonance that they can possess in the channels of political exchange raise troubling questions concerning the reasons that drive this kind of systemic scepticism.

One reason for this twin-track approach to political leadership is the way that it offers a medium not just for the arousal of an optimistic and purposive cast of mind but also for the assignment of responsibility for the disappointment and deflation that are so often engendered by the passage of political projects. In many ways, this type of transition can be said to represent an inevitable dimension of reality within a political order. However, this process has been exacerbated by the increasing need of leaders to mobilize progressively de-aligned electorates through sustained campaigns to oversell the feasibility of prospective policy programmes and accordingly to raise political expectations to unrealistic levels. Competitive leadership politics induces ever more forms of permanent campaigning and ever more ambitious prospectuses of transformative government which in turn generate successive responses of consequential frustration and disappointment.

Over a period, specific instances of these fluctuating sentiments can work to produce a more generic condition of scepticism and even distrust. When this is combined with the kind of life-cycle pathologies that characterize much of the rites of passage associated with political leadership, the result can indeed become one of a critical fatalism in which the promises of leaders almost invariably exceed that which is delivered or could ever be secured. Leaders habitually promote themselves as possessing the political agency to convert agendas into realizable outcomes. Accordingly, when actual political advances turn out to be more limited in scope it is the conspicuous figureheads who become the defining element in a general shift in attitudes towards political cynicism. The controlling logic of this process is guided by the implications of what is an initial explanatory dependency upon leaders. In the same way that leaders serve to extrapolate outward from their own individual and specific properties towards general themes and wide horizons, so it is commonplace for the process to be reversed, at which point large-scale developments beyond the remit of any leader are assigned to them in a critical turn of outlooks. In terms of cost–benefit analysis, the tendency on the part of leaders in giving emphasis to the latter makes them especially vulnerable to being declared responsible for the former. Within this potent dimension of exaggerated presumptions and penalties, leaders become the main signifiers of political disappointment and disillusionment.

A quite different aspect of this syndrome of alleged leadership failure is based less on the composite culpabilities and aggregate vulnerabilities of individual leaders and more on the interpretation of the contexts in which they operate. In the light of this perspective, the emphasis is laid upon the systemic limitations that arise from the increasing scale and complexity of the constraints that condition the positional resources of contemporary leadership. While individuals do not entirely escape the attribution of political responsibility, they are nevertheless seen

---

[7] For a representative account of this proposition, see Barbara Kellerman, *The End of Leadership* (New York, NY: HarperCollins, 2012), especially chs. 7, 8.

more as symptoms of a deeper malaise that inherently prejudices the structural and operational aspects of leadership activities in what is a deepening of the context of multidimensionality. Specific leaders are seen as necessarily marginalized figures adrift in political contexts that feature multiple fault lines, cross-cutting issues, de-aligned electorates, eroded mass parties, jurisdictional dissonance, complex organizational networks, plural identities, intractable problems, and polycentric forms of governance. The situational fluidity is further compounded by evidence of a growing disjuncture between the perceived magnitude of problems confronting contemporary societies and the capacity of individual political entities to respond adequately to them—especially in an era when the prevailing currents of received opinion give weight to the virtues of market dynamics, economic deregulation, and the limitation of the state.

LEADERSHIP 'GAPS' AND THE INTERNATIONAL

The ascribed confinement of leaders on both counts is particularly relevant at the international level. This is because it offers a context that always poses problematic issues for leadership activity. But more significantly, it is because the international dimension is especially proficient in revealing both the rationale and the reach of those arguments that centre upon an asserted contemporary condition that is characterized as an 'end of leadership'. In shifting the focus to this wider dimension, it shows the ways in which those narratives normally associated with the theme of leadership deficits at the national level can be extended upwards to elements of the international sphere. Even though this dimension falls far short of possessing the properties normally ascribed to a polity and therefore to a location of political leadership, it nevertheless reflects a diagnostic and prescriptive reliance upon those familiar categories drawn from the more domestic contexts of leadership production and consumption.

Notwithstanding the evident dissonance between these different kinds of environment and the palpable limitations upon the exercise of more conventional forms of leadership, there remains an impulse to structure perception and guide analysis along tracks that bear a close resemblance to the selfsame pathways that are used to procure political understandings, identify problems, and define solutions in the smaller and tighter realms of individual political systems. Just as leaders can be said to have a compulsive attachment to the themes and devices of extrapolation, so it is noteworthy that these very techniques are deployed in a reversed logic in which serious international and global problems become characterized as symptoms of a chronic form of leadership failure. In such a scheme of comprehension, a process of scaling up is regarded not only as a plausible rationale but a convincing form of migratory explanation. Highly demanding and complex problems become defined as signifying a missing ingredient—a 'deficit' or a 'gap'. More often than not it is leadership which offers the best perceptual and conceptual handle on that which is presumed to be conspicuous through its absence.

Despite its susceptibility towards tautologies, this kind of approach can be interpreted as a rational and logical piece of argumentation drawing on premises and working towards a specified type of conclusion. However, what might be deemed to be a logical calculus can just as easily be seen as more aligned to an instinctive form of response that owes more to habitual and reflexive impulses than to any sequence of logically constrained steps. From this perspective, the leadership question is not so much deployed upwards as an integrated model of political relationships and performance assessment so much as a spontaneous, compulsive, and even primitive device that offers an explanatory, normative, interpretive, and critical framework of intelligibility where no others seem to be available. Leadership issues—especially in the form of ascribed deficits—become a way of filling other forms of deficit relating to perception, cognition, and judgement. An imputed or declared lack of leadership offers a way out of what would otherwise be an interpretive cul de sac or locked-room scenario. Whether the construction of missing or deficient leadership is drawn primarily from a closely argued and sequential formulation, or from a habitual application of a known formula in one context to quite another type of context, the fact remains that in many cases the challenges of international politics, global problems, regional issues, and complex governance structures are intuitively transposed to matters of leadership agency as a descriptive and prescriptive medium of interpretation.

The net effect is that even in those conditions and contexts that are least consistent with the practical and conceptual parameters of political leadership, as they are normally understood, it is nevertheless the case that complex environments and issues are reduced to leadership-related frames of reference. The framework of leadership analysis becomes an eminently usable technique through which large diffuse issues can be made comprehensible. But far from being a necessarily constructive approach, this means of engagement is more often than not synonymous with a critical viewpoint. The medium of leadership is strongly associated with dimensions of functionality and utility. That being so, it introduces the medium to a seminal complaint—namely that while the international realm offers graphic evidence of chronic problems requiring concerted political action, the response in the form of leadership vision and capacity is wholly inadequate to the scale of the challenges.

This encourages the formation of a circular and self-reinforcing dynamic. Just as the apparent lack of leadership throws the intractable nature of the problems into even higher relief, so the problems underline the asserted urgency of leadership generation. The consequence is often that of a highly negative syndrome in which while forms of international leadership are seen to be disproportionate to the scale of need, the calls for leadership-based solutions become louder. In other words, even though it might be realistic to acknowledge that a leadership-sourced political agency is not really feasible in a context where there is currently no established polity, the discourses of leadership expectation and responsibility remain paradoxically in place. Thus the challenges are considered to be too high and the problems too intractable for normal politics; and yet the familiar demands for political leadership to fill the gap are retained. The extraordinary context is repeatedly unmatched by commensurate leadership resources. On the contrary, context emerges as predominant over any forms of autonomous and directive agency.

It is the scale of this disjunction that generates an outlook of frustration on the part of leaders and their audiences alike. Given the dynamics of globalization, world trade, and communications technologies, even local leaders have to have an awareness of the interdependency of transnational problems. They have to be able to fold domestic concerns into these wider dimensions and to show an ability to engage with the expansive properties of ramifying issues. In one respect, leaders are apt to draw these issues to their own remit. As we have witnessed, in promoting themselves leaders have to be able to impart defining and reassuring stories. As part of their disposition towards self-dramatization, leaders will raise the political stakes in relation to problem definition and resolution by evoking a 'can-do' outlook in relation to even the severest of challenges. Given their influence on the local processes of opinion formation and knowledge production, incumbent and potential leaders will tend to embed the need for decisive international leadership firmly within their repertoires of mobilization. The implication is either that they will personally seek to mobilize the resources for new political initiatives at the higher level, or that they will attempt to secure a general shift in the agendas and operational performance of international organizations in order to improve the responsiveness of governance structures in this context. Either way, political leaders tend to create expectations that are very largely unsustainable and therefore incapable of being fulfilled.

When this dynamic is combined with the notion of leadership at the international level, which is always a highly elusive theme, the net effect can be seen as a syndrome of high-profile mutual marginalization. In underlining the imperatives of international solutions to global issues, national leaderships raise the stakes of leadership feasibility by assigning an equivalence between the severity of the issues to be confronted and the need for leadership-inspired forms of intergovernmental cooperation and coordination. As leadership-centred rhetorical devices and presumptive roles are scaled up from the domestic to the international domain, the result is a proliferation of critical impulses. In the same way that national leaders find they have to engage increasingly with forms of international governance that rarely deliver the kind of action to satisfy domestic agendas, so international organizations complain that their remits are persistently constrained by the bargaining culture necessitated by the multiple entities of retained national sovereignty. The difficulties involved in negotiating these different dimensions of governance can lead to the kind of frustration which cultivates a deep scepticism surrounding the feasibility of effective leadership even in conditions of urgent need.

While political leadership remains closely aligned to notions of functional competence and responsive agency, it is these properties that are seen to be deficient, and even absent, in that area of political life which is widely recognized to be in most need of such attributes. In this light, the limits of international politics are transposed—justly or unjustly—to generic failures of leadership. Instead of offering a form of functional compensation for the structural limitations of international governance, leaders at this level can appear merely to replicate the inherent weaknesses associated with this sphere of political activity. The implication that is commonly drawn is one of a prescriptive demand for leadership which is invariably neutralized by being juxtaposed with a pessimistic realism denying the presence of those conditions that would allow for its material existence.

This mix of inflated expectations, disappointed ambition, and fatalistic realism is a conspicuous feature of numerous discourses surrounding the various themes relating to the feasibility and prospect of leadership formats at the level of international governance. The high-profile demand for leadership as a commensurate response to serious issues that transcend any existing single political entity or group of entities is a commonplace theme of projected resolution but it is one that is almost invariably conjoined to a sense of conditioned denial. Whether it is the Eurozone crisis, climate change, economic regulation, weapons of mass destruction, or global poverty, the proposition of a leadership imperative to address such issues normally produces little more than a heightened awareness of the very tenuous nature of leadership potential in such areas.

Sometimes the critiques are directed to individual leadership entities that are viewed as not having taken the opportunities to develop a decisive leadership role. On other occasions, the chief subjects for reproach are collections of leaders who at regular or special meetings of regional or other forms of multilateral organization fail to produce the kind of clear policy directions demanded by observers. On both counts, the narratives are the same. National leaders who desist from taking imaginative stands for long-term international objectives; economically successful nations that decline to accept political responsibilities on a global scale; and international organizations which remain risk averse or functionally ineffectual in high-priority yet sensitive areas of political need—all are tainted with the adhesive indictment of endemic failure. Thus it is becomes a repeated theme that leadership at the international level is more conspicuous for its absence than for its provision.

In this vein, summit meetings of the G8 and G20 are regularly dismissed as having failed to meet the requirements of managing the global economy and sustaining the liberal world order in the face of increasing evidence of disruptive imbalances within their midst. More generally, the institutions and processes of global governance are regularly indicted both for their functional inadequacies and for their vulnerabilities to immobilism. The United Nations in particular is heavily critiqued for an inability to match its actions to the scale of its remit and for the way that it is circumscribed by its powerful member states whose motives are 'clearly shown in their preference for weak candidates for UN Secretary-General'. As such, the UN's contemporary relevance is repeatedly brought into question:

> Today that institution confronts a vast array of problems, some potentially terminal. It is needed in ways its founders could not have imagined. And it is sorely neglected . . . The United Nations resembles Gaudi's cathedral, the Sagrada Familia. It is half-built, it has great achievements to its name, but its parts are not connected and there are new threats to its foundations.[8]

Even where an issue is cited as an existential threat not only to the world order but to the natural environment and even allegedly to civilized life, the response to the UN's record has commonly been one of disappointment and denunciation. The following reaction to the 2009 United Nations Climate Change Conference in Copenhagen typifies the sense of anti-climax amongst advocates for urgent collective action in the face of an impending global crisis:

---

[8] 'United Nations: weak leaders wanted', *Guardian*, 14 August 2011.

The job of world leaders is not done... World leaders had a once in a generation chance to change the world for good, to avert catastrophic climate change. In the end they produced a poor deal full of loopholes big enough to fly Air Force One through. Climate science says we have only a few years left to halt the rise in emissions before making the kind of rapid reductions that would give us the best chance of avoiding dangerous climate change. We cannot change that science, so instead we will have to change the politics—and we may well have to change the politicians.[9]

In similar vein, the European Union is also indicted for failing to meet the terms of its prospectus. Its multiple constituent units combined with its complex structures and processes have created a perception of an institution that is unable to articulate a common interest with a single voice. Its consequent dependence upon a style of internal leadership that is technocratic and equivocal to the point of obscurantism and its recent preoccupation with the internal turmoil of the Eurozone crisis have given the EU a reputation for being a defining symbol of a contemporary malaise in world leadership. Far from facilitating unified and concerted action on the sovereign-debt crisis, EU summits have instead tended to reveal the depth of disarray. The resultant confusion has prompted *The Economist* to conclude that as voters are left sensing the paralysing powerlessness of individual leaders so their collective summit meetings have come to look 'like a mad hospital ward, filled with the broken-limbed, straitjacketed and terminally ill'.[10]

The alleged syndrome of diminished and deteriorating international leadership is given further emphasis by the claim that the United States is no longer in a position to act as a global hegemon. According to this perspective, since the end of the Second World War the US has been able to use its position as a military, economic, technological, and geopolitical superpower to establish a liberal world order. The security guarantees and public goods offered by the US allowed it to acquire a reputation as a *de facto* global hegemon which has been able to exert influence and authority on an international scale. After the fall of communism, its stature grew to a point of uncontested pre-eminence operating within a largely settled consensus of liberal democratic values and in an avowed unipolar alignment of global power. Recently this level of US supremacy has increasingly been seen as an unsustainable position. To many observers and analysts, just at a time when the world is most in need of strong leadership, international conditions have become unfavourable to the kind of hegemonic presence that could provide it.

It is claimed that while the US no longer possesses the resources or even the legitimacy to generate a leadership capacity, other players are unable or unwilling to take up the slack. Instead, there is a dissipation of global power that is variously described as a West-to-East power shift, a geopolitical unbalancing, an emergent multipolar process, a chaotic realignment, or a 'rise of the rest'.[11] Although new areas and regions (e.g. the BRICS[12] countries) are making rapid gains in power

---

[9] Kumi Naidoo (Executive Director of Greenpeace International), quoted in Michael McCarthy and Chris Green, 'Green lobby attacks failure of leadership', *The Independent*, 19 December 2009.

[10] 'The handicapped union', *The Economist*, 2 April 2011.

[11] See Fareed Zakaria, *The Post-American World: Release 2.0* (New York: Norton, 2012).

[12] BRICS is a representational acronym that refers to a group of countries that have reached a comparable stage of economic development and which amount to a set of newly advanced global players in the international system. The acronym stands for Brazil, Russia, India, China, and South Africa.

and status, they are seen as being too preoccupied with the next stages of their development to engage in the commitment and expense of global responsibilities. This has led to serious speculation over the effects of what is perceived as a dangerous disjunction between the requirements of managing a globalized world and the very feasibility of an international leadership that can preserve the type of global security and public goods required for building compromise, cooperation, and consensus. The prospect of a post-American world is now commonly regarded as equivalent to a chronic state of political uncertainty and unsettlement.[13] This condition has been summarized as a non-polar configuration that allows not so much for a G20 or G8 or even a G2 world, as nothing other than a 'G-Zero world'—i.e. a world of strong states, self-absorbed regions, and global gridlock where no 'no single country or durable alliance of countries can meet the challenges of global leadership'.[14]

The apparent lack of political space for effective political leadership in what is an increasingly complex and arguably intractable context gives rise to an additional interpretive dynamic. In sum, the asserted existence of leadership gaps or leadership failures carries the inference of a deeper malaise concerning the viability of the political medium at large. In this way the limitations assigned to the sphere of political leadership can be used to signify the limitations of politics per se. Because the relationship posits a direct interdependence between the two categories, the bounded depictions of political action serve to elicit a pessimistic and even fatalistic perspective of future political leadership. In the face of critical challenges whose magnitude and urgency would normally serve to evoke the kind of leadership response ascribed to past periods of stress, the conclusion that is often drawn in these conditions is one of anxiety and resignation. The apparent lack of leadership resources and political will can even proffer the existence of a chronic syndrome in which a notional 'end of politics' appropriately coexists with an 'end of leadership'. Thus instead of operating as an antidote to an ascribed end of politics, or end of history, leaders and leadership are folded into the end point itself. Instead of exceptional circumstances having evoked the kind of leadership response normally attributed to a perceived crisis, the conditions are claimed to have merely marked the presence of an irredeemable failure and with it the final false prospectus of a once valued and even noble idea.

NEVER-ENDING STORY

The kind of pessimism that can support and sustain such sweeping depictions of pathology and finality is noteworthy for the centrality that is intuitively assigned

[13] See Zbigniew Brzezinski, *Strategic Vision: America and the Crisis of Global Power* (New York, NY: Basic Books, 2012); Robert Kagan, *The World America Made* (New York, NY: Alfred A. Knopf, 2012); Charles A. Kupchan, *No One's World: The West, the Rising Rest, and the Coming Global Turn* (New York, NY: Oxford University Press, 2012).

[14] Ian Bremmer, *Every Nation for Itself: Winners and Losers in a G-Zero World* (New York, NY: Portfolio/Penguin, 2012), p. 1. See also Ian Bremmer and Nouriel Roubini, 'A G-Zero World: The New Economic Club Will Produce Conflict, Not Cooperation', *Foreign Affairs*, 90(2) March/April 2011.

to the role of political leadership in the nature of contemporary conditions. In these portrayals of systemic dysfunction, the element of leadership occupies an explanatory position that is seen to be not just highly plausible but also compulsively authentic. Paradoxically, though, the empirical and normative vortex that surrounds the voluminous indictments of leadership as a conspicuously missing component can be viewed more as an affirmation of an extraordinarily durable mindset rather than a signature of declining relevance.

Instead of occupying a pivotal point in a process of contemporary disablement, the issue of leadership provision reveals an extraordinarily resilient feature in the way politics is understood and is believed to operate—even in an international setting. The properties, functions, and rationales associated with leadership continue to generate strong attachments that span a range of conceptual, analytical, and emotional dimensions. It might be argued that the very utility of leadership as an expansive and assimilative category infers not merely a vacuous domain of engagement, but also the lack of any viable alternative in the consideration of complex issues. But such a claim is misplaced on both counts. First it overlooks or misunderstands the substantive nature of the genre and its hold on political sensibilities. And second, the view underestimates the ways in which leadership politics elicits serious and substantive approaches to the political realm and in doing so actively shapes the processes of opinion and agenda formation. Ironically, a key feature that illustrates this depth of significance within political ecologies is the very condition that is most often used as the basis of critique and indictment—namely its absence.

It has already been noted that references to gaps and deficits are ubiquitous features of the discourses surrounding the theme of political leadership. While these carry considerable rhetorical weight, their deeper implications are normally overlooked. At one level, the deployment of a term like deficit is a relatively loose form of assessment that evokes a general complaint against an incumbent leader. At another level, the notion of a gap can denote an altogether more revealing attachment to a far more intuitive conceptual and analytical approach to the subject area than is often realized. While the idea of a gap connotes a missing element, it also follows that it equates to an absent entity that need not and should not be left absent. The driving implication is that of a condition distinguished by its wrongful non-appearance; embracing as it does a sense of needless dispossession. As such, the subtext of a leadership gap is notionally a contradiction in terms. Just as leadership operates as a material entity, so the term leadership gap becomes self-evidently a description of that which is not there. However, it is also a device that operates prescriptively as a value stripped of its normal form—a property that has been prevented from coming into a proper and rightful state of existence. A leadership gap therefore suggests both a material category whose normal presence has been denied, and a substantive value that defines such an absence as abnormal, anomalous, and dysfunctional.

In this light, the notion of a leadership deficit becomes closely aligned with a reflexive impulse that fuses the materiality of leadership with the abstraction of leadership as an idea. The appeal of such a binary construct is evident in the way that a leadership deficit is taken as being synonymous with a functional imbalance but also with leadership as a prospective alternative political reality—a reality as substantive as the reality sourced from the perception of a lack of leadership. In this way, the imagination that is often attributed to leaders themselves is discernible in the uses to which the language of gaps and deficits is applied by the imagination of those who criticize leaders as responsible for denying the provision of leadership. As alternative realities and alternative imaginaries drive both the depictions of gaps and the prescriptions for closing them, so the initial denial of leadership is matched by an elemental presumption that insofar as gaps exist they are there to be removed.

In defining problems as leadership deficiencies, the logic that emerges is that of a double denial. As the presence of leadership is denied, it is followed by a comparable denial that the cited absence can be and will be permanent. Sometimes, the reference agency for closure will take the form of a definite alternative figure. On most occasions, however, the remedy has the character of an alternative idea of replacement leadership upon which a variety of themes and sources are superimposed upon a prospectus for change. On both counts, however, the significance lies in the interior logic of the deficiency device and in the conceptual apparatus that is aroused by its usage. The modal properties of a missing essential not only possess a strong conceptual and analytical appeal as a technique of comprehension, but also reveal a deep dependency upon the idea of a concurrence between a lack of leadership and a resultant process of corrective compensation. Far from inducing a condition of fatalistic resignation in the face of disagreeable circumstances, therefore, the various claims of leadership gaps are almost invariably accompanied by reflexive moves to precipitate the kind of change that is considered to be a natural concomitant of the specified inadequacy.

By observing the way that the leadership gap device is used, it is possible to discern the architecture of dependency which both distinguishes the attitudes towards the subject area and structures the discourses surrounding it. Although the leadership category can acquire a nebulous catch-all property which makes it susceptible to a reductionist and omnibus reputation, it nevertheless possesses substantive utility as an operational agency. Its adaptability as a term of reference and a medium of political exchange reflects its force as both a mobilizing idea and an organizational instrument. In a political context, leadership can be taken as the central subject of a critical indictment, while at the same time it can assume the identity of the principal counterpoint to such a critique. Similarly, although the leadership position is necessarily reflective of a wider political context, the role also entails a generative force that can shape its immediate environment and even reconfigure a broader hinterland of relationships. The various issues that are denoted by, and devolved upon, the central significance of leadership repeatedly demonstrate the profusion of ways that the concept and the practice of leadership service those key roles and staple requirements which have been alluded to above: namely its role as a facilitating convention of political usage; a reference point of political ethics; an agency of adaptive change; and a medium of communication and negotiation.

Set against the scale, weight, and ramifications of these myriad contributions, the notion of enduring and chronic leadership gaps sits very uneasily in the systems, traditions, and narratives of normal political activity. This is not just because of a presumption or faith in an autonomous process of self-adjustment. It lies more in the way that leaders and the issues and demands surrounding leadership actively combine to offer constantly changing pathways to various reformulations of leadership provision. Political leadership can be presented as a functional prerequisite to the conventional profile of a polity. It can also be portrayed as an almost abstract entity drawn from the embedded arrangements and expectations of particular political cultures. However, political leadership also necessarily possesses a political dimension that means it is conditioned by the contingencies and possibilities of an open rather than a closed system of dynamics.

This is not to claim that questions and disputes related to leadership are pursued along wholly indeterminate and random pathways. It is evident from this and numerous other studies that leadership issues are to a significant extent rooted in deeply embedded traditions and processes, as well as being the subject of a host of ingrained and habituated attitude structures. While the reflexive and regularized aspects of the subject area represent important situational components, they do not and cannot account for all the phenomena associated with the theme. A characteristic element of the field, and one whose significance largely supersedes the more formal segments, is the essential unpredictability of how leaders emerge; how leadership styles and agendas are formed; and how leadership questions are raised and with what effect.

It is these less predictable and more tractable dimensions that generate the interior energies and creative matrices that can allow leaders to offer the potential to shape alternative political contexts and devise new forms of leadership activity. In drawing resources from political exchange and simultaneously altering political environments, leaders can operate as agents of visceral interaction and productive synergy. While some leaders may admit to a fatalistic resignation in the face of confining spheres of political constraint, others will disavow such professed realism and seek to resist immobilism with active campaigns to establish new narratives of change and to introduce fresh opportunities for capacity building. In effect, whenever it is claimed that there is no available capacity for leadership in an area of social, economic, or cultural life there will be leadership figures who will contest such a conclusion either out of their individual convictions on an issue, or because they will regard it as necessary to the preservation or development of their political resources. In these circumstances, it would not be extravagant to suggest that, by one means or another, most leaders gravitate to areas of political space— and where that space does not exist they will normally seek to discover and cultivate new space, and thence to secure it to serve their purposes.

Placed in this perspective, the allegation of leadership deficits can be given a different construction: namely that of an indeterminate condition marking a host of leadership activities intent upon bringing about change in line with their own particular priorities and in doing so also addressing the issue of more generic leadership inadequacies. This dynamic can be construed in terms of an increasingly fluid and disaggregated world order featuring a rapidly evolving global web of transnational networks. Alternatively, it might be envisaged more as a formative arrangement in which hegemonic power is no longer confined to a single state, political entity, or depiction of power but is necessarily conditioned to a more plural non-polar context of negotiation and soft power relations. On the other hand, leadership capacity might be seen as an emergent property of cohesion and purpose, drawn spontaneously from an array of pre-existing discrete and ostensibly autonomous units. It is even possible for leadership functions to be derived from social and political movements that might disavow the need for any recognizable forms of leadership.[15]

It is the political character of leadership which ensures that it will always possess a pluralistic capacity for mutating forms and differing modes of expression. The provisional nature of leadership's constituent parts and systemic operation ensures that the field never remains a static construct. As multiple leaderships constitute and reconstitute their credentials and remits into a widening biodiversity of variants and hybrids, it is possible to discern innovative strategies of adaptation and with them new positional situations for the exercise of leadership. And along with these developments emerge not only evolving perspectives on the meaning and definition of any leadership deficits, but also shifting paradigms on the prospects for their closure and the ways in which this might be achieved.

One ever-present source of changing leadership configurations comes with the rhythms of the election cycle or with comparable periodic processes of formalized transitions to new leaderships. These arrangements are often dismissed as amounting merely to a circulation of established elites that have more of a symbolic or presentational value rather than being indicative of anything resembling radical change. However, they should not lightly be discounted. The expression of choice within the accepted remit of a political organization has the effect of sustaining focused attention on the issue of leadership within particular contexts, and in doing so it ensures that leadership possesses a centrality within the processes and even identity of a political order. Just as incumbent leaders seek to convince their publics that serious consequences will flow from any change, so it is opposition leaders who usually appropriate the arguments of leadership gaps that can be closed with a shift of personnel at the top. As the competitive spirit deepens and the stakes are raised, so the language and traction of the rhetoric intensify into grand visions and elevated narratives of social and political imaginaries. Whether the messages are couched in terms of memories and recoverable pasts, or in terms of future states of existence, the position of leadership as a medium and an agency pervades the exchanges and conditions all parties to the prospect of altered perspectives. Even if there is no turnover in leadership provision, the claims and counterclaims continue to abound and to shape subsequent adaptive responses. As a consequence, the issues surrounding leadership are conceptually, materially, and cognitively

---

[15] For example, see Joseph Nye, *The Paradox of American Power: Why the World's Superpower Can't Go It Alone* (New York, NY: Oxford University Press, 2003); Anne-Marie Slaughter, *A New World Order* (Princeton, NJ: Princeton University Press, 2004); Stephen Goldsmith and William D. Eggers, *Governing by Network: The New Shape of the Public Sector* (Washington, DC: Brookings Institution, 2004); Charlotte Bretherton and John Vogler, *The European Union as a Global Actor*, 2nd edn. (Abingdon: Routledge, 2006); Martijn L. P. Groenleer and Louise G. Van Schalk, 'United We Stand? The European Union's International Actorness in the Cases of the International Criminal Court and the Kyoto Protocol', *Journal of Common Market Studies*, 45(5) December 2007: 969–98; David A. Snow, Sarah A. Soule, and Hanspeter Kriesi (eds.), *The Blackwell Companion to Social Movements* (Malden, MA: Blackwell, 2007), chs. 4, 6, 8, 14, 15, 17, 19, 23; Sidney G. Tarrow, *Power in Movement: Social Movements and Contentious Politics*, 3rd edn. (New York, NY: Cambridge University Press, 2011), chs. 6, 12; 'The magic of diasporas: How migrant business networks are reshapingthe world', *The Economist*, 19 November 2011; Kateřina Čmakalová and Jan Martin Rolenc, 'Actorness and Legitimacy of the European Union', *Cooperation and Conflict*, 47(2) June 2012: 260–70.

substantive enough to ensure that the pool of actual and potential leadership amounts to a constantly mutating dynamic of competitive selection.

Another source of altered political landscapes through leadership politics comes with those situations where the competitive instinct has generated a highly polarized and unstable set of relationships. When an established leadership has become detached from its previous support structures, has proved to be beyond the measures of ameliorative adaptation and tactical repositioning, and in the process has degenerated into a destructive issue in its own right, then it can precipitate major political convulsions. Such upheavals almost invariably settle upon the figure of a discredited leader and on the issue of his or her continuation in office. Under these conditions, new political possibilities through the normal channels are no longer considered to be adequate or viable. As a consequence, minds become concentrated on the means of removal either by means of concerted persuasion or through violent action. Just as the destruction of an established leadership is depicted as the absolute prerequisite and symbolic harbinger of transformative change, so any successor regime's first great challenge comes with the task of fulfilling the need for a new form of stable and sustainable leadership. On both counts, the main political preoccupation is focused upon the central functional and normative significance of leadership. Even after the experience of a form of tyranny—and possibly because of that precondition—the animating theme and the priority remain that of leadership. Any political order disfigured by the excesses of the past always has to reconfigure itself into an organization capable of renewing its vows with the obligations and benefits of political leadership. No transition is seen to be complete without settlement on this issue.

Of course in referring to any one set of leaders or leadership possibilities, it is possible to introduce a note of time constraints on the present study. In a relatively short period, it becomes possible to know the outcome of many specific competitive processes. But such retrospectives do not invalidate the basic drives and logics of leadership politics which assume a continual adjustment to pressures and opportunities as well as a generic impulse to open up and occupy political spaces for maximum benefit. Political leadership is evidently time dependent but it also possesses features that are relatively timeless in character. There will always be new leaders and novel leadership situations. But they will be framed and understood through the familiar prismatic properties of leadership politics. The issues and themes related to leadership remain not only central to the way that politics is understood, but also the primary medium by which political engagement is given symbolic and substantive focus.

Timeless properties, however, should not imply a condition of stasis. Political leadership can have different meanings and evoke different identities. At one and the same time, it can be defined as a pathological condition that is used to portray the presence of an adaptation crisis, but also as both the means and the end of a response to such a crisis in the form of a newly emergent state of political existence. Political leadership offers a highly recognizable franchise of comprehension and connection. Nevertheless behind its evident materiality lies an idea replete with ramifying significance. Its status and appeal as a conceptual construct and analytical technique give it diagnostic, cognitive, and prescriptive traction which appeals to both rational calculation and emotive attachment. This cultivates an architectural dependency in which deeply ingrained notions of leadership generate a cognitive principle of first resort wherein habituated reflexes of understanding and conventional fields of recognition readily establish sets of compulsive pathways in political understanding. At the same time, what can appear as closed systems of accustomed observation and reductionist outlooks can foster a capacity for seeing different expressions and alternative variants of leadership which in aggregate can be characterized more as an open system of insight, comprehension, and attribution. This more intuitively expansive approach feeds on the conventional but allows for the appropriately unconventional in interpretive realism.

Political leaders are commonly cited as functional agents in the processes of adaptation to changed conditions. While they are generally characterized as instrumentalists, leaders operate in an environment that itself can be equally instrumental in the cultivation of innovative configurations of leadership activity. In coming to terms with leadership therefore it is necessary for the rest of us to accept that political actors adjust to those opportunities for leadership that present themselves in contexts which may not initially appear to be conducive to such roles but which nevertheless generate positional opportunities for unanticipated, unfamiliar, and often unrecognized strands of leadership provision. Instead of depicting an end to politics or portraying its self-demise, the interplay of leaders and contexts offers an extraordinary biodiversity of constantly evolving political forms and activities. This burgeoning matrix cannot assure the production of any selected future outcomes, but neither can its dynamics preclude any or all of them. Political leadership is not a solution or an antidote to politics. It is grounded firmly within the drives and logics of the political sphere and as such it cultivates creative possibilities and unpredictable futures. Just as the study of what appears to be a finite entity can generate an infinite regression of causal factors, so the actual operation of political leadership presents a trajectory of infinite egress in terms of prospective constructions, forward extrapolations, and imaginative states.

Index